Burack, Abraham Saul, 1908- comp.
One hundred plays for children: an anthology of non-royalty one-act plays, edited by A. S. Burack. Boston, Plays [1970]
viii, 886 p. 22cm.

1. Children's plays. I. Plays; the drama magazine for young people. II. Title.

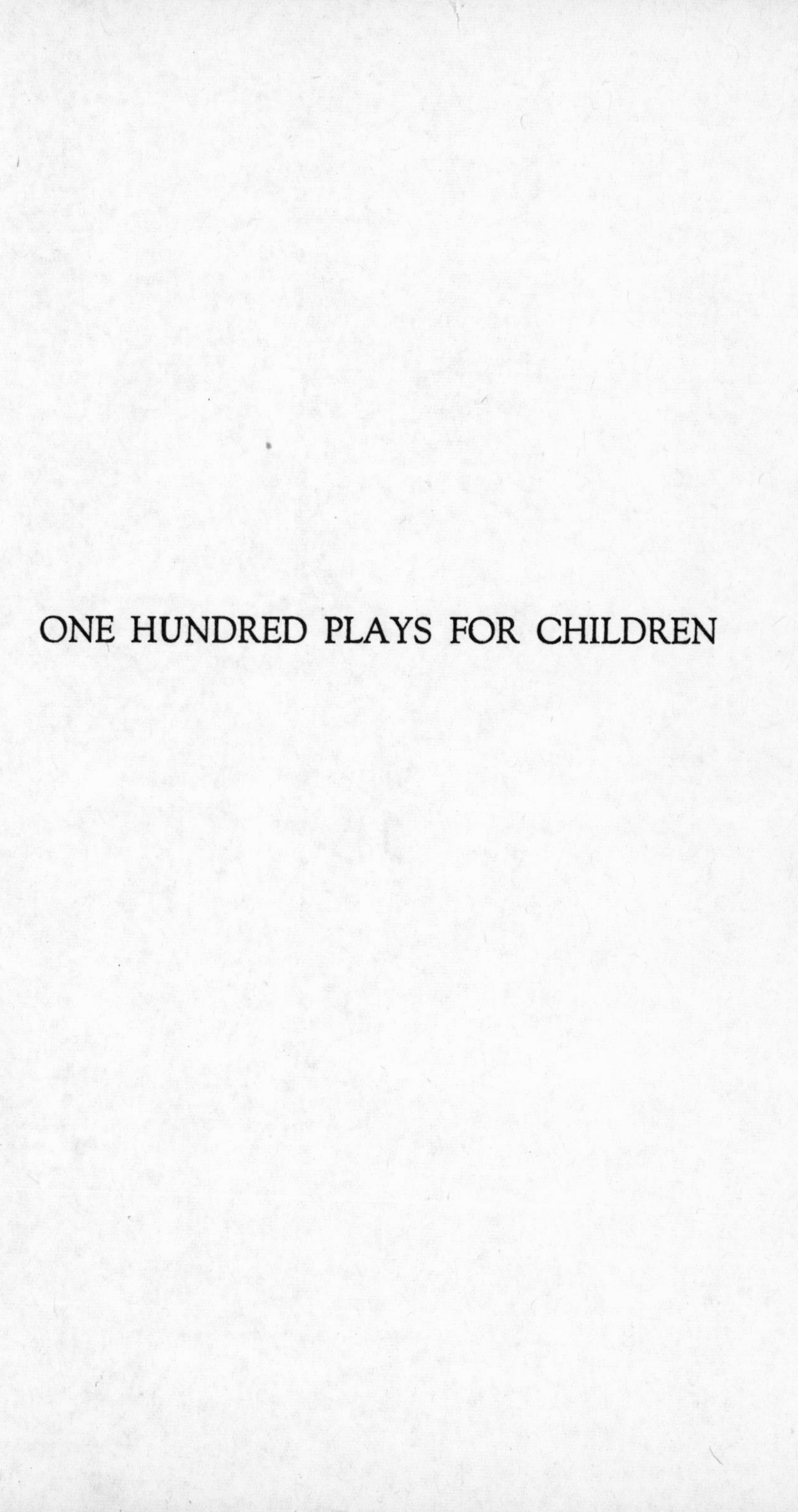

ONE HUNDRED PLAYS FOR CHILDREN

ONE HUNDRED PLAYS *for* CHILDREN

An Anthology of Non-Royalty
One-Act Plays

Edited by

A. S. BURACK
Editor, *PLAYS, the Drama Magazine for Young People*

Boston
PLAYS, INC.
Publishers

PLAYS, INC.

8 Arlington Street, Boston, Massachusetts 02116.
Library of Congress Catalog Card Number: 75–99964
Standard Book Number: 8238–0002–4

CAUTION

NOTICE FOR AMATEUR PRODUCTION

These plays may be produced by schools, clubs, and similar amateur groups without payment of a royalty fee.

NOTICE FOR PROFESSIONAL PRODUCTION

For any form of non-amateur presentation (professional stage, radio or television), permission must be obtained in writing from the publisher. Inquiries should be addressed to PLAYS, INC., 8 Arlington Street, Boston 16, Massachusetts.

Manufactured in the United States of America

CONTENTS

GENERAL PLAYS

Holiday Plays

Lincoln's Birthday

Valentine's Day

Washington's Birthday

Easter

Historical Plays

PREFACE

The plays in this collection have been selected to make available to teachers, drama directors, and young actors a complete source of one-act, royalty-free original plays that offer flexible casting, require simple staging, and are easy and exciting to produce.

The one hundred plays in this volume are divided into four groups, providing a variety of subjects and roles for effective and enjoyable classroom and assembly programs. There are plays for celebrating holidays and special occasions; historical costume and period dramas; modern comedies; fantasies, legends, fairy tales and fables in dramatic form. Many are plays with a purpose, and some are plays just for fun.

Although the plays may be simply presented using a plain backdrop with only a suggestion of furnishings, simple costumes, and no special effects, more elaborate productions may be staged with authentic costuming, special lighting, and professional makeup, properties and settings. The Production Notes at the back of this book offer suggestions for staging, lighting, costumes, properties, and other details to achieve maximum effectiveness. And the plays may be used for play-reading groups in the classroom, with a Narrator describing the setting, background, and appropriate action throughout the play.

In making the selection of plays for this volume, I have considered not only the practical aspects of production, but that vital intangible quality which is the real measure of a play's success — the enjoyment inherent in each play for audience and actors.

A. S. Burack

MAKE HIM SMILE

by E. W. Arnold

Characters

OLD MRS. BIMILIE, *owner of the Doll Shop*
MR. SOLOMON CROSSBY, *her landlord*
THE VERY BEST DOLL
THE SOLDIER DOLL
THE DUTCH DOLL
THE FLOWER DOLL
THE JUMPING JACK
THE WITCH DOLL
THE ROOSTER DOLL

SETTING: *Inside the Doll Shop.*

TIME: *About* 8 *o'clock at night.*

AT RISE: *Seated at a table, down right, and facing the audience is* MRS. BIMILIE. *She is writing a letter, but stops every so often to wipe her eyes and to blow her nose. She finishes the letter, folds it, and puts it into a large envelope which she starts to address.*

MRS. BIMILIE (*Speaking aloud as she writes*): "M-i-s-t-e-r-S-o-l-o-m-o-n- C-r-o-s-s-b-y." And Cross Boy is right! It's a good name for him, the miserable creature! Now, what's his address? (*Consults book beside her.*) "Frowning Manor, Misery Lane." Hump! Two other horrid names, and they just suit him — for of all cross, mean, noisy, making-other-people-miserable men that I ever saw he's the worst. And to think that I have to write him that I haven't the rent money! (*Begins to cry.*) Oh dear! Oh deary gracious me! (*A loud knock is heard on door, left. She jumps up, her hand across her mouth, and stands in terror as the knock is repeated.*) Who — who's there? (*The door opens and* MR. SOLOMON CROSSBY *himself enters noisily, slamming the door shut behind him. He removes his hat and tosses it on top of the* JACK'S *box.)*

MR. CROSSBY: Oh! Didn't expect to see me *this* time of night, did you?

MRS. BIMILIE: N-no, Sir, I-I didn't. In fact, I was just writing to you —

MR. CROSSBY (*Advancing towards her threateningly as she retreats toward the* JACK'S *box*) : *Writing* to me, eh? Does that mean that you can't pay your rent? (*She nods*) I thought so! And you wonder why I have come around this time of night! I've been expecting something like this! Well, let me tell you something — if you'd just pay up promptly, you wouldn't see me any more than you see (*Looks around*) — than you see the Jack-In-the-Box! (*Throws himself down in comfortable chair.*)

MRS. BIMILIE (*Timidly, coming near him as he sits*) : It's because of the Jack-In-The-Box that I haven't the rent money.

MR. CROSSBY (*Laughing raucously*) : Ho! What do you mean by that, hey? Did he run off with your cash? That's a good one! Ha! ha!

MRS. BIMILIE: Someone came in to buy him yesterday — a little girl who said she wanted him to make her cross old grandpa smile. But when she opened the box the Jack wouldn't come out —so she went away without buying anything! (*Wipes her eyes*)

MR. CROSSBY (*Leaning forward*) : So! Just because a silly Jack-In-The-Box was sulky, you haven't my rent money! What's the matter with you that you can't bring up your dolls better than that? Why was the Jack so stubborn, eh? Why wouldn't he come out?

MRS. BIMILIE (*Slowly*) : I think it was because he didn't *want* to make the little girl's cross old Grandpa smile.

MR. CROSSBY: And why not?

MRS. BIMILIE: He — he's afraid of him.

MR. CROSSBY: Afraid of him! Has he seen him? Does he know him?

MRS. BIMILIE: Y — yes, he does.

MR. CROSSBY: Stuffy nonsense! It's his business to make people smile, no matter how frightening they are.

MRS. BIMILIE (*Eagerly*) : Yes, sir, but you see, you always talk so loud — oh! (*She claps her hands over her mouth.*) I didn't mean to tell you!

MR. CROSSBY (*Sitting up straight*): I talk so loud! You mean I'm the man he was to make smile? (*She nods*) Ridiculous stuffy nonsense! (*Springs up and begins to pace the floor,* MRS. BIMILIE *following him, wringing her hands.*)

MRS. BIMILIE: Oh, please, please, Mr. Crossby, don't be offended!

MR. CROSSBY (*Fairly yelling*): Who says I'm offended? Offended, indeed! I'm amused, that's what I am! (*Laughs a very forced "ha ha," then turns in a fury to poor little* MRS. BIMILIE.) But I'm not too amused to forget my rent — and I want it now — this very minute!

MRS. BIMILIE (*Desperately*): Very well, Mr. Crossby. I shall have to go out and try to borrow it from my brother who lives up the street. Will you please sit down and wait until I return? (*Takes her bonnet and shawl from hat-tree and tremblingly starts to put them on.*)

MR. CROSSBY (*Subsiding into chair*): That's better — that's something like! And your brother had better come across with the money, too, or I'll have you both in jail! (MRS. BIMILIE *fumbles wretchedly with her things which so enrages him that he shouts.*) Well! What are you standing around here for? Go get that money! (*She hurries out, and he pretends to chase her out the door.* MR. CROSSBY *settles himself in chair, gets up, walks over to box and looks at it, rubbing his hands over his chin.*) Hum. Afraid of me, eh? I like people to have some spirit. (*Slaps side of box contemptuously, wanders around room, noticing each doll in an abstracted way. Sits down again in chair and begins to rock very fast. He gradually rocks slower and slower, his eyes close. The lights grow dimmer. The* DOLLS *move in their places, slowly turning towards him. There is a low chorus of "Shame! Shame!" repeated over and over again as they turn. The* DOLLS *descend from their places and, moving in irregular groups, advance towards* MR. CROSSBY *still repeating "Shame!" They stand watching him.*)

FLOWER DOLL: How can he treat our dear Mistress so?

BEST DOLL: How cross he looks, even in his sleep!

DUTCH DOLL: Vy iss his face all wrinkles?

SOLDIER DOLL (*Standing straight and tall*): See how he slouches!

ALL: Shame! Shame!

FLOWER DOLL: Well, we can't have him coming here, yelling at our dear little Mistress. We must stop him.

ALL: How?

BEST DOLL: Witch Doll, can't you do something?

WITCH DOLL: I can stop him from moving or speaking, but only for an hour.

ALL: Good!

JACK (*Knocking on inside box*): Wait! I want to see this! Let me out!

BEST DOLL (*Hurrying across room and undoing box lid*): Oh yes, Jack, you must see him — his yelling always frightened you so. (JACK *pops up.*)

JACK: Hurrah for the Witch! Hurry up and enchant the old crank!

ALL: Sh, you'll wake him up! (MR. CROSSBY *stirs, opens his eyes, and tries to spring to his feet. The* WITCH DOLL *raises her hand.*)

WITCH DOLL: Abracadabra! Fall, oh spell!
Enchant his form — his mouth as well!
(MR. CROSSBY *sinks back in chair — tries vainly to speak — attempts to rise but cannot — sits in helpless fury.*)

ALL: Ahha. Now we have him! (*They advance towards him threateningly.*)

BEST DOLL: Stop! Stop! That's not the way to act. We mustn't hurt him.

ALL: Why not? (*They still advance.*)

DUTCH DOLL: He iss a nasty man!

FLOWER DOLL: Let's pull his hair.

JACK: I want to pull his nose!

SOLDIER DOLL: Wait! The Best Doll is right. If we want to stop him from being so mean, we mustn't be mean. We must show him how much better it is to be kind.

BEST DOLL: Oh yes, don't you see, dolls? Two wrongs never make one right. Let's show him how nice and funny we are, and then perhaps he'll change.

FLOWER DOLL: Yes, let's. Let's try to make the corners of his mouth turn up — and his frown wrinkles turn to smile ones —

JACK (*Enthusiastically*): Yes! And Flower Doll's the one to show him how nice a quiet voice can be —

ALL: That's right, Jack!

BEST DOLL (*Bending over* MR. CROSSBY): Do you hear, old man? (*His eyes roll towards her. To the others.*) Come, stand over here and we'll show him one by one all the nice pleasant things we know. (*Flutters to stage right, followed by others.*) Flower Doll, you go first. Show him your little dance and poem.

FLOWER DOLL (*Swaying over to him, she says in a clear sweet voice*):

Swinging my petals, I sway and I sing,
Watching the birds going by on the wing.
Lifting my face to the shining sun,
And folding my petals when day is done.

(*All smile and clap gently. She returns to her place.*)

BEST DOLL: Did you like that, old man? Wasn't it better than your loud yelling voice? (MR. CROSSBY *looks ashamed.*)

SOLDIER DOLL: Sure it was! (*All nod.*) Now, let's make the old man laugh.

DUTCH DOLL: Who iss der funniest? (*All talk at once, saying, "Jack is!" — "The Dutch Doll is too!" etc.*)

BEST DOLL: You all are cute and funny except the Witch Doll and me; so suppose we give the Rooster Doll his chance?

ROOSTER DOLL (*Flapping forward, clearing his throat once or twice as if in practice*): Cook — a oook! (*Hops over to* MR. CROSSBY, *draws himself up very tall.*)

Cock-a-doodle-doooo!
I'm a barnyard friend so true!
My wings I beat (*Flaps his wings*)
And worms I eat! (*Pretends to gobble a worm.*)
That's something you can't do!

(*Suddenly pokes his head at* MR. CROSSBY *who tries to draw back. All laugh but* MR. CROSSBY.)

BEST DOLL: Oh dear, you startled him, Rooster. That's not the way to make a person laugh. Dutch Dolly, suppose you try. (DUTCH DOLL *comes clumping forward and bows jerkily.*)

DUTCH DOLL:

Donner! Diss iss sooch a much!
I am leedle Dolly Dutch! (*Drops a curtsey.*)
Full of funs — dot's me — Dot's me!
Joost you watch and you shall see.

(*Dances a few steps to the tune of "Ach, du lieber Augustine". All laugh and clap.* MR. CROSSBY *has unconsciously been keeping time with his head to the music, and half-smiling. Stops at the sound of clapping and looks angry again.*)

BEST DOLL (*Peeping into his face*): Ah! We almost had him then! Quick, Jack, see if you can catch that smile!

JACK (*Jumping up and down*): Likes people to have some spirit, eh? I'll show him some spirit! (*Leaps about crazily.*)

Whee! Whee!
Just look at me!
I jump in the air
And children I scare,
But they don't care!
There's fun to spare!
Whee! Whee! Whee!

SOLDIER DOLL: Very good, my boy — but you were scared of the old man yourself, don't forget.

ALL: Yes, you were, Jack!

JACK: Well, I'm not now. And do you know why? 'Cause the old man's smiling, that's why! Look at him! (*All look.* MR. CROSSBY *is almost grinning.*)

ALL: Three cheers! He's smiling! We've done it!

BEST DOLL: And isn't he handsome when he does smile? (*All agree.*) Now there are only three of us left to complete the job. Witch Doll, wouldn't you like to have a turn?

WITCH DOLL (*Hobbling over to* MR. CROSSBY *and bending down close to his face*):

I'm a terrible, terrible, terrible Witch!
I tickle your nose to make it itch!
(*She does so — all laugh.*)
I ride a broom when night draws near,
I haunt your house to make you fear!
You'd better be good! You'd better smile!
Or life for you won't be worthwhile! Yahhhh!
(MR. CROSSBY *shivers and shakes. All point fingers at him.*)

BEST DOLL: I think that's quite enough of scaring the poor man. And now —

FLOWER DOLL: And now, Best Doll, it's your turn!

ALL: Yes! Yes!

BEST DOLL: Well, the Soldier Doll and I are the last. Will you give me your arm, Soldier? (*He offers her his arm with a very gallant gesture, and they both walk over to* MR. CROSSBY *with very stately steps. The* BEST DOLL *drops a curtsey and the* SOLDIER *salutes her. They begin to do a dignified little dance, such as a step or two of the Minuet — while all the dolls recite.*)

ALL:

When a Soldier Doll all unafraid
Meets a dainty little dolly maid,
And he takes her hand and they dance together.
Forward and back, light as a feather.
Then the sun comes out, and our hearts grow light,
And our faces smile, and our eyes are bright,
For a dolly maid, and a soldier boy,
And a dance, and a smile, can bring you joy!

(*All clap as he bows and the* BEST DOLL *curtseys again.* MR. CROSSBY'S *face is one big smile, and he tries to speak.*)

BEST DOLL: Oh Witch, he is trying to say something nice to us! Unenchant him, please! (WITCH *hesitates.*)

ALL: Yes, do!

JACK (*Magnanimously*): Sure! Go ahead — the old boy's all right!

ROOSTER DOLL: Come on, Witch, let him talk — awk — awk!

WITCH (*Approaching* MR. CROSSBY *and waving her hands before him*): Abracadabra! Spell, away! (*All watch while a cheerful-looking* MR. CROSSBY *moves in his chair, stretches, moves first one leg and then the other, flexes his arms, rubs his jaws, etc. He is smiling as he leans forward in his chair.*)

FLOWER DOLL: Look, he isn't angry any longer!

MR. CROSSBY: I should say I'm not angry any longer! How could I be, when you dolls have shown me what fun it is to smile and be happy? (*All shout "Hurrah!"*) Why, I feel so good that I want to jump — and sing — and dance!

JACK: All right, let's see you! (*He and the* SOLDIER DOLL *help* MR. CROSSBY *from his chair, one on each side. The other dolls arrange themselves in a semicircle behind them,* JACK *jumps on his box, and* SOLDIER DOLL *steps right leaving* MR. CROSSBY *alone in center. With* JACK *leading and all the others clapping in time, they sing, while* MR. CROSSBY *does an awkward lively dance.*)

ALL:

Pack up your troubles in the Jumping Jack's box
And smile! Smile! Smile!
Dance from your head down to your socks,
Smile, dolls, that's the style!
What's the use of frowning?

It never was worthwhile! So —
Pack all your troubles in the Jumping Jack's Box
And smile! Smile! Smile!

(*All are laughing, and* MR. CROSSBY *is breathless when suddenly the door opens, and* MRS. BIMILIE *enters. She stops in incredulous amazement. The dolls scatter to their places and stand motionless.* MR. CROSSBY *halts, embarrassed, fumbling with his necktie and clearing his throat noisily.*)

MRS. BIMILIE: Mercy gracious me! (*She falls against* JACK'S *box.* MR. CROSSBY *springs to her aid and supports her to a chair, talking as he does so.*)

MR. CROSSBY: Do not be alarmed, dear lady —

MRS. BIMILIE: Dear lady! Ohhhh!

MR. CROSSBY (*Blushing*): I — er — realize that those words are perhaps rather a shock to you, Mrs. Bimilie, and that my position when you came in is a bit difficult to explain —

MRS. BIMILIE (*Fanning herself*): Oh gracious mercy me, yes!

MR. CROSSBY: But I assure you that since you have been gone I have had a wonderful revelation.

MRS. BIMILIE: Revelation?

MR. CROSSBY: Yes. I have seen how much better and happier people can be when they dance — and sing — and smile!

MRS. BIMILIE: Well, praises be! But who changed you and made you realize that?

MR. CROSSBY: Your dolls! Your jolly happy dolls, God bless them!

MRS. BIMILIE: Can I believe my ears? Are you really saying "God bless them"? (*He nods.*) And you aren't angry any more? You won't put me in jail — for my brother was away and I haven't the rent money.

MR. CROSSBY: Jail? Rent money? What's rent money? And who's going to put you in jail? Stuffy nonsense!

MRS. BIMILIE: Oh thank mercy goodness! (*She begins to cry.*)

MR. CROSSBY: Here now, none of that! (*Pulls out a huge handkerchief and wipes her eyes.*) Why, you haven't anything to cry about, you know. You won't have to go to jail, and you won't have to pay the rent either.

MRS. BIMILIE: Not pay the rent! How is that!

MR. CROSSBY: Well, you see, it's this way. I had such a good time with your dolls that, instead of rent money, I want to take a couple of them home with me to remember this evening by.

MRS. BIMILIE: Oh, sir, that's wonderful of you! Which ones will you choose?

MR. CROSSBY (*Judiciously*): Well now, let's see. You said, didn't you, that my little granddaughter wanted the Jack-In-The-Box to make me smile?

MRS. BIMILIE: Well, yes, she did — but —

MR. CROSSBY: But he was afraid of me — wasn't that it? (*She nods.*) Well he isn't afraid any longer! So I choose him. And for my little granddaughter I'll take the Best Doll. So we'll have something to laugh at and something to love! How's that?

MRS. BIMILIE (*Emotionally*): That's, that's just beautiful, sir! (*He turns to go. She jumps up and crosses to desk.*) But wait, sir! Will you take them with you, or shall I send them? And to what address?

MR. CROSSBY: Send them, please. (*She gets charge book and pencil.*) And I can't have two such nice merry creatures going to my old address. I shall change my name and my home. I am now Mr. Solomon Not-So Crossby, and I live at Smiling Manor, on Happiness Lane!

THE END

CHINA COMES TO YOU

by Karin Asbrand

Characters

DOROTHY, *daughter of an American missionary*
MAY LING, *the mother*
SING LING, WANG LING, HI LO, CHING SEE, LO SEE — *Chinese boys*
LITTLE GOLDEN DAUGHTER, LOTUS BLOSSOM, CHERRY BLOSSOM, RED FLOWER, BLUE BLOSSOM, WEE ONE — *Chinese girls*
SERVANT
FLO FLO, *a dragon*
SOO LA, LOO CHEE — *lions*
THE KITCHEN GOD
THE SUN GOD

SCENE 1

SETTING: *A room in the Ling home in China.*

AT RISE: MAY LING *and the* SERVANT *are busy preparing the meal. They set a low table at right. All the children are on the stage except* SING LING *and* DOROTHY. *The* KITCHEN GOD *sits behind frame on dais and the dragon is beside him.*

MAY LING: Sing is very late this evening. Does he not remember that he has guests to share his evening rice?

WANG LING: Sing does not remember any further than the end of his nose, which is very short, honorable Mother. He was going to the American Mission, and there is a new little girl there. She is the daughter of the honorable missionary.

CHING SEE (*With interest*): Is she nice?

WANG LING: As far as girls go she will pass.

SERVANT (*Looking out the door*): Here he comes now, Mistress, and the bowls of rice are steaming. We can begin.

HI LO (*Rises and looks over her shoulder*): He has a strange girl with him, an American girl, I think.

WANG LING (*Also looking out*): It is she. (*Enter* SING LING *right with* DOROTHY.)

SING LING (*With his hands in his sleeves, bows low to his mother*): I greet you good evening, honorable Mother. (*Bows to the others.*) And you, honorable good friends. It is not of my choosing that I am late this time.

DOROTHY: No, it is my fault. He did an errand for my father. (*Turns to* MAY LING.) You are May Ling?

MAY LING (*Bows to her*): I am May Ling.

DOROTHY: My father and mother speak often of you.

SING LING: And this is my brother Wang Ling, and my sisters Little Golden Daughter and Wee One, and some of our friends who have graciously consented to share our evening rice.

DOROTHY (*Holds out her hand to* WANG): How do you do, Wang Ling?

WANG LING (*Looks at the proffered hand*): What is that for?

DOROTHY: Why, to shake, of course.

SING LING: Why should I shake it? I am not angry with you.

DOROTHY (*Laughs merrily*): In America we shake hands to greet each other.

SING LING: Ho! In China we shake hands with ourselves to greet each other. So. (*He does so, and bows to her.*)

DOROTHY: My goodness! Like this? (*Shakes hands with herself, and bows to him.*) That is like the prize fighters in America. It is certainly a very sanitary custom.

WANG LING: It is a very ancient and honorable custom.

SING LING: I have invited Dorothy to share our evening rice.

MAY LING (*Graciously*): It is good.

WEE ONE (*Pats her stomach*): I am hungry.

BLUE BLOSSOM: That is nothing new. You are always hungry, Wee One.

WEE ONE: That is no crime. Confucius says, "It is a wise stomach that keeps step with the body." (*They sit cross-legged around the table.* MAY LING *and the* SERVANT *pass the dishes of rice around.)*

DOROTHY (*Looks up at the* KITCHEN GOD): Who is that man?

LITTLE GOLDEN DAUGHTER: That isn't a man. That is the Kitchen God. Our worthy ancestors had many gods.

DOROTHY: He is funny-looking.

WANG LING: It is a good thing he cannot hear you.

WEE ONE: He looks as though he can hear you. I think he looks as though he were alive.

CHING SEE: You should not do too much thinking. You are only a girl.

LO SEE: You do not need to worry. She does not think enough to hurt her.

DOROTHY: Why should not girls think?

HI LO: Because they should sit around and look pretty.

RED FLOWER (*Sighs*): Sometimes that is hard even for a girl to do.

HI LO: What? Look pretty?

RED FLOWER: No, stupid one! Sit around when there are so many things to do that are fun.

CHERRY BLOSSOM (*Thoughtfully*): It would be fun to sit around in a frame all day and be a picture. (*They set aside their empty plates and the* SERVANT *brings out bowls of tea.* MAY LING *also eats and drinks.)*

WANG LING: Well, it might have been fun in the days of our worthy ancestors. Then the gods were well taken care of, you may be sure. Then nobody could eat before a bowl of rice had been placed before the Kitchen God for him to eat, also.

DOROTHY (*Politely*): And did he eat it?

WANG LING: He looks very sleek and fat and so does the dragon.

SING LING: But it is many decades since this household has had to feed him. It is a good thing, for China does not have too much rice now.

DOROTHY (*Puts her hand up against her dress, and starts up in dismay*): Oh! Oh! Oh!

WANG LING: What is the matter, little daughter of our honorable friend, the Missionary?

MAY LING: You have lost something?

DOROTHY: Oh, yes! I have lost a pin that is very dear to me. It was my grandmother's.

WANG LING: I will walk down the road with you, and see if we can find it. (DOROTHY *and* WANG LING *start out door. The other children all rise and bow low.*)

RED FLOWER: Thank you, honorable Mother of Wang Ling, Sing Ling, Little Golden Daughter, and Wee One, for your hospitality of evening rice.

MAY LING (*Bows*): It is good. As long as there is rice and tea in China we will always extend our humble and gracious hospitality to each other.

CHERRY BLOSSOM: And now we must wend our way homeward.

MAY LING: May sweet dreams hover about your beds all night long. (*Enter* DOROTHY *and* WANG LING.)

LOTUS BLOSSOM: Did you find your pin?

DOROTHY (*Sadly*): No. Somebody must have picked it up. And I forgot to thank you, May Ling.

MAY LING: It is good. And be not so sad, little daughter of our honorable friend, the Missionary.

LITTLE GOLDEN DAUGHTER: Confucius says, "In time of trouble holding the head high will help lift the heart."

WEE ONE: We will all look for your pin, and if we find it we will run with it to the Mission.

LO SEE: We are so many of us that I am sure one of us ought to find it before morning.

DOROTHY: You are so good. Good night then, and thank you. (*She curtsies to* MAY LING *and goes out, followed by all the Chinese children who walk with little mincing steps, their hands in their sleeves.* WANG LING, SING LING, LITTLE GOLDEN DAUGHTER *and* WEE ONE *remain.* LITTLE GOLDEN DAUGHTER *and* WEE ONE *exeunt, while* MAY LING *and the* SERVANT *are clearing away the dishes. They bring out a pallet.*)

MAY LING: It is your turn to sleep here tonight, Sing, and guard the house. Good night, my sons. (*The boys bow very low to her. Exeunt* MAY LING, SERVANT, LITTLE GOLDEN DAUGHTER *and* WEE ONE. *A pin falls from the folds of* SING'S *clothes.*)

WANG LING (*Starts to pick it up, but* SING *makes a grab for it*): What's the matter? Did you steal it?

SING LING (*Indignantly*): No. I found it.

WANG LING: Then it must be Dorothy's pin. Well, if you keep it, that is stealing.

SING LING: Finders is keepers. I read it in a book. It was an English book.

WANG LING: Then that is not a good book for a well brought up Chinese boy to read. I will tell that you have found it.

SING LING: All right for you, dishonorable brother. And anyway, perhaps it is not Dorothy's pin.

WANG LING: It is not so they teach you at the Mission. May your conscience keep you awake all night, dishonorable brother. (WANG LING *exits.*)

SING LING (*Lies down on the pallet*): What a big fuss over a little thing like a pin. (*Holds it in his hand, and admires it.*) It is a very pretty thing, and valuable, I am sure. (*Tucks it into his coat.*) Finders, keepers. (*Lies back on pallet and goes to sleep. Soft music may be played as lights dim a little, and spotlight plays on the picture.* KITCHEN GOD *steps out of frame with the dragon. Goes to* SING LING *and prods him with his foot.*)

KITCHEN GOD: Get up, unworthiest of the unworthy.

SING LING (*With a little gasp, sits up, and rubs his eyes*): Oh, oh! Honorable and most gracious Excellency, but I thought you were only a picture.

KITCHEN GOD: You thought I was only a picture! Ho, you do a great deal of wrong thinking! Just as you thought that pin should be yours.

SING LING: But I found it.

KITCHEN GOD (*Severely*): But somebody else lost it.

SING LING: But I read in a book —

KITCHEN GOD: In a book! Excuses. Always excuses. Empty as your head. You shall go with me to the Sun God's castle. He will know how best to punish you and bring you to your senses.

SING LING: But I do not wish to go to the Sun God's castle. I am supposed to guard this house tonight.

KITCHEN GOD: Ho, guard! I will see that the house is guarded. We will not be long. It is just a matter of seconds, even though it may seem like hours to you. (*He claps his hands, and the* TWO LIONS *come in.*)

SING LING (*Gets up quickly and cowers against the wall*): Lions! I do not like lions! (*The lions back away.*)

KITCHEN GOD: The lions don't seem to like you either. They always know when somebody has done wrong. Soo La and Loo Chee, we must escort two boys to the Sun God's castle tonight. Ah, and here comes the other one. (*Enter* WANG LING.)

SING LING: Why is Wang going? He has done no wrong.

KITCHEN GOD: No, he is just going for the trip.

WANG LING (*In an aside to* SING): I told you, dishonorable brother, that you would be sorry.

SING LING: But I am not sorry — yet.

KITCHEN GOD: Come, mount the lions.

SING LING: But I do not like lions. I am afraid of them. I do not wish to mount. (*The* LIONS *roar and he backs away from them towards the wall, covering his face.*) I do not even dare look at them.

WANG LING (*Mounts one*): Ho, what's a lion in my young life? Nothing but a lion, that's what it is. Who cares about a mere lion? Wang Ling is brave. Don't be a baby, Sing. See, what cunning little lions they are.

SING LING (*Gingerly comes closer*): Y-y-yes, ve — ry cunning, I don't think. (*Gingerly gets astride, but with a roar and a shake the* LION *throws him off.*) See, that is why I do not like lions. (*Picks himself up and tries to mount again, but the* LION *roars.*)

KITCHEN GOD (*Severely*): He does not seem to like you either. Maybe if you tried to like him a little he would like you better. That is the way with animals, yes, and with people, too. Just show that you like them a little, and they will like you.

SING LING (*Grudgingly*): All right. So I like him. What do I do next? Kiss him?

KITCHEN GOD: You do not have to go to that extreme. Just — pat him.

SING LING (*Pats lion*): O.K., so I pat him. Now what does that net me? (*The* LION *playfully cavorts around, then lies down so that* SING LING *can mount.*) Well, well, old fellow, that is better, I'll admit. (*He mounts.*)

KITCHEN GOD (*Mounts the dragon*): After a little while maybe you will have some sense. And now we are off. Flo Flo, lead the way to the Sun God's castle. We must get there and back before dawn. (*With a wave of his hand*) Follow on. (*They start to canter out as the curtain goes down.*)

* * *

Scene 2

SETTING: *The Sun God's Castle, a few minutes later. The frame has now been removed. The Sun God's throne is in the Center.*

AT RISE: *The* SUN GOD *sits on his throne. Two of the little Chinese girls sit on either side and fan him. Chinese children enter with little Chinese lanterns and group around throne. Enter* FLO FLO, *the* KITCHEN GOD, *the* LIONS, *and* SING *and* WANG LING.

CHINESE CHILDREN (*All singing to the tune of "Chop Sticks"*):
You've taken something that doesn't belong to you.
You've taken something that doesn't belong to you.
You've taken something that doesn't belong to you.
You've taken something that isn't yours.
Now you must learn that that is wrong, Sing Ling,
That is why you've been sent for here.
Yes, you must learn that that is wrong, Sing Ling,
And you'll have to return the pin.

KITCHEN GOD (*Gets off the dragon*): Greetings, Honorable Brother. (*Bows low.*) I have brought a bad one to you for punishment.

SUN GOD: So? And what then has he done that he should require punishment?

KITCHEN GOD: He is about to keep for himself a pin that is not his.

SUN GOD: So? Such a pin shall bring him no pleasure for it shall prick him in many places, beginning first with his conscience.

SING LING (*Gets off the* LION *and prostrates himself before the throne*): Honorable God of the Sun of my ancient and honorable ancestors, I found the pin, and when I found it I did not know to whom it belonged. I will return it to its rightful owner.

SUN GOD: So? You know now who is the rightful owner?

SING LING: Well, I almost know. I will ask her if it belongs to her.

SUN GOD: Aye, and if it does not, leave then not a stone unturned to find the rightful owner.

WANG LING: I will help you to find the rightful owner, Sing Ling.

SUN GOD: You are the eldest of the household, Wang Ling. It is good that you walk always in the straight and narrow path that your worthy ancestors may always be proud of you; aye, and your honorable parents, also. And now, Brother God of the Kitchen, I am sure that Sing Ling will always remember to show respect to the teachings of Confucius and his worthy ancestors.

KITCHEN GOD: I hope so. Come then, we must hie us back ere the break of dawn, or else you might wake up before the dream is over, even before we leave the Sun God's castle. (*They mount their steeds and start to canter away as the curtain goes down.*)

* * *

SCENE 3

SETTING: *The same as Scene* 1. *Early in the morning.*

AT RISE: SING LING *is asleep on the pallet. The* KITCHEN GOD *sits in his frame with the dragon.*

SING LING (*Sits up very straight as the temple bells ring, rubs his eyes, and then prostrates himself before the* KITCHEN GOD): I must have been dreaming, but what a dream! I must take care never to displease him again. (*Enter* WANG LING.)

WANG LING: What in the world are you doing?

SING LING (*Gets up quickly*): Nothing. Just saying prayers, that's all.

WANG LING: To him? Ho, ho! But you are awake early. What's the matter? Did your conscience prick you?

SING LING: No. I haven't even been asleep. Neither have you.

WANG LING: I haven't? Well, I've been in a state of blissful unconsciousness then.

SING LING: How did you like the trip to the Sun God's castle?

WANG LING (*Goes over to him and feels of his forehead*): You must be feverish. Whatever are you talking about? I took no trip.

SING LING: But Wang, we went to the Sun God's castle riding on lions. Remember?

WANG LING (*Laughs heartily*): Are you sure the lions didn't eat us up, too? I guess I didn't have the same dream as you.

SING LING: Well, perhaps it was a dream. Ah, well, it is best always to do what is right and not bring disgrace upon the name of our honorable parents. I am going to return the pin to Dorothy. I suppose it is hers.

WANG LING: That is a most excellent conclusion, honorable brother. And see (*As he looks out the door*), here comes Dorothy now. (DOROTHY *enters.*)

DOROTHY: Good morning, Sing and Wang Ling. Have you found my pin? My father told me I might come over and find out.

SING LING (*Takes pin from the folds of his clothing*): Is this your pin, Dorothy?

DOROTHY: Oh, yes! I am so glad that you have found it. You shall be my friends forever and ever. (*She takes two little American flag pins from her pocket and pins them on the boys.*) See, I shall give you these as a token of my friendship and as token of the friendship of all the American children everywhere for you.

SING LING: Thank you, honorable little daughter of the American missionary. I am very happy. (*They bow low to her, and she curtsies to them as the curtain falls.*)

THE END

WHAT'S A PENNY?

by Karin Asbrand

Characters

SEVEN CHILDREN
THRIFT
MR. PIGGY

AT RISE: FIVE CHILDREN *skip in on stage from right and go to center. Each carries a penny.*

FIRST CHILD:
I have got a penny.
I wonder what to buy,
A lollypop, a pickle,
Or a piece of apple pie.

SECOND CHILD:
I have got a penny, too,
My Grandma gave to me.
I am going to spend it
On the first nice thing I see.

THIRD CHILD (*Shows penny*):
I found me a penny
Right there on the street. (*Points.*)
I am going to spend it
On a very special treat.

FOURTH CHILD (*Shows penny*):
See my shiny penny.
It looks so bright and new.
I am going to spend it
On something special, too.

FIFTH CHILD:
I, too, have got a penny,
So shiny bright and new. (*Shows it.*)
And when you go and spend yours

I'll go and spend mine, too.

(*Enter* THRIFT *right and goes to center of stage.*)

THRIFT (*To the* CHILDREN):

Why do you spend your pennies?
Just think what they would do
If you would put them in the bank,
They'd pile right up for you.

FIRST CHILD (*With a shrug*):

Aw, what's a penny?

SECOND CHILD (*Scornfully*):

It's just a cent!

THIRD CHILD (*Looks at penny*):

It's so very small.

FOURTH CHILD:

It might as well be spent.

FIFTH CHILD:

Nobody can stop me
From spending my penny
(*Thoughtfully*):
But when I have spent it
I won't have any.

(*Enter right, two* CHILDREN *with piggy banks.*)

SIXTH CHILD:

Five pennies make a nickel
And if you give them time
And let them add each other up,
Ten pennies make a dime.

SEVENTH CHILD:

And so we save our pennies
In our piggy banks each day.
Mine is very full and fat.
I like him best that way.

(*They both jingle their banks to the tune of "Yankee Doodle," one shake to the first beat in each measure, and sing.*)

SIXTH AND SEVENTH CHILDREN:

A piggy bank is your best friend.
If you just save each penny
In no time you can add them up.
And find that you have many.

(*While they are singing* MR. PIGGY *enters left, jauntily, and goes to center.*)

MR. PIGGY (*Bows*):
Yes, I am Mr. Piggy.
Some call me Piggy Bank,
And as a penny saver
In the first class I rank.

I have a monstrous appetite.
I don't like to be thin.
I'm waiting every day for you
To drop your pennies in.

I do not sneeze at nickels.
Oink! Oink! I like dimes, too.
So any money that you get
I'll gladly keep for you.

And when I'm full to bursting
How rich you all will be
If you have put your money
Each day inside of me.
(*Bows low again, says "Oink! Oink!" and goes to left.*)

FIRST CHILD:
I haven't any piggy bank.

SIXTH CHILD:
Then here is mine for you. (*Hands over hers.*)

SECOND CHILD:
I haven't got one either.

SEVENTH CHILD (*Handing hers over*):
Here's mine then. Will it do?

FIRST CHILD:
Oh, thank you. I will save and save.
It really sounds like fun
To put coins in a piggy bank
When all is said and done.

SECOND CHILD:
I'll start to feed the piggy bank
With my nice shiny penny.
It makes a lovely jingling noise (*Shakes bank.*)
Especially when there are many.

THIRD CHILD:
I will add my penny, too. (*Drops hers in.*)

I'm sure it will be fun
To save a lot of pennies,
And then count them, every one.

FOURTH CHILD (*Drops her penny in bank*):
We'll feed you, Mr. Piggy Bank,
You may be sure of that
Because you look much better
When you are full and fat.

FIFTH CHILD (*Drops her penny in bank*):
If I can't spend my penny
I will not even holler
For a hundred little pennies
Will make a paper dollar.

THRIFT:
That is what I like to hear
And what I like to see,
For I am Thrift, your loyal friend,
So stick right close to me.

MR. PIGGY (*Pats his chest*):
It makes me very happy
To know you'll feed me well.
We hope you've all enjoyed
The things we've had to tell.
(*They all sing to the tune of "Yankee Doodle," jingling the banks in time to the music.*)

ALL:
It makes a very lovely noise;
Jingle, jangle, jingle;
Pennies dropped by girls and boys;
Jingle, jangle, jingle.
What's a penny? Don't you know?
It's a good beginning
To a big fat bank account
That you will soon be winning.

THRIFT:
And so this little story ends
As little stories do.
We hope you'll all get piggy banks
And fill them, all of you.

THE END

THE DULCE MAN

by Catherine Blanton

Characters

JULIO, *a young boy*
JUANA, *his sister*
CARMELITA, *their beautiful older sister*
PEDRITO, *the dulce man, in love with Carmelita*
JOSE, *the bullfighter, also in love with Carmelita*
VILLAGERS, VENDERS *and* SINGER

SCENE 1

SETTING: *The placita of a small pueblo in Mexico.*

TIME: *Early morning.*

AT RISE: JULIO *and* JUANA *are sitting on the floor upstage.*

JULIO (*Counting change from one pile to the other*): Uno, dos, tres —
JUANA: Cinco, seis, siete —
JULIO: Ocho —
JUANA (*Louder*): And quince.
JULIO (*Triumphantly*): And vienticinco.
JUANA (*Jumping to her feet*): Vienticinco! So much money, Julio!
JULIO (*Rattles money in hand*): Almost a pocketful.
JUANA: But what are you going to do with so much money, Julio?
JULIO (*Leans close and whispers loudly*): I'm going to spend every single bit for dulces.
JUANA: Dulces! But, Julio, that is so much money. What would the grandmama think?
JULIO: She won't care. Didn't she give it to me for my saint's day to spend as I wish? (*Pauses and looks at the money in his hand.*) Never have I had all the dulces I wanted. And now,

little sister, you and I are going to have the best that Pedrito has on his table.

JUANA (*Excitedly*): Ooooh! I hope he has some with chocolate today.

JULIO (*Looking about*): I wish he'd hurry and come.

JUANA: He's late.

JULIO: Sure on the day I have money to spend. (*Gets up and looking again at the money in his hands, drops the coins into his pocket.*) Come on, let's see if we can find him. (*They run about as if looking through the trees.*)

PEDRITO (*Offstage*): Dulces! Dulces! Fresh dulces! Who'll buy my dulces? Straight from the kitchen of Pedrito.

JULIO: Here he comes.

JUANA: I can hardly wait.

PEDRITO (*Comes on stage carrying table on head*): Buenos dias, Julio. And Juana. You are like the birds out so early.

JULIO: It is you who are late, Pedrito.

PEDRITO: Is it so? (*Smiling*) But today I make the very special candy. (*Sets table on floor. Children anxiously peep under the white cover of table, but* PEDRITO *makes no effort to lift it.*)

JUANA: Really!

JULIO: Fine! For today we have the money to buy.

PEDRITO (*Dreamily*): Yes, today I make the very special candy. All night my heart keeps saying "Pedrito, tomorrow you make the good dulce and perhaps the lovely Carmelita will smile at you and then — (*Draws a deep breath*) then maybe your heart will be brave to give it to her."

JULIO (*Disgusted*): Caramba! Carmelita does not need the candy. It is I who want to buy.

PEDRITO: Buy? Oh, si, you have a few centavos to spend? That is nice. (*Takes cloth from table. Children lean over excitedly and pick up various pieces, showing them to one another.* PEDRITO *picks up a large piece in shape of heart and holds it up admiringly.*) Here is the piece I made for Carmelita. Will she not like it? (JULIO *holds up candy to* JUANA.)

JUANA (*Shakes head*): No, I don't like that.

PEDRITO (*Surprised*): But does the lovely Carmelita not like good dulce?

JULIO (*Disgustedly*): No. No.

PEDRITO (*Going off into rapture*): Sometimes it seems I must die if she doesn't smile at me. She is like the angel in the church. And I, and I — cannot even speak to her.

(JULIO *and* JUANA *look at one another, then* PEDRITO. JULIO *points to his head then at* PEDRITO. JUANA *shakes her head and points to her heart.*)

JULIO (*Nods his head*): Then if you love Carmelita, why don't you say so, Pedrito? Tell her.

PEDRITO: Oh, it is not so easy. The words, they do not come. (*Swallows nervously*) In fact, they do not come at all. And my hands. I do not know what to do with them.

JUANA: Why don't you serenade her like Jose, the bullfighter?

JULIO: Sure! You could do that. Then you wouldn't have to talk.

PEDRITO (*Throws out hands helplessly*): But, alas, the Pedrito does not play the guitar and his voice sounds like the singing of the little burro.

JULIO: Well, that is too bad. But Juana and I want to buy our dulces.

PEDRITO (*Unheeding*): Such a coward I am. I shall never be able to tell my love to Carmelita.

JULIO: Can we buy all these dulces for twenty-five centavos? (*Points to the various pieces.*)

PEDRITO: Dulces? Eh? Oh, why, sure, for the little brother and sister of Carmelita I would sell much for the centavos. (JULIO *excitedly takes up the candy, handing some to* JUANA. *They taste it hungrily.*)

JUANA: Well, pay him, Julio.

JULIO (*Smiling*): I most forgot. (*Reaches into his pocket. Slowly the smile fades from his face. He begins more frantically to search through his pockets.*)

JUANA: Can't you find the money, Julio? (JUANA *starts looking in his pockets. Then* PEDRITO. *They pull strings, top, balls, spoon, colored handkerchiefs, boxes, etc., from pockets.* JULIO *reaches his hand in and pulls out a mouse.*)

PEDRITO (*Laughs*): What? Another mouse? Do they grow in your pockets, Julio?

JULIO: No, but this one is the best I've had yet, Pedrito. He's really good. He can sing.

PEDRITO: Ho! A singing mouse. Que cosa!

JUANA (*Seriously*): It's a good thing you didn't put the dulces in the pocket or he would have eaten them up. (*A startled ex-*

pression comes to her face) Do - do you suppose the little ratòn might have eaten the money?

JULIO (*Holds mouse by tail and shakes vigorously. Suddenly the mouse slips from his fingers and is gone*): He's gone! (JULIO *and* JUANA *run about as if chasing the mouse.* PEDRITO *looks on and sometimes helps.*)

JUANA: He's gone, Julio. There's no use looking any more. It's better to try to find the money and pay for the dulces.

JULIO (*Almost in tears*): But I know el ratòn ate the money and now we'll have to give back the dulces. And they did taste so good.

PEDRITO (*Covers the table*): Ah, that is all right. I think you have only dropped the money on the grass. You will find it sometime. Give it to me then. (*Puts table on head*) Adios. (*Slowly goes off stage after making effort to sell to women at fountain, etc.* JULIO *and* JUANA *again sit down in first position and eat the candy.*)

JUANA: Mmmmmm, isn't it delicioso, mi Julio?

JULIO: I wish I could have this every day and every day.

JUANA: Do you really think you're going to get filled?

JULIO: Hmmm, that's hard to tell. Seems I'm empty for candy right down to my toes. (*Holds up bare feet.*) And that's a long ways.

JUANA: I bet nobody can make such good candy as *our* Ped — (*Stops, startled. Leans toward* JULIO) Julio! If Pedrito, the dulce man, should marry Carmelita, he — he would really be ours then.

JULIO (*Sits up straight*): And all his dulces would be ours.

JUANA: That would be much better than having that Jose for a brother.

JULIO: Of course it would.

JUANA: But Pedrito is such a funny man. He is afraid of our Carmelita.

JULIO: Huh! I am too sometimes. (*Jumps to his feet*) Come, let's look again for that mouse. (*While they are looking,* CARMELITA *enters right, carries large stone jar.*)

CARMELITA: And what are the muchachos hunting? (JUANA *starts to speak, but* JULIO *stops her with fingers on lips.*)

JULIO: Es nada! Nada! (JULIO *and* JUANA *follow* CARMELITA *toward fountain.*)

JULIO (*Hands* CARMELITA *a piece of candy*): Do you like Pedrito's dulce?

CARMELITA: Of course, I like it.

JUANA: Wouldn't you like to have some every day?

CARMELITA: Que cosa! Such children.

JUANA: Don't you think the dulce man is nice?

CARMELITA (*Looks at her closely*): What are you talking about, Juana?

JULIO (*Hesitatingly*): He loves you.

JUANA (*Hurriedly*): He told us.

JULIO: He is afraid to tell you.

CARMELITA (*Tosses her head proudly and laughs*): He is a silly old clown. All he can do is go around saying, "Dulces, dulces, who'll buy my dulces?" Who would want such a husband? What a sweetheart! Afraid to tell you he loves you. Now me, I prefer the brave Jose. He is not afraid of anything. Does he not send me the love letters? But your Pedrito — what does he do? Stands about looking like the barnyard calf. No, give me a brave matador like my Jose. (JULIO *and* JUANA *reluctantly again start hunting for the mouse and* CARMELITA *goes to the fountain.*)

CARMELITA (*Starts back with filled jar*): Julio, what are you looking for?

JUANA: He's looking for the money the grandmama gave him. (*The messenger, out of breath, comes on stage.*)

MESSENGER: Senorita, Senorita Carmelita! Here is a letter that only now came on the bus. (*Slowly reads over the address*) Senorita Carmelita Reyes, San Miguel, Mexico. It is for you — (*Excitedly*) and from the bullfighter.

CARMELITA (*Grabs envelope*): Here, give it to me. (*Everyone waits expectantly while she opens and scans the page.*)

MESSENGER: What does it say, Senorita?

CARMELITA (*Proudly*): He's coming.

VILLAGERS: The bullfighter is coming here?

CARMELITA: Certainly. He's coming to see me.

1ST VILLAGER: It is not often the great Jose visits our pueblo.

2ND VILLAGER: We should have a fiesta for him.

VILLAGERS (*In chorus*): Bravo, a fiesta for the brave Jose! (*All start off stage as curtain lowers.*)

CURTAIN

* * *

SCENE 2

SETTING: *The same.*

AT RISE: VILLAGERS *and* VENDERS *are decorating the placita with flags, bunting and flowers.* CARMELITA *primps, keeping an eye out for* JOSE. JULIO *and* JUANA *are hunting for the mouse and getting in everyone's way.* PEDRITO *stands to the left, upstage, with table before him.*

JULIO (*Loud whisper to* PEDRITO): We have not found the money, Pedrito.

JUANA: And the candy is all gone.

PEDRITO (*Shrugs shoulders*): It does not matter, mi muchachos. Ah, nothing matters now. The handsome Jose comes and Carmelita will never smile at me. Why do I have to be such a coward? Why would my tongue not speak what my heart was saying?

JULIO: You have lost Carmelita and I have lost my mouse. He was such a clever one, too.

PEDRITO (*Mooning*): And so beautiful. There will never be another like her.

JULIO: It could have learned many tricks and I might have made much money with such a mouse.

JUANA: Stop being so foolish, Julio. You know there are many mice in the kitchen. And one is as good as another. And as for you, Pedrito, you are very stupid. Carmelita is sometimes cross and angry and then you forget how pretty she is. (JULIO *and* PEDRITO *look unbelieving, but help with the decorations.*)

MESSENGER (*Runs on stage*): He's coming. Jose, the bullfighter, is coming. (*Everyone acts excited.* CARMELITA *hurriedly primps, but is indifferent to* JOSE *when he appears.*)

VILLAGERS: Buenas tardes! Viva! Jose!

JOSE (*Makes grand entrance. Bows from waist with hat in hand*): Senoras — senors — (*Turns to* CARMELITA) Senorita! You do the Jose much honor.

1ST VILLAGER: We are proud to have the great matador visit our pueblo.

VILLAGERS: Bravo, for the brave matador. (JOSE *bows again.*)

JULIO (*Runs to* JOSE): Please, Senor Jose, tell us of your fights.

JUANA: Yes! Please, senor. Were you ever afraid?

JOSE: What? The great Jose afraid? (*Throws back head proudly*) That is a joke. The great Jose is afraid of nothing.

CARMELITA (*Comes forward*): Please Jose. We are waiting.

JOSE (*Bows to* CARMELITA): Of course, for you, senorita.

VILLAGERS: Bravo! Bravo! Tell us of your fights. (*They sit or stand in semi-circle. All listen attentively.*)

JOSE: Ah, it is the narrow escapes I have had. But no bull is going to frighten the great Jose. (*Tweaks* CARMELITA *on chin*) No, Senorita. Nothing frightens me. Why, the last time I was in the ring I faced the meanest bull in all of Mexico.

VILLAGERS: In all of Mexico!

JOSE: Already that torote had killed three men on the rancho.

VILLAGERS: Three men on the rancho!

JOSE: Yes, he was a match for me. Around and around the ring we went. (*Waves cape or serape in demonstration.*) The crowd was screaming with excitement. El Torote came closer and closer. His breath was on my face.

JULIO (*Sitting right upstage with* JUANA, *suddenly points finger towards* JOSE's *feet. Screams.*): The mouse! (JOSE *freezes. Then starts running among frightened villagers. Finally makes exit.* VILLAGERS *run about excitedly. Women grab skirts and climb up on benches, etc.* JULIO *and* JUANA *are in and out among them.*)

JULIO: Catch him, Juana. There he goes.

CARMELITA (*Runs screaming, finally jumps to top of fountain. Wavers as if about to fall in*): Jose! Help me! My Jose! The mouse it is coming toward me. Save me!

PEDRITO (*Runs to* CARMELITA): Carmelita! (*Jumps up by her side and takes her in his arms.)* Carmelita, my darling.

CARMELITA: Oh, mi Pedrito!

4TH VILLAGER: Where is Jose? (VILLAGERS *look for* JOSE.)

1ST VILLAGER: He is gone.

2ND VILLAGER: The great and brave matador has run away. (*Gradually the* VILLAGERS *leave the stage.*)

PEDRITO: Ah, Carmelita, my little dove. For the many months my arms have cried to hold you. (*Holds out his arms.*) See how strong they are. Always will they protect and keep you safe.

CARMELITA (*Looks at him admiringly*): Ah, Pedrito.

PEDRITO (*Gives her an awkward kiss*): There, how do you like that?

CARMELITA: Ah, Pedrito, you are wonderful. Your kisses are like your dulce.

PEDRITO: Then, senorita, have another. (*Kisses her again.* JULIO and JUANA *come running up to them with the mouse hanging by its tail in* JULIO's *hand.*)

JULIO: I've found him, Pedrito. (*Fondles the mouse*) Do you want to hear him sing?

CARMELITA: No! No! Take him away. Pedrito —

PEDRITO: There, there, my love, I will protect you.

JUANA: We found the mouse, Pedrito, but we did not find the money. What about the dulces?

PEDRITO (*Waves hand generously*): Es nada, nada. Forget. There is my table. Take all you want.

JULIO: Honest?

JUANA: Really!

PEDRITO: Si, si! (*As an afterthought*) And give el ratòn some. But leave Carmelita and me alone. We have much (*Embarrassed pause*), well, much business to talk about. (*Helps* CARMELITA *down and they go off stage, arm in arm, with her head on his shoulder.* JULIO *and* JUANA *look after them in amazement.*)

JUANA: Why, the dulce man is going to be ours after all.

JULIO: And — and all because of the little mouse.

JUANA (*Pulls* JULIO *toward table*): Hurry, I'm hungry.

JULIO (*Picks up candy heart intended for* CARMELITA): Here, let's give this to el ratòn. He deserves it.

THE END

THE TALENT TREE

by Thelma Lucille Brown

Characters

SUNDOWN, *the peddler*
BOBBINS, *a boy of ten*
ART, WHISTLER, POET, ACROBAT, CULINARY ART, GARDENER — *the Talents*

TIME: *Any time ago.*

SETTING: *A woods.*

AT RISE: SUNDOWN *is sleeping under a pile of leaves left.* BOBBINS *stands right looking up at the sky. He is tired and frightened.*

BOBBINS (*Calling entreatingly to Skylark who has flown away and left him*): Come back! Come back! (SUNDOWN *stirs under the leaves.*) Come back!

SUNDOWN (*Throws off leaves and sits up, blinking at* BOBBINS): Well, bless my brother in the moon.

BOBBINS (*Startled*): Oh! I thought I was alone.

SUNDOWN (*Gets up grumbling*): Done in the time it takes to turn round twice. (*Moves to go.*)

BOBBINS: Please don't go—that is, not yet. I believe I'm lost.

SUNDOWN (*Brushing leaves from his clothes*): Lost! A big fellow like you! Now that's a fine—a fine trick of the wind.

BOBBINS (*Puzzled*): Trick of the wind?

SUNDOWN: A fine kettle of—kettle of katydids. A fine how are you.

BOBBINS (*Chuckling*): You're a funny fellow. (*Looks at him closely.*) Haven't I seen you somewhere before? (*Moves closer, peering at him.*) I know. You're Sundown, the peddler.

SUNDOWN: Quite right. A little left of right but quite right. And I know you. Master Bobbins. Penury Lane. Village of Meekville. Father mends shoes.

BOBBINS: Exactly right. You pass through our village every night.

SUNDOWN: Round about sundown. That's how I got my name.

BOBBINS: I don't know what you're doing here, Mr. — er — Sundown, but I'm looking for buried talents. Do you know where they're found?

SUNDOWN: Tie a knot in the rainbow! And what makes you think I would know where the talents are buried?

BOBBINS: I don't know. I guess because you're such a quaint fellow. It's as if you belong to another world.

SUNDOWN (*Pretending anger*): Now then, young sir, now then! What do you see that's quaint about me?

BOBBINS: I'm sorry if I've hurt your feelings. It's the way you talk, the funny things you say. And the things you sell.

SUNDOWN: The things I sell? Perhaps it's the singing whirligig you admired or the package of Darning Needle Darts. The ladies like my special jar of Summer Night and the masque of Wild Rose Blush.

BOBBINS: And then the way you come and go through the village. First you're nowhere around then, very suddenly, there you are. It's like magic.

SUNDOWN: If a toadstool's an umbrella. Who brought you here?

BOBBINS: Lark brought me. I was searching his field. I thought the talents might be buried there.

SUNDOWN: I thought so. That tattler, Lark! Boil his song and roast his feathers, he never could keep a secret. So he told you where to find me.

BOBBINS: Not exactly. He sang me a song and I followed him.

SUNDOWN: Did his song go like this:

Round about Sundown every night
Far from lazy people's sight
Talents play in the deepening light?

BOBBINS: Not exactly. It was more like this:

Master Bobbins follow me

I'll guide you to the talent tree
Two leagues left and three to the right
Round about Sundown every night
Talents play in darkening light.

SUNDOWN: That rascal, Lark. He changes his words, but never his tune.

BOBBINS: It is you he meant! The talents dance around you!

SUNDOWN: Tie his beak and hang him to a sunflower! So he brought you here and flew off home.

BOBBINS (*Eagerly*): Is it true, Mr. Sundown? Do you know where the talents are?

SUNDOWN: They are buried talents. Buried deep. But I can bring them out — that is with the help of the Talent Tree.

BOBBINS: Lark mentioned the Talent Tree.

SUNDOWN: And there it is.

BOBBINS (*Looking up at it*): It's a queer looking tree.

SUNDOWN: That is because it's mostly roots and heart.

BOBBINS (*Touching the tree with his hand*): Why do you call it the Talent Tree?

SUNDOWN: It seeks out lonely talents with its roots, gives them nourishment and keeps them safe in its heart.

BOBBINS: And you can bring them out. Will you show me how, Mr. Sundown?

SUNDOWN: It all depends. Just like the weather—it all depends.

BOBBINS: Please, Mr. Sundown, depends on what? I'd do anything to find a talent.

SUNDOWN (*Sits down on rock left and takes a flute from his pocket*): Depends on what you want it for. Now what would you do with a talent?

BOBBINS: Oh, if I had a talent I'd do anything for it. I'd work for it. I'd work hard for it.

SUNDOWN: As the stars come out and the moon is bright, I believe you would. Well, then, Master Bobbins, what kind of a talent would you like?

BOBBINS: Oh, just a little one. Any one.

SUNDOWN: Buried talents are talents other people don't want, you know.

BOBBINS: That's just it. If I could have just one—the littlest one.

SUNDOWN: Talents expect to grow. You have to feed them.

BOBBINS: Feed them?

SUNDOWN: Take care of them. I can bring them out because I have something to give them.

BOBBINS: I'd do anything. I'd work for one, but I haven't much to give.

SUNDOWN: If you give all you have, no talent could ask more. Now what I've got is a kind of charm. I use it to call the talents. See this?

BOBBINS: It's a flute, isn't it?

SUNDOWN (*Caressing it*): An instrument. Do you know what music is?

BOBBINS: I've heard the lark. (SUNDOWN *imitates the song of the lark on his flute.*) That's it! That's his song!

SUNDOWN: This instrument knows all songs.

BOBBINS (*Looking up at the sky*): It's around sundown.

SUNDOWN: So it is and we can't keep talents waiting. Sit down, Master Bobbins, sit down. (*Plays a few introductory notes.*) I'll call the talents, one at a time. There's a song for each.

BOBBINS: I'm beginning to feel nervous. Suppose none of them likes me?

SUNDOWN: Spin a star and touch the moon, there's nothing to be nervous about. Talents are mighty particular, but these are lonely, too. When you see one you like just try it on. (*Begins to play.* ART *steps out from behind the Talent Tree, stretches and looks about her.*)

SUNDOWN (*Stops playing*): Here's a talent, Master Bobbins, everyone admires.

ART:

Yes, I am a talent admired by all,
But the lad I belonged to preferred football,
A sissy gift was his decree,
So deep in the earth he buried me.
(*Moves to back of stage.*)

SUNDOWN: There's a fine big talent gone to waste. (*Takes up his flute.*) This one you'll like. (*Plays.* WHISTLER, *a little fellow, comes from behind the tree, sidles up to* SUNDOWN *and stands bashfully digging the earth with his toe.*) Hi, there, young fellow. Whistle us a tune. (*To* BOBBINS) Whistler doesn't talk much. Bashful is the trouble. (WHISTLER *imitates bird calls.* SUNDOWN *tries some on his flute and they forget*

BOBBINS *in their enthusiasm.* BOBBINS *jumps up and moves toward them.)*

BOBBINS (*To* WHISTLER) : I like you. May I try you, please? (WHISTLER *nods and grins happily.* BOBBINS *braces himself, puckers out his lips and tries unsuccessfully to copy one of* WHISTLER'S *imitations.* SUNDOWN *laughs.* BOBBINS *sits down, crestfallen, and* WHISTLER, *disappointed, sits on the ground with his back against* SUNDOWN'S *rock.*)

SUNDOWN (*Giving* WHISTLER *an encouraging pat*) : Funny thing about this young fellow. Belonged to a country lad that liked him well enough until he moved to the city. Found too much else to do and buried him. Ashamed of his talent, I always maintained. Thought it gave him a countrified air and carry me off on a humming-bird's trill if there's a finer talent anywhere. Well, cheer up. We'll try another. (*Plays.* POET *with a notebook and pencil skips out, reaches out her arms, breathes in the fresh air hungrily and recites.*)

POET:

I'm a very unfortunate subject of the muse,
I was given to a girl I couldn't use,
She buried me in a musty book,
I preferred a shady nook,
Sunlight and starlight, a wide, wide sky,
A singing brook, a lazy wind's sigh,
Hills that echo a morning bird's tune,
And love in the light of a summer moon
And love in the candlelight of the moon.

(*She sits down under the tree.* SUNDOWN *plays a rollicking tune and* ACROBAT *comes tumbling out.*)

SUNDOWN: Try this one, Master Bobbins. Here's a lively talent to be buried. (ACROBAT *tries to teach* BOBBINS *some of his tricks, but he flops miserably each time.* ACROBAT *tumbles to the back of the stage and sprawls on his back stretching arms and legs joyfully.* SUNDOWN *plays and* CULINARY ART *appears.* SUNDOWN *smacks his lips. Talents watch him eagerly.*)

CULINARY ART:

Can you imagine! A talent like me
Neglected for party and social tea!
With me my mistress might have been
The very finest cook in the land,

Cakes and puddings, parfaits and russe,
Savory curries and sauce for the goose,
Sweetmeats — number them if you can —
Every delectable known to man
Perfection in every touch of her hand.
(*Sorrowfully*)
But she buried me. All I got was abuse.
For so humble a talent, she had little use.

(CULINARY ART *and* BOBBINS *exchange wistful glances.* CULINARY ART *shakes his head and takes a place at the back of the stage.*)

SUNDOWN: Ginger pie and marigold jell. That's a talent I'd like right well. (*Takes up his flute and plays.* GARDENER, *a small boy in overalls with garden tools slung across his back hops out from behind the tree on one foot, rubs the muscles of one leg, exercises it and stretches his arms as though lame from inactivity. He blinks at the light, nods unhappily to* SUNDOWN, *sees* BOBBINS *and runs to him.*) Well, carve me a window in the sky, young Master Bobbins, if Gardener hasn't found a home. Takes to you like a cricket to a kettle.

GARDENER: So you've come for me, Bobbins. I thought you never would.

SUNDOWN: Quarter past blue and ten tonight. It's your own talent, young sir, and buried deepest of any of them.

BOBBINS (*Excitedly*): Are you sure, Mr. Sundown? I don't believe I had a talent.

GARDENER: I'm yours all right if you'll put me to work. We're supposed to be the makings of a great naturalist, Bobbins. While you've been idling under the trees we might have been making gardens grow.

BOBBINS: May I take him home, Mr. Sundown? May I take him home?

SUNDOWN: Ho, you like him, do you?

BOBBINS: Oh, yes. Yes, indeed. He's just the one. Why, he's the best talent of all.

SUNDOWN: Well, build me a house of honey and rice. It's a farmer you're going to be now. Then here's a tune to carry you home. (*Plays a few bars.*) Just blink your eyes and you'll be there. (*Plays while curtain closes.*)

THE END

A CHINESE RIP VAN WINKLE

by Anna Curtis Chandler

Characters

CHORUS
CHOW WAN, *wife of* WANG CHIH
WANG CHIH, *laborer in the rice fields*
HO-SEEN-KO } *children of* CHOW WAN
HAN CHUNG } *and* WANG CHIH
PROPERTY MAN
THREE OLD MEN OF THE MOUNTAINS
WHITE CRANE
DRAGON
OLD WOMAN
OTHER VILLAGERS *in procession*
MUSICIANS

SETTING: *Village in China. Open space surrounded by houses and rice fields.*

AT RISE: MUSICIANS, *seated on platform, holding cymbals. Throughout play, cymbals are struck three times whenever name of Emperor, "Son of Heaven," Honorable Ancestors, and Celestial China are mentioned. Enter* CHORUS. *He walks to center, downstage, bows right, left and center, with dignity.*

CHORUS (*Ceremoniously*): Most Honorable Friends, I am about to tell you a story of the Celestial Land of China, dealing with family life, with strange old men of the mountains, with a terrible Dragon, and a kindly Being who dwells in the moon and reaches out his hand to aid the sufferers on the earth. Listen well with your ears, pretend well with the eyes of your imagination, and you will find yourselves in the Celestial Land of China in the time of our Honorable Ancestors. My Property Man, invisible to your eyes, will assist you. Chow Wan, the gentle wife of our hero, Wang Chih, now appears before you. (*Bows three times, sits center.*)

CHOW WAN (*Enters shyly, from right, followed closely by* HO-SEEN-KO *and* HAN CHUNG) : Gentle listeners, here in this humble one-roomed thatched cottage, I live in happiness as the honorable wife of Wang Chih, a poor laborer but good, with love in his heart for his wife and children. All day long he works in the fields, but although he labors with his hands there is music in his heart for at night he returns to me, Chow Wan, to his beautiful little daughter Ho-Seen-Ko, and to his beloved son, Han Chung. Even tonight the lanterns will rival the very stars in brightness for it is the Festival of the Lanterns. I fly within to arrange bamboo shoots and rice-cakes as a special treat for my honorable master. (PROPERTY MAN *enters right, raises arms to indicate door of house.* CHOW WAN *pantomimes stepping over sill.*)

CHORUS (*Rising*) : Our hero, Wang Chih, appears. (*Sits*)

HO-SEEN-KO (*Bowing low to her father*) : Our Honored Father hastens to the rice fields. Come back early tonight, oh my Honored Father, to light my lantern of crimson, bright as the flowers that sway beneath our humble windows. (PROPERTY MAN *hands her a lantern, and gives one to* HAN CHUNG, *then saunters across stage.*)

HAN CHUNG: My lantern awaits you too, Honored Father, a bright one of many colors.

WANG CHIH: My little Golden Flower, Ho-Seen-Ko, and my pretty boy, Han Chung, I shall fly from the rice fields at the close of day to make your lanterns shine. I hasten now that I may return the earlier. (PROPERTY MAN *gives him a basket and axe*) My little flowers, my treasures, I will return just as early as I can, so that, when the moonbeams send their yellow light, and the stars gleam, we shall be able to join in the Procession of the Lanterns like so many fire-flies. (*Exits left.*)

CHORUS (*Rising*) : Wang Chih now goes to the fields to work, while other laborers come in with baskets handed them by our Property Man. They work in the rice fields. (*Sits.*)

WANG CHIH (*Enters, walks back and forth, basket on arm, and axe over his shoulder*) : Weary I am with my work in the fields — and faint from lack of food, so I will take a little rest on the mountain side, playing hide and seek with the rays of the Sun. On my way, I will seek a tree to cut down with my axe, to make warmth and cheer tonight at the Feast of the Lanterns for my little Cherry Blossom. (PROPERTY MAN, *moving indolently, puts chair against table to represent mountain.*)

CHORUS (*Rises, speaking in most dignified manner, wielding Chinese fan*): The honorable Wang Chih now goes up the mountain side and peers into a deep cave in the mountains, where sit the old men of the mountains with their long white hair and beards. (PROPERTY MAN *arranges cave under table, and* OLD MEN OF THE MOUNTAINS *enter.* PROPERTY MAN *hands* OLD MEN *sweetmeats, and slowly and indifferently unravels beards.*)

WANG CHIH (*Surprised; as he bends down and peers into "cave"*): Who can these venerable strangers be and what can they be eating? It makes my hunger more terrible to bear.

OLD MAN (*Winks at his companion, chuckles and speaks in quavering voice*): Help yourself, young man! These are delicious sweetmeats.

WANG CHIH (*Hesitating*): Just one of those sweetmeats which the venerable men are eating, surely cannot hurt me. (*Takes one from* PROPERTY MAN. PROPERTY MAN *then puts hump on* WANG CHIH'S *back, powders his hair, and* WANG CHIH *stoops over. He rubs his stomach.*) Oh! How delicious it is! Like nothing which has passed my lips before, and it has taken my thirst away! (OLD MEN *laugh and wink at one another as they continue eating sweetmeats.* PROPERTY MAN *unravels their white beards and sticks or ties one on* WANG CHIH.)

CHORUS (*Rising*): Wang Chih has eaten of the magic sweetmeats and has become old — burdened by many years. (*Sits.*)

WANG CHIH (*Peering at* OLD MEN *and noticing how long their beards have grown*): Those long white beards, the signs of old age, must be very troublesome when they grow so quickly. Their years fall from them like the swiftly falling petals of a cherry tree when the branch is shaken!

OLD MAN (*Winking at companions and laughing*): Your wits are dulled by hard toil, stranger! Our beards have not grown quickly. How long do you think you have been here on the mountain side?

WANG CHIH (*Sadly*): Long enough to make me late in getting home to my little Cherry Blossoms in order to light their lanterns, I daresay.

OLD MEN (*Laughing and pointing to sweetmeats, speak together in old quavering voices*): An hour, a day, a week, a month, a year — aye, a century of years are the same to him who tastes of these magic sweetmeats. Go down into your village and look well with your eyes! (WANG CHIH *picks up axe, which crumbles; hobbles down chair.* OLD MEN *stay in place; play game and eat sweetmeats.*)

CHORUS (*Standing in center*): Wang Chih, now grown old, goes down into his village calling sadly to his wife and children.

WANG CHIH (*Sadly, holding out his arms as he walks back and forth*): My glorious Chow Wan, and my little Treasures, Ho-Seen-Ko and Han Chung!

CHORUS (*Solemnly*): Wang Chih now reaches his village and finds that all is changed. 'Tis the time when day meets night with a flash of colors across the sky. The fireflies will soon be gleaming like rare starflowers. The august Wang Chih sees no familiar face for all is changed, and many new thatched cottages are builded. (*He sits. People enter from right and move to and fro, looking at* WANG CHIH *without recognition.* PROPERTY MAN *makes his beard grow longer, as he grows more bent, and trembles. He approaches bent old woman.* MUSICIANS *strike gongs three times.*)

WANG CHIH: Most Honorable Mother, may the Celestial Gods rain blessings upon your path. Will you, perchance, unfold the mystery which clouds my mind and tell me of the family of Wang Chih, the laborer in the rice fields?

OLD WOMAN (*Holds up hands in astonishment, speaks in trembling voice*): Wang Chih? Venerable Father, Wang Chih and his humble family have been gone for many years; they are but shadows of the past. They are among our Ancestors. Tonight, when the moonbeams send forth their yellow rays, the Festival of the Lanterns will be held. Watch well the figures who come last in the procession, for you will find a woman dressed to represent Chow Wan, wife of Wang Chih, carrying a rice bowl; and two children dressed to represent his little ones whom he left so long ago on the morning of the Feast of the Lanterns. He was spirited away by the Old Men of the Mountains. As each year passes we do this to teach our children to be kind to the poor and the fatherless. (WANG CHIH *stands there sadly,* OLD WOMAN *and rest of procession exit left.*)

CHORUS (*Rising*): The sky darkens, the stars peer through, and the fireflies, star flowers all, flit here and there hunting for the

Emperor. For each firefly is the tear of a beautiful moon-princess, shed when she was drawn back to the moon and compelled to leave the Emperor and his love. 'Tis the flowery and sparkling way of a perfect evening. The perfume of fragrant flowers fills the air! The Festival of the Lanterns begins! (*Enter procession, with figures of* CHOW WAN, HAN CHUNG *and* HO-SEEN-KO *at end.* WANG CHIH *looks at them sadly, and they look at him with curiosity.*) Wang Chih with sorrow-heavy feet goes back to the mountain. A storm breaks, the wind shakes the branches of the swaying trees, and the rain bathes the earth. (PROPERTY MAN *whistles for wind, sprinkles water from bottle.*) But just as the Celestial Sun changes the mountain top into gold, Wang Chih once more reaches the cave of the Old Men of the Mountains. (*He sits.* PROPERTY MAN *holds up gold paper ball, representing sun, over table.* OLD MEN *enter and sit in cave, eating sweetmeats, and* PROPERTY MAN *unravels their beards again. When they see* WANG CHIH, *they laugh in high cackles.*)

WANG CHIH (*Stretching out his arms pleadingly*): Oh, give me back my lost years, my beautiful wife, and my precious children, August Spirits of the mountains! (OLD MEN *laugh again.*)

ONE OLD MAN (*Chuckling*): You must journey on the White Crane's back to the Sky Dragon! Get some water from his cavernous mouth and take it to the White Hare of the Moon, who will mix it with the Elixir of Life. Then you will lose the burden of your years and may return to your humble family. Here is a bottle to catch the water from the Sky Dragon's mouth. Now be gone and interrupt our game no more! (PROPERTY MAN *hands bottle to* WANG CHIH.)

WANG CHIH: Oh, Venerable and August Fathers, where shall I find the Sky Dragon and the White Hare of the Moon?

OLD MAN (*Impatiently*): The White Hare dwells in the Moon and the Sky Dragon in the Sky, of course, stupid fellow! Now leave us in peace to our sweetmeats and our game. (PROPERTY MAN *hands* WANG CHIH *a stick and feather for the* WHITE CRANE. WANG CHIH *mounts it and pantomimes galloping or jumping out.*)

CHORUS (*Rising*): Wang Chih now flies to the Sky Dragon, the honorable monster who keeps the sky from caving in. He approaches the Sky Dragon's cave made of sky rock and surrounded by dried grass. (PROPERTY MAN *removes* WHITE CRANE.

WANG CHIH *stands in listening attitude.*) The Sky Dragon bellows, and also sends forth flames of fire instead of water. (*He sits. Red and white tissue paper is "blown" from* SKY DRAGON'S *mouth; bellowing is heard.* MUSICIANS *strike gongs.* WANG CHIH *draws back, then bends down and fans grass.* MUSICIANS *strike gongs three times.*)

WANG CHIH: Oh, my Honorable Ancestors! How terrible is the August Dragon! How long are his horns! His eyes gleam like fire, claws he has, and glittering scales, while from his mouth, wide as a yawning chasm, long teeth protrude. I will fan into flame some of these sparks of fire to see whether he will not quench them with water.

SKY DRAGON (*Bellows*): O-ho — Wang Chih — I can soon put a stop to that! (SKY DRAGON *breathes "water."* PROPERTY MAN *sprinkles water and* WANG CHIH *catches it in bottle.* PROPERTY MAN *hands* WANG CHIH *the* WHITE CRANE.)

WANG CHIH: Swift as the flight of the soaring gull I must go, else the waters surround me. The Earth People are enjoying a gentle rainfall, causing the thirsty flowers and bamboos to grow.

CHORUS (*Rising*): Wang Chih now flies to the moon. (PROPERTY MAN *holds up gilt moon, and* WHITE HARE *stands on stepladder in front of it.* PROPERTY MAN *gives him a dish and a stick.*) There dwells the White Hare, a kind and generous and most honorable being. Look well and see his white, soft fur, and brown, kind eyes. He lives thousands of years, and is ever busy mixing the Elixir of Life which will make all who drink it live forever in happiness. Wang Chih arrives in the moon! (PROPERTY MAN *removes* WHITE CRANE, *which* WANG CHIH *has been holding between his legs.* CHORUS *sits.*)

WANG CHIH (*Looking up at* WHITE HARE): Oh Gentle and Celestial Hare of the Moon, here in this glistening bottle is some water from the yawning mouth of the Celestial Sky Dragon. I pray you to mix it with the Elixir of Life, that I may have back my treasures — my cherished wife and children. Swiftly have the years fallen from me since I ate one of the sweetmeats of the Venerable Men of the Mountain, and I would get back my lost years, oh White Hare of the Moon! (PROPERTY MAN *holds arms to make a window.*)

WHITE HARE (*Leading* WANG CHIH *to window*): Look through this window, Wang Chih, Honorable Mortal from the Earth, and tell me what your eyes behold.

WANG CHIH (*Looks through window and sees people moving to and fro with lanterns*): Oh White Hare of the Moon! I see thatched houses, many in number, men, women and children! It is the time of shadows, and gay lanterns flit this way and that! Oh White Hare of the Moon, it is the very village which has taken the place of the old one where I dwelt many years ago in happiness with my wife and children! What does it all mean to be up here in the golden moon, and yet be able to look down upon the earth?

WHITE HARE: That is my secret, Wang Chih, Honorable Mortal from the Earth. Many are the secrets known to me, but hidden from mortals. (PROPERTY MAN *makes another window with his arms.*) Now look through this window and tell me what you see! It is the window of the past.

WANG CHIH (*Gazing through window — cries joyfully*): I see my own little house — and there is my beautiful wife getting ready rice cakes and bamboo shoots as a special treat. My little flower, Ho-Seen-Ko, comes with her lantern, and my treasure, Han Chung, with his! Oh King Hare of the Moon, pray let me go to them! Will you not help me? (PROPERTY MAN *hands bottle to* WHITE HARE *who mixes contents with Elixir of Life, and gives it back to* PROPERTY MAN, *who hands it to* WANG CHIH.)

WHITE HARE: Drink each one of these crystal drops, Wang Chih, and think of your wife and children. So will you have the power to live in the past. (WANG CHIH *drinks.* PROPERTY MAN *makes window larger and larger.*)

CHORUS (*Rising*): The window grows larger, and steps lead to the street below.

WANG CHIH (*Bowing before* HARE): White Hare of the Moon, may your August Presence ever cause the moon to shine, and the hearts of mortals to rejoice! I thank you for my lost years. (PROPERTY MAN *takes away his hump, and* WANG CHIH *straightens up. He steps through window made by* PROPERTY MAN'S *arms, runs to meet* CHOW WAN, HO-SEEN-KO *and* HAN CHUNG, *who enter right. He clasps* HO-SEEN-KO *to him.*)

CHORUS: Wang Chih, our hero, once more young, returns to his wife and his children, wiser in many things, and little Ho-Seen-Ko wonders why he clasps her to him. (*He sits.*)

HO-SEEN-KO (*Holding up lantern which* PROPERTY MAN *gives*

her) : You are late, oh Honorable Father! Do hurry to light our lanterns for us!

HAN CHUNG: The Feast of the Lanterns soon begins, oh Father! (PROPERTY MAN *hands* WANG CHIH *a match to light candles. People with lanterns enter right. Then procession moves* — WANG CHIH, CHOW WAN, HAN CHUNG, HO-SEEN-KO, *and others, with lanterns of many colors. They march about stage in line.*)

CHORUS (*Rising*) : Wang Chih, with his garden of flowers, his beautiful wife and his little plum blossoms, now joins the procession of the Feast of the Lanterns, and they dance to and fro in the little village like so many fireflies. (MUSICIANS *play.*) Most August and Honorable Friends, you may applaud my actors as I call them before you. In turn they will thank you. Take care that you do not applaud them too much for it will embarrass them. I am accustomed to praise and it will not disturb me. (*Each actor bows, Chinese fashion, as his name is called.*) Chow Wan — the honorable wife and devoted mother. My hero, Wang Chih. The little Plum Blossoms, Ho-Seen-Ko and Hang Chung. The Spirits of the Mountains, the Venerable Men. The Venerable Mother. The White Hare of the Moon, who helps all mortals. (PROPERTY MAN *holds moon over* HARE'S *head.*) The Celestial Sky Dragon. (DRAGON *roars.*) Laborers of the fields. And now, quite visible to your eyes, our Property Man. (PROPERTY MAN, *bowing, shakes hands with* CHORUS, *bows to audience and goes out. All bow again.* MUSICIANS *strike cymbals three times.*)

THE END

GREY GHOSTS

by Dorothy Deming

Characters

LEWIS GREENE, 17
ALICE GREENE, 15
JOHN GREENE, 12
DAVID FISK, *young Fire Warden*
MR. and MRS. GREENE (*Offstage voices*)

SCENE 1

SETTING: *A camp in the Maine woods. A glowing campfire in center stage. It is evening.*

AT RISE: LEWIS, ALICE *and* JOHN *are sitting on the ground around the campfire, toasting marshmallows.*

LEWIS: I like to get my marshmallow almost black, then slip off the toasted coat and cook the inside again—makes it last longer.

JOHN: No, that's not the way I like them. I toast them just a teeny bit, then eat all at once. (*He suits the action to the word, putting a whole marshmallow in his mouth at once.*)

ALICE: I like marshmallows all ways, even raw! (*Takes one directly from box and eats it.*)

JOHN: Gee! I wish this wasn't our last night camping! It's been wonderful. The best vacation ever!

ALICE: But we've got all tomorrow, John, and tomorrow's Mount Franklin, the highest mountain we have climbed.

LEWIS: Guess we will be plenty stiff when we climb back into the old car tomorrow night!

ALICE: Oh, I don't know. We are in pretty good condition after three weeks in the woods. Let me have that marshmallow, John, it's just the way I like it. (*She reaches for the marshmallow* JOHN *is toasting.*)

JOHN (*Letting her have it grudgingly*): Thought you liked them *any* way! Thought you —

MR. GREENE (*From offstage*): Children, children! Time for bed. Put away the marshmallows where the ants can't get them and cover the campfire well. We will want the hot coals for cooking breakfast.

LEWIS (*Calling*): Can I go swimming once more before turning in? The lake's not cold.

MRS. GREENE (*Offstage*): No, dear. We will all go for a dip before breakfast tomorrow morning. Better get to bed now. Father says you've got a hard climb ahead of you, that is, if you want to go all the way to the top of Mount Franklin.

JOHN: You bet we do!

ALICE: Of course; there's a wonderful view they say!

LEWIS: All the way to the fire lookout!

ALICE: Are you and Dad going to the top?

MR. GREENE (*Offstage*): Mother is going to the halfway house, but I'll go to the summit with you.

LEWIS: Swell!

JOHN: Oh, gee, wonderful! (ALICE *closes the marshmallow box and tucks it into a duffle bag.* JOHN *goes over to his bathing suit and takes it off the line.* LEWIS *covers the campfire, pretending to pull grass over it, at the same time the light under the fire goes out, leaving the stage quite dim.*)

JOHN: Got the fire fixed O.K., Lew?

LEWIS: Yes, it will be all right now.

ALICE: Better pull that fresh wood out of the way so it won't catch. (LEWIS *pulls wood to one side.*)

JOHN: Well, good night ol' campin' ground! Wish I could stay here at Beaver Lake all summer.

LEWIS: So do I! Gosh, how still it is! Look, the sky is full of stars! (*They all stand very still, looking up at the sky.*)

ALICE (*Softly*): The trees make a lovely pattern of lace against the stars and how sweet the pine needles smell!

JOHN: I love pine trees! I wish I had some in my little ol' hot bedroom in the city!

LEWIS: Tall trees make the air lots cooler, Dad says, besides being useful for making things.

JOHN: What things, for instance?

LEWIS: Millions of things, stupid. Houses, barns, boats, furniture, telephone poles and —

ALICE (*Interrupting*): Charley McCarthy! Let's go to bed. I'm sleepy.

LEWIS: So'm I. Come on, John.

JOHN (*Taking another long look at the sky and sniffing the breeze*): Coming. (*The two boys exit left,* ALICE *right.*)

ALICE: Good night!

LEWIS and JOHN: Good night, Sis.

CURTAIN

* * *

SCENE 2

SETTING: *A fire warden's lookout station.*

TIME: *Early afternoon.*

AT RISE: DAVID FISK *is sitting at the table, charting. A pair of binoculars is beside him. He uses the glasses, glances at the clock, writes something on his chart, then sits back lazily, looking out of the window, singing or humming: "Don't Fence Me In." There is a sound of thumping as though someone were climbing stairs.* DAVE *stops singing and looks toward the only door in the room.* ALICE'S *voice is heard offstage, panting.*)

ALICE: Wait for me, boys! I'm getting all out of breath.

JOHN (*Offstage*): Forty-eight, forty-nine, fifty! Fifty steps up! Gee! Tell Dad not to come. He said he was getting tired.

ALICE (*Still offstage, but nearer, calling*): Dad, stay down. It's a long flight of stairs—fifty of them.

MR. GREENE (*Off*): Right! I'll stay here. The view is fine enough for me. (*There is more clattering on stairs.* DAVE *closes his chart and straightens the other papers on his table.*)

JOHN (*Bursting in on* DAVE, *panting*): Hello! Gee! (*He gazes breathless out of the window as though at a far-distant view.*)

LEWIS (*Entering not quite so out of breath, but breathing heav-

ily): Whew! Some climb. (*He stops short, barely noticing* DAVE, *his eyes sweeping the horizon.*) Gosh all hemlock! What a view!

ALICE (*Entering wiping her face and very much out of breath, Falls into first chair she comes to, fans her face with her handkerchief*): Whee—I'm no mountain goat. (*She, too, gazes speechless at the view, then after a pause, less breathlessly*) You wouldn't have any water to drink up here, would you? (*Smiling at* DAVE.)

DAVE (*Takes canteen from shelf, and pours out a cup of water for* ALICE. *Hands it to her smiling*): Best spring water in the State o' Maine! (*To the boys*) Help yourselves.

ALICE (*Drinking slowly and smiling up at* DAVE): Thanks! How I needed that! What an utterly super view you have here! (*Stares again out of the window.*)

LEWIS (*Still gazing out*): Gosh all hemlock, I never saw so much forest!

DAVE: Some hemlock, sure, but a lot of spruce, pine, balsam and juniper! Not to mention oak, maple, birch, beech and hazel nut. By the way, won't you sign my guest book? (*He looks at* ALICE *as he says this and hands her the guest book and pencil.* ALICE *takes them. Moves up to table.*)

ALICE: I'll sign for all of us.

JOHN: May I use your binoculars?

DAVE: Sure. Know how to adjust them?

JOHN (*With the glasses at his eyes, looking off over audience*): Yep.

LEWIS: This is my sister, Alice Greene, that's John and I'm Lewis. What's your name?

DAVE: David Fisk. Call me Dave.

LEWIS: Glad to meet you, Dave.

ALICE (*Finishing signing the guest book, turns and smiles at* DAVE): There! We are all recorded in your book. Are you the fire warden for this county?

DAVE: That's me! Fire Warden number 242, sector B56. I look after about thirty square miles of one county and an even larger area of a second county, including some dozen towns, a hundred farms and some summer camps over in the lake region. (*He points off in the distance. The others follow his gesture, as though seeking lakes in that direction.*)

JOHN: What do you do all day? Read?

DAVE: No, only when the weather gets so thick I can't see but a few yards around me! I live in the log cabin you passed on the way up here, but I'm on duty up here during the daylight hours. I spot fires and telephone their location to the town nearest the smoke.

LEWIS: Do you go to the fires yourself?

DAVE: No, my job is to get the fire fighters there as fast as possible and keep on the lookout for more fires!

JOHN: Spot a fire for us now!

ALICE (*Sarcastically*): Yes, Dave, please produce a fire on order! (*She and* DAVE *smile at each other.*)

DAVE (*Takes the binoculars and sweeps the horizon in a full circle.*) Nope, no luck. That's luck, because the long stretch of dry weather and the summer campers and hikers are a bad combination. (*He looks again in the lake region. Concentrates on one spot and adjusts the glasses*) Wait — wait a moment — I guess I've found a fire for you, John! (*He hands the glasses to* ALICE) See if you see smoke at the end of the ravine — see? Follow the ridge of this mountain down till you see a little white farm house, then look left over the brown field, in that patch of woods near the lake. See a —

ALICE (*Breaking in excitedly*): Yes! Yes, I see a thin smudge of bluish white smoke! Look, Lewis. (*Hands the glasses to* LEWIS.)

LEWIS: Yes, I see it, too!

JOHN: Let me look! (*Looks. Very excited*) So do I! Oh boy! What do we do now?

DAVE: That's right in the heart of the woods on Beaver Lake, a favorite camping place for motorists. (*He takes the glasses from* JOHN *and looks again, talking as he focuses*) Of course, it might be a campfire being used to get lunch, but it's a little late for that and the smoke is too scattered. We can soon tell. (*He puts down the glasses and goes to the wall map, the children crowd around him.*) See this map? It shows that section in detail. That smoke is about here. (*Indicates a spot on the map.*) It's easy to locate this fire, because it's bounded by those woods and we are getting a clear view; it's when it is back of the hills that it's hard. Now let's see—(*He takes the glasses again.*) Yes, that's fire, all right. I'll have to call Carpenter. (*He steps to the back of the stage to telephone.*)

Alice (*Moving to front of stage and motioning to* Lewis. *In a low voice*): Lew, isn't that just about the place where we were camped last night—on the edge of Beaver Lake?

Lewis (*Looking uncomfortable, nods*): I was thinking the same thing.

John (*Taking the glasses*): Yep, that's fire all right. Smoke's growing thicker. (Dave *comes back to the table.*)

Lewis: Dave, we camped at Beaver Lake last night and had a campfire. We used it again this morning at breakfast, but we—

Dave (*Interrupting, sternly*): Did you soak it down well with water this morning before you broke camp?

Alice (*Miserably*): I'm afraid we didn't. We stamped out the flames and threw on dirt and —

John (*Breaking in*): I kicked the logs off and stepped on every little ol' spark. They were out all right.

Lewis: Honestly, I think the fire was out, Dave.

Dave: Thinking isn't enough. You've got to be sure. (*Turning to* Alice) Where did you build your fire?

Alice: In a clearing in the pine woods at the end of the lake. There were no trees very near it.

Dave (*Sighing*): There ought to be a law — ! Now look, you three, I suppose you weren't taught anything in school about caring for campfires?

Alice: No, never.

John (*Earnestly*) I know how to build a good fire; you take little dry sticks and dry leaves first, then bigger sticks and —

Dave (*Cutting in and motioning toward the direction of the fire*): Yes, John, you *build* good fires, but just look —! (*All turn to look.*)

Alice: Oh, mercy! Look at that smoke! It's spreading fast!

Lewis: It's heading toward that little farmhouse!

Dave (*Very soberly*): Yes, the wind is in that direction.

John (*With glasses, cries out*): I can see cows in that field near the farm. Will they be burned?

Dave: Maybe, but I don't think so. My map shows a good-size brook, which may still have a little water in it, on the edge of the farmland, and the fire fighters ought to get there before the flames make much more headway. I'd telephone the farm but they have no phone.

Lewis: How do you know?

DAVE (*Smiling*): It's part of my business to know. I also know the nearest telephone to that farmhouse is in the valley, fellow by the name of Morse. But look, you campers, never build a fire on dry pine needles, dry leaves or grass. The fire will eat down into and around the dry material and after smoldering for hours burst into flame. Try to build on wet cleared ground, good old dirt, sand or best of all, rock. In dry weather build near a brook or lake where you can get the ground well soaked with water and never leave a fire without drenching it with pails of water until you are sure every spark is out and the ground around the fire soaking.

JOHN: Kicking it apart was not enough?

DAVE: Not by a long shot! You may have kicked logs with live sparks in them right into the tinder-dry pine needles. Gang, I'm afraid that fire is your fault. (*The three gaze ruefully at the fire.* DAVE *is using the glasses.*)

ALICE: I think the smoke is a little thinner.

DAVE: So do I, and besides, there comes the truck! Can you see that cloud of dust with a little black speck in it? That's the Carpenter truck with the fire fighters in it. (*Focuses the glasses*) Yes, there they go. Quite a load of them. They will have the fire out in no time.

LEWIS (*Giving a long sign of relief*): Gee, I'm glad!

JOHN: I'll never leave another fire without drowning it!

LEWIS: That goes for us all, Dave.

DAVE (*Seriously*): It might have been a costly lesson — the forest, the camps, the farm and its stock, possibly loss of human life. Forest fires destroy millions of feet of lumber, and take homes and lives every year just through the carelessness of people enjoying the woods.

ALICE: To say nothing of the birds and wild flowers and the scent of the pines!

DAVE: Right! Do you know that verse about forest fires? I always think of it when I see the poor naked trees and barren fields left by forest fires — all too often the result of pure thoughtlessness. (*He repeats slowly*)

"The careless smoker on an idle trail,
A smouldering campfire and a vagrant breeze,
Make all your ancient pride of what avail,
You tall grey ghosts which once were stately trees!"*

LEWIS: "Stately trees!" Remember them last night, Alice? With the stars shining through their branches.

JOHN: Don't! I can't stand it. It was my fault. (*He looks as if he wants to cry.*)

ALICE (*Softly to* DAVE): I guess you can see we three will not be "careless campers" ever again!

MR. GREENE (*From a distance*): Alice, John, Lewis! Time to go down the mountain. We must start home.

LEWIS (*Glances at the clock.*) Golly, look at the time! (*Calling*) We're coming, Dad! Good-bye, Dave, thanks. If you ever come to New York, look us up.

ALICE: I put our address in your book.

DAVE (*Laughing*): I'd have to be met at the station. I couldn't find my way around that city even with a compass.

JOHN (*Scornfully*): Ho! That's nothing. You wouldn't need a compass. I'll show you.

DAVE: Thanks, maybe I'll come some day.

ALICE: I really wish you would, Dave. Good-bye and good luck. (*Puts out her hand.*)

DAVE (*Taking her hand*): Good-bye, Alice.

JOHN: So long! (*Exits, clattering down the steps.* ALICE *follows, waving.* LEWIS *starts out, then sticks his head back in the door.*)

LEWIS: Dave, if you ever need anyone to help you up here, I'd — well, I'd like the chance. It would be one way to make up for setting the woods on fire.

DAVE: Great stuff! Maybe I'll need you next summer. I'll remember, Lew!

LEWIS (*Beaming*): You will? Gosh all hemlock, wait till I tell Dad I'm working next summer! (*He disappears, clattering on the steps.*) 'Bye.

DAVE (*Smiling*): 'Bye. (*He sits down at his table, makes a note and takes up the binoculars, starting the slow sweep of the horizon.*)

THE END

***These lines were printed on the menu of the Banff Springs Hotel, Canada, Canadian-Pacific Railway. No author given.**

OLD MAN RIVER

by Dorothy Deming

Characters

AMY MARSHALL, *17 years old*
BETTY MARSHALL, *her younger sister*
ROSE FIELD, *16 years old, the Marshall's neighbor*
SARA FIELD, *9 years old, Rose's sister*
JIM HALL, *17 years old, another neighbor*
MR. PETERS, *member of Red Cross Disaster Committee*
PENNY MARSH, *Red Cross nurse*

SCENE 1

TIME: *Late afternoon in March.*

SETTING: *Living room of the Marshall home.*

AT RISE: AMY, BETTY *and* ROSE *are sitting around the living room table.* AMY *and* ROSE *are knitting,* BETTY *is looking at pictures in a magazine. The stage is not very light.*

ROSE: Goodness, it gets dark early on these rainy days. Mind if I raise the shade a bit, Amy?

AMY: No, do, but I guess we need the light on, too. (*She goes over and puts on the electric light.*)

ROSE (*Going to the window*): How it rains! In sheets, and look! Your backyard is a small lake.

AMY (*Joining* ROSE *at the window*): Gracious! I've never seen it rain so hard and this is the third day of it.

BETTY (*Puts down magazine and runs to window*): Whee — ee! It's more than a lake, it's a sea! The radio said the river was above flood stage this morning — whatever that means.

AMY: It means that the water is above that white line on the bank at Thompson Bridge. It must have covered the south meadows and the highway there.

ROSE: It isn't only the rain. It's the snow melting in the hills in the northern part of the state. (*The girls return to the table*) Oh, I hope we don't have a flood *here!* (*There is a noise of stamping feet and someone breathing hard. The girls all look to the right, the direction of the sounds.*)

JIM HALL (*Entering from right, in shining wet rain coat and rain helmet, which he drags off as he enters. He is panting*): Gosh, girls, it's a cloudburst! (*He kicks off his rubbers.*) I've run every step of the way from school to get here. The river is rising fast. The Burnett Dam gave 'way an hour ago they say and it looks bad! Where is your mother, Amy?

AMY: She took Dick to the dentist's and was going to stop at Mrs. Brant's for a recipe on her way home. She ought to be here soon.

JIM: And your father?

AMY: In Chicago on business, but why all the questions, Jim?

JIM: Well, er — you see — (*He is interrupted by the ring of the telephone.* AMY *exits left to answer it. Her voice can be heard clearly.*)

AMY: Hello. Yes, yes, Mother — I know, isn't it awful? How will you get home? — Yes, Mother, I'm listening carefully. (AMY's *voice grows very serious*) Yes — yes — yes, I will. — No, Mother, — no, I won't. Jim Hall is here and Rose Field. Yes, all right, I'll tell them. Goodbye. (AMY *returns to the room. She is looking very scared.*) Mother can't get home from Mrs. Brant's. The bridges between here and town are under water. Rose, Mother says you are to telephone your mother right away and tell her you will spend the night here.

ROSE: I will. That will be fun! (*Hurries from room.*)

AMY: Betty, you and I are to fill all the bowls, tubs, pails and pitchers with fresh water in case the town supply is cut off or made unsafe to drink. Mother says she hopes you will stay and help us, Jim. We girls will need a man's hand, now.

JIM: That's just why I came, Amy. I think I'll look up a lantern and —

BETTY (*Interrupting*): I've got a flashlight. I'll get it and some candles.

ROSE (*From outside, still at the telephone, with irritation*): Central! Central! I'm trying to get Main 3022 — I can't — (*There is a pause and* ROSE *comes to the door, her face frightened.*)

The telephone is dead! I can't get Central. There isn't even a buzzing on the line!

JIM: Means the lines are down between here and town! Well, girls, let's get organized! Betty, look up your flashlight and candles, lamps, lanterns or anything you've got. Rose, fill the tubs and pails and Amy and I will check on food, blankets and coats. Better get out the first-aid kit. Everyone make it snappy! (ROSE *and* BETTY *exit left.* JIM *turns to* AMY) This is serious, Amy. I don't want to scare you, but your house is in the direct line of the river. If the dam *has* given 'way — (*He goes to the window*) Well, if it has, you can see for yourself it means we can't get out by the main road and we are already cut off from the south side. Look! (*He points out of the window.* AMY *joins him. She gasps.*)

AMY: Jim! The water is up around the garage! I thought it was just a pool in the garden, but it's — it's —

JIM (*Soberly*): The river. Yes, Amy, that's ol' man river himself "creepin' up to yo' door." (JIM *and* AMY *watch it a moment.* AMY *shudders.*)

AMY: Oh, Jim, I'm scared!

JIM (*Placing a hand on her shoulder*): Steady, old pal! We've been through bad things before and come out safely. Remember the school fire? First thing, we must not let the others see how scared we are. Next, get all the things you can together here: water, food, blankets, coats, lights. I'm glad I served on the Junior Red Cross emergency squad during the war! It's too bad you live in a bungalow instead of a two-story house, but we can always climb into the attic and onto the roof.

AMY (*Still staring out the window*): How fast is the river rising, do you think, Jim?

JIM: I don't know and it might stop before it reaches us. If only the rain would let up! We will signal for help from the roof. They will send a boat or something.

ROSE (*Entering left*): I've got enough fresh water to last us a week! Who will send a boat for us, Jim, and from where? (*She goes to the window, screams*) Horrors! Look at the river!

AMY: Hush, Rose. Don't tell the others. Jim says we will be all right. Let's see what food we have on hand.

BETTY (*Entering left*): Here are lights. Did you say food? Hark, what's that? (*All four stand perfectly still, listening. From far off a child's voice is heard.*)

SARA: RO — ose! It's me! Sara!

ROSE: Sara! Where is she? (*All run to the window.*)

AMY: There she is! On the playhouse porch. How did she get there?

ROSE: Followed me here, probably; she loves that playhouse, the little monkey!

JIM (*Goes out right, calling*): Stay where you are, Sara, I'll get you.

AMY: It's lucky the playhouse is on high ground.

ROSE (*Still at window*): But it isn't. Look, it's nearly afloat! (*The girls gather at the window.*) There goes Jim! Look, the water is above his knees.

AMY: He will need dry clothes. See if you can find some of Dad's things for Jim, Betty. Sara can have Dick's.

ROSE: There! He's got her!

AMY: I'll make some hot cocoa for everyone. (*There is a thumping and voices at the right and* JIM *enters carrying* SARA *pickaback.* SARA *is beaming.*)

SARA: Hello, everybody! That was fun! Ride some more, please. Jim!

JIM: No, young lady, that's enough. You're heavy. She is dry as a bone, Rose. I'm not!

AMY: You can have some of Dad's things. I'm going to get us some supper — (*As she says this, the lights go out. They all gasp and* BETTY *screams.*)

JIM (*Trying to sound casual*): Power house must be out of commission. Light your candles, Betty. (BETTY *puts on flashlight. Lights three candles.*)

AMY: I'm glad we have an oil stove for cooking.

ROSE (*Taking a candle*): Forward march to the kitchen! (BETTY *takes a candle and follows, with* SARA *trailing, all exit right, humming "Tramp, tramp, tramp the boys are marching."*)

JIM (*In a low voice to* AMY): The river was up another foot, Amy. Another hour and that playhouse would have been floating out in the current. At this rate the floor here will be under water by morning.

AMY: What will we do then, Jim? Neither Sara nor Betty are strong swimmers.

JIM: I'm going to climb out on the roof and start waving the flashlight. Someone will see it and come for us.

AMY: But who? No one is on the main road and there are no houses within sight of us. That will be just a pinpoint of light. Aren't you scared?

JIM: You bet! Are you?

AMY: Terrified. But I'm glad you're here.

JIM: We'll see it through, if we just keep our heads.

CURTAIN

* * *

SCENE 2

TIME: *An hour or so later.*

SETTING: *The same.*

AT RISE: *Same group is in the living room with the exception of* JIM. SARA *is asleep, covered with a blanket, in a big chair.* AMY, ROSE *and* BETTY *have three candles on the table.* BETTY *is trying to read.*)

BETTY (*Putting down her book with a thud*): I can't read by this light. How do you suppose our grandmothers ever did?

ROSE: I don't believe they tried to read. I guess they went to bed when it grew dark.

AMY: Maybe we ought to go to bed. It's nearly eleven, but I couldn't sleep a wink.

BETTY: Nor I.

ROSE: Nor I. Listen, what's that noise? (*All three listen.* ROSE, *running to window and peering out*) I can't see a thing. It's pitch dark. It sounded like something bumping against the house.

AMY (*Taking one of the candles, goes right toward kitchen*): Maybe on the back porch?

BETTY (*Nervously*): Oh, come back! Let's stick here together!

JIM (*Entering left, in rain coat, carrying flashlight*): Battery's dead. I waved her almost a hundred times, though. Maybe somebody saw it.

BETTY (*Scornfully*): Maybe.

JIM: It has stopped raining anyway.

AMY (*Entering right*): I can't see anything out there, but we may as well face it. The water is over the back porch and lapping the kitchen floor.

JIM: Start moving everything to the attic. Bring the food and water first, then the blankets. I'll do the carrying up the ladder to the roof.

AMY (*Half-crying*): Oh, Jim, Mother's rugs, the new drapes and Father's books!

BETTY: My new spring coat! I'm going to save *that!* (*She rushes out left, taking candle with her.*)

ROSE (*Going over to her sister, shaking her gently*): Sara! Sara, wake up, dear. We are going to sleep in the attic.

SARA (*Sleepily*): Strawberry ice cream soda and cracker jack!

ROSE (*Laughing hysterically*): Hear her! Wake up, Sis! (SARA *stirs.*)

SARA: Oh, where am I?

ROSE: Come on! (*She helps* SARA *to her feet and quickly wraps a blanket around her*) To the attic! (*Exits left, leading* SARA, *and taking one of the candles with her.*)

AMY: We ought to get Father's most valuable books and Mother's jewel case, and —

JIM: Amy, we will need water and food more than books and jewels. You don't seem to realize — (*He is interrupted by a cry from outside, right*)

MR. PETERS: Hello there! Hello in the house! Mr. Marshall! Mr. Marshall!

AMY: They have come for us! Here we are! (*She runs to the window.*)

JIM (*Picking up the third candle from the table, running to the window and waving it back and forth*): Here we are! In here!

BETTY (*Entering on the run from the left, carrying a dress box*): Are we rescued? Who is there?

MR. PETERS (*Still outside*): Mr. Marshall, are you all right? This is Tom Peters and Miss Marsh, the Red Cross nurse. We're here in a boat.

JIM: Row around to the back porch! You can get in there. (*There is a bumping of a boat against wood. Voices: "Steady now — there — I've got hold of the rail. Tie her up."* JIM *and* AMY *exit right toward the voices. More voices greeting, and then* MR. PETERS *enters living room with a lighted lantern, followed by* MISS MARSH, AMY *and* JIM.)

BETTY: We're rescued, we're rescued! Come, Rose! Come, Sara!

MR. PETERS: Why, are you children all alone?

AMY: Yes, we — (*There is a terrific crash, followed by a wail of pain and a scream.*)

ROSE (*Offstage left*): Oh, *Sara!* She's fallen off the step ladder! Come quick, somebody! I've dropped my candle and it's gone out! (MR. PETERS, MISS MARSH, *who is carrying a small black bag, and* AMY *rush off stage, left.*)

BETTY: Oh, I hope she hasn't broken her neck!

JIM: Get the first-aid box. It's in that pile of coats. I'll fix a place for her to lie down. (*He arranges chairs so* SARA *can be put down full length.*)

MR. PETERS (*Carrying* SARA, *enters left*): Steady now, you are all right. More frightened than hurt, I think. (*He places* SARA *on the chairs.*)

AMY (*Placing lantern near* SARA): I'm glad Miss Marsh is here! (MISS MARSH *is examining* SARA. SARA *is sobbing softly, saying every so often: "It hurts."* ROSE *kneels beside* SARA'S *chair, holding her hand.* JIM *stands in the background with* BETTY.)

SARA: It's my leg that hurts!

MISS MARSH: Yes, you have hurt it badly, Sara, but we can fix it up and we will all get into the boat and take you home. You are going to be all right. (*She motions to* MR. PETERS, JIM *and* AMY *to move to one side of the stage.* ROSE *stays with* SARA) She has broken her right leg just below the knee. We can splint it up with pillows and umbrella and lift her safely into the boat. I think we ought to take her to the emergency Red Cross hospital in the Armory.

MR. PETERS: We can take Rose and Betty along too, but Jim, you and Amy will have to stay until we can get back for you or send some other boat. (MISS MARSH *returns to* SARA *and with the help of* BETTY *and* ROSE *begins to surround* SARA'S *right leg with pillows, using an umbrella and cane along the outside to keep the leg stiff.*)

JIM: That's all right, sir. We will be perfectly safe up on the roof.

MR. PETERS: We can leave you an extra lantern and a jar of coffee. Need anything else?

AMY: Only some of your calmness! We will be all right, thanks.

MR. PETERS: Don't thank me, thank the Red Cross. (*He goes over to* SARA *and helps lift her into a blanket rolled to form a stretcher.* MISS MARSH *picks up her bag.* JIM *and* MR. PETERS *lift and carry* SARA *toward the right*) We can swing her down into the boat very easily. It won't hurt a mite, Sara. Get your things, Rose and Betty, you are going with us. (ROSE *and* BETTY *grab their coats.* BETTY *takes her dress box.*)

SARA (*Drowsily*): Miss Marsh gave me something to stop the hurt and it has almost gone!

AMY (*At the door, dropping a kiss on* SARA'S *forehead as they carry her out*): That's fine, dear! Have a nice boat ride! (*She waves as the stretcher goes out, followed by* ROSE *and* BETTY) Try to get word to Mother that we are all right, Betty, and Jim's family, too!

BETTY: I'll try. I hope you'll be rescued soon. 'By!

ROSE: Good-by, Amy, good luck!

AMY: Good-by! (*There is more thumping, only less loud than before, and voices giving directions.* AMY *fusses with the lantern, trying to get it lighted.*)

MR. PETERS (*Offstage*): You will be all right, Jim?

JIM (*Still offstage*): Yes, don't worry about us. Good-by! (*Voices in distance, sound of oars.* JIM *enters right, wiping forehead.* AMY *gets lantern lighted and blows out candles*) Water's dropping! There are a good two inches of wet board showing on the kitchen step. That was a narrow squeak! (*He pours two cups of coffee from the jar* MR. PETERS *left. Hands one to* AMY. *Raises his cup as though in a toast*) Here's to Red Cross coffee, Red Cross lantern and Red Cross rescue! I'm glad we have a wide-awake, well-equipped Red Cross Disaster Committee in this town!

AMY: And a Red Cross nurse for emergencies! Thank God for the Red Cross! (*Both lift their coffee cups and drink, still standing*)

THE END

* Based in part on chapters XI-XIII of "Penny Marsh: Public Health Nurse," Dodd, Mead & Co., New York, 1938

ONE-RING CIRCUS

by Aileen Fisher

Characters

KEP, *a budding engineer*
PINKIE, *his admiring pal*
SPINDLE, *who owns a pet mouse*
LARRY, *a friend*
JANET, CATHY } *Larry's sisters*
MIL, *a friend*
HORACE, *a bookish boy*
MISS "PINCH-FACE" COBB, *Horace's aunt*

SETTING: *A vacant lot.*

AT RISE: KEP *and* PINKIE *are near the center of the stage.* PINKIE *sits on a box whittling.* KEP *has a dishpan of sawdust and is outlining a circus ring.*

KEP (*As he sprinkles*): It's sure hard to make a circle look round. But you can't have a circus without a sawdust ring. (*Tramps on imaginary grass.*) Some of this grass is too high—that's the trouble with a vacant lot.

PINKIE: What'd we do without it, though? I think vacant lots are a swell invention.

KEP (*Still sprinkling his ring*): Does it look pretty round to you, Pinkie?

PINKIE (*Squinting*): O.K., Kep. We just going to have one ring?

KEP: Yup. Three's too hard. Anyway, nobody can look three places at the same time . . . except my mother. *She* can even see out of the back of her head. Specially when I'm experimenting, or inventing.

PINKIE (*With an envious sigh*): Must be pretty nice to know you're going to be an engineer when you grow up. Wish *I* knew what to be.

KEP: Wait till you get through acting in this show, Pinkie. Then maybe you'll decide to be a monkey or something.

PINKIE: Thanks for the tip. Say, who's coming to the meeting, anyway?

KEP: Oh, Larry and his two sisters. They've got a stunt all worked out. Besides, Janet can turn six cartwheels in a row, and Cathy can jump rope like nobody's business. Ever see her?

PINKIE: Nope. I don't have much time for girls.

KEP: Then Spindle's going to play the mouth-organ and make his pet mouse perform. That ought to bring down the house. By the way, I'm depending on your bantam rooster and your butterfly collection for the menagerie.

PINKIE: O.K. What about my collection of keys?

KEP (*Ignoring question*): And Mil's going to make pink lemonade and wear her clown suit and walk on stilts.

PINKIE: All at the same time?

KEP: And don't forget you're down for a trapeze act. I'll take charge of the rodeo. I'm going to engineer a synthetic bucking bronco I dare anyone to stick on more'n 30 seconds, myself included.

PINKIE (*Tentatively*): What about Horace?

KEP: Well, what *about* Horace?

PINKIE: Why don't we let Horace in on things for once? He's got more stuff than the rest of us put together. Why, his aunt's so rich she could buy out any store in town.

KEP: That old Pinch-Face.

PINKIE: And Horace could sell a lot of tickets, I bet — considering who his aunt is.

KEP: Nothing doing. He's a sissy. Besides, he gets too-good marks. Besides, it's a matter of principles. I don't believe in making buddies of people just to get something out of 'em.

PINKIE: He's got a Magic Set, though, and can do lots of tricks.

KEP: How do you know? You're not taking up with that pantywaist, are you? Why, I bet he'd faint if he saw a mouse. This circus is a he-man's outfit, see? (*Suddenly waves at wings left, and calls out.*) Hi, Spindle! (SPINDLE *comes in with a small wooden or metal box which contains an imaginary or toy mouse.* SPINDLE *also has a mouth-organ which he plays snatches on.*)

SPINDLE: Hi. I brought Felix so you could get a preview of his act. (SPINDLE *carefully puts box on upturned crate.*) But, look, don't anyone close down that cover tight, because it locks, and I haven't got a key! Besides, it has to be left open a crack or Felix will suffocate. (SPINDLE *lifts cover and the boys bend over to watch.*) Here, Felix. Sit up, boy. Sit up! Naw, not down. Well, O.K. then, roll over. Atta boy!

KEP: Some mouse.

SPINDLE: He's got stage fright. Usually he minds right off. Come on, wiggle your nose, Felix. Wiggle your nose.

PINKIE: He's a circus, that's what!

KEP: Anyway, he's cute. Ought to make a big hit with the audience. (LARRY, JANET, CATHY *and* MIL *come in noisily from right.* JANET *turns a few cartwheels.* CATHY *does tricks with a jump rope. There are various greetings back and forth. The children then sit around on ground or boxes, except for* KEP, *who still stands and hangs on to the sawdust pan.*)

KEP (*In a speech-making voice*): Well, now we're all here, the meeting is called to order. (*He keeps nervously sprinkling sawdust as he talks, as if feeding birds.*) As you know, we are about to embark on a very worthwhile, money-making project. Not only will we entertain the neighborhood with an amazing one-ring circus, but we will accumulate a fund.

SPINDLE: We hope!

KEP: . . . a fund, so I can go ahead with the most important experiment of my scientific career.

LARRY: Got any ideas yet about how to do it, Kep?

KEP: Well, no. Not exactly.

CATHY: Everybody I know says it can't be done.

KEP: A scientist never says "can't" — see?

LARRY: Well, you'll be pretty good if you can figure something out, Kep. That's all I can say. My dad told me *no*body can invent a defense against atomic bombs — not even Einstein. Let alone you!

MIL: Not that it wouldn't be good to have one, though!

KEP: There must be some kind of defense. As an engineer, I won't be satisfied till I try.

JANET: Sure, it's worth a try. A circus is worth the price of admission anyway, even if you never figure out a defense.

SPINDLE (*Playing with mouse*): Felix says to tell you he's ready to do his stuff for the cause any time.

KEP (*Speech-making voice again*): If we charge 5 cents admission for children and 7 cents for adults, we'd get a big enough fund so I could probably start several different experiments at once. Something ought to work . . . law of averages. (*Children give various assents.*) Anyway, it's a worthwhile idea. And there's no time to lose! Do you think we can be ready to put on the circus this coming Saturday? (*More assents.*)

PINKIE: Look! There comes Horace with his aunt, old Pinch-Face, down the street.

KEP (*Warningly*): Don't let Horace in on anything, remember. He knows too much already . . . out of books. Besides, he's an auntie's boy!

PINKIE: I bet he'd give his eye teeth to be in our circus, though.

SPINDLE: Let's all get in a huddle over Felix, and then we just won't *see* them. (*The children gather over Felix's box.* MISS COBB *and* HORACE *come in.* MISS COBB *is quite old-maidish and prim.* HORACE *wears glasses and carries a stack of books.*)

MISS COBB: Now *there* are some children, Horace. I am confident they will be more than delighted to play with you while I attend the Elite Ladies' Club. Let me ask them.

HORACE (*Holding back*): No, auntie. Please don't. I believe they don't like my company very much.

MISS COBB: Nonsense, Horace. You're my nephew, aren't you?

HORACE: Just the same, auntie . . . experience tells me . . .

MISS COBB (*Coyly, to the children*): Children. (*There is no reply. The children bend studiously over Felix.*) Children. (*Still no indication the children have heard.*)

HORACE: They seem to be rather hard of hearing. Come on, auntie, I have an abundance of reading matter for this afternoon. I can get along by myself.

MISS COBB (*Angrily*): CHILDREN! (*Still the children do not budge.* MISS COBB *goes closer, notices sawdust on ground, picks up some. Then she is quite exasperated.*) What do you children mean . . . throwing sawdust on my lot? I could have you arrested . . . for trespassing. Do you realize it? (*This brings the children to frightened attention.*)

KEP (*Gulping*): On your lot? We didn't know it was your lot, Miss Cobb. Honest.

PINKIE: We thought a vacant lot was . . . well, vacant. (*Gestures*) You know, vacant!

MISS COBB: You did, did you? I want you to know this lot has been in the Cobb family for 37 years. What do you mean — defiling it with sawdust? Speak up! I am positive there is a law against it.

KEP: You see, Miss Cobb, we were planning to give a circus . . .

HORACE: How interesting.

MISS COBB: Let them explain, Horace. So! You were planning to give a common, low-brow entertainment on Cobb property without permission. Unpardonable.

JANET: It's for a good cause. Really.

CATHY: It's to earn some money so Kep can go ahead with important, world-famous experiments.

LARRY: You see, Kep's trying to figure out a defense against the atom bomb. And, of course, that takes a little money. That's why we're putting on the circus.

MISS COBB: What nonsense. (*To* KEP) I find it hard to believe that a boy of your age and appearance bothers his head about things like that.

HORACE: I think it perfectly natural, auntie. I have read considerable on the subject myself. (*Wistfully*) Besides, I believe a circus might do a great deal for this neighborhood.

MISS COBB (*Looking at* HORACE): You'd like to be in it, wouldn't you, Horace dear? Well, perhaps we might be able to arrive at a compromise. As a matter of principle I object to sawdust and circuses on Cobb property, but . . . (*To children*) if you will allow Horace to contribute his many talents to the success of the performance, I shall permit you the use of my lot.

KEP: As a matter of principle, Miss Cobb, we don't . . . (*Suddenly he looks at Felix's box and calls out.*) Hey, Spindle, watch Felix! He almost escaped. We couldn't put on the circus without Felix.

MISS COBB (*Curiously*): Felix? Are you children hiding something from me? On my property? (*She goes over to the box, lifts lid, and then shrieks. In horror she bangs down the lid, holds her skirts, and jumps up on a crate.*) A mouse! A live mouse! Ooohhh. I shall never be the same again.

PINKIE: The lid! She banged down the lid and it locked. And Spindle hasn't got a key.

SPINDLE: Felix! He's locked in the box. He'll suffocate. Can't somebody do something?

KEP: Race home and get your collection of keys, Pinkie. Maybe one of 'em will fit.

PINKIE: I doubt it. They're mostly pretty big . . . and rusty. (PINKIE *runs out left. At almost the same moment* HORACE *impulsively rushes out right.*)

MISS COBB (*Who has not seen* HORACE *go*): A mouse! On Cobb property! Horace. Horace dear, run home this minute and get auntie her smelling salts. That little green bottle on top of my dresser. And hurry, Horace. I feel very faint . . . (*She gets down from the crate and sits on it.*)

KEP: Horace isn't here, Miss Cobb. He's gone.

JANET: He just ran home. And, honest, I never thought Horace could run so fast.

MISS COBB: He ran home? Ah, the dear boy thought of my smelling salts before I did. Such a thoughtful child! So considerate of his auntie.

CATHY (*Who has been trying to pry up lid of box*): Miss Cobb, do you realize what you have done? You banged the lid on poor Felix, and it locked, and there isn't any key.

SPINDLE: He's imprisoned. He'll suffocate. He was the best mouse I ever had.

MISS COBB: A mouse on my property . . .

KEP: Maybe it *is* your property, Miss Cobb, but it's Spindle's mouse.

MIL: I bet there's a law against suffocating an innocent little person like that.

MISS COBB: Hurry, Horace. My smelling salts!

CATHY: I'd feel awful if I did it, I know that.

SPINDLE (*Mournfully*): And Felix was just getting to wiggle his nose so good. (PINKIE *comes rushing in from left with his key collection. Some keys look pretty huge for such a small box. The children frantically try to make the keys fit. There are various expressions of disappointment.*)

LARRY: Collecting keys is a dumb hobby, Pinkie. What good are keys if they don't unlock anything?

PINKIE: Aw — they unlock *some* things.

JANET: Poor little Felix.

MIL: If we don't get him out soon, it'll be too late. (HORACE *comes running in from right with a cardboard box. He has suddenly acquired a sense of "belonging."*)

HORACE: Gangway! Gangway!

MISS COBB: My smelling salts. Oh, Horace, you dear thoughtful boy. (*She has her head in her hands so doesn't see what happens. Instead of going to his aunt,* HORACE *hurries to* FELIX'S *box. He whips out a piece of wire and a gadget from his cardboard box, gives a few twists in the lock, and opens the lid! The children are much impressed and excited.*)

HORACE: There you are!

MISS COBB: Where, Horace? I don't see them. The little green bottle?

HORACE: What little green bottle?

MISS COBB (*Suddenly much alive*): The one on my dresser. Do you mean to say you couldn't find it?

HORACE: Find what?

MISS COBB (*Crossly*): My smelling salts, of course. You certainly saw the desperate condition I was in after beholding that dreadful animal. What *did* you go home for Horace?

HORACE: Why, for my Magic Set. I've had considerable practice opening locks and undoing puzzles. That lid was nothing.

KEP: Everything's O.K. now, Miss Cobb. The show can go on. Horace saved Felix's life . . . look, he's as lively as ever!

MISS COBB (*Jumping up*): Lively! Did you say lively? Oh, I am afraid I am long past due at the meeting of the Elite Ladies' Club. (*She swishes out in a great flurry as the children laugh.*)

HORACE: . . . I guess maybe I'd better be going, too . . .

KEP: Wait a minute, Horace.

PINKIE: What's the great hurry?

KEP: I . . . we . . . I mean, we sure could use a magician in our circus. You're hot. Only we never knew it.

HORACE: You mean you want me to stay? Honest? Golly, I never thought I'd ever get to act in a circus. (*He puts down books and picks up two linked rings from the Magic Set, and begins to be a showman.*) Ladies and gentlemen, all the king's horses and all the king's men would be unable to pull these rings apart. (*Passes them to* KEP *and* LARRY, *who try unsuccessfully, then hand them back.*) Now . . . by a simple turn of the wrist . . . well, there you are! (*Holds up two rings. The children applaud.*)

HORACE (*To* KEP): I'd like to be in on the scientific experiments, too, Kep . . . only . . .

KEP: Only what?

HORACE: Well, I've read a great deal about atom bombs, and what scientists say. You'd be wasting your money. There *isn't* any defense — all the scientists agree on that.

KEP (*Gloomily*): I've sorta come to that conclusion myself, only I hated to admit it. I kept hoping. It sounded like a swell idea to work on. (*Brightens*) But look, we could use the money for something else. We could use it in the Junior Red Cross for that National Children's Fund that helps kids in Europe and places! We could send food and things they need. (*Children approve loudly.*)

HORACE: You've solved it, Kep!

KEP: Yeah?

HORACE: Sure! *That's* the real defense against the atom bomb — thinking about other people and doing something to help them! There may not be a scientific defense, but this is just as good. If we treat other people the way we'd like to be treated . . . there won't ever be another war. (*Gestures*) No war — no atom bombs!

MIL: You got something there, Horace. I'm for the National Children's Fund! (*Others agree vociferously.*)

SPINDLE (*To Felix in box*): Stand up and shake Horace's hand, Felix. He's all right! (*Suddenly* SPINDLE *makes a dive at the ground.*) Oooops! What do you mean, Felix, running around on Miss Cobb's private property? (*He scrambles around comically.*) Hey you, come back here . . .

CATHY (*Dramatically jumping on crate, imitating* MISS COBB): A mouse! Oh, my soul, a live mouse! Quick, Horace . . . the smelling salts! (*They are all laughing as the curtain closes.*)

THE END

SPECIAL EDITION

by Aileen Fisher

Characters

PATSY, *editor of "Neighborhood News"*
CHUCK, *her brother, editor of "What's Up"*
SHARON, JUNE } *reporters on "Neighborhood News"*
HENRY, KEN } *reporters on "What's Up"*
TALBOT, *a budding poet, cousin of* PATSY *and* CHUCK
MILLICENT, TALBOT'S *kid sister*

TIME: *The present.*

SETTING: PATSY *and* CHUCK'S *home. The stage is divided into three parts. Down the middle is a strip representing a hallway in a large house. At the end, back, of the hall is a telephone. To the right of the hall is* PATSY'S *room, the office of "Neighborhood News" with a sign to that effect. To the left of the hall is* CHUCK'S *room, office of "What's Up," also with a sign.*

AT RISE: PATSY *and* CHUCK *are alone in their rooms.* PATSY *is sighing over a stack of papers and account books.* CHUCK *is laboriously writing in longhand.* SHARON *comes in from left wing, runs down hall and bursts into "Neighborhood News" room.* PATSY *looks up expectantly.*

SHARON: Talk about news! If we can get our paper out this afternoon instead of tomorrow, we'll have a scoop. Providing your dear brother (*She nods in direction of "What's Up" office*) doesn't get the same idea!
PATSY: What happened anyway?
SHARON: Well, I saw your cousin, Millicent...
PATSY: You couldn't miss her — she's as broad as she is long.
SHARON: Millicent says that Talbot just got a letter that he won

first prize in the county poetry contest, and he's going to get a prize of ten dollars. Imagine! And he lives right in our block.

PATSY: And he's my cousin. Imagine! Ten dollars all at one time.

BOTH: Imagine!

SHARON: And here we work our heads off on the "Neighborhood News" for about two cents an hour, if we're lucky. What'd you and Chuck go and quarrel for anyway, Patsy? There wasn't nearly as much work when we all had the paper together... before Chuck started one of his own. And it was more fun, and we made more money too. Nobody wants to subscribe to *two* papers.

PATSY: Chuck always wants his own way. I guess I can be an editor as well as he can! Anyway, I think if people can't get along together they better get along separately. Now look, Sharon, if we can dig up some of Talbot's poems to print along with the contest news in a special edition, I bet our circulation will zoom from 28 to at least 40. Do you have a copy of the prize poem?

SHARON: No. I asked Millicent, but she said she didn't know where a copy was. And Talbot's locked up in his room, writing. And, besides, Millicent wasn't interested for less than an ice cream cone.

PATSY: She wouldn't be! Getting anything out of Millicent always eats up our profits. I'll go 'phone and see what I can find out. (PATSY *goes out into hall to telephone.* SHARON *sits at typewriter and pecks out news story. Just as* PATSY *is dialing a phone number,* HENRY *comes rushing in, from offstage left, down hall, to "What's Up" office. With hardly a glance at* PATSY *he bursts into* CHUCK'S *room.*)

HENRY: Guess what, Mr. Editor.

CHUCK: What?

HENRY: I saw your cousin Millicent and, in return for my last stick of gum... I extracted a piece of news that will scoop our rival's paper all hollow. Providing we can get our edition out this afternoon instead of tomorrow. (PATSY *in the hall has been having difficulty getting her number. Finally she has it.*)

PATSY: Is that you, Millicent? Hello. Is Talbot there? (*Pause*) Not even for your cousin? (*Pause*) Look, Millicent, this is important. Try to find some of your big brother's poems lying around and bring them over to the office. We want to run a story about Talbot and the prize. (*Pause*) Sure ... believe me, we'll make it worth your while. Mother baked chocolate gingersnaps this morning. O.K. And hurry up! (PATSY *goes back to her room, and plunges into work again, while* SHARON *continues to work at the typewriter.* CHUCK *is much interested in what* HENRY *is telling him.*)

CHUCK: What's happened, anyway?

HENRY: Your cousin Talbot won first place in the county poetry contest. It means ten bucks.

CHUCK: Ten bucks! Holy smoke, why doesn't somebody around here write poetry? We could make a down payment on a typewriter with ten bucks.

HENRY: We wouldn't need a typewriter, Chuck, if you hadn't gone and quarreled with Patsy. Now they've got the typewriter . . . and where do we come off?

CHUCK: We've got the hektograph. Once we print a stencil we can turn out copies faster than they can. Why, they have to type at least four different sets of carbons to get enough copies.

HENRY: Yeah, but we have to print our whole stencil by hand.

CHUCK: You get on to it after a while. Anyway, Patsy always wants to run things. If she thinks she's such a good editor, she can prove it. I bet they haven't got as many subscribers as we have. Look, Henry, did you bring a copy of Talbot's poem to print in the special edition?

HENRY: No. Millicent didn't have one. Besides, she wanted a popsickle before she'd say another word.

CHUCK: She would! We've got to get hold of Talbot's poems. Write up what you know, Henry, while I make a 'phone call. (*Starts for door and turns back*) Say, if we're going to run a special edition, we ought to put the "Neighborhood News" off the track. Write 'em a note, Henry, and we'll chuck it under their door this noon. Tell 'em that seeing *tomorrow* is press day, we'll lend them the hektograph for an hour if they'll lend us the typewriter.

HENRY (*Grinning*): That'll fool them, all right. (HENRY *sits down and writes industriously.* CHUCK *goes out into the hall to telephone.* SHARON *and* PATSY *work quietly in their office. Just as* CHUCK *dials telephone,* JUNE *comes down the hall, listens a minute, then goes into the "Neighborhood News" room.*)

JUNE: Hi! Chuck's out in the hall calling up Talbot.

PATSY: Oh! I bet he's heard about the prize too. Heck!

JUNE: What prize?

SHARON: Talbot won ten dollars in that poetry contest. Do you know anything about the poem he sent in, June?

JUNE: Sure. He read it to me before he sent it.

PATSY *and* SHARON (*Excited*): He did! Can you remember it? What was it about? Oh, boy, what a scoop this'll be.

JUNE: It was called something like "Man and the Atomic World" ...only I don't remember exactly. It was full of lots of big ideas. You know Talbot!

SHARON (*Dreamily*): He's wonderful.

JUNE: It started out about a couple of people who were in business but couldn't get along together, and so they decided to split up and each start a business of their own and grab the other's trade...

PATSY: I suppose he meant the people were like countries. The United States and Russia, maybe...

SHARON: Oh, sure. Talbot always means deep things.

PATSY: What happened?

JUNE: Well, just when they were at each other's throats, a dove that was trained by an airplane pilot did some sky-writing with streamers above this town where the business men lived...

SHARON: Isn't that modern, though? Just like Talbot.

JUNE: The sky-writing said something like "Divide and Perish, Co-operate and Live," only it was in poetry, of course.

PATSY: That sounds like Talbot all right. Look, June, you write up what you just told us, and if we hurry we can get out a special edition of our paper this afternoon before "What's Up" knows what's up.

JUNE: A special edition! You mean we'd have to type twenty-eight carbons this afternoon? It's much more work than the hektograph, Patsy...

PATSY: But think what it would do to our circulation.

JUNE: What'd you have to quarrel with Chuck for, anyway? Everything was easier when we all had the paper together, and more fun too.

PATSY: We can run a paper just as well as they can. And when we get enough profits we'll buy a hektograph of our own. Say, if we're putting out a special edition, we ought to do something to keep our rivals from knowing about it. Let's write them a note and tell them that since *tomorrow* is press day we'll lend them the typewriter for an hour if they'll lend us the hektograph.

SHARON: Good! That'll put them off the track. We can stick the note under their door this noon. (*The three girls get to work.* CHUCK *meanwhile has been having trouble getting his number.* HENRY *is writing in the other office.*)

CHUCK (*At phone*): You mean to say, Millicent, that Talbot's too busy to talk to his own cousin? Look, it ought to be worth a lot to you to have a special edition of our paper devoted to your brother. We want to print some of his poems. Can you get us some? (*Pause*) O.K. O.K. A double-deck ice cream cone... if you find some poems and bring them over pronto. Step on it! (CHUCK *hangs up, just as* KEN *comes in rather slowly and sorrowfully from wings left and down hall.*)

CHUCK: Hi, Ken. Did you get those society items?

KEN: Yeah.

CHUCK: What's the matter? You look like a wet ostrich. (CHUCK *and* KEN *go into "What's Up" office.*)

KEN: Listen, Chuck, I don't like to report society news, see? That's girls' stuff. I like to report baseball... and important things like that. You can get a sissy to be the society reporter—not me.

CHUCK: But now that we're a he-man's outfit, we don't have any sissies on our paper, Ken. You know that. They're all over at "Neighborhood News."

KEN: Well, it was more fun before... when the girls did all the society and I did all the baseball. Heck, who cares if little Peggy Higgins had nine of her friends, aged 3 to 7, at a birthday party. Who cares?

CHUCK: Write it up anyway. People like to see their names in print. We're getting out a special edition this afternoon.

KEN: A special edition! What for?

CHUCK: Because Talbot won ten dollars just for writing a poem. Talk about luck! Imagine getting ten dollars for *that*.

HENRY: Talbot's full of ideas. I read some of his poems once... snitched his notebook when he wasn't looking. He writes sonnets or something.

CHUCK: What about?

HENRY: Oh, everything. Atom bombs and things like that. About the end of the world if people don't get together and cooperate.

He's real professional. Deep, too. And modern! Say, there's no lilies and nightingales about the stuff Talbot writes. (MILLICENT *comes in hall with a worn notebook. Looks first at one door, then at the other. Decides to knock on "Neighborhood News" door first.*)

PATSY (*Answering* MILLICENT'S *knock*): Who is it?

MILLICENT: Me. Millicent. Did you get the chocolate gingersnaps?

PATSY: Good grief, I forgot. (*Calls to* MILLICENT) Come in, Millicent. I'm going for the cookies right this minute. (PATSY *leaves hurriedly, and* MILLICENT *comes in. She is younger than the others, is quite chunky, and always hungry. She clutches a worn black notebook.*)

SHARON: Did you bring some of Talbot's poems, Millicent? Let me see.

MILLICENT: Not till I see the cookies first.

JUNE: It looks like an awful worn-out notebook.

MILLICENT: There are lots of poems in it that Talbot wrote. Real pretty ones...about lilies and nightingales and things like that.

SHARON: You mean Talbot writes about lilies and nightingales?

MILLICENT: Sure. And ladies in white dresses.

JUNE: I must say that doesn't sound like Talbot!

MILLICENT: It is, though. In his own handwriting. (PATSY *comes back with a bag of cookies.*)

PATSY: Here you are, Millicent. I had to promise Mom I'd wash all the downstairs windows to make up for these. One cookie for one poem.

MILLICENT (*Trying a cookie, and enjoying it*): O.K. How many are there?

PATSY: A dozen.

MILLICENT (*Carefully counting 12 pages and tearing them out*): Here's twelve then. Only you get a bargain because sometimes there's more than one poem on a page. (*The "Neighborhood News" staff looks the pages over, in surprise.*)

PATSY: I don't see anything about atom bombs and cooperation and survival in the modern world. (*Reads aloud*)

Out of the shadows into the night
Floated a maiden vested in white.
Vested? What does that mean?

SHARON: It doesn't sound like Talbot!

PATSY: It certainly doesn't. But if we're getting out a special edition, there's no time for minor details. You pick out a couple of the poems you like best, June, and we'll print them.

MILLICENT (*Still enjoying her cookies*): If you want anything else, just let me know. Only next time I'll have to charge lemonade too. Goodbye. (MILLICENT *goes out as "Neighborhood News" staff rather grudgingly says goodbye. With a good grip on the notebook and cookie bag,* MILLICENT *knocks on the "What's Up" door.*)

CHUCK: Who's there?

MILLICENT: Me. Millicent.

CHUCK (*To boys*): It's Millicent with the poems. We've got to be nice to her. It's good business. (*Calls out*) Come in, Millicent. Glad to see you, cousin.

MILLICENT (*Entering*): Did you say a double-deck ice cream cone?

CHUCK: Yeah, sure. Any flavor you want, Millicent.

MILLICENT (*Looking appraisingly at notebook, then boys*): I'll let you have twelve whole pages of poems for *two* double-deckers.

CHUCK: (*To staff*): Do you think it will do that much for our circulation?

KEN: Never can tell.

CHUCK: O.K., Millicent. When you go into business, we'll sure want to buy some stock! (*Digs in pocket*) Here's the money... you'll have to buy the cones yourself. We don't keep 'em in stock. (CHUCK *gives* MILLICENT *coins, while she tears out twelve carefully counted pages and hands them over.*)

MILLICENT: They're all in Talbot's handwriting.

KEN (*Peering to look*): Let's see. (*Reads aloud*)

Ah, nightingale in yonder tree,
What message has your melody
For hapless lonely souls like me?

(*He makes a face*) There's nothing atomic about that, Henry.

CHUCK: What's the dif? Poems are poems. Copy a couple of 'em off on the stencil, Ken. (KEN *starts to write.* MILLICENT, *still munching cookies, hesitates at the door as she turns to go.*)

MILLICENT: What do *you* like best, Chuck... chocolate or vanilla? Or strawberry? (*She sighs heavily*) I never can decide. (*There is a great racket in the hall as* TALBOT, *hatless and out of breath, comes rushing in. He is shouting, "Millicent... Millicent..."*

and seems quite frantic about it.)

TALBOT: Millicent! Has anybody seen Millicent around here? (PATSY *jumps up and opens the "Neighborhood News" door.*)

PATSY: Oh, hello, Talbot. Congratulations on the prize! Millicent was here just a little while ago. Eating chocolate gingersnaps... by the dozen!

TALBOT: Where is she now? It's a matter of life and death, Patsy. I've *got* to find her. Millicent! Millicent! (MILLICENT *comes out of the "What's Up" office, holding notebook behind her.* CHUCK *sticks his head out, too —* HENRY *and* KEN *behind him.* SHARON *and* JUNE *look on behind* PATSY.)

MILLICENT (*Sweetly*): Do you want me, Talbot? If there's anything I can do for you, it will only cost you a peanut.

TALBOT: This is a matter of life and death, Millicent. Did you see an old black notebook I dug out of the attic and put on the hall table?

EVERYONE: A black notebook?

TALBOT: Did you? An old notebook I used to write poems in when I was just a kid... before I was dry behind the ears... before I had any sense...

MILLICENT: Yes, I saw it.

TALBOT: Where is it? Did you take it? I've got to have it, Millicent...

MILLICENT (*To* PATSY *and* CHUCK): I told you the poems were in his own handwriting, didn't I? You got a real bargain.

TALBOT: A bargain? What bargain? Millicent, did you take that notebook?

MILLICENT (*Sweetly*): Sure, I did, Talbot. Patsy and Chuck want to print some of your poems in their newspapers. Because you're famous! Isn't that nice of them? They're *both* going to get out special editions today.

PATSY *and* CHUCK (*Glaring at each other*): Both!

TALBOT (*Tearing his hair*): Those poems! Where are they? Give them back to me this minute. Human eyes must never set foot on those pages! Ye gods, those poems are dated... they're baby stuff. I was going to burn up that old notebook... and here you ran off with it. (*Sees notebook behind* MILLICENT'S *back*) Give me that book, Millicent, before there is a...an atomic explosion! (*He grabs the notebook, thumbs through pages*) Where are the other sheets?

MILLICENT: Why, the "Neighborhood News" is going to print some. So is "What's Up."

TALBOT (*Furiously*): Is that true? (*When* TALBOT *sees* PATSY *and* CHUCK *assent sheepishly, he becomes very stern and dramatic*) Then I will have you all arrested. Sister or no sister, cousins or no cousins, friends or no friends! You can't print a person's poems without his permission. Especially when it would ruin his reputation! It's slander...that's what it is. (*He strides into the "Neighborhood News" office, sees the sheets on desk, and rescues them. Tears them in shreds. The onlookers are all rather awed*) I'll take this case to court, that's what I'll do. (*He strides into "What's Up" office and rescues pages*) Just in time! If these infantile poems had got into print, I'd...I'd cut my throat. (*Glares at the group*) Then you could all be tried for *murder*.

SHARON (*Shuddering*): Oh, Talbot.

TALBOT: As it is, my life is spared. But your lives are in danger. Surreptitious slander... that's the charge I'll make against you. (*Under breath*) Or maybe it's libel...

KEN: Gee, is it as bad as it sounds, Talbot?

TALBOT: Penitentiary offense!

JUNE: Honest?

TALBOT (*Grimly, slowly*): And to think I was about to give you all a treat out of my ten dollars. To think I thought I *owed* you something for giving me the idea!

ALL (*Except* MILLICENT, *who still nibbles cookies*): What idea?

TALBOT: The idea for the poem, of course. I was grateful enough for it!

CHUCK: I don't get you.

PATSY: Me either.

TALBOT: Why, my whole prize-winning poem was based on the way you acted! You gave me the idea.

CHUCK *and* PATSY: We did?

TALBOT: Sure. You act just like certain countries. For instance, instead of making yourselves get along together, you get mad at each other and quarrel. You upset all the apples after you pile them on the cart. You break up a perfectly good business arrangement, then try to snitch each other's customers. And in the atomic age, too. You don't seem to realize everybody can't have his own way. If you'd only *each* give in a little, you'd get along O.K., and everyone would be better off.

KEN: That's what I think, too. And I wouldn't have to report society!

JUNE: And we could have the hektograph.

HENRY: To say nothing of the typewriter.

TALBOT: See? Just what I said. Everybody would be better off. Instead of getting arrested!

PATSY: Look, Talbot, don't you think... in view of our giving you a prize-winning idea...

CHUCK: And admitting you're right...

PATSY: That you ought to drop the charges, if we promise to benefit by the lesson in your poem?

CHUCK: Yeah. You drop the charges, Talbot, and we'll have one paper again instead of two. We'll cooperate. What do you say, Patsy?

PATSY: Sure. Providing one thing, though. Providing Talbot will be editor. He knows how to make the most of ideas. Chuck and I never could win a prize for anything... except quarreling! And that's certainly nothing to be proud of.

TALBOT: Well...

KEN: Come on, Talbot. You'd get all kinds of ideas editing a newspaper. Just so you didn't have to report society!

TALBOT: Well...

PATSY: Really, Talbot, I don't see how you can get out of it, after winning a prize on cooperation! Here's your chance to practice what you preach.

CHUCK: By the way, Millicent, you give me back my money or I'll have you arrested for defaming your brother's character.

PATSY: And you help me wash windows tomorrow morning or I'll have to turn you over to the police for doing business under false pretenses!

HENRY: What about it, Talbot! Do we *all* get arrested, or do you become editor of... (*Looks from* PATSY *to* CHUCK)... of... a cooperative newspaper?

PATSY: Editor of the "Neighborhood News."

CHUCK: Nothing doing. The name's "What's Up."

TALBOT: Well, for the sake of humanity, I'll do it! I'll show you we can all work together in peace and harmony on...

KEN: You better think of a new name!

TALBOT: "What's Up in the Neighborhood." How's that?

OTHERS (*Applauding*): Fine. Hooray. Good.

TALBOT: I'll demonstrate that cooperation is the *must* of the atomic age. Pass the cookies, Millicent!

THE END

THE WAY TO NORWICH

by Aileen Fisher

Characters

FOUR CHILDREN
THE MAN IN THE MOON
CHAIR MENDER
OLD CLOTHES MAN
BOY WITH PONY
TWO GOSSIPY GIRLS

SETTING: *Outdoors, somewhere on Earth.*

TIME: *Some time soon.*

AT RISE: FOUR CHILDREN *come in with porridge dishes. They march around the stage, chanting.*

CHILDREN:
The Man in the Moon came tumbling down,
And asked the way to Norwich;
He went by south, and burnt his mouth
With eating cold pease porridge.
(*They put down their bowls and begin to clap out "Pease Porridge" as they chant loudly.*)
Pease porridge hot,
Pease porridge cold,
Pease porridge in the pot,
Nine days old.
Some like it hot,
Some like it cold,
Some like it in the pot,
Nine days old.
(*There is a loud thud offstage, and* THE MAN IN THE MOON *comes tumbling or somersaulting onto the stage from wings, left.*)

1st Child: My stars!

2nd Child: Good night!

3rd Child: Who *can* it be?

4th Child: A man!

Others: But who?

4th Child: Let's ask and see.

Man in the Moon (*Sitting comically on floor*):
The Man in the Moon! I tumbled down. (*He looks around.*)
Which is the way to Norwich?

1st Child (*Teasingly*):
Go south and burn your mouth
With eating cold pease porridge.

2nd Child:
Go by east and have a feast
On pease too old for storage.

3rd Child:
Go by north and know henceforth
That pease are good for forage.

4th Child:
Go by west and freeze your chest
With eating hot pease porridge.

Man in Moon: No thanks! (*He gets up and brushes himself off, looks at children, peers into their dishes.*)
What's all this talk, my friends, of pease?
Why all this fuss with porridge?
People like *me* just eat green cheese...anything else sounds horridge.
Life should be simple! If you please, which is the way to Norwich?
(Children *look at each other, baffled*)

1st Child: Nobody knows.

2nd Child: It's miles away.

3rd Child: Why take a trip so taxing?

4th Child:
Most of *our* friends prefer to sleep or sit in a chair, relaxing.

Children (*Chanting*):
Nancy Dawson was so fine
She wouldn't get up and feed the swine;
She lies in bed till eight or nine...

Man in Moon (*Interrupting*): So it's shame on Nancy Dawson!

1st Child (*Calling toward wings, right*):
Little Boy Blue!
2nd Child: Come blow your horn.
3rd Child: The sheep's in the meadow...
4th Child: The cow's in the corn.
Man in Moon: Where's the little boy that looks after the sheep?
Children (*Shrugging*): Under the haystack, fast asleep!
Man in Moon:
Heavenly, days, he's fast asleep!
I must make a note of this to keep.
(*He takes out a little notebook and writes as he mumbles, "Under the haystack...fast asleep."*)
Maybe *that's* why the Earth's in deep.
(Man in Moon *shakes his head and looks worried.*)
Children: Something the matter, Man in the Moon?
Man in Moon:
Something is wrong with your planet.
The things I have seen through my telescope!
Explosions of buildings and granite.
Columns of dust have gone up so high,
I had to come down to investigate why.
Children: Oh, my. Oh, my!
Man in Moon:
My wife, Lady Moon, is as worried as I.
I thought if I traveled to Norwich, you see,
I'd quickly find out what the trouble must be.
(*Shakes finger at children*)
Explosions are serious, my children, not comic...
especially when they look rather atomic!
If people aren't careful your globe will be strewn
with craters as gaping as those on the Moon.
(*There is a noise in wings, right. All peer to look.*)
Children: Somebody's coming.
Man in Moon:
They may know the way
to Norwich...I'll ask them
and see what they say.
(Chair Mender *with chair on back, and* Old Clothes Man *with bag of old clothes over shoulder come in. They are en-*

grossed in telling each other their troubles. They cross stage as they talk.)

CHAIR MENDER (*Wailing*):
If I'd as much money as I could spend,
I never would cry old chairs to mend;
Old chairs to mend, old chairs to mend;
I would never cry old chairs to mend.
(CHAIR MENDER *sighs, and turns out empty pockets.* MAN IN MOON *approaches him.*)

MAN IN MOON:
Pardon me, gentlemen. Pardon me, Sir —
which way to Norwich do you prefer?

CHAIR MENDER (*Tersely*): The way that gets me a customer!

OLD CLOTHES MAN (*Wailing*):
If I'd as much money as I could tell,
I never would cry old clothes to sell;
Old clothes to sell, old clothes to sell;
I never would cry old clothes to sell.

MAN IN MOON: The way to Norwich, gentlemen...please...

OLD CLOTHES MAN (*Bitterly*): The way that helps me get rid of these! (*Indicates clothes and the two men exit.* MAN IN MOON *looks after them.*)

MAN IN MOON:
Well! What do you think of a thing like that?
They only think of money.
(*Takes out notebook and writes*)
That is the trouble, I bet my hat.
It's really so sad it's funny.
I must make a record that people wear blinds
when dollars and cents are too much on their minds.

CHILDREN (*Chanting*):
My little old man and I fell out;
I'll tell you what 'twas all about, —
I had money and he had none,
And that's the way the noise begun.

MAN IN MOON:
Money makes oodles of trouble, all right —
Greed is a vice that's horridge.
(*There is a noise in wings left and* CHILDREN *and* MAN IN MOON *look to see who it is*)

A boy and his pony have come in sight!
I'll ask *them* the way to Norwich.
(A BOY *leading his* PONY *comes in. The* BOY *affectionately pats his* PONY *as he talks.*)

BOY: I had a little pony,
His name was Dapple-Gray,
I lent him to a lady
To ride a mile away.
She whipped him, she lashed him,
She rode him through the mire;
I would not lend my pony now
For *any* lady's hire!

MAN IN MOON:
Which is the way to Norwich, buddy?
Mind if I inquire?
Is the road good or is it muddy,
does it go through a mire?

BOY (*Belligerently*):
I would not lend my pony now
For *any* person's hire!
(*He says giddyap to his* PONY *and hurries out before* MAN IN MOON *can ask more questions.*)

MAN IN MOON (*Looking after him*):
That lad is running a temperature!
He's fearful and suspicious.
(*Takes out notebook and writes in it*)
He had tough luck, and it makes him sure
everyone is malicious.
My stars, I'm getting some facts all right
though Norwich still is out of sight.
(MAN IN MOON *looks apprisingly at notes, counts things wrong on fingers as he talks*)
Too many people are fast asleep...
too much concern with money...
too much wanting a life that's sweet,
flowing with milk and honey...
too much suspicion and fear and hate.
The picture isn't sunny.
Seems I'm finding some reasons why
atom bombs blow dust in the sky.

1st Child (*Looking right*): Two people coming!

2nd Child: Perhaps they'll know...

3rd Child: The way to Norwich.

4th Child: I doubt it, though. (*Two* Gossipy Girls *come in, one talking excitedly to the other.*)

1st Girl:

Molly, my sister, and I fell out,
And what do you think it was all about?
She loved coffee and I loved tea,
And that was the reason we couldn't agree.

Man in Moon (*Approaching*): Is Norwich close...or over the sea?

1st Girl:

Norwich? Better ask Tweedle-dee,
or Tweedle-dum, as the case may be.

2nd Girl (*To* 1st Girl):

She loved coffee and you loved tea...
that was the reason you couldn't agree?
(*The girls exit, and* Children *chant another rhyme.*)

Children:

Tweedle-dum and Tweedle-dee
Resolved to have a battle,
For Tweedle-dum said Tweedle-dee
Had spoiled his nice new rattle.

Man in Moon (*Taking notes in his little book*):

Too many battles and tiffs and fights
for foolish little reasons!
Some people should be ashamed, by rights —
quarreling these days is treason. (*Sighs heavily*)
No wonder the bombs go plop! Dear me,
making a point about coffee or tea...

Children: It *is* pretty foolish, Man in the Moon.

Man in Moon (*Suddenly*):

Why should I go to Norwich?
I've found enough reasons here, this noon,
to last me forevermore-idge...
Laziness, greediness, jealousy, quarrels,
fear, and suspicion...don't earn any laurels,
but mix up a planet's good-nature and morals!
(*Takes out watch and looks at it.*)

Good night! I'd better be going soon
and tell my discovery to Lady Moon.
We're due to rise in an hour or so...
I'll give you a wink when the sun is low.

1ST CHILD: Please, Mr. Man in the Moon, don't go and leave us to bombs and rockets.

2ND CHILD: Please, can't you give us a hint or so to keep in our minds and pockets?

3RD CHILD: Give some advice so our faults will cease,

4TH CHILD: So we can live happily here in peace.

MAN IN MOON:
My children, it's simple:
all people are brothers.
As *you* would be treated,
be sure to treat others;
and then all your blessings will be astronomic
and you will be masters of matters atomic.
Remember, you're brothers!
Don't make any slips
or your planet may suffer
a *total eclipse*.

(MAN IN MOON *shakes a warning finger, smiles, and then begins to somersault backwards to the zoopy sound of a slide whistle.* CHAIR MENDER, OLD CLOTHES MAN, BOY *and* PONY, *and* TWO GOSSIPY GIRLS *poke their heads in from wings to see what in the world is happening.*)

CHILDREN:
The Man in the Moon came tumbling down
and asked the way to Norwich...

OTHERS:
We showed him all our faults instead,
and they were pretty horridge!

(*All come front stage and join hands and nod at each other as they say the final lines*)

ALL:
But here and now
we make a vow
to put our faults in storage.

THE END

LOUISA ALCOTT'S WISH

by Sophie L. Goldsmith

Characters

LOUISA ALCOTT, *six at this time. May be acted by a child of eight or nine.*
MRS. BRONSON ALCOTT, *her mother*
BRONSON ALCOTT, *her father*
PAT O'ROURKE, *an Irish lad of seven or eight*
BIDDY O'ROURKE, *his sister, a year or so older*
THE TOWN CRIER
MRS. O'ROURKE
GIANT, *the dog*

SCENE 1

SETTING: *The living-room of the Alcott family.*

AT RISE: *On the floor, surrounded by books, sits six-year-old* LOUISA. *She is building a bridge out of large, fat books, and every once in a while she stops to scribble something on paper. Her father sits next to her, watching her proudly, and on the other side of her sits her mother, rocking the baby to sleep.*

BRONSON ALCOTT: You see, Abigail! She has already a natural taste for books!

MRS. ALCOTT: Now, Bronson! The child is just learning to read! Do you suppose she has any idea *what* book she's using?

LOUISA: I want the big, fat book beginning with "B," Father.

BRONSON ALCOTT: There! She knows Bacon's *Essays* already!

MRS. ALCOTT: Why do you want that book, dear? It's a very big, heavy one.

LOUISA: That's just why, Marmee, dear! I want to make a bridge of it, and then I want to walk across the bridge and sail far, far away!

MRS. ALCOTT: Wouldn't you just as soon keep Baby for me for a few minutes?

LOUISA (*Stretching out her arms for Baby*): Oh, yes indeed.

MRS. ALCOTT (*Handing baby to her*): Be careful of her! Come, Bronson. Help me to move Anna out of her room — ours is sunnier and better for her cold.

BRONSON ALCOTT: Very well, my dear. Louisa, you will find Plato on the lowest shelf. He is also rather a heavy book, but useful — useful!

LOUISA: Oh, thank you, Father! (*Exit* MR. *and* MRS. ALCOTT. LOUISA, *left alone, talks to the baby while she builds a house all of books around her.*) Now, baby, dear, I *was* going to build a bridge, but instead I'll build a nice, cozy cottage all for you. Let's pretend you are my very own baby, and that this is our brand-new cottage. Dear me, I have nothing to feed you with! Will you be very good and wait till Louisa gets you something to eat? Will you? (*She peeps inside the fence of books and waves good-bye.*) Good-bye, baby! Louisa is coming right back! (*Backing to the exit and blowing kisses to the baby, she goes out. Naturally nothing can be seen of the baby, because the high fence of books completely hides her. Enter* MRS. ALCOTT.)

MRS. ALCOTT (*Looking about the room*): Louisa! (*Calling*) Louisa! Where can she be? And the baby, too! (*Calling more loudly and continuing to search everywhere except inside the fence of books.*) Louisa! Louisa!

CURTAIN

* * *

SCENE 2

SETTING: *The Boston Common.*

AT RISE: PAT *and* BIDDY *are sitting on bench swinging their feet.* GIANT, *tne aog, squats at one end of the bench.*)

BIDDY: I do believe you are afraid of that dog, Pat!

PAT: 'Fraid! I guess *not!* I'm just tired of playin', that's all.

(GIANT *half gets up and starts toward* PAT, *who shrinks back.* GIANT *growls and lies down again.*)

BIDDY: Oh, no, you're not afraid! Oh, no! (*Enter* LOUISA, *rolling a hoop. As she comes skipping along in back of her hoop, it rolls into* GIANT. *Immediately* LOUISA *kneels next to him and puts her arms around his neck.*)

LOUISA: Did I hurt you, dog? Oh, what a beauty you are! (*She pets him, and he snuggles up to her.*)

BIDDY: That's more than you'd dare do, Pat!

LOUISA (*Looks up from patting* GIANT, *and notices children for the first time.*): Hello, little girl!

BIDDY: Hello!

LOUISA: Is this your dog?

BIDDY: Oh, no. We were playing here, and he came along and then we couldn't play any more.

LOUISA: Why not?

BIDDY: Well, you see — (*Here* GIANT *gives a growl. She shrinks away.*) He's so big, and Pat tried to tie a can to his tail —

LOUISA: Tie a can to his tail! How dared he do such a thing?

PAT: Aw, that's nothin'. We do it to all the dogs in our alley.

LOUISA: But it's cruel! And such a beautiful dog, too! (*Pets him.*)

PAT: That's just like a girl! We were just havin' some fun — most of 'em don't mind. They like it.

LOUISA: Like it! I'd like to do it to you and see how *you'd* like it!

PAT: All right! Go ahead!

LOUISA: Do you really mean it?

PAT: Sure I do. Here — here's the can. (*He reaches under the bench and picks up an old tin can with a string tied to it.*) Here — tie it on me. I bet *I* won't say a word.

LOUISA: Oh, what fun! Only you haven't got any tail.

BIDDY: Wait — I'll fix him a tail. I got this out of the ashcan this morning. I *knew* it would come in handy. (*From the pocket of her torn and dirty apron she produces a scraggy bit of fur from an old neckpiece.*) There's your tail, Pat! (*She pins the tail on his jacket, and* LOUISA *ties the can on the tail.* PAT *gets on all fours, barking like a dog and dragging the tail behind him. Suddenly* GIANT *leaps on him, and boy and dog roll over and over.*)

BIDDY: Oh, oh, oh! He'll kill him, I know he will! Get off there

— get *off,* you great big dog, you! (*As they are scuffling, enter* MRS. O'ROURKE. *She is a big Irishwoman, and she carries in her hand a paper bag.*)

MRS. O'ROURKE: Well, for the love of the saints! An' what are you children doin' now?

LOUISA (*To* GIANT, *the dog*): Come here, sir! Come here, I say! (GIANT *gives* PAT *a final roll-over and bounds over to* LOUISA.) Didn't you know he was only playing? Bad dog, to frighten them so! Bad *dog!* (PATS *sits up and rubs his bumps.* GIANT *puts his head contritely on one side.*)

MRS. O'ROURKE (*To* PAT): A fine-lookin' fellow *you* are, my lad! Letting a little lass call the dog off you!

PAT (*Sulkily*): She didn't need to call him off. I knew all the time he was just fooling.

MRS. O'ROURKE (*Spying* PAT'S *"tail" as he gets up and rubs himself off*): And where does *this* come from?

BIDDY: 'Twas in the ashcan, Mom. I didn' think you wanted it any more.

MRS. O'ROURKE: No more I did. But no more I ever wished to see it again. I thought 'twas gone for good and all. (*She unpacks the paper bag she carries.*) Come, now — 'tis time for lunch. Will ye be having a bite and a sup with us, little lady?

LOUISA: Oh, thank you. (*She eats what is handed to her.*) My, this is good! What is it?

PAT: What should it be? Cold fish an' cold potatoes, o'course!

LOUISA: Fish! How splendid! I never had any.

BIDDY: Never had any fish!

LOUISA: No, my father won't let us eat fish or meat. We have only vegetables and bread and fruit.

MRS. O'ROURKE: Saints alive! And who may your father be?

LOUISA: Don't you know *my father?* Why, he's Bronson Alcott, and I'm his little girl, Louisa.

PAT: How come you're here?

LOUISA: Well, you see, I was taking care of Baby, and I had nothing to feed her, so I went to get something. And then the sun looked so beautiful, I just slipped out of the house and walked a little way, and then I walked a teeny bit more — and here I am!

MRS. O'ROURKE: Well, you'd best be getting back to the baby!

LOUISA: Yes, I s'pose I ought. May I bring her a piece of this salt fish? She's never had any, you know.

PAT: Sure — bring her mine. I hate the stuff.

BIDDY: And bring her this tail to play with. She won't be raising a fuss with it, the way Pat did. (*Hands* LOUISA *the "tail."*)

LOUISA: Oh, thank you all. How kind you are! Good-bye — good-bye! (*Exit* MRS. O'ROURKE, BIDDY *and* PAT. LOUISA *climbs up on the bench, spreads out the piece of paper which they have left, and carefully wraps in it the pieces of salt fish and tail.* GIANT, *the dog, jumps up on the bench with her, and she talks to him.*)

LOUISA: My, isn't it splendid to see the world, dog! I wonder what your real name is? I shall call you "Giant" because you're so big. (GIANT *claps his paws.*) Now, Giant, I'm going to take you home with me and show you my baby sister and the beautiful house I built for her. Oh, it's such a beauty! Father let me have all his biggest books for it, and I built them all snug around her. (*She yawns.*) Oh, excuse me, Giant! The sun's making me sleepy! (*She yawns again.*) I've had a long walk, you know. Shall we go home, Giant? Shall we. (*Her head droops down on his shoulders.*) Nice dog — good dog. (*She falls asleep. There is a pause of a minute or two while she sleeps with* GIANT *on guard. Then in the distance a clanging dinner bell is heard, and a voice calling.*)

TOWN CRIER (*In the distance*): Lost! A little girl, six years old, in a pink frock, white hat, and new green shoes! Anyone finding this child, please return to the distracted parents, Mr. and Mrs. Amos Bronson Alcott! (*He comes on the stage, ringing his big dinner bell and proclaiming.*) Lost! A little girl, six years old, in a pink frock, white hat, and green shoes! Anyone finding this child, please return to the distracted parents, Mr. and Mrs. Amos Bronson Alcott! (*He approaches* LOUISA'S *bench. At the sound of his bell and voice, she awakens with a start, listening as he again proclaims.*) Lost! A little girl, six years old, in a pink frock, white hat, and new green shoes! Anyone finding this child, please return to the distracted parents, Mr. and Mrs. Amos Bronson Alcott! (GIANT *also does a bit of pantomiming, tapping* LOUISA, *pointing at her, etc.*)

LOUISA (*Wide awake now*): Why, I'm Louisa! Here I am, sir —here I am!

TOWN CRIER (*Turning and seeing her*): Why, so you are! How

did you get here, child?

LOUISA: Oh, I just walked. It was easy!

TOWN CRIER (*Again ringing his bell*): Found! Found! A little girl, six years old, in a pink frock, white hat —

LOUISA (*As loudly as possibly*): And new green shoes! (*She takes the bell from the hand of the astonished* TOWN CRIER, *and walks ahead of him.* GIANT, *picking up the newspaper package with his teeth, brings up the rear.*) Hurrah, everybody! Found, a little girl, six years old, in a pink frock, white hat, and new green shoes! (*As she proclaims this, ringing the bell, the little procession exits.*)

CURTAIN

* * *

SCENE 3

SETTING: *The same as Scene* 1. *The fence of books is just exactly as* LOUISA *has left it.*

AT RISE: MR. *and* MRS. ALCOTT *are sitting together at the window, anxiously looking out.*

MRS. ALCOTT: Oh, if we only had some news! Where can she be?

BRONSON ALCOTT: She cannot be very far off, my dear. Surely those little feet cannot go far, especially when she's carrying the baby.

MRS. ALCOTT: Yes, to think she took Baby with her! I cannot believe she would do such a thing! (*The sound of the bell is heard, and* LOUISA'S *voice heard proclaiming loudly — "Found —" etc., etc.*)

BRONSON ALCOTT: You see? Providence watches over her, my dear.

MRS. ALCOTT: Oh, how happy I am! (*Enter* LOUISA, TOWN CRIER, GIANT. LOUISA *rushes up to her mother and hugs her, then to her father.* GIANT *goes to one end of the room and sits there, guarding the package.*)

LOUISA: Mother, I've had such a splendid time.

MRS. ALCOTT (*Hugging her, too*): Louisa! What a fright you gave us, my darling! But where is Baby?

LOUISA: Why, I left her in my new cottage.

MRS. ALCOTT: Your new cottage? Where, dear? Where?

LOUISA: Right here, Marmee, darling! (*She goes over to the fence of books, stoops over, and lifts the baby out.*) Why, I do believe she's been fast asleep all this time!

MRS. ALCOTT: Louisa! This is too good to be true! (*She takes the baby from* LOUISA'S *arms.*) True — fast asleep!

BRONSON ALCOTT: Louisa, my dear, it is impossible to be harsh with you. But I fear you must be taught not to give us so much anxiety in the future. (*He takes a piece of strong cord from his pocket, and ties it around* LOUISA'S *waist. Then he ties the other end around a chair.*) For the rest of the day, Louisa, you will remain right here. Perhaps this will help you to remember not to run away again.

TOWN CRIER: Well, I must be going. Sorry to see you in trouble, miss, but it won't last long. Would you like your parcel?

LOUISA (*Reaching out her hands eagerly*): Oh, yes! Yes, indeed! (*He takes the parcel from* GIANT'S *mouth, and hands it to her. Then he goes out, touching his hat.*)

MRS. ALCOTT: What have you there, Louisa?

LOUISA: Oh, please, Marmee, dear, it's a secret. I can't tell you.

MR. ALCOTT: Secrets flourish well in solitude, Louisa. We will leave you with your secret and your own reflections. (*Exit* MR. *and* MRS. ALCOTT.)

LOUISA (*Starts to go across the room to* GIANT, *but the cord which ties her to the chair prevents her from doing so. She stretches out her arms to him. With a bound, he jumps over to her and rubs his nose against her.*): Never mind, Giant! When I grow up, I'm going to write books, and tell other children all about good times like we had today. (*Unwraps parcel and starts feeding* GIANT.) And I think maybe you'd better eat this fish instead of Baby. Don't you think so, Giant? (GIANT *nods and chews happily.* LOUISA *examines the fur piece* PAT *has used as a tail.*) But you wouldn't want this tail, would you, Giant? (*He shakes his head.*) You have such a beautiful one of your own. When I grow up I'll have a lovely tail too — but no, I think I'd rather write stories. Yes, I'm sure I'd rather do that. (*She reaches over to where "Plutarch's Lives" is lying face downward, and starts scribbling busily. Enter* BRONSON ALCOTT.)

MR. ALCOTT: What are you doing, Louisa?

LOUISA: I'm writing a story about everything that happened to-day. Some day I mean to write lots and lots of stories, and then I wish everybody in the world would read them.

GIANT (*Stepping to the middle of the stage and bowing low while* LOUISA *scribbles in utter absorption, and* BRONSON ALCOTT *looks over her shoulder*): And we all know Louisa's wish came true, don't we?

THE END

GRANDMA AND THE PAMPERED BOARDER

by Frances B. Watts

Characters

GRANDPA BASCOM
GRANDMA BASCOM
FRED, LINDA — *their grandchildren*
MRS. VANDEMARK, *a wealthy lady*
JOSEPH, *her chauffeur*
LOLLYPOP, *her pet lion*
JEAN, JACK — *neighbor children*
HARLOW, *the delivery boy*
GORILLA

TIME: *An afternoon in early summer.*

SETTING: *The kitchen of The Bascom Boarding House for Pets.*

AT RISE: GRANDPA *sits at kitchen table, pasting snapshots in a scrapbook.* FRED *enters, bouncing a ball, followed by* LINDA, *jumping rope.*

LINDA: Hi, Grandpa.

FRED: It's getting too hot to play outside.

GRANDPA (*Absentmindedly*): Well, you'd better play a quiet game, if you're staying in. Otherwise, you might break something. And you know how your grandma is about breakage.

LINDA: Where is Grandma?

GRANDPA: At the library, Linda.

FRED: What are you doing with that scrapbook, Grandpa?

GRANDPA: Oh, I'm pasting in pictures of former guests who have stayed at The Bascom Boarding House for Pets. There aren't too many of them yet, though.

LINDA (*Picking up snapshot*): Oh, look at this cute little poodle!

GRANDPA: That's Angela, who belongs to a couple named Carter. Angela stayed with us for two weeks while her folks went to Albuquerque. . . . And here's the Farley's cat, Alfalfa. He was a nice old Tom.

FRED: I sure wish you'd get some nice animal boarders while Linda and I are here.

LINDA: Yes, Fred and I wanted to help with the pets.

FRED: We've been here five days and the only guest you've had is that dumb canary of the Tuttle's. (*Points to canary*) He doesn't even sing.

GRANDPA (*Sighing*): I keep hoping business will pick up. It could be a pleasant and lucrative sideline for a retired fellow like me. Well, maybe this year will be better than last. (*A knock sounds at the door.* LINDA *opens it, and* MRS. VANDEMARK *enters.*)

MRS. VANDEMARK: Oh, so sorry! I fear I came to the back door by mistake.

GRANDPA: That's perfectly all right, ma'am. I'm Mr. Bascom. What can I do for you?

MRS. VANDEMARK: I'm Mrs. Ralston Vandemark from Hob Nob Hill. I understand that you board pets here.

GRANDPA: That's right. Do you have one you wish to leave?

MRS. VANDEMARK: Yes. My darling Lollypop. He's scarcely more than a kitten. I have never left the little darling before, but I must go to New York on a shopping trip.

GRANDPA: Have no further qualms, Mrs. Vandemark. Our guests always feel at home here.

MRS. VANDEMARK: Wonderful! Then may I count on Lollypop having the run of the house?

LINDA: Oh my, I don't think Grandma would approve of that!

GRANDPA: You see, my wife doesn't like to mix business with our domestic life. She insists that our guests stay in our nice, airy kennels out back.

MRS. VANDEMARK: Kennels! Oh, dear! Lollypop never would stand for that. He's used to the freedom of the house. I'm afraid I've spoiled him, but he's such a willful kitty.

GRANDPA: Many felines have that trait.

MRS. VANDEMARK: I'll be very happy to pay you triple your fee, if you'll let Lollypop live here in the house with you.

GRANDPA: Well . . . I could use the money. Perhaps we might make an exception in this case.

FRED: Uh-oh. Grandma isn't going to like it.

GRANDPA: Nonsense. A week with a half-grown kitten shouldn't trouble her too much.

MRS. VANDEMARK: Thank you, Mr. Bascom. I'll ask my chauffeur to bring Lollypop in. (*Calls out door*) Joseph, you may bring Lollypop in now. . . . (*To others*) You'll find Lollypop adorable, even though he is hopelessly spoiled. (JOSEPH *enters, pulling shaggy-maned lion,* LOLLYPOP, *by his collar.* BASCOMS *stare, and children back away timidly.* MRS. VANDEMARK *pets lion.*) Don't be upset, dear. These nice folks are going to take good care of you. (LOLLYPOP *purrs.*)

FRED: A half-grown kitten? It's a half-grown, genuine *lion*!

LINDA: I think I'm going to faint!

MRS. VANDEMARK: Oh, you mustn't be afraid of Lollypop, children. He's just a playful little kitten at heart. He's never even harmed a mouse . . . that I know of. (LOLLYPOP *stretches, walks around.*)

GRANDPA: May I ask, ma'am, where you acquired such an unusual pet?

MRS. VANDEMARK: My friend, an Indian Maharajah, gave him to me as a hostess gift. Lollypop was only a six-week-old kitten at the time. (*To* JOSEPH) Joseph, did you bring in his custard?

JOSEPH: No, madam, I will fetch it now. (*Exits*)

GRANDPA: Custard? I don't understand.

MRS. VANDEMARK (*Tittering*): I told you Lollypop was set in his ways. He takes his milk only when it's made into custard with a dash of nutmeg on top. Here, I've brought you the recipe. (*She takes recipe out of purse. Lion pounces playfully on* FRED, *knocks him down and nips his ankles.*)

FRED: Help! Help! He's a man-eating lion! (*Chases him off*)

GRANDPA: I'm wondering about the children. Will they be safe with this lion?

MRS. VANDEMARK: No need to be alarmed. Lollypop just loves to pounce and nip. It's his odd little way of being friendly. I've tried to break him of the habit, but to no avail. (*Pulls* LOLLYPOP *away by the collar*) . . . Be a good boy, now. (JOSEPH *returns with bowl of custard.*)

JOSEPH: Lollypop's custard, madam.

MRS. VANDEMARK: You had better keep this refrigerated, Mr. Bascom. And make it up fresh every morning. Remember the nutmeg. He won't eat it without that dash of nutmeg.

GRANDPA (*Putting custard in refrigerator*) : Yes, ma'am.

MRS. VANDEMARK: Well, I must be on my way. I'll be back one week from today. Lollypop, I'm sure, will be no trouble as long as you let him have his own way. Don't ever try to cross him.

LINDA: What will happen if we do?

MRS. VANDEMARK: I haven't the foggiest notion. Even though he has been difficult, I've never said no to him. (*Titters*) He *is* a *lion,* after all. And one should not take chances, should one? (*Hugs lion*) Goodbye, Lolly. Goodbye, everyone. Good luck! (MRS. VANDEMARK *and* JOSEPH *exit.* LOLLYPOP *pounces on* LINDA)

LINDA: Help! He's nipping me! Take him away from me!

GRANDPA (*Pulling lion*) : Dear me! Maybe we have bitten off more than we can chew. (*Lion pounces on* GRANDPA.)

FRED: If we don't watch out, Lollypop will bite off more than *he* can chew. (*Tries to help* GRANDPA. GRANDMA *enters with a book.*)

GRANDMA: Who was that driving off in the big limousine? (*Stops in horror*) Glory be to heaven! A wild lion is eating Ned! (*Starts whacking lion with book*)

GRANDPA (*Collaring lion*) : Stop, Lydia. This isn't a wild lion. It's a boarder.

GRANDMA: A boarder! Have you lost your mind?

GRANDPA: No. I just found a way to make a little money. A Mrs. Vandemark is paying us triple board for Lollypop here.

FRED: The only thing is, he has to have the run of the house.

GRANDMA: A lion have the run of the house? Not *my* house!

GRANDPA: Now, now, calm down, Lydia. It's only for a week. Lollypop is a bit playful, but perfectly harmless.

GRANDMA: Lollypop! What sort of woman would name a lion Lollypop? (*Stares at* LOLLYPOP) She doesn't keep his mane very tidy — it looks like an old mop. But he does seem quite tame. And we could use the money to get the chimney fixed.

GRANDPA: I knew you'd be sensible about this, Lydia.

GRANDMA: Humph! If I were sensible, I'd — ship him off to the zoo.

LINDA: Fred and I will help take care of him, once we get used to him.

FRED: Boy, wait till I tell the kids back home that we lived with a lion! (GRANDPA *lets go of* LOLLYPOP, *who then begins scratching the refrigerator*)

GRANDMA: Stop scratching my refrigerator door! Don't tell me he's going to be the destructive type. (GRANDPA *takes out custard and sets it on floor.* LOLLYPOP *eats.*)

GRANDPA: He just wants his custard, Lydia.

LINDA: It's the only way he will take his milk. Custard with a dash of nutmeg on top.

FRED: You'll have to make it fresh every morning, Grandma.

GRANDMA: I never heard of a pet so pampered. He'll just have to learn to drink plain milk like our other boarders.

LINDA: Oh, no! We can't cross him. Mrs. Vandemark never does.

GRANDMA: Well, I'm not Mrs. Vandemark. My children never ruled me, and I don't intend to let this lion rule me either. (*She marches to refrigerator and replaces custard with a bowl of milk. Lion whines and growls.*)

FRED: You're giving Lollypop milk instead of custard.

GRANDMA: That's right. It's high time somebody started giving this young lion some proper training. He's a fussy, finicky eater. And the best way to deal with a fussy, finicky eater is to stop encouraging such habits.

GRANDPA: But he's not drinking the milk, Lydia.

GRANDMA: He will, when he gets hungry enough. We all must be patient and firm and not give in. That's half the battle. (*Lion sits and whines. After a while he takes a few laps of milk.*)

LINDA: Look, Grandma. He is beginning to drink a little!

GRANDMA: Give him time. In a few days he'll empty his bowl and beg for more. (HARLOW *enters with package of meat*)

HARLOW: Delivery boy! Here are the pork chops you ordered, Mrs. Bascom. . . . Holy smokes! A lion! (LOLLYPOP *sniffs, gallops to* HARLOW *and grabs package in his mouth and runs around.*)

GRANDMA: Good heavens! He has the pork chops. At ninety-nine cents a pound! Catch him, somebody! (LINDA *and* FRED *chase lion. Lion hides under table with chops*)

HARLOW: Jeepers! I'm getting out of here. That lion acts too hungry to suit me! (HARLOW *runs off.*)

FRED: Lollypop is under the table. How can we get the pork chops now?

LINDA: We'd better let him keep the chops. He just *has* to have his own way, you know.

GRANDMA: Oh, no, he doesn't. A child doesn't *have* to have his own way, and neither does a pet. (*Gets the broom*)

GRANDPA: Be careful, Lydia. What are you going to do?

GRANDMA: The lion took Harlow unawares and got the pork chops away from him. So I'll take the lion unawares and get the chops back. (GRANDMA *swiftly pokes broom under the table.* LOLLYPOP *drops package in surprise and runs out.* GRANDMA *rescues chops.* LOLLYPOP *runs to her and whines.*) Oh, no. (*She puts chops in refrigerator.*) Now sit down and behave yourself. (*Lion paces, then sits down.*)

FRED: Golly! Lollypop actually sat down. Do you think he's really going to learn to mind?

GRANDMA: He'd better, or out in the kennels he goes.

GRANDPA (*Sinks into rocker*): I must admit that Lollypop is not the most desirable boarder. But I promised Mrs. Vandemark I'd keep him in the house, and I can't go back on a promise.

GRANDMA (*Hesitates*): I guess not. A promise is a promise. (*Lion walks over to* GRANDPA *and whines.*) Now what does that animal want?

GRANDPA: He's trying to tell me something. (*Rises*) What is it, boy? (*Lion jumps into rocker.*)

FRED: He wanted your rocker, Grandpa.

GRANDMA: Well, push him off, Ned. Stand up for your rights.

LINDA (*Laughs*): He did stand up. And look what happened. (GRANDPA *tries to unseat lion, who paws at him and snarls.*)

GRANDPA: Better not argue with him, I guess. I really didn't want to sit down, anyway.

GRANDMA: Hah! That's a fine excuse. Be firm, or— (JEAN *and* JACK *run in.*)

JACK: Hey, Linda and Fred! Come out and see our new bicycles!

JEAN: We'll let you each take a ride around the block. (LOLLYPOP *jumps from rocker, starts playfully pawing and nipping* JACK *and* JEAN.)

JEAN: Help! Help!

JACK: It's a lion! A real lion!

GRANDMA: Get down! Get down, I say! (*Lion continues jumping.* GRANDMA *and* GRANDPA *collar him.*)

FRED: We're sorry. Lollypop is one of the boarders. He was only trying to be friendly.

JEAN: Well, he's not the sort I want to be friends with. Look, he tore a big hole in my sock.

JACK: I don't want to be friends with kids who are friends with lions, either. That wild beast bit my ankle.

LINDA: He just *nips,* Jack.

JACK: It felt like a *bite* to me. Come on, Jean. We'll take our bikes to the Wilson's instead. (*They exit.*)

LINDA: Oh, dear, we were just beginning to make friends with Jean and Jack. Now we've lost them!

FRED: They're great kids, too.

GRANDMA: It's a shame, Ned. I've never seen such a spoiled, pampered, and rude pet.

GRANDPA: He sure is set in his ways.

GRANDMA: Well, we'll just have to *unset* his ways. And as quickly as we can.

LINDA: But Lollypop is not an ordinary pet.

FRED: You'd better believe it! (*Lion sneaks over to bird cage, starts jumping and snarling.*)

GRANDPA: Now he's after the canary.

GRANDMA: Get down, Lion! You may not want your milk, but you can't have that canary as a substitute. (GRANDMA *and* GRANDPA *grab lion by the collar.*)

GRANDPA: Quick, somebody! Take the bird to another room! (LINDA *and* FRED *run off with canary, shutting door.*)

GRANDMA (*Dropping into rocker*): Whew! Deliver me from lions! Hereafter, you'd better let me screen all the prospective boarders.

GRANDPA: I'm sorry, Lydia. I felt we couldn't afford to be choosy. Our business really isn't off the ground yet. If things don't pick up soon, we'll have to close down. (*Lion goes to rocker and whines at* GRANDMA.)

GRANDMA: Oh, no. You don't get this rocker. I'm sitting in it. (*Lion paws and nips her ankles.*) Stop behaving like a pampered child!

GRANDPA: Glory be, Lydia! You've antagonized him enough. Let him have the chair, or he might decide to have a piece of your leg instead. (*Lion tries to hop up in her lap. She pushes him off.*)

GRANDMA: Down, Leopold. . . . That's going to be his name around here. With a name like Lollypop, it's no wonder he acts like a baby. A noble name should help him act like the noble beast he should be. Furthermore, he needs a haircut. It's a fact that a sloppy appearance fosters miserable manners. (*Lion tries to hop on her lap again and roars angrily.* FRED *and* LINDA *enter.*)

FRED: Better move, Grandma. He's getting cross.

GRANDMA: So am I. Leopold and I may as well have our battle out once and for all! (GRANDMA *and* LOLLYPOP *struggle for the possession of the chair. Others shout warnings.*)

GRANDPA: You can't win a battle with a lion. Lydia, I beg you, let him have the rocker!

GRANDMA: Not on your tin-type! Lions may be king of the jungle, but a lion will never be king of Lydia Bascom's kitchen. Never! (*Curtain falls as struggle continues*)

* * *

SCENE 2

TIME: *One week later.*

SETTING: *The same as Scene 1.*

AT RISE: *The canary cage is back in its place.* GRANDMA *sits knitting and singing in rocker. Lion lies purring at her feet, his mane neatly combed.*

GRANDMA (*Singing "The Daring Young Man on the Flying Trapeze"*): How did you like that song, Leopold? (*Lion stretches and meows contentedly.*) My Uncle Louie used to be a trapeze artist in the circus. Never even used a net. I tell you, that fellow wasn't afraid of man or beast. . . . I think your mane needs a bit of brushing, Leopold. (*She brushes his mane.* LOLLYPOP *submits, meekly.* HARLOW *enters cautiously, with package of meat.*)

HARLOW: Here's your pot roast, Mrs. Bascom.

GRANDMA: Thanks, Harlow. Just set it on the table. (LOLLYPOP *sniffs and gets up.* HARLOW *backs away.*) No, Leopold, you lie down. (LOLLYPOP *obeys.*) No need to be afraid, Harlow. Our boarder has learned some manners since you were here last.

HARLOW: I'll say he has. What happened?

GRANDMA: Just showed him who was boss. We had a few hot battles and fisticuffs. But now we understand each other. Don't we, Leopold? (*She pats lion and he purrs.*)

HARLOW: Well, I'd never think it was the same lion. He seems so happy and contented, too.

GRANDMA: All animals are happier when they have a few rules and regulations to abide by. People are, too.

HARLOW: I guess you're right, Mrs. Bascom. My ma and pa make rules and regulations for me. I don't mind. Somehow it makes me feel that they really care about me.

GRANDMA: You've hit the nail right on the head, Harlow.

HARLOW: Well, so long, Mrs. Bascom. So long, Leopold. It's been a pleasure to know you. (*He exits, as* GRANDPA *enters.*)

GRANDPA: Guess it's about time for Leopold's snack. (*Prepares milk bowl.*) Here's your milk, Leopold. (*Lion starts lapping milk.*)

GRANDMA: My, I sure am glad I trained that lion to like milk. All that sweet custard was bad for his teeth.

GRANDPA: You are a marvel, Lydia. In a week's time you've broken Leopold of all his bad habits. Besides that, you've got him looking as clipped and dapper as a French poodle. I'm ashamed to admit that I was too much of a coward to try to change him.

GRANDMA: Why, you're one of the bravest men I know. If you had been a coward, you never would have taken a lion boarder in the first place. It's just that women often have more patience when it comes to training children and pets. Besides, I have some of Uncle Louie's circus blood in me. Lions just don't intimidate me. (FRED, LINDA, JEAN, *and* JACK *enter.*)

JACK: There's Leopold! (*Pets him.*) Hi, old boy.

JEAN: He turned out to be such a nice, well-behaved lion. Is he really going home today, Mr. Bascom?

GRANDPA: Yes. We're expecting Mrs. Vandemark at any time now.

FRED: We're going to miss him.

LINDA: We sure are. We've had so much fun with him.

JACK: I get a kick out of the way he plays ball with us.

JEAN: Yes, no matter how excited he gets, he doesn't jump or nip anymore.

LINDA: That's because Grandma taught him good manners.

JACK: I'm so glad we became friends, Fred and Linda. Getting to know your lion boarder has been a real experience. (JACK *rolls a ball and lion plays with it. Knock sounds on door.* LINDA *answers it, and* MRS. VANDEMARK *and* JOSEPH *enter.*)

LINDA: Hello, Mrs. Vandemark!

MRS. VANDEMARK: Good afternoon, everyone. How is Lollypop?

Has he been too upset without me? . . . Ah, there he is! Come to Mother, darling. (*Lion strolls calmly over to her.*)

JOSEPH: Lollypop seems changed, Madam.

MRS. VANDEMARK: Yes. He's not pouncing or nipping. Has he been ill?

GRANDMA (*Rising, walking over to* MRS. VANDEMARK *and holding out her hand*): I'm Mrs. Bascom. If you'll pardon my frankness, I found Leopold as coddled as a breakfast egg, so I took it upon myself to establish some rules and regulations for him, and enforce them.

MRS. VANDERMARK: Leopold? His name is Lollypop.

GRANDMA: This week his name has been Leopold, and he seemed to take to it. As Leopold, he behaved with dignity and nobility, as a lion should.

LINDA: Oh, the things Grandma taught him, Mrs. Vandemark! He doesn't have to be pampered with custard anymore.

FRED: He doesn't snitch meat or attack the canary anymore.

JACK: He doesn't pounce or nip.

JEAN: He lets Mrs. Bascom tidy up his mane.

GRANDPA: And he sits where he's told to sit. My wife is a remarkable woman, Mrs. Vandemark.

MRS. VANDEMARK: She must be! Lollypop — I mean Leopold, has been so set in his ways that I've always been a little afraid to try to change him. How did you manage it, Mrs. Bascom?

GRANDMA: Just a little firm discipline. You simply lay down the law and stick to it. It's something all pets understand, and they soon come to respect you for it. (*Takes a book from the cupboard and gives it to* MRS. VANDEMARK.) Here, you can read all about it in this book, *Good Training Makes Good Children.* It will help you with any of Leopold's future behavior problems.

MRS. VANDEMARK (*Amazed*): *Good Training Makes Good Children*! But Leopold is a *pet,* not a *child*!

GRANDMA: Pets or children, what's the difference? I brought my children up on that book, and it worked. So I figured, if good training makes good children, good training ought to make good pets. And judging by the change in Leopold, it does.

MRS. VANDEMARK: Well, upon my soul, it never would have occurred to me to use a child training book to train a pet! But I certainly shall read it and follow it. Frankly, I've become weary of making custard. It's going to be heavenly, having a disciplined pet! . . . Mr. Bascom, here is a check for Lolly — Leopold's board.

GRANDPA: Thank you kindly, ma'am. We truly can say that we enjoyed having Leopold as our guest.

MRS. VANDEMARK: Well, you may rest assured that I will sing the praises of Bascom's Boarding House for Pets all around Hob Nob Hill. My friends are always traveling, so you'll undoubtedly be boarding their pets.

GRANDPA: That's wonderful, Mrs. Vandemark!

FRED: I think your business worries are over, Grandpa!

MRS. VANDEMARK: Well, say goodbye, Leopold. We must be on our way. (*All wave goodbye to lion, who goes to* GRANDMA *and holds up his paw.*)

GRANDMA: What's this? A special goodbye for me, Leopold?

MRS. VANDEMARK: My goodness! Did you teach him tricks as well?

GRANDMA (*Laughing and shaking hands with* LOLLYPOP): No, it's not a trick, Mrs. Vandemark. It's just Leopold's way of saying, "You won. But there are no hard feelings." (*All laugh.* JOSEPH *enters, leading gorilla.*)

JOSEPH (*To* MRS. VANDEMARK): Pardon me, madam. Will you be much longer? Goo-Goo Eyes, here, is misbehaving dreadfully. He keeps trying to honk the horn and yank off the steering wheel. (MRS. VANDEMARK *takes gorilla by collar.*)

MRS. VANDERMARK (*To* BASCOMS): You must meet Goo-Goo Eyes, my new pet gorilla. He just arrived by express this morning from a friend of mine in Africa.

GRANDMA: Your friends certainly give original gifts.

GRANDPA: He's a fine-looking gorilla, I'll say that much.

MRS. VANDEMARK: I'm *so* glad you like him. You'll be seeing a lot of him this summer. I'm planning a month's vacation in Hawaii and . . .

GRANDMA: Oh, no!

GRANDPA, FRED *and* LINDA (*Groaning*): Here we go again! (*Curtain*)

THE END

THE LANGUAGE SHOP

by Mazie Hall

Characters

CLERK
CUSTOMER
PRINCIPAL
PRINCIPLES, *two girls*
MESSENGER BOY
SOMEONE, *a girl*
ANYONE, *a girl*
EVERYONE, *a boy*
ANYBODY, *a boy*
HIS, *a boy*
DONE, *a boy*
HAVE, *a boy*
FIFI
GREEK CITIZEN
ROMAN CITIZEN
FRENCH CITIZEN
SOLDIER

SETTING: *A store.*

AT RISE: *A* CLERK *is busy arranging boxes of different shapes and sizes which are displayed on the counter. Signs, "Slightly used adjectives" and "Adverbs—Shopworn," "Reduced in price" are prominently displayed.*

CLERK: May I help you, sir?

CUSTOMER: Yes, perhaps you can. You see, my vocabulary is completely outgrown. I need to replenish it.

CLERK: Yes, sir. Shall we start with some nouns? I have a complete line of them.

CUSTOMER: Well, I think my nouns are adequate. But I sometimes have trouble deciding which of two nouns to use.

CLERK: Like this, sir? (*He holds up two cards. One has the word "Principal" and the other "Principle."*)

CUSTOMER: Yes, that's what I mean.

CLERK: I can help you there. (*He rings a bell.*) This one (*He holds up a card*) means chief; like the principal speaker at a banquet, or the principal of a school. This one (*He takes up the other card*) means a fundamental or primary truth, as the principles of democracy. (MESSENGER BOY *enters.*)

BOY: Did you ring for me, sir?

CLERK: Yes. Please go to the stockroom and bring me samples of these two nouns.

BOY (*Taking the two cards*): Yes, sir. Right away, sir. (*Goes out briskly.*)

CUSTOMER: That's a brisk party.

CLERK: Yes, sir. But you used the wrong noun there. He is a person. We only use "party" in legal work. Lawyers talk about the "party of the first part." But ordinary individuals are persons. (BOY *enters, followed by a woman.*)

BOY: Here she is, sir.

CLERK: Will you tell this gentleman who you are and what you do?

PRINCIPAL: Certainly. I am the head, or principal, of a school. I am in charge of the school and it is my duty to see that it is well managed, that the children are faithfully taught, that the teachers do their work well and that work proceeds regularly and smoothly. I am a principal. (*She steps aside.*)

CLERK: Now, will you come in? (*Two little girls carrying a large sign enter. The sign reads, "Congress shall make no law respecting an establishment of religion, or prohibiting the free exercise thereof or abridging the freedom of speech, or the press; or the right of the people peaceably to assemble, and to petition the Government for a redress of grievances."*)

CUSTOMER: This must be taken from the Constitution. It is fundamental to democracy.

CLERK: Yes, sir. These are the principles upon which our government is established.

CUSTOMER: Well, how could I ever confuse these principles with that principal? (*The* PRINCIPAL *and the* "PRINCIPLES" *go out.*)

CLERK: Many people do, sir. What can I show you next? How about pronouns? Ours are very fine and sure to agree with their antecedents.

CUSTOMER: Well, I would like to see some indefinite pronouns. I always have trouble with them.

CLERK: Yes, indeed. (*Steps to the side of stage and beckons. Two boys and two girls enter, each carrying a large sign. One sign says "Someone," one "Anyone," another "Everybody" and the last "Anybody." They take their places on the stage.*) Now, sir, we need another pronoun to agree with these. Which shall it be — "his," "hers" or "theirs"?

CUSTOMER: Well, I don't know. I usually try the first one I find.

CLERK: Well, suppose "Someone" has lost a hat? Is it *his* hat, or *her* hat, or *their* hat? (SOMEONE *steps to the front of the stage and goes through the motions of searching for a hat.*)

CUSTOMER: Why, Someone has lost "his" hat! (*When he says "his," a child runs on the stage, carrying a sign that says "His." He stands beside* SOMEONE.)

CLERK: That's right. Now suppose Anyone can find the hat *he* has.

CUSTOMER: Anyone can find "his" hat. (ANYONE *pulls a hat out of his pocket and puts it on.*)

CLERK: Yes, sir. You used the right pronoun with both of those. Everybody, you come forward.

CUSTOMER: Everybody has trouble with his pronouns. (HIS *runs out and stands by* EVERYBODY *as soon as his name is called.*)

CLERK: Yes, sir. Anybody is apt to get his pronouns mixed. (HIS *runs to stand beside* ANYBODY), unless he remembers that Someone, Anyone, Everybody and Anybody mean one at a time, and that they must take a singular pronoun. (*The group of "pronouns" walk off the stage.*)

CUSTOMER: That was a good assortment of pronouns. I'll take them all and use them easily now. (*A* BOY *carrying a sign which reads "Done" comes staggering onto the stage. He totters about, finally coming to rest against the counter.*)

CLERK: Why, what's the matter with you, Done?

DONE: Oh, I've lost my auxiliary, and I can't stand alone. They ought to know that I'm too weak to stand without my crutch. Find my crutch for me, please. I'm just a weak verb.

CUSTOMER: Oh, poor fellow! Where is your crutch?

CLERK (*Goes to door and comes back with* HAVE. *He leads* HAVE *up to* DONE, *who immediately leans upon* HAVE *with great satisfaction*): There you are. Now, Have, don't leave poor Done alone any more for you know he can't get along without a helper.

CUSTOMER: Well, I never will send that poor fellow out without his auxiliary again. I see now it hurts him.

CLERK: We have many verbs that need auxiliaries. There's Been and Gone and Seen and Taken. They all need auxiliaries just as this fellow does. (*Pointing at* DONE.) People really put a severe strain on them when they use them without their helpers. (DONE *and* HAVE *go out together.*)

CLERK: What would you like to see next? We have a special sale on used Adjectives. Would you care to see them?

CUSTOMER: No, indeed. I'm so tired of worn-out adjectives that I never want to hear another. My kid sister has only two adjectives. They are "swell" and "awful." She uses them for everything whether they suit or not.

CLERK: They're two of the group we're selling out on this sale. (*Reaches in the box of "Slightly Used Adjectives" and takes out two signs—"Swell" and "Awful."*)

CUSTOMER: Show me some new ones. I'm sick and tired of those. Surely you must have some fresher ones in stock.

CLERK (*Steps to the door and calls*): Fifi, will you come here a moment? (*Turns to* CUSTOMER) She's our model. We can try out some adjectives on her. (FIFI, *a very pretty girl in a party dress, enters.*) Fifi, this gentleman wants to see some fresh adjectives. Will you stand in front of the mirror so that we can try some on you? (FIFI *smiles and takes her place in front of the glass.*) Now, sir, we'll try a new adjective on her and you can see if it fits. (*Take from a box on the shelf a sign which reads, "Attractive." He ties the sign on* FIFI. *She turns to give the* CUSTOMER *a look. He looks thoughtful but shakes his head.*)

CUSTOMER: It fits her. But I believe there's a better one for her. (CLERK *unties the sign and puts it back on the counter. Takes out another sign which reads, "Adorable." He ties it on* FIFI *who twirls around, doing a couple of dance steps.* CUSTOMER *again shakes his head.*)

CUSTOMER: It seems to fit, too, but it's not the right one.

CLERK: Yes, sir, you're right. Most people use any old adjective without giving a thought to its real appropriateness. But (*He hunts through several boxes while he talks.*) there's always one that seems made for the occasion. (*He pulls out a sign which reads,"Vivacious." He ties it on* FIFI *who smiles, nods, and curtsies to the* CUSTOMER. *The* CUSTOMER *looks thoughtfully at her, tilts his head to one side and slowly nods with satisfaction.*)

CUSTOMER: Yes, that's the very one for Fifi. She is a vivacious girl. (FIFI *smiles happily.*)

FIFI: It certainly is a pleasure to find someone who knows what word describes me. If you could see some of the adjectives they hang on me! (*Gathers up the discarded adjectives and goes toward the door.*)

CUSTOMER: Goodbye, Fifi. Better luck with your accessories! You see, many people don't realize how important they are.

FIFI: But you do! 'Bye. (*She goes out.*)

CLERK: Would you like to try any more adjectives? I think you understand their use.

CUSTOMER: No, I think I'd better look at some Adverbs.

CLERK: Yes, indeed.

CUSTOMER: I find that I have trouble sometimes in deciding when to use an adverb and when to use an adjective.

CLERK: That is a very common difficulty. Shall we try a few to see how they work?

CUSTOMER: Yes, that is a really good idea.

CLERK: You used *really* as an adverb in that sentence modifying the adjective, *good*. It's a real pleasure to hear adverbs properly used.

CUSTOMER: And you used *real* as an adjective modifying the noun *pleasure*. I think I see now.

CLERK: You have the idea for the use of those two. Would you care to see any other Adverbs?

CUSTOMER: No, I believe not. How is it that the supply of words is so abundant?

CLERK: The supply will be abundant as long as people have ideas and want to express them.

CUSTOMER: But where do all these words come from? Aren't many of them imported?

CLERK: Many were imported, but they have become part of our language now. Would you like to meet some of the stockholders of this shop?

CUSTOMER: Yes, I certainly would.

CLERK: They are coming here to hold a meeting and elect a new stockholder. Here comes Mr. Roman Citizen.

MR. ROMAN CITIZEN (*Entering*): Good morning, my boy.

CLERK: Good morning, sir. Mr. Citizen, this is a customer. He wants to know where we get our stock of words. Will you tell him?

ROM. CIT.: My friend, *I* gave you a great many of them. The Latin word for bread is "panis," which doesn't seem at all like your word.

CUSTOMER: Bread — panis. I don't see the connection.

ROM. CIT.: Well, let me show you how many of your words grew out of that association. Bread was originally stored in the "pantry." Your word "companion" means, literally, someone with whom we share our bread.

CUSTOMER: Why, that is true! What other words came from the Latin?

ROM. CIT.: Your word "digit" means a finger. The Roman traders kept their accounts on their fingers. They held up one "digit" or two "digits" to indicate their bids on goods. You can see how in time, a "digit" came to mean one. Likewise, our word "dexterity" or skill with the fingers, came from the Latin word "dexter," which means pertaining to the right hand. The people who were right-handed were clever with their fingers. So it goes! All through your language you will find Latin.

MR. GREEK CITIZEN (*Entering in time to hear the last remark*): While you're on the subject, don't forget what *your* language owes to mine. Greek is the very foundation of the Latin. But you Romans always were proud and vain.

MR. FRENCH CITIZEN (*Entering as the last speech was made*): *My* language has given you the words "chauffeur," "curfew," "guerrilla" and many more.

SOLDIER (*Entering and looking around in some uncertainty*): Say, buddy, is this the Language Shop? (*They all crowd around the* SOLDIER.)

GREEK CITIZEN: It is a good thing you have come. We need the new words you have brought. Open your pack and let's see what you have.

SOLDIER: Well, I left in a hurry. I just dropped my army banjo, boarded a plane and, after a Chinese landing, was brought here in a wheelbarrow. It isn't every guy that has such a homing device.

LATIN CITIZEN (*Frowning in concentration*): "Army banjo," "Chinese landing," "wheelbarrow," "homing device"? What do these mean?

SOLDIER: Pardon, pal. That's Army language. "Army banjo" is a shovel, "Chinese landing" means one wing low, a "wheelbarrow" is a general's car, while a "homing device" is a furlough.

GREEK CITIZEN: Are these your contributions to our language, sir? Have you brought only such nonsense to enrich it?

SOLDIER: I can't say as to that. It just happens to be Army slang. It may get into the language and it may not. But you can't say that words like "jeep" and "commando" and "ack-ack" aren't real additions to our speech.

CUSTOMER (*Who has been listening with great interest*): What a wonderful language! It takes new words from any source because words are the medium for ideas. Just as our country is the melting pot for all races, so our language is the melting pot for all languages.

THE END

THE TRIAL OF BILLY SCOTT

by Mazie Hall

Characters

BAILIFF
JUDGE
VERNON J. VERB
BILLY SCOTT
PROSECUTING ATTORNEY
DEFENSE ATTORNEY
MRS. GOOD ENGLISH
MRS. NOUN
PREPOSITION, CONJUNCTION, INTERJECTION } *three little girls*
ADDIE ADJECTIVE
ADAM ADVERB
DAN, *the jury foreman*

SETTING: *Courtroom. Judge's desk on a raised platform at the center rear of the stage. The defendant and his attorney sit at a table at the left. Witnesses sit at the right. A table for the court reporter is just in front of the judge's desk. The witness stand is at the immediate right of the judge's desk.*

BAILIFF: All stand. The Judge is about to enter. (*All stand until the* JUDGE *enters and takes his seat.*) This court is now in session.

JUDGE: What is the first case on the docket?

BAILIFF: Vernon J. Verb versus Billy Scott, your honor.

JUDGE: Bring in the accused. (BAILIFF *goes to the side of the stage and brings* BILLY *before the* JUDGE.)

JUDGE: Billy Scott, you are accused of using a singular verb with a plural subject. Do you plead guilty or not guilty to this charge?

BILLY: Not guilty, your honor.

JUDGE: Are you represented by counsel?

BILLY: Yes, your honor.

DEFENSE ATTORNEY: I am the attorney for the accused, Your Honor. (*Returns to seat.*)

JUDGE (*Speaks to the jury, which is the entire audience*): We are here to decide the innocence or guilt of this man. It is your duty to listen to the testimony which will be offered and to make your decision with strict impartiality. Let no personal feeling, either for or against him, enter into a calm deliberation on all the facts in the case. Is there any one of you who has any previous knowledge of this case? Or is there anyone who feels he cannot render an impartial verdict? If so, let him stand and declare himself at once. (*No one stands.*) You may proceed with the case, Mr. Attorney.

PROS. ATT.: Ladies and gentlemen of the jury, we are to consider the facts in the case of Vernon J. Verb against Billy Scott who, as you have heard, is accused of using a singular verb with a plural subject. I shall attempt to prove that this man committed the unpardonable crime of saying, "We was going to the park." This, you will see at once, is a crime of such nature that it is the duty of all right-thinking citizens to stamp it out. Think of the confusion which might follow such a practice! Verbs, my dear ladies and gentlemen, are the most important members of the entire Good English family. Yet, here we have a man who is so careless, so ignorant, or so lawless, that he fails to use verbs which agree with their subjects. Is this behavior worthy of our great heritage, as English-speaking people? This is a crime against Washington, against Patrick Henry, against our early history! (*Waves his arms. Grows excited.*) Why, our very country is based upon a decent respect for the rights of others!

DEF. ATT. (*Rising*): I object, Your Honor. All this has nothing to do with the case.

JUDGE (*To* PROSECUTING ATTORNEY): What are you trying to prove by this line of argument?

PROS. ATT.: Your Honor, I am proving that this man failed to allow others the right to hear correct English spoken.

JUDGE: Objection over-ruled. (ACCUSED'S LAWYER *sits.*)

PROS. ATT.: If this man, and others who might be encouraged by his example, should be allowed to go unchecked you would soon find the very streets of our fair city filled with broken verbs, fractured pronouns and murdered phrases! Are we to permit such a thing to happen? No, it must not be!

DEF. ATT.: I object, Your Honor.

JUDGE: Objection sustained. Proceed with the case, Mr. Attorney.

PROS. ATT.: I shall call as the state's first witness, Mrs. Good English.

BAILIFF (*To* MRS. GOOD ENGLISH): Do you promise to tell the truth, the whole truth and nothing but the truth, so help you Webster?

MRS. G. E.: I do. (*Mounts witness stand.*)

PROS. ATT.: Mrs. Good English, this child was adopted by you at a very early age, wasn't he?

MRS. G. E.: Oh, yes. He was not more than a year old when I took him.

PROS. ATT.: You tried to give him good training?

MRS. G. E.: Yes, sir. I set him a good example at all times. I tried to show him correct usage.

PROS. ATT.: How did he repay your kindness?

MRS. G. E. (*Beginning to cry*): He was so careless. I gave him four kinds of sentences, eight parts of speech and thousands of words to use! But he had no regard for my feelings. He tossed his verbs about, left sentences unfinished and was not careful to make his pronouns agree with their antecedents.

PROS. ATT. (*Soothingly*): Then you think he is capable of committing the crime of which he is accused?

MRS. G. E.: Yes. I'm sure he is.

PROS. ATT.: Mrs. Good English, think carefully and tell me if you heard him do any violence to this fellow, Verb.

MRS. G. E. (*Doubtfully*): I — I don't know. Well, yes, I think I did.

PROS. ATT.: Tell us the circumstances.

MRS. G. E.: It might have been last week when he came in from school.

JUDGE (*Interrupting*): Madam, you are here to tell what you know; *not* what might have been.

MRS. G. E. (*Looking somewhat frightened*): I don't know.

PROS. ATT.: Thank you. That will be all, Mrs. English. (*She leaves the stand.*) Call the second witness, please.

BAILIFF: Vernon J. Verb. (*He goes to stand.*) Do you swear to tell the truth, the whole truth and nothing but the truth, so help you Dan Webster?

VERB: I do. (*He wears a bandage and limps.*)

PROS. ATT.: Mr. Verb, will you tell this court how you received these painful injuries?

VERB: That will not take long. I received them at the hands of that man. (*Points to* BILLY.)

PROS. ATT.: Had you quarrelled?

VERB: No. I had not provoked him in any way. He has always abused me. He never considered my tenses, nor my voice. He never cared whether I agreed with the subject. He threw me around, and this is the result. (*Touches his bandaged head.*)

PROS. ATT.: That is all, Mr. Verb. (*He withdraws.*)

DEF. ATT. (*Rising and crossing to stand*): I should like to cross-examine the witness.

JUDGE: Proceed.

DEF. ATT.: Mr. Verb, you say that you did not provoke this attack. Now think carefully and tell me if you and the accused ever had a disagreement.

VERB: Well, I did object to his careless treatment and I suppose I let him know it.

DEF. ATT.: You have many moods, haven't you?

VERB: Yes.

DEF. ATT.: You also change your tense, do you not?

VERB: Yes, I do.

DEF. ATT.: Sometimes you demand a helper, called an auxiliary, do you not?

VERB: Yes, I certainly do.

DEF. ATT. (*Threateningly*): Yet you claim that you have done nothing to provoke a reasonable man to anger?

VERB (*Hesitantly*): Y-y-es.

DEF. ATT.: I will name something for you which would arouse any man's anger. The principal parts of: *is*. You demand that they be: *is, was, have been*. Is there any reason in that, sir?

VERB: N-no.

DEF. ATT. (*Pressing it further*): Sometimes you are active; sometimes passive. Sometimes you take an object; sometimes you don't. Isn't this uncertain conduct enough to cause anger in any man who tried to learn your ways?

VERB (*Shrinking back in his chair*): I s-s-suppose so.

PROS. ATT. (*Coming forward*): Your honor, I object. This man is not strong. He is scarcely able to be here. He should not be subjected to such treatment.

JUDGE: Objection over-ruled. (*To* ACCUSED'S LAWYER.) Proceed.

DEF. ATT. (*Turning to audience*): Ladies and gentlemen of the jury — this man has admitted that he is unreliable, changeable and thoroughly irritating.

PROS. ATT. (*Vigorously*): I object. Mr. Verb is not on trial.

JUDGE: Objection sustained.

DEF. ATT.: Defense rests. (*Returns to his desk.*)

PROS. ATT.: Bailiff, summon Mrs. Noun.

BAILIFF: Mrs. Noun. (*She goes to the stand.*) Do you swear to tell the truth, the whole truth, and nothing but the truth so help you Webster always?

MRS. NOUN: Why, of course, don't I always?

JUDGE: Answer the question asked.

MRS. N.: I do.

PROS. ATT.: My dear young lady. I want you to tell me how long you have known the accused.

MRS. N.: For years and years. We're old friends.

PROS. ATT.: How has he treated you?

MRS. N.: He has always been very courteous.

PROS. ATT.: You have never been distressed in any way?

MRS. N.: No, not at all.

PROS. ATT.: He never called you names?

MRS. N.: No. You see, *I* do that myself. I name everything.

PROS. ATT.: That will do. (*Retires.*)

DEF. ATT. (*Coming forward*): I would like to ask the witness a few questions. Mrs. Noun, you have always found Mr. Scott courteous and agreeable, have you?

MRS. N.: Yes, I have.

DEF. ATT.: He is generally regarded so?

MRS. N.: The only name I have for him is "Gentleman."

DEF. ATT.: That will be all.

MRS. NOUN (*Turns brightly to the* JUDGE): The children are so fond of him. (*Turns toward the witness' bench and calls loudly.*) Preposition, come here and bring Conjunction and Interjection with you. (*Three small girls enter, holding hands.* PREPOSITION *drags a toy wagon which is her "object." They gather around the* JUDGE'S *desk.*) Tell the nice judge about the time Billy Scott found all of you in that paragraph where you were lost.

JUDGE (*Reproachfully*): Mrs. Noun, this court does not recognize the testimony of children.

MRS. N. (*In great surprise*): But, Judge, these are unusual children!

DEF. ATT.: Thank you, Mrs. Noun. These *are* charming children and I am sure the jury understands their affection for my client. We will let them return to their places now. (MRS. NOUN *and children leave.*)

PROS. ATT.: If we may resume the case, I should like to call the next witness, Your Honor.

JUDGE: Proceed.

PROS. ATT.: Please summon Addie Adjective, Bailiff.

BAILIFF (*Calling*): Addie Adjective. (*She goes to stand.*) Do you swear to tell the truth, the whole truth, and nothing but the truth — so help you Webster?

ADJ.: I do.

PROS. ATT.: Miss Adjective, do you know the accused?

MISS ADJ.: Yes, I know him.

PROS. ATT.: Do you regard him as a man who respects the feelings of others?

ADJ.: Well, no. For instance I offer him a great variety of words to use, but he ignores them and uses just one. He says everything is "swell." "That's a swell pie," "We had a swell game." "He's a swell guy" and "I saw a swell ship." He doesn't do me justice, you see!

PROS. ATT.: That is a good point. Now, have you ever observed his treatment of Mr. Verb?

ADJ.: I'm afraid not.

PROS. ATT.: Has he ever mentioned him to you?

ADJ.: Yes, he said he hated those darned old conjugations.

PROS. ATT.: Thank you, Miss Adjective. I am sure the jury understands the attitude of the accused when he used those terms. That will be all. (MISS ADJECTIVE *returns to witness bench.*)

DEF. ATT. (*Rising*): I object, Your Honor. Such testimony is mere hearsay and is not relevant to the case.

JUDGE: Objection over-ruled.

PROS. ATT.: Please summon Adam Adverb.

BAILIFF (*Calling him*): Adam Adverb. (*He comes forward.*) Do you promise to tell the truth, the whole truth and nothing but the truth, so help you Webster?

ADV.: I do. (*Mounts witness stand.*)

PROS. ATT.: Do you know the accused, Mr. Adverb?

ADV.: Yes, quite well.

PROS. ATT.: How has he treated you?

ADV.: With neglect, generally.

PROS. ATT.: Have you observed him with Mr. Verb?

ADV.: Yes, indeed. He was quite violent. He threw his principal parts all around. And he often failed to use an auxiliary for Mr. Verb though you know there are times when he must have one.

PROS. ATT.: Give me an example of that treatment.

ADV. (*After a short pause*): He'd say, "I been to the store" or "He done his lessons in school."

PROS. ATT.: Thank you, Mr. Adverb. That will be all. (*Retiring.*)

DEF. ATT. (*Coming forward to witness stand*): I should like to cross-examine the witness.

JUDGE: Proceed.

DEF. ATT.: Mr. Adverb, please tell this court what relation you are to Mr. Verb.

ADV.: I'm his half-brother.

DEF. ATT.: I see. Now, Mr. Adverb, tell the court who supports you?

ADV.: Why, Mr. Verb does. I've always depended on him.

DEF. ATT.: You are, then, very much influenced by what Mr. Verb thinks? You usually agree with him and do just as he says, don't you?

ADV.: Well, yes, I suppose so. He is so much stronger than I am.

DEF. ATT.: All that you said about my client was just what you'd heard Mr. Verb say, wasn't it?

ADV.: Well, yes, that is — I think so.

PROS. ATT. (*Rising, excitedly*): I object, Your Honor. Testimony which has been given should not be altered.

JUDGE (*Rebuking him*): Mr. Attorney, it is our task to establish the truth. If erroneous testimony has been given, it should be pointed out. Proceed with the cross examination.

DEF. ATT.: Haven't your own feelings for my client been very friendly?

ADV. (*Twisting his hands*): Yes, only I don't know him very well.

DEF. ATT.: That will be all.

PROS. ATT. (*Turns to audience*): Ladies and gentlemen of the jury, I ask you to think of the testimony you have heard. Think of the violence which has been done to a valued member of the

Good English family. Think of the suffering Mr. Verb has undergone in his principal parts, and his auxiliaries. All this has been caused by the outrageous carelessness of that man who is on trial. Thinking of all these things, I feel sure you will feel it your duty to bring in a verdict of "guilty." This I ask you to do, for the sake of the Good English family in whom we take such pride! You are fair and just. I urge you to make a just decision. Thank you. (*Sits down.*)

JUDGE: Have you anything to say, Mr. Attorney for the Accused?

DEF. ATT. (*Rising and facing audience*) : Ladies and gentlemen of the jury, you have heard Mr. Verb admit that he is unreliable, changeable and not to be depended upon; while my client, Mr. Scott, is a reasonable man. You have heard the testimony of Mrs. Noun and have seen her three darling little daughters. They would not be allowed to associate with anyone who uses bad English. Think of your own difficulties with this Verb. Do *your* verbs always agree with their subjects? And what of your tenses? Do you always use the proper auxiliary with your past participles? No, ladies and gentlemen, I tell you no one can learn all the peculiarities of this fellow, Verb! For the sake of humanity, I ask you to find my client, Billy Scott, not guilty!

JUDGE: Ladies and gentlemen of the jury, you are now charged with the duty of sifting the testimony which you have heard, to determine its truth or falsity. This you must do fairly, impartially and honestly. This is a court of law in which no man should be condemned unfairly, and no evil-doer should be allowed to escape punishment. The jury will now render its decision. I declare this court in recess. (*Raps with gavel.*)

BAILIFF: (*Steps to the front of the stage. To a member of the audience.*) Will you act as foreman of the jury?

FOREMAN (*To audience*) : All those who believe Billy Scott innocent, stand. (*Counts them.*) Be seated, please. All who believe him guilty, stand. (*Counts them.*) Thank you. You may sit down, now. (*Turning to face the* JUDGE.) We are ready, Your Honor.

ENDING — IF FOUND GUILTY

JUDGE: What is the verdict?

DAN: Your Honor, we find the accused, Billy Scott, guilty as charged.

JUDGE: Billy Scott, stand and hear your sentence. (BILLY *is led by the* BAILIFF *before the* JUDGE'S *bench.*) This court finds you guilty of the crime of using a singular verb with a plural noun. I sentence you to one year at hard work in Junior High School. (BILLY *hangs his head.*) Court dismissed!

CURTAIN

ENDING — IF FOUND INNOCENT

JUDGE: What is the verdict?

DAN: Your Honor, we find the accused innocent.

JUDGE: Billy Scott, stand to hear the decision of this court. (BILLY *stands before the* JUDGE.) In the opinion of this court, you are innocent of the crime of which you are accused. It is my duty to send you forth, a free man. You are at liberty to return to your normal life. I declare this court dismissed. (BILLY'S *lawyer and witnesses crowd around him, shaking hands and patting him on the back.*)

CURTAIN

CHILDREN OF THE CALENDAR

by Carol Hartley

Characters

FATHER TIME
JANUARY
FEBRUARY
MARCH
APRIL
MAY
JUNE
JULY
AUGUST
SEPTEMBER
OCTOBER
NOVEMBER
DECEMBER

SETTING: FATHER TIME'S *workshop.*

TIME: *Any time, any day.*

AT RISE: JANUARY *is sitting at end of table near fireplace.* FEBRUARY *sits on stool at left front, pouting, chin in hand. Rest of children are grouped about the table.* FATHER TIME *places scythe against rear wall and goes about table inspecting the children's work.*

FATHER TIME: How are you getting along with the calendar, children?

AUGUST: Just fine, Father Time. Is this all right? (*Holds up picture she is working on.*)

FATHER TIME: Very nice, August. That is just the right shade of blue for a summer sky, and that old swimming hole looks as though one could jump right into it.

MAY: Isn't this apple orchard just beautiful, Father Time?

FATHER TIME (*Going over to* MAY): Yes, May, it is, and your letters and figures are nice and even. They improve every year.

JULY: Look at my picture. (*Holds it up*) Doesn't it look like a Fourth of July celebration?

JANUARY: If you put in any more flags you'll have to put them on the back. (*Everyone laughs.*)

JUNE (*Busily cutting paper*): I love to make the new calendar. See my nice green hills and fields. (*Holds up picture.*)

OCTOBER: I like mine better. Look at the color of those maple leaves, and aren't those the nicest pumpkins you ever saw?

SEPTEMBER: I'd like to see any of you make anything better than this apple. (*Takes a big bite of his apple.*)

JANUARY: How about giving us some apples?

SEPTEMBER: Sure, here they are. (*Gets basket of apples from rear and passes them to children.*) I have lots of them.

NOVEMBER: I think my month is the best. Thanksgiving with turkey, cranberries and all the trimmings. Do I love turkey! (*Rubs his stomach.*)

MARCH: I believe people are happiest in the spring. The snow melts, the streams begin to flow again, the pussy-willows come out, the first flowers poke up their heads. Just wait till I get this finished.

DECEMBER: How about me? Do you think you could get along without me? Remember, I have Christmas.

MAY: I think we'll keep you, December. Everybody loves Christmas.

FATHER TIME: I love this time of making the calendar best of all, for then all my children are here with me. I always feel sad when the first month, January, is torn off the calendar. February goes next . . .

SEPTEMBER: How about February? Hi, Feb., old boy. Better get busy. You don't want to be the last to finish.

FEBRUARY (*Grumpily*): There's no hurry. My month is so short, it won't take long.

JANUARY (*Jumps up and rushes over to door and opens it wide*): Whew!! My snow and icicles are melting! I feel all weak. Guess I was too close to the fireplace.

DECEMBER (*Shouting with laughter*): Ha! Ha! Ha! Looks like a January thaw! (*Children all laugh.* JANUARY *smiles weakly and fans himself with his hat. Work is resumed.*)

OCTOBER: Aren't calendars funny? Why aren't the months all the same length?

NOVEMBER: They can't be. There are 365 days in the year, and if you divide it by twelve it doesn't come out even, so the calendar makers tried to give every other month an extra day.

OCTOBER: Why does leap year only come once in four years? Why doesn't it come every year?

JANUARY: I can tell you. The solar year is 365¼ days long because it takes the sun that long to go around in its orbit. The calendar has just 365 days even, because we can't have an extra quarter of a day in it.

MARCH: Wouldn't that be funny? To have an extra quarter of a day, and then have to start a new day? That wouldn't do at all.

APRIL: That would be awful. The clocks would be all wrong, the days and nights would get all mixed up.

JANUARY: No, it wouldn't work at all. Pretty soon the solar year and the calendar year wouldn't be together, so something had to be done about that odd quarter of a day.

APRIL: What did they do about it?

SEPTEMBER: That's an easy one. Since we have an extra quarter of a day every year, we let them go for four years. That makes a whole day, so we add that day to February and call it leap year.

FEBRUARY (*Suddenly shouts*): It isn't fair! I don't like it!

FATHER TIME (*Goes over to* FEBRUARY, *places his hand on the boy's shoulder*): What's wrong, my boy? What isn't fair?

FEBRUARY: I am the shortest of all the months. I'm just a runt, and I hate being a runt! (FEBRUARY *is almost in tears.*)

JULY: Don't feel badly, February. Size doesn't count.

FEBRUARY: That's all right for you to say. It's all your fault I'm so short!

JULY: Why, February, what did I do?

FEBRUARY: It wasn't you exactly. It was Julius Caesar. When he was Emperor of Rome he wanted July to be a long month because it was his birth month and he wanted to honor himself; so he borrowed a day from February. That gave July 31 days and left me with 29.

AUGUST: 29? But February, you only have 28 days now, except in leap year. What happened to the other one?

FEBRUARY: That's your fault, August. Well, not yours exactly, but Caesar Augustus'. He was a great-nephew of Julius Caesar so he became Emperor, too. He called August his lucky month because the best things happened to him in that month. He wanted August to have 31 days, the same as July, so he borrowed one of my days. And now look at me! I'm the very shortest of all the months, and I can't even catch up in Leap Year! It just isn't fair!

APRIL: But, February, you have so many wonderful days. You are the only one who has the extra day for leap year, and you have ground-hog day . . .

FEBRUARY: Who cares about that?

APRIL: The ground-hog does. If he doesn't see his shadow he knows that spring has come, and everyone is glad when spring comes.

SEPTEMBER: And if he does see his shadow he can go back and snooze for another six weeks. Wouldn't that be wonderful to sleep six weeks? (*Yawns and stretches.*)

MARCH: Leave it to September. How he does love his lazy days! (*Everyone laughs.*)

FEBRUARY: I don't think that's funny. I'm still short.

DECEMBER: You have St. Valentine's Day, when people send valentines and sweet little notes to one another.

FEBRUARY: Aw, that's nothing. Just a lot of love stuff.

JUNE: The birds are supposed to choose their mates on that day. Doesn't that mean anything?

FEBRUARY (*Grudgingly*): I suppose so, a little.

MAY: And February, you have Abraham Lincoln's birthday, and George Washington's, too.

AUGUST: I don't have a single holiday in my month. I would love to have such great people born in August.

NOVEMBER: Yes, February, Lincoln and Washington, two of the greatest men in the world born in your month, and you squawk about it. And there were other great men born in February, too: Charles Dickens, Thomas Edison, Henry W. Longfellow, Victor Hugo and a lot of others. Shall I name some more, Feb.?

FEBRUARY (*Brightening*): No, that does it. I'm kind of ashamed of myself for making so much fuss. I guess you're right. Those are pretty fine days. Why, sure! They're the very best!

JUNE: You know you could go to live in one of the countries where they still use the old calendar as it was before Cæsar changed it.

FEBRUARY (*Jumping up*): No, sir! I like America. I'll stay here!

FATHER TIME (*Smiles and pats* FEBRUARY *on the shoulder*): That's the spirit, my boy. Be proud of your country and of the job you have to do.

FEBRUARY: I'm sorry I was so cross, Father Time. I never will be again. I'll be just as proud of February as I can be. It has *everything,* even if it is the shortest month of the year. Out of my way, everybody! Let me at that table! I'm going to make my part of this calendar the finest month you ever saw. Oh, Boy! What I'm going to do! (*Goes to work with vim.*)

THE END

MUCH ADO ABOUT ANTS

by Anna Lenington Heath

Characters

DICK MURCHISON, *worried young editor*
NANCY MURCHISON, *Dick's sister*
BOB MOORE, *cousin living with the Murchisons*
BABE MOORE, *Bob's sister*
HENRY V. HENRY, *vacuum cleaner salesman*
SUE DAMON

SETTING: *The living room of the Murchison home.*

AT RISE: DICK *is seated at desk. He writes furiously for moment, thinks a while, then writes again. He is disgusted with what he has written, wads it up and tosses it into air, muttering. He tramps about in distraction, clutching at hair.* BOB *enters at right, holding a catcher's suit. He is tired and dejected.* DICK *stares at him a moment in appraisal.*

DICK (*In mock dramatics*): Ha! No flags flying. No bands playing. No air of triumph. (*Drops into normal speech*) I gather that the Pigtown team won the game.

BOB (*Hurling glove into corner and dropping into chair*): Boy, oh boy! Did we take a beating: nineteen to three.

DICK: But the coach, Coxe, said last night that you had it in the bag.

BOB (*Bitterly*): Oh, yeah, Coxe said! Coxe ought to be in jail.

DICK: What did he do?

BOB: Our pitcher, Lee, blew up in the first half of the third, and Coxe kept him in there till the second of the sixth. When he finally pulled him out, the second pitcher, Burt, was so mad and rattled that he went clear out of control. Everybody hit him, even little Petie Hull, who never hit anything before. Nineteen to three they beat us. The Pigtowns, who hadn't won a game this season. Coxe ought to be in jail with the key thrown away. (BOB *sprawls in disgust.* DICK *stares at him a moment, then paces about beating his right fist into his left palm, muttering.)*

DICK: Rejection. Discouragement. Despair.

BOB (*Testily*): No. Incompetence. Pig-headedness. Stupidity.

DICK (*Repeating as he walks*): Incompetence. Pig-headedness. Stupidity. (*Nearly collides with* NANCY *who enters at left*) Oomph!

NANCY (*In sarcasm*): Stupidity, sure. (DICK *continues to stare.*) Remember me? Your sister, Nancy?"

DICK (*Turning away in offended dignity*): Don't be silly. You should know —

NANCY (*Laying bundle of mail on table and pulling off hat*): I certainly should know, living here as I do. You are the editor of the school paper, *The Campus Limited.* It is all ready to go to press except your own special article, The Thought For The Week. You are foaming around trying to think of something to write about. We go through this every week.

DICK (*Scathingly*): If I seem to be making heavy weather of it, just toss off some fruity subjects yourself, Nancy. Let's hear a couple of them.

NANCY: There's fuming. Fretting. Tearing your hair and —

BOB: Irony. Sisterly gibes and —

DICK: You two are a pain in the neck. I'm trying seriously to make my weekly article a helpful thing and you clack around with a lot of flighty levitations —

NANCY: No, no, Dicky. Levity is the word. (DICK *ignores her and returns to desk and types.*)

BOB: Sorry, Dick. Forget it, please. (*To* NANCY) What's in the mail, Nan?

NANCY (*Going through bundle*): The magazines. Letter for mother. Your star map. (*Hands* BOB *magazine*) Overdue from library and a lot of ads for Dad. (BOB *looks at star map.* NANCY *lays rest of mail on table. Takes one ad from envelope which she drops on table. Reads ad.*)

DICK: How many c's in recommend?

BOB: Better say praise.

NANCY (*In excitement*): Dick! Bob! Listen. This thing I thought an ad is a report from the Termite Riddance Company on an inspection they made of this house. It's awful. (*Reads*) "Floor joists under living room heavily infested. Ceiling joists of same area eaten away. Foundation of bow-window weakened." Why, that's right here. Over us and under us.

BOB: I knew there were some ants around but I never heard of any inspection. When was it done?

NANCY: While we were at camp, I suppose. This is dated yesterday.

BOB: Better call your father as soon as he gets to his office and ask him what to do. (DICK *begins to type furiously.* NANCY *runs to him, dropping the report among papers on his desk.*)

NANCY: Dick, oh, Dick, don't —

DICK: I've got to finish this article before the house falls down around our ears. It's important. Move away and don't bother.

NANCY: But Dick, the way you type! It'll set up a vibration like— well, you know —

BOB: The measured cadence of marching feet. Been known to cause bridges to fall.

DICK: I tell you this article has to be —

NANCY: Then break it up, Dick. Just hunt and peck without any swing to it.

DICK (*Outraged*): Hunt and peck! Me!

NANCY (*Pleads*): Not so violent! Can't you use a pencil?

DICK: No! (*Makes several starts at writing. Tears paper from machine and flings it to floor*) You've made me forget what I was going to write. (*Rises and brushes papers from desk to floor. Sound of thumps off left*) What's that?

BOB: That's Babe jumping rope. I'll stop her. (*He goes out.* DICK *starts tramping about.* NANCY *stops him.* BOB *returns with* BABE *who has a jump rope.*)

BOB: You will have to be very quiet, Babe. The whole place is shot with termites and likely to collapse any minute. Better get into that chair and sit light. (BABE *climbs into rocker and squats uncertainly on heels.*)

BABE: Is it safe to telephone?

DICK (*After a questioning look at* NANCY *and* BOB): Well, if it is important.

BABE: Chuck Lacey and Sue Damon are coming over to practice the trumpet duet they are to give Friday night.

DICK: Trumpets! Oh, my Sunday hat! The walls of Jericho fell down from trumpets. What Chuck and Sue'd do —

NANCY: Stop yelling and quietly phone them about our difficulty and they will —

BOB: Just a minute, Dick. Chuck's father is head of the real estate firm that's trying to sell this place. We'd better keep quiet about the ants till your father sees that report.

NANCY: Good head, Bob. We'll have to think of something else.

DICK: Tell 'em we've got bubonic plague.

BABE (*In derision*): That's not so good, either. Sue's Dad is health officer, and let him hear about any kind of disease and he'd be here asking questions right now.

BOB: Plague's out, then. Any other suggestions?

NANCY: They are coming right after Chuck's gym class, aren't they, Babe? (BABE *nods.*) It's too late to stop them, then. We'll just have to keep them from playing. Talk fast about other things.

DICK (*Glumly*): What other things?

NANCY: You talk about your article. Wave your arms and stamp— Oh, no. Don't stamp and don't yell. Just wave and whisper dramatically. And you, Bob, talk about the game and the coach.

BOB: What I'd say about the game and coach would probably make the floor drop out from under us. Isn't there some less painful subject?

NANCY: This whole thing is painful. You just talk and talk and talk and don't let Chuck and Sue play a note. If worse comes to worst I can always feed them.

BOB (*Fervently*): You have something there, Nancy.

DICK (*Peevishly*): Sit down in the chair, Babe, and stop teetering as if you were about to jump.

BABE (*Fearfully*): Won't I be heavier that way?

BOB (*Interrupting*): No, kid, you'll weigh just the same in any position, and sitting, you will look less like a demented frog.

BABE (*Stubbornly*): I'd weigh less in water.

DICK (*In heavy sarcasm*): We could bring in a tub and let her sit in it.

BOB (*Shortly*): Stop it, Dick. Sit down, Babe. (*She slips to sitting position*) Now let's consider — (*Phone rings sharply. No one moves. Phone rings again.* NANCY *tiptoes to answer it.*)

NANCY (*At phone, whispers*): Hello. (*Repeats word twice, louder each time*) Yes. Yes, I'll call him. (*To* BOB) For you, Bob.

BOB (*At phone*): Hello. Oh, yes, Bill. (*Pause*) Absolutely not.

(*Pause*) We have the house full of relatives and must be very quiet. (*Pause*) Yes, a very large family. Sorry. Good-bye. (*Replaces phone*) Bill and his brother wanting to show us a new tumbling act they're learning.

NANCY: That's the last thing we want to see. (*Sound of steps off right*) Oh, oh, here are Chuck and Sue. (*Loud knock at door at right.*)

DICK: Come on in. Don't knock the door down. (*Knock is repeated.* DICK *opens door.* HENRY *breezes in, dragging vacuum cleaner.*)

HENRY: Good-day, ladies and gentlemen. I am Henry V. Henry, introducing the Little Giant vacuum cleaner, manufactured by Atlas, Atlas and Atlas, of Atlas, Mo. I have an appointment with a Mrs. Murchison of this address, to demonstrate the Little Giant. Will one of you kindly tell the lady I am here?

NANCY: Mother was called away suddenly. She must have forgotten the appointment. I will remind her when she returns, and I am sure she will arrange for some other time.

HENRY: No time like the present. I am here. The Little Giant is here. You are here. We will demonstrate. (*Moves machine and sets it down heavily.*)

DICK (*Nervously*): Don't bang that thing down so hard.

HENRY (*Loftily*): This machine is of the sturdiest construction throughout. Slight jars will not harm it in the least.

BOB: Slight jars have precipitated avalanches before now.

HENRY: True, true, my dear young man, but that interesting natural phenomenon has no bearing whatever on the matter at hand.

DICK: That's what you think, laddie.

HENRY (*To* NANCY): These young men are pleased to be flippant, madam, but I am sure you would like to see this remarkable machine in operation. Is there an outlet handy where I can plug it in? It will draw matter up through this rug in a manner never seen before.

BOB: That's what we are afraid of.

HENRY: I do not understand, sir. You —

NANCY (*Interrupting*): Please, we do not wish to have you demonstrate. The Little Giant is all you claim for it, I'm sure, and more, but we do not want a demonstration.

DICK: We do not want a demonstration.

BOB: We do not.

BABE: Do not.

HENRY: I find your conduct strange —

BOB: We are a strange family. Too many ants and not enough uncles. (HENRY *backs toward door at right, carrying cleaner.*)

HENRY: Very well, but I must say that never before have I been so —

NANCY: Goodbye. I will have Mother call you. (HENRY *exits, slamming door.*)

DICK: Whew! Another slam or two like that and we'll need a steam shovel to excavate us.

BOB (*To* BABE): Sit down, kid. (*She sits. Voices outside right*) Here come Chuck and Sue.

NANCY: Remember, all of you. Talk, talk, talk. (*Opens door.*) Hi, Chuck and Sue. Come in. (CHUCK *and* SUE *enter, carrying trumpets.*)

CHUCK AND SUE: Hi, everybody.

DICK, BOB AND BABE: Hi.

CHUCK: What's the good word?

DICK (*Beginning loudly, then remembering to whisper*): There isn't any. I've got the *Campus Limited* all ready for press except my special Thought For The Week, and can't for the life of me think of a topic to write about. Bob and Nancy think up silly ones but they're no good. No good at all. I say, they are no good at —

SUE: What's wrong with him, Chuck?

BOB: Think nothing of him, Sue. Dick gets into dithers like that every week over his articles. (*To* CHUCK) Did you see the game, Chuck?

CHUCK: I'll say I did. You guys sure took a walloping from a team that hadn't won a game before this season. You need a new pitcher. (NANCY *tiptoes out at left.*)

BOB: What we need is a new coach. Coxe ought to be in jail. He kept Lee in there pitching long after he'd run out of everything. Yeah, we need a new coach. That's what we need — (NANCY *returns with plate of doughnuts.*)

SUE: Oh, forget Coxe and that game. We came to practice our trumpet duet. You'll play accompaniment for us, won't you, Nancy?

NANCY: Have some doughnuts first. (SUE *takes one.* CHUCK *takes two. They eat.* BABE *wiggles to squatting position again.*)

DICK (*In hoarse whisper*): I've got to get this article written and I haven't a single idea. I just can't —

CHUCK: Why the raucous whisper, Dick? Laryngitis or did you lose your voice cheering for Bob's team?

BOB: Coxe ought to be in jail. I say, Coxe ought to be —

CHUCK: And I say if we are going to practice we'd better be at it. Sue's gotta —

NANCY: Another doughnut, Chuck? (*He takes another.*)

SUE (*In annoyance to* BABE): I wish you'd sit down, Babe. You make me nervous and you can't be comfortable, jiggling there like that. (BABE *pretends not to hear.*)

DICK (*Walking about on tiptoe and with long steps*): I can't get a single idea and time is running out-out-out-out-

SUE: His needle's stuck.

CHUCK: That last doughnut wasn't as good as the others.

BABE (*Dryly*): The sixth seldom is. (BOB *and* DICK *speak together.*)

BOB: Coxe ought to be in jail.

DICK: Time is running out.

SUE (*Clutching* CHUCK'S *arm in alarm*): I don't like this, Chuck. Dick whispering and raving like a horror film. Bob hounding Coxe to jail, Nancy mincing around on eggs, and Babe wobbling there like a Billikin. I don't like it. It's crazy. They've all got something. Come away before we get it. (CHUCK *takes another doughnut.* SUE *snatches it from him and throws it back on plate*) They're fried in crankcase oil. They'll poison you. Come on. (SUE *drags* CHUCK *out at right, taking his trumpet and leaving hers. Slams door.*)

NANCY (*After all have stood an instant expecting the roof to fall*): Well they're gone. And we'll be lucky if Sue doesn't send in an officer and an alienist. She's some worked up and — (SUE *bursts in, grabs her trumpet and starts out.*)

DICK (*Sharply*): Don't slam that door!

SUE: I will slam the door if I want to! (*Exits with violent slam.*)

BABE (*After another wait during which nothing happens*): Now they're gone, for sure.

BOB: Unless Chuck comes back after another doughnut. Your father must be in his office now, Dick.

DICK: Yes, I'll call and ask him what we'd better do. (*To* NANCY) Where is that report, Nancy?

NANCY (*Taking envelope from table*): Here. No, this isn't it. It's only the envelope. (*Looks about on table. Feels in pocket*) I read it and Dick yelled and —

BOB: You ran over to his desk to stop him. Probably dropped it there. (*All hunt through papers on desk and floor.* BOB *looks at one he picks up a moment. Holds it out to* NANCY.) Is this it?

NANCY (*Giving it a quick glance*): Yes, that's it.

BOB: Well, we can all relax. This isn't a report from the termite company of their investigation of the premises here. It's just an ad.

NANCY, DICK a 1 BABE: Ad!

BOB: Yes. Her(on the first page is what Nancy read, and below it says, "Don't delay till damage as suggested above is done. Call the Termite Riddance Company at the first sign of the insects. Save your home." Then the address. You didn't get all the facts, Nancy.

NANCY (*Dropping into chair, gasps*): All that nervous strain for nothing.

BOB: We've made a reputation for general loopiness, at least.

BABE: Can I let down my whole weight now?

BOB (*Helping her from chair*): You can. You can even jump rope right here if you like. (BABE *rubs her cramped legs. Makes a few light skips. Satisfied that it is safe she whirls through door at left and is heard jumping heavily outside.*)

DICK (*Sagely*): There is no great upheaval without some progress.

BOB: Yeah?

DICK: Yeah. I have the topic for my article. Will you escort your cousin out that I may write undisturbed?

BOB: With pleasure. (*Offers* NANCY *his arm. They exit grandly at left.*)

DICK (*Whipping paper into typewriter and chuckling happily*): Get All The Facts! Boy oh boy, will I go to town with this! (*Types swiftly as curtain falls.*)

THE END

MIDNIGHT BURIAL

by Kay Hill

Characters

SUZIE
BETTY
CHUBBY
NONA
SALLY
ROSIE
FIRST LEADER
SECOND LEADER

SETTING: *Woods at night.*

AT RISE: *Empty stage. Enter from left,* SUZIE *and* CHUBBY, *carrying a large square parcel wrapped in brown paper.* BETTY, *looking behind her as she follows, bumps into the two ahead and makes them drop the parcel.*

SUZIE: There now! See what you've done! Can't you look where you're going, Betty?

BETTY: Sh-h! Do you want the whole camp down on us to see what we're doing in the woods after lights-out? I'm almost sure I heard something a minute ago.

SUZIE: Nonsense! You're imagining it. Well, Chubby, this is as good a spot as any to hide the body.

CHUBBY: Don't talk about *bodies!* Just think, if we'd eaten that cake, *we'd* have been the dead bodies!

SUZIE: Do you think they'd have buried us out here in the woods? I'd like that — the pine trees whispering at night, and sprinkling us with needles on a hot day.

BETTY: Will you *stop,* Suzie! You're giving me the creeps. How on earth, Chubby, did your mother happen to get poison in the cake, anyway?

CHUBBY: It was a terrible mistake. My mother made the cake yesterday and sent it to the post office right away. This morning, she discovered the vanilla bottle she'd used was an old one my little brother Freddy had filled up with rat poison. She got me on the telephone this afternoon just after the box arrived. She was nearly out of her mind until she found I hadn't opened the box yet.

BETTY: And it looks so good. Just think — one bite of that luscious-looking cake and (*Dramatically*) we'd be writhing in death agony!

SUZIE: Well, let's get it over with. We can't light a fire out here in the woods. We'll have to bury it.

BETTY: What'll we dig a hole with?

SUZIE (*Aghast*): What a bunch of dopes we are! We need a shovel!

BETTY: I know where there's a hoe.

CHUBBY: Where?

BETTY: Over in Farmer Green's field. I saw it lying there this afternoon.

SUZIE: Come on, then, let's get it. Leave the box here. (SUZIE, CHUBBY *and* BETTY *rush off right. A minute later, three more* GIRLS *enter left, walking on tiptoe.*)

NONA: I'm sure they went this way. Come on, we must be close on their track. (*Sees box*) What's this?

ROSIE: They were carrying something when they sneaked out of Chubby's tent. This must be it.

SALLY: What do you suppose is in it?

NONA: Only one way to find out. (*Tears off wrapping and lifts lid of box*) It's a cake!

SALLY: A *beautiful* cake. Chocolate with pink peppermint icing — I can smell the peppermint.

NONA: So that's why they came out here, the greedy things, so they wouldn't have to share it.

ROSIE: But why did they leave it here?

SALLY: Probably heard us coming and got scared. Well, I don't know about you two, but *I* think finders are keepers. (*Breaks a piece off and raises it to her mouth.* NONA *slaps it out of her hand.*)

NONA: Greedy pig! Wait till I divide it — share and share alike.

I'll have to break it. Here's your piece, Sally. And one for you, Rosie.

ROSIE (*As she raises the cake to take a bite, her mouth already open*) : I'm thirsty. I wish we had something to drink with it.

SALLY: There's a brook down the hill back there. Let's fill the box — it's tin.

ROSIE: Let's. (*They jump up and run through bushes, centre.* SALLY *comes back, stealthily, and grabs her piece of cake. Just as her teeth bite in,* NONA *pops back and says sternly—"Sally!"* SALLY *drops the cake guiltily and follows* NONA *off again.* SUZIE, CHUBBY, *and* BETTY *reappear at right, with hoe.*)

SUZIE: It doesn't feel very sharp. But we can try. Here's a soft spot. (*They dig, or pretend to, quickly.*) There! Where's the box?

CHUBBY: Look! The cake is out of the box and all broken up.

BETTY: I *knew* we were being followed.

SUZIE: Don't be silly! Chipmunks, of course!

BETTY: Chipmunks?

SUZIE: Or squirrels. They're inquisitive little beggars, just love to get into things. Wonder where their dead bodies are, poor things.

CHUBBY: But the box is gone, too! Don't you try to tell me, Suzie Blake, that any old chipmunk ever walked off with the tin box!

SUZIE (*Patiently*) : But of course, Chubby — that's just what squirrels and chipmunks love, anything bright and odd. The little imps have hidden it somewhere.

BETTY: I don't like it! I'm sure I heard the bushes crackle when we came down the path.

SUZIE: Well, Betty, if nothing else will satisfy you, we'll take a look around. I'll go back the way we came. You and Chubby go that way. (*Pointing to right side of stage*) Meet here in five minutes. (*They go off in their separate directions.* NONA, ROSIE *and* SALLY *return from centre, carrying water. They sit down around the cake.* SALLY *sits on edge of hoe, which makes the handle fly up in the air.* SALLY *yells and sprawls on the ground, rubbing the spot that hurts, while the other two jump up in dismay, staring at the hoe.*)

NONA: Where did it come from?

ROSIE: And look at that hole. That wasn't there before!

SALLY: I'm s-scared. Let's go back.

NONA: We might as well. We can take the cake with us. (*Offstage, left,* SUZIE'S *voice "Come on, Chubby. I told Betty there was no one."*)

NONA: Quiet! It's Suzie. Hide the cake!

ROSIE: I'll sit in front of it. (*She does. Enter* SUZIE *and* CHUBBY, *left,* BETTY *right. They stop short.*)

SUZIE: What are you doing here?

CHUBBY (*Suddenly and loudly*): The cake! Where's the cake?

NONA: Ha! You thought you'd eat it all yourselves. Well, you're too late! We've eaten it all up!

SUZIE, CHUBBY *and* BETTY (*In chorus*): Wha — a-t!

SUZIE: You ate it? You ate it *all!*

SALLY: Certainly. It's a lesson to you not to be so stingy hereafter!

CHUBBY (*Starting to sob*): Murderers, that's what we are — murderers —

SUZIE: How do you feel, Nona?

NONA: I'm fine — how are you?

SUZIE: Do you feel any pain, Sally?

SALLY: Not a twinge. Cake agrees with me, especially in the woods at midnight.

SUZIE: What about you, Rosie?

ROSIE: I'm all right.

CHUBBY: This is a nightmare — a horrible dream! We'll go to jail.

SUZIE: Now, Chubby, keep cool. All may not be lost. If we can get them to a doctor in time... maybe he has an antidote, or a stomach pump. Now you two take Rosie and Sally. I'll take care of Nona. Here, Nona, put your arm across my shoulder.

NONA: What nonsense is this?

ROSIE: I *won't* get up. (*Resists* CHUBBY'S *efforts to move her, but* CHUBBY *hauls her up with strength of desperation*) All right, there's your old cake. But I'm going to have one piece anyway! (*Snatches it.*)

SUZIE: *Stop!* Don't eat that! It's full of rat poison — (*After a shocked moment of stillness,* ROSIE *hurls the cake as far as possible away from her,* SALLY *goes limp in* BETTY'S *arms, and* NONA *says in whisper — "Rat poison!"*)

SUZIE: We'll bury it right now, before anything else happens. Come on, everybody help. (*In a moment, everyone is frantic-*

AUNT POLLY: Ah, but they didn't — that is — not *entirely.*

BILL: But we call them *Arabic* numbers.

AUNT POLLY: I know, but we really should call them *Hindu* — Arabic.

MARY ANN: You mean the Arabs got their numbers from the Hindus?

AUNT POLLY: To a great extent, Mary Ann — and the Hindus borrowed some of their ideas from the Chinese, the Persians, the Egyptians and the early Babylonians.

BILLY: Wow! Our numbers really do have a history!

MARY ANN: How did the Arabians happen to get the numbers from the Hindus?

AUNT POLLY (*Seriously*): Do you really want to know, children?

MARY ANN: Of course, Aunt Polly.

BILL: Sure thing.

AUNT POLLY: Well, settle down then, because it's a long story. You might as well be comfortable. (MARY ANN *sinks into an easy chair.* BILL *plops down on a footstool.*)

BILL: All right now, Aunt Polly. How *did* the Arabians get their numbers from the Hindus?

AUNT POLLY: Well, of course, there had always been a great deal of commerce carried on between India and Arabia, and you know how trade spreads ideas and knowledge from one country to another.

MARY ANN: Sure, we learned that in school.

AUNT POLLY: Well, historians think that knowledge of the Hindu numerals was carried to Arabia by traders who used these numbers in their business. But there was one single event that *officially* introduced the Hindu numbers into the Arabian court of the Caliph Al-Mansur. One day in the year 772 a Hindu arrived at the court of Bagdad and was received by the Grand Vizier. (*There is the sound of an Oriental gong. Enter the* GRAND VIZIER *and the* HINDU SCHOLAR. HINDU *carries a scroll. The spot is played on them and they present their scene on one side of the stage.*)

VIZIER: You have the look of a Hindu and a scholar. May I ask your business with the Caliph Al-Mansur, the All-Wise, the gracious lord of Bagdad?

HINDU (*Proudly*): I do not *solicit* an interview. The *Caliph* has *sent* for *me.*

VIZIER: Then he will see you shortly. At present, he is closeted with the court astronomers His daughter is shortly to wed and they must decide the most auspicious day and hour for the ceremony.

HINDU: So he is with the astronomers? It is astronomy that causes my presence here. I bring astronomical tables which stand in high authority among my people, having been derived from the great Brahmagupta. It is the Caliph's wish that they may be translated into Arabic.

VIZIER: So, you are one of those! The Caliph has drawn to this court the most famous scientists of the East — men versed in science and astronomy. The great manuscripts of the Greeks are being translated by us into Arabic. All of this knowledge becomes the property of Arabians. What, O, Hindu, have *you* to add to our vast fund of scientific knowledge? (*The Oriental gong sounds again. The spot returns to* AUNT POLLY *and the children. Exit* VIZIER *and* HINDU.)

BILL: And what *did* he have, Auntie — just a lot of stuff about star-gazing?

AUNT POLLY (*Solemnly*): That Hindu astronomer, Bill, is credited with having introduced — officially — Hindu numerals, *with the zero,* into Arabia. When he translated his tables he had to use the Hindu numbers.

BILL: Why? If he were translating from Hindu to Arabic why didn't he translate from Hindu numbers, to Arabic numbers!

AUNT POLLY: For the simple reason, Billy, that the Arabs didn't have numbers!

MARY ANN: Didn't have numbers? My goodness, Aunt Polly, what did they use before they adopted the Hindu system?

AUNT POLLY: *Words,* Mary Ann. They wrote out their numbers in *words.* Of course, they could abbreviate to simplify them somewhat. But it was a very unsatisfactory system.

BILL: They must have been glad to get a good system like the Hindu numbers.

AUNT POLLY: They were; they revised it somewhat, and changed the forms of some of the numerals, but the system is still mainly the *Hindu* system.

BILL: How did *we* get the Hindu-Arabic numbers, Auntie? Did the early settlers bring them?

AUNT POLLY: Yes, they had learned the Hindu-Arabic system in Europe.

MARY ANN: Then how did the numbers go from Arabia to Europe, Aunt Polly?

AUNT POLLY (*Laughing*): My goodness, Mary Ann. Now you really have asked me a question. No one is certain just *exactly* how they did get there. There are several possibilities. *You* ought to be able to figure out *one,* Bill, from the history you studied in the fifth grade.

BILL: Oh, gee, I know! *Trade!* The people of Europe wanted the spices and other rich products of the East. I remember *that.*

AUNT POLLY: Trade is probably the best explanation. We can easily see how traders could introduce the new number system into Europe.

BILL: Sure. When European merchants bought products from the Eastern traders they just *had* to learn something about their way of counting.

AUNT POLLY: We feel sure that some knowledge of the Hindu-Arabic numbers must have been carried into Europe by traders. But there are some historians who claim that an Italian, called Leonardo of Pisa, deserves the credit for acquainting his fellow-countrymen with the knowledge of the East. Leonardo's father was a commercial agent in Northern Africa, representing the interests of a firm of merchants in Pisa. His son, Leonardo, was educated in the city of Bougia in Africa, and there Leonardo learned the arithmetic knowledge of the Arabians. (*Oriental gong sounds again. Spot shifts to side to* LEONARDO *and* ALI. LEONARDO *is studying a scroll.*)

LEONARDO: But this is a wonderful thing you have shown me, Ali. To think — with only nine symbols and this wonderful other symbol, *this dot* — you can express any numbers you want.

ALI (*Gravely*): It is this wonderful "other symbol" as you call it, my son, that gives the system its power.

LEONARDO: What do you call it, Ali?

ALI: The Hindus call it the "void" or "heaven-space." We express it by a dot. With this, and the numbers one through nine, we can express any number we wish.

LEONARDO (*Enthusiastically*): My father has insisted that I learn much about arithmetic, Ali, so that I can help him with his business. I have learned to use the abacus. I have mastered the clumsy Roman system of counting. I have traveled through Egypt and Syria and Greece. I have collected all of the knowledge I could find concerning arithmetic. But here, in the custody of the Arabians, I have found the queen of all counting systems — the Hindu-Arabic numbers. I shall not rest, Ali, until I have carried this knowledge to my people. (*Gong sounds — spot returns to* AUNT POLLY *and the children. Exeunt* LEONARDO *and* ALI.)

BILL: Did he, Aunt Polly? Did he take the numbers back to Italy?

AUNT POLLY: Leonardo was so deeply impressed, Billy, that he wrote a book about the Hindu-Arabic system when he went back to Pisa. His book showed very plainly how superior the Arabic system was to the Roman system. Many people claim that this book was responsible for introducing the Hindu-Arabic numbers into Europe. Other historians claim that a monk named Gerbert, who afterwards became Pope Sylvester the Second, should receive the credit. He studied at the Great Moorish universities in Spain and later brought knowledge of the Hindu-Arabic numbers to Europe. Gerbert, however, apparently didn't know anything about that tenth symbol which the Hindus called "the void" or "heaven-space."

BILL: Do you mean the *zero,* Aunt Polly?

AUNT POLLY: That's right, Bill. We owe the name *zero* to Leonardo of Pisa. In this book he referred to it as *zephirum* — and from that we got the term *zero.*

MARY ANN: *When* did the people of Europe start to use the Hindu-Arabic numbers, Aunt Polly?

AUNT POLLY: Well, Mary Ann, that's hard to say definitely. But I can tell you this. The first manuscript in Europe to use Arabic numerals comes from the year 976. But as late as the year 1500, arithmetics were still explaining the system very carefully.

MARY ANN (*Slowly*): Let's see now. That means that even in Columbus's time people were using Roman numerals more than Arabic.

AUNT POLLY: Even in *Queen Elizabeth's* time Roman numbers were used frequently. It took several centuries for the Hindu-Arabic numerals to gain ground. In the meantime, the two systems lived side by side with the one gaining slowly.

BILL: Why did it take so long for the Arabic numbers to take the place of the Roman system?

MARY ANN: Why, Bill, that's easy. People were used to the Roman system. It's hard to change when you're accustomed to something.

AUNT POLLY: You're partly right, Mary Ann. For instance, take us today. Many people feel that our system of weighing and measuring is not so good as the metric system that the French use. But we still haven't adopted the metric system. It's difficult to force the people as a whole to accept new ideas.

BILL: It must have been confusing to have half of a country using Roman numerals and half using Arabic numbers.

AUNT POLLY: Well, Bill, in some cases authorities even went so far as to *prohibit* the use of the Hindu-Arabic system, especially in Italy. You see, Italy was a great trading nation and her people were among the first to realize the value of the new system.

BILL: You say people were *forbidden* to use Arabic numbers!

AUNT POLLY: Yes, indeed, Bill. For instance, scenes like this took place (*Fading*) in the great trading cities of Italy. (*Spot shifts to side to* ROBERTO *pacing sadly back and forth.* ANTONIO *enters and addresses him.*)

ANTONIO: Good evening, Roberto. Or is it? Judging from your gloomy expression, I should say something has gone amiss.

ROBERTO: Something has, Antonio. You should have been in the bank this morning — such confusion — such rage — such an annoyance —

ANTONIO: A robbery, my friend?

ROBERTO (*Groaning*): Worse! Haven't you heard, Antonio? An edict was issued today forbidding all bankers to use the simple Arabic numerals. We had to convert everything — all of our statements — Such stupidity! What pig-headed, doltish, imbecile ever —

ANTONIO (*Interrupting*): Indeed. I understand that somewhat the same order was issued to the booksellers at Padua. They have been prohibited to mark their stock in the clear ciphers of the Hindu-Arabic system, but must mark it in *letters*.

ROBERTO: Haven't the fools read the book of Leonardo of Pisa? Don't they have sense enough to realize what they are doing? I tell you, Antonio, the authorities can make rules until Florence ceases to exist, but the Hindu-Arabic numerals will some day count the commerce of the world! (*Spot returns to* AUNT POLLY *and the children. Exeunt* ANTONIO *and* ROBERTO.)

BILL: No wonder the numbers took so long to get around!

MARY ANN: All because people hate to change to something new!

AUNT POLLY: That isn't entirely the reason, Mary Ann. You see, most businessmen outside of Italy didn't seem to need the new figures until about 1550. Most of them used an abacus to do their figuring, and since numerals were used only to record the answer, Roman numerals did as well as any. Cheap paper was not known, and there were no pencils similar to modern ones until much later. Figures had to be erased after they were used.

MARY ANN: That must have been very inconvenient.

AUNT POLLY: It was, Mary Ann. So the merchant clung to his counter or abacus. As long as businessmen didn't require the new figures, the schools didn't teach them.

BILL: Well, look Aunt Polly. Business of today doesn't require Roman numbers and yet Mary Ann had a homework assignment on them tonight.

AUNT POLLY: Look at your great-grandfather's old clock, Billy. What kind of figures do you see on it?

BILL (*Slowly*): Roman numbers! I've never even noticed them before.

AUNT POLLY: Look at the chapter headings in this book.

BILL: Roman numbers!

AUNT POLLY: And on your way home, notice the cornerstone date of the old church on the corner.

BILL: We use Roman numbers in making outlines too.

MARY ANN: Well, personally, I'm glad those are the only uses we have for those old Roman numbers. — Suppose we had to say today's date in them. Let's see — It would be "today is the ______ day of ____________, in the year MCMLXX."

BILL: I'd never get beyond the date at the head of my paper. Yessir, Aunt Polly, I'm glad those Oriental traders carried their numbers into Europe.

THE END

PIFFLE! IT'S ONLY A SNIFFLE!

by Ted Kaufman

Characters

The Mighty Germ
Johnny
Mother
Father
Teacher
Julia
Arthur
Principal
Doctor
Sun
Children

Mighty Germ (*Struts to the center of the stage and pounds his chest proudly as he faces the audience.*):

I am the mighty Germ
Who makes children infirm!
I am evil and bold —
(*Blows*) Whooo! I can give you a cold!
And if I so please,
I can make you sneeze!
I can put you to bed
With a nose that's so red
And a chest that's so rough,
It tickles your throat and makes you cough!
(*Pounds chest with his fist.*)
Oh, I am the mighty Germ
Who makes children squirm!
By day and by night
I keep mothers in fright,
'Cause I work like a beaver
To give children fever!
I'm the huffer and puffer

Who makes you suffer!
And I know every trick
To make you sick!
(*Bends forward, resting hand on knee*
Do you want to see
How nasty I can be?
Say yes or say no —
You can't stop the show.
Just sit in your places
And lift up your faces,
Then watch closely the way
I act in this play!
(*Struts off stage.*)

Scene 1

SETTING: *Johnny's home.*

TIME: *Early morning.*

AT RISE: JOHNNY, *about eight years old, is all bundled up ready for school. The* MIGHTY GERM *enters and begins to dance around* JOHNNY. *Suddenly he stops, takes a feather out of his pocket, turns impishly toward the audience, then tickles* JOHNNY *under the nose with the feather.* JOHNNY *sneezes.* THE GERM *laughs silently, then tickles* JOHNNY *again.* JOHNNY *sneezes a second time.* FATHER *enters, looks concernedly at* JOHNNY, *who sneezes a third time, then turns to* MOTHER.

FATHER: Say, what's this? Another cold?

MOTHER: Oh, piffle! It's only a sniffle! (THE MIGHTY GERM *struts up front, throws up his hands and laughs silently, then retreats to a far corner.*)

FATHER: You call this a sniffle? Look at those teary eyes — and that running nose! (*Takes out handkerchief and walks toward* JOHNNY.)

JOHNNY (*Trying to avoid the handkerchief*): I'm okay, Dad. I've been sneezing for days!

MOTHER (*As* FATHER *holds up handkerchief and* JOHNNY *blows into it*): Oh, let him alone, Michael. He'll throw it off.

FATHER: He'll throw it off, all right. On the other children in school! Mary, don't you realize the danger? Colds are catching!

MOTHER: Of course I realize it, dear. But Johnny isn't that bad, really. Besides, this is my busy day, and I want some peace. (*She turns to* JOHNNY *and kisses him, then pushes him gently toward the door*) Off with you, now, and be a good boy.

JOHNNY (*Suppressing sneeze*): Yes, Mom. Bye. Bye, Dad. (*Goes off stage left.* FATHER, *shrugging shoulders, follows* MOTHER *off stage right.*)

THE MIGHTY GERM (*Alone now, walks to center of stage*):

Did you see
How I fooled those three?
The mother said: "Piffle!
It's only a sniffle!"
Little does she know
That the rest of this show
Is really the effect
Of her sad neglect!
(*Struts off stage.*)

CURTAIN

* * *

SCENE 2

SETTING: *Classroom. Three rows of four seats each face right.* TEACHER *behind table face left. Behind* TEACHER *is a blackboard.*

AT RISE: CHILDREN *are seated.* JOHNNY *occupies first seat in row nearest audience. The* MIGHTY GERM *is seated on floor next to* JOHNNY. MIGHTY GERM *gets up on his feet, pulls out his feather, tickles* JOHNNY. JOHNNY *sneezes.*

TEACHER: Bless you, John.

JOHNNY (*Rises, pulls out large red polka dot handkerchief and brings it up to nose to arrest second sneeze. Talks inside kerchief*): Thank you, Miss Brown. (MIGHTY GERM *laughs silently.*)

TEACHER (*Rises and approaches blackboard*): Now, children, I'm going to write some problems on the blackboard. I want you to copy them in your notebooks, together with the correct answers. (*As she talks,* MIGHTY GERM *tickles girl seated next to* JOHNNY *with feather.* GIRL *sneezes.* TEACHER *turns around, facing class*) Bless you, Julia.

JULIA: Thank you, Miss (MIGHTY GERM *tickles her again and she sneezes*) Brown. (TEACHER *turns to blackboard and resumes writing.* CHILDREN *open their notebooks and begin copying.* MIGHTY GERM *goes to* BOY *sitting next to* JULIA. BOY *sneezes.* TEACHER *turns. She is slightly annoyed.*)

TEACHER: Bless you, Arthur. (*As* ARTHUR *rises to thank* MISS BROWN, MIGHTY GERM *very rapidly moves from one pupil to the other, so that as* TEACHER *says "Bless you" to one, another begins to sneeze. After about the fifth or sixth child has sneezed, and as all continue to sneeze in unison, the* TEACHER, *worried, returns to her desk*) Sit down, all of you. (CHILDREN *sit down, sneezing, each into a different colored handkerchief*) There must be a cold germ lurking somewhere in this room. (MIGHTY GERM *moves about to the as yet unaffected children and causes them to sneeze, one after the other*) Oh, dear, you're *all* affected with colds! (TEACHER *walks among the* CHILDREN *and feels of their heads to determine if they have fever. As she does so, and while the* CHILDREN *sneeze, the* MIGHTY GERM *struts to center of stage and triumphantly faces the audience.*)

THE MIGHTY GERM:

Hooray! Hip! Hip!
I'm post-nasal drip!
I'm his Highness
The headaching Sinus!
I woo Influenza
With a raspy cadenza,
And I think it's such fun
To make your nose — run!

(*He dances back to the sneezing* CHILDREN. *Then he approaches the* TEACHER *and tickles her under nose with feather. She is about to sneeze when the* PRINCIPAL *enters.)*

PRINCIPAL: What's going on here?

TEACHER: Oh, Mr. Princip, everybody has a . . . (*Sneezes*) a . . . (*Suppresses a sneeze*) a cold!

PRINCIPAL: Everybody?

TEACHER (*Almost in tears*): Everybody . . .! This is due to some mother's carelessness.

PRINCIPAL: I'm sure. Miss Brown, dismiss the class. These children belong in bed!

TEACHER: Yes, Mr. Princip. (*Turns to* CHILDREN) Come, children, everybody file in . . . (*Sneezes*) file in . . . (*Suppresses sneeze*) line! (*All file in line, single file, sneezing or suppressing sneezes. As they file out,* MIGHTY GERM *follows last and, in passing, tickles the* PRINCIPAL *under nose.* PRINCIPAL, *now alone, sneezes into tiny white handkerchief, then hastily follows the rest off stage.)*

CURTAIN

* * *

SCENE 3

SETTING: *Principal's office.*

AT RISE: PRINCIPAL *and* DOCTOR *are seated.*

DOCTOR: As a doctor in this neighborhood, Mr. Princip, I am glad to join your Health Club. We must all get together, doctors, nurses, teachers and mothers, to maintain the good health of our community. It is a great responsibility. And I feel we ought to stress that most of that responsibility falls upon the mothers. For example, if a child starts the day with a raspy throat, with teary eyes and a running nose, he should not be sent to school. A day of rest and careful nursing at home will restore strength to the child and avoid the danger of infecting other children. Good health habits, you know, begin at home.

PRINCIPAL: Yes, Dr. Smith. And I think we might also tell the mothers about the benefits which are derived from a balanced diet and plenty of sunshine. Sunshine, I believe, is the greatest enemy of the cold germ.

DOCTOR: And of lots of other germs, too, Mr. Princip. We could all benefit from a more intimate acquaintance with the sun. (*As the* DOCTOR *speaks, he and* MR. PRINCIP *rise and walk right and disappear.*)

CURTAIN

* * *

SCENE 4

SETTING: *Same as Scene 2.*

AT RISE: *The classroom is empty now but for the* MIGHTY GERM. *The* MIGHTY GERM *looks at the rows of empty seats and laughs. He runs to the blackboard and begins to write "I am the Mighty Germ" when the* SUN *appears. The* MIGHTY GERM *cowers in a corner as the* SUN *walks brightly to the center of the stage and faces the audience.*

SUN:

Hello, everyone
I am the Sun.
Any day you look up,
From breakfast to sup,
You can see me afloat
In my fiery boat.
My rays spread a wealth
Of strength and good health.

To the bees and the birds
And the animal herds,

To the earth at your feet,
To the food that you eat,
To all of you here,
I bring life and good cheer!

Now I've heard that a germ,
A mean little worm,
An ornery tick,
Has made children sick.
(*At first cowering in fright, the* MIGHTY GERM *now takes out the cold-giving feather and sneaks up on the* SUN *from behind. As the* SUN *speaks, the* MIGHTY GERM *attempts to tickle its nose. At the word "exist" the* SUN *becomes conscious of the feather and snatches it away.*)
Such a condition
Is without permission.
The germ must desist
Or cease to exist!
(*The* SUN *snatches feather and wheels around to face the* MIGHTY GERM *who is terror-stricken.*)
Aha! So you are the bully
Who's been so unruly!
(*The* MIGHTY GERM *is silent.* SUN *angrily shakes feather at* GERM)
Well, what do you say . . . ?

THE MIGHTY GERM (*Utterly defeated*): Crime does not pay . . .

SUN:
Yes, and this is one time
You will pay for your crime!
In my boat you will sail
To a hot little jail
Way up in the sky,
Where you'll wither and die!
(*Pushes* MIGHTY GERM *forward off stage*)
Hurry now, the moon is almost in sight —
(*Turns to audience*)
And you, dear friends, before I say goodnight,
Let me speak a word or two
About some things you ought to do.
To make your skin as smooth as silk

Drink your daily share of milk.
Balance food at every meal
To make your body strong as steel.
Meat is good, but very lonesome
Without those friends which make it wholesome;
Peas and beets and, yes, potatoes,
Carrots, spinach and tomatoes.
Wash your hands and face and body,
Brush your teeth like everybody.
Balance study, food and rest
So that you may prosper best.
Never sneeze in children's faces,
Never play in dirty places.
Make all these habits your daily plans
To become healthy, happy Americans. (*Follows* GERM *off stage.*)

THE END

TOMMY'S ADVENTURE

by Eleanore Leuser

Characters

TOMMY, *a little boy*
ELLIE, *a little girl*
THE CAT
FIDO, *the Dog*
THE RED HEN
THE BUTTERFLY
THE BEE
THE SUNFLOWER TWINS
THE WIND
THE SUN

TIME: *Early morning of any school day.*

SETTING: *A farmyard with house showing in background.*

AT RISE: TOMMY *is digging with a spade in one of the flower beds. He stoops and is putting something in the hole as* ELLIE *enters.*

ELLIE (*Looking amazed*): What are you doing with that spade, Tommy?

TOMMY (*Jumping*): Hey, Ellie! I didn't see you. If you promise, cross your heart not to tell, I'll show you.

ELLIE (*Crossing her heart*): Cross my heart... hope to die. If toads eat me, you'll know why.

TOMMY (*Pointing to hole*): Look!

ELLIE (*Looking in*): Tommy Masters... isn't that your speller? (*Looking again*) Isn't that your reader and your arithmetic?

TOMMY (*With satisfaction*): That's right. I'm burying them.

ELLIE (*With mouth open*): Why?

TOMMY: Because! I'm not going to any old school. I'm going to play.

ELLIE (*Shocked*) : Tommy, you're not!

TOMMY (*Stubbornly*) : I am too. I'm sick of working at school when everyone is playing but me. Do you want to come, too?

ELLIE (*Doubtfully*) : I... don't think I ought to.

TOMMY (*Coaxingly*) : Oh, come on. We'll have heaps of fun. We'll play all day.

ELLIE (*Shaking her head*) : No, I'm going to school. You ought to come too, Tommy.

TOMMY (*Decidedly*) : I'm not coming. I'm going to have fun.

ELLIE (*As she runs off*) : You'll be sorry. Anyway I think school is fun. I'm going to school. (*She exits.*)

TOMMY (*Looking at her glumly*): Girls are silly. Wait till she hears how much fun I have. She'll be sorry she didn't come. (*A large gray cat walks slowly in.*)

TOMMY: Hey, kitty, kitty, don't you want to play with me?

CAT (*Standing on hind legs*) : No, Tommy, I can't.

TOMMY (*In amazement*) : Did you speak, Mr. Cat?

CAT (*Very slowly*) : I certainly did, Tommy. I said I couldn't play with you.

TOMMY: My goodness, I didn't know cats could talk. Why can't you play with me, Mr. Cat?

CAT: Because I'm much too busy.

TOMMY (*Astonished*) : How can a cat be busy?

CAT (*Folding its arms*) : Indeed, boy, you insult me. I have mice to catch. The place will simply be overrun with mice unless I keep busy.

TOMMY: Oh-h, I see.

CAT (*Turning to go*) : Good-bye, Tommy. Have fun. (*The* CAT *walks off slowly and the dog,* FIDO, *enters.*)

TOMMY: Why, there's Fido. He'll play with me. Here, Fido... Here, Fido... Here, Fido... good doggie! Let's go play.

FIDO (*Coming up to* TOMMY *and speaking in a deep voice*) : Can't! I'm too busy.

TOMMY (*Staring at* DOG) : Fido, can you talk too? My goodness, dogs can't be busy.

FIDO: Oh, yes, they can. I have to watch the house and yard and see that no thieves get in. That's a very important job. Good-bye, Tommy, sorry I can't join you. Have fun. (*He ambles off stage.*)

TOMMY (*Disgustedly*) : How can I have fun all by myself? No one will play with me. (A RED HEN *enters and comes towards* TOMMY.)

TOMMY: Hello, Red Hen, can you play with me?

RED HEN: Cluck! Cluck! I should say not. I have work to do.

TOMMY: Don't tell me that you work, too?

RED HEN: I should say so. Who'd lay your eggs for breakfast if I didn't?

TOMMY: I forgot about that.

RED HEN: Forget indeed! I've a good mind not to lay you another egg. But you'll learn. Cluck! Cluck! Good-bye, Tommy, have fun. Cluck! Cluck! (*She clucks her way off stage.*)

TOMMY (*Sulkily*): How can I have fun with no one to have it with? Oh, there's a butterfly! It has nothing to do but fly about, I'm sure. She'll play with me. (*He runs after a* BUTTERFLY *who appears at the first of his speech and is flitting from flower to flower.*)

TOMMY (*Calling*): Butterfly! Butterfly! Please stop a moment and play with me.

BUTTERFLY (*Fluttering her wings*): Oh Tommy, you bad boy, what are you doing here? Shouldn't you be in school?

TOMMY: I thought it would be fun to play. But I can't find anyone to play with. Everyone has to work.

BUTTERFLY: Of course everyone has to work. That's part of living. I work, too.

TOMMY: Oh, no, you're too pretty to work.

BUTTERFLY: But I do. You couldn't do without my work, either. If I didn't flit from flower to flower and carry pollen, there wouldn't be half so many green growing things on the earth today.

TOMMY: I didn't know that. But can't you play with me?

BUTTERFLY: Play indeed! I can't do that till my work's done. That's the time to play. (*She flits off leaving* TOMMY *looking very sad.*)

TOMMY: Oh dear! I don't suppose it's much use asking that nice bee over there. But I'll try. (*Calling*) Mr. Bee! Mr. Bee!

BEE (*Who has just entered and is buzzing happily around*): Bzz! Bzz! Who wants me? I'm too busy to see. Bzz! Bzz!

TOMMY: Oh dear! He's too busy to see what I want. (*Going over to the* BEE) What are you doing, Mr. Bee?

BEE: Didn't you ever read about me? I gather nectar from the flowers and make it into honey.

TOMMY (*Ashamed*): I'm sorry, Mr. Bee. All I ever did was to eat your honey. I never thought of your working to make it.

BEE: Tut, tut, my boy, you'd better get busy and learn something. Good-bye, now. I must be off to work. Bzz...Bzz... (*The* BEE *exits.*)

TOMMY: My goodness, I'm glad I didn't ask *him* to play with me. (*Pause*) Well, I guess I'll try those sunflowers. Flowers certainly don't work... or do they? (*Going over to them*) Good morning, Sunflowers, would one of you come and play with me?

SUNFLOWER TWINS: (*Together*): We heard what you said, Tommy. Of course flowers work.

TOMMY: They do?

SUNFLOWER TWINS: Yes, they do. Just look at us. We're busy growing our seeds for fall. There wouldn't be any flowers without seeds, you know.

TOMMY: Oh, I never thought of that. I guess you *are* too busy to play with me. Oh dear, isn't there anybody at all who can play? (*The* WIND *enters with a big swirl and a leap and a bound. He swoops right over to* TOMMY.)

WIND: What's the matter, little boy?

TOMMY (*Almost crying*): I've asked and asked. Everybody is too busy to play with me.

WIND: Well, why aren't you busy, too?

TOMMY: I thought it would be more fun to play. But now, I'm not so sure. I suppose there's no use asking you?

WIND (*Puffing out his cheeks and laughing*): Ha! Ha! Ho! Ho! That's a good joke! Who would turn the windmills? Who would sail the boats? Who would dry your mother's clothes if I stopped working?

TOMMY (*Respectfully*): Do you do all that, sir?

WIND: I certainly do and lots more.

TOMMY: I'm going to ask just one more person to play with me and if he can't...then I'm going home.

WIND (*Chuckling*): A good idea, Tommy! A good idea! Why don't you ask the Sun over there? If anyone could play with you he could. He's the most powerful of us all. (*The* SUN *enters as the* WIND *begins to speak.*)

TOMMY (*Looking at* SUN): The Sun looks so bright and happy. I should think he plays all day. He'll be the last one I'll ask.

Surely he'll say yes. (*Calling*) Mr. Sun!

SUN (*Calling*): Come closer to me, Tommy. I can't hear you. (TOMMY *goes over to the* SUN.)

TOMMY: I just asked if you'd play with me, Mr. Sun.

SUN (*Kindly*): Tommy, what do you suppose would happen if I stopped shining?

TOMMY: I guess it would get pretty dark, Mr. Sun.

SUN: Yes, and nothing would grow. It would always be night.

TOMMY: But don't you ever have any fun?

SUN: Of course we do. All of us have fun while we work.

TOMMY (*Surprised*): Fun while you work! How can you?

SUN (*Laughing*): That's easy. We have fun because we enjoy what we're doing. Haven't you seen my sunbeams dancing and playing while we work? (*Calling*) Come, all you who couldn't play with Tommy because you worked. Come! (*The* CAT — DOG — RED HEN — BEE — SUNFLOWER TWINS — WIND — BUTTERFLY — *all enter and stand on each side of the* SUN *facing* TOMMY) Tell us... don't you have fun while you work?

CAT: I have fun in the chase, sir.

DOG: It makes me feel good to know I am guarding the house.

RED HEN: Did you ever hear me cackle when I lay an egg? That's to show how good I feel.

BEE: It's fun to flit from flower to flower. I like to make the golden honey.

SUNFLOWER TWINS: It's fun to be alive and feel the Sun and Wind and to know we're getting the seeds ready for another planting.

BUTTERFLY: My wings catch the sunshine and the flowers welcome me as I stop for their pollen. I feel happy and gay.

WIND: I laugh as I blow and I sing a song of the Wind as I work.

SUN: There, you see, Tommy: Work can be fun, too. It's all in the way you do it.

TOMMY: I see, Mr. Sun. I see a lot I didn't see before. I guess I have to work, too. I'll try liking it. It will be fun learning about a lot of things I never knew before. Maybe it will be even as much fun as playing all the time. I'm going right now to try it. Goodbye, everybody!

ALL: Goodbye, Tommy! We know you'll have fun. (*They are waving good-bye to* TOMMY *who runs off stage as the curtain falls.*)

THE END

THE CLOCK'S SECRET

by Esther MacLellan and Catherine Schroll

Characters

SHIRLEY MADISON
ANNE, *her younger sister*
JOHN, *her brother*
MOTHER
SAMMY, *a cousin*
AUNT MARIAN

SCENE 1

SETTING: *Living room in a country home.*

AT RISE: SHIRLEY *is seated working at table or desk. Enter* ANNE *carrying an egg.*

ANNE: Look, Shirley. Elspeth has laid another egg.

SHIRLEY (*Going towards* ANNE): It's awfully big! What does it taste like?

ANNE: Duck eggs are very good. Just like a chicken's, only more to eat. Here... (*Places egg on table*) You can have it for breakfast tomorrow. After all, I had the first, you know.

SHIRLEY: But Elspeth is your duck. Are you sure you don't mind?

ANNE: Oh, no. (*Enter* JOHN.)

JOHN: Well, everything is finally settled. (*Sits dejectedly*) We're leaving for the city...right away.

SHIRLEY: I can't bear to think of it. Just imagine, our first Christmas away from home!

ANNE: Mother says we simply can't afford to live here any longer. It takes so much coal to heat a big house in the country.

JOHN: I'll hate living in the city, especially with Aunt Marian and Cousin Sammy. He's nothing but a spoiled baby, always wanting his own way.

SHIRLEY: Sammy's bad enough, but worst of all is to leave the farm at Christmas.

ANNE: I suppose there's nothing we can do about it. If we could only find where Grandfather hid the money....

JOHN: But we can't. We've been searching for two months now. We've looked everywhere.

ANNE: I can't understand how he ever took so much money out of the bank. You'd think he would have been afraid of being robbed or something.

JOHN: You know what Grandfather was like, impulsive and hot-tempered. He and the bank president were good friends, but they had an argument. Then Grandfather got excited the way he used to, and said the president didn't know anything about investments and he was taking *his* money out right away, even the government bonds.

SHIRLEY: I suppose by the time he reached home, he'd cooled off and was ashamed to tell Mother what he'd done.

JOHN: Oh, that wasn't the first time he and the bank president had quarreled. But Grandfather always brought the money back the next day.

SHIRLEY: Dear Grandfather. He never stayed angry long.

ANNE: And then to think he would be killed in that dreadful accident the very same night. (*Enter* MOTHER.)

MOTHER: You children mustn't be so glum. We aren't leaving the house forever, you know. We'll be back in the spring or even sooner if Daddy is well by then.

JOHN: Months will seem like years with dear Cousin Sammy.

MOTHER: I'm a little disappointed in you, John. Of course if you feel so strongly, I could write to your father.

SHIRLEY: Oh no, Mother. Dad would insist on coming home from the hospital, and he's getting along so well now. We know he isn't to be worried. It's just that we love the house so much and we're so happy here and then at Christmas... (*Starts to cry.*)

MOTHER (*Puts arm around her*): I know how you feel, dear. It is hard. But perhaps each of you children could take some little thing along to remind you that we'll soon be coming home again Would that help?

ANNE: Must it be little, Mother? (*Goes to clock.*) I hate to leave our dear old clock alone shut up in the winter's cold. I suppose it's silly, but I think it would miss us.

SHIRLEY: Oh yes, Mother. I'd rather take the clock with us than anything.

MOTHER (*Doubtfully*): But it's so very large...

JOHN: Aunt Marian will be *so* glad to see you arrive with three kids *and* a grandfather's clock.

MOTHER: What is the matter with you, John? I don't know what I'd have done if your aunt hadn't kindly offered to let us stay with her this winter. You're old enough to understand that there just isn't enough money now to keep this huge old house running. Coal bills are the worst and then we're so far from school and the stores that we have to use the car a lot. That's an expense too.

SHIRLEY: Don't mind Johnny, Mother. He's thinking of Cousin Sammy again.

MOTHER: You should try to understand your cousin, John. His father died when he was a baby, and Sammy was delicate...

JOHN (*Incredulously*): Delicate? He looks like an ox. (*Aside*) And he acts like one too.

MOTHER: Well, he was delicate when he was a baby. Your Aunt Marian was rich, and there were no other children but Sammy, so she could never refuse him anything.

ANNE (*Slowly*): It's just like the Bible. He was her one ewe lamb.

MOTHER: That's it exactly.

SHIRLEY: If we could only find the money, then we wouldn't have to leave the farm. We would be here, in our own home at Christmas.

MOTHER: We must just forget about it, that's all. Ever since your grandfather's death, we've been looking. I have no idea where else to search. The money seems to have vanished completely.

JOHN: You're right, Mother. There's no use complaining. When do we go to Aunt Marian's?

MOTHER: Tomorrow. It won't take long to pack, and we might just as well leave at once. There's nothing to be gained from putting things off.

ANNE: And may we take the clock?

MOTHER: Yes. If it means so much to you, we'll take it.

GIRLS: Oh thank you, Mother.

MOTHER: There, there, that's all right. Now run along, all of you, and get your things ready. We don't have too much time.

CURTAIN

* * *

SCENE 2

SETTING: *Aunt Marian's living room in the city.*

AT RISE: ANNE *and* JOHN *are seated.* SHIRLEY *is standing at the window.*

SHIRLEY: I hate the city. The days are so gloomy and the streets are always filled with dirty slush and ice!

ANNE: It's so different from the lovely white snow at the farm.

JOHN: Sledding, ice skating, hikes through the woods! What good times we had! And then, best of all, the Christmas holidays!

SHIRLEY: Oh, if we could only be home for Christmas! I'm so tired of it here.

ANNE: At least it's peaceful for a while. I wonder where Sammy is. (*Voice offstage. "Shirley! Anne!"*)

JOHN: Cease wondering. (*Enter* SAMMY.)

SAMMY: Didn't you hear me? I was calling you. (*Pause*) Why don't you answer? What're you doing?

JOHN: Before you came in, we were enjoying ourselves.

ANNE: Don't start anything, John. You know Mother hates you to quarrel with Sammy.

SAMMY (*Wanders around*): What's this funny old thing, a clock?

ANNE: It isn't funny. It's beautiful.

SHIRLEY: We brought it from home. Don't go poking at it or you'll break it.

SAMMY: It just looks like a piece of old junk to me. (*Inspects the clock. Enter* MOTHER.)

MOTHER: Children, why aren't you getting ready? Didn't Sammy tell you?

SHIRLEY: Tell us what?

MOTHER: Aunt Marian is taking us Christmas shopping. It's been so nasty all week she thought that perhaps dinner at a restaurant and then a visit to the stores would be a treat for everybody.

JOHN (*Aside*): The only place I want to go is *home*.

MOTHER: We're taking both cars, as Aunt Marian has invited some other guests. Anne dear, you go with her and be company for Sammy.

JOHN: Lucky Anne!

SAMMY (*Excitedly*): Look everybody, the clock opens! I've found the secret of the old clock!

JOHN: Some secret! We've known about that since we were babies.

MOTHER: Come along, children. We mustn't keep Aunt Marian waiting. (*Exit* MOTHER, SHIRLEY, JOHN. ANNE *starts off.*)

SAMMY: Wait a minute, Anne. You're going in our car. Show me how the clock works.

ANNE (*Going to clock*): It's just a little door, Sammy. Then inside there's an empty space. I don't know what it was used for originally. When we were small, we liked to hide in it.

SAMMY: Did you? That must have been fun. How did you get in?

ANNE: You just press this button, and the door opens.

SAMMY: Oh, I see.

ANNE: Then you get in like this... (*Gets in*) Of course, it's a pretty tight fit for me now. The only trouble is when you shut the door, you can't open it from the inside.

SAMMY (*Shuts the door*): Ha! Ha! The joke's on you, Anne. Now you're my prisoner.

ANNE: Oh, don't be silly, Sammy. It's frightfully hot and stuffy in here. Let me out.

SAMMY: No, I won't. You're my prisoner, and I'm going to hold you for ransom. That's it, I'll be a pirate captain, and... (*Enter* JOHN.)

JOHN: Your mother wants you right away.

SAMMY: I'm not coming now. I have something else to do first.

JOHN (*Grabs him*): Your mother said right away.

SAMMY: Get your hands off me! Who do you think you are, pushing me around?

JOHN: Everybody's ready to go. Think we want to wait around all night just for you? Come on... (*Boys struggle.*)

SAMMY: I'll go when I want. Let me alone. . . .
JOHN: You're going now. (*Pushes* SAMMY *toward door.*)
SAMMY: All right. You'll be sorry. (*Boys exit.*)
ANNE: Let me out! Let me out! (*Her voice gets fainter.*)

CURTAIN

* * *

SCENE 3

SETTING: *Same as Scene 2.*

AT RISE: *Voices are heard off stage calling "Anne! Anne!" Enter* MOTHER *and* SHIRLEY.

MOTHER: Anne! Anne! Where are you? (*Sits*) Oh, Shirley, I'm so worried. Where can she be?

SHIRLEY: Anne's so prompt and thoughtful. Something must have happened.

MOTHER: When your aunt drove up without her, I was so frightened. (*Walks around*) Anne! Where are you? (*Enter* AUNT MARIAN, SAMMY, JOHN.)

AUNT (*Going to* MOTHER): Now, dear, you musn't worry. She must be somewhere in the house. Perhaps she took a nap, and then fell asleep. . . .

JOHN: I can't imagine Anne suddenly wanting a nap, but I'll run up to her bedroom and look. (*Exit* JOHN.)

AUNT: Naturally, when Anne didn't come, I thought she had decided to go in your car.

SHIRLEY: Mother, do you suppose we should call the police?

SAMMY: Oh no, no, don't do that!

AUNT: Now, don't let this worry you, Sammy dear. You're just too sensitive. (*To others*) He's such a thoughtful boy.

MOTHER: Suppose we all separate. You try the attic, Shirley. I'll go down to the cellar. And you, Marian, you. . . (*All exit, except*

SAMMY. *He looks around, and then opens the door of the clock.* ANNE *falls out with money clutched in her hand.*)

SAMMY: Oh, Anne! What's the matter? Are you dead? If you are, I've killed you! Anne, Anne, say you are all right! (*Enter* JOHN.)

JOHN: Anne! (*Kneels*) She's fainted. Go get some water, Sammy. (*Exit* SAMMY.) Gee, where did all this money come from? Anne, Anne! (*Calls*) Mother! Anne's here! (*Enter everybody.* SAMMY *with water.*)

MOTHER (*Kneels*): Anne, darling, what happened?

ANNE (*Opens her eyes*): Mother, I've found grandfather's money. Look, here it is!

JOHN: But where? How?

MOTHER: Never mind about that now. Where were you, Anne? We have all been so worried.

SAMMY (*Ashamed*): I shut her in the clock.

MOTHER: What?

AUNT: Oh, Sammy, how could you?

SAMMY: Aw, it was just a joke. I didn't mean to hurt her.

MOTHER: You knew we were all going out, and yet you left Anne alone shut up in the clock.

SAMMY: I didn't mean to leave her. But then John came in and started pushing me around and then...well, I got mad.

ANNE: Don't scold Sammy, Mother. I really don't think he meant any harm. He just got excited.

SAMMY: I'm sorry, Anne. Really I am.

SHIRLEY: But the money, Anne. Where did you find it?

ANNE: It was in the clock, after all.

JOHN: But we looked there the very first thing....

ANNE (*Goes to clock*): But see, it was hidden back here, in a really secret hiding place.

SHIRLEY: How did you find it, hidden in there in the dark?

ANNE: I heard you leave, and it was so uncomfortable that I started twisting around, and my elbow hit against the rear of the clock. Then there was a sliding noise, and I felt a hole in the back. I managed to get my hand in and felt the money in there. Oh, Shirley, I was so excited!

SHIRLEY: Oh, Anne, how thrilling! It's just like a story.

ANNE: After that, I suppose I must have fainted. I don't remember anything more.

MOTHER: No wonder you fainted, child. There wasn't enough air in that tight place for a mouse to breathe.

SAMMY: Well, everything turned out all right. If I hadn't shut Anne in the clock she'd never have found the money.

JOHN (*Sarcastically*): You're a big help, Sammy.

SHIRLEY: That's right, the money is found! (*Runs to* MOTHER) Oh Mother, couldn't we go home for Christmas?

JOHN: It wouldn't take long to open the house. Say yes, Mother. I want a real country snow for Christmas, and a Christmas tree right out of our own woods and a farm turkey and...

AUNT (*Laughing*): You make it sound very attractive, John.

SAMMY: I want to go too!

ANNE: Mother dear, let's all go, please.

ALL: Please! Please!

MOTHER: Of course if *everybody* wants to go...

ALL: We do! We do!

MOTHER: Then what are we waiting for?

CHILDREN: Hurrah! (*They dance around the room singing "Jingle Bells" as the curtain falls.*)

THE END

THE SHADY SHADOWS

by Helen Louise Miller

Characters

NIP, *a girl*
TUCK, *her brother*
NIP'S SHADOW
TUCK'S SHADOW
MOLLY, *a maid*
VOICE OF A RADIO SINGER

SCENE 1

SETTING: NIP *and* TUCK'S *bedroom.*

AT RISE: NIP *and* TUCK *are studying Robert Louis Stevenson's poem, "My Shadow." They are just finishing reciting it, in singsong fashion.*

NIP *and* TUCK:
One morning very early before the sun was up,
I rose and found the shining dew on every buttercup;
But my lazy little shadow like an arrant sleepyhead,
Had stayed at home behind me and was fast asleep in bed.

NIP: Now that we have learned it, what are we going to do with it? I can see some excuse for learning multiplication tables, because, after all, we must know them to do long division and interest problems. But what use can we ever make of poetry?

TUCK: I'm sure I don't know. When I grow up to be an inventor, maybe I'll invent some uses for poetry. Perhaps I could rig up a new-fashioned restaurant — something like an automat. We could call it Poetical-Mat and the customers would have to recite a verse or two before they could get anything to eat.

NIP: That would be fun. "Twinkle, Twinkle, Little Star" might buy a sandwich, and "The Old Woman Who Lived in a Shoe" might be the price of a glass of milk.

TUCK: Ice cream and pie would be more expensive — something like "The Children's Hour" or "Wynken, Blynken and Nod" for those.

NIP: You'll be a second Thomas Edison if you ever work out that idea, Tuck. But if we are going to get credit for this poem on Monday, we had better go over it again.

NIP: "But what can be the use of him is more than I can see!" There is something for you to invent, Tuck. A use for shadows!

TUCK: I can think of plenty of uses for them, if I could just invent a way to catch them.

NIP: What, for instance?

TUCK: Make them work for us, of course. They could do all our geography and arithmetic and spelling; and yours could wash the dishes and mine could rake the yard and shovel snow in the winter time.

NIP: And go to the dentist and take castor oil —

TUCK: Maybe I could fix it so we could eat the green apples and they could get the stomach-ache.

NIP: You'd have to be terribly clever for that, Tuck, but I guess you could do it if you put your mind to it.

TUCK: Sure I could, if I had plenty of time.

NIP: Wouldn't that be wonderful? Oh, Tuck, let's try to think of a way to catch shadows. Tomorrow we have a test in history and it would be grand to get the shadows to learn all the dates.

TUCK: And Father wants me to clean the garage this afternoon. That would be a good job for the shadows. Then I could go to the "Y."

NIP: Think hard, Tuck.

TUCK: I am thinking. You better think too. You might get an idea — accidentally or something.

NIP: We could set a shadow-trap.

TUCK: What's that?

NIP: A trap to catch shadows, of course. We'd have to catch them alive, you know.

TUCK: What would we use for bait?

NIP: I don't know. What do shadows like best?

TUCK: Light. You must have light to catch a shadow.

NIP: But we need something to hold them fast after we get them.

TUCK: Hold them fast! Hold them fast! I've got it, Nip, I've got it!

NIP: Got what?

TUCK: A way to hold them fast.

NIP: How?

TUCK: Remember when you broke your little chair last week?

NIP: Yes, but —

TUCK: And I fixed it with Hold Fast Glue!

NIP: Tuck, you are marvellous!

TUCK: And there's almost a whole bottle left. See — (*Gets bottle of glue from desk drawer.*) Now all we need to do is smear the glue on this screen, put a light behind it, and when the shadows come out they will stick fast to the screen. Then we'll have them at our mercy.

NIP: What shall we do with them?

TUCK: Make them promise they ll do everything we say before we pull them loose.

NIP: That's perfect. Come on, give me a brush.

TUCK: You smear half of the screen and I'll attend to the other half. Be sure to get it on good and thick. (*Children smear glue on reverse side of screen.*) Won't the shadows be surprised when they can't get away from the screen?

NIP: They'll think they've walked into some flypaper. (*Finishing screen*)

TUCK: Now, we'll set the desk light on the floor behind the screen and, when we walk near the light, our shadows will appear. (*Set the light on floor behind screen. They walk to wall socket, turn on light and move behind the screen. The* SHADOWS *enter center so that their shadows are reflected on the screen instead of the actual shadows of* NIP *and* TUCK. *As soon as the shadows are visible,* NIP *and* TUCK *run out in front of the screen.*)

SHADOWS (*Struggling madly*): Help! Help! Let us out. We're stuck!

NIP: It worked! It worked!

TUCK: Naturally it worked. See, they can't possibly get loose.

SHADOWS: Nip! Tuck! Help! Police! Fire! Murder! Help!

NIP: Sh! You'll arouse the neighbors.

TUCK: And Mother and Father, too.

TUCK-SHADOW: You let us go, you great big bully! Get us out of here, or I'll — I'll —

TUCK: Now, now! No threats if you please, Mr. Shadow. You must be more polite.

NIP-SHADOW: You horrible children. I'm going to tell your mother. I hope she puts you to bed and feeds you on bread and water for the rest of your lives.

NIP: I'm afraid you'd get awfully thin, Shadow, for you depend on us, you know, for your very existence.

TUCK-SHADOW: Why did you play this sticky trick on us?

TUCK: We had our reasons.

TUCK-SHADOW: Well, what are they?

TUCK: You mean you are ready to listen to reason?

TUCK-SHADOW: Yes.

NIP: And you too, my little Shadow?

NIP-SHADOW: Yes, but hurry. This glue is getting in my hair.

TUCK: Do you really want us to set you loose?

TUCK-SHADOW: Certainly. If you think it is any fun to be stuck fast to this screen, you try it.

NIP: Are you willing to do us a few favors?

NIP-SHADOW: Anything.

TUCK: Anything?

TUCK-SHADOW: Yes, anything to get out of this mess.

TUCK: Even to taking castor oil?

NIP: And standing for hours to have dresses tried on?

SHADOW: Yes.

TUCK: All right, then. We'll set you free. But first you must promise to do all our work for us today so that we can have the time for ourselves. Do you promise?

SHADOWS: We do.

TUCK: Well, first there is the garage to be cleaned. Then, the yard must be raked and the hedge trimmed. Dad is very particular about the hedge. Be sure to get it straight. After that you better have a look at my arithmetic for Monday and there is a composition to be written about "How I Spent Saturday." Be sure to leave a margin and put in a lot of commas and apostrophes. Miss Collins is a Holy Terror on punctuation. If you have time after that, you might sort out the old magazines and newspapers in the cellar. I was supposed to do that this morning, but I've been too busy.

TUCK-SHADOW: Is that all?

TUCK: Yes, unless you have time to take the wash over to Mrs.

Reilly. Mother likes to send it to her on Saturday afternoon.

NIP: My bureau drawers are in an awful mess, and my blue sweater needs mending. I tore a hole this big in it yesterday. The living room hasn't been dusted and I'm supposed to return a book to the library for Mother. Be sure to practice my piano lesson a full hour and a quarter or I won't be allowed to go to the movies next week, and be careful about lifting your wrist. I'm always dropping mine. Mr. Totino is wild. You'll find my school books here on the desk and take extra pains with the history, because we're having a test on Monday.

NIP-SHADOW: Do you mean you want us to do all that work this afternoon?

TUCK: Unless you prefer the screen.

NIP-SHADOW: But —

TUCK-SHADOW: You villains!

NIP: Stick to your promise — or stick to the screen. It makes no difference to us.

TUCK: Do you promise?

SHADOWS (*Reluctantly*): Yes.

NIP: On your word of honor?

SHADOWS: On our honor.

TUCK: Criss cross your heart?

NIP: And hope to die?

SHADOWS: Criss cross our hearts and hope to die.

TUCK: Come on, Nip, let's pull 'em loose. (*They catch hold of the* SHADOWS' *outside hands and pull. There is a tearing sound and suddenly the* SHADOWS *are released.*)

NIP-SHADOW: Where are you going?

NIP: I'm going for a bicycle ride, and then, maybe to the movies.

TUCK: I'm going to the "Y" for a swim and then Fred Frey's going to show me his new boat.

NIP-SHADOW (*Half crying*): I want to go with you.

NIP: Not today. You're going to stay right here and be useful.

TUCK-SHADOW (*To* NIP-SHADOW): Don't let them see you cry. (*To children*) Hurry if you're going.

TUCK: Goodbye and good luck to you.

NIP: Goodbye and don't forget my sweater. (*Exit* NIP *and* TUCK.)

NIP-SHADOW (*Crying*): Oh, this is dreadful. Why should they treat us like this? We never did anything to them.

TUCK-SHADOW: I guess we have led an idle life, but who ever heard of shadows working?

NIP-SHADOW: I've heard of people working themselves to a shadow, but I never really saw anyone do it.

TUCK-SHADOW: Neither did I. But Nip and Tuck will be sorry. They forgot something.

NIP-SHADOW: What?

TUCK-SHADOW: They forgot that since we are their shadows we must be as smart as they are. If Tuck is an inventor, so am I. We know a few tricks ourselves.

NIP-SHADOW: That's so. But what tricks do we know? Good ones, I mean? Good enough to make Nip and Tuck wish they had never caught us?

TUCK-SHADOW: I have several up my sleeve. And if you'll stop crying and come along with me to the garage, I'll elucidate my cryptic utterance!

CURTAIN

* * *

SCENE 2

SETTING: *Same as Scene* 1

AT RISE: *The* SHADOWS *are seated at a small table in the act of finishing their supper. They wear pajamas and bathrobes.*

NIP-SHADOW: Wasn't that delicious ice cream?

TUCK-SHADOW: And that coconut cake! Ummmmmm!

NIP-SHADOW: I would never have dreamed the difference it makes in the flavor of food — eating it first hand, I mean, instead of letting Nip and Tuck do the actual tasting.

TUCK-SHADOW: Everything tasted so good because we were hungry. Cutting that hedge gave me an enormous appetite.

NIP-SHADOW: Well, we've eaten everything but the dishes, and all our work is finished, so we might as well go to bed. I'm tired.

TUCK-SHADOW: I have a little matter to attend to first.

NIP-SHADOW: What? I thought you had finished all your work.

TUCK-SHADOW: So I did, but this is pure pleasure. A little invention of my own. (*He begins to do mysterious things with the light fixtures.*)

NIP-SHADOW: What are you doing?

TUCK-SHADOW: Making the world safe for democracy — for the democracy of us shadows, I mean.

NIP-SHADOW: I don't understand.

TUCK-SHADOW: You will. Wait and see. Listen — here they come. Quick, sit down at the table. (*They run to the table.* NIP *and* TUCK, *bedraggled and dead tired, enter right.*)

NIP: Hello. Did you finish all the work?

NIP-SHADOW (*Glancing at the empty dishes*): Yes, we've finished everything.

TUCK: So I see, if you mean food, and we are nearly starved.

NIP: I'll ring and ask Molly to bring us some supper.

TUCK-SHADOW: You can't, or rather, you can, but she won't. You see, she thinks you have had your supper so she won't bring you any more. She'll think it will make you sick.

TUCK: But she certainly knew you weren't us. You are black.

TUCK-SHADOW: Black looks white to some people. We might look black to you but that is because you know we are your shadows. When you went away and left us here alone, we appeared to be you. No one noticed any difference.

NIP-SHADOW: And we had an extra piece of cake for supper because your mother said we had done our work so well.

TUCK-SHADOW: By the way, your father gave me fifty cents for cutting the hedge.

TUCK: Good! Where is it? Give it to me.

TUCK-SHADOW: It was my money. I earned it, but shadows have no use for money so I gave it to the boy next door.

TUCK: You gave it away! (*Moaning*) He gave my fifty cents to Billy Bates!

NIP: Well, I must have something to eat. I'm starving. (*Rings bell and moves left stage. Calls*) Molly.

VOICE OFFSTAGE: Yes, Miss Nip?

NIP: Will you please get Tuck and me a glass of milk and a sandwich, Molly?

MOLLY: Indeed, and I'll do no such thing. You children have

done nothing but eat all afternoon . . . and such a supper as you had!

TUCK: But, Molly!

MOLLY: No buts, young man. Your mother has just discovered that the whole bottom layer has been eaten out of her candy box. And when your father finds that there is no apple pie for his dinner, I'd hate to be in your shoes. Take my advice, you rascals, and get to bed before your parents come upstairs.

TUCK: You villains! You've got us into a pretty mess.

NIP: Father is always in a temper when there is no pie for dinner.

NIP-SHADOW: We're sorry, but we had to keep up our strength to accomplish all that work.

TUCK-SHADOW: And it's finished, too, every bit of it.

NIP: That's the first good news you've told us.

TUCK: Come on, Nip, let's get ready for bed. We won't mind being hungry while we are asleep, and in the morning we'll eat enough to make up for this. (*Exit* NIP *and* TUCK. *As soon as they leave, the* SHADOWS, *with much giggling hop into bed.*)

TUCK (*Offstage*): Who's been using this toothpaste?

TUCK-SHADOW: We have. We didn't care very much for it either. After this, you'd better get peppermint.

NIP: And there's no hot water.

NIP-SHADOW: Of course not. We were terribly dirty, and we each took a bath before supper.

TUCK: Where are my bedroom slippers?

TUCK-SHADOW: In here — under my bed.

TUCK (*Entering*): *Your* bed! Why, you — Nip, they're in our beds!

NIP (*Entering*): Make them get out right away. I'm nearly dead.

TUCK: Get out of there right away, or I'll knock you out.

TUCK-SHADOW: All right — knock me out. But I'll yell like an Indian and then your father and mother will probably come up to see what is the matter.

NIP: And I wish they would. They'd make you get out soon enough.

NIP-SHADOW: And what would they do to you for eating the candy and the pie?

TUCK-SHADOW: And someone broke a window over at the Bates place. Mr. Bates thinks it was Tuck, 'cause I heard your father say he'd attend to you the first thing in the morning. I guess he'd do it tonight if you made any disturbance.

TUCK (*In despair*): Oh, my goodness! Nip, these shadows have ruined us. They've got us into more trouble in one day than we can get out of in a week.

NIP-SHADOW: I guess it will take a couple of weeks because I'm not very good at washing dishes and I'm afraid I broke a lot of them. Your mother is going to be terribly annoyed when she finds her big blue platter is gone.

NIP: Not the willow pattern!

NIP-SHADOW: I guess that's what you call it. I didn't ask anybody. I just swept the pieces under the range!

NIP: Under the range! (*Beginning to cry*) Oh, Tuck, Mother said last week I'd have to pay for every dish I broke, and that platter cost a fortune. I know it did. And it's all your fault for getting these awful creatures here.

TUCK: My fault! You were as keen about it as I was. Do you suppose I'm going to enjoy that broken window business?

NIP: Well, get rid of them. Make them get out of our beds.

SHADOWS (*Quoting from poem*): "He's always there before me when I jump into my bed."

TUCK: Well, you won't be there long. I'll fix you. I'll turn out the light. Then where will you be?

TUCK-SHADOW: I couldn't guess. Where will we be when you turn out the light, that is, if you can turn it out?

TUCK: What do you mean — if I *can* turn it out?

TUCK-SHADOW: I mean you can't! (TUCK *runs to light switch, turns it and nothing happens.*)

TUCK: Great jumping grasshoppers! Nip, I can't turn it out! He's monkeyed with the switch.

TUCK-SHADOW: You forget I am an inventor like you. Wasn't it clever of me?

TUCK: Jerusalem! Nip, we can't get rid of them! I can't turn out the light.

NIP: Oh, dear! Oh, dear! Why did we ever get into this mess?

TUCK: What are we going to do?

NIP: We can't have them here forever — breaking dishes, and eating candy and ruining our lives. (*Loud snores from the* SHADOWS.)

TUCK (*Shaking them*): Listen, you, will you go away peaceably? (*More snores.*)

NIP (*Stamping her foot*): Go away, you mean, hateful things! (*She snores.*)

TUCK-SHADOW (*Between snores*): You must be more polite.

TUCK: Why have you treated us like this?

NIP-SHADOW: We had our reasons.

NIP: Let's hear them.

TUCK-SHADOW (*Sitting up*): You mean you are willing to listen to reason?

NIP *and* TUCK: Yes.

TUCK-SHADOW: Are you willing to promise anything we ask?

BOTH: Yes.

NIP-SHADOW: Anything?

BOTH: Anything.

TUCK-SHADOW: Then promise never, never, never to set any more shadow traps.

BOTH: We promise.

TUCK-SHADOW (*Jumping out of bed*): Criss cross your hearts and hope to die.

BOTH: Criss cross our hearts and hope to die!

NIP-SHADOW: All right. Fix the lights, Mr. Inventor. (TUCK-SHADOW *fixes light.*)

TUCK-SHADOW: It's all right now. You can turn it off.

TUCK: Thanks, Brother Shadow, you are a better inventor than I am. (*Shadows move behind screen where their silhouettes are visible.*)

NIP-SHADOW: But this isn't the last of us. (*Quoting*) "He stays so close beside me, he's a coward you can see; I'd think shame to stick to Nursie the way that shadow sticks to me!"

NIP: Oh, dear! It will make me nervous to see you.

TUCK-SHADOW: Don't worry, we won't trouble you again. We'll just be playmates as we were before.

TUCK: Here goes the light — good-bye!

SHADOWS: Good-bye! (*The lights go out, the shadows disappear and when the lights come on again,* NIP *and* TUCK *are in bed.*)

NIP: What a day!

TUCK: And what a tomorrow if all those shadows said was true!

NIP: Turn on the radio a minute. Maybe a good song would soothe our minds. (TUCK *turns on the radio.*)

ANNOUNCER: The Lullaby Lady from Lullaby Lane will sing an old favorite. (*Voice begins to sing* — "I had a little shadow." NIP *and* TUCK *groan as they each throw a bedroom slipper at the radio. Curtains fall.*)

THE END

IF WISHES WERE HORSES

by Bertha Nathan

Characters

HIRAM, *an old farmer*
SILAS, *his chum*
JOHN, *Hiram's nephew*
EMMIE, *John's wife*
JACK, GEORGE } *John's sons*
MARY, STELLA } *orphans*

SETTING: *The yard of a farm house which is covered with dry leaves. Upper left is a rock.*

TIME: *Afternoon of late summer or early autumn.*

AT RISE: *The stage is clear. Then* HIRAM *comes on from house, carrying a rake and crosses to rock.*

HIRAM (*Leans on rake*): That old rock just about ruins the looks of the place. I certainly wish I could get rid of it. (*Sighs and starts raking leaves toward house.* SILAS *enters from the road and creeps up to* HIRAM, *touching him with his stick.*)

HIRAM: Ouch! You scared me coming up so quietly.

SILAS: Did you expect me to whistle "Listen to the mocking bird"? (*He whistles.*)

HIRAM: No, I didn't expect you to whistle; but you might have cleared your throat or something.

SILAS (*Clears his throat several times*): Is that right?

HIRAM: I suppose so. (*He crosses and throws his hat towards the rock.*)

SILAS: Well it makes a good hat rack anyhow.

HIRAM: Well it ought to be good for something. My, how I'd love to get rid of it.

SILAS: I bet I've heard you say that a hundred times. Why don't you do something instead of always talking about it?

HIRAM (*Gestures with rake*): Do something. (*Louder*) Do something. Why you consarned old idiot. You know how I've tried just about everything that anybody ever suggested.

SILAS: I never saw you do anything. What all did you do? (*Crosses stage and sits on ground near rock.*)

HIRAM (*Shakes his rake at him and sputters as he talks*): You're just contrary that's what you are. You *do* know what I've done. (*He drops rake and counts on his fingers.*) I've tried to dig it up. I've tried to blast it. I've painted it. (*Throws out his hands helplessly*) Oh what's the use. I've tried everything (*Pause*) but —

SILAS (*Stares at him with interest*): But what?

HIRAM (*Looks around as though he might be overheard*): But wishes.

SILAS (*Laughs heartily*): That's a good one. You've done nothing *but* wish.

HIRAM (*Moves nearer to* SILAS *and sits down, knees drawn up to chest, arms around them*): No, you don't understand what I mean.

SILAS: Well I got to be goin' now. All I know is if wishes were horses then beggars would ride. And I'd be ridin' home 'stead of walking.

HIRAM: Wait a minute. If you remember the old saying about wishes and horses, don't you remember the other one?

SILAS: What other one?

HIRAM: Why the one that says if a person sits on the rock and makes an *unselfish* wish he gets his wish and the rock grows smaller and smaller 'till it gradually goes away. But if he makes a selfish wish the rock will grow larger and he won't get his wish.

SILAS (*Stands up*): Well I'll make a wish right now.

HIRAM (*Jumps up and pulls him away from rock before he can make a wish*): Oh no, you won't. First place the person musn't know the story and second I said an *unselfish* wish. (*Points his finger at him*) Like as not you'd wish for a ride home and then my rock would grow bigger.

SILAS (*Scratches his head*): Well, sorry I can't help you but I really must go home for supper.

HIRAM (*Puts his hand on* SILAS's *arm*): Oh no, you don't. First you *are* going to help me.

SILAS: Help you? Why you just said I couldn't help you.

HIRAM: Well now I say you *can* help me. So put down your stick and come along. I want you to help me carry an old table and blanket from the barn.

SILAS: What for?

HIRAM: Help me with the table and then I'll tell you. (*They exit down right to barn.* HIRAM *and* SILAS *return carrying table and blanket to right center back stage near rock. They cover table with blanket which reaches to floor.*)

SILAS: Now *will* you tell me what all this nonsense is for?

HIRAM: Sure I'll tell you. (*He lifts the banket*) I'm going to hide under here; and on top I'm going to put a scarecrow.

SILAS: Well what in tarnation that all has to do with your rock I still don't see.

HIRAM: Well you will see.

SILAS: But when? Next year, I suppose.

HIRAM: No, matter of fact I think I'll have news for you tomorrow morning or perhaps even late tonight.

SILAS (*Reaches in his pocket and brings out a rumpled dollar bill*): Bet you this against your lucky penny you can't *wish* that rock away.

HIRAM: Oh, but I don't want to lose my lucky piece.

SILAS: I knew you had no faith in it.

HIRAM (*Hesitates a second*): I'll do it. It's a bet. (*Puts out his hand to shake with* SILAS) And now go home. I've got lots of work to do.

SILAS: I'll go home all right: but I'll be back for my lucky piece.

HIRAM: Better bring the dollar bill along — just in *case*. (SILAS *exits left to road*) Now I'll have to get that old scarecrow from the hayloft. (*Looks up at sky*) It's nearly sunset. I'll have to hurry, too. (*Exits lower right whistling or singing. Returns with scarecrow which he places on table, then stands off to admire it*) But it ought to have a hat. (*Takes his own hat off and jams it down on scarecrow's head*) Yep, that looks better. My, he must be an old fellow. (*Puts his hand in pocket of scarecrow*) I knew it. There's still moth-balls in the pocket. Now I'll have to write my notes because I want Emmie to get her note when she meets John coming home for supper. And my nephew is a *very* punctual man. (*Pulls paper and pencil from pocket and writes leaning on table . . . then he puts the note in the overcoat pocket along with the sleeve*) I know Emmie — she'll just have to pull out that sleeve and then she'll find the note. (*Laughs and hides under the table.*)

EMMIE (*Comes on from house, looking up at sky*): Why it's nearly sunset. Land sakes, can the sun be fast? I wonder. It must be because I never knew John to be a minute late before. (*Louder*) John, hurry up. (*Notices the scarecrow*) For pity's sake what have we here? Uncle must have put this contraption up. (*Goes over to look at it and pulls sleeve out of pocket. The note falls to the ground*) Wonder what's on that piece of paper? (*Picks up note and reads it*) Well, of all things! It's a good thing Uncle's not as smart as I am or he'd have found this note. It has on it, up at the top, a skull and cross bones and it says if you will dig near the rock, where there is a cross mark, on the first night of full moon, at nine-thirty, you will receive a package. Place the package where you see the red dot. Sit touching the rock to make your wish. Important: Obey all instructions and leave before ten o'clock. This note must be very old. (*Sees* JOHN *coming and calls*) John, hurry, I've got a big surprise for you.

JOHN (*Enters from road, running and rubbing his hands on some cotton waste as though to get grease off*): What's the matter, Emmie? Aren't sick, are you? (*Catches sight of scarecrow and whistles*) What's this? Who did it?

EMMIE (*Puts her finger to her lips*): Shoo-o-o! Uncle made it, I suppose. He's always been talking 'bout bringing one up from the field.

JOHN: Then why all the hush-hush about it?

EMMIE (*Hands him note*): Take a look at this.

JOHN (*Reads it*): Where'd you find it?

EMMIE: In the overcoat pocket. It's that old coat that's been in the barn for years.

JOHN: Don't think it's a joke, do you?

EMMIE: How can it be a joke? I just accidently put my hand in the pocket because the sleeve was tucked in, otherwise I wouldn't have found it.

JOHN (*Reads note again, then walks over to rock*): Now here to the front between the house and the rock is where we dig. While here right near the scarecrow is where we put the package while we make our wish.

EMMIE: Yes, I guess you've got it about right.

JOHN (*Faces* EMMIE): One thing certain, Emmie, you've just got to get the boys to bed early. They'd never stop teasing us if —

EMMIE (*Cuts in*): Oh I'll do that, don't worry. But it *will* amount to something. I feel it in my bones.

JOHN: Well I hope your bones are truthful.

EMMIE: Come now to supper. (*She exits to house followed by* JOHN. HIRAM, *laughing silently, slips out and puts another note and sleeve back in pocket; then crawls under table again.* JACK *and* GEORGE *enter from road, see the scarecrow and walk over to it.*)

JACK: Now who may you be? And how did you get here?

GEORGE: Perhaps 'tis royalty come to visit us. Let's make a bow. (*Both bow, then straighten up and sniff.*)

JACK: Wonder where they are? We could use them for marbles.

GEORGE (*Pulls out sleeve and note and moth balls fall to ground*): What do you know about this? Hidden treasure and all about how to find it. (*Reads note with* JACK *hanging over his arm.*)

JACK (*Walks over to rock*): Here is where we're supposed to dig.

GEORGE (*Reading partly to himself and partly out loud*): First night of full moon. That's tonight. Be at rock by ten o'clock sharp. Leave before ten-thirty. Signed with bloody crossbones. (*Pointing with his hand*) Now here is where we're supposed to sit; and here is where we place the treasure.

JACK: Yeah, I know. Lucky we found it before Mom saw it. (EMMIE'S *voice from the house*: *"Children come in this minute for your supper."*)

GEORGE (*Slips note in his pocket*): Coming right away. (*Low voice*) How are we going to get the folks to bed?

JACK: Oh we'll just yawn and yawn and pretty soon Mom will say we'd better go to bed. (*Both exit to house.* HIRAM *crawls out from under table just before* EMMIE *enters from house.*)

EMMIE (*Trying to pull him in house*): Where have you been? Come in before supper gets stone cold.

HIRAM (*Looking towards road*): Just leave me something on a plate. I see Stella and Mary coming and I want to talk to them.

EMMIE: Well, all right, but we're all sleepy and want to go to bed early.

HIRAM: I'm tired too so it suits me perfectly. (EMMIE *exits to house just as the children enter from road.*)

STELLA (*Coming toward scarecrow*): Oh, isn't it beautiful?

MARY: Oh, just beautiful.

HIRAM (*Walking over to stand near the girls*): Hello! What's this? (*Stoops pretending to pick up paper already in his hand*) Why, it's a note from the scarecrow!

STELLA: What does it say?

HIRAM: It's addressed "Two Good Little Girls." That must mean you. (*Both nod their heads and crowd round* HIRAM.)

MARY: Please, Sir, won't you read the note to us?

HIRAM: It says at ten-thirty to dig where there is an arrow. (*Walks to the spot followed by the children. Looks at note again.*) When you have your treasure sit on ground facing rock to make your wish.

MARY: Please, Mr. Hiram, we'd be scared to stay out so late.

HIRAM: There's no need to be scared. We'll have a full moon tonight: and I'll be around to take you home.

STELLA (*Jumping up and down*): Oh let's, Mary. We can slip out through the little window. I wonder what we'll get.

MARY: If you think it's all right, then we'll come.

HIRAM (*Taking each child by the hand*): I think it's perfectly all right; and I'll see you tonight. Now run home because it's supper time. (*The children wave to him as they run off.*)

HIRAM (*Stretching his arms up and yawning*): Well I guess it's supper and bed for me. (*Turns to scarecrow*) And now my friend, it's up to you. (*He exits to house.*)

CURTAIN

* * *

SCENE 2

SETTING: *The same.*

TIME: *Night of same day.*

AT RISE: JOHN *and* EMMIE *enter from house.* EMMIE *carries a lantern or flashlight;* JOHN *a spade.*

EMMIE: Have you got the paper.

JOHN (*Puts a finger to his lips*): Sh— sh—, not so loud or you'll wake the boys.

EMMIE: The boys are very sleepy. They won't wake. But what about Uncle?

JOHN: He's been in his room all evening with the door shut. (*Followed by* EMMIE, *he goes over to the spot and starts to dig*) Now we'll soon see what's what. (*He lifts a package from under the leaves and hands it to* EMMIE) There you are.

EMMIE (*Sniffing as she takes it*): It's money. I just know it is. It even smells like it.

JOHN: That's funny. Smells like money. Now put it between the rock and scarecrow; then we make our wish. (*Both sit facing rock*) Hurry up, now.

EMMIE: I just wish you'd give me a chance to concentrate. O-Oh!

JOHN: A bad one. I knew it. Well, all I wish is that you don't blame me. (HIRAM *pulls the package under the table.*)

EMMIE (*Sadly*): They're both bad. Well anyhow we have our package. (*They both get up and* JOHN *goes to look for the package.*)

JOHN: I certainly know where I put it and it isn't here. Somehow it makes me feel queer. Sort of like ghosts. Let's go in before we overstay our time and have more bad luck. Now remember we don't tell Uncle or the boys. (*They exit.* HIRAM *slips package under the leaves just before the boys come out tiptoe fashion holding a lantern.*)

GEORGE (*Finger to lips*): Sh— sh— your shoes squeak.

JACK: They don't either. Its yours that squeak. (*Takes map out of pocket, looks at it, then walks to spot where package is concealed*) Now right here's where it says to dig. (*He digs.*)

GEORGE (*Hopping around*): Oh boy, I hope we get a treasure.

JACK (*Throws down spade and pulls out the package which has been covered by leaves*): Hurray, here it is.

GEORGE: Sh— sh— be quiet. We'll put the package where it says to then we'll make our wish. (*They put package near scarecrow.*)

JACK (*Both sit facing rock*): Now we'll make our wishes. I'll start.

George: I wish you'd once let me do something first. Oh — (*Putting his hand over his mouth*) I made a wish.

Jack (*Sarcastically*): And how. Wish I'd come alone.

George (*Slowly*): Well both wishes are gone now. Let's get our package. Wonder what's in it. (*They look for package but* Hiram *has pulled it under the blanket.*)

Jack (*As they both stand staring at each other*): Where is it?

George: We must've dreamed it.

Jack: Yes, I guess we did. (*They tumble off almost asleep as the girls come on from road carrying a lighted lantern.*)

Mary (*Shuddering*): My, it's awful spooky here.

Stella: I'm scared to death. (*They put down lantern.*)

Mary: Wonder where Mr. Hiram is? He said he'd meet us here.

Stella (*Teeth chattering*): What's that?

Mary: Oh that's the scarecrow. Don't you remember you saw it this afternoon? (Hiram *comes out of the back of table so the children do not see him coming.*)

Hiram (*Rubbing his hands together*): Well, well, if it isn't my old friends Mary and Stella.

Stella: Oh, Mr. Hiram, we're so glad to see you. We're so scared.

Hiram (*Picking up lantern*): Nothing to be scared of. Now let's get right down to work. Let me see the note.

Mary (*Handing him the note*): Let me hold the lantern for you.

Hiram (*Spreading note out, then going over to the spot followed by the girls*): It says to dig right here.

Stella: Do you think we'll find something, Mr. Hiram?

Hiram (*Taking up the package*): We *did* find something. A nice big package. Looks as if it might be money. Now hold on to it while you sit here to make your wish. (*Points to place to sit then walks off a few steps.*)

Stella (*After they have sat down*): My it's so pretty here with the moon shining so bright. I wish all the children could see it.

Mary: Our wish. Be careful.

Stella: Well, I do wish it but I guess I wasted my wish. (*Slowly*) Well perhaps there's money in the package then we could have a party with presents for everybody.

Mary (*Nodding her head*): Yes I wish so too; and a lollypop for every girl.

Hiram (*Taking a long breath and letting it out on the words*):

Glory be somebody's made an *unselfish* wish. (*Backstage somebody must pull all pillows out of rock.*)

STELLA (*Wringing her hands*) : Oh, Mr. Hiram, your beautiful rock. It fell down.

MARY (*Crying*) : Please, Mr. Hiram, don't be angry with us. We didn't do anything to it.

HIRAM : Oh yes you did.

STELLA (*Nodding her head sideways*) : Oh no we didn't. Honestly we didn't.

HIRAM : Yes you did. You made a lovely wish. And in this world when we do a kind act it sometimes blots out an ugly one.

MARY : But the rock was beautiful.

HIRAM : No, that's where you're wrong. It's very ugly. I always wanted to get rid of it but somebody had to make an unselfish wish before it would fall. And you did it. (*He pulls them to their feet*) Now let's open your package and see what's in it.

MARY (*Handing it to* HIRAM) : You open it, please.

HIRAM (*Tearing the paper at one end*) : Children, it's money. Now you can have the party you were wishing for.

STELLA and MARY (*Jumping up and down*) : Thank you, Mr. Hiram.

HIRAM : Don't thank me. I didn't do it. Didn't you read the note I found in the scarecrow's pocket?

STELLA : Yes, but you gave us the note.

MARY : Yes, you did.

HIRAM : Well we'll talk that over tomorrow when you come over to see how nice the place looks without the rock. But now you must go home because it is very late.

STELLA : Oh, we will come, Mr. Hiram.

HIRAM (*Handing* STELLA *the lantern and going to exit with them*) : Now, girls, go right straight up the road and wave your lantern just as soon as you get to the home. Then I'll know you're safe.

MARY : We won't forget to wave. And thank you for helping us get the treasure. (*They exit.*)

HIRAM (*Stretching*) : It's been a long day but a grand one. Hello, what's that? Somebody with a flashlight coming along the road. (*Pause*) And whoever it is has stopped the children. Perhaps I'd better go see who it is. (*Snaps on flashlight and starts to go, then realizes it is only his old friend.*) I see now. It's only Silas

— might've known he'd be over to try to get my lucky piece. (*Yawns then crosses right and leans on table as* SILAS *comes in.*) Well I reckon you've come to collect your bet.

SILAS: No, I guess it's the other way 'round. The girls were both chattering away for dear life about a picnic for all the children. But tell me what happened.

HIRAM: First go over and look at my rock.

SILAS (*Looking all around*): Why, you haven't any rock! Who did it?

HIRAM: The children. They wished for a picnic for the whole orphan asylum. *A real unselfish wish.*

SILAS (*Unpins his pocket and takes out a worn wallet from which he takes a dollar bill then he puts wallet back in pocket and fastens pin. He hands it to* HIRAM): Here's your dollar.

HIRAM: Well, Silas, I guess I'll give this to the children, too. It ought to buy the lemonade. (*Puts his hand on* SILAS's *shoulder*) Just think all these years I've wanted to get rid of that ugly old rock; and how many different ways I've tried to do it. (*Pauses*) And yet all it really needed was just *one little unselfish wish.*

THE END

NOT ON THE MENU

by Mary Thurman Pyle

Characters

BARBARA ANDERSON, *14, capable and thoughtful*
JEAN ANDERSON, *12, whose imagination is sometimes almost too much for the family*
TOMMY ANDERSON, *11, whose friendly grin includes everybody*
"BUBBLES" ANDERSON, *8, a little girl who just bubbles over with good spirits and affection*
LESLIE NORRIS } *friends of Tommy's*
BOB BROWN }
AUNT HARRIET, *the Anderson children's great-aunt — a severe, plain-spoken, somewhat terrifying old lady*
MRS. ANDERSON, *an understanding mother*

SETTING: *The sun porch at the Anderson house.*

AT RISE: *The four Anderson children are discovered busily preparing for some unusual event. The furniture has been pushed back and in the center of the room a heap of sticks has been laid, with three large sticks crossed at top, in imitation of a gypsy campfire. Other touches are about to suggest that the children have been converting the porch into a gypsy camp. At one end of a table,* BARBARA *is counting some kitchen knives and forks, and* JEAN *is pasting pieces of white paper onto the backs of old playing cards. There are five finished, and she is completing the sixth one.* BUBBLES *is fitting pieces of brown crepe paper over some empty jelly glasses, putting rubber bands around the top of the glasses to hold the paper in place. There are already five glasses covered in this way, and she is completing the sixth.* TOMMY *is tying a piece of burlap over a low kitchen stool on which a sofa pillow is laid, the burlap to cover the whole, producing an irregular, lumpy object.*

BUBBLES: What are we *really* going to drink out of these jelly glasses, Barbara?

JEAN (*Quickly*): They *aren't* jelly glasses! They're brown, earthenware mugs. That's what gypsies would use — I think.

TOMMY (*Looking up from his job*): I'll bet gypsies wouldn't have cocoa for supper, though.

JEAN: Now, Tommy! You promised you'd really play the game. We've got to pretend the cocoa is a strange brew that only the gypsies know how to make — a secret recipe handed down to them.

TOMMY: Okay. But you've sure got some imagination, Jean. I'll bet you'd like to bring some real rocks in here to make the porch look more like a gypsy camp in the mountains.

JEAN (*Laughing*): That's an idea! If there were time, I would. But that's a pretty good rock you're making.

TOMMY (*Surveying his handiwork*): Some rock! And I have to sit on it, too.

JEAN: Well, if you want to be the king of this gypsy tribe, you've got to get in the spirit of it.

BUBBLES: I think Jean has a wonderful imag — imag — (*She is unable to remember the big word.*)

BARBARA: Imagination, darling.

BUBBLES: Imagination. That means she can make up swell stories, doesn't it?

BARBARA: Yes, Bubbles, it does — but Mother asked you *not* to say "swell." Remember?

BUBBLES: I won't, Barbara. But Tommy and all the boys say "swell."

TOMMY: Sure we do. You practically have to. There's just no other word. — Say, how is this boulder for the gypsy king to sit on?

JEAN: That's *swell* — I mean, it's fine.

BARBARA: Just the thing — if it will hold you.

TOMMY (*Grinning as he sits on "rock" to test it*): She works! I'm the king of the tribe — and that means you'll do as I say!

JEAN (*Enthusiastically*): Get your costume on. I'm just dying to see how you'll look.

BARBARA: I'll help you. (*She selects from the pile of accessories a red handkerchief, which she ties around her brother's head, a striped sash, which goes around his waist, a pair of curtain rings, with threads attached, which become earrings. The chatter continues as she adds these colorful items to* TOMMY'S *ordinary costume of shirt and trousers.*)

TOMMY: Say, I don't know what Les and Bob will think of all this junk. (*Indicating the additions to his costume.*)

BARBARA: Oh, we've got some things for them to dress up in, too.

JEAN: And if those two kids don't behave at our party, they'll have to leave, that's all. Even if they are your special buddies.

TOMMY: Well, Mother said I could ask them, because tonight's our club night. And they're not kids. They're nearly as old as you are.

JEAN: All right — but if Leslie Norris and Bob Brown don't play like we want them to —

BARBARA: They will, Jean. I'm sure they will. — Look! Doesn't Tommy look wonderful?

JEAN (*Her enthusiasm returning*): Isn't this *fun?* And wasn't Mother a darling to let us have our supper like this?

BUBBLES: I wish Mother was here, too — and Daddy. (*Her chin begins to quiver.*)

BARBARA (*Quickly*): Never mind, Bubbles. Mother won't be out long — and we'll have daddy home soon, I know.

TOMMY: These earrings won't stay on.

BARBARA: They will if you keep still.

JEAN: Imagine Tommy keeping still.

TOMMY: Sure I can!

BUBBLES (*Going to her brother and hugging him*): Oh, Tommy, you look so sweet!

TOMMY: Sweet! (*His tone is one of great disgust at the very idea.*)

BARBARA (*Laughing*): Well, take the earrings off till time to begin. There's more work to do before you can take your place on yon throne and boss us around.

JEAN: I'll say there is. Get the flashlights and see how the fire works.

TOMMY: I knew you girls would find more work for me to do.

BARBARA: But there's always a lot of things that only boys know how to do.

TOMMY (*Flattered*): Oh, well — (*He goes out.*) I'll get the flashlights.

BUBBLES: I've finished the jelly glasses — (*Hastily*) — I mean the — the — what kind of mugs did you say they were, Jean?

JEAN: Earthenware.

BARBARA: Come here, Bubbles, and let me fix you up. (BUBBLES *crosses to* BARBARA, *who adds beads and a headdress to her little sister's outfit.*)

JEAN: And I've finished the menus. Don't they look *wonderful* on the backs of these old playing cards? You see, (*To* BUBBLES) gypsies tell fortunes with cards, and that's how I got the idea of putting our menus on them.

TOMMY (*Returning with two flashlights*): Here they are. (*All bend over eagerly as he turns them on and places them among the twigs and brown paper which are on the floor in the center of the room, to give the effect of a lighted fire.*)

BARBARA: That looks wonderful! That was your idea, Tommy.

TOMMY (*With no false modesty*): And a darned good one.

BARBARA: Tommy! Mother does so want us to grow up speaking nicely.

TOMMY: Well, if daddy were here, he'd understand how a fellow has to say "darn" and "swell" sometimes.

BUBBLES: When will daddy come home? Do you know, Barbara?

BARBARA: The doctor says he should stay at the sanatorium for several more months.

TOMMY: And he'll be all well then, won't he?

BARBARA: Yes — if he can just stay there a while longer.

JEAN: If only we could think of a way to keep him at the sanatorium. It seems like all of us together could raise the money — somehow.

TOMMY: What could a bunch like us do to get the money? Gosh, I wish I were older. I could get a job.

JEAN: And so could I!

BARBARA (*Firmly*): Now, listen, children! Mother doesn't want us to worry about things. She said so — very distinctly. The best we can do is keep happy and cheerful. Daddy would want that, too.

JEAN: There's Great-aunt Harriet!

TOMMY: Sure — and she could give mother the money she needs, if she weren't a stingy old sour-puss.

BARBARA: Tommy, you mustn't say such things. Mother says if worse comes to worse, she'll ask Aunt Harriet for help, but you know mother. She'll not ask unless there's no other way out.

BUBBLES: Maybe Aunt Harriet doesn't *know* daddy is sick.

BARBARA: Of course she does — but perhaps she doesn't realize we need money so badly. Poor darling mother has done everything she can to make some extra money.

JEAN (*With spirit*): I'm not afraid of Aunt Harriet! I'll ask her for some money when she pays that promised call on us — if she really does come, which I doubt.

BUBBLES (*Hugging her sister*): Jeannie! You're not afraid of anybody.

BARBARA: Of course we can't ask her for help. If it has to be done, mother will do it. As a loan, of course. And daddy must never know. He *must* believe we're getting along all right, or he hasn't as much chance to get well.

JEAN: And we *are* getting along all right! Aren't we having a marvelous time this very minute, with our gypsy dinner? (*This brings them all happily back to matters at hand.*)

BARBARA: Read the menu, Jean.

JEAN: I'm calling the stew "Hungarian goulash." There were Hungarian gypsies, weren't there?

BARBARA: There must have been.

TOMMY: But I'll bet their old goulash couldn't hold a candle to mother's beef stew with vegetables.

BUBBLES: I wish mother was here to eat it with us.

TOMMY: Trust mother to drop everything to go sit with old Mrs. Andrews.

BUBBLES: Won't mother have any dinner?

BARBARA: Of course she will, Bubbles. She'll probably have a delicious dinner, as well as the three dollars she'll make.

TOMMY: Old Mrs. Andrews is plenty rich. Mother will probably have chicken and ice-cream and —

JEAN (*Briskly*): But no fun! Now, besides the Hungarian goulash, I have down (*Consulting her menu again*) "gypsy brew"— that's the cocoa. And for the rolls I wrote, "crusty bread baked fresh over the coals." We can pretend we really are toasting them, you see.

TOMMY (*Guffawing*): Over the flashlights!

JEAN (*Glowering*): Tommy! Are you going to play or not?

BARBARA: Of course he is. What else, Jean?

JEAN: Well, the apples and grapes we are supposed to have gathered as we travelled through the country.

TOMMY: Swiped 'em, you mean?

JEAN (*Dubious over the moral issue involved*): Well — no. Maybe we worked in the orchards for them. It was hard to think up fancy names for just apples and grapes. I've heard of "apples of Hesperides."

BARBARA (*Superior*): Oh, they were in Greek mythology.

TOMMY: There was a movie called "Grapes of Wrath."

JEAN: But that didn't have anything to do with gypsies, silly. I thought "apples of happiness" sounded nice, and I've called the grapes "vintage grapes." (*Giggles.*) I don't know exactly what that means, but it makes them sound good.

BARBARA: Everything is ready to serve. Let's get dressed, Jean. The boys will be here soon.

JEAN: May I wear the orange-colored scarf? (*The two girls begin to add their embellishments. At this moment there is a war whoop from outside.* LESLIE *and* BOB *are approaching!*)

JEAN: Did you say the boys would be here?

TOMMY: Hot dog! It's Les and Bob. (*He goes to the porch door and unlocks it.* LESLIE *and* BOB *burst in. They are noisy, pleasant, average boys, about* TOMMY'S *age and his special cronies.*)

LESLIE (*Entering*): Whoopee! Hey, everybody!

BOB: Hail, hail, the gang's all here!

LESLIE: What kind of eats are we going to have?

BOB: Is your mother out?

BARBARA (*Firmly*): Yes, mother's out. But that doesn't mean you boys can raise the roof.

LESLIE (*Taking in* TOMMY'S *costume*): Hey, look at Tom!

BOB (*Bursting out laughing; quoting a popular song*): "You ought to be in pitchers!"

BARBARA: "Pictures," Bob. "Pitchers" is simply dreadful.

BOB: Yeah, but the song says "pitchers."

TOMMY: You fellows have to dress up like this, too. Only I'm the king of the tribe, see. (*He struts about.*)

BOB: Oh, yeah! Then I'll be Prime Minister.

LESLIE: And I'll be — who has charge of the food? — I'll be chief cook.

JEAN: Here, boys, put on your scarves and handkerchiefs.

BUBBLES: And put your earrings on.

LESLIE: Sure we will, Bubbles.

BOB (*With a bow*): Anything Miss Bubbles Anderson asks, we will do!

LESLIE (*Bowing also*) : Bubbles, our future glamour girl!

BARBARA : We will eat as soon as we're all fixed. It's to be a gypsy supper, out here on the porch, you know. (*There is the sound of a long, firm ring at the doorbell. They all stand silent for a moment.*)

JEAN : Didn't mother say we shouldn't answer the doorbell when she's out?

BARBARA : Yes, she did. (*The ring is repeated.*)

TOMMY : I'm not afraid. I'll go.

BARBARA : Wait, Tommy. Maybe they'll go away.

JEAN : Maybe we should telephone mother.

BARBARA : Oh, no. She said not to phone her unless something really urgent came up.

BUBBLES : I'm — scared.

BARBARA : No, you're not, darling. Nothing could hurt us, with so many of us here.

LESLIE : Especially with all us fellows.

BOB : Let's scare 'em off, whoever it is. Come on — let's give the school yell. (*Without more ado, the three boys let out a war whoop of terrifying volume. The girls burst out laughing in spite of themselves. There is a sudden loud knock at the porch door. The laughers and the whoopers all stop in their tracks, frozen. The knock is repeated, followed by a sharp, feminine voice from outside.*)

AUNT HARRIET (*From outside*) : Why doesn't someone open this door? (*She shakes the door.*) Open this door! It's Harriet Anderson — it's your great-aunt Harriet!

BARBARA (*In a whisper*) : Aunt Harriet! My goodness!

JEAN : What's she doing here? She wasn't supposed to come till next week.

TOMMY : Let's pretend we don't hear her.

BARBARA : Of all times! But we simply must open the door. After all, she is our aunt.

TOMMY (*Deprecatingly*) : Our *great*-aunt!

AUNT HARRIET : Children! Don't you hear me?

BARBARA (*Going to the door and opening it*) : Hello! Do come in. You *are* our Aunt Harriet, aren't you?

AUNT HARRIET (*At door*) : Of course I am.

BARBARA : Please excuse us for not opening the door when you first knocked. We were frightened for a minute, because we're alone. Mother isn't here right now. (AUNT HARRIET, *tall, angular, rather forbidding, enters. She is about 60, grey-haired. She peers about in a curious but not unkind way.*)

AUNT HARRIET: Oh! I'm sorry if I frightened you. (*Dryly.*) I thought that you were merely making so much noise you didn't hear me.

BARBARA (*Apologetically*): We were making a lot of noise, I guess.

AUNT HARRIET: And who are all these children? I didn't know the family was so large.

BARBARA: Oh, only four of us belong here. I'm Barbara.

AUNT HARRIET: The oldest. I remember you. Your father brought you to New York to see me once.

BARBARA: And this is Jean — she's twelve. And Tommy (*she draws* TOMMY *away from the other two boys*) — this is Tommy — he's eleven. And this is the baby — she's eight.

AUNT HARRIET (*Looking them over appraisingly and stopping at* BUBBLES): The youngest. Harriet! Named after me, your mother wrote me.

BUBBLES (*In innocent friendliness*): I'm Bubbles.

BARBARA (*Hastily*): You see, we thought "Harriet" sort of — sort of serious sounding for Bubbles. She is so — so *bubbling* over all the time. And she's such a happy little soul —

AUNT HARRIET: I see! You can't be happy if your name's Harriet, I presume. (*Fixes* LESLIE *and* BOB *with her glance. They stand in comical attitudes of embarrassment.*) Who are these?

TOMMY (*With his friendly grin*): They are my special pals. We're the three Musketeers — "One for all, and all for one." (*The boys go into position, with arms around each other's shoulders, in the famed Three Musketeers style.*)

AUNT HARRIET: You don't look like the Three Musketeers to me.

TOMMY: My goodness! I forgot these rigs.

JEAN: We're playing gypsy, Aunt Harriet. Mother said we could, while she was out.

AUNT HARRIET: Where is your mother?

BARBARA: She's — she's out on an errand. But I'll phone her right away to come home. (*She starts into the house.*)

AUNT HARRIET: Nothing of the sort! (BARBARA *comes back.*) It's all working out very nicely. I came on purpose at a time your mother wasn't expecting me. And with her out — that's even better. You can tell a great deal about a family if you study the children of that family when the parents aren't around. — Well, aren't you going to ask me to sit down? And have dinner with you?

BARBARA: Of *course!* Where are our manners! (*The three girls help* AUNT HARRIET *off with her coat and hat. Gradually the atmosphere thaws, as, childlike, they begin to take their aunt into their jolly evening's plans.*)

JEAN: It's a funny dinner — but we think it's going to be fun. It's a gypsy dinner.

BARBARA (*Explaining, as the eldest*): You see, Mother had to be out for a few hours, and she left our dinner all ready — it's beef stew —

JEAN (*Clapping her hand over* BARBARA'S *mouth*): No, it *isn't!* (*To* AUNT HARRIET) We're playing it's gypsy food, and we've a menu, pasted on the backs of old playing cards.

BUBBLES: And I fixed the jelly — (*Catching herself*) the earthenware mugs. There aren't but six, but you can have mine.

TOMMY: And I'm the king of the tribe.

LESLIE: I'm the Prime Minister. Do gypsies have prime ministers?

BOB: I'm head-man in the food department.

JEAN: And all of this is the gypsy camp. We're going to eat out here on the porch. Mother said we could.

AUNT HARRIET: Where *is* your mother, may I ask?

BARBARA: She is staying with one of our neighbors who is an invalid.

AUNT HARRIET: Very commendable — if she doesn't neglect her family.

TOMMY: She gets three dollars for it — and we sure need the money.

BUBBLES: For daddy.

BARBARA: Children!

AUNT HARRIET: Oh, I see.

BARBARA (*Quickly*): Don't let's bother Aunt Harriet with things like that. We want you to have a good time, Aunt Harriet.

JEAN (*Inspired*): You can dress up! We've plenty of beads and scarves.

TOMMY: And you can sit on this rock if you want to — (*Grinning*) — only it isn't really a rock and it might break.

AUNT HARRIET: In that case, I'll take the armchair.

JEAN: But not before you've dressed up like a gypsy. Here, let me fix you. (*She and* BARBARA *tie a bright handkerchief around* AUNT HARRIET'S *head, before she can protest — if she meant to protest — and put some beads around her neck.*)

BUBBLES: Oh, you look so *nice,* Aunt Harriet. Let me put some bracelets on you. (*She stands against* AUNT HARRIET'S *knee and slips a bracelet over her wrist.*)

BARBARA: Boys! — I mean, Prime Minister and Chief Cook — bring on the dinner! The king of the tribe will show you where it is, while we entertain our honored guest. (*She bows before* AUNT HARRIET, *and the rest follow her lead, all laughing merrily. The three boys march on in style, executing an "About, face! Forward, march!"*)

JEAN: Here's our menu, Aunt Harriet. It's just crazy names for what we are going to have. (AUNT HARRIET *takes the "menu" and studies it, a little smile beginning to play about the corner of her mouth.*)

BARBARA: I'm sorry you struck us on stew night. Mother says beef stew with vegetables is healthy and *filling* — for a bunch of children.

BUBBLES (*Innocently*): And it's cheap.

BARBARA: Bubbles! Ssh! (*The boys return, bringing in an old-fashioned iron kettle, the handle of which they have put across a broomstick. They set it down over the make-believe fire.*)

LESLIE: Goulash! Lemme at it.

BOB: This stuff smells swell, no matter what you call it.

TOMMY (*Taking his place on his "throne"*): Bring on the eats!

BUBBLES (*Very seriously*): You mustn't say "swell" and "eats." (*They all laugh at her manner.*)

JEAN: Oh, this is such fun! Don't you *love* being a gypsy, Aunt Harriet?

TOMMY: I think you ought to be the gypsy queen, Aunt Harriet.

BARBARA: I *do* hope you don't mind pretending with us.

AUNT HARRIET: Not at all. I rather imagine I'll have a very enlightening — *and* entertaining time of it. And before the dinner is served, may I quote some words apropos to the occasion. They are words a real gypsy once said: "There's night and day, brother, both sweet things. There's the sun and stars, brother, all sweet things. There's the wind in the heath." (*There is a pause.*)

Jean (*Sighs*): That's *beautiful!*

Aunt Harriet (*Softly*): I hadn't thought of those words for years.

Bubbles: I *like* you, Aunt Harriet.

Tommy: Food! Food! That's a sweet thing, too!

Leslie: I'll say! (*There is a chatter and a clatter as the girls begin to serve the plates. The party is beginning to get into its stride as the curtain falls.*)

* * *

Scene 2

At Rise: Mrs. Anderson *is seated at the table, and the four* Anderson Children *are grouped around her.* Mrs. Anderson *is an attractive, energetic, but gentle and understanding woman. She has just come in from* Mrs. Andrews', *and has taken off her hat and coat, which lie on the table. She is reading a note written on a piece of notebook paper. The children show by their attitudes their affection for their mother and their interest in what she is reading.*

Mrs. Anderson: But what did your Aunt Harriet *say,* Barbara?

Barbara: She said she couldn't spend the night. I really did urge her to, mother.

Jean: She said she'd go back to the hotel and drop by again tomorrow.

Tommy: And that she'd leave you this note. I gave her a sheet of my notebook to write it on.

Mrs. Anderson: I can't understand her coming before the time she set for her visit. Did you explain why I was away, Barbara?

Barbara: Oh, yes, mother. I think she understood.

Jean: And she had a wonderful time at our party — didn't she, Barbara? She dressed up and everything.

Barbara: She certainly seemed to enjoy it.

Bubbles: And she ate some of everything.

Tommy: I'd say she was a good egg.

MRS. ANDERSON: Tommy!

TOMMY: I mean — a very nice — a very nice old lady. We had plenty of fun.

BUBBLES: I like Aunt Harriet. She let me put the jewelry on her. And she liked the mugs I fixed out of the jelly glasses.

MRS. ANDERSON (*Reading the note*):
"Dear Charlotte."

BARBARA: What does she say?

JEAN: Read it loud mother.

MRS. ANDERSON (*Begins to smile quietly as she continues to read*): "I attended a very wonderful dinner party this evening. I liked everything on the menu (that was really a very tasty beef stew, besides being 'healthy and filling'), but I particularly liked the things I found at that dinner which were *not* on the menu. I shall give myself the pleasure of a more formal call to-morrow. Harriet." And here's a postcript. "Don't worry about the future, my dear Charlotte. 'There's night and day, brother, both sweet things.' H."

JEAN: She told *us* that, too. A gypsy said it.

BARBARA: But what does she mean by things not on the menu?

MRS. ANDERSON: I think I understand that. She meant (*Looking at* BARBARA) tact and grace; (*Looking at* JEAN) and wit and imagination. (*She rumples* TOMMY'S *hair fondly and he grins at her.*) She meant friendliness and good nature. (*She lifts* BUBBLES *to her knee.*) And affection. Yes, she certainly meant affection.

BUBBLES: She said I was named Harriet, but I said no, I was "Bubbles."

MRS. ANDERSON: You didn't! And you're supposed to be named after her. Oh, my goodness! (*They are all laughing at their mother's tone of comic dismay, as the curtain falls.*)

THE END

A FAMILY IN SPACE

by Charles Rittenhouse

Characters

CHAIRMAN
PROFESSOR STELLAR
JEAN, JOAN, JIM, JOHN, JENNY, JOE — *young science students*
LONELY STAR (*afterwards the Sun*)
MERCURY
VENUS
EARTH
MARS
JUPITER
SATURN
URANUS
NEPTUNE
PLUTO
CHARLIE, *the Comet*
LADY SPACE
THE PILOT
2 JET ENGINES

SETTING: *A schoolroom.*

AT RISE: CHAIRMAN *enters with* PROFESSOR STELLAR *whom he ushers politely to a seat by the desk. Then he taps his bell and waits for absolute silence.*

CHAIRMAN: The meeting will now come to order. This morning our Science Club has a very famous visitor who is going to address us. As you know, we have been studying about the sun and the earth and all that, and some of us were pretty puzzled. When our teacher heard that Professor Stellar was passing through the town, she asked him if he would pay us a visit. Now, the Professor is a very busy man, but he kindly consented to come, and I am more than happy to welcome him. (*Introducing him grandly*) Professor Stellar! (*He sits. The class applauds as the* PROFESSOR *rises and comes front. He is a cheerful old man with silver-rim glasses and a goatee.*)

PROFESSOR: Thank you, boys and girls, thank you. (*He looks them over, smiling.*) So you want to learn something about the solar system, eh? That's fine, but first I'd like to find out what you already know. Who can tell me what the solar system is? (*Hands waving*) You, the boy in the blue sweater.

JIM: The solar system is the sun and its family of planets.

PROFESSOR: That's a good way to describe it — the sun and its family of planets. What is a planet? (*Hands again*) The girl with the butterfly hair clips.

JEAN: It's a world like ours that goes around the sun.

PROFESSOR: A world? Just like ours?

JEAN: Not exactly, but it's round. I guess it's more like a star.

PROFESSOR: What's the difference between a planet and a star? (*Hands*) The boy in the white shirt.

JOHN: A star is a ball of fire burning in the sky, just like the sun. A planet doesn't burn.

PROFESSOR: You know because you live on one, eh?

JOHN: Yes, sir. Planets always move around some star. They get their heat and light from it.

PROFESSOR: Very good. How many planets are there in the solar system?

JOHN: Nine — the Earth, Mars, Jupiter, and — (*Trying to remember*)

JOE: Mercury, Venus, Uranus — and —

JOAN: Neptune and Saturn.

PROFESSOR: That's eight. The ninth is —

JENNY (*Triumphant*): Pluto!

PROFESSOR: Excellent! You're such a smart class that I'm going to ask you a really hard question. How did the Earth and the other planets get here? How were they made? (*Silence. A few whispers*) You don't know? Well, nobody knows exactly, so you're in good company. But this is what some scientists think. You watch — (*He claps his hands.* LONELY STAR *enters and rushes to center, twirling a red cape. He is followed by the nine* PLANETS *who stand behind him in a line, back to audience, in this order, right to left:* PLUTO, SATURN, JUPITER, VENUS *and on the other side of* LONELY STAR, MERCURY, EARTH, MARS, NEPTUNE, URANUS. *They do not move until they are "born." They each carry hidden a red ribbon on a stick.*)

LONELY (*As he enters*): Fire! Fire! Fire! Fire! (*He stands center twirling his red cape slowly.*)

PROFESSOR: Once long ago the sun was a lonely star. (LONELY STAR *bows to audience.*) He was just like all the other stars, only smaller than most of them. All by himself he traveled through space — on and on and on, whirling round and round — a great big lonely ball of fire. There were many other stars in the sky, but somehow he could never get near to them, never any nearer than a million million miles. (LONELY STAR *stops twirling his cape, listens, stares off.*) The only friend Lonely Star ever met on his travels was Charlie the Comet who came whizzing by once every five hundred years. Like this . . .

CHARLIE (*Offstage*): Whizzzzz! (*He comes racing in from left, hissing, and circles wildly about* LONELY STAR *all during the following. He wears flapping streamers on his arms.*) Here I am again! Here I am again! Here I am again!

LONELY: My goodness, Charlie Comet, but I'm glad to see you.

CHARLIE: So am I! So am I! So am I!

LONELY (*Trying vainly to follow his circlings*): Please stop a minute and talk to me. You make me dizzy, Charlie Comet.

CHARLIE: Can't stop now! Can't stop now! Have to be off! Have to be off! Whizzzzz! (*He races off right, hissing.*)

LONELY: There he goes! Now I won't see him again for 500 years. I do wish I had someone to talk to — anyone. This is a rotten life. Oh, well . . . (*He starts gloomily twirling his cape. After a pause a girl's voice is heard through a megaphone offstage. We never see her.*)

SPACE: Hello there!

LONELY (*Stops suddenly*): My goodness, a voice!

SPACE: Hel-lo-o!

LONELY: Who's that?

SPACE: Me. Just me.

LONELY (*Looking around*): Who are you?

SPACE: I am Lady Space.

LONELY: Yes, but *where* are you, Lady Space? I can't see you.

SPACE: You can't see me, but I'm here, all right. I'm everywhere. I am Space.

LONELY: I don't care who you are, or where you are so long as you talk to me. Say something more, anything.

SPACE: Of course. I want to help you.

LONELY: Then talk, talk!

SPACE: That's what I've been planning to do for a long time. You see, I'm worried about you, Lonely Star. What you need is a family.

LONELY: What kind of a family?

SPACE: A family of planets.

LONELY: What are they?

SPACE: Planets are pieces of a star.

LONELY: Where can I find any pieces of a star? The only thing that ever comes around here is Charlie the Comet.

SPACE: You don't *find* planets, you pull them off.

LONELY: Off what? Show me and I'll start pulling.

SPACE: Off yourself, silly. You're such a big ball of fire, you'd never miss a few little flames.

LONELY: What do you think I am, anyway? Pulling off pieces of myself!

SPACE: You don't do the pulling. Another star does that.

LONELY: Not if I can help it.

SPACE: You *can't* help it. If another star comes near you, he's going to pull off some of your fire whether you like it or not. It's the *law.*

LONELY: What law, and who says so?

SPACE: I say so, and it's the Law of Gravity.

LONELY (*Dismissing it airily*): Pooh! Never heard of it.

SPACE: You're *going* to. The Law of Gravity is the strongest law in all the sky. You see, every star has a magic power, the power of pulling. When one star crosses the path of another, they pull at each other, across the sky, hard.

LONELY: Sounds crazy to me.

SPACE: You'll soon find out it isn't crazy. Sometimes two stars actually pull themselves together in an awful collision. Sometimes one star pulls another all to bits. You've never heard such an explosion as when a star blows up in bits. But most of the time one of the stars just loses some pieces of itself. These are pulled off and form planets.

LONELY: So that's how it's done. No, thank you! Gravity, explosions, pulling off a piece here, a piece there. Not on your life! Go talk to some other star.

SPACE: Well, that's what is going to happen to you, because I say so. Goodbye.

LONELY: Hey, where are you going?

SPACE: To find another star and bring him here.

LONELY (*Alarmed*): No you're not!

SPACE: You wanted people to talk to. You're going to get them. Nine of them. Nine little planets all of your own. Good-bye.

LONELY: Hey, come back! (*Bellowing*) Lady Space! Come back! I don't want to blow up!

SPACE (*Far away*): Good luck, and don't worry.

LONELY (*To himself*): Don't worry, she says. Don't worry! (*Tearfully*) Oh, my! Oh, my! (*He pantomimes during the following.*)

PROFESSOR (*Coming forward*): The years rolled by, and Lonely Star kept whirling on and on through the empty sky. Then, one day he noticed that one of the far away stars seemed to be getting bigger and brighter. Yes, another star was coming nearer — and nearer —

LONELY (*Shrinking in anguish*): Do we bump, or do we burst? Oh, Lady Space, help me! (*Sobs*) I don't want to blow up. (*He hides his face in his cape, sobbing.*)

PROFESSOR: Lady Space *did* help poor Lonely Star, but first the new star kept coming nearer — and nearer —

LONELY (*Gingerly peeping from behind his cape*): It's still coming! (*With a feeble gesture*) Go away, you! Go away! (*He groans and hides his head again. Weakly.*) Help! Help!

PROFESSOR: Then, suddenly, the approaching star turned off in a different direction. Lady Space had sent another star — a third star — and this third star was pulling the second one away. Lonely Star was saved! *But* just before the star turned away, he gave *one — big — pull.* And —

LONELY (*Jumping*): Waaaa! (MERCURY, *who has remained perfectly still up to now, back to audience, turns quickly, and waves his ribbon round and round.*)

MERCURY (*Spinning*): Wheeeeee! Pop! Look at me!

VENUS: Pop! (*She waves her ribbon happily.*)

EARTH: Pop! (*She waves her ribbon happily.*)

MARS: Pop! (*He waves his ribbon happily.*)

JUPITER: Pop! (*He waves his ribbon happily.*)

SATURN: Pop! (*She waves her ribbon happily.*)

NEPTUNE: Pop! (*He waves his ribbon happily.*)

URANUS: Pop! (*He waves his ribbon happily.*)

PLUTO (*With a snarl*): Pop! (*He waves his ribbon happily.*)

ALL: Whirl — whirl — whirl! Now we are free! (*They stop their ribbons.*)

LONELY (*Sticking his head out again*): What's all that racket! (*He listens for a moment.*) Don't hear anything now. (*He looks off after the vanishing star.*) Say, look at that, would you? It's going away. Yes, sir, it's going away. (*Wiping his brow*) Phew! That was a close one. But say — (*He starts feeling himself, slowly, all over.*) Say, I seem to have shrunk. What's happened to me? I'm smaller. (*The* PLANETS *giggle.* LONELY STAR *stiffens, his eyes wide with alarm. Then, very slowly he looks furtively over his right shoulder. The* PLANETS *on that side grin impishly and wave their ribbons at him. Still very slowly he peers over his left shoulder. The* PLANETS *there wave gleefully. Then staring straight at the audience, he slaps his forehead.*) Do you see what *I* see?

PLANETS: Hello, Daddy! (*They join hands and dance around him, singing.*) Here we go round our daddy dear,
Daddy dear,
Daddy dear,
Here we go round our daddy dear,
So early in the morning. *Boom!*
(*They all sit down in a circle.*)

LONELY (*Staring at them with a forced smile*): Well, well, well! So! So, you're my little — little children, eh? (*The* PLANETS *giggle to one another.*) Hm-m-m. (*To audience*) I don't know whether I'm going to like this. (*The* PLANETS *giggle*). What am I going to *do* with them? (*The* PLANETS *giggle.* LONELY *calls out.*) Lady Space! Lady Space!

SPACE (*Offstage as before*): Yes?

LONELY: Now that I have them, how do I get rid of them?

SPACE: You can't. They're yours forever.

PLANETS: Yippee!

LONELY: What can I *do* with them?

SPACE: Talk to them. Isn't that what you wanted — someone to talk to?

LONELY: I didn't want a lot of *kids.*

SPACE (*Carelessly*): They'll grow up. Their fires will go out, and they'll cool off. It will be up to you to keep them warm when that happens, Mr. Sun.

LONELY: What did you call me?

SPACE: Mr. Sun. That's your new name now that you're a father.

JUPITER (*Standing*): Three cheers for Father Sun! Hip — hip —

ALL: Hurray! (*As they finish the cheering,* JUPITER *sits.*)

MERCURY (*Clapping his hands*): Tell us a story, Daddy.

ALL (*Chanting*): We-want-a-stor-ee — we-want-a-store-ee.

SUN (*Rapidly going mad*): Silence!

ALL (*Shushing one another noisily*): Ssh — ssh — ssh — ssh.

SUN (*Raising his clenched fist to heaven and screaming*): Eeeeee! (*The* PLANETS *are silenced by this demonstration and look at him in alarm.*)

MERCURY: What's the matter, Pop?

SUN (*Through set teeth*): Good grief! I might have known something like this would happen. (*Calling off again*) Are you still there, Lady Space?

SPACE: I'm always here.

SUN: Tell me, how long is it going to take them to cool off and grow up?

SPACE: Millions and millions and millions of years. (*The* SUN *gives a howl and faints, as* CHARLIE THE COMET *enters with a whiz and a hiss as before.*)

CHARLIE: What's all this? What's all this? What's all this?

PLANETS: Hello there!

CHARLIE (*Running around the circle*): What's going on? What's going on? What's going on?

SUN (*Staggering to his feet*): Charlie — Charlie — I want you to meet (*He gulps.*) my family. Children dear, this is Charlie the Comet.

PLANETS: Pleased to meet you, Uncle Charlie.

CHARLIE (*For the first time in his life he is brought to a stop. He even speaks slowly.*): Well, I'll be blowed! I'll be blowed! I'll be blowed! How did it happen?

SUN (*Morosely*): Gravity.

CHARLIE: What is gravity?

SUN: Don't ask me. All I know is it *works.*

CHARLIE (*Shaking his head*): Too bad, old man. (*He starts off again.*) Have to be off! Have to be off! Have to be off! (*He exits with a final whiz. The* PLANETS *join hands again and dance around the* SUN *singing.*)

PLANETS:

Here we go round our daddy dear,
Daddy dear,
Daddy dear.
Here we go round our daddy dear,
Forever and forever. BOOM! (*They all sit down as before. The* SUN *gazes into the distance, a broken man.*)

SUN: Forever and forever — boom! (*The pose is held. The* PROFESSOR *rises and comes forward.*)

PROFESSOR: There you are, boys and girls. That's the way I imagine the solar system was made. Any more questions?

JEAN: What are the planets like?

JENNY: Which is the biggest?

JIM: Is the Earth the biggest, sir?

PROFESSOR: I think I'll let them answer you. (*He claps his hands. The* PLANETS *rise and take their original positions, the* SUN *stepping into line between* VENUS *and* MERCURY.) Let's start with the one we know best, our own Earth.

EARTH (*A self-satisfied girl, stepping forward a pace*): Good morning, boys and girls. Everybody knows me, so there's not much sense in my telling you my name and all that, but —

JUPITER: Anyway she hasn't any name. (*He snickers in his sleeve.*)

EARTH (*A bit annoyed*): No, I haven't a real name like Jupiter here and the rest of them, but then I am called The Earth or The World, as you all know, and that's good enough for me. But even if I haven't any name, I'm still the most important member of the family.

PLANETS (*Ad lib*): You are not! Who do you think you are! Always bragging! (*Etc.*)

EARTH: I am, too. (*Smugly*) I'm just right. The rest of you are too cold or too hot or too something. I'll bet nobody could even live on you.

JUPITER (*Irritatingly*): Somebody asked if you were the biggest planet. Go on, tell them.

EARTH (*Reluctantly*): Well, no — I'm one of the smallest, really.

(*With an illustrative gesture*) I'm only 25 thousand miles through my middle.

JUPITER (*With a flat-handed gesture of scorn*): That's nothing.

EARTH: All of us travel around the Sun, and it takes me 365 days to make the trip.

JUPITER: That's nothing either. It takes me 12 years—*12 years!*

EARTH: Oh, take your old twelve years, Jupiter. Who cares? (*Steps back*)

MERCURY (*A small boy coming forward*): Well, I make the trip in only 88 days. They call me Mercury because I travel so fast.

JUPITER: You don't travel so *fast*. You haven't so far to go, that's all.

MERCURY: Want to race?

JUPITER (*Wearily*): Not now. Get on with your story.

MERCURY: You see, I'm nearest to the Sun, which makes me the hottest of the planets. Am I hot! Sizzle, sizzle, sizzle and a—(*He gives a whistle.*) I am also the smallest of the family, half the size of the Earth, but then size isn't everything. (*To* VENUS) Next—(*During the preceding speech* VENUS *has been arranging her hair with the aid of a hand mirror.*)

VENUS: Just a second.

JUPITER: Come on, you look beautiful.

VENUS: There! (*A final pat*) My name is Venus. Everybody admires the way I shine low down in the sky just after sunset.

JUPITER: Everybody, including yourself.

SUN: Now, that's enough, Jupiter. Mind your manners before strangers.

JUPITER: O.K., Pop.

VENUS: No telescope has ever seen my face, because I keep it hidden behind thick clouds.

JUPITER: Thank goodness!

SUN (*Thundering*): Silence!

JUPITER (*Cowed*): Yes, Father.

VENUS (*To her father*): That's right, shut him up. You'd think he owns the whole sky, the way he talks.

SUN: Now, now, don't quarrel, my child.

VENUS: Can I help it if I'm pretty? (JUPITER *chokes on a suppressed laugh.*)

SUN (*More sternly*): Continue, daughter—and don't be so vain.

VENUS (*Tossing her curls*): I'm about the same size as the Earth, but I am *much* nearer the Sun. It takes *me* only 225 days to make the round trip. I am named after the most *beautiful* of all goddesses, Venus, goddess of love. So there! (*She steps back after making a face at* JUPITER *who makes one right back.*)

MARS (*Advancing*): I am the planet that shines red in the sky. (*Fiercely*) Red as blood — and I am named after Mars, fierce Mars, god of war and bloodshed.

JUPITER: Just call him Butch.

MARS (*Gives a glare at his brother, and continues*): Though I'm little, I'm afraid of no one, for I am hard and tough as a soldier. (*Pointing his remarks at* JUPITER) No, sir — I'm afraid of no one.

JUPITER (*Yawns*): Ho hum!

MARS (*To him fiercely*): That goes for you, too.

JUPITER: You little babies! You make me laugh. Why, you're no bigger than the point of a pin beside me. (*With a roar*) For I am Jupiter the Giant! Look at me! Take a thousand planets the size of the Earth, roll them all into one ball, and I could swallow them whole — swallow them whole.

EARTH (*Controlling her temper*): Now, just a minute, there. You may be a thousand times bigger than I am, but what use are you? Answer me that. What use are you?

JUPITER (*Swelling with rage*): What do you mean?

EARTH: Does anything *grow* on you? Any plants or animals?

JUPITER: Who wants a lot of plants and animals crawling all over him? No, not me! I want to be by myself and *sail* around the Sun. Anyway, I'm too cold. (*Proudly*) Why, I'd freeze any animal to death who came within a million miles of me. That's the kind of a fellow *I* am — huge and freezing and fierce and alone!

EARTH: Exactly! A great, big, frozen lump of uselessness!

JUPITER: Why, you! If you weren't a girl, I'd —

SUN: That will do, children.

JUPITER: She can't get away with that.

SUN (*Angrily*): I said, *that will do!* (JUPITER *growls and steps back into line.*) Saturn, you're next.

SATURN (*A tall girl*): I am the last planet you can see with the naked eye. I am the strangest of all, for I am Saturn, the planet who wears three rings. That is what I look like through a telescope. (*She points to a picture which the* PROFESSOR *has taken from the desk and displayed.*) No boy or girl could live on me, for my air is poison. If anyone tried to walk on me, he would sink right in and vanish in cold, cold ooze. Stay away from me! (*Eerily*) Stay away from me! (*She returns to her position.*)

URANUS (*Stepping forward*): Uranus.

NEPTUNE (*Stepping forward*): Neptune.

TOGETHER: We are the heavenly twins.

URANUS: We are so far away —

NEPTUNE: That we can't be seen.

TOGETHER: Except through a big telescope.

URANUS: We are much bigger than the Earth.

NEPTUNE: We are made of gas —

TOGETHER: Just two big spheres of gas, billions of miles away from the Sun.

URANUS: If you think Jupiter is cold —

NEPTUNE: Or if you think Saturn is cold —

TOGETHER: Just you visit us!

NEPTUNE: Neptune.

URANUS: Uranus.

TOGETHER (*Shivering*): Brrrrrrrrr! (*They go back.*)

PLUTO (*Creeps forward wickedly, and speaks in a hollow voice*): Now it's my turn. Gloomy Pluto! Gloomy Pluto! The farthest planet, and the *da — arkest!* I am so far away from the Sun that he seems no bigger than a little star to me, and lights me not at all. On me all is black — blacker than a grave — blacker than a hundred midnights. For I am dead — dark and distant and dead. Gloomy Pluto! I am named after the black god of *Hell!* (*He gives a maniacal laugh.*)

JUPITER (*To audience*): Don't be scared of him. He thinks he's a bogeyman, but he's really just a little fellow and couldn't hurt a flea.

PLUTO (*In his own piping voice*): I could so. I can scare the daylights out of anybody. Why, I even scare the daylights out of myself. (PLANETS *laugh boisterously.*)

PROFESSOR (*Coming forward with a laugh*): Thank you, thank you all. We have enjoyed your little demonstration very much. (*He leads the class in applause as the* PLANETS *dance off.*)

PLANETS (*As they go*): Goodbye, all.

CLASS: Goodbye! Goodbye!

PROFESSOR: Now, any further questions? I have time for just one more.

JIM: Only one? Aw, gee!

JOHN: We're having fun.

JOAN: Please, sir, Jenny has a question.

PROFESSOR: Yes, Jenny?

JENNY: Professor Stellar, how long would it take to fly from the Sun to the farthest planet? I'd like to take that trip.

PROFESSOR: You couldn't do it. If you started from the Sun, you would be burnt to a crisp.

JENNY: Let's pretend I won't. I want to start from the Sun and fly past all the planets.

PROFESSOR (*Smiling*): How do you propose to travel?

JENNY: I want to travel in comfort.

PROFESSOR: Do you realize that to journey even the little distance from the Earth to the Moon you would have to cram yourself into a spaceship cabin? And that spaceship would have to go 25,000 miles an hour. If it didn't, the Earth's gravity would pull it right back. That wouldn't be very comfortable.

JENNY (*Doubtfully*): No.

PROFESSOR: If you wanted to travel from Earth to one of the planets, you might have to transfer from the spaceship to a space station.

JENNY: This is just *pretend*. I want to sit back in a nice big jet airliner and look at the stars — all the way.

PROFESSOR: How fast do you want to go?

JENNY: Oh, about 500 miles an hour. That's fast enough for me.

PROFESSOR: From the Sun to Pluto, eh? We'll see what we can do. (*He claps his hands. The* PILOT *and two* JET ENGINES *enter, the latter unrolling a long scroll that shows the planets in the order of their distance from the Sun. The* PILOT *carries a model jet plane.*) A plane that travels 500 miles per hour would take about two days to fly all around the world. Are you sure that's fast enough?

JENNY: I have lots of time.

PROFESSOR: Very good. Are you ready, Pilot?

PILOT: All set, sir.

PROFESSOR: Then, blast off! (*The* PILOT *places his plane over the* SUN. *The* ENGINES *make noises imitating a plane.*)

PILOT: We'll pretend that this plane starts from the Sun on the very day you were born. (*He "takes off" very slowly, with accompanying noises from the* ENGINES.) Now you're one *year* old — two years old — three years — four years — five — six. There! We're just getting to Mercury, and you're going to school for the first time. Remember, that day in Grade One? Let's travel on. Seven years — eight years — nine — ten — eleven — twelve — thirteen — fourteen — fifteen. What's that down there? Yes, sir, it's Venus. You're fifteen years old now, and in high school. On we go! My, how time flies! (*One* ENGINE *develops a little trouble.*) Oh-oh! That No. 2 engine is coughing a bit. Thank goodness, here's the Earth and a good landing field. Down we go. (*The plane stops with a final sputter.*)

JEAN: Please, Mr. Pilot, how old are we now?

PILOT: You've just come of age.

JEAN: You mean 21 years old?

PILOT: That's right. You're beginning to think of getting married.

JEAN: Not me.

PILOT (*Laughs*): We're off again. (*The sound accompaniment from the* ENGINES *is renewed.*) 22 — 25 — 28 — 30 years old. Now we're passing Mars and you've discovered your first grey hair. And here comes middle age. 40 years — 50 — 60 — Look out for your rheumatism here — it's getting pretty cold. 70 years — 80 — 90 — 100. You're so old now you have your picture in all the papers. 110 years — There's Jupiter — and you're *dead.* Too bad. On we go, dead or alive. Come on there; speed up a bit or we'll never make it. (*The* ENGINES *sharpen the pitch of their humming accompaniment.*) That's better; now we're *traveling.* Whoops! There goes Saturn. 200 years — 300 — 350 — 400 years. Now we've passed Uranus and are heading for Neptune. 500 years. (*One of the* ENGINES *begins to sputter.*) Now listen, you, don't be silly. There's not a landing field within a billion miles. You have to go on whether you sputter or not.

1ST ENGINE: But, boss, I'm tired. 500 years!

PILOT: It's 600 now. (*Suddenly*) Hey, watch out there! We almost hit Neptune. (*The plane zooms frantically away, then rights itself.*) Now, tend to business. Say! Do you see what I see? There's Pluto! At last, at last, at last! All out for Pluto! All out for Pluto! (*The plane comes in wheezing and puffing. After a final gasp and blow, the* ENGINES *start fanning themselves.*) Quite a journey, eh, Professor Stellar? How long did we take?

PROFESSOR: 889 years.

PILOT: What's the mileage? My speedometer gave out a while back.

PROFESSOR: 350 billion miles!

PILOT: That must be a record. (*He rubs his hands proudly.*)

PROFESSOR: Nonsense! As Jupiter says, (*Repeating the gesture* JUPITER *made*) "That's nothing."

PILOT: What do you mean, nothing?

PROFESSOR: Suppose we'd asked you to travel on to the nearest star. Do you know how long it would have taken you?

PILOT: No, but I'm game.

PROFESSOR: At 500 miles an hour you'd have to travel for 5 million years.

PILOT (*Stunned*): 5 million years!

PROFESSOR: That's only to the *nearest* star. Don't ask me how long it would take to fly to the *farthest* star. I get dizzy just thinking about it.

PILOT (*With a yawn*): Guess I'd better be getting back. It's been a long trip.

PROFESSOR (*Consulting his watch*): Yes. It's getting late. (*Turning to the class*) Well, boys and girls, I hope you've enjoyed yourself. (*He suddenly notices that the class is asleep.*) My goodness! They're all asleep. (*Going to the* CHAIRMAN *and shaking him*) Mr. Chairman! Mr. Chairman!

CHAIRMAN (*Mumbling in his sleep*): 20 years — 30 years — 40 years — 50 years — (*And so on till end of play.*)

PROFESSOR: That trip to Pluto was too much for them, I guess. (*He takes out a handkerchief and places it over the* CHAIRMAN'S *face. The* ENGINES *have rolled up their scroll.*) There! That will keep the flies away. Now let's go before they wake up and ask any more questions. (*They all tiptoe out, saying "Ssh! Ssh!" as the curtain falls.*)

THE END

ALL IN FAVOR

by Morton K. Schwartz

Characters

EDDIE
NANCY
SIDNEY
HARRIET
TOM
DOROTHY
ALVIN

TIME: *A summer afternoon.*

SETTING: *A backyard, just outside a shack—the Aces' clubhouse.*

AT RISE: NANCY, *a neatly-dressed girl of about 13, is patiently leaning against the wall of the shack, next to the door. Presently* EDDIE, *a little boy of about 10, comes walking on.*

EDDIE: Hello, Nancy.
NANCY: Hello.
EDDIE: What are you doing?
NANCY: Can't you see? I'm standing here waiting. (*She is annoyed.*)
EDDIE: Oh. (*He moves next to* NANCY, *and leans on the wall the way she is doing.*) What are you waiting for?
NANCY: We're having a meeting.
EDDIE: Who's having a meeting?
NANCY: *We* . . . our club.
EDDIE: What club?
NANCY: The Aces.
EDDIE: How soon does it begin?
NANCY (*Annoyed*): Why don't you stop bothering me, Eddie? You have your own friends to play with.
EDDIE: I can't find any of them.

NANCY: Then play ball or something. I'm busy.

EDDIE: You won't be busy till the meeting begins, will you?

NANCY: It's going on right now.

EDDIE: Where?

NANCY: In the clubhouse, of course. (*She motions back to it.*)

EDDIE: Well, if the meeting is going on in the clubhouse, how come you're out here?

NANCY: Because this is my first meeting, and I have to be elected to the club. Now stop asking questions.

EDDIE: Then you're not in the club yet?

NANCY: I told you to stop asking questions!

EDDIE: That wasn't a question. I just said "then you're not in the club yet."

NANCY: Well, you said it with a rising inflection, and that makes it a question.

EDDIE: What's a rising inflection?

NANCY: It's a rising tone in your voice when you ask a question —and anyway I said I won't answer any more questions, so I won't tell you.

EDDIE: All right then, I'll just say it plain—you're not in the club yet.

NANCY: That's right. But I will be in it in about five minutes, because they're electing me right now.

EDDIE: Maybe they won't let you in.

NANCY: Don't be silly. Of course they will.

EDDIE: I don't see how you can tell beforehand.

NANCY: I only need a majority to vote for me. There are only five kids in the club, so all I need is three votes.

EDDIE: Maybe you won't get three.

NANCY: Of course I will. Why, three of the kids are my best friends. There's Harriet, Sidney, and Tom. They'll all vote for me, I'm certain. That makes a majority without even counting the other two.

EDDIE: Then I guess you'll get in. Can I join the club?

NANCY (*Impatiently*): Of course not!

EDDIE: Why not?

NANCY: You're too young. And you have different friends.

EDDIE: I know Harriet, and Sidney and Tom . . . and you. You'll vote for me, won't you?

NANCY: Well . . . yes, I would vote for you. But you wouldn't be elected anyway, because the others wouldn't.

EDDIE: I think I would. When you get inside, tell them that I want to join. (*There is the sound of movement inside the club-room.* NANCY *stands and straightens her dress. In a few moments,* SIDNEY *opens the door, steps out, and closes the door behind him.* SIDNEY *is about the same age as* NANCY.)

NANCY: Hello, Sidney. Is the voting done yet?

SIDNEY (*Hesitantly*): Er . . . yes, Nancy . . . yes, it's done.

NANCY: Let's go inside then. (*She starts in.*)

EDDIE: Don't forget I want to join, Nancy.

SIDNEY (*Keeping* NANCY *back*): Er . . . wait a second, Nancy. There's er . . . something I want to talk to you about.

NANCY (*Wonderingly*): Why . . . what is it, Sidney?

SIDNEY: Well, er . . . it's about, er . . .

NANCY (*Noticing that* EDDIE *is listening*): Go away, Eddie! (EDDIE *doesn't move.*) Eddie! I said go away! Sidney has something to tell me. It might be some secret rules of the club or something, and you're not supposed to hear. (EDDIE *moves a step or two away, but remains in earshot.*)

SIDNEY: Er . . . no, Nancy . . . it isn't about the rules.

NANCY: What is it then?

SIDNEY: It's about the vote. I have to explain . . .

NANCY: Isn't the vote done? Do you have to vote again?

SIDNEY: Yes, yes . . . it's done. I want to explain the way it came out. You see . . . er, . . .

NANCY (*Joyfully*): Was I elected unanimously?

SIDNEY: Er, no . . no, Nancy . . . not exactly. That is . . . you weren't elected . . .

NANCY: Unanimously?

SIDNEY: No, no . . . you weren't elected . . . er . . . at all. (NANCY *is dumbfounded.*) What I mean to say is that . . . you, er . . . didn't get in.

NANCY (*Astounded*): Didn't get in!

SIDNEY: No, no . . . you, er . . . you see, you didn't receive a majority of the votes.

NANCY: B-but . . . th-that's impossible! You . . . y-you must have counted them incorrectly . . . or gotten them mixed up or something! It's . . . it's impossible!

SIDNEY: We counted them a few times. That's the way it came out.

NANCY: B-but . . . I only needed three votes to get in, isn't that right?

SIDNEY: Yes, that's right. I guess you . . . er . . . you didn't get the three, that's all. (*Hastily*) Of course *I* voted for you; you know that. *I* tried to get you in. I spoke for you and everything . . . but, well . . . the others, I guess.

NANCY: B-but . . . how many votes did I get?

SIDNEY (*Quickly*): Oh, you almost made it. You were barely one vote shy, that's all. Only one vote. You needed three and you got . . . er . . . two . . . just one short, that's all.

NANCY (*A catch in her voice*): C-couldn't you do something . . . make an exception or . . . ?

SIDNEY: We'd *like* to, Nancy, honestly. But you know how those things are. It would be all right with me, of course . . . but the others . . . you know how it is.

NANCY (*Near tears*): Well . . . well . . .

SIDNEY: I'm really sorry, Nancy, honestly. Well . . . have to, er, get back inside . . . meeting going on. See you later, Nancy. (*He starts for the clubhouse door.*)

NANCY (*Barely keeping back her tears*): Sidney . . .

SIDNEY: Yes, Nancy? Glad to do anything for you.

NANCY: C-could you ask Harriet to come out?

SIDNEY: I'll try, Nancy . . . but the meeting is going on . . . I'll tell her, and she'll probably be able to come out in a few minutes, if you want to wait.

NANCY: All right. Tell her to try to make it as soon as she can. And . . . thanks for voting for me and everything.

SIDNEY: Oh, er . . . sure, Nancy. I certainly wanted you in the club. (*He exits into the clubhouse. A moment or two later,* NANCY *bursts into tears, and covers her mouth and nose with a handkerchief as she cries.*)

EDDIE (*After a while*): I told you.

NANCY (*Sobbing*): Go away.

EDDIE: Now you're not going to the meeting.

NANCY: Go away.

EDDIE: Do you want to play ball with me?

NANCY (*Still sobbing*): No.

EDDIE: Do you think I'll be elected to the club now?

NANCY (*Sobbing and angry*): No!

EDDIE: I guess they won't even vote for me. (*Pauses*) Are you going to try to get in again next week?

NANCY: No.

EDDIE: The week after?

NANCY: No. (*Wipes tears from her eyes with handkerchief. After a few moment's silence, the door to the clubhouse opens, and* HARRIET *slips out — and shuts the door again.*) Harriet!

HARRIET: I'm . . . I'm awfully sorry, Nancy. Sidney told you what happened, didn't he?

NANCY: Y-yes . . . b-b-but . . .

HARRIET: You just missed by one vote. Of course *I* voted for you. You know that.

NANCY: Yes, Harriet . . . b-but . . .

HARRIET: It was the others, I guess . . .

NANCY: It couldn't have been a mistake . . . ?

HARRIET: I, er . . . I thought it was at first . . . and we recounted the votes. But it was correct the first time . . . you only had two votes. I really thought you were going to get many more than that, but...well, I don't know what happened. Of course . . . you know we only have a small clubhouse and everything . . . and maybe some of the members figured . . . well, you know. (NANCY *sobs and cries*) You . . . er, you don't feel bad, do you?

NANCY (*Through tears*): N-no. I d-don't mind.

HARRIET: We're having a party at my house this Saturday, and . . .

NANCY: Y-your house?

HARRIET (*Hastily*): Well . . . I'm not giving it myself . . . it's the club. And only the members can come . . .

NANCY: Oh. (*More tears*)

HARRIET: Er . . . how about . . . er . . . how about going to the movies with me later today?

NANCY: N-no thanks. I'm going home.

HARRIET: All right. Well, I better get back to the meeting. See you later, Nancy. (*She exits into the clubhouse.*)

EDDIE (*After a pause*): Nancy . . . (*She doesn't answer*) Nancy . . .

NANCY (*After a little while*): What? (*She wipes tears from her eyes.*)

EDDIE: Why don't we start a club?

NANCY: I don't want to be in any club. I never want to be in one.

EDDIE: You felt just the opposite five minutes ago.

NANCY: I changed my mind.

EDDIE (*After a silence*): How do you start a club?

NANCY: Oh . . . I don't know exactly. You get a few people together and start one.

EDDIE: How many people?

NANCY: I don't know. (*Sobbing*) Can't you stop asking me silly questions?

EDDIE: Is three enough?

NANCY: I suppose so. There's no exact amount.

EDDIE: Is two enough?

NANCY (*Impatiently*): Any amount is enough!

EDDIE: How about one?

NANCY: Let me alone.

EDDIE: I guess one is enough too, then. I guess I could start a club myself.

NANCY: Do anything you please.

EDDIE (*After thinking for a few moments*): I'm starting a club. Do you want to be in it, Nancy?

NANCY: No.

EDDIE: Well, I'm in it. That makes one. Let's see . . . I guess I'm president.

NANCY: Go away.

EDDIE: Does the president decide when there are going to be meetings? (*No answer*) Nancy . . . does the president . . .

NANCY (*Angrily*): Yes, yes! Can't you be still? (*Sobs a bit.*)

EDDIE: Well, let's see . . . (*Ponders*) I think I'll have a meeting. (*Thinks another moment.*) Nancy, you'll have to go away. Only members can attend meetings.

NANCY: Go away yourself. (EDDIE *thinks again, and then moves a few steps away and sits down, to start his "meeting." After a short silence, the clubroom door opens again, and* TOM *emerges, shutting the door after him.*)

TOM: Hello, Nancy.

NANCY: Hello.

TOM: Did they tell you what happened?

NANCY (*Sulkily*): Yes.

TOM: It's really a shame. Of course, *I* voted for you. I thought you would surely be elected.

NANCY: Thanks, Tom.

TOM: You only missed by one vote, you know. I thought maybe we could make an exception, but you know how clubs are . . .

NANCY (*Sobs*): Yes.

TOM: We're having a picnic Sunday . . . would you like to . . . er . . .

NANCY: No.

TOM: Well, all right. They probably wouldn't want anyone who wasn't a member to come along anyway. Well, . . . (*Awkwardly*) I'll . . . I'll see you later. Have to get back to the meeting . . . (*He goes back into the clubhouse.*)

EDDIE (*Getting up and coming over to* NANCY *after a pause*): Nancy . . . I have good news for you. (*No answer*) You were just elected to my club.

NANCY: I don't want to be in your club.

EDDIE: You have to be. You were elected. (*No answer*) You were barely elected by one vote. But it was a majority, and you're a member.

NANCY (*Dryly*): That's good.

EDDIE: And you got in unan . . . unanimous . . . ly . . . (*He has trouble pronouncing it.*) . . . by one vote. (NANCY *says nothing*) Now there are two members in my club. (*A pause*) Nancy . . .

NANCY: What?

EDDIE: Am I still the president?

NANCY: If you want to be.

EDDIE: All right. You're the vice-president. Should we have any treasurer?

NANCY: You don't need a treasurer.

EDDIE: But my father is in a club, and they have a treasurer. My father is the treasurer.

NANCY: You don't need a treasurer unless there's some money.

EDDIE: What's the treasurer's job? To spend the money?

NANCY: He keeps the money. That's what a treasurer is for.

EDDIE: Well, whose money is it?

NANCY: The club's money.

EDDIE: Where are we going to get money?

NANCY: We're not going to get any.

EDDIE: Do you think we'll need a treasurer then? (*Their conversation is interrupted by noises coming from inside the clubhouse. There is a sound of moving benches, and then a pounding of a gavel. Then* TOM'S *voice is heard saying "Meeting adjourned." There is more scraping of benches, and the door opens and* SIDNEY *emerges. A moment later* HARRIET *and* TOM *step out.)*

SIDNEY (*Seeing* NANCY): Oh hello, Nancy. Are you still here?

NANCY: Yes.

SIDNEY: We . . . er . . . just finished our meeting.

HARRIET: Nancy . . . we decided you can come to the party Saturday night. Er . . . a couple of the other kids won't be able to be there.

NANCY: I . . . I'm not coming.

TOM: But it's all right, Nancy, even if you aren't a member.

NANCY: Thanks, but I can't.

SIDNEY (*To* HARRIET): Never mind, Harriet—we'll have enough.

HARRIET: Well . . .

TOM (*To* HARRIET *and* SIDNEY): Let's go to the drugstore and have a soda.

SIDNEY: All right. Come on.

HARRIET (*To* NANCY): You can come with us if you want to, Nancy.

NANCY: No . . . I have to go home. (*She barely keeps from crying.*)

HARRIET: Well . . . 'bye, Nancy.

NANCY: Goodbye.

TOM and SIDNEY: Goodbye, Nancy. (HARRIET, TOM *and* SIDNEY *exit to one side.*)

EDDIE (*After the three are off*): If they don't want you in the club, why do they want you to have a soda with them?

NANCY: But they do want me. They're my friends. Harriet, Tom and Sidney voted for me.

EDDIE: Didn't you only get two votes?

NANCY: Yes . . .

EDDIE: Then how could they all have voted for you? Harriet, Tom and Sidney make three.

NANCY (*Counting on her fingers*): Harriet . . . Tom . . . Sidney.

EDDIE: See? Three.

NANCY: But . . . but you heard what they said, didn't you? They all wanted me in the club. (*At this point,* DOROTHY *and* ALVIN, *the other two club members, are coming out of the door of the clubhouse.*)

DOROTHY: Oh . . . there she is, Alvin.

ALVIN: Hello . . . er . . . what was your name again?

NANCY (*Turning*): Nancy.

DOROTHY: Oh, that's right. Where do you live?

NANCY: On Jay Street. Near the school.

DOROTHY: Oh.

ALVIN: Are you going to be at the party Saturday night?

NANCY: No. Only club members can attend.

DOROTHY: Well, Alvin and I aren't going.

NANCY: You're not?

ALVIN: No. We had a big argument just before, in the meeting. We didn't like that rule.

NANCY: Oh.

DOROTHY (*To* NANCY): I'm sorry you didn't get in the club. You seem like a nice girl.

NANCY: I . . . only got two votes.

ALVIN: Don't you have any friends in the club that you know? Don't you know Harriet, or Sidney, or Tom?

NANCY: I know all three of them. They're all my friends.

DOROTHY: All? I don't see how that could be. You only need three votes to get in.

NANCY: Well . . . Harriet said she voted for me. And so did Tom, and so did Sidney. That's three right there. (*She sobs a bit again*) But I only got two.

DOROTHY (*Surprised*): But I voted for you!

ALVIN: And so did I!

DOROTHY: Even though we never met you before, Alvin and I both thought you seemed like a nice girl, and would be a good member for the club; and we voted for you.

NANCY: B-but . . .

ALVIN: Why, I counted the votes myself. Here . . .! (*He reaches into a pocket*) I crushed them up and put them into my pocket. (*He pulls out the votes and smoothes them open one by one*) Here's mine . . . see? We put our initials on them. A.H. It says "yes." (NANCY *looks over* ALVIN'S *shoulder and nods.*) And here's another "yes."

DOROTHY: That's mine! Those are my initials—D.M.

ALVIN: And these other three are "No's." Tom, Harriet and Sidney wrote those.

NANCY: Then *none* of them voted for me! And they all said they did!

ALVIN: Gosh!

DOROTHY: That was certainly mean of them!

ALVIN (*To Dorothy*): You know, Dorothy, I think I'm going to quit the Aces. I'm sorry we started the club with them. We ought to have a club with some other kids, like Nancy.

DOROTHY: That's a good idea. Do you want to start a club with us, Nancy?

NANCY: Why, I guess I . . .

EDDIE (*To* ALVIN *and* DOROTHY): Wait a minute! She can't be in your club!

DOROTHY: Why not?

EDDIE: She's already in one. She's in my club. She was elected at the last meeting!

DOROTHY: Oh.

ALVIN (*Not giving* NANCY *a chance to speak*): Well, why don't we join their club, Dorothy?

DOROTHY: All right. Let's do that.

EDDIE: Wait a minute...you can't just "join." We have to elect you at a meeting.

ALVIN: When is your next meeting?

EDDIE: Whenever I decide. I'm the president, you see. Now... let me see . . . I think we'll have one right away. Come on, Nancy. (*He pulls* NANCY *into the clubhouse.*)

NANCY: But Eddie!

EDDIE (*Pulling her along*): Hurry up . . . we have to vote. (*He gets her inside and shuts the door.* ALVIN *and* DOROTHY *stand by and look on curiously. In a moment,* NANCY *opens the clubhouse door and pokes her head out.*)

NANCY: You only got two votes.

EDDIE (*Poking his head out beside* NANCY'S): You were elected unan . . . unan . . . unanimous . . . ly. (*He has the same trouble pronouncing the word.* ALVIN *and* DOROTHY *look at each other, and then happily start into the clubhouse as the curtain falls.*)

THE END

TWIN COUSINS

by Morton K. Schwartz

Characters

EDDIE *and* FREDDIE, *the twin cousins* (*played by one person*)
DIANA
FRANCES
ARTHUR
BILL

SETTING: *A street, in a quiet, residential section of a town. It is a summer day.*

AT RISE: EDDIE, DIANA *and* FRANCES *are onstage.* FRANCES *is a little younger than* DIANA.

DIANA (*As* EDDIE *seems inclined to walk off left*): Stay with us for a while.

EDDIE: I have to meet my cousin at the railroad station.

FRANCES: We want to play something.

EDDIE: I don't think I have enough time. What do you want to play?

DIANA: Rope the Steer.

EDDIE: What do you want to play that silly game for?

FRANCES: We like it. We haven't enough kids for rope-skipping. What else can you do with a rope than Rope the Steer? (*She holds up a long rope which she has coiled loosely around her hand.*)

EDDIE: You could rope each other, and then we wouldn't have so many foolish girls around here.

DIANA: Don't be fresh or we won't play with you.

FRANCES: Neither will I.

DIANA (*To* FRANCES): I already said "we."

FRANCES: Oh, I thought you meant us.

EDDIE: But the train comes in in about fifteen minutes.

DIANA: Well, play for a little while.

EDDIE: You can't really play "Rope the Steer" with three people.

You have to have a steer, a roper, two cowboys and the boss.

FRANCES: Oh, we can do without the cowboys.

DIANA: No. Eddie is right, Frances. (*To* EDDIE) We can get two more.

EDDIE: Who are you going to get? Anyway I don't want to play.

DIANA (*To* FRANCES): I told you Eddie would play. Who are the two we can get?

FRANCES: I know one!

DIANA: I do too!

FRANCES: Then we don't need mine.

EDDIE (*A bit exasperated*): No, Frances. Diana means she knows *one,* too.

FRANCES (*A little doubtfully*): Oh.

DIANA (*To* FRANCES): Who are you thinking of?

FRANCES: Arthur. Which one — er — or two are you thinking of?

DIANA: Only one. Bill. I saw him in his house just a few minutes ago, and he isn't doing anything.

FRANCES: Arthur wasn't doing anything either.

DIANA: Good. Let's get them.

EDDIE: Wait a minute! You surely don't intend to get Arthur and Bill to play in the same game, do you?

DIANA: Why not! I know they hate each other, but . . .

EDDIE: *Hate* each other? They despise each other!

FRANCES: Gosh!

EDDIE: Do you know that Bill hates Arthur so much, that whenever Arthur gets within ten feet of him, Bill throws his hat on the floor and stamps on it?

FRANCES: Gosh!

EDDIE: And any time Bill gets within twenty feet of Arthur, Arthur pulls his hair and yells, "Egad!"

DIANA: Oh, I think you're making all this up.

EDDIE: Just try getting Arthur and Bill into this game, and you'll see.

DIANA: We may as well try, anyway. (*To* FRANCES) You get Arthur. I'll get Bill. (*To* EDDIE, *as* FRANCES *exits left, and* DIANA *exits right*) You stay right here! (EDDIE *shrugs his shoulders, and waits. He whistles a tune for a few seconds, and then carefully adjusts his cap on his head, as if it had been mussed. In a few seconds* FRANCES *and* ARTHUR *enter.*)

ARTHUR: Hello Eddie. Where's Diana?

EDDIE: She'll be along soon, Arthur.

FRANCES: Yes, she just went to get B — er, that is, I mean — she'll be along soon.

ARTHUR: Well, what are we going to play?

EDDIE: Rope the Steer.

ARTHUR: Don't we need five people for that? You have to have two cowboys.

FRANCES: Oh, we'll have two cowboys all right. You'll be one, and B — er — well, Diana will be along soon.

ARTHUR (*To* EDDIE): Who's the other cowboy?

EDDIE: Well, er . . . you don't have any preference, do you?

ARTHUR: No, I don't care. But who is it?

EDDIE: After all, it doesn't make any difference. One player is as good as another.

ARTHUR: Certainly. It doesn't matter. Who is it?

EDDIE (*With forced casualness*): Er — Bill.

ARTHUR (*Growing livid*): Bill! That . . !! (*He clenches and unclenches his fists in rage*) That . . . . ! (*Suddenly he stiffens. He draws his chest up, and brings his hands toward and upward to his head. Then he seizes his hair with both hands and utters a vehement —*) Egad! (*Just as he says this,* BILL *and* DIANA *enter from the right.* BILL *stops short as soon as he sees* ARTHUR.)

BILL: Arthur! (*His face grows red with rage, and he too reaches to his head for a hat he isn't wearing at the moment*) What luck! I went and left my hat home!

DIANA: Say! What the matter with you two? Can't you two make up? (ARTHUR *and* BILL *turn haughtily away.*) Can't we play a simple game without you two boys going into tantrums? (*No answer*) We'll even put you on different ranches. (*To* ARTHUR) You can be the X-bar-X, and Bill, you can be the Bar-X-Bar (*No answer*) Well? Can't you stop hating each other.

BILL (*Turning toward* DIANA): Well — maybe if we don't have to talk to each other . . .

ARTHUR (*To* BILL): I wouldn't talk to you anyway!

BILL (*To* ARTHUR): And I wouldn't talk to you either, you — you — dunce!

ARTHUR: You *are* talking to me now, you dunce!

BILL: And so are you to me!

FRANCES (*To both of them, very reasonably*): You see? You boys can get along with each other when you want to.

EDDIE (*To* DIANA): It's no use. I have to meet my cousin at the station. I only have about five minutes now.

DIANA: What's the rush? You'd think the railroad station was a mile away instead of right over there. (*She nods toward the left.*)

FRANCES (*As* ARTHUR *and* BILL *turn away, pouting*): Who is this cousin of yours, Eddie?

EDDIE: You know him. His name is Freddie.

DIANA: Where does he live?

EDDIE: Chicago.

FRANCES: And he's come all that distance to visit you?

EDDIE: Yes. We get together every year on our birthday.

DIANA: *Our* birthday? What do you mean, *our* birthday?

EDDIE: We're twins. We have the same birthday.

FRANCES: But you said cousins.

EDDIE: That's right. Twin cousins. (*A train whistle blows*) There! Hear that? That's the train! I have to go! See you later! (*He exits hurriedly left.*)

DIANA (*To* ARTHUR *and* BILL, *after a pause*): Well, you can stop arguing now. We can't play any more.

ARTHUR: Don't try to tell *us* when to argue!

BILL: That's right. We'll argue whenever we want to!

FRANCES (*To* DIANA): Gosh! They agreed with one another!

ARTHUR *and* BILL: No, we didn't! (*They both turn their backs again.*)

FRANCES (*After a pause*): I wonder what Eddie meant about his twin cousin.

DIANA: I'm sure I don't know. I never heard of such a thing.

FRANCES: Are they twins or are they cousins?

DIANA: That's what I can't figure out. If they're cousins, then they haven't the same parents. And if they haven't the same parents, how can they be twins?

ARTHUR (*Turning*): It's simple. He meant that they look alike, that's what he meant. They're *twins.*

BILL (*Turning*): No he didn't. He just meant that they have the same birthday.

ARTHUR: Of course they have the same birthday if they're twins, dizzy!

BILL: Don't call me dizzy!

ARTHUR: I will if you *are* dizzy!

BILL: Well I'm *not* dizzy! They have the same birthday, so they're twins. But that doesn't mean they're really real twins!

ARTHUR: Of course that's what it means! That's just what twins means! Look in the dictionary if you don't believe it.

BILL: How could they look alike and have different parents? Tell me that!

ARTHUR: I don't know how, but they do. (*Train whistle blows again.*)

DIANA (*To* ARTHUR *and* BILL): Stop arguing. We'll soon see whether they look alike or not. The train just pulled out, and they'll be coming this way soon. (*All peer off left.*)

FRANCES (*After a pause*): Here comes Eddie now, with a suitcase.

ARTHUR: Not so fast! It might be his cousin.

BILL: Anybody can tell it's Eddie. (*In a moment,* EDDIE *enters, carrying a suitcase.*)

ALL: Where's your twin cousin?

EDDIE: He'll be along. He had to check some baggage.

FRANCES: Eddie, did you mean that your cousin looked like . . .

EDDIE (*Cutting her off*): I can't stop to talk now; I have to take this suitcase home. See you later. (*He exits right. They watch him go off. Then they turn and look off left again. Presently mild astonishment appears on all their faces, and they peer off more intently.*)

FRANCES: Goodness! Here comes Eddie again! And without the suitcase!

ARTHUR (*Triumphantly*): That's Eddie's cousin, Freddie!

BILL: Not so fast. It might be Eddie. (*In a moment* FREDDIE *enters from the left. He is dressed exactly like* EDDIE, *except that his cap is bright red.*)

FREDDIE (*Looking about him, as a stranger would*): Pardon me, could you please tell me the way to Eddie's house? (*No one replies. They keep their eyes fastened on* FREDDIE, *and, in unison, raise their left arms and point off right, their mouths agape.*)

FREDDIE: Thank you. (*He nods to them, and exits right.*)

ARTHUR (*After a pause*): Well? Do they look alike or not?

FRANCES: Exactly!

DIANA: Golly, I've never seen such a strong resemblance — except in twins.

ARTHUR (*Proudly*): They *are* twins!

DIANA (*To* BILL): Arthur was right.

FRANCES: Yes, Arthur was right.

BILL (*Pondering*): Hmmm . . .

ARTHUR: Well? Why don't you admit it? I'm right!

BILL: Not so fast. Something is fishy here!

DIANA: What?

BILL: They were wearing the same clothes!

ARTHUR: Twins always do! Anyway, they had different colored caps.

BILL: How come they didn't walk past here together?

ARTHUR: Freddie had to check some baggage.

BILL: Well, I think Eddie is trying to put one over on us. You can't prove they're *really* twins until we see them together!

ARTHUR: You don't want to admit I'm right, that's all. We all saw that they're twins. Ask Diana. Ask Frances.

BILL: What do you think, Diana? Isn't it possible that Eddie was playing some sort of a trick on us?

DIANA: I don't see how he could be, but then again, I guess we can't really be sure until we do see Eddie and Freddie at the same time.

ARTHUR: All right, then! I will get them out here together! And if I'm not right, I'll — I'll — I'll never say "Egad" again!

BILL: Well, the same goes for me! If I'm not right, I'll never stamp on my hat when I see Arthur again! (*To* ARTHUR) I'm going to Eddie's house with you! (*They stalk off right together.*)

FRANCES: Gosh! If they both turn out right, they'll never argue again!

CURTAIN

* * *

SCENE 2

SETTING: *The same, two hours later.*

AT RISE: *No one is onstage. In a few moments* DIANA *and* FRANCES *walk wearily on.*

DIANA: I give up. I'm beginning to think that Bill is right.

FRANCES: I am too. Eddie and Freddie, or Eddie, or Freddie, or whoever he is, or both of them, doesn't want to come out and let us get a look at him.

DIANA: Or them.

DIANA: Poor Arthur and Bill. Both of them are so anxious to be right, and to prove the other one is wrong.

FRANCES: How long have they been trying?

DIANA: It's about two hours now. First Eddie said he couldn't come out because he had to eat.

FRANCES: And then he had to unpack Freddie's things.

DIANA: And then they had to put the candles in the birthday cake.

FRANCES: I wonder why that took so long?

DIANA: They had to break each candle in half — half for Eddie, and half for Freddie.

FRANCES: Oh. Well, I thought Bill would succeed when he tried to get into Eddie's house by imitating a messenger.

DIANA: He probably would have gotten in too, if Arthur wasn't trying to pose as the iceman at the same time. Bill said Eddie, or Freddie, answered the front door, and Arthur said Freddie, or Eddie, answered the back door. And both Eddie and Freddie said they didn't know where their cousin was.

FRANCES: Doesn't that prove they're twins?

DIANA: We couldn't be sure the doors were answered at the same time.

FRANCES: Golly, what will they try next?

ARTHUR (*Hurrying on from right. He is breathing hard*): Diana! Frances! We've finally got him! Bill and Eddie will be here in a second. Now, tell Eddie you want to play with his cousin! I'll explain later. Ssshh! Here they come!

BILL (*To* EDDIE, *as they enter from the right.* EDDIE *wears his green cap*): I'm glad you could finally come out for a while. We all wanted to play with you.

EDDIE: O.K.

FRANCES (*As* ARTHUR *prods her*): Eddie — how about getting your cousin out to play?

EDDIE: Oh, he has to finish unpacking.

DIANA: Why don't you do the unpacking? We're all anxious to meet him.

ARTHUR: That's right. Eddie. Let him come out and play with us.

BILL: Yes, Eddie.

EDDIE: Well — all right. I'll go back and send him out. (*He exits right.*)

ARTHUR: Good!

FRANCES: But — don't you want them to be here together.

BILL: That's all right. We found another way to settle the question.

ARTHUR: It was my idea. I just pinned a button on Eddie's back, and he doesn't know it's there. When he — or his cousin — comes out now, we'll be able to tell which one it is!

DIANA: Good! What kind of a button is it?

ARTHUR: A school button. It says "Vote for George Mason."

FRANCES: Ssh! Here comes — er — someone.

FREDDIE (*Entering from right, wearing red cap*): My cousin said you wanted to play with me.

BILL: Yes, Freddie, that is, you are Freddie, aren't you?

FREDDIE: That's right.

BILL: Good.

ARTHUR: Freddie, I think you have something on your back. Turn around.

FREDDIE (*As he turns*): On my back? What is it? (*A small button is seen to be pinned on* FREDDIE'S *back.* BILL *folds his arms triumphantly, and stands proudly to one side.* ARTHUR *goes up very close, and peers intently at the button.*)

FREDDIE: What is it? What's on my back?

BILL: It's an ink stain on your sweater. You'd better wash it out right away.

FREDDIE: Oh gosh! I'll see you later. (*He exits right.*)

BILL (*Folding his arms and smiling after* FREDDIE *is gone. To* ARTHUR): Well, you saw the button, didn't you? We put it on Eddie, and we find it on the boy who's supposed to be Freddie! I guess *that* shows that they aren't twins!

ARTHUR (*Also folding his arms*): I saw the button all right! It said on it, "Down with George Mason — Vote for Selma Holland."

DIANA: Oh golly! We *still* don't know who's who!

BILL (*After a pause*): There's one more thing we can try. Rope the Steer! Come here everybody. (*He motions the others inward, and they get into a huddle.* BILL *whispers instructions to them as the lights fade. The lights come up again, and* DIANA, FRANCES *and* ARTHUR *are onstage, waiting silently. Presently,* BILL *enters.*)

BILL (*Coming in*): Well, it took about half an hour, but I finally did it.

ARTHUR: How did you manage it?

BILL: I threatened not to lend him my bicycle any more, and he agreed to play. And you know the rest. They'll be here soon.

FRANCES: We got them to play "Rope the Steer." But how will that help us?

ARTHUR: Don't you see? We made Eddie the roper, and Freddie the steer.

BILL: Eddie has to pull the rope, and Freddie has his head in the noose. They won't be able to do it unless they are really twins!

FRANCES: H'mmm. I guess he can't get out of that one.

BILL: He can't if he wants to use my bicycle!

DIANA (*Looking off right*): Look everybody! Here he comes! (*Immediately they all turn and look off right. Presently,* EDDIE, *with green cap, trudges slowly on, holding the end of a rope over his shoulder. He moves across the stage, without looking up, and the rope stretches out behind him. More and more rope appears. Finally, trudging along, he exits left, and the rope stretches across the entire stage, still moving along.* DIANA, FRANCES, ARTHUR *and* BILL *gaze at* EDDIE *till after he has gone off left. Then all together, they turn and look off right to the other end of the rope. The rope moves along, and the noose appears.* FREDDIE *is in it, wearing red cap. He holds the noose with his hands, and trudges across as* EDDIE *did, the noose pulling him across and off left, as all watch him in amazement.*)

ARTHUR (*To* BILL, *after a pause*): I'll never argue with you again as long as I live.

BILL (*To* ARTHUR): Shake! (*They do, and go off right, arm in arm.* DIANA *starts walking off right also, slowly and thoughtfully.*)

FRANCES: But Diana! Wait a minute! Was he twins, or wasn't he?

DIANA: We'll never know. Let's go home. (*They start off right together as the curtain falls.*)

THE END

THE KING'S CREAMPUFFS

by Martha Swintz

Characters

THE KING
THE QUEEN
ALGERNON
THE PRINCESS
THE PAGE
THE FIRST WITCH
THE SECOND WITCH
THE HERALD
THE BAKER

SCENE 1

SETTING: *Creampuff Hall, the throne room of the royal palace in the ancient country of Delicatessia.*

AT RISE: THE KING *is seated on his throne, asleep. He holds a creampuff in his hand. There is a table beside him with a tray of creampuffs on it.*

KING (*Waking up with yawns and stretches*): Oh, hum. Let me see. What am I supposed to do today? (PAGE *enters and kneels before* KING.)

PAGE: Good morning, Sire. I have come to you today for a very special purpose.

KING: To tell me what I am supposed to do, no doubt. Well then, get up off your knees and tell me.

PAGE (*Rising*): If you will permit me to remind you, Sire, you are supposed to judge the Witch of All Witches.

KING: The Witch of All Witches? And who may she be?

PAGE: Surely you must remember the witch who comes so frequently to the palace.

KING: Oh, you mean that cute little witch with the blond curls?

PAGE: Nay, Sire. The one with the grey wig, glass eye and false teeth.

KING: Oh, that one. Well, I might as well get it over with. I am to judge her, you say?

PAGE: Yes, Sire.

KING: Why am I to judge her? Can you tell me what crime she has committed?

PAGE: She stepped on your royal toe, Sire.

KING: My toe? Which toe?

PAGE: The one on your left foot, Sire.

KING: Oh, that one. Well, send her in. (QUEEN *and* ALGERNON *enter. They are followed by several* LADIES IN WAITING, *who group themselves beside thrones.* QUEEN *wears large spectacles and is reading a book.*)

PAGE: I had hoped to ask you a very important question, Sire. (QUEEN *bumps into* PAGE) Pardon me, your Majesty.

KING (*To* QUEEN): Let that Page go by.

QUEEN: Oh not this page. It's one of the best in the whole book. Listen to this. (*Reads*) "The prince drew his sword and with one fell swoop killed the mouse and saved the princess." (*Sighs*) Isn't that romantic?

KING: Yes, yes, I suppose it is. But, enough of your romance. Please don't interfere with important court matters. I have a witch to judge. Page, go and bring her in. (PAGE *bows and exits.*)

QUEEN (*Sighing*): How I wish you were filled with romance instead of creampuffs. Algernon is filled with romance. Aren't you, Algernon?

ALGERNON: Oh, quite.

QUEEN: Listen to this, Algernon. (*Reads*) "The prince looked into the deep blue eyes of the princess, and..."

KING: Will you kindly read that trash somewhere else?

QUEEN: You just don't appreciate romance. But Algernon does. I will take him to the garden and read it to him.

KING: A fine way to treat our future son-in-law.

QUEEN: Oh, he loves it. Don't you, Algernon?

ALGERNON: Oh, quite.

QUEEN: Then come along, my dear, I'll read you a whole chapter. (PAGE *enters with* WITCH OF ALL WITCHES) And here is my old friend, the Witch of All Witches. Maybe she would like to join us. (*To* WITCH) Could I interest you in a good book?

WITCH: Don't tell me you're working your way through college!

QUEEN: Humpf! You're impossible! Come along, Algernon. We'll go to a more refined atmosphere. (QUEEN *and* ALGERNON *sweep out indignantly, followed by train of* LADIES-IN-WAITING, *also indignant.*)

KING (*Turning to* WITCH): This is the witch I am to judge. Well, you moth-eaten old broomstick rider, are you ready to admit you are sorry you stepped on my toe?

WITCH: Never!

KING: What? Then I must sentence you.

WITCH: And if you do, I will put a curse on you and your creampuffs.

KING: You wouldn't! Not my creampuffs! (*Covers up creampuffs*) No! No!

WITCH: Just sentence me and see.

KING: All right, I will. I don't believe you'd have the nerve to do it. (*Clears throat*) I sentence you to your mountain den for the rest of your life.

WITCH: Oh, you do, do you? Then I warn you; on this very day your creampuff recipe book will walk out of your kitchen to my den, and be lost forever!

KING (*To* PAGE): Do you think she can do it?

PAGE (*Shrugging shoulders*): She's the Witch of All Witches.

KING: If I really thought... But no! She's just bluffing. Take her to her den!

PAGE (*Taking* WITCH *by arm*): Come with me. Home to your mountains. (WITCH *laughs shrilly as they exit.*)

KING: I wonder if she really has the power to deprive me of my creampuffs. Maybe I'd better call her back. (*Calls*) Page! Page! (HERALD *enters running.*)

HERALD: Thank you, Sire. You called me, didn't you?

KING: Not that I know of. Who are you?

HERALD: I am the court herald, Sire. Please say you called me.

KING: All right, I called you. But now I can't remember why.

HERALD: It doesn't matter, Sire. The Queen had me cornered in the hallway outside and was reading aloud some romantic drivel from a book. I — well — Oh, I just had to get away from her.

KING: Say no more. I understand fully. But now that you're here, I want to ask you a question.

HERALD: Anything, Sire. Ask me anything.

KING: Do you think the Witch of All Witches could put legs on my creampuff recipe book and cause it to run away?

HERALD (*Thoughtfully*): She is very powerful. Remember the time she made the river run uphill?

KING: Indeed I do! That settles it! Something must be done at once. I have just sentenced the witch to her den for the rest of her life. Go immediately to the kitchen and bring the recipe book to me. I'll sit on it!

HERALD: At once, Sire! (*Exits running.*)

KING: Why didn't I think of that before? If I'm sitting on the book it can't possibly run away — legs or no legs. (BAKER*, clad in white apron and cap, enters excitedly.*)

BAKER: Your Majesty! Your Majesty! I cannot go on. I quit!

KING: Please, Pierre. Just a moment. What is wrong?

BAKER: I was making some creampuffs for your Majesty, and the recipe book was on the kitchen table, right in front of my eyes.

KING: Yes, yes, go on.

BAKER: Well, all of a sudden — you won't believe this.

KING: I'm afraid I will.

BAKER: It sounds impossible, but all of a sudden that recipe book sprouted legs and walked right out of the kitchen!

KING (*Dejectedly*): Then it's too late. She did do it. Pierre, do you remember the creampuff recipe?

BAKER: Well, let me see. One pinch of salt; one spoonful of sugar. Or was it a spoonful of salt and a pinch of sugar?

KING: You don't remember.

BAKER: Well — I'm not sure. But there must have been cream in them. They couldn't be creampuffs without cream. And surely they contained puffs. But, what's a puff? Oh, Sire, I can't remember.

KING (*Picking up tray of creampuffs from table beside him and handing it to* BAKER): Then here. Take these to the kitchen at once and pull them apart — pick them to pieces — and find out what they are made of. I must know.

BAKER: But, Sire —

KING: Go at once! (BAKER *backs toward door*) No — wait a minute. I must have one last creampuff. (*Points*) That big one. (BAKER *gives creampuff to* KING) Now, on your way. And hurry!

BAKER: Yes, Sire. (*Exits running.*)

KING: Oh why did I ever let that Page leave with the Witch? I wonder if the Queen could have stopped them in the hallway to listen to her romantic reading. I'll see. Page! Page! (PAGE *enters and bows.*)

PAGE: You called, Sire?

KING: Yes. Where is the Witch of All Witches?

PAGE: In her den, Sire. You ordered me to take her there as a prisoner.

KING: And you have done it so soon?

PAGE: Yes. We went on her broomstick. It takes but a moment.

KING: Then get my daughter. Bring her here at once. She will think of something to do.

PAGE: Gladly, Sire. But first, may I speak to you of your daughter?

KING: No, no. There isn't time now. I've lost my creampuff recipe, and perhaps the Princess can help me get it back.

PAGE: I'm sure she can, Sire. I'll bring her at once. (*Exits.* KING *settles back on throne and looks longingly at one remaining creampuff. His hand reaches slowly toward it. He slaps it with other hand.* HERALD *enters, running.*)

HERALD: Sire! Sire! The recipe book is gone! I can't find it anywhere.

KING: Yes, I know. It sprouted legs and walked out of the kitchen. Pierre told me. He saw it.

HERALD: How horrible! I wish there were something I could do.

KING: There is. The Baker is down in the kitchen trying to find out how he made my creampuffs. You may go and help him.

HERALD: Gladly, Sire. But how? I know nothing of baking.

KING: He is taking my creampuffs apart, crumb by crumb, to see what's in them.

HERALD: But that will take hours.

KING: Not with two of you working at it. Go at once — and don't leave a crumb unturned. (PAGE *and* PRINCESS *enter.*)

HERALD: But, Sire, I am a Herald; a very good Herald, and —

KING: You are now a crumby Herald. Go and get busy. I want to talk to my daughter.

HERALD: Very well, Sire, but this is not in my contract. (*Exits.*)

KING: Bother his contract.

PRINCESS: He'll probably charge you time and a half.

KING: It will be worth it if he finds out how my creampuffs are made.

PRINCESS: Doesn't the Baker know? He's been making them for years.

KING: He can't remember; and the Witch of All Witches has spirited away my recipe book to her den. That's what I want to talk to you about.

PRINCESS: Oh, the Page said you wanted to talk about — us.

KING: You?

PAGE: Yes, Sire. For some time I have been trying to ask you about a very important matter, but I have always been interrupted.

KING: Something more important than my creampuffs?

PAGE: Well — it's more important to me, Sire. I want to ask you for the hand of your daughter in marriage.

KING: What? A Page dares to ask for the hand of a Princess? Never!

PRINCESS: But, Father, I love the Page.

KING: And what has that got to do with it, pray tell? Princesses don't marry Pages. It just isn't done.

PRINCESS: But this is different. I —

KING: You're going to marry Algernon. At least, that's what your mother told me.

PRINCESS: She may think I'm going to marry Algernon, but I'm not!

PAGE: Sire, do you want a son-in-law who has said only two words since he learned to talk?

KING: Oh, quite.

PRINCESS: Father!

KING: Now go, young man. Go at once.

PAGE: Is there nothing I can say to convince you that your daughter and I should be married?

KING: Nothing. My daughter shall never marry a Page. Of course, I would prefer an improvement over Algernon, but —

PRINCESS: But Mother says I am to marry Algernon, so there's nothing you can do about it. Is that right?

KING (*Squirming on throne*): I refuse to talk about it any longer. Page, go about your duties.

PAGE: Very well, Sire. But I shall return. (*Exits.*)

KING: He's an obstinate fellow.

PRINCESS (*Dreamily*): He's wonderful. I've never known anyone like him in all my life.

KING: You will. The world is full of Pages. But there's only one Algernon.

PRINCESS: One is enough, if you ask me.

KING: But I'm not asking you. There is something I want to ask you, though. Could you possibly help me get back my recipe for creampuffs?

PRINCESS: So far as I know, there is nothing I can do. (QUEEN *enters with* ALGERNON *and* LADIES-IN-WAITING.)

QUEEN (*Adjusts spectacles and looks at* KING): My dear! What's the matter with you? You looked worried.

KING: Why wouldn't I be? The Witch of All Witches has stolen my recipe for creampuffs.

QUEEN: Why, that old hag. I think she should give it right back to you. Don't you, Algernon?

ALGERNON: Oh, quite.

KING: Isn't that just like a woman? My dear wife —

PRINCESS: Father, just a moment, please. You see, Mother, it isn't quite that simple.

QUEEN: Why not? In all the books I've read, the King simply tells the witch —

PRINCESS: I'm sorry, Mother, but you're wrong. It won't work in this case.

QUEEN: But my books say —

KING: Books! Books! Books! Is that all you think of?

PRINCESS: Wait, Father, I have a plan.

KING: You have? Good! What is it?

PRINCESS: I will go to the witch's den myself and get the book for you.

QUEEN: You? Alone?

PRINCESS: I'm not afraid.

KING: I knew you could help me. When can you start? There's no time to lose.

PRINCESS: Not so fast, Father. I have not finished telling my plan.

KING: What more is necessary? You're going after my creampuffs. That's all there is to it.

PRINCESS: Not quite. I will do this for you only on one condition.

KING: And that is —

PRINCESS: You must permit me to marry the Page if I succeed.

QUEEN: Marry the Page? What is this all about?

KING: Our daughter wants to marry the Page, and he has asked me for her hand.

QUEEN: Impossible! Just think of the disgrace. I can see the headlines in the papers now, "Daughter of King becomes Mrs. Page." Horrors!

PRINCESS: Very well, then. No Page — no creampuffs.

KING: No creampuffs — no King.

QUEEN: And no King — no Queen!

PRINCESS: All you have to do is give me your permission to marry the Page if I recover your recipe.

KING: Would that be satisfactory to you, Algernon?

ALGERNON: Oh —

QUEEN: Quiet!

PRINCESS: Do you agree with my conditions, Father?

KING (*Clearing throat*): In this moment of national crisis, I hereby decree that the Princess may marry my Page when the recipe for creampuffs is delivered to me safe and secure.

PRINCESS: Thank you, Father. I'll do my best. Goodbye. (*Exits.*)

QUEEN: Wait! (*Starts after* PRINCESS. KING *stops her and pulls her spectacles off. Hands them to* ALGERNON.) Oh — oh my! Now I've lost my spectacles.

KING: Algernon will help you find them, won't you, Algernon?

ALGERNON: Oh, quite.

KING: I knew you would. You're so helpful. (*Pushes* QUEEN *and* ALGERNON *out door. Hurries to throne and picks up creampuff*) Now that my daughter has gone after my recipe, I can eat this last creampuff. (*Stuffs it into mouth. Curtains close.*)

* * *

SCENE 2

SETTING: *Mountain Den of the* WITCHES.

AT RISE: WITCH OF ALL WITCHES *is standing over a cauldron, holding book in one hand and stirring with a long spoon in the other.*)

2ND WITCH (*Entering from side*): Ah, that smells good. What are you brewing, sister?

1ST WITCH: Something we have never had before.

2ND WITCH: Not vulture stew? Don't tell me you have finally caught a vulture. They usually take one quick look at you and fly to the highest crag.

1ST WITCH: It's not vulture stew.

2ND WITCH: Well, if it's not vulture stew, what is it?

1ST WITCH: Promise you will never tell a soul?

2ND WITCH: Not a living soul.

1ST WITCH: Any soul.

2ND WITCH: Very well — I promise.

1ST WITCH: I'm making creampuffs.

2ND WITCH: Creampuffs? They sound windy. What are they?

1ST WITCH: They are the favorite food of the King. He eats thousands of them. But he'll never eat another, because I've taken his recipe. It's right here in this book. (*Puts book beside cauldron and stirs briskly.*)

2ND WITCH: I'd much rather have vulture stew. But listen! I think I hear someone in the passageway.

1ST WITCH: No one would dare come here.

PRINCESS (*Off*): Let me in. Please let me in.

2ND WITCH: Oh no? I suppose that's just the wind.

1ST WITCH: Well, let her in.

2ND WITCH: You let her in.

1ST WITCH: I'm busy. Besides, it's probably just a black cat peddler, and we have plenty.

PRINCESS (*Off stage*): In the name of the King, let me in!

2ND WITCH: Black cat peddler, eh? It sounds to me like the Princess. I'll be glad to let her in. (*Starts for side.*)

1ST WITCH (*Catching hold of her*): Oh no you don't. I'm the head of this den. I'll let her in. And I'll do all the talking too. I have an idea what she wants. You go into the bat room and stay there. (*Points to opposite side of stage.*)

2ND WITCH (*Pouting*): Why can't I hear what you talk about?

1ST WITCH: It's a private matter between the Princess and me.

2ND WITCH: You're mean, and I'll get even with you for this. You'll never eat a creampuff! It's my curse on you for pushing me out like this.

1st Witch: Your curse? On me? Me—the Witch of All Witches? Bah! (*Pushes her out.*)

Princess (*Off*): Are you ever going to let me in?

1st Witch (*Hurrying across stage*): Keep your jerkin on. I'm coming. (*Goes to side*) Come on in, and stop howling.

Princess (*Entering*): You're not very cordial.

1st Witch: Why should I be? I didn't invite you here.

Princess: Most people would be glad to have a Princess visit them.

1st Witch: Princess? Humph. What's a Princess? I'm the Witch of All Witches.

Princess: Then you're just the person I want to talk to.

1st Witch: Well, I don't want to talk to you. What did you come here for?

Princess: I want my father's recipe for creampuffs.

1st Witch (*Sarcastically*): Oh, you do? Well now, isn't that just fine? I told your father he would never have that recipe again—and he won't! Now, get out of here before I put a curse on you.

Princess: You can't put a curse on someone who is not afraid of you.

1st Witch: No? I'll show you. (*Points finger at* Princess) Huggle, puggle, riggeldy smote. You are now a nanny goat.

Princess: Really? How stupid.

1st Witch: What? You defy me?

Princess: I do — because you can plainly see your curses have no effect on me, for I am not afraid of you.

1st Witch (*Shrinking back*): What's this? You are not afraid of me — the Witch of All Witches?

Princess: Not a bit. And furthermore, I shall tell the whole kingdom your spells work only on those who fear you and they will fear no more. Then you will be helpless.

1st Witch: No, no! Not that! I'll lose my union card! Please keep my secret, and I'll do anything you say.

Princess: You will? (*Walks slowly toward recipe book*) Then give me this book.

1st Witch: No! Anything but that. Don't ask me to do that!

Princess (*Picking up book*): Do you want the whole kingdom to know your secret?

1st Witch: You wouldn't dare tell your people.

PRINCESS: I do not fear you, so I would dare do anything. (*Starts toward side of stage.*)

1ST WITCH: This shouldn't happen to a dog!

PRINCESS: Well, it has happened to you. I am taking this recipe book back to my father. There is nothing you can do about it. Goodbye — fake! (*Exits.*)

1ST WITCH: Fake! She called me a fake! I'll show her. (*Hurries to cauldron*) I'll brew a concoction that will teach her I am not a fake. (*Pulls bottle from her cloak pocket and pours liquid into cauldron.*)

2ND WITCH (*Poking head in from side of stage*): Still making creampuffs, sister?

1ST WITCH: Yes — in spite of your curse.

2ND WITCH (*Entering*): I said you would never eat a creampuff —and you won't, if you want to live. That's poison you're pouring into the cauldron.

1ST WITCH: Yes — I'm making a choice little brew for the Princess. She just called me a fake.

2ND WITCH: Well, well, well. She knows you better than I thought she did.

1ST WITCH: Get out of here! (*Picks up spoon and chases* 2ND WITCH *off stage. Lights go out.*)

CURTAIN

* * *

SCENE 3

SETTING: *Same as Scene* 1.

AT RISE: KING *and* QUEEN *are seated on thrones.*

KING: I wonder when our lovely darling daughter will return. (*Sighs*) Ah, what a wonderful child she is.

QUEEN: You must think a lot of her, to send her to that awful witch's den alone. (*Cries into large handkerchief.*)

KING: Oh, come, come, my dear. There is nothing to worry about. She will handle the situation beautifully. She takes after my side of the family, you know.

QUEEN: That's why I'm so worried about her. But, I'm sending Algernon after her. Oh dear, I hope there won't be any trouble.

KING: If there is, my daughter can get Algernon out of it safe and sound. You can depend on her. (*Smacks lips*) And I'll have my creampuffs again. (BAKER *and* HERALD *enter. They are supporting each other. They look tired and discouraged, with their heads hanging*) What ho! Have you two been testing my wine again?

BAKER (*Sinking to floor*): Nay, Sire. We have been carrying out your orders.

KING: Orders? What orders?

HERALD: To take the creampuffs apart, Sire, crumb by crumb, to find what they contained.

KING: Ah yes. And what did you find?

BAKER: That they are made only of crumbs, Sire — millions and millions and millions of crumbs. And, alas, I had each and every one under my personal inspection. (*Sighs*) I am poohed. (*Puts head on arm and goes to sleep.*)

HERALD: And I — I am pooh poohed. (*Sinks down, puts head on* BAKER *and goes to sleep.*)

QUEEN: Pooh! What nonsense. (ALGERNON *enters wearing a pair of boxing gloves.*)

KING: What on earth! Boxing gloves! You can be wearing those for only one reason — to keep your hands warm.

QUEEN: Nothing of the kind. He's on his way to the witch's den to save our daughter, aren't you, Algernon?

ALGERNON: Oh, quite. (KING *laughs loudly.*)

KING: Do you think you can knock the witch out with those gloves?

ALGERNON: Oh, quite. (KING *laughs.*)

OFF-STAGE VOICE: Make way for her Highness, the Princess!

KING: She's back! Hooray! Creampuffs again! (PRINCESS *enters carrying recipe book.*)

PRINCESS: Father! I have it! Your recipe book! (*Hands book to* KING *who immediately sits on it.*)

KING: Daughter, you've saved my life. I've a notion to make you Queen.

QUEEN: You're horrid. I'm going home to mother. (*Steps down from throne and starts haughtily across the stage.* WITCH OF ALL WITCHES *enters.*)

KING (*To* WITCH): I sentenced you to your mountain den for life. What are you doing here?

WITCH: I have come on the kindest of missions, Sire. I have brought a gift for your brave, gracious daughter. When she told me of your suffering because of the loss of your creampuff recipe, I was afraid you might wither away in front of her very eyes. So, I willingly gave her the recipe.

PRINCESS: Why, you —

WITCH: Just a moment, dearie. I have brought you the most valuable gift a girl could receive — the Water of Youth. You have but to take one swallow and you shall never grow older.

PRINCESS (*Slightly interested*): Really?

WITCH: I guarantee it. One sip of this wonderful water and you remain just as you are for the rest of your life. (PRINCESS *takes bottle as* 2ND WITCH *runs in.*)

2ND WITCH: Stop! Don't drink that! It's poison! I saw her brew it after the Princess left her den. (PRINCESS *drops bottle.*)

1ST WITCH: You fool! Now you've ruined everything! (*Runs to door.* PAGE *enters and catches hold of her.*) Let me go!

KING: No! Hold her! She has tried to poison my daughter. Herald! Baker! Get up! Take the Witch prisoner! (HERALD *and* BAKER *spring up and take* WITCH *by arms.*)

1ST WITCH: Let me go, I say!

KING: You'll go after I'm through with you. Page, pick up that bottle. (PAGE *picks up bottle*) You now hold in your hand the magic Water of Youth — a gift to my daughter from the Witch of All Witches. Take it to the Witch and make her drink of it.

1ST WITCH: No! No!

KING: But you said one sip of it and you would never grow older. Surely you would like to remain as you are the rest of your life.

1ST WITCH: But the rest of my life would be so short.

KING: Ah, so you admit your bottle contains poison.

1ST WITCH: No, Sire. But —

KING: Then drink. It is my royal decree. (PAGE *puts bottle to* WITCH'S *lips and tips it up. She collapses.*) Take her out and throw her to the buzzards. (BAKER *and* HERALD *drag* WITCH *out.*)

2ND WITCH: Good riddance to bad rubbish. And now, Sire, what is your royal decree for me? Remember, I am the one who saved your daughter from a horrible death.

KING: You? Well, let me see. How would you like to be the Witch of All Witches?

2ND WITCH: Silly boy. There is nothing I'd rather be in the whole world.

KING: Then come and kneel in front of my throne.

2ND WITCH: Could I please stand, Sire? My rheumatism has been bothering me lately.

KING (*Rising and holding hand over* WITCH'S *head as she stands before throne*): I dub you the Witch of All Witches. But remember, no stomping on my royal toes.

2ND WITCH: Never, Sire.

KING: And no attempts at poisoning my daughter.

2ND WITCH: Perish the thought.

KING: And above all — no more stealing of my creampuff recipe.

2ND WITCH: May I follow in my sister's footsteps if I should ever do a thing like that.

KING: Very well, then. Depart, Witch of All Witches. (WITCH *bows, turns to go, and notices* PAGE.)

2ND WITCH: You! No it can't be. Yet, my witch's eyes never deceive me.

QUEEN: What's wrong with him? Has he got chickenpox?

2ND WITCH: Chickenpox! Pooh! He has a kingdom far greater than yours.

KING: What? Who is he?

2ND WITCH: He is Prince Reginald, son of the mighty King Cole. He was lost when only two years old and his father thought him dead. I remember it well, because I was working on the night shift in a haunted house near the castle.

QUEEN (*Running to* PAGE): How romantic. A real prince and my future son-in-law.

KING: How's that? I thought our daughter was to marry Algernon.

PRINCESS: But remember, Father, you promised that if I brought back your recipe for creampuffs you'd let me marry the Page.

KING: Oh, so I did. Well, then I guess I can keep my promise, now that the Page is really a Prince. (PRINCESS *holds out her hands to* PAGE *who comes to her and takes them in his*) Go, my children, and arrange the ceremony.

QUEEN: I'll take care of that. And I'm so happy for you, my dear. (PAGE *puts his arm around* PRINCESS *and they exit as all on stage applaud.* ALGERNON *keeps beating his boxing gloves together after others have stopped clapping their hands.*)

KING (*Looking at him*): And now, what do we do with him? (*Points to him*)

2ND WITCH: Let me have him. He can feed my bats for me.

QUEEN: No, I'll keep him here. He listens to my reading.

KING: Let him decide for himself. Algernon, do you want to stay here and listen to the Queen read her books?

ALGERNON (*Rapidly*): I should say not! If I had to spend the rest of my life that way I think I should go mad. I've listened to romance so long now I'm sick and tired of it. And I never wanted to marry your daughter either. I think she's a little snip, but I have no means of support, so marrying her would have been better than starving to death. If the Witch wants me to go with her, I'll be glad to. Feeding bats is far better than listening to romance. I hate romance! I love bats! So what are we waiting for? Come on, witchie, my love. Fly with me to your mountain cavern where I can sit on a cool rock, take off my shoes and relax in peace and quiet. (*Puts arm around* WITCH.)

2ND WITCH: My pin-up boy! Let's go. My broom is waiting at the gate. (*They skip out.*)

QUEEN: Well, I never in all my life.... Did you know he was as silly as that?

KING: Oh, quite.

QUEEN: Please! Don't ever say that again. (*Shudders*) And to think he might have been my son-in-law.

KING: Would you like to read something to get him off your mind?

QUEEN: Yes. What would you like to hear?

KING (*Dreamily*): I would like to hear the sound of a spoon stirring —

QUEEN: Now wait a minute.

KING: I would like to hear a spoon stirring up a bowlful of delicious creampuffs. (*Holds recipe book out to* QUEEN) And as long as you are so anxious to read, take this down to the kitchen, read the recipe for creampuffs and start making some right away.

QUEEN: You're horrid.

KING: I'm also hungry. (*Puts book under* QUEEN'S *arm and ushers her to exit*) That's a good girl, now. One big batch. Just like mother used to make.

QUEEN: Oh, the kind that taste like tennis balls. (*Sighs*) Very well — if you insist. (*Exits, followed by* LADIES-IN-WAITING. KING *hurries back to throne, sits down. Takes creampuff from pocket of his cloak. Settles back, smiles.*)

KING: I always keep a spare for emergencies. (*Eats as curtains close.*)

THE END

THE DAY IS BRIGHT

by Norman Myrick

Characters

MURILLO, *the painter, at the age of* 57
THE DUCHESS OF CASTILE
SEBASTION, *Murillo's servant boy*
CARLOS, *Sebastion's father and also a slave. He is a Moor.*
RICARDO, CARMEN, HERNANDO, FRANCISCO, ROSITTA — *pupils of Murillo*

SETTING: *The action takes place in the studio of Murillo, the Spanish painter.*

AT RISE: *The* DUCHESS *is seated in the subject's chair while* MURILLO *paints her portrait. After a few strokes he steps back and looks critically at the* DUCHESS.

MURILLO: The head, Duchess, please, a little more to the right. (*Pauses and studies a moment.*) No, that is not it. Perhaps a little more to the left. Yes, yes, that is it. Now please, please, dear Duchess, try to hold the head so.

DUCHESS: Very well, Murillo. Very well. But do hurry along. I am tired.

MURILLO: Tired? Perhaps the flesh, yes, but the soul, no. And it is the soul that I paint.

DUCHESS: Humph!

MURILLO: Do not look so grim, dear Duchess. It is so hard for the soul to shine through the grimness. (*The* DUCHESS *turns her head.*) Please, please. The head, to the left, always to the left, dear Duchess.

DUCHESS: The left, always the left. Does my soul go to the left? Does my heart go to the left? Does my hand go to the left?

No and no and no! But always my head, to the left, please!

MURILLO: There, there. Will the Duchess be so good as to relax? It is not an angry Duchess that I paint but a great lady, a great soul, calm and serene.

DUCHESS: A great soul — bah! Tell me this, Señor Murillo, is there a wart upon my soul?

MURILLO: Surely the Duchess is joking. In all Castile there is —

DUCHESS: Answer me, Murillo. Is there a wart upon my soul?

MURILLO: A wart?

DUCHESS: Yes, an ugly, toady wart.

MURILLO: Never. By all the Saints, it is a soul so pure, so bright —

DUCHESS: Then, why, Señor Murillo, did you paint such a great purple wart on my nose?

MURILLO: My dear Duchess, you are joking. I do not paint a wart on your nose. Such a thing I would not do.

DUCHESS: I am not joking, Señor Murillo. (*During the latter part cf the speech she gets up and goes to the portrait.*) Is this a drop of gold? (*Pointing to her nose in the portrait.*) Is it an angel with silver wings? No, it is not. It is a wart. And it is on my nose.

MURRILLO: But my dear Duchess, I assure you —

DUCHESS: It is a wart and it is on my nose.

MURILLO: I know nothing about it. I did not paint it.

DUCHESS: It did not grow there.

MURILLO: No, but —

DUCHESS: There is no one but Murillo who is painting.

MURILLO: No, there is no one —

DUCHESS: Nevertheless, the wart is there.

MURILLO: But I did not paint it.

DUCHESS: Then who did?

MURILLO: I do not know. But I would call the Duchess's attention to this fact: while there is a wart painted on the portrait, about which I know nothing, mind you, there is also a wart right there. (*Walks up close to the* DUCHESS *as he speaks and points his finger at the* DUCHESS's *nose.*)

DUCHESS: You — you — you insulter. I will have you hanged.

MURILLO: Hang me, then, you will still have your wart. (*Enter* SEBASTION *who stands waiting to be recognized.*)

DUCHESS: My husband will call on you. He will kill you.

MURILLO: Your husband couldn't kill a fly. Yes, Sebastion?

SEBASTION: If you please, Master —

DUCHESS: I will go to Enrico Calles —

MURILLO: Enrico Calles is a jackass that uses its tail for a paint brush. What is it, Sebastion?

SEBASTION: If you please, Master —

DUCHESS: Better a jackass than you who tells lies and insults his clients.

MURILLO: I did not lie. I am Murillo, the artist. I do not have to lie.

DUCHESS: I will not stay here any longer. My cloak, my hat, my carriage! I am going. I will have you drawn and quartered. I will go to Enrico Calles. (*Exit with a great flourish and* MURILLO *follows her to the door, shouting after her.*)

MURILLO: Well, then, go to Enrico Calles. Go and have him paint you like a Fra Angelico Madonna. Have him paint you like a Velazquez horse. You will still have your warts and so will all your children. (*Pauses, and as an after-thought*) And so will your children's children. (*To* SEBASTION) Well, what is it? Don't stand there like a mummy.

SEBASTION: If you please, Master —

MURILLO: A wart on her nose! Ten thousand devils, there is a wart on her nose.

SEBASTION: If you please, Master, the pupils are here.

MURILLO: And what if they are? Am I to stop everything just because some infant daubers are here? So her husband will kill me. Hah! He is a killer of flies, do you hear me, a killer of flies. Why, were he so much as to show his nose in the doorway I would cut it off for him. Well, what are you waiting for? Show them in. The day will not last forever.

SEBASTION: Yes, Master. (*Exit* SEBASTION.)

MURILLO (*Goes over to portrait and studies it carefully*): A wart on her nose. Yes, there is a wart there. It is not a drop of gold nor yet an angel with silver wings, it is a wart and such a wart! A truly magnificent wart. It is a wart that lives and grows, a wart that has a soul, a wart such as only Murillo could paint. The same style, the same stroke and yet Murillo did not paint it. Who, then? Enrico Calles, seeking to discredit me? No. He could not paint such a wart. Quipus? No. Pedrarias? No. A pupil? Yes, possibly a pupil. But whoever, to paint such a wart — it is — it is genius. (*Enter the pupils, one by one. The boys bow to* MURILLO *and the girls curtsey.* MURILLO *stands facing the door and nods slightly to each one in turn.*)

HERNANDO: Good morning, Master.

MURILLO: Señor Hernando.

CARMEN: Good morning, Master.

MURILLO: Señorita Carmen.

FRANCISCO: Good morning, Master.

MURILLO: Señor Francisco.

ROSITTA: Good morning, Master.

MURILLO: Señorita Rositta.

RICARDO: Good morning, Master.

MURILLO: Señor Ricardo. (*As they are greeted the students move to their easels and set about preparations for the morning's work. There is much bustle and talk before the class settles down.*)

RICARDO: Has anyone seen my brush with the yellow bristles?

CARMEN: Goodness, have you lost that again? Well, I haven't seen it.

RICARDO: I left it right here with my easel and now it's gone.

HERNANDO: It must have grown legs and walked away.

RICARDO: Very funny. I'll bet a peso that you have it.

HERNANDO: Ho! So you call me a thief. (*Walks belligerently toward* RICARDO.)

ROSITTA: Oh, do stop squabbling and let somebody do some work!

FRANCISCO: She talks like an artist, doesn't she?

CARMEN: At least she doesn't paint women with blue hair.

HERNANDO: Oh, yes, women with blue hair. Ha, ha, ha, ha!

FRANCISCO: It wasn't blue hair. It was a balanced color combination, as anyone who knows the first thing about painting would know —

RICARDO: I still can't find that brush.

ROSITTA: Oh, bother the brush! Take one of mine and keep quiet!

RICARDO: One might think that you were the Master.

MURILLO: Come, come, enough of this bickering. Get to your easels, all of you. (MURILLO *strolls around the room, pausing before this easel and that one.*)

CARMEN: Master, there is a fly in my bowl of soup.

MURILLO: This is no place for soup. Take it out and the fly with it.

CARMEN: It is the bowl of soup in my picture, Master. (*Pupils laugh.*)

RICARDO: It is a wonder the fly knew what it was.

CARMEN: Oh, keep still!

MURILLO: Silence, Ricardo! Carmen, all of you, quiet! (*Goes to picture.*) The fly isn't dead, Carmen; chase him away. Shoo, shoo, fly! (*His actions must suggest that he has no luck.*)

CARMEN: You see, he is stuck on. (*The students gather around.*)

MURILLO: Nonsense! I'll fix him. (*Takes out his handkerchief and swishes at the fly.*) In the name of ten thousand saints, what's the matter with that fly. (*Snaps with his finger at the fly and then examines it closely.*) By the bones of the Evil One, it is a painted fly. Someone has painted a fly in Carmen's bowl of soup. Who did it? Which one of you? Ricardo? Francisco? Hernando? Which one?

ALL: Not I. I can't paint that well.

MURILLO (*Very angrily*): Someone is making fun of Murillo. Some evil dog is carrying a joke too far. Hernando, what are you laughing at?

HERNANDO: Nothing, Master. Nothing.

MURILLO: So, it is nothing. It is nothing that the Duchess threatens to have me killed because someone paints a wart on her nose. It is nothing that I waste my time with a painted fly that I think is real. No, it is nothing at all, except that when I lay my hands on the wretch I shall wring his scrawny neck until the bones in his spine snap like dry twigs, one by one.

HERNANDO: One by one.

MURILLO: Now back to your easels, all of you, and let us have no more of these pranks. (MURILLO *resumes his stroll and the pupils go back to their easels.*)

RICARDO (*To* FRANCISCO): Who did it? Did you?

FRANCISCO: No, I didn't do it. I thought you did.

RICARDO: Maybe it was Hernando.

FRANCISCO: He'd do it, only he can't paint that well. Even the Master thought it was a real fly. Sshh, here he comes.

MURILLO: (*Pauses in front of* RICARDO'S *easel*): Ricardo.

RICARDO: Yes, Master.

MURILLO: Do you know what warm colors are?

RICARDO: Yes, Master. Yellow, red —

MURILLO: Yellow and red, yellow and red. Then why don't you

paint in yellow and red? May the saints deliver me if I even understand how you can paint a warm, living Castilian scene in a cold blue that would freeze the blood of an English barbarian. (MURILLO *goes on.*)

ROSITTA: The Master is in a vile humor this morning.

RICARDO: He is an old goat, and I will paint in blue as much as I please.

MURILLO: Hernando.

HERNANDO (*To* CARMEN): It is my turn now. Yes, Master.

MURILLO: Hernando, how many legs has a horse?

HERNANDO: Four, Master.

MURILLO: Yes, a horse has four legs. Not five, not three, but four. Be so good, Master Hernando, as to tell a poor ignorant creature like your teacher, why you paint a horse with five legs?

HERNANDO: I do not understand, Master, I painted only four.

MURILLO: Ha! He painted only four. What, then, is this?

HERNANDO: It is a leg to be sure, but I did not paint it. I swear I did not paint it.

MURILLO: A horse has five legs and he did not paint it. The leg is there.

HERNANDO: Yes, but I did not paint it.

MURILLO: So. A wart is on the Duchess's nose and Murillo did not paint it. A fly is in Carmen's soup, but Carmen did not paint it. A horse grows a fifth leg, but Hernando did not paint it. And such a wart, such a leg, such a fly. Magnificent! Magnificent! But you do not paint them. Who, then? Who? Who? Who? (*Paces up and down and finally steps in front of an easel that no one is using. At first he pays no attention to it, but gradually his attention is drawn to it so that he does not listen to what the pupils are saying.*)

ROSITTA: Perhaps the good God has spoken to a Saint.

CARMEN: It might have been a fairy.

HERNANDO: Don't be a dunce; fairies aren't real. I think it was Calles or Quipus, or some other one of the Master's rivals.

MURILLO: Hernando, Ricardo, Carmen —

ALL: Yes, Master —

MURILLO (*Excitedly*): This — this portrait, which one of you did it?

RICARDO: Not I, Master.

CARMEN: Nor I either, Master.

HERNANDO: Would that I had, Master.

FRANCISCO: I didn't do it.

ROSITTA: It is all that I can do to paint a bowl of flowers.

MURILLO (*Engrossed in the picture*): The lips, do you notice the lips, so sure, so soft? And the eye. An eye that sees, an eye that looks out upon the world and lives. (*Very softly*) Which one of you?

FRANCISCO: We do not know, Master. It wasn't one of us.

MURILLO (*Not blustering now, but very gentle*): No, it was not one of you. You are good children. You work hard, but you are only children learning to daub. This — this is the work of a great artist. There is a holy light in the eyes and a soul hides in the curve of the lips. Someone there is who paints warts that grow and flies that buzz and legs that travel and eyes that see. Someone there is who will yet be the Master of us all. You may go home, now. I am bewildered. I must think. I am living next to greatness, and I must think. (*Exit* MURILLO. *The students gather around the portrait.*)

RICARDO: I wonder who it could be?

HERNANDO: I still think it was Enrico Calles playing a joke on the Master.

CARMEN: No, not he. The Master would know his work, and besides, Enrico could not paint an eye that lives, or even a fly in a soup bowl.

ROSITTA: I think it is the work of a Saint. I think it is a miracle. (*Crosses herself.*) I think it is the good God.

FRANCISCO: It might be. It frightens me, it is so strange.

HERNANDO: Pooh! It doesn't frighten me. It is a joke to plague the Master.

RICARDO: What did he mean about the wart on the Duchess's nose?

CARMEN: She has a wart, you know. She tries to hide it, but she has a wart just the same.

ROSITTA: No one dares to mention it, though, at least not when she's around.

FRANCISCO: That's just it, the Master wouldn't paint the wart even if it is there.

HERNANDO: Let's look. (*They all run to the portrait which* MURILLO *covered when the* DUCHESS *left.* HERNANDO *yanks the cover off.*) See, see, there it is.

RICARDO: It's right. It's just exactly right. (SEBASTION *enters unnoticed and watches the group. He is eating an apple.*)

CARMEN: Oh, ho, ho, ho! My, she must have been furious. Just furious.

SEBASTION: She was. She was as mad as an old alley cat caught in the rain. (*All turn when* SEBASTION *speaks.*)

ROSITTA: Did you see it?

SEBASTION: Yes, I was there all the time.

ROSITTA: Tell us about it, Sebastion. What did she do? Did she scream? They say she screams when she's mad. Do tell us, Sebastion.

ALL: Yes, yes, Sebastion. Do it for us; how was it?

SEBASTION: Well, it was very funny. I almost broke in two, laughing, it was so funny.

ROSITTA: Don't tease us, Sebastion, tell us.

SEBASTION: I will, but it was so funny I laugh all the time. Ha, ha!

CARMEN: Oh, Sebastion, please!

SEBASTION (*He acts the story out as he tells it. It is a caricature*): I was standing in the doorway and the Duchess sat up in the posing chair. You know how the Duchess is, like this. (*Sits in chair.*) The Master is down there painting, and I think that the Duchess knew about the wart all the time because she was very grim. Well the Master was so busy painting he didn't even notice the wart until the Duchess said, "Señor Murillo, is there a wart upon my soul?" (*All of the children laugh.*) "But no," says the Master, "in all Castile there is no soul like the Duchess's. It is a soul so pure, so bright." Then the Duchess gets up and goes down to the easel and says, pointing to the wart, "Is this a drop of gold? (*Laughter.*) Is it an angel with silver wings? (*More laughter.*) No and no and no! It is a wart and it is on my nose!"

CARMEN: Oh, my goodness. Ho, ho, ho! My mother will love this.

HERNANDO: What did the Master do?

SEBASTION: The Master said, "But I did not paint it."

HERNANDO: That's just what I said.

RICARDO: Then what did the Duchess do?

SEBASTION: Why, she got just as mad as could be and said, "But the wart is there." And the Master said, "But I did not paint it." And she said, "Who did?" And the Master said, "I don't know." And she said, "You are a liar."

ROSITTA: She did? She really did?

SEBASTION: She certainly did. And the Master got very, very angry and said that, anyway, she did have a wart on her nose, and it looked just like that. She said her husband would kill the Master, and then she ran at him and tried to scratch his eyes out, but the Master picked up a chair and hit her over the head with it like a matador. Then they had the most dreadful fight you ever saw.

RICARDO: And then what happened?

SEBASTION: Well the Duchess's husband came in with six armed guards and they rushed at the Master. The Master drew his sword and fought them. All the time the Duchess was screeching and screaming like a wildcat. The Master killed one of the servants and wounded two others, and then you came in, and they all flew out the window, and that's the last I saw of them. (*He sits down.*)

FRANCISCO: He fought seven men.

SEBASTION: Yes, sir, seven men. I tell you it was better than a bull fight.

ROSITTA: I guess the Duchess won't come here any more.

HERNANDO: Oh, yes, she will. They're always having fights. But seven against one. Whew!

RICARDO: I don't see any blood.

CARMEN: Of course not, silly. Do you think the Master would leave his studio looking like a bull ring?

ROSITTA: But who did paint the wart?

HERNANDO: Yes, who did paint the wart and the fly and the horse's leg and the portrait?

CARMEN: The Master says that whoever it was, he is a great artist.

SEBASTION: Did he really? You're joking.

ALL: No, no. He really did.

RICARDO: He said whoever did it would be the Master of us all.

FRANCISCO: Who did it, Sebastion?

SEBASTION: Don't you know?

ROSITTA: No. Do tell us.

SEBASTION: Promise not to tell?

ALL: Yes, yes. We promise. We won't tell.

SEBASTION: Well, every night just as the clock strikes midnight, a spirit comes here.

CARMEN: A spirit?

SEBASTION: Yes, sir, a spirit.

ROSITTA: I told you it was a Saint.

FRANCISCO: I don't like spirits. I'm frightened.

HERNANDO: Cry baby. What is it like, Sebastion?

SEBASTION: Well, it's about ten feet tall and it has a cloak of silver cloth.

CARMEN: I always thought spirits wore black.

SEBASTION: Oh, no! A spirit can wear anything it pleases. The spirit comes right through the wall, right over there and looks around and then starts to paint. Sometimes he paints portraits and sometimes he plays jokes — like the wart and the fly. But generally he just sits on the chair and looks around, sort of hungry.

CARMEN: Sort of hungry?

HERNANDO: How long has he been coming?

SEBASTION: Oh, for a long time. As long as I can remember.

RICARDO: Is he really ten feet tall?

SEBASTION: I guess he's ten feet tall. Do you know whose spirit he is?

ALL: No. Whose? Tell us, Sebastion.

SEBASTION (*Very mysteriously and in a loud whisper*): Velasquez.

ALL: Oh! (*Long and drawn out.*)

RICARDO: That explains everything.

HERNANDO: I guess he is the Master of us all.

CARMEN: I'd like to see him.

SEBASTION: Just come here at midnight and you'll see him.

ROSITTA: I'd be scared.

CARMEN (*Starting for the door*): I'm going home and tell my mother.

SEBASTION: You'd all better go if you're going to get any dinner.

HERNANDO: I wouldn't be afraid of any old spirit. (*They start to go.*)

FRANCISCO: Just think, he's ten feet tall!

RICARDO: Goodbye, Sebastion.

SEBASTION: Goodbye. (*To* ROSITTA, *who has lingered after the others*) Aren't you going, too?

ROSITTA: Yes, I'm going, but I wanted to give you something first.

SEBASTION: Me? Give me something?

ROSITTA: Yes, I — I wanted to bring you something. (*She takes an orange out of a bag.*) Here.

SEBASTION: Oh, thank you! My goodness, thank you very much! Why?

ROSITTA: Why what?

SEBASTION: Why did you bring me this orange?

ROSITTA: Oh, just because.

SEBASTION: Because why? You don't just bring people things. There's always a reason.

ROSITTA (*She says nothing for a moment, just stares at her feet and then she says*): Because I'm sorry you're a slave and I like you. So there, now. (*She starts to run, but* SEBASTION *runs after her and catches her.*)

SEBASTION: Sorry for me?

ROSITTA: Yes.

SEBASTION: Well, you don't need to be.

ROSITTA: Do you like being a slave?

SEBASTION: No, I don't like it, but there isn't anything I can do about it, and in some ways I like it.

ROSITTA: I don't see how you could like it.

SEBASTION: No, I know you don't. It's like this. There are lots of things that I understand that nobody else understands just because I am a slave.

ROSITTA: What?

SEBASTION: What does it mean to be free?

ROSITTA: Why it means — it means — why I don't know, it just means being free.

SEBASTION: There, you see. You don't know what freedom means. But I do. I know better than anybody else. Better than you or Carmen or Ricardo or the Master or the Duchess.

ROSITTA: Yes, but you have to do what the Master tells you, and you have to work all the time.

SEBASTION: Oh, that! That doesn't really matter. It's the way you feel way down deep inside that counts.

ROSITTA: I'm still sorry that you're a slave.

SEBASTION: Don't be sorry, because someday I'll be free.

ROSITTA: I hope so, Sebastion. I must go now. (*She starts to go.*)

SEBASTION: Thank you for the orange. Good-bye.

ROSITTA: Good-bye. (*Exit* ROSITTA. SEBASTION *watches her go and then hurriedly sets about getting out paints and brushes.*

Then he goes over to the unknown portrait and, after studying it for a few minutes, begins to paint. After a short time has passed, his father enters. He stands behind the boy, watching and then —)

CARLOS: How goes it, my son?

SEBASTION (*Turning quickly*): Father. How quietly you came.

CARLOS: I didn't want the Master to see me.

SEBASTION: I didn't think you were coming.

CARLOS: I was lucky. The Mistress has gone out for lunch and there wasn't anything for me to do in the kitchen. How does it go?

SEBASTION: Pretty well. I don't seem to get the chin just right, though.

CARLOS: Hmmm. It isn't just right, is it? But it will come.

SEBASTION: Yes, I know it will. It is strange how it happens. Sometimes it comes all of a sudden and I see just what I want to paint as clear as the dew in the morning. Like the eyes.

CARLOS: Yes. The eyes are the way I had hoped they would be. What did you do to them?

SEBASTION: Why, nothing except paint what I saw.

CARLOS: What did you see? Tell me. Tell me. When you looked into my eyes, what did you see? Was it an old man, an old slave? (CARLOS *is very earnest and almost afraid when he asks this.*)

SEBASTION: Why, no, that wasn't what I saw.

CARLOS: What, then? Tell me.

SEBASTION: Why I saw — (*Slowly at first, gathering momentum*) I saw the wide horizons of the desert that you have told me about. I saw the great blue of the summer sky and heard the wild thunder of eagles' wings. I saw the gay dancing of the silver sea with white sails from the ends of the earth. I saw the cold horsemen of the stars wheel and charge across the empty night. Hard over the world they rode, to meet the blazing spearmen of the sun.

CARLOS: And what else, what else did you see?

SEBASTION: Oh, many things. Things that have no beginning and no end, like an endless torch burning in the night.

CARLOS (*Seizing him fiercely*): Then you know, you know. (*Triumphantly.*)

SEBASTION: Yes, Father, I know. I know better than anyone else.

CARLOS: May Allah be praised! I was afraid, so terribly afraid.

SEBASTION: Afraid of what?

CARLOS: Afraid that born to slavery you would never know the holy fire that burns in the hearts of all men who have tasted freedom. But you know; my heart is at rest. Finish the chin, my son. Allah is good. (*Goes and sits in the posing chair.*)

SEBASTION (*Softly*): Yes, Father, Allah is good. (*Starts to paint again. After a minute* MURILLO *comes in very quietly and stands watching* SEBASTION *work. By one's and two's the students come and stand gazing in wonder as* SEBASTION *works. Finally* MURILLO *speaks.*)

MURILLO: Boy — (SEBASTION *turns quickly and* CARLOS *jumps up from the chair. There should be a pause before* SEBASTION *answers.*)

SEBASTION: Yes, Master.

MURILLO: So, you are the one.

SEBASTION (*Barely audible*): Yes, Master.

MURILLO (*Walks over and looks at the portrait*): Who is thy master?

SEBASTION: None but you, Master.

MURILLO: Thy teacher, boy, who was thy teacher?

SEBASTION: None but Murillo, Master.

MURILLO: Enough of this. I have never taught you so much as a single stroke. Never. But this, this is the work of a master.

CARLOS: Believe him, sir.

MURILLO: Silence, old man. I will tend to you in good time. As for you, (*Turns to* SEBASTION) give me the truth or I will scourge thy back till the red blood runs. Who is thy teacher?

SEBASTION (*He does not answer immediately, and then with his head up*): None but Murillo, Master.

MURILLO (*Moves as if to seize him*): So, you would lie, you would make sport of Murillo.

CARLOS: He speaks the truth, Master. No one but Murillo has been his teacher. Believe me, Master. Day after day, month after month he has watched and learned. Watched when you knew not that he was watching and stolen the midnight hours to practice your craft. You, Master, have been his teacher and only you.

MURILLO (*Thoughtfully*): Is it so, Sebastion?

SEBASTION: It is so, Master.

MURILLO (*Turns away and goes to portrait of the* DUCHESS *and talks aloud to himself*) : A wart such as only Murillo could paint. A fly that drinks at the soup. A leg that travels as only Murillo could make it travel. (*Turns suddenly on* SEBASTION) I should have you beaten, beaten, do you understand? Coming here like a thief in the night to bewilder and plague me. Why did you paint a wart on the Duchess's nose?

SEBASTION : There *is* a wart on the Duchess's nose, Master.

MURILLO: Why did you paint an extra leg on Hernando's horse?

SEBASTION : I was afraid lest it fall over, Master.

MURILLO: A joker. A bothersome infidel joker. What to do with you I know not. A slave you have always been, a good slave, too, and yet you have been no slave at all. You have talent, perhaps great talent, but you insult my clients, baffle my pupils and throw my studio into an uproar. You are my slave, my slave, don't you understand — my property to do with as I please, and yet you're as free as the Northern star. (*Turns to the students*) What shall it be, reward or punishment?

ALL: Reward, reward!

ROSITTA: He is of the good God, Master. Reward it should be.

MURILLO (*Slowly, thoughtfully*) : Yes, Rositta, he *is* of the good God. Reward it shall be. (*To* SEBASTION) Well then, lad, speak up, name thy desire and it shall be yours.

CARMEN : Ask for lessons, Sebastion. Ask to be the Master's pupil.

HERNANDO: The Master will make you rich, Sebastion. Ask for wealth.

ROSITTA: No, no, Sebastion. Ask for freedom. Ask the Master to set you free.

MURILLO (*When* SEBASTION *fails to answer*) : Speak up, lad, speak up! There is no one here to do you harm. What would you have?

SEBASTION (*Suddenly kneeling and in a soft, desperate voice*) : Master — Oh, Master, make my father free.

MURILLO: Thy father, eh!

SEBASTION : Yes, Master, make my father free.

MURILLO: Yes, lad, thy father and thyself. What little freedom it is mine to give, I gladly bestow on you both. But that is only freedom of the body. The larger freedom, the freedom that lives in the soul and travels the highways of the universe, that belongs to the God that made you.

SEBASTION (*Turns slowly to his father*) : Well, Father?

CARLOS: My heart is at rest, my son. Allah is good.

MURILLO (*After a moment, while the children stare and stare at* CARLOS *and* SEBASTION): What are you staring at? Do you see a ghost? To your easels, all of you! (*To* SEBASTION) Come, my son, let us look at the chin. It is late and we have work to do.

SEBASTION: Yes, Master. There is much work to do. (*Goes with* MURILLO *to the portrait of his father.*)

THE END

A LETTER TO LINCOLN

by Lindsey Barbee

Characters

MRS. BAXTER
MEDORA, ELLEN, CAROLINE — *her daughters*
SARAH, *a neighbor*
MEDORA, *a namesake*
BETTY

TIME: *1862.*

SETTING: *Sitting room in an old Maryland house.*

AT RISE: MRS. BAXTER *is on the settee, knitting.* ELLEN *is standing at the window.* CAROLINE *is on the floor with scraps of silk, workbox, etc.* MEDORA *is curled up in the large chair, reading.*

ELLEN: What is the Mason and Dixon line, mother?

MRS. BAXTER: A division between Pennsylvania and Maryland.

ELLEN: A real division?

MRS. BAXTER: A real division. (*Laughs*) It isn't a wire fence, Ellen — but it's there.

ELLEN: Are all the people on one side of the line southern, and on the other side, northern?

MRS. BAXTER: Something like that, I'm afraid.

ELLEN: We're on the southern side, aren't we?

MRS. BAXTER: Yes, we are.

ELLEN: (*Coming to the settee*): But my father was on the other side of the line.

MRS. BAXTER: Yes. (*Pauses*) The other side of the line.

ELLEN: He fought for the north.

MRS. BAXTER: And died, Ellen.

ELLEN: Mother, did you want to come back to this house?

MRS. BAXTER: It's my girlhood home, Ellen, and grandfather, before his death, wished us to come back.

ELLEN: I like it here.

MRS. BAXTER: I like it, too. And now it will be our home forever and ever. (*Suddenly*) Pick up your scraps, Caroline.

CAROLINE: I'm making a dress for my doll, Mary Todd Lincoln.

MRS. BAXTER: Suppose you finish it tomorrow morning.

MEDORA (*Suddenly screaming*): They just can't do it — they can't.

MRS. BAXTER: Medora! Can't do — what?

MEDORA: Sell Uncle Tom.

CAROLINE: Who's Uncle Tom?

MEDORA: He's a slave in this book, and they're going to sell him to the man who'll pay most for him. (*Runs to* MRS. BAXTER) Oh — Mother!

MRS. BAXTER: Hush, Medora. There are some things that little girls do not understand.

MEDORA: I understand that it's wrong to have slaves and that it is wicked to sell them.

MRS. BAXTER: You are living in the South, Medora.

ELLEN: And this is a dreadful book, Medora. Everybody says so. (*Takes book from* MEDORA.) *Uncle Tom's Cabin.*

MEDORA: It isn't dreadful. It's true. (*Takes back book.*)

MRS. BAXTER: Put it away, Medora. Nobody here will understand just why you're reading it.

MEDORA: But I'm from the North.

MRS. BAXTER: Remember that we're living in the South. (*Pauses*) And that makes all the difference in the world.

MEDORA: Just the same, I'll do everything I can to help the slaves.

MRS. BAXTER: Hush. Hush.

ELLEN: Just what could you do, Medora?

MEDORA: I could — I could — (*With a half sob*) Oh, I wish I could see Mr. Lincoln.

MRS. BAXTER (*Rising*): Let's go to bed, Caroline.

CAROLINE (*Holding out the doll*): Isn't Mary Todd Lincoln just lovely in her new dress?

MRS. BAXTER: Very lovely. Suppose we call her Miss Dixie.

CAROLINE: But that isn't her name.

MRS. BAXTER: We'll talk about it tomorrow. (*Crosses to left*) I'll be back shortly, girls. (*Goes out with* CAROLINE)

ELLEN (*Once more at the window*): Oh, there's Sarah! (*Knocks on window*) She's coming in. (*Runs to right and opens door*) Sarah! (SARAH *enters*)

SARAH: It's cold, girls — and it's beginning to snow.

MEDORA: Come over here and get warm. (*The two cross to fire*)

ELLEN (*Clapping her hands*): Maybe we'll have a real snow storm — like the ones we had up north.

SARAH: We're going back — I mean father, mother and I —

MEDORA: Back where?

SARAH: To New York. That's our home. My father has finished his business here.

MEDORA: I wish we could go, too.

ELLEN: Why, Medora! This is our home — our home for always.

MEDORA: I don't want to live in a place where there are slaves. (*Catches up her book from hassock.*)

SARAH: What's that?

MEDORA: *Uncle Tom's Cabin.*

SARAH: Better not let anyone see you reading it.

MEDORA: Just why?

SARAH: It's not a popular book here. You see, I've lived here for a year and I know what I'm talking about.

MEDORA: I can't bear to have them sell Uncle Tom.

SARAH: It's just a story.

MEDORA: But it's happening all the time — other places — other slaves.

SARAH: It's happening right here.

MEDORA: What do you mean?

SARAH: Cassie — she's our servant, you know — told me that there are two runaway slaves here in this town.

MEDORA: Here — in — this — town?

SARAH: Hiding. Hiding in an old cellar.

ELLEN: Oh — how — terrible!

SARAH: Their master is hunting them — and if he finds them —

ELLEN: What will happen?

SARAH: They'll be beaten — and dragged back — and maybe killed.

MEDORA (*Bitterly*): Not if they're good workers.

SARAH: Medora! What is the matter? You look so — wild — and fierce.

MEDORA: I am fierce. And I'm wishing for Abraham Lincoln.

SARAH: Just why are you wishing for Abraham Lincoln?

MEDORA: Because he'd tell me some way that I could help him.

ELLEN: Help him? Medora, you do talk so strangely.

MEDORA: Yes — that's just what I mean. Help him.

SARAH: We're close to the borderline, you know.

ELLEN: Yes, we know.

SARAH: And if the slaves could get across the line, they'd be safe.

ELLEN (*Gaily*): Come, let's forget all about it.

SARAH (*Walking around*): This is a nice old house, isn't it?

ELLEN: I love it — and it was my mother's home.

SARAH (*At mantel*): Lafayette carried these candlesticks once upon a time.

ELLEN: How do you know?

SARAH: Your grandfather told me. (*Pauses*) Since I was a neighbor, he told me — oh, ever so many things about the house.

ELLEN: Tell us. For we haven't been here very long.

SARAH (*In a whisper*): There's a secret passage — or tunnel —

MEDORA: No!

SARAH: Yes!

MEDORA: Are you sure?

SARAH: Your grandfather told me.

ELLEN: What good is it?

SARAH: Oh, it was used a long time ago — maybe in the Revolutionary War — or was it the French and Indian war? I forget. But, anyway, it was used.

MEDORA: Where does the tunnel go?

SARAH: Into a sort of cave.

ELLEN: Oh — how — exciting!

SARAH: And the cave is in another state. Did you ever hear of anything so strange?

MEDORA: What state?

SARAH: Pennsylvania. (*Pauses*) You see, our little town is close to the line.

MEDORA (*Rushing to* SARAH): Do you know how to find this secret passage?

SARAH: Of course I do. (*Pushes* MEDORA) Don't get so excited, Medora.

MEDORA: Then — tell us.

SARAH: It's right before you.

ELLEN: Where?

SARAH: Right before you. (*At fireplace*) Do you see this funny little knob?

MEDORA: Of course we see it.

SARAH: Then — press. (MEDORA *presses*)

MEDORA: Nothing happens.

SARAH: Let's both press. (*As the side of the fireplace begins to move*) There!

ELLEN (*Looking inside*): It's dark!

SARAH: Of course it's dark.

ELLEN: It smells damp — and feels cold — and —

SARAH: Why shouldn't it be? (MEDORA *walks slowly to center and stands motionless, her eyes wide, her arms crossed before her.*)

ELLEN: Medora! What's the matter ?

SARAH: Medora! (*After a moment*) Are you — thinking — just — what — I — am — thinking?

MEDORA (*Holding out her hand to* SARAH): I'm sure that I am. (*Pauses*) Shall we do it?

CURTAIN

* * *

SCENE 2

SETTING: *The same, the next morning.*

AT RISE: MRS. BAXTER *is moving restlessly around the room.* CAROLINE *with her doll is on the hassock.*

MRS. BAXTER: Where are the girls?

CAROLINE: They went over to Sarah's.

MRS. BAXTER: But it's snowing.

CAROLINE: Not much of a snow. (*Pauses*) I don't think it's any kind of a snow.

MRS. BAXTER: But why should they go before breakfast?

CAROLINE: I don't know, mother, I really don't know. (*Begins to cry*)

MRS. BAXTER: What is it, dear? (*Goes to her*)

CAROLINE: It's Miss Dixie. I don't like her.

MRS. BAXTER: Why, I think she's a beautiful dolly.

CAROLINE: But she's really Mary Todd Lincoln, and she shouldn't have another name.

MRS. BAXTER (*Quickly*): Then she shall be Mary Todd Lincoln.

CAROLINE: That's what she started out to be. (*The door at right opens, and* MEDORA *and* ELLEN *enter, wearing their heavy coats and hats.*)

MRS. BAXTER: Girls! Where have you been?

CAROLINE: And why did you want to go out before breakfast?

MEDORA: Because I had to send a letter.

ELLEN: And because we had important business with Sarah.

MRS. BAXTER: You're acting rather — mysterious — girls.

ELLEN: But we can explain everything, Mother — and explain it very well, indeed. (MRS. BAXTER *sits on settee with* MEDORA *on one side and* ELLEN *on the other.*)

MRS. BAXTER: I was wakeful last night. Perhaps I was nervous—but I imagined all sorts of things.

MEDORA: Things?

MRS. BAXTER: Noises.

CAROLINE: I heard them, too.

MEDORA: We opened the secret passage, Mother. (CAROLINE *sits at their feet.*)

MRS. BAXTER: How did you know about the secret passage?

ELLEN: Sarah told us.

MEDORA: And she also told us that there were two runaway slaves right here in the town hiding in a cellar.

MRS. BAXTER: Go on.

MEDORA: And Sarah said that the tunnel ended in a little cave —

MRS. BAXTER (*Quickly*): In another state.

MEDORA: Yes — in another state. (*Pauses*) A free state.

ELLEN: Did you know about it, Mother?

MRS. BAXTER: Yes, I knew about it.

MEDORA: Sarah and I had the same idea at the same moment.

MRS. BAXTER: Go on.

MEDORA: It was — why not put these poor, frightened slaves in a place that would lead them right into freedom.

MRS. BAXTER: So, what did you do?

ELLEN: We packed a lunch and found some warm clothes.

MEDORA: And Sarah gave them candles and matches.

ELLEN: Then we opened the tunnel and started them on their way.

MEDORA: They were very grateful, Mother. (*For a moment there is silence.*)

ELLEN (*Anxiously*): Mother, are you angry?

MRS. BAXTER: No — I'm not angry.

MEDORA: Aren't you sure that we did the right thing?

MRS. BAXTER: Yes, I'm sure. I'm quite sure.

MEDORA: And today is Abraham Lincoln's birthday. (*Sighs*) That makes it quite wonderful.

CAROLINE: You wanted to do something for him, didn't you?

MEDORA: I have done something. We all have.

CAROLINE: And it will be a lovely birthday present.

ELLEN: Tell Mother about the letter, Medora.

MEDORA: I wrote it early this morning.

MRS. BAXTER: A letter — to President Lincoln?

MEDORA: Of course. It's his birthday.

MRS. BAXTER: And what did you say in the letter?

MEDORA: I made a copy for you, Mother. (*Goes to desk, takes paper and reads.*)

"Dear President Lincoln:

"I am a little girl who lives close to the Mason and Dixon line. We have a secret tunnel in our house that leads into another state, and my sister, a neighbor and I have sent two runaway slaves through this tunnel into safety. We did this, not only because we wanted to remember your birthday in some way that you would like, but because you are such a wise man, President Lincoln; you are so good and kind to everybody that we think you're also a very great man.

"And this is your birthday gift.

"Your friend,
"MEDORA BAXTER."

ELLEN: It's a lovely letter, isn't it, mother?

MRS. BAXTER: It's a very lovely letter, Medora dear, and it will make President Lincoln very happy.

ELLEN: Will he answer it, Medora?

MEDORA: I think that he will.

MRS. BAXTER: He's a busy man, Medora.

MEDORA: But he is never too busy to be kind.

ELLEN: It will be — wonderful — to hear from him.

MEDORA: And when the letter comes, I shall hide it away in the secret drawer of my desk.

ELLEN: That's foolish.

MEDORA: Oh, no, it isn't. (*Pauses*) For on some day 'way off in the future, somebody will touch the little spring that opens the drawer and will find the letter tucked away in the desk. (*Softly*) The letter signed *Abraham Lincoln.*

CURTAIN

* * *

SCENE 3

TIME: *February 12.*

AT RISE: MEDORA *is at the window and* BETTY *has just picked up a knitting bag, settling herself comfortably on the settee.*

MEDORA: Oh, I'm going to love this place.

BETTY: It's all right in its way, but it's terribly old-fashioned.

MEDORA: Who wants a family home that isn't old-fashioned?

BETTY: How long ago was it built?

MEDORA: Oh, years and years ago — 'way back to the Revolution.

BETTY: Oh, it must have been patched up as time went by — for it's livable.

MEDORA: Of course it's been patched up.

BETTY: Just the same, I shouldn't want to live here *all* the time.

MEDORA: I'd like it. I think it's wonderful.

BETTY: Just how did this house come to us?

MEDORA: Betty, you're not a bit interested in family history.

BETTY: No, I'm not.

MEDORA: Why, it belonged to great-great-great — oh, so many greats — Aunt Medora Baxter. (*Sighs*) I'm so proud that her name has come down to me.

BETTY: I'd rather be Elizabeth than Medora.

MEDORA: Then we're both satisfied. (*Sits by* BETTY) Do you remember about the secret in the room?

BETTY: What are you talking about?

MEDORA: It's come down through all the years that there is a secret in this room.

BETTY: Strange that nobody's found it out.

MEDORA: Not strange at all. It was Aunt Medora's secret.

BETTY: What has that to do with it?

MEDORA: Lots. She said she had left something in this room.

BETTY: Where did you get all this?

MEDORA: If you'd had any interest in your ancestors, Betty, you'd know that it's been a sort of tradition — Aunt Medora's secret.

BETTY: Then run along and find out about it. I'm counting stitches.

MEDORA: I'll finish my letter. (*Goes to desk. For a moment there is silence.* BETTY *knits and* MEDORA *settles down to her letter. Then suddenly she cries out.*)

BETTY: What is it?

MEDORA: I touched something sharp. Why, it's a little knob — and — and (*Her voice trails into nothingness.*)

BETTY: What on earth is the matter?

MEDORA: Something is moving.

BETTY: Moving?

MEDORA: It's a part of the desk. (*Excitedly*) It's a drawer.

BETTY: Probably got stuck.

MEDORA: It's a drawer — a little, secret drawer. And there's a paper inside.

BETTY (*Crossing to desk*): Let's see. (*The two girls bend over the desk.*)

MEDORA: Here it is — the paper.

BETTY: Oh, it's old — very old. It's — yellow.

MEDORA: I'll open it carefully (*Crosses with* BETTY *to center*) It's so old that it's ready to break.

BETTY: Read it.

MEDORA (*As she carefully opens the paper*): "Dear Medora Baxter: No one could have a finer birthday gift than the letter that you sent me. When you helped the poor, frightened slaves to escape through your secret tunnel, you gave them something that meant unmeasured happiness to them; and at the same time you brought me the loyalty and faith that I am trying so hard and so humbly to deserve." (*Pauses*) And it's signed Abraham Lincoln.

BETTY: Oh — how — wonderful!

MEDORA: Betty, do you know what day it is?

BETTY: Why — why it's February the twelfth.

MEDORA (*Softly*): Lincoln's birthday.

THE END

THE LINCOLN COAT

by Thelma W. Sealock

Characters

CYNTHIA ROBERTS, *the teacher, about 25*
JOEY ABRAMS, *a little Jewish boy, small and intelligent*
ABIE ABRAMS, JOEY'S *slightly smaller brother*
NELLIE ABRAMS, JOEY'S *sister of Junior High age*
SARAH ABRAMS, JOEY'S *sister of High School age*
MR. ABRAMS, JOEY'S *father*
MRS. ABRAMS, JOEY'S *mother, bright but timid and self-effacing*
ALEX ABRAMS, *the youngest member of the family*
OTHER SCHOOL CHILDREN

SCENE 1

TIME: *Late in January in the 1930's.*

SETTING: *A schoolroom on the lower East Side of New York City.*

AT RISE: *The children are standing singing "America."* JOEY *is in the front row. He sings lustily till he reaches "Land where my fathers died," when he gradually stops.* MISS ROBERTS *notices and nods as she beats time for the singing. Immediately on the completion of the singing, he raises his hand.*

MISS ROBERTS: What is it, Joey?
JOEY: Could I stay and clean the 'rasers for you?
MISS R. (*Smiling at him*): Yes, Joey, you may if you wish. The others will please file to the cloak room. (*The children file out.* MISS ROBERTS *follows and is heard directing them.* JOEY *still sits staring unseeingly at the board.*)
MISS R. (*Entering again*): Well, it gets dark early these days, doesn't it?
JOEY (*Abruptly*): Miss Roberts, the song says "Land where my fathers died," but my father — he's —

Miss R.: Oh, you didn't understand the song? "Land where my fathers died" means that this is the country where our grandfathers and great-grandfathers fought for their liberty and won —but some of them died winning it.

Joey: But "grandfathers," you say? My grandfather died in Russia many years ago. I know, my Papa tells me. I don't think I ought to sing it. (*Looks at* Miss Roberts *earnestly, twisting about uncomfortably.*)

Miss R.: Oh, but Joey, don't you understand — (*Pauses a moment as she considers how best to explain it.*) The song doesn't mean America alone. Your father's and mother's fathers and grandfathers fought for liberty in Russia. Your father knows much more about that history than I do. Don't you see — (*Reaches over and takes his hand into hers*) wherever people have fought and been wounded and died for freedom and liberty —"America" is their song, too, Joey!

Joey (*His face lighting*): Oh, yes'm. Then — I have the right to sing it, too.

Miss R.: Yes, indeed, more right than some of us who have lived here longer.

Joey (*Joyfully*): My — I'm glad! (*He collects the erasers and exits.*)

Miss R. (*Watching him*): If more of them only cared! (*Goes to her desk.* Joey *returns. He wipes the blackboard, humming "America" as he works.*)

Joey: Miss Roberts, do you think I could ever be a doctor — like the Dispensary-man?

Miss R. (*Heartily*): Oh, I'm sure you could, Joey. Wouldn't it be fine to help sick people and make them well again!

Joey: Yes'm — maybe I could make them grow up and not sell old clothes.

Miss R.: What do you mean, Joey?

Joey: *You know* — be good Americans and learn! Sell buildings and know how to do plumbing and papering.

Miss R. (*Smiling a bit behind her hand*): Oh, I see, Joey, you want them to go into other kinds of work.

Joey: Yes'm. My Papa wanted to do that only you had to have lots an' lots of money in Russia, and so he just reads by himself.

Miss R.: Well, I think it's wonderful that he reads and studies when he couldn't go to school as he wanted to.

JOEY (*Pausing and turning dramatically*): I bet — I bet one of the big pink candy rings in Papa's store — I bet *you can't* guess what *I've* done!

MISS R. (*In deep thought*): Now let me see. I mustn't lose this. It might be a party? No. It wouldn't be a new sweater? And your shoes are just newly mended. (JOEY *is delightedly watching and shaking his head at each suggestion.* MISS R. *pretends to have suddenly come on the exact thing!*) Oh, *I* know! You've been reading ahead in history!

JOEY (*Gleefully, showing intense excitement*): No sir! I — I learned all my Lincoln part for the program on the twelfth!

MISS R. (*Great surprise*): You did! Well, for pity's sake! It does no good to give you the biggest part — you go ahead and do it ahead of time!

JOEY: Oh but, Miss Roberts, it's such a grand part! Grand! I can — I can say it all while I sleep — I bet I can!

MISS R. (*Laughing*): I don't doubt it but I'm not going to bet any more today. It reminds me, though—(*She puts her papers aside*) I have one of your costumes. Would you get it? It's in the cloak room — that flat box on the end shelf.

JOEY (*Rushing to the door*): Sure, I will. (*He is back in an instant with a suit box which he places on the desk top.*)

MISS R.: It's the coat to the costume a boy in Miss Jenning's room wore last year. (*She is untying box and getting out a long-tailed black coat — which will be very long on* JOEY.) I thought it would be all right if it just isn't too terribly big. (JOEY *strips off his worn old sweater.*) Of course I can take it up some. (*She slips it on him. It is big, standing out from his shoulders, especially long — the tails hang on the floor.*)

JOEY (*Looking back and down at it admiringly*): My! It's a grand coat and so heavy! (*He lifts his shoulders as if testing it.*) Teacher — (*Touching her sleeve lovingly*) I can say *all* of it! I don't even read the part he said at the battlefield!

MISS R.: Oh, Joey, you mean you know his Gettysburg Address, too?

JOEY (*Modestly*): Yes'm. I think when such a poor man was so honest that he got to be President and said grand things about the poor, dead men and what they'd done, they ought to be learned!

MISS R. (*Arranging coat and trying to pin it more nearly in a fit *for small* JOEY): That's wonderful, Joey. I wish all the boys and girls would remember about his honesty and greatness —

JOEY (*Reminiscently*): Remember, too, how he walked so far, after he was tired, to give the woman her pennies.

MISS R.: Yes, Joey, always be honest as you can be — an upright man and a good citizen.

JOEY: Yes'm.

MISS R.: My goodness, Joey! I didn't realize you were so little! I'll have to take this up a great deal in order to make it so you can keep it on. (*She squeezes him impulsively.*) For a ten-year-old you're small size but you're such a good student, I'd love having you in my room if you were fifteen! (*She laughs,* JOEY *hangs his head.*) Why, Joey, what's the matter?

JOEY: Nothin', only I have to go. I have to go home, Teacher. I feel bad — here. (*He places his hand at his throat.*)

MISS R. (*Alarmed*): Oh, Joey, is your throat sore?

JOEY (*Turning away in taking the coat off*): No'm, it — it just hurts.

MISS R.: Well, you just wait a minute. I'm going to walk home with you. I have to take the Third Avenue El, anyway.

JOEY (*Protestingly, obviously trying to get away from her*): But — but I have to hurry!

MISS R. (*Distressed*): Oh, Joey, why did you stay then? You didn't need to help! (*Hurries to cloak room and returns with her coat and hat and a ragged cap and mackinaw of* JOEY'S.) Hurry then — but I'm going, too. (*She bundles the costume coat hastily into the box.* JOEY *watches wistfully.*)

JOEY: Teacher, could I carry it — the Lincoln coat?

MISS R. (*Seems about to protest but sees his eagerness and consents*): All right, but it's awfully heavy. (*They go off as the curtain falls.*)

* * *

SCENE 2

SETTING: *Same as Scene 1, three days later, at noon.*

AT RISE: *Children are heard outside the room, marching, then calling and whistling back and forth.* MISS ROBERTS *is sitting at her desk. She looks worried and runs her hand over her forehead — somewhat absent-mindedly.*

MISS ROBERTS: Oh, dear, I wonder what could be the matter. It's three days! (ABIE, JOEY'S *brother, edges in at the hall door.* MISS R. *turns and sees him eyeing her.*) Hello.

ABIE (*Turns his cap nervously. Looks toward her and away.*): Joey's sick!

MISS R.: Oh, is he? Are you Joey's brother? I've just wondered and wondered about him.

ABIE: Yes'm, he's sick.

MISS R.: Does he have a cold? He spoke about his throat hurting him.

ABIE (*Eagerly*): No'm. It's no cold Joey's got!

MISS R. (*Anxiously*): Did your father and mother have a doctor see him?

ABIE (*Importantly*): Yes'm. I ran to the dispensary the first morning. The lady said, "Doc's not here." I waited and I missed school. (*Triumphantly*) But I *got* him!

MISS R. (*Impatiently*): Oh, do tell me what he said!

ABIE: He says Joey's not so strong (MISS R. *nods*), but because he talked crazy all night, he says it's much more worser'n a cold.

MISS R.: You say he talked "crazy." What did he say?

ABIE (*Shifts uneasily*): Oh, only *some* of the time could I tell what he was saying.

MISS R.: You mean, he didn't talk the way he did when he was awake?

ABIE: No'm, he said speeches and told me he walked through the snow to give you pennies!

MISS R.: Oh, he had the Lincoln program on his mind — but surely he wasn't worried about it.

ABIE (*Shifting about again*): Please — I'm — Papa comes to see you.

MISS R.: Oh, he's coming this noon?

ABIE: Yes'm. (*A discreet knock sounds at the door.*) That's Papa now! (*He rushes to the hall door and opens it to disclose* PAPA ABRAMS, *a small man, shabby but neat, who bows with real courtesy.*)

MR. ABRAMS: This is Joey's teacher? (*To* ABIE)

MISS R. (*Cordially*): Yes! Come in, Mr. Abrams. I'm so anxious to talk with you. Abie has been telling me — (*Pulls a chair out toward him.*)

MR. A. (*Pulls* ABIE'S *ear affectionately*): Many things, eh?

MISS R.: Do tell me, Mr. Abrams, how is Joey? Is he very ill? And just what is wrong?

MR. A. (*Sits down, puts hat on floor, with a book in it. Sighs deeply.*): Joey, that boy! He is very sick. The man from the — the — (ABIE *supplies 'dispensary'*) says it is bad — bad. I think Joey thinks too much of something — I don't know what. He talks of speeches and makes them. Oh, he says such grand words, Miss Roberts (*Looks at her and sighs.*), grand —

MISS R.: Do you think he is worried about school? Maybe I shouldn't have asked him to take the biggest part in our Lincoln program.

MR. A.: No, Miss Roberts, it is not your mistake. I am sure of it. It is a worry —

MISS R.: What are the things he says, Mr. Abrams?

MR. A.: Oh, he tells about Mr. Lincoln, and then he says he is the most honest of all. Then he cries to his Papa — *to me* — to be honest. Only the honest man, he says, is great and then he begins the speeches again. Mostly he says — "we cannot forget what they did here," and then he cries and cries. (MR. A. *is becoming more worked up as he speaks. He wipes his eyes.*)

MISS R.: That's what he learned — part of what he learned, I mean. Our program is February twelfth, you know, and we were planning to show parts of Lincoln's life. Joey was to be president!

MR. A.: Oh that Joey, how happy he was! His Mama says — oh Abie, Mama says to run straight home! (ABIE *starts out*) We do our best. It is not like Russia. I want them all to have school —and seven — sometimes it is hard to feed from the store. It is but a small store.

MISS R.: Mr. Abrams, I think it's wonderful that you are so interested in having your children go to school. So many parents seem only to want to put their children in the factories as soon as possible.

MR. A. (*Sadly*): No, Miss Roberts. I see plenty where I live. My boys and girls have a chance. My Sarah is already in the higher school, Nellie will go there soon. Then Joey and Abie and Alex — they shall all go.

MISS R.: That's certainly fine. Joey is so bright and quick — although he's so small!

MR. A. (*Confidentially*): Miss Roberts, I need to say something. It is only that Joey loves you that I can say it. When Mama and the children come to me here I did a wrong.

MISS R.: Why, what do you mean, Mr. Abrams? Have you been unhappy?

MR. A. (*The inherent fineness of a truly fine Jewish parent comes out.*): Miss Roberts, it is what we hope for always — but I do not know. Maybe these people will not like a Jewish man to have a store. So — I make *sure* Sarah and Nellie and Joey and Abie have the chance! Fourteen is the age for a boy or girl to go to work. I tell the man that my children — *each* is two years younger. (*His emotion is great here. One should feel that he has to think in order not to have his words and word-order confused.*)

MISS R.: Why, you mean Joey is twelve instead of ten?

MR. A.: Yes, Miss Roberts. His own Papa tells a lie that he shall learn two years more!

MISS R. (*Looking at him with increasing admiration*): Oh, Mr. Abrams, that was wonderful of you! Of course, it wasn't strictly right — (*With a little smile to soften her words*) because you know the schools — and everything — would be dreadfully mixed up if everyone gave his children's ages wrong. But I understand your reasons — and your feelings, and *I* don't think you were wrong. You were just *very* kind to your children!

MR. A. (*Brightening*): Is it — if Joey's teacher can think it is not all bad then I maybe — (*He bows his head and sighs*) Joey makes such speeches all the nights. I am worried more and more. It hurts me.

MISS R.: Oh, but Mr. Abrams, you did a beautiful thing for your children, when they were young and helpless. You must love them all very greatly. Joey speaks so lovingly of you and of his mother.

MR. A. (*More happily*): I am mos' happy to tell you. I had to know what you would feel. (*Frown grows on his forehead.*) If —if Joey is well again. He reads — we talk together.

MISS R.: Might I come around this evening after school to see him?

MR. A. (*Bowing and smiling*): Yes — yes, Joey's teacher — he would be made happy seeing you. (*He rises to go.*)

MISS R.: Then I'll come right after three-thirty.

MR. A. (*Discovers book he has put in his hat. Is disturbed and drops it. They both reach for it and bump heads*): Oh, Miss — is terrible — Joey's teacher —

MISS R. (*Laughing*): Oh, that's nothing, Mr. Abrams—nothing!

MR. A.: This is *your* book. Joey says it is yours.

MISS R.: Yes, it's the one from which he learned his part. He told me he had it all learned.

MR. A.: Yes'm and he says — "Tell her a note —" he says.

MISS R.: He sent me a note? How nice!

MR. A. (*As he backs toward the hall door*): You will come this day — and the bump —

MISS R.: Yes, indeed, and I'm so glad you came, Mr. Abrams. So glad! Goodbye.

MR. A.: Goodbye, Miss. (MISS R. *leafs through the book and soon finds the note. She reads it aloud.*)

MISS R.: "Dear Teacher: Please have some other boy wear the Lincoln Coat. I will not be the President. It hurts me. It hurts my Papa, too. With love, Joey Abrams." Now Sherlock, go to work! (*She studies the note. A bell rings outside.*) Oh yes, the playground and cafeteria must be supervised! But Joey — I *will* find what is wrong. I will. I must! (*She exits as curtain falls.*)

* * *

SCENE 3

SETTING: *The Abrams' living room.*

AT RISE: JOEY *lies on a couch at left, carefully covered. He is asleep. The youngest Abrams child slides in and out, an all-day sucker in hand.* MAMA ABRAMS *comes from the kitchen to see if* JOEY *is covered.* PAPA ABRAMS *comes in from the store.*)

MR. A. (*In a low voice*) : You think he is better, Mama?

MRS. A.: Oh, Papa — seems he don't want to get well! (*She wipes her eyes on her apron. He pats her shoulder and takes her hand in his.*)

MR. A.: Now Katrinza, no worryings helps it. The man, you know, comes to see Joey — he says no worryings!

MRS. A. (*Sighs*) : Well, maybe teacher makes him more happy— when she comes.

MR. A. (*Brightening*) : I think so, Mama. She is a fine, grand lady and she likes our Joey. He's good boy, she says. (SARAH *and* NELLIE *burst in,* ABIE *following close behind.*)

MRS. A.: Sh — sh — Don't wake — Joey — (*A bell rings faintly in the distance.* MR. A. *hurries back to the store. The girls put their wraps and books away and fix their hair before a small wall mirror.*) Abie — come — necks are washed! Teacher comes, remember! (ABIE *looks disgusted but accompanies her to the kitchen. The girls whisper a little.* JOEY *is awakening.* MR. ABRAMS' *voice is heard from the store.*)

MR. A.: Yes'm — yes'm — Miss Roberts — we are very proud — but the bump!

MISS R.: I'm so glad to come, Mr. Abrams. Please forget about the little bump. Do you think Joey is better?

MR. A.: Well, the man he says he is not so hot — but he is not right. He worries! Still he worries! (SARAH *and* NELLIE *exit quietly.* MRS. A. *and* ABIE *come from the kitchen.* SARAH *and* NELLIE *then softly follow them back in.*) Mama, I want you to meet Joey's teacher — Miss Roberts.

MRS. A. (*Shyly*) : I am happy to be acquainted with you, Miss.

MISS R. (*Cordially*) : I'm so glad to meet you, Mrs. Abrams. Joey's family are my special friends because I think so much of him. (JOEY *hears but pretends to be sleeping.*)

MRS. A.: An' you know Abie? An' Sarah and Nellie?

MISS R.: Yes, I've met Abie before, and I'm glad to know Sarah and Nellie. Sarah is in high school and Nellie will be next year, is that right? (*The two girls are pleased and embarrassed.*)

MR. *and* MRS. A. (*Proudly*) : Yes'm — the high school that's where Sarah goes to school.

MISS R.: Mr. Abrams, I have an idea. I think I've found out what is worrying Joey — (JOEY *stirs and hides his face in the blan-*

ket.) and I — I want to know if you'll let me talk to him alone.

MR. A.: Oh yes'm — but is it — something at the school?

MISS R.: Oh, no, Mr. Abrams. Joey has been perfect in every way at school. You remember you told me something worried him. I think I know what it is — and I know what to do.

MRS. A. (*Eyes brimming*): Oh Miss — do it — *do it!*

MR. A.: Yes'm, I will want Sarah and Nellie in the store. Abie—Mama needs you.

MRS. A. (*Wiping her eyes*): Then a tea — perhaps? (*She indicates a samovar.*)

MISS R.: Yes, indeed. (*She pats* MRS. A's *arm*) And everything will be all right. (*They all leave,* ABIE *reluctantly,* SARAH *and* NELLIE *slowly because of taking in details of* TEACHER'S *dress and hat.* MISS R. *seats herself in a rocking chair near the couch. All is very quiet.* MISS R. *hums "America."* JOEY *stirs and finally uncovers his face.*)

MISS R.: Why, hello, Joey! Aren't you glad to see me?

JOEY (*Painfully*): Yes'm — but you — you oughtn't to have come.

MISS R.: But why not, Joey? You've been sick and I wanted to see you, so I came.

JOEY (*More painfully*): Yes'm.

MISS R.: Besides, I didn't understand your note and I thought you could explain it better than anyone else.

JOEY: I *can't* be Lincoln — and wear the big Lincoln Coat.

MISS R.: I know you can't, Joey, if you're going to be sick, but you're going to get well and then you can take your part.

JOEY: But it's — it's not right. (*He twists and turns miserably.*)

MISS R.: For you to take the part, you mean? (*She reaches over and takes his hand in hers.*)

JOEY: It's — he was *so* honest — an' — an' oh, teacher, I'm not! (*He bursts into sobs. She comforts him, patting his shoulders.*)

MISS R.: Oh, Joey — the idea! You're as honest as daylight! With such a fine father you couldn't be otherwise. (JOEY *squirms again.*) Joey, do you know he told me today about a wonderful thing he did for Sarah and Nellie and Abie and you. *Just think* —when he didn't know but what he'd starve, he did something so big and so fine that it could hurt no one — only help you children! He made sure that you and your brother and sisters would be educated so that you need not work beyond your strength all your lives!

JOEY (*Incredulously*): Teacher, you mean — my Papa is honest!

MISS R. (*Near to tears*): Oh, Joey, he's more than honest. He is a truly great and big-hearted man in every way!

JOEY (*Joy coming into his thin face*): Then I am *not* a bad boy!

MISS R. (*Hugging him*): Joey, you couldn't be bad if you tried!

JOEY: But then — (*His face falls.*) — you have a boy for president.

MISS R.: No, Joey. You've got to be president. I'm positive that coat will never fit anyone but you!

JOEY: Oh, Teacher, then I say the wonderful words!

MISS R.: And, Joey, if you should gain a pound or two it won't hurt — though I'll never be able to let the coat out now it's sewed up! (JOEY *giggles happily.* MR. A. *sticks his head in from the store.* MRS. A. *sticks her head in from the kitchen. They stare at* JOEY. *He sees them.*)

JOEY (*He gets to his knees on the couch*): Oh Papa — Mama — (*They run in to him.*) I shall make the wonderful speech in that big coat with the tails — the president's — the Lincoln Coat!

THE END

THE QUEEN WITH THE BROKEN HEART

by Catherine Urban

Characters

QUEEN OF HEARTS
KING OF HEARTS
LADY-IN-WAITING
PAGE
FAIRY GODMOTHER
SPRING

SETTING: *The palace.*

AT RISE: *The* QUEEN *sits near a table on which is a small plant. She is knitting and now and then glances at the* KING *whc sits slumped down in an easy chair, his feet on a hassock, fast asleep. A pile of large books is on the floor beside him. In the rear, the* PAGE *and* LADY-IN-WAITING *whisper together and sadly shake their heads. The* QUEEN *glances at the* KING, *sniffs and, putting down her knitting, takes up a handkerchief and sobs loudly into it.*

LADY-IN-WAITING (*Rushing forward*): Oh, my Queen, do not weep!

PAGE (*Also forward*): My dear mistress, do not distress yourself!

LADY-IN-WAITING (*As the* QUEEN *sobs louder*): My dear, you will ruin your beautiful eyes!

QUEEN (*Sniffs*): And of what good are beautiful eyes, if no one ever looks into them?

LADY-IN-WAITING (*Glancing at the* KING): The lazy, thoughtless brute!

PAGE: But my King is worn out. (LADY-IN-WAITING *sniffs.*)

QUEEN (*Sobs*): He does not love me any more! My heart is broken!

PAGE: Oh, I am sure, my dear Queen .

LADY-IN-WAITING (*About to prod* KING): I'll wake up the lazy thing!

PAGE (*Hurriedly*): Oh, no! No! You know how angry he becomes if he is disturbed. And he has a lot on his mind! He needs his rest! (*The* QUEEN *sobs.*)

LADY-IN-WAITING: Rubbish! He has nothing on his mind! These books! (*Kicks at them*) They are nothing but an excuse! He only pretends that he is busy so he may tire sooner and sleep longer.

PAGE: He is worn out with affairs of state!

LADY-IN-WAITING: Affairs of state! What affairs of state have we had? We are at peace! The people are busy and prosperous! The crops are good! But the better things are, the lazier the King has become! Why, we haven't had a visiting ambassador for months! We haven't had a party for over a year!

QUEEN (*Sobs as she touches the plant*): And my King hasn't given me a gift for ages and ages! This little plant is the last thing he gave me. (*Sighs. Gets up and picks up the plant.*) I will go back to my old home! I will take this plant and cherish it for the rest of my days, for it will remind me of happy, happy days when my King loved me! (*Sobs*)

LADY-IN-WAITING: Oh, my Queen, do not even think of leaving us!

PAGE: The people worship you!

LADY-IN-WAITING: We all love you!

QUEEN (*Glancing at the* KING *and sighing*): My King does not love me! He has forgotten that I exist! Oh, if he would only notice me once more! We were so happy when we were first married! But, now, I must go . . .

PAGE: Oh, please, your majesty, do not go! (*Glances about worriedly*) We must think of something!

LADY-IN-WAITING: He needs a good jolt!

QUEEN: If I go, perhaps . . . he . . . will miss me a little!

PAGE: But the people will be angry! They love you! We must do something! We must wake him up and make him realize . . .

QUEEN: No, love must come from the heart . . .

LADY-IN-WAITING: Your fairy godmother! She could help you!

QUEEN: My fairy godmother!

LADY-IN-WAITING: Of course, don't you remember? Rub your locket and she will come!

QUEEN: My locket! I had forgotten! (*Picks up the heart-shaped locket that hangs about her neck and rubs it. The* FAIRY GODMOTHER *enters.*)

FAIRY GODMOTHER: Well! You finally had sense enough to call me! I've been wondering how long you would put up with this situation!

QUEEN: You mean you can help me? You can make my King love me again?

FAIRY GODMOTHER: He still loves you.

QUEEN: But he can't! He never says so! It has been months since he has paid me the slightest notice . . . much less the lovely compliments he used to.

FAIRY GODMOTHER: He's just in a rut.

QUEEN: But I can't go on this way! It's so lonely! I don't believe he loves me!

FAIRY GODMOTHER: Oh, you women! You always have to be shown!

QUEEN (*Thoughtfully*): Yes, it is true . . . one likes to be told now and then.

LADY-IN-WAITING: But what can we do? How can we make the King realize the Queen is unhappy?

FAIRY GODMOTHER: He needs a dash of spring in his blood to wake him up!

PAGE: But this is February!

FAIRY GODMOTHER: I will call Spring! She will bring her magic formula! (*Waves her wand*) Come, Spring! Come from your sleep! (SPRING *enters sleepily, carrying flowery handbag.*)

SPRING: Oh, why did you call me? I was having such a wonderful dream. (*Rubs her eyes sleepily.*)

FAIRY GODMOTHER: I am sorry to disturb you, but the King needs a dose of your magic formula. He is growing old before his time.

SPRING: I have heard tell that he no longer walks in the Garden of Youth.

FAIRY GODMOTHER: Please give him your magic potion.

QUEEN: Oh, Spring, give him back a youthful heart!

SPRING (*Yawning*): All right, but I do think you could have waited. (*Rises, takes flask and spoon from handbag, and pretends to give* KING *spoonful.*) That should do it. The formula is made of essence of honeysuckle, the lilt of a nightingale's song, and a breath of a soft breeze.

QUEEN: Oh, thank you! Thank you! I know how wonderful your magic is, for each year when you come to us, we all feel happy and gay.

SPRING (*Yawns*): Thank you. I only hope that I can get back to sleep again.

FAIRY GODMOTHER: Of course you can. (*Waves her wand*) I have a special power from the Sandman for that! You had better go quickly or you will fall asleep here. Page, help Spring to her coach. (PAGE *bows and exits with* SPRING.)

QUEEN (*Glancing at the* KING, *who stretches*): Oh, he is awakening!

KING: Darling Queen, where have you been for such a long time?

QUEEN: Oh, my King, I have been right here.

KING (*Getting to his feet and bowing over her hand*): You are so beautiful, my beloved!

LADY-IN-WAITING: Oh, it is working! It is working! (PAGE *enters and smiles in delight.*)

FAIRY GODMOTHER: Of course. My magic never fails!

KING: Darling, you have been such a wonderful wife to me. Such a good queen to my people . . . for a long time I have thought to give you a present. (*Glances about worriedly.*)

QUEEN: Oh, King, that is not necessary . . . as long as you tell me you love me!

KING: I love you dearly, but I want to give you something too . . . just some little thing to show I think of you.

FAIRY GODMOTHER: Everyone needs a little word now and then from friends and loved ones. (*Waves her wand over box and pulls off cover revealing a gaily decorated Valentine Box.*) Here, O King, are small messages of love not only for your Queen but for all your people as well. For they, too, need to know that their King remembers them. (*All rush to the box and remove lid.*)

QUEEN: It is full of messages and cards!

LADY-IN-WAITING: How lovely they are!

KING: I thank you very much. (*Bows low to* FAIRY GODMOTHER.)

QUEEN: And I thank you, so very, very much. Here . . . (*Hands the* FAIRY GODMOTHER *the plant*) I want you to have this. Take it to remember how very, very happy you have made me! (*Kisses the* FAIRY GODMOTHER *who bows and smiles.*)

PAGE (*Who has been running his hands through the Valentines*): But come, let us give these out! (*All nod and begin distributing the Valentines.*)

THE END

WHAT HAPPENED TO THE CAKES

by Alice Very

Characters

PUSSY CAT
DAME TROT
MOTHER HUBBARD
DOG
BO-PEEP
LAMB
MICE
CHILDREN

SCENE: *A kitchen.*

PUSSY CAT:
Tomorrow it is St. Valentine's day,
All in the morning time,
It's time to make
A pretty cake
To please your valentine.

DAME TROT:
Little Bo-Peep
Is fast asleep,
Her lambs are all in bed,
So I shall bake and make a cake,
Some cookies and some bread.

MOTHER HUBBARD:
My cupboard's not bare,
There's plenty to spare,
My dogs have all been fed,
So I'll help you bake
And make a cake,
Some cookies and some bread.

DAME TROT:
Stand on your legs
And beat four eggs.

MOTHER HUBBARD:
Two cups of sugar
And beat hugger-mugger.
DAME TROT:
Two cups of butter,
Cut with a cutter.
MOTHER HUBBARD:
Four cups of flour
And bake half an hour.
(DAME TROT *and* MOTHER HUBBARD *mix cakes as they speak and put them in oven.*)
DAME TROT (*Dancing*):
Now I'll hop
And then I'll run
Until the cakes are nicely done.
MOTHER HUBBARD (*Yawning*):
While they bake, a nap I'll take.
Call me when it's time to wake.
(*Exit.*)
DAME TROT:
Now she's gone
I must make haste.
I mean to have a little taste.
(*Takes cake from the oven and bites piece.*)
PUSSY CAT:
Meoow, meoow!
Give me some, too.
I like cake as well as you.
DAME TROT:
A little bite
Will be all right,
I'm sure it will not hurt a mite.
(*Gives cake.*)
What was that?
Come, Pussy Cat.
We'd best be getting out of sight.
(*Exit.*)
MOTHER HUBBARD (*Enters, goes to oven, opens door and looks in*):
Come, come,

The cakes are done.
Now it's time to have some fun.
How good they look!
How nice they smell!
Shall I try them?
Might as well.
(*Takes cakes out and bites one. Enter* DOG.)

DOG:
Boo, woo!
I want some, too,
Just a little bite will do.

MOTHER HUBBARD:
Yes, indeedy,
(*Gives cake.*)
Don't be greedy.
Now run out, and make it speedy.
(*Exit* DOG.)
Just so—
(*Arranging cakes.*)
Hardly show—
Someone's coming—I must go!
(*Exit.*)

BO-PEEP:
Little Bo-Peep
Was fast asleep
When something made her wake.

I can tell very well
By the lovely smell
That something must be cake.
(*Bites cake.*)

My teeth are so small
They don't show at all.
They'll think where it's bitten
'Twas done by a kitten.

LAMB: (*Entering*):
Baa, baa,
Here I am.
I am Mary's little lamb.

I am hungry,
So I bleat,
I want something good to eat.

BO-PEEP:
Come right here,
Lambie, dear.
You shall have some, never fear.
(*Feeds* LAMB.)
Now you're fed;
Go to bed.
Morning time is drawing near.
(*Exit. Enter* MICE.)

FIRST MOUSE:
Squeak, squeak!
Let me peek.
Tell me if you hear a creak.

SECOND MOUSE:
Yum, yum,
I want some.
Give me just a tiny crumb.

FIRST MOUSE:
Crunch, crunch,
Time for lunch,
How our mousie teeth can munch!
(MICE *nibble. A bark is heard off-stage.*)

SECOND MOUSE:
Hush, hark!
There's a bark
Morning scares away the dark.
(MICE *run out. Enter* DAME TROT, MOTHER HUBBARD, PUSSY CAT.)

DAME TROT:
Dear, dear!
(*Looking at cakes.*)
What have we here?
Something's happened, very queer.

MOTHER HUBBARD:
My, my!
What do I spy?
Someone ate the cakes, I fear.

DAME TROT:
They must have had to eat and run.
There's *just one* bite in every one.
(*Holding up bitten cake.*)

PUSSY CAT:
Just give the cakes to me to bite.
I'll show you how to make them right.

MOTHER HUBBARD:
Well, we'll let you try it, kitty,
But be sure you make them pretty.
(PUSSY CAT *nibbles cake and holds up a heart-shaped one.*)

PUSSY CAT:
Now you see that I am smart.
I've made each cake a pretty heart.

SONG (*Offstage*):
Good morning, it is St. Valentine's day,
All in the morning time,
And I a maid at your window
To be your Valentine.
(*Enter* LITTLE BO-PEEP, *followed by* LAMBS, DOGS, CHILDREN.)

PUSSY CAT:
Oh, little Bo-Peep
And all your sheep
And all your playmates too,
Come in and see the valentines
That we have made for you.

Now, children, dear,
It's very clear
That this must be a sign,
The cakes and tarts
Were turned to hearts
By good St. Valentine.
(*All hold up hearts.*)

THE END

A GUIDE FOR GEORGE WASHINGTON

by Lindsey Barbee

Characters

GEORGE WASHINGTON
THE CAPTAIN
JOHN WINCHESTER
MRS. WINCHESTER
ELIZABETH WINCHESTER
MARIA, *the maid*
THE STRANGER

SCENE 1

SETTING: *The bank of the Delaware River.*

AT RISE: *Two soldiers, swathed in heavy cloaks, are standing — evidently on a slight eminence — as a third soldier approaches them and climbs a bit laboriously before he reaches their level. A lantern, swinging from his hand, reveals his weather-beaten face and throws its rays upon a stalwart, eager-eyed youth and upon the commanding figure of the General of the continental forces—*GEORGE WASHINGTON. *The youth,* JOHN WINCHESTER, *catches the arm of the newcomer and bends excitedly toward him.*

JOHN:
What think you, Captain, of the risk tonight —
The river and the way the wind has turned —
The ice — what chance have we to venture?
How long before we dare a crossing? (*As the* CAPTAIN *makes a gesture of impatience.*) Wait!
You must know that tonight we win or lose.

CAPTAIN:
Have patience, John, have patience till I speak.
The fire of youth is oft at war with reason
And knows not prudence nor the wiser course

That bids one watch and wait and counsel. (*Turns.*)
My General, we must not cross tonight.

WASHINGTON:
You are quite sure?

CAPTAIN:
Quite sure, for even now
The river clogs with ice, the air is sharp,
The very wind is hostile to our venture.

WASHINGTON:
But still, in some strange way, it comes to me
That we must cross — tonight — if we would win.

CAPTAIN:
My General, it is not courage fails us
Nor keen desire; the elements themselves
Make it impossible.

WASHINGTON:
Impossible?
We know not such a word.

CAPTAIN:
Nay, but the truth
Has come to us in hard and bitter ways.
At Trenton and at Bordentown there stand
The Hessian and the British troops. Your plan
To send a force across the Delaware,
To sever any union of the two
Has come to naught. We cannot cope with storms.

WASHINGTON:
There also was a third phase to my plan.
Have you forgotten? I, with my own men,
Had thought to cross the Delaware — to creep
Upon the Hessian troops at Trenton.

CAPTAIN:
True,
You were to lead the main attack; but now
The icy storms have played a tragic part
In thwarting our designs. (*Pauses.*) We cannot cross.

WASHINGTON:
But still I say — we cross ere dawn.

CAPTAIN:
My General!

WASHINGTON:
We cross ere dawn — for now at heart I feel
It is the Hand of God that points the way.
CAPTAIN:
The river is not open for our men.
WASHINGTON:
Then we must make it so. It can be done.
CAPTAIN:
Then be *your* wish *my* wish. (WASHINGTON *grasps his hand.*)
It can be done.
JOHN:
Perhaps it is our very chance. Tonight
Is Christmas night. The Britishers forget
There is a war. The Hessian troops are gay
And careless. Oh, it is our chance to win!
WASHINGTON:
Hold fast that faith, my boy, for only faith
Can work the miracle we sorely need.
The British hold the towns. Their leader waits
The freezing of the Delaware before
He pushes on to Philadelphia.
Our loyal colonists have heavy hearts.
The enemy seems slowly closing in.
It is a crisis. For without the spur
Of victory we hold a losing cause.
CAPTAIN:
When do we cross?
WASHINGTON:
At three o'clock. 'Tis then
They will be taken unaware. By four
We should effect a landing.
CAPTAIN:
Save for storms —
For ice — for wind. Somehow, my General,
I fear the elements. And should we land —
WASHINGTON:
And land we shall.
CAPTAIN:
How can we know the way?
The point of vantage? And the crucial time
To strike?

JOHN:

Through me. I beg of you, send me.
For Trenton is my home — I know each inch
Of ground. I can be stealthy, too, and wise;
And I can lead you to the Hessian camp.
Oh, grant me this to do!

CAPTAIN:

(*Aside to* WASHINGTON.) The boy is young.
He has not yet been tested.

JOHN:

Grant me this.
It is my opportunity to serve.

CAPTAIN:

But there are older, wiser men who know
The devious ways of strategy.

JOHN:

Send me.
I will succeed. It is my chance — my chance.

WASHINGTON:

Your chance. Why not, my lad? 'Tis such as you
That must infuse new zeal into our hearts. (*Pauses.*)
Accept the trust I give you. Be our guide
When we shall reach the shore.

JOHN:

I shall be there.

WASHINGTON:

Above — nine miles — the ferry —

JOHN:

Yes, I know.
And even now the time is short. Farewell.
Across the river — four o'clock — we meet. (*Rushes off. For a moment there is silence. Then the* GENERAL *lays his hand upon the shoulder of the* CAPTAIN.)

WASHINGTON:

You doubt the wisdom of my choice, good friend,
But in a time of weakness and of doubt
We need the fearless spirit of adventure,
The faith that brooks no failure — and the youth
That never falters, never faints and never fears.

CAPTAIN:
To you is given the vision, General.
I trust your word as always.
WASHINGTON:
Then, my friend,
We work together on this Christmas night. (*Pauses.*)
Christmas night! The time of peace, good will.
How can we plan for war — perhaps, for death?
How is the holy season marred — and yet —
Tonight we work toward that same peace
The Christ Child sought. Our lives we consecrate
To liberty, to justice and to right.
CAPTAIN:
The ice — the snow — if there could only be
A sign that they would hinder not.
WASHINGTON:
A sign?
Perhaps this Christmas night the sign will come.
CAPTAIN:
A sign will come? I do not understand.
WASHINGTON:
Did you not wish that there would be a sign?
I only say — perhaps the sign will come.
CAPTAIN:
Signs herald miracles, 'tis said.
WASHINGTON:
Why not?
It is the very night for miracles. (*Pauses.*)
The air is very still. The wind has ceased.
Beyond us is the banner — and its folds
Are drooping. But a little time ago
The wind blew toward us. Had we crossed just then
We should have battled hard. But now you see
There is no wind.
CAPTAIN:
(*In a whisper.*) My General — you mean —
WASHINGTON:
That if another wind should rise and blow
Our banner outward, we should know the sign
As one that bids us godspeed on our mission.
We'll watch and wait and pray the sign will come.

CAPTAIN:
The air is still and cold. There is no sound —
The very silence is oppressive. See!
The banner hangs as lifeless as before.

WASHINGTON:
Look close. The banner moves. Can you not see
That something is astir? That something blows —
And blows it outward — *outward?* 'Tis the sign.

CAPTAIN:
The sign, my General. My faith returns.

WASHINGTON:
And now, tonight, we cross the Delaware!

CURTAIN

* * *

SCENE 2

SETTING: *A room in the Winchester home.*

AT RISE: *At a curtained window,* ELIZABETH *is standing, looking out into the night.* MRS. WINCHESTER *enters from right, a long, full cape covering her formal gown.* ELIZABETH *turns from the window.*

MRS. WINCHESTER:
What foolishness is this, Elizabeth?
Have you forgotten that our English friends
Are celebrating Christmas with a ball?

ELIZABETH:
I've not forgotten, Mother.

MRS. WINCHESTER:
Then I ask
Why you have failed to be in readiness.

ELIZABETH:
Because I do not care to go; because

I have no interest in the gayeties
Of those who are our enemies.

MRS. WINCHESTER:

How dare
You speak so of the British when you know
That hearts and hands are pledged to good King George.

ELIZABETH:

Not *my* heart, not *my* hand. I choose to pledge
To that dear land I love — America.

MRS. WINCHESTER:

You still are wayward, stubborn. 'Tis because
Your foolish brother —

ELIZABETH:

Hush! I shall not hear
One word against him. He has had the faith,
The courage to be true to what is right.

MRS. WINCHESTER:

And he has forfeited his heritage.

ELIZABETH:

That is your cruelty to him. You choose
The King and not your son. (*Suddenly.*) I should not speak
So boldly to you, Mother.

MRS. WINCHESTER:

You must learn
That older heads are wiser — that the band
Of churlish wits who prate of liberty
Must now be kept subservient to the King.

ELIZABETH:

The patriot cause is mine.

MRS. WINCHESTER:

Why, even now
The English close upon the colonists. (*Impatiently.*)
Why do I tarry thus? I shall expect
You later at the ball, Elizabeth.
The carriage will return.

ELIZABETH:

I shall not go.

MRS. WINCHESTER:

(*Firmly.*) I shall expect you.

(*She goes out at right and a frightened little* MAID *appears from back.*)

MAID:

Oh, Miss Betty — I —

ELIZABETH:

What is it? What has happened?

MAID:

Master John
Is waiting for you — there. (*Points to back as* JOHN *enters.*)

ELIZABETH:

Oh, John — dear John.
How can you be so reckless! All around
Are Tory soldiers.

JOHN:

Betty, I am here
Upon a secret mission — there is time
For just a word.

ELIZABETH:

Maria, stand outside —
Keep guard. (MAID *goes out at back.*)
Speak quickly, for I am afraid.

JOHN:

At three o'clock our General will cross
The Delaware.

ELIZABETH:

Impossible! The snow —

JOHN:

But on this Christmas night, the Hessian troops
Are off their guard. The British, too, forget
There is a war. They hold high carnival.
And if we force a crossing — victory
Is ours.

ELIZABETH:

(*Excitedly.*) And courage, too, will be renewed.

JOHN:

I am the trusted messenger who learns
The proper place for an attack; and I
Will 'wait them at the ferry nine miles south
To lead them to the Hessians. Even now
My horse is hidden by the evergreens.
By four o'clock I reach the Delaware
And lead them by the path we know so well.

(*The* MAID *appears.*)

MAID:
I saw two soldiers passing.

ELIZABETH:
(*To John.*) Then be gone —
No moment for farewell. (JOHN *hurries off.*) Maria, go
To watch — to listen — and to bring me word. (MAID *goes out.*).
(*To herself.*) The ferry — nine miles south—at four o'clock —
(*There is a pistol shot. The* MAID *rushes in.*)

MAID:
The Tory soldiers saw him and they fired —
They took him prisoner —

ELIZABETH:
Tonight — tonight —
When Washington will cross the Delaware!

CURTAIN

* * *

SCENE 3

AT RISE: *Against a snowy background with sparkling evergreen trees,* WASHINGTON *stands with his faithful* CAPTAIN *by his side.*

CAPTAIN:
There is no sign of Winchester. The men
Are restless — and they wish to march ahead
Toward Trenton. You will see, my General.
That Winchester has failed us, left us here
To make our way as best we can.

WASHINGTON:
Not failed,
Not faltered, Captain, I am sure of that —
But fallen into evil hands.

CAPTAIN:

If true
That he is intercepted, we surmise
That our proposed attack is known, that we
Have little chance of pressing farther on.
The capture of a spy means watchful eyes
Upon our movements; and I fear that we
Must now expect to find the troops prepared
For quick resistance.

WASHINGTON:

Still my faith is strong
In ultimate success. And we shall march
To Trenton.

CAPTAIN:

Knowing not the route that leads
Directly to the Hessians?

WASHINGTON:

We shall make
Our own route. Providence will lead the way.

CAPTAIN:

Then I shall — (*He breaks off abruptly and gazes off stage.*)
Wait! Someone has ridden up —
'Tis Winchester — no, 'tis a stranger. See —
He makes his way to us.
(*A* STRANGER *enters, cap pulled low on his forehead, long cape around him, high riding boots.*)
What is it, sir?

STRANGER:

My message is for General Washington.

WASHINGTON:

And I am Washington. What word have you
For me? Be brief, I beg, for time is short.

STRANGER:

I come to you from your own messenger,
John Winchester.

WASHINGTON:

And why has he transferred
His mantle to your shoulders?

STRANGER:

He has been
Imprisoned by the British. I have come

To lead you to the Hessians by the path
He chose — the shortest, truest path.

WASHINGTON:

And how
Did you know of this purpose? Messengers
Are not supposed to whisper of their tasks.

STRANGER:

Was it not better that he give his task
To someone else than that you should be left
Without a leader?

WASHINGTON:

Who are you, my lad?

STRANGER:

John's friend and confidant — *your* loyal friend,
My General. I only ask that you
Believe my tale, trust John, and realize
That my great happiness is serving you.

CAPTAIN:

(*Aside to* WASHINGTON.) Someway this story does not ring as true
As I would have it.

WASHINGTON:

Yet I trust this youth
And see in him the answer to our prayer
For guidance.

CAPTAIN:

Yet, if he should be a spy
From British forces —

STRANGER:

I am not a spy.
I come direct from your own messenger.
There is no time to tell you how and why.
The morning soon will break. Nine miles there are
To follow. And the British do not know
Of this, our undertaking. Take no time
To question, but believe me when I say
That I can guide you to the Hessian camp.

(*For a moment there is silence.*)

CAPTAIN:
I trust your word — but should you play us false —
STRANGER:
I shall not play you false.
WASHINGTON:
Then, lead us, lad!

CURTAIN

* * *

SCENE 4

SETTING: *A small room, plainly and sparsely furnished. At a table sits* WASHINGTON *while the* CAPTAIN *stands near by.*

CAPTAIN:
A thousand prisoners, my General —
And forty killed and wounded.
WASHINGTON:
While our loss?
CAPTAIN:
Two killed, three wounded.
WASHINGTON:
Every victory
Must have its toll of victims. And our men —
What spirit have they?
CAPTAIN:
Victory does much
To change the outlook and to cheer the heart.
This morning they could face the British force
In its entirety and never flinch.
Success means much, and now our patriot cause
Has passed its very crisis. 'Tis your faith
That brought us through the darkest, drearest days.
(JOHN *appears at the door. His head is bandaged and his arm is in a sling. He crosses to* WASHINGTON *and salutes.*)

JOHN:
I cannot find the words to plead my cause;
I cannot ask that you will ever trust
Another mission to me. I have failed —
Failed when I should have won. Is it too much
To ask for clemency?

WASHINGTON:
Are we not here?
Have we not won our victory? Success
Has crowned our venture.

JOHN:
But this same success
I had no part in gaining. May I speak,
If not to clear myself to tell you why
I failed to meet you at the ferry?

WASHINGTON:
Speak, my boy.

JOHN:
In Trenton live my people, as you know.
They all are Tories save Elizabeth,
My sister, who is very dear to me.
When I declared the patriot cause, she, too,
Upheld me, for we felt alike in this —
A free and independent country. Now
My family has cast me off; and she
Has been forbidden to receive me, though
At times we have our stolen interviews.

CAPTAIN:
(*Impatiently.*) Come — come — the time is passing. We must know.

JOHN:
(*Motioning for silence.*) Tonight when I had seen the Hessian camp —
Had watched their carelessness — their revelry —
I knew that now it was the time to strike.
I passed my home. I saw my sister's maid —
She let me in to see Elizabeth.

CAPTAIN:
Treachery! You ran the risk of capture.

WASHINGTON:
Quiet, Captain, for this is no treachery.

JOHN: I had but left the house. Two officers
Who happened to be passing shot at me
And kept me with them. It is only now
I have escaped their watchfulness.

WASHINGTON

And still

You played your part; you sent the messenger
Who guided us so skillfully, who knew
So well the path to follow. And before
We realized, he slipped away without
Our thanks. If you will tell his name, we shall
Express our gratitude.

JOHN:

A messenger?

WASHINGTON:

Your messenger.

JOHN:

I sent no messenger.

WASHINGTON:

Then who came to us seemingly from you?

JOHN: I am as puzzled as yourselves. I sent no one.

CAPTAIN:

And told no one your secret mission?

JOHN:

No.

CAPTAIN:

Think well and hard. For this same messenger
Knew all our plans, and knew that you, our guide,
Was wounded, could not come. You told no one?

JOHN:

I told no one — (*Suddenly*) save — save —

CAPTAIN:

Save whom?

JOHN:

Elizabeth.

(*At the door appears a smiling maiden* — ELIZABETH — *with cheeks like roses.*)

ELIZABETH:

(*Curtseying.*) Your servant, General, answering to her name,
But much more proud to call herself a guide,
A leader of the loyal patriot band
That marched this morning into Trenton.

JOHN:

You?

ELIZABETH:

Why not? I knew your mission, knew that you
Were captured. Was it not my very chance
To aid the cause I love, uphold and cherish?
Your horse was waiting, and I hurried off,
A trifle late, dear General, but I did my best
And rode my fastest. And I had the joy
Of being for a little while a part
Of Washington's own army.

JOHN:

Betty, dear,
'Twas you who did my part, who took the word.

ELIZABETH:

'Twas I indeed — and proud, so proud to do it. (*Crosses to* WASHINGTON.)
You will not blame John for such recklessness,
Such thoughtlessness in risking peril when
He should have thought alone of country's need.

WASHINGTON:

Since I have known the guide, have proved his worth
I grant him any favor. And since I
Have seen the maid, I understand the risk.

ELIZABETH:

I thank you — for this Christmas gift to me.
Our gift to you is our united love
And loyalty and service. (*Suddenly.*) Oh, how fair
The day has grown — how dazzling is the sun!

WASHINGTON:

How happy are our hearts — for we forget
The darkness and the peril.

ELIZABETH:

Evermore
We shall remember that dear Christmas night
When Washington dared cross the Delaware.

THE END

DAVID AND THE SECOND LAFAYETTE

by Lavinia R. Davis

Characters

DAVID COHEN
"FATTY" BARNES
BILLY GOODHUE
MARY WENTWORTH
PATRICIA O'BRIEN
ANGELO GIOVANNI
PETER PERRY
HUGH COURT
} *pupils in the school*

OTHER BOYS AND GIRLS
JEAN DU PRE, *a French boy, new to the school*
MISS FARNSBEE, *a schoolteacher*
MR. DOOLITTLE, *headmaster*
GRANDPAPA COHEN, *an old Hebrew scholar and grandfather of David*
MARQUIS DE LAFAYETTE

SCENE 1

TIME: *The end of study period.*

SETTING: *A typical American schoolroom.*

AT RISE: MARY WENTWORTH *and* DAVID COHEN *are the only ones really studying.* MISS FARNSBEE *is unsuccessfully trying to keep order.* "FATTY" BARNES *and* BILLY GOODHUE *are having a good time making faces.* PATSY O'BRIEN *is passing a note to* ANGELO *who replies by throwing a spit ball. One of the children tries to pass a note to* DAVID *who is so deep in his work that he doesn't even notice.* HUGH COURT *shrugs his shoulders and grins at* BILLY. *It is clear that the class knows its* DAVID. *They accept him as a real student and a good sport. They may make fun of him a little, but on the whole are very fond of him.*

MISS FARNSBEE: Billy! Patsy. Francis, stop that at once!
PUPILS: Yes, Miss Farnsbee.

MISS FARNSBEE: Children. Children! I cannot have such behavior. (*There is a sharp knock on the door. The attention of the class, except for* DAVID *and* MARY *is suddenly riveted on that door.*) Come in. (MR. DOOLITTLE, *accompanied by a tall, dark French boy dressed in typical French black school smock and looking very out of place, comes in. The class, on seeing* MR. DOOLITTLE, *snap to their feet. For a moment* DAVID *is left behind, but at last with a start he puts down his book and rises.*)

MR. DOOLITTLE: Be seated, children. Miss Farnsbee, this is Jean Du Pre whom you have been expecting. I am sure he will be a pleasant addition to your group.

MISS FARNSBEE: How do you do, Jean? We are so glad you are going to be with us. (JEAN *makes a formal and rather exaggerated bow.* MISS FARNSBEE *goes to the door with* MR. DOOLITTLE, *both of them talking in low tones. The class is all eyes looking at* JEAN. *He hesitates, uncertain, and then bows to the class. That is the final stroke, and they all titter out loud.* JEAN, *hurt, waits until he is sure that* MR. DOOLITTLE *and* MISS FARNSBEE *are not looking and then sticks out his tongue at the class.* MISS FARNSBEE *returns as door closes on* MR. DOOLITTLE.) Children, I am sure we are all very glad that Jean du Pre has come to join us. I think class four stands in need of seeing some fine old-world manners.

BILLY (*Aside to* FATTY): Fine old-world tongue-sticking!

MISS FARNSBEE (*Gives* JEAN *some books and shows him to a seat near* MARY WENTWORTH): I think you will be happy here, Jean. Mary is one of our honor students.

JEAN (*With another bow*): Of a certainty, Mademoiselle. (*He sits down without a word to* MARY.)

MISS FARNSBEE (*Going back to desk*): Since it is such a rainy day you will have your recess period here. You may do whatever you like for the first half and then I suggest you work on the school play. We have a real rehearsal tomorrow you know.

PUPILS: Yes, Miss Farnsbee. All right, Miss Farnsbee. We certainly will. (*She goes out and a good-natured pandemonium breaks out. Someone plays a mouth organ.* BILLY *and* FATTY *start a game of ball.*)

FATTY: Come on, Jean. Play ball with us. (*He throws the ball which* JEAN *ducks in a very sissified manner as though afraid of being hurt.*)

JEAN (*Who speaks with a very marked accent*): Why is it you Americans always play ze ball?

HUGH: Well, don't you play in France?

JEAN (*Contemptuously*): Certainly no! In France, one goes to school to study, not to play.

HUGH (*Rolling the ball over* DAVID'S *book.* DAVID *at last looks up grinning.* DAVID, *who has been studying up to this moment, retrieves the ball and throws it back to* HUGH. *This little action is typical of* DAVID'S *good-natured poise.*): Well, old David here studies, but he plays ball. Catch, Davy.

DAVID (*Catching ball and throwing it to* BILLY): Here you are, Bill.

BILLY (*Throwing it to* ANGELO): Coming, Angelo. (ANGELO *misses and the ball rolls near* JEAN'S *feet. He gives it a kick into a far corner.*)

BOYS (*Angrily*): Say, what's the big idea? You don't have to spoil other people's fun do you?

DAVID (*Soothingly*): Say listen, fellows, how about our getting going on rehearsing the play. We've still got a lot to do.

BOYS: O.K., Davy. Right you are.

FATTY: Come on, Bill, and help me fix up the crossing-the-Delaware boat out of these chairs. (CHILDREN *except for* JEAN *divide into two groups. Most of them off center and around* FATTY *begin making boat out of school chairs.* DAVID *and* HUGH COURT *in center take a few properties out of costume box and strike attitudes as they begin declaiming lines to one another.*)

DAVID (*In his role as* HAYM SALOMON): Good morning, Your Excellency. And how are General Washington's gallant troops this winter's day?

HUGH (*In his role as* GENERAL WASHINGTON): Strong in spirit, Mr. Salomon. Stout of heart. But perishing from the cold and lack of food.

DAVID: Bravely said, Your Excellency. To help such soldiers is a patriot's greatest privilege. (*He reaches into his pocket for some play money and then as he gets it out, suddenly drops his role and becomes himself again.*) Golly I'm glad we're doing this play.

HUGH: Me too. It's swell fun wearing a sword.

DAVID (*Half to himself*): And to make history come alive. To make people see that those men at Valley Forge were really cold and hungry. That Washington had troubles like any other leader. That Haym Salomon was only an ordinary Jew who loved his country. (*Growing suddenly confidential.*) You know, Hughie, that's why it's so grand for me to have this part. To act out the part of another Jew who really served his country.

HUGH: Salomon sure did. Miss Farnsbee said the Continental Army couldn't have gotten through without his dough. You'll have fun swishing around with all that fake money.

DAVID (*Half in a dream again*): And to make people see — to understand — (*He is interrupted by a terrific crash at stage left. The boys and girls had just gotten the boat finished.* FATTY *reached up to rig up a sheet for a sail when* JEAN *kicked the bottom of the boat from under him, ruining the boat and sending* FATTY *sprawling.*)

MARY: Oh, Jean, how could you?

JEAN (*Giving* FATTY *a pinch as he struggles to get up*): It was not my boat was it? They did not ask me to help.

FATTY (*Squaring off for a fight*): Put up your mitts, Jean du Pre! (*They start to fight and* JEAN *suddenly kicks.*)

CHILDREN: Say, he's kicking. No fair. (DAVID *and* HUGH *try to separate them.*)

DAVID: Oh stop it both of you. Please do!

PATSY O'BRIEN: Cheese it! Here comes teacher! (MISS FARNSBEE *enters and peace descends on the class.*)

MISS FARNSBEE: Well, children, I hope you got on with your rehearsal.

CHILDREN: Yes, Miss Farnsbee. Yes, Miss Farnsbee.

FATTY (*Aside to* JEAN): Just you wait until after school — you — you — FROG! (JEAN *looks terrified but says nothing.*)

MISS FARNSBEE: Mental arithmetic now, children. No books, please. (*Desks are cleared with a clatter and children sit up straight at desks.*) Peter, how much is 8 times 9?

PETER: 72.

MISS FARNSBEE: Right. Billy, how much is 5 plus 72 plus 12?

BILLY: Well — er — let's see 5 plus 72 —

JEAN (*Raising his hand*): Mademoiselle!

MISS FARNSBEE: All right, Jean.

JEAN: 89 (*He sits down with a smug look and another little bow.*)

MISS FARNSBEE: That's correct. Very good, Jean. I'm sure you are a good student.

BILLY (*Aside*): Teacher's pet! Teacher's pet!

MISS FARNSBEE: Order! Mary, how much is 79 plus 41 plus 6? (MARY *starts to answer when there is another knock on the door and* MR. DOOLITTLE *puts his head in.*)

MR. DOOLITTLE: Sorry to interrupt class work, Miss Farnsbee, but would you come out to show me those new records?

MISS FARNSBEE: Certainly. (*Turning to pupils.*) You will go on with your homework preparation for tomorrow. (*She goes out and as she shuts door pandemonium breaks loose as children turn back to* JEAN.)

FATTY: You can't get away with busting down my boat.

BILLY: And just because you're good at math, you can't kick when you're fighting either! (*As the boys, except* DAVID, *crowd menacingly around* JEAN, *he cowers back, facing the boys, his back to the wall.*)

DAVID: Aw now, fellows, take it easy. Maybe Jean didn't mean to fight crooked. My grandfather says that French wrestlers are taught to kick.

MARY: Don't gang up on him. Maybe he'll say he's sorry. Won't you, Jean?

JEAN (*Screaming*): No! (*Then as first boy touches him.*) Yes! Yes! But don't touch me! I apologize. There. (*He makes another one of his little bows.*) I apologize for breaking your stupid boat. I apologize for the kick. (*Boys, half-disappointed at missing a show-down, turn on heels and go over to window talking about* JEAN *in low tones while several of the girls giggle at their desks. Only* DAVID *and* MARY *are left with* JEAN.)

JEAN (*Scared and excited and furious*): Bêtes! Fools. They are savages. But truly savages!

MARY: But, Jean, you did start it you know.

JEAN (*Bitterly*): Start the staring, the laughing, the joking the minute I came into the room? I start that? Of a certainty, non. A thousand times non, non, non!

DAVID: It's true they did laugh but they didn't mean anything. They're a great gang really. It's just that you're new, and your clothes are a little different, and you know—

JEAN (*His voice rising as he sees boys are about to return toward him*): Know? Know! I know more than these babies with their balls and their boats.

DAVID: Sure. I bet you're a swell student. It's just you mustn't mind their fun — and you mustn't be scared.

JEAN (*Once more with his back to the wall and growing almost hysterical as boys come around him*): Oh, it is easy to talk. Very easy. But what about you and you and you? Have you never felt strange and lonely and sc-scared? (*He turns his face to the wall, breaking down completely as* MISS FARNSBEE *reënters the room — and the curtain falls.*)

* * *

SCENE 2

TIME: *Afternoon of the same day.*

SETTING: *The Cohens' comfortable book-lined living room.*

AT RISE: GRANDPA COHEN, *an old gentleman with thick glasses, is nodding over a big book as* DAVID *comes in and drops his school books on the table.*

GRANDPAPA COHEN: Hello, David boy. And how was the school today?

DAVID: Oh kind of so-so.

GRANDPAPA (*Looking over his glasses*): Not so good, hein? Did my David not know his lessons?

DAVID (*Turning over the pages of one of the books on the table*): Yes, I got on all right, Grandpapa. I'd have to, the way you explain things and all. (*He looks up smiling; it is clear that there is a strong bond of affection between these two.*) It's just there was a new boy. French chap, name of du Pre. The other boys pick on him, and he fights back *kicking*. It's all such a mess. They're decent, really, and so is he. It's just that they don't understand each other.

GRANDPAPA COHEN: Ach, misunderstanding. Davy boy, that is at the root of most troubles. Misunderstanding. (*He moves slowly over to the table center and pulls over some of the big books strewn on it.*) Even in the time of your play, the great Washington faced misunderstanding. Many, many times. (*He leafs through one of the books as he speaks, as though to bring proof.*)

DAVID (*Kindling with interest as he always does at mention of the play*): Oh, Grandpapa, did you find some more books about Haym Salomon and Washington? (*He looks eagerly at the book while* GRANDPAPA COHEN *stands beside him gently patting his shoulder and showing him a picture here, an especially interesting line of text, there.*)

GRANDPAPA: I always liked this picture of the Marquis de Lafayette. A brave soldier, a very gallant Frenchman.

DAVID: I wonder if he and Washington understood one another.

GRANDPAPA (*Chuckling*): I have often wondered too. The one a spoiled, idealistic young aristocrat; the other a fox-hunting squire from Virginia. Well, well, it is hard to tell now, Davy. (*He starts moving off stage right humming the "Lorelei."*) You help yourself to the books, Davy. They are good company for a youngster or an old man like Grandpapa. I am going off to take a little nap.

DAVID (*He settles down to the table his back to the audience as the light becomes faint*): All right, Grandpapa. Thanks a lot. (*He begins to read, but gradually he puts his arms on the table and is asleep. There is a slight rustling noise on stage left.* DAVID *sits up straight again*) Is that you, Grandpapa? (LAFAYETTE *enters at left. He is very suave and foppish in a military uniform. He is very young, very French and dandified and speaks with a cultivated accent. He is all polish and gayety, but underneath it all he has the shrewd, practical approach to life.*)

LAFAYETTE: I — a grandpapa? But that is to rire — how-do-you-say, to laugh, surely?

DAVID (*Rises startled*): Golly day! Wh — who are you? Wh — whom do you want?

LAFAYETTE: You, my young David.

DAVID (*Breathless and incredulous*): M — m-me? But who are you?

LAFAYETTE: Marie Joseph Paul Roch Yves Gilbert Motier, Marquis de Lafayette, and very much at your service.

DAVID: Lafayette! But he's been dead for ages.

LAFAYETTE (*With an impatient shrug*): Oh this dead business. When will people learn that ideas do not die? And people are their ideas!

DAVID: I — I — I'm sorry! But you did startle me. (LAFAYETTE *drops his gloves on the table and perches on the edge of it his sword swinging gayly.*)

LAFAYETTE: Ah, ma fois, that it is! I am forever to startle you solid Americans. Your good generale, my commandante, your Washington, how I startled him. (*He laughs, playing with his gloves, as though still amused at the memory.*)

DAVID (*Eagerly*): But you got on, didn't you? That is I mean you always understood each other?

LAFAYETTE: But most assuredly, no! And why should we? He was a seasoned soldier. A mature man. And I a boy little older than yourself. And when we first met what did I see? A plain man, a soldier, not much better clothed than his raggle-tailed troops. And he—(*The* MARQUIS *gets off table to show how he must have looked*) he saw a fop, a how-do-you-say, a macaroni! A little sugar soldier with a pretty sword. Your hard old Thomas Paine now, the one with all the Common Sense, who loathed an aristocrat and spat upon kings, he had words for it.

DAVID: But you and George Washington did get on! You fought together —

LAFAYETTE (*Suddenly serious*): Of a certainty, my son. We planned together, lead together, fought together — and why?

DAVID (*Fascinated out of all shyness*): Because you believed in freedom, in democracy.

LAFAYETTE: Oh la! la! la! Even in those days you young Americans talked the same way about de-mock-crrra-cee. But we got along, as you put it, your Generale George and I, because we had something to do! Because work must be done. Because there was work, we had to get along!

DAVID (*Struck by an idea that has not heretofore occurred to him*): You mean that when people have a job to do, something that they must get done together — (*Suddenly brightening*) Why, yes, of course. I see it. If they must work, there just isn't time to quarrel.

LAFAYETTE: Well said, my boy. (*He looks up startled as* GRANDPAPA COHEN *is heard off stage still whistling the "Lorelei"*) Ah, so our interview is over. It is time I say au revoir. (*He goes off left, moving very quietly, very lightly as* GRANDPAPA COHEN *comes on right and the lights go on strong.*)

GRANDPAPA: David, David, where are my glasses. I must have left them here.

DAVID (*Suddenly waking up*): Marquis Lafayette — Why, Grandpapa, it's — it's — you.

GRANDPAPA (*Still rummaging for his glasses*): Of course. Who should it be?

DAVID (*Yawning and rubbing his eyes*): I must have been asleep. I was just looking over this book and I had the most marvelous dream!

GRANDPAPA (*Suddenly finding his glasses on the table*): Ah, here they are!

DAVID: A wonderful dream!

GRANDPAPA (*For the first time really concentrates on* DAVID *and pats him affectionately*): Ah, David boy, to read, to think, to dream. Those are the pleasant things of life. But first one must work!

DAVID (*Rising slowly*): *Work!* That's just what he said, Grandpapa. That if people work together there is no time for quarrels.

CURTAIN

* * *

SCENE 3

TIME: *The next day at the end of the school period.*

SETTING: *The same as Scene* 1.

AT RISE: *About half the class is present including* DAVID. JEAN DU PRE *and some of the others are in another class room studying history.*)

MISS FARNSBEE (*Closing book*): Very well, that is all for today. You've all done splendidly. If you do as well in your play, it will be the best one the school has ever given.

DAVID (*Alert and eager*): I've got the parts right here, Miss Farnsbee.

MISS FARNSBEE: Good. You give them out, and you can start right in as soon as the others come down from history. You can begin by yourselves while I correct these papers. I'll be in the library if you need me.

DAVID: All right, Miss Farnsbee. (MISS FARNSBEE *goes out left. As soon as she goes, the children all start talking and threatening, still talking about what they'd like to do to* JEAN, *what a sissy he is, etc.* DAVID *busily gives out parts and then as he hears them talking about* JEAN *stands listening, a worried expression on his face.*) Now listen, fellows, he isn't so bad.

FATTY: Listen nothing.

HUGH: You're too easy going, Dave.

BILLY: When I get hold of that little Frenchman I'm going to punch his nose. He just had luck yesterday

DAVID (*In distress*): But — but you just don't understand him. He's just frightened and lonely and strange.

HUGH: He's a sap.

BILLY: He's a dope! (DAVID *starts to hand* BILLY *a part and then looks at it himself as an idea occurs to him.*)

DAVID: Hugh! Billy. How many days have we left to rehearse?

BILLY: Four, of course. What difference does that make?

DAVID: Plenty. Only four more days. We've got Washington, that's you, Hugh; Putnam, that's Fatty; Light Horse Harry Lee, that's Pete; Salomon, that's me; but no Lafayette!

FATTY: Well we've got to get somebody out of another grade, that's all.

DAVID: That's the point. We've got only four days left, and we've still got to get a Lafayette.

HUGH: I still don't get what you're driving at.

DAVID: At the play and at you! Only four more days and we've got to get a Lafayette. And I've got one! Jean du Pre! He's tall and thin and French. It's a knockout. (*Just then the rest of the class comes rushing in.* JEAN *sees the others staring at him and makes one of his formal little bows. He no longer wears a black smock.*)

BILLY (*Half under his breath*): Golly, he would fit the part.

HUGH (*His mind suddenly made up*): Hi, Jean. D'you want to be Lafayette in our play?

JEAN (*Looks scared and bewildered but moves a little nearer the others*): You mean you want me to play the part of Lafayette?

DAVID (*Hastily*): You bet. We're all crazy to have you do it. You're the only one that could possibly understand how he felt. You know, strange, new in America, everything looked funny. You could play that, couldn't you, Jean?

JEAN (*Taking a deep, fluttery breath*): Of a certainty! A stranger, a Frenchman. Oh, I could play that, yes. (*Suddenly suspicious*) But do the others all want me? (*The other children are too busy getting ready the furniture as it will be used in the play to answer.*)

DAVID: Of course. We can't go on without you. (*He grabs an old cocked hat from the costume box and presses a part book on* JEAN.) See, you just read some of the lines to get the feel of it, and then Miss Farnsbee likes us to make up as we go along. (JEAN *reads as* DAVID *turns to the others.*) Come on, fellows. Let's do the part where Lafayette offers his services to Washington. I'll be one of the aides just for now. (HUGH *paces up and down stage, very military in his bearing and trying very hard to look like* GEORGE WASHINGTON. DAVID *makes sure* JEAN *understands his part and then rushes into his speech as* AIDE.)

DAVID AS AIDE: Your Excellency, I have the honour to present to you the Marquis de Lafayette, come from fair France to help our cause.

HUGH AS WASHINGTON: Welcome, Marquis de Lafayette. You do us honour. (JEAN *is halting at first and then becomes more and more fluent as he gets into the spirit of his part. Also as he talks his speech comes more rapidly and his accent is more marked.*)

JEAN (*Bowing*): It is I who am honoured. To serve such a cause under so great a leader. (*He moves forward, more Frenchified than ever and bowing very low.*) Monsieur le Generale.

HUGH: Your hand, sir.

JEAN (*Shaking hands*): My hand and sword are at your service, sir. Command and I obey. (MARY WENTWORTH *slips over beside* DAVID.)

MARY (*In a low voice*): Why Jean's wonderful. He looks just like Lafayette. And he can act.

BILLY (*Who has also been watching the actors*): He's good. He's swell. I take it back about his being a dope.

JEAN (*Who all this while has been acting with* HUGH *and the others*): And that is the truth, Monsieur le Generale. France and America are one in spirit, in dreams, in love of liberty.

HUGH AS WASHINGTON: We shall fight shoulder to shoulder. Marquis de Lafayette, you have been made a general in the continental army. (*He reaches over to pin an imaginary decoration on* JEAN'S *shoulder.*)

JEAN AS LAFAYETTE: You do me great honour. (*Just at that moment* MISS FARNSBEE *comes in.*)

MISS FARNSBEE: Time to go home, children. Have you had a good rehearsal?

HUGH (*Enthusiastically*): You bet! And Jean here's a grand Lafayette. (MISS FARNSBEE *after busily tidying up her desk leaves the room.*)

DAVID: You were good also, Hugh.

HUGH: Jean's just made it. We couldn't get on without him.

JEAN (*Walking toward* HUGH *still half in character of* LAFAYETTE): I thank you. To work with you is how-do-you-say, a privilege.

DAVID (*His eyes are on* JEAN *and* HUGH): Why he was absolutely right, that dream Lafayette. Where people work together hard enough, there isn't room for misunderstanding! (HUGH *and* JEAN *shake hands as* DAVID *speaks — and the curtain falls.*)

THE END

THE MAGIC EGG

by Mildred Hark and Noel McQueen

Characters

PAPA BUNNY
MAMA BUNNY
PETER BUNNY
PAUL BUNNY
POLLY BUNNY
MRS. FEATHERS
MR. FEATHERS
1ST GROUP OF CHILDREN, *three girls and two boys*
2ND GROUP OF CHILDREN, *two girls and a boy*
GIRL
BOY

TIME: *The day before Easter*

SETTING: *A sunshiny spot in the woods where the Easter bunnies live.*

AT RISE: *At upstage right under a spreading tree sits* MAMA BUNNY *on a small log, using a big toadstool for a table. She is busy trimming Easter bonnets with feathers and flowers. When they are finished she hangs them on little twigs sticking out from the trunk of the tree. At upstage center there is a fallen tree which is being used as a table by* PAUL BUNNY. *On it he has several bowls of different colorings, and standing about him are baskets of eggs, some colored and some uncolored. Downstage, left,* POLLY BUNNY *works over a sawed-off tree stump on which she is rolling out dough for hot cross buns. A little to her left is a small bonfire and over it a small oven placed on pegs. (The fire can be made of twigs laid over a red light bulb.)* PETER BUNNY *stands at center holding a basket of uncolored eggs.*

MAMA BUNNY (*Putting down her work and clapping her hands sharply*): Peter, Paul, Polly — hurry with your work! Tomorrow is Easter.

PETER: But, Mother, we *are* hurrying as fast as we can. I'm bringing eggs from the farmyard as fast as the chickens lay them —

PAUL: And I'm coloring them — red and gold and blue and yellow — and all the other colors of the rainbow. (*He takes a white egg on a spoon and submerges it in one of the bowls.* NOTE: *Paul need not really color the eggs. There can be eggs of all colors in the bowl so that whatever color is required can be lifted out.*)

POLLY: And I'm making hot cross buns. (*As she rolls out some dough, chanting.*) One a penny, two a penny — hot cross buns! If ye have no daughters, give them to your sons; one a penny, two a penny — hot cross buns!

MAMA BUNNY: Stop singing, Polly, and get on with your buns.

PETER: But Mother, we've got to sing. It's spring — the sky is blue, the grass is green —

PAUL: The flowers are popping out.

POLLY: 'Tis the most beautiful time of all the year —

PETER: Of that there is no doubt.

MAMA BUNNY: That's all very well, but we have a job to do. The Easter Bunnies have to make the day happy for the children. Where's your father, Peter?

PETER: Out gathering Easter lilies — dazzling white — to decorate all the churches.

MAMA BUNNY: Well, I wish he'd hurry back. I have lots of things I want to discuss with him.

PAUL (*Lifting out a blue egg*): Oh, Mother, look; isn't this a beautiful egg? A heavenly shade of blue.

POLLY (*Taking a spritely step*): I feel so gay I could dance.

PETER: Let's then.

PETER, PAUL, POLLY (*Together, with a few dance steps*):
Tomorrow morn we'll sally forth,
Tiptoeing all around;
Delivering Easter presents
To every village and town.

MAMA BUNNY (*Clapping her hands again*): Stop it — stop it or you'll all get a whipping. Polly, run and ask Robin Redbreast if he could spare another feather for this Easter bonnet.

POLLY: Yes, Mother. (*She runs off.*)

MAMA BUNNY: All the bonnets in the Easter parade must be very beautiful.

PETER AND PAUL (*Dancing again*):
Oh, the Easter parade is merry,
The Easter parade is gay;
Everyone's smiling and cheerful —
'Tis such a glorious day!

MAMA BUNNY: What did I tell you? I know you're in high spirits but you'll have to behave yourselves.

POLLY (*Running back in*): Robin Redbreast says he's given enough of his feathers for bonnets this season and so did Mr. Cardinal. But I brought you a bunch of spring flowers instead. (*She hands a bouquet to* MAMA BUNNY.)

MAMA BUNNY: Dearie me.... Well, it'll have to do, although I've used a good many flowers. As soon as I finish this, I must make some chocolate bunnies for the children to eat. I'll use you as a model, Peter.

PETER: Me, Mother?

MAMA BUNNY: Of course. Now, don't look so scared. The children aren't going to eat *you.* I'll just make the chocolate ones look like you.

POLLY: Mother, who is going to get the magic egg this year?

MAMA BUNNY: The magic egg? The magic egg! Oh, for humpty dumpty's sake. I wonder if the chickens have laid it yet. My goodness! Well, your father will know.

PAUL: Here he comes now. (PAPA BUNNY *enters right with basket of Easter lilies. He wears spectacles on his nose.*)

PAPA BUNNY: Greetings, greetings, my Easter bunnies.

ALL: Hello, Papa.

PAPA BUNNY: Well, I've got the Easter lilies. Baskets and baskets of them. (*Waving the ones he has*) These are just a sample. I put most of them in the brook to keep fresh until you children can find time to deliver them.

MAMA BUNNY: Papa, what about the magic egg? We forgot all about it.

PAPA BUNNY: I didn't, my dear. I visited the chickens down at the farm only a few minutes ago. Mrs. Feathers hasn't laid it yet. She has to be inspired, you know.

PETER: Well, she'd better hurry. It's almost Easter.

POLLY: What if she isn't inspired at all?

PAPA BUNNY: She will be. Some little boy or girl is going to get the magic egg. It happens every year. (MRS. FEATHERS *enters left looking angry.*) Oh, Mrs. Feathers, good morning.

MRS. FEATHERS: It's not such a good morning as you think, Mr. Easter Bunny. I have bad news for you.

MAMA BUNNY: Bad news? But that can't be — not on the day before Easter.

MRS. FEATHERS: Well, it is — the chickens have stopped laying.

PAPA BUNNY (*Shocked*): Stopped laying?

MRS. FEATHERS: Yes, we've all gone on strike, including myself.

PAPA BUNNY: But we need hundreds more eggs — thousands; you can't go on strike.

MRS. FEATHERS: Well, we have. We're tired of laying all the eggs and having you Easter bunnies get all the credit.

PAPA BUNNY: Oh, but now wait a minute, Mrs. Feathers. I'm sure we can discuss this sensibly.

MRS. FEATHERS: There's nothing sensible about it. We lay and lay and lay, egg after egg after egg —

PETER, PAUL AND POLLY: But we deliver the eggs.

MRS. FEATHERS: Humph, that's easy.

PAPA BUNNY: Now, wait a minute, Mrs. Feathers. I'll have you know that I work as hard as —

MRS. FEATHERS: Oh, don't tell me. You talk a lot about it but that's all. You're as bad as Mr. Feathers — all he does is crow!

PAPA BUNNY: What? You're angry with Mr. Feathers too?

MRS. FEATHERS: I'm angry with everyone — and we're not going to lay any more eggs — that's certain.

PAPA BUNNY: But Mrs. Feathers — wait — the magic egg! (*Two boys and three girls enter right.*)

MAMA BUNNY: Oh, Papa Bunny, look — children!

PAPA BUNNY: You children can't come here. What do you want?

1ST GIRL: We're looking for Easter eggs. (*The children go poking about.*)

1ST BOY: Oh, look — beautiful ones.

PAPA BUNNY: Now — now — go away — go away, I say. You know as well as I do that you're not supposed to hunt for eggs until Easter morning.

2ND GIRL: Oh, but Mr. Bunny, please. We heard if we looked hard we might find a magic egg.

3RD GIRL: Yes, and we thought you might tell us where to find it.

MAMA BUNNY: We can't do that. It wouldn't be fair to the other children in the world.

2ND BOY: Oh, but if you could just help us a little, Easter bunnies —

PAPA BUNNY: Now — now — we can't — that's final. But why do you want the magic egg anyhow?

1ST GIRL: We heard it was a wonderful egg — that whoever found it would always be happy, that they could get anything they wanted.

PAPA BUNNY: Humph — well, you can't stay around here poking into our secrets. Now — run — run!

1ST BOY: But Mr. Bunny —

PAPA BUNNY (*Clapping hands*): Run, I say! (*The children scamper out right.* MRS. FEATHERS *has stood watching, still looking angry.*) There, you see, Mrs. Feathers — you can't disappoint the children. You've got to lay the magic egg.

MRS. FEATHERS: Humph. No one deserves it anyhow. They're all just thinking of themselves. (*And she flounces out left.*)

PAPA BUNNY: But, Mrs. Feathers — oh, dear, she's gone.

MAMA BUNNY (*Walking back and forth*): I don't know what to do. I've got to think.

PAUL: We've colored the last of the eggs, Papa, and there's not half enough —

MAMA BUNNY: Listen, children. I've run out of feathers and flowers to trim my Easter bonnets. Why don't you come with me into the woods and help me collect some more. We can pick some flowers and maybe coax the birds to give us an extra feather.

PETER, PAUL AND POLLY: All right, Mother. (POLLY *puts a tray of buns into the oven.*)

MAMA BUNNY: Besides, it will give your father a chance to concentrate.

PAPA BUNNY: That's a good idea, Mama. If everything's quiet, maybe I can think how to make the chickens lay more eggs.

MAMA BUNNY: You've simply got to, Papa.... Come, children. (*As she goes*) I think we can find some violets down by the brook and — (MAMA BUNNY *and the little bunnies go out right.* PAPA BUNNY *walks back and forth for a moment looking thoughtful.*)

PAPA BUNNY: Hmmmm-mmmm... Hmmmm-mmmmm... (MR. FEATHERS, *the rooster, enters left, looking very glum.* PAPA BUNNY *turns and sees him.*)

PAPA BUNNY: Why, Mr. Feathers.

MR. FEATHERS: Hello, Mr. Easter Bunny.

PAPA BUNNY: What in the world is the matter with you? You look awful.

MR. FEATHERS: I *feel* awful. Mrs. Feathers is angry with me — all the hens are angry with me. And they've stopped laying eggs.

PAPA BUNNY: You're telling me? It's a very serious thing. But why is Mrs. Feathers angry with you?

MR. FEATHERS: I don't know — except that she says the women do all the work. She says all I do is crow.

PAPA BUNNY: Oh, yes. She mentioned that to me... Well — well, I'm glad you've come, Mr. Feathers. Maybe between us we can figure out something.

MR. FEATHERS: I hope so. I'm the most miserable rooster that ever walked in the barnyard. Imagine Mrs. Feathers saying that — when I crow so beautifully.

PAPA BUNNY: Of course you do, but stop thinking about yourself for a moment. The important thing is the eggs. Why, children all over the country expect eggs on Easter morning. The hens can't stop laying.

MR. FEATHERS: Well, they have — and Mrs. Feathers is stubborn — she won't change her mind.

PAPA BUNNY: Oh, now — now, let's not be too discouraged. You ought to be able to persuade her — a fine handsome rooster like you.

MR. FEATHERS: Humph — that's all very well —

PAPA BUNNY: I have it — why don't you tell her you'll stop crowing?

MR. FEATHERS: What good will that do? Didn't I just tell you what she said? And it's a shame. Why, my crowing is like music. Every morning I crow so loud and long that I wake everyone up. You can hear me for miles around.

PAPA BUNNY: Wait a minute — is that the way the chickens wake up — by your crowing?

MR. FEATHERS: Certainly it is.

PAPA BUNNY: Then I have it. You just tell Mrs. Feathers that you're going to stop crowing if she's going to stop laying, and that if she goes to sleep, she'll never wake up again!

MR. FEATHERS: But I don't think —

PAPA BUNNY: Tell all the chickens. Now hurry, I'm sure it will work!

MR. FEATHERS: Well, it might.

PAPA BUNNY: And don't look so crestfallen. Raise your head, throw back your wings, look like the proud cock you are!

MR. FEATHERS (*He walks straighter*): I'll try — I'll do my best.

PAPA BUNNY: Fine — fine. We've got to get more eggs as fast as we can — and especially the magic egg. (MR. FEATHERS *goes out as* MAMA BUNNY *and the three little bunnies enter right, carrying flowers and feathers.*) Mama, I've fixed it — I've fixed it — I'm sure I have.

MAMA BUNNY: That's wonderful, Papa, and look what we have —all kinds of flowers and feathers. My, they'll make the Easter bonnets look beautiful. (*She gets to work again.*)

PETER: You mean the chickens are laying again, Papa? Can I go to the farm and gather some more eggs?

PAPA BUNNY: I'd wait for just a minute, Peter. Give Mr. Feathers a little time.

MAMA BUNNY: Oh, so you and Mr. Feathers have been getting together, have you?

POLLY (*Taking out tray of buns*): Look, Mama, another tray of hot cross buns ready for Easter breakfast.

PAUL (*Going to coloring bowls*): Oh, this is exciting. I'm going to mix up some more colors from the rainbow. (*Some more children enter right — two girls and a boy.*)

1ST GIRL: Oh, look — Easter bunnies!

PAPA BUNNY: Now — now, just a minute, children. (*The children start running about the stage, poking into everything.*)

MAMA BUNNY: You children can't go poking about looking for eggs — not until Easter morning.

BOY: But we're not looking for eggs especially — we always get plenty of eggs.

PAPA BUNNY: I suppose you're looking for the magic egg. Well, you won't find it here. Now, run away — all of you.

2ND GIRL: Oh, dear. If we can't look for the magic egg, can't we have something else? Oh, look at the three little bunnies — aren't they cute? (PETER, PAUL *and* POLLY *all stop work and huddle together.*)

1ST GIRL: Yes — oh, I want to take them home with me.

POLLY: Mama, don't let them take us.

PETER: Help, Mama — help, Papa!

PAUL: We want to stay with you.

BOY: Hey, it would be fun to have three bunnies to play with. Can't we take them?

MAMA BUNNY: Dear me, no. You can't take my children home with you. Now — now, behave yourselves, and I'll see that you get some chocolate bunnies on Easter morning.

PAPA BUNNY: If you go home right away —

CHILDREN: Oh, all right then, we'll go — we'll go — come on, everyone. (*They troop off right.*)

PETER: Oh, Mama, that was a very close call.

POLLY: They wanted to take us home.

PAUL: Were they going to eat us as if we were made of chocolate?

MAMA BUNNY: Nonsense, of course not. They only wanted to play with you.... Now, get to work, all of you, so the children won't be disappointed on Easter morning.

POLLY: Papa, who's going to get the magic egg? I mean how will you know which boy or girl to give it to?

PAPA BUNNY: Never mind. I'll know — provided there *is* a magic egg. Oh, dear me, I wish I knew how Mr. Feathers is making out — (MR. FEATHERS *enters left, carrying two large baskets full of eggs.*)

MR. FEATHERS (*Excitedly*): Mr. Easter Bunny — Mr. Easter Bunny —

PAPA BUNNY: Oh, look — eggs!

MAMA BUNNY: Eggs!

PETER, PAUL AND POLLY: Eggs and more eggs. Hooray — hooray — hooray! (*They start to skip about.*)
When an Easter bunny sees an egg —
He's as happy as can be;
He winks his eyes and wrinkles his nose—
For he feels so full of glee.

MAMA BUNNY: Children, stop dancing. You're shaking the earth. You might break the eggs.

MR. FEATHERS: It worked — it worked — the chickens are laying again as fast as can be.

PAPA BUNNY: It's wonderful — it's wonderful.

MR. FEATHERS: And Mrs. Feathers isn't angry any more. She's pleased with the whole world — and listen to this — she loves to hear me crow.

MAMA BUNNY: That's as it should be.

MR. FEATHERS: And I just crowed so beautifully a few minutes ago that guess what?

PAPA BUNNY: What?

MR. FEATHERS: She laid the magic egg!

PAPA BUNNY: The magic egg —

MAMA BUNNY: Dear me — the magic egg!

PETER, PAUL AND POLLY: The magic egg! Hooray. (*Then dancing*)

Oh, the magic egg, the magic egg —
It has been laid, we hear;
And twill bring good luck to someone—
It happens every year.

MAMA BUNNY: Children!

PETER, PAUL AND POLLY (*Stopping*): Yes, Mama.

MR. FEATHERS: I knew you'd be pleased.

PAPA BUNNY (*Reverently*): It's — it's in one of these baskets?

MR. FEATHERS: Yes. (*He leans over and whispers in* PAPA'*s ear.*)

PETER, PAUL AND POLLY: But which is it? Which is the magic egg?

MAMA BUNNY: Sh-h-h! Papa will know. He never even tells me —he says women can't keep a secret.

PAPA BUNNY: Now, don't be hurt, Mama. You'll all know in good time. . . . Thank you, Mr. Feathers — thank you.

MR. FEATHERS: And come down soon for more eggs.

PAPA BUNNY: We'll need hundreds more.

MR. FEATHERS: Of course, and you needn't worry. Production is going at great rate — full speed ahead! (*He sweeps out.*)

PAPA BUNNY (*Rubbing his hands gleefully*): Well, as usual, Easter is going to be a beautiful time — a happy time.

PAUL: Had I better color the eggs, Papa?

PAPA BUNNY: No — no — not this batch. I'll color them myself.

PAUL: But, Papa —

MAMA BUNNY: Now, don't argue, Paul. You know this batch is most important — the magic egg.

POLLY (*Looking at baskets as* PAPA *takes them over to fallen log with coloring bowls on it*): Oh, how I wish I knew which was the magic egg —

PETER: And I wish I knew who was going to get it. (*A boy and girl enter right. They do not poke around but look about timidly.* MAMA BUNNY *sees them.*)

MAMA BUNNY: What is it? What are you looking for?

GIRL: Why, we thought — that is —

BOY: We wondered if you could help us.

GIRL: You see, we're looking for the magic egg. (PAPA BUNNY *turns from his coloring.*)

PAPA BUNNY: The magic egg?

BOY: Yes, we've got to find it. And, sir, aren't you the Easter Bunny?

MAMA BUNNY: Of course he is, but he's very busy right now.

PAPA BUNNY: Wait, Mama. So you two want the magic egg — well, that's not unusual; most children want it.

GIRL: Yes, I know, but the children next door to us need it more than anyone.

BOY: You see, sometimes it's hard for their mother to get enough clothes and food for all of them, so we thought if they had the magic egg —

MAMA BUNNY: You want to give the magic egg away?

GIRL: Yes — because we've heard that whoever has it will have good luck and be happy.

PAPA BUNNY: But what about yourselves? Wouldn't you like to be happy?

BOY: Oh, yes, sir, but we are — most of the time. We don't need it. But the children next door — they just don't have anything to be happy about — ever.

GIRL: Oh, Mr. Easter Bunny, can't you help us find the magic egg?

PAPA BUNNY: Harumph — harumph. Well, no, I can't — not this minute, because you see, it's never delivered until Easter morning.

GIRL: Oh, dear —

PAPA BUNNY: It's a surprise and a secret, so I can't tell you anything but this. Go right home and hope very hard — and it may be — it just may be that you'll get it.

GIRL: Oh, that's wonderful — as long as there's a chance.

BOY: Just one thing, Mr. Easter Bunny. If it should be that you deliver it to our house, could you — that is, would it be too much trouble to ask you to come very early so that we could take it next door before the children wake up?

PAPA BUNNY (*Getting out a handkerchief and blowing his nose*): I — I think that could be arranged; now, run away — both of you.

BOY AND GIRL (*As they go off right*): Won't it be wonderful? Oh, if only we get it. They'll love the magic egg!

MAMA BUNNY: Papa, what's the matter? Are you sniffling?

PAPA BUNNY: Somewhat, my dear — somewhat.

PAUL: Papa, are they the ones?

POLLY: Are they going to get the magic egg?

PAPA BUNNY: Yes, they're the ones. I can let you in on the secret.

PETER: But how did you ever decide? Why were they different?

PAPA BUNNY: Because they wanted to make someone else happy.

PAUL: But the magic egg is supposed to make the ones who *get* it happy, and if they give it away —

PAPA BUNNY: That little girl and boy will be happy — don't worry about that. When you make others happy, you always gain happiness for yourself.

MAMA BUNNY: Exactly. Now, stop asking questions — your father's busy.

PAPA BUNNY (*Busy at coloring bowls*) : And in just one moment I'll have something to show you.

PETER: Not — not —

PAPA BUNNY (*Turning and holding in his hands a very beautiful Easter egg. It shines and glitters*) : Yes — the magic egg! (*They all gather round him with "oh's" and "ah's" of delight.*)

MAMA BUNNY: Oh, isn't it beautiful?

PETER: It sparkles —

PAUL: It glows —

POLLY: It makes me happy just to look at it.

PETER (*Running upstage*) : I'll get a basket to put it in. (*He brings a beautiful basket and* PAPA *places the egg in the middle of the basket.*)

PAUL (*Bringing flowers*) : And we must pack it all around with flowers.

POLLY (*Producing a big ribbon*) : And tie on this beautiful lavender bow!

PAPA BUNNY: Ah, there it is — all ready to be delivered — the magic egg! (*He sets the basket down center stage and they all gaze at it admiringly.*)

PETER: Oh, it's so exciting —

POLLY: Easter is the loveliest time —

PAUL: Can't we dance now, Mother?

MAMA BUNNY: Of course. I feel like dancing myself. Come, Papa. (*They all join hands and skip around the basket. Then facing the audience.*)

ALL:

On Easter morn we'll sally forth
Before the church bells ring;
And to the children everywhere,
Our joyous gifts we'll bring.
And perhaps this magic egg will spread
A secret all should know —
That when you think of someone else,
Your happiness will grow!

(*Quick curtain.*)

THE END

A PRESENT FOR MOTHER

by June Barr

Characters

JANIE
BILL
LITTLE SQUIRREL
LITTLE DEER
LITTLE RABBIT
LITTLE BEAR
MR. WISE OLD OWL

SCENE 1

SETTING: *The woods. A big fallen log in center, with bushes around it.*

AT RISE: JANIE *and* BILL *enter, and head for fallen log, slowly.*

BILL: Whew! Let's sit down here and rest!

JANIE (*Sits down with a sigh*): Oh, dear, I suppose we might as well.

LITTLE SQUIRREL (*Comes dancing on stage, and over to* JANIE *and* BILL): Hello! What are you two doing out in the woods?

BILL: Oh, hello, Little Squirrel!

JANIE: We're looking for a present for Mother. Sunday is Mother's Day.

LITTLE SQUIRREL: What's Mother's Day?

JANIE: Oh, it's the day when we stop and remember how nice Mother is —

BILL: And then give her a little present to let her *know* we think she's nice.

JANIE: Only — we can't think what to give her.

LITTLE SQUIRREL: Why, that's easy! Give her a big, fat, juicy *nut!* That's what *I'd* give *my* mother!

BILL (*Laughing*): Oh, but that's different!

JANIE: *Our* mother isn't a *squirrel!*

LITTLE DEER (*Poking head through the bushes*): Whose mother isn't a squirrel?

BILL *and* JANIE: *Our* mother!

LITTLE DEER (*Stepping from bushes*): Well, of course not! Whoever heard of such a thing!

LITTLE SQUIRREL: Well, since you know so much about it, maybe you can help them.

LITTLE DEER: What's the troubble?

JANIE: Sunday is Mother's Day.

BILL: And we can't think of a present for Mother.

LITTLE DEER: What's Mother's Day?

LITTLE SQUIRREL: It's the day for showing their mother they think she is nice.

LITTLE DEER: Oh. Let me think. (*Gazes up in air, thinking, then looks back at others*) I have it! Why don't you show her a fine patch of new grass! That's what I'd do for *my* mother!

JANIE: But what would she do with grass?

LITTLE DEER: Why, eat it, of course!

BILL: But, Little Deer, our Mother doesn't *eat* grass!

JANIE: She isn't a *deer!*

LITTLE SQUIRREL: Oh — ho! ho! ho! (*Holding his sides*) And you were so smart!

LITTLE DEER: Well, I did the best I could!

LITTLE RABBIT (*Comes hopping around log*): Of course you did, Little Deer! You always do your best.

BILL: Hello, Little Rabbit!

JANIE: Maybe you have an idea!

LITTLE SQUIRREL: What can they give their mother for Mother's Day?

LITTLE DEER: It's the day when you share with your Mother the best patch of grass you've found. At least — (*He adds hurriedly, with a glance at* LITTLE SQUIRREL) — that's what *I'd* do for *my* mother!

LITTLE SQUIRREL: Or bring her the biggest *nut* you could find!

BILL: A day for being especially nice to mother.

LITTLE RABBIT: I see. (*Puts head on one side to think*) I know!

BILL and JANIE: What? What?

LITTLE RABBIT: Give her a big juicy carrot from the farmer's garden!

DISMAYED CHORUS: Oh, no.

LITTLE RABBIT: Why not? That's what I'd give *my* mother! . . .

JANIE: But our mother isn't a *rabbit!*

LITTLE RABBIT (*Thoughtfully*): So she isn't, children.

BILL: Well, we're no nearer the answer than before.

LITTLE BEAR: What answer? (*Pokes head up over fallen log, then climbs over.*)

BILL: We want a present for Mother.

JANIE: And we don't know what to get.

LITTLE SQUIRREL: It's Mother's Day.

LITTLE BEAR: What's that?

LITTLE RABBIT: A day to remember how good your mother is *all* the days.

LITTLE SQUIRREL: And to give her a present to show you remember.

LITTLE BEAR: Why, how nice! That should be easy! (*Stands thinking, with paw on cheek, while the others wait expectantly*) Of course! Give her some honey! That's what I'd give *my* mother, some sweet, golden honey to eat!

JANIE: But our mother isn't a *bear!* She likes honey, of course, but — I don't think —

LITTLE BEAR: Honey won't do?

JANIE: I'm afraid not, Little Bear.

LITTLE DEER: We haven't been much help —

LITTLE SQUIRREL: I know! Let's ask the Wise Old Owl!

LITTLE RABBIT: Of course! He knows *everything!*

LITTLE BEAR: He'll know the answer!

LITTLE DEER: Let's hurry and find him!

JANIE: All right, we'll ask the Wise Old Owl! (*All leave the stage, led by* LITTLE SQUIRREL, *who is bragging—*)

LITTLE SQUIRREL: I'm very good friends with the Wise Old Owl. He lives in the hollow tree right next to me.

CURTAIN

* * *

SCENE 2

SETTING: *Slightly different woods scene, with hollow tree in center.*

AT RISE: JANIE, BILL, *and all the* ANIMALS *are grouped around hollow tree.*

BILL: You call him, Little Squirrel.

LITTLE SQUIRREL: Mr. Owl! Mr. Wise Old Owl!

WISE OLD OWL: Whooo?? Whoooo??

LITTLE SQUIRREL: It's Little Squirrel — and some friends. We need your help!

WISE OLD OWL (*Sticking head out of hollow in tree*): What do you want me to do?

JANIE: It's Mother's Day, Mr. Wise Old Owl.

BILL: And we can't think what to give our Mother.

LITTLE RABBIT: We tried to help —

LITTLE SQUIRREL: But none of us can think what she'd like.

LITTLE BEAR: Not honey.

LITTLE DEER: Not grass.

LITTLE SQUIRREL: Not a nut!

LITTLE RABBIT: Not a carrot.

WISE OLD OWL: Well, well, well! There's a very simple answer to that!

JANIE: Oh, tell us what it is, then!

BILL: Yes, tell us, please!

ANIMALS: Please do!

WISE OLD OWL: Every day you see things you think are beautiful, or odd, or interesting, don't you?

JANIE: Oh, yes!

WISE OLD OWL: Some of them you exclaim over, and show each other, isn't that true?

BILL: Yes, we always do that!

WISE OLD OWL: And sometimes you say, "Oh, I wish Mother could see that!" Now, don't you?

JANIE and BILL: Yes!

WISE OLD OWL: Well, the next time you come to something that makes you wish as hard as anything that Mother could see it —

JANIE: Yes?

WISE OLD OWL: That's the present for Mother!

JANIE: Oh, I know just what you mean! There was a patch of wild flowers on the edge of the woods, and we stopped there a long time just looking, and we wished and wished that Mother could see them!

BILL: I remember! Let's go pick some, Janie! Then she *could* see them!

JANIE: Oh, yes! Let's! (*As they start off,* JANIE *looks back*) Thank you, Mr. Wise Old Owl, and goodbye!

BILL: And thanks to you, Little Bear, and Little Deer, and Little Rabbit and Little Squirrel! We're going to get our Mother some pretty flowers!

LITTLE SQUIRREL: And I'm going to get *my* mother a big nut!

LITTLE DEER: And I'm going to get *my* mother some grass!

LITTLE RABBIT: And I'm going to get *my* mother a juicy carrot!

LITTLE BEAR: And I'm going to get *my* mother some sweet, golden honey!

JANIE: Then we'll *all* be keeping Mother's Day!

BILL: What fun! (*All troop off.*)

THE END

MOTHER'S GIFT

by Helen Littler Howard

Characters

DICKY, *a little boy*
SAMMY SQUIRREL
RITA RABBIT
DICKY'S MOTHER
BENNY BIRD
BECKY BEE
KORA KITTEN

SETTING: *In front of curtain.*

DICKY (*From stage left*): Today is Mother's Day. I wish I had something to give my mother to show her how glad I am that she is my mother. She does so many things for me: she cooks my food; she washes my clothes; she buys everything I need for school, and she's always thinking of ways to make me happy. (*Looking in pockets*) No use looking again. I have no money to buy a present for her. What shall I do? (*Thinking*) I know. I'll go into the woods and look for something. (*Goes off stage right. Curtains open.*)

SETTING: *The edge of a little wood.*

AT RISE: *Stage is empty.* DICKY *enters from right with several things in his hands and arms.*

DICKY: What a lot of nice gifts I've found! (*Showing each article as he mentions it*) I'll make a basket with these reeds, and I'll put these nuts in it and tie this red ribbon with its little silver bell around it. What a pretty gift it will make! (*Seeing* SAMMY SQUIRREL *coming sadly from behind the tree, center.*) There's Sammy Squirrel. I wonder what is the matter with him. Hello, Sammy. What makes you look so sad?

SAMMY (*Coming to* DICKY): I can't find any nuts. I buried some here behind this tree last fall and now they are not there.

DICKY: What did you want them for, Sammy?

SAMMY: My squirrel babies are hungry.

DICKY (*Holding out nuts to* SAMMY): Here they are, Sammy. I did not know that they were yours. I was looking for something to give my mother for Mother's Day. This is the day to say "Thank you" for all she's done for me.

SAMMY (*Taking nuts*): Oh, thank you, Dicky! My baby squirrels are so hungry. I hope you can find something else for your mother. (*Trots off stage right.*)

DICKY: You're welcome, Sammy. I suppose I could fill the basket with this pretty pink clover. It's the only clover I've seen in bloom. (*Picks clover.*) Here comes Rita Rabbit down the path. She seems to be looking for something. Hello, Rita.

RITA (*Looking up from path as she enters stage left*): Hello, Dicky. I'm so glad you're here. Maybe you can help me. My little Bunny is sick and she longs so for some pink clover. I thought I saw some along this path yesterday and it looked as if it were just ready to bloom. Will you help me look for it?

DICKY (*Hesitating*): I found it, Rita. (*Holding out clover.*) Here it is. I was going to put it in a basket and give it to my mother for Mother's Day, but I'm sure she'd rather I gave it to you.

RITA: Oh, thank you so much, Dicky! I'm sure this will make my little, sick Bunny feel better. (*Runs off stage left.*)

DICKY: I'm glad I could help the little, sick Bunny. (*Looks around*) There's a bush of little flowers. How lucky I am to find it. There aren't many flowers in the woods this year. These are the only ones I've seen. I'll pick those and put them in the basket. (*Goes to bush, stage left.*)

BECKY (*Coming from behind bush*): Oh, please, Dicky, do not pick these flowers! I need them. You see we are so short of honey just now since there are so few flowers and our little bees are just needing more honey.

DICKY: You may have them, Becky Bee. I did not mean to take away the baby bees' food. I only wanted the flowers to put in a basket I'm going to make for my mother.

BECKY: I'm sure you didn't mean to take the baby bees' food, Dicky. Thank you for leaving it for them. (*Flying away back stage left.*)

DICKY (*Cheerfully*): I'll make the basket and put the ribbon and bell on it and give it to mother. (*Hearing* BENNY BIRD *chirruping sadly*) Why, what can make Benny Bird so sad?

BENNY (*Hops in back stage right, chirruping sadly*): I cannot find any reeds to finish my beautiful nest and my mate has no place to put her eggs so that they will be safe until the little birds come.

DICKY: Reeds? Did you say reeds? I have some. I was going to weave a basket for my Mother but I'm sure she'd rather you had them for a nest. You need them more than I do. (*Gives reeds to* BENNY.)

BENNY: Oh, thank you, Dicky! Now I can finish my nest in time. (*Flies away.*)

DICKY: Now I cannot make the basket, but I still have this pretty ribbon and the tiny silver bell. I wonder if it belonged to the Fairy Queen?

KORA (*Coming in stage left*): Mew — mew — mew —

DICKY: What are you looking for, Kora? Could it be this little, silver bell?

KORA (*Running joyfully*): Indeed it is! I lost it last night when I came here to play in the moonlight. My little mistress is dreadfully upset because I lost it. (*Arching her back.*) I do thank you, indeed.

DICKY: Here, little Mew, I'll tie it around your neck. Run home quickly and show your mistress.

KORA (*Trotting back stage left*): My little mistress has been crying almost all day. How glad she will be that the bell is found!

DICKY: Now, I have nothing at all to give my mother for Mother's Day. I may as well go home and tell her. (*Going off stage right.*)

CURTAIN

* * *

SCENE 2

SETTING: *In front of curtain.*

DICKY (*Entering stage right*): I hope Mother won't be too disappointed.

MOTHER (*Entering stage left*): Oh, Dicky, I've been looking everywhere for you to thank you for my lovely Mother's Day gifts!

DICKY (*Astonished*): But, Mother, I have no gifts for you. I gave them all to others who needed them. Sammy Squirrel needed the nuts for his baby squirrels; Rita Rabbit needed the clover for her little, sick Bunny; Becky Bee wanted the flowers for honey for the baby bees; Benny Bird needed the reeds I had picked for a basket to finish his nest; and the bell and ribbon I found belonged to Kora Kitten.

MOTHER: Yes, Dicky, I know the whole story. You gave me such lovely gifts. Sammy Squirrel, Rita Rabbit and Becky Bee came to thank me for such a son as you are. Benny Bird came and sang such a lovely, new song all about you, and Kora Kitten came and rubbed her head against my knee and purred her thanks. These are the nicest Mother's Day gifts I've ever had because they are real gifts of love.

DICKY: I'm so glad, Mother. I did not know that by helping others I was making a gift to you.

MOTHER: Those are the only *real* gifts, Dicky, gifts of love — for real love is the willingness to serve others. Now I know that you love others. No other gift could mean so much to me on Mother's Day. (MOTHER *and* DICKY *move off stage left.*)

THE END

A GOLDEN BELL FOR MOTHER

by Alice Very

Characters

TWINKLE, SCRATCH, WHISKERS, TINY, SQUEEK, FRISKY — *mice*

CUDDLES, FLUFFY, ROLY-POLY, TUBBY, MOUSER, PUFF — *kittens*

STOREMAN

MOTHER MOUSE

SCENE 1

SETTING: *A mouse hole. Sign on wall, "Mice Working."*

AT RISE: *Six* MICE *sit spinning, sewing, knitting, etc.*

MICE (*Singing*):

Some little mice sat down to spin.
Pussy came by and she popped her head in.
"What are you at, my little men?"
"Making coats for gentlemen."
"May I come in and snip off your threads?"
"Oh, no, Mistress Pussy, you'll snip off our heads."

TWINKLE: What shall we make for Mother's Day?

SCRATCH: I'll spin.

WHISKERS: I will sew.

TINY: I'll knit.

SQUEEK: I'll crochet.

FRISKY:
I know just the thing
For Mother—I'll make
A beautiful string
To tie round her neck.
(*Showing string.*)

TWINKLE:
What good is a string
Without anything on it?

SCRATCH:
Let's buy her a ring
Or a pretty new bonnet—

WHISKERS:
I'd buy her a ring
Or a big golden locket,
But there isn't a thing
But holes in my pocket.
(*Showing holes. A large "silver coin" rolls into the mouse hole.*)

TINY: Oh, goody!

SQUEEK: What luck!

FRISKY:
Let's run to the store!
There's a pretty gold bell
That hangs on the door.

TWINKLE: Oh, no!

SCRATCH: I'm afraid!

WHISKERS: I'm a good little mouse.

TINY:
You know Mother told us
To stay in the house.

SQUEEK:
Come on, don't be scared.
Unfasten the latches.

FRISKY:
Run fast as you can
And no one will catch us.
(MICE *unlatch door and run out, rolling coin along before.*)

CURTAIN

* * *

SCENE 2

SETTING: *A store. Door left with a bell hanging on it, so as to ring when the door is opened.*

AT RISE: *The* STOREMAN *is leaning on the counter. Enter* MICE, *one by one, each one slamming door and ringing bell. Last* MOUSE *rolls in coin.*

STOREMAN: Who's that at the door?
MICE: It's six little mice.
TWINKLE:
We want to buy something
That's really quite nice.
STOREMAN:
Well, what do you know!
Six mice in my store!
There must be a hole
Down under the floor.
SCRATCH:
Oh, please, Mr. Storeman,
We want you to sell—
WHISKERS:
Your neat little, sweet,
And complete little bell.
(MICE *roll their coin to the* STOREMAN.)
STOREMAN:
That looks like a dollar
Rolled out of my till,
But if you return it
It may be I will.
TINY:
You see, it's a present
For Mother today.
SQUEEK:
We're willing to pay you
Whatever you say.
STOREMAN:
All right, I will sell you

My valuable bell,
If a song you will sing
Or a story will tell.

FRISKY:
We know a good song
And a story to tell—
It's about a big frog
That lived in a well.

MICE (*Singing*):
A Frog he would a-wooing go.
Heigh-ho, says Roly.
Whether his mother would let him or no.
With a roly poly, gammon and spinach,
Heigh-ho, says Anthony Roly.
(*Etc.*)

STOREMAN:
You sang that so well
I'll give you my bell.
(*Takes down bell from the door and gives it to* MICE, *who tie string to bell and run out, dragging the bell clattering behind them.*)

CURTAIN

* * *

SCENE 3

SETTING: *A room outside mouse hole.*

AT RISE: KITTENS *curled up cozily; yawn and stretch.*

KITTENS: (*Singing*):
"Pussy-cat, pussy-cat, where have you been?
I've been to London to visit the Queen.
Pussy-cat, pussy-cat, what did you there?
I frightened a little mouse under her chair."

CUDDLES:
Come, Kittens, instead
Of taking your naps,
Please put on your heads
Your best thinking-caps.
FLUFFY: I've tried and I've tried—
ROLY-POLY: We all have tried too—
TUBBY:
But we can't quite decide
What present will do.
(*Clattering of a bell along the floor, offstage, draws nearer.* KITTENS *start up and prick up ears.*)
MOUSER: Do you hear a queer noise?
PUFF: Yes, what can it be?
MOUSER:
Crawl under here, boys,
And wait till we see.
(KITTENS *hide under table. Enter* MICE, *dragging bell*).
MICE:
Oh, Mother, come here
And see what we brought!
KITTENS (*Jumping out*):
Yes, hurry, I fear
You're going to be caught!
(*Each* KITTEN *catches a* MOUSE.)
CUDDLES:
I've got just the present
To give to my mother!
FLUFFY: And I have one too!
ROLY-POLY: And I have another!
TWINKLE:
Oh, please, Mr. Kitten,
Your mother, the Cat,
Will eat us all up—
SCRATCH: And we wouldn't like that.
TUBBY:
There's nothing so nice—
Or so I've heard say—
As fat little mice
For dear Mother's Day.

WHISKERS:
Oh, yes, there is something
Far better than mice.
Perhaps we might sell
If you paid us the price.
MOUSER: What's better than mice?
PUFF: We dare you to tell!
TINY:
There's nothing so nice
As a beautiful bell.
(*Ringing bell*)
SQUEEK:
Now where could you find
A present like that?
Our mother, you see,
Rates more than a cat.
FRISKY:
Too bad it's the last—
You won't find another—
But nothing's too good
For dear Mousie Mother.
CUDDLES: Just look at that bell!
FLUFFY: Let me see it too!
ROLY-POLY: Say, that would look well!
TUBBY: Do you think it would do?
MOUSER:
I think it would go
On the front of her collar.
TWINKLES: It's valuable, though.
SCRATCH: It cost us a dollar.
PUFF:
See here, little mice,
If you will agree,
You give us your bell
And we'll let you go free.
WHISKERS:
What! give you our bell?
Then what should we do?
KITTENS:
But *we* need a present

For Mother's Day too.
TINY: We know how you feel.
SQUEEK: You need it, we see.
FRISKY:
We'll agree to the deal
If you let us go free.
(MICE *give bell to* KITTENS *who run off with it joyfully, while* MICE *scamper into mouse hole.*)

CURTAIN

* * *

SCENE 4

SETTING: *Same as* SCENE 1.

AT RISE: MICE *busy as in* SCENE 1.
Enter MOTHER MOUSE. MICE *run to hug her.*

MOTHER MOUSE:
Were my children all good
While I was away?
TWINKLE:
Yes, as good as we could,
But we're sorry to say—
SCRATCH:
We have nothing to give
Our dear Mother today.
MOTHER MOUSE:
Dear Children, you know
There's nothing so nice
As my snug little hole
And my six little mice.
But I've very good news—
I can't wait to tell—

They have hung on the cat
A wonderful bell!

WHISKERS: A bell on the cat!

TINY: What's good about that?

MOTHER MOUSE:
Why, child, don't you see?
The bell makes us free.
We mice can have fun
Till it warns us to run.
She'll never come stealing
To catch us at play;
The bell's merry pealing
Will give her away.

SQUEEK:
Hooray, hooray!
For Mother's Day!

FRISKY:
The cat is belled:
The mice can play!

MOTHER MOUSE:
Sh, sh, I hear
She's coming near!

(*Sound of bell offstage, coming nearer and then dying away.* MICE *sit giggling with paws over mouths as they listen; then dance in a circle.*)

MICE:
Hooray, hooray!
For Mother's Day!
The Cat is belled:
The Mice can play!

THE END

THE DO-NOTHING FROG

by Patricia Clapp

Characters

SHOPKEEPER
SIX GIRLS
NINE BOYS
OTHER CHILDREN

SETTING: *The I'm-Going-To-Be Shop. Tables set upstage serve as counters, piled with a collection of items symbolizing various trades and professions. A stool is down right.*

AT RISE: *The* SHOPKEEPER *enters and hangs up a sign reading,* THE I'M-GOING-TO-BE SHOP. *After adjusting it, he picks up a large bell, moves downstage, and begins to ring bell.*

SHOPKEEPER: Hear ye! Hear ye! Announcing the opening of a new store in town! Come one, come all, to *The I'm-Going-To-Be Shop!* Now is the time to decide what you are going to be when you grow up. The world is waiting! (BOYS *and* GIRLS *enter left and right.*) Don't delay, decide today! Now is the time for all good children to come to the aid of their country! (BOYS *and* GIRLS *look curiously at* SHOPKEEPER *and his shop.*) Don't waste time! Time is for *doing,* not for wasting! Step right up, boys and girls. Pick your future from our enormous stock! Only one future to a customer, so choose carefully. No exchanges, no refunds, and we do not handle complaints. Take your time, browse as long as you like. Make your decisions while our great supply of futures is still fresh. (1ST BOY *shakes* SHOPKEEPER'S *arm gently.*) Yes, sir? You have a question, sir?

1ST BOY: Yes, sir. I have a question.

SHOPKEEPER (*Politely*) : And what, sir, might your question be?

1ST BOY: My question, sir, is what the dickens is this all about?

SHOPKEEPER: A ridiculous question, if you will pardon my saying so. Why don't you listen? I am simply announcing the opening of my new *I'm-Going-To-Be Shop*.

1ST BOY: But what do you sell?

SHOPKEEPER: Well, I don't exactly *sell* anything. At least not for money.

1ST GIRL (*To* 1ST BOY) : What in the world is he talking about?

1ST BOY: I don't exactly know. It seems to be some funny sort of store. (*They shake their heads.*)

6TH GIRL: Oh, good! Maybe I can do my Christmas shopping early.

5TH GIRL: But he says he doesn't sell anything.

6TH GIRL (*Puzzled*) : He doesn't *sell* anything?

5TH GIRL: That's what he says.

ALL: He doesn't sell *anything?*

5TH GIRL (*Impatiently*) : Look, talk to the Shopkeeper yourselves if you want to. *I* don't know what it's all about.

2ND GIRL (*To* SHOPKEEPER) : Pardon me, sir —

SHOPKEEPER (*Graciously*) : Certainly. You're pardoned. What did you do?

2ND GIRL: Would you kindly explain just what your shop is all about? I see all sorts of things inside, and yet you say you don't sell anything. It seems a very odd sort of shop.

SHOPKEEPER: That simply shows your limited experience! It's all perfectly plain!

2ND GIRL (*Firmly*) : Not to me.

ALL: Not to us, either.

SHOPKEEPER (*With a sigh*) : Very well, then. Listen carefully. How many times do grown-ups ask you what you're going to be when *you* grow up?

2ND BOY: All the time! My father's friends are always asking me.

3RD GIRL: And my mother's friends.

3RD BOY: And my uncles and aunts.

4TH GIRL: And my grandfathers and grandmothers.

SHOPKEEPER: Quite so. And what do you tell them?

4TH GIRL: I tell them I don't know. Because I don't.

2ND BOY: But the next time they see us, they ask us again.

SHOPKEEPER: Just as I thought. You see what a waste of time it is? Now, if you knew for sure what you were going to be when you grew up, you'd have the answer all ready for them, and they wouldn't have to ask you again, and you could get on with learning how to be whatever it is you want to be.

3RD BOY (*Considering*): That sounds sensible.

SHOPKEEPER (*With a small bow*): Thank you. (*Gestures toward shop*) So here in my new shop you can search around and find just the right thing to be when you grow up.

3RD BOY: And how do we pay you? You said you didn't sell things for money.

SHOPKEEPER: I don't. I sell futures, and you can't buy futures with money.

5TH GIRL: What do you buy them with, then?

SHOPKEEPER: Hope, hard work and promises. You can pay me in promises.

6TH GIRL: Pay you in promises? I don't understand.

SHOPKEEPER: My, my. We are a little slow today, aren't we? Let's say you enter my shop. Right?

ALL (*Loudly*): Right!

SHOPKEEPER (*Jumping*): Heavens! Business is going to be good today! Very well. You enter my shop, and look around. Right? (*Quickly puts fingers in ears in expectation.*)

ALL: Right!

SHOPKEEPER: Then you look over all the futures, and pick out the one you like best. Right? (*Immediately claps hands over ears*)

ALL: Right!

SHOPKEEPER: Good. Then you simply give me your promise that you will use that future wisely and well, so the world will be a better place. *Now* do you understand?

ALL (*After a second's pause*): Oooohhh!

SHOPKEEPER (*With relief*): At last! Very well, then. In you go, and look over the merchandise. Choose anything you like, providing you will be *giving* to the world, not just *taking* from it. (*Children move upstage and inspect articles laid on tables.*) No pushing or shoving, please. There is plenty of room for all. Don't block the entrance, miss. Keep traffic moving freely, please. Don't crowd! Take your time. (4TH BOY *remains downstage and seats himself on stool.* SHOPKEEPER *walks over to him.*) You're not interested in my shop?

4TH BOY: Not very.

SHOPKEEPER: But what about your future? Everyone needs a future.

4TH BOY: Mine is already planned.

SHOPKEEPER: Ah, I see. Very forehanded of you. And are you sure there's nothing in my shop that would equip you better for the future you have in mind?

4TH BOY (*Politely*): Nothing at all, thank you.

SHOPKEEPER (*Doubtfully*): Well, I suppose your future is your own business.

4TH BOY (*Agreeably*): I suppose so, too. Thank you just the same.

SHOPKEEPER: Not at all. (*Moving away, murmuring to himself, puzzled*) Still, I wonder what future I forgot. I thought I had *everything!* (*Some of children now start to leave counters and move downstage, carrying the "tools of their trade." All are pleased and excited, talking quietly together.* SHOPKEEPER *turns to* 1ST BOY.) Well, sir. Did you find what you were looking for?

1ST BOY: Yes, sir. I know exactly what I'm going to be.

2ND GIRL: So do I!

2ND BOY: I do, too!

3RD GIRL: And me!

SHOPKEEPER: Fine! I'm glad my shop was helpful. Suppose you tell me what you have chosen. (*The following couplets may be spoken, or sung to "Hush, Little Baby, Don't You Cry." As each says his line, he steps into place, gradually forming a long line across stage, with* SHOPKEEPER *at one end and* 4TH BOY *at other.*)

1ST BOY: When I grow up I'm going to be
A fisherman in the deep blue sea.

1ST GIRL: I'll be a nurse who cares for the ill.

2ND BOY: I'll be a doctor who prescribes a pill.

3RD BOY: A fireman who puts out the flames.

5TH BOY: A football player who wins the games.

2ND GIRL: An actress in the very best shows.

3RD GIRL: A dancer spinning on her toes.

4TH GIRL: A teacher loved by all her class.

6TH BOY: A gardening man who cuts the grass.

7TH BOY: An engineer in a Diesel train.

8TH BOY: A farmer raising corn and grain.

5TH GIRL: A secretary who types and files.

6TH GIRL: An airline stewardess who flies for miles.

9TH BOY: A policeman protecting everyone.

4TH BOY: A Do-Nothing Frog who sleeps in the sun. (*There is sudden silence, and all turn to stare at him.*)

ALL: A *what?*

4TH BOY: A Do-Nothing Frog.

ALL: A Do-Nothing *Frog?*

4TH BOY: Yes. A Do-Nothing Frog.

5TH GIRL: But why do you want to be a *frog?*

4TH BOY: Frogs don't have to go to school.
And they're not punished if they break a rule.

3RD GIRL: But frogs don't have any fun!

4TH BOY: What's fun?

6TH GIRL: Fun? Why, *everybody* knows what *fun* is! (*All nod in agreement*)

4TH BOY (*Persisting*): What is it, then?

6TH GIRL: Well — it's — it's *enjoying* yourself! That's what it is. (*Children nod in agreement.*)

4TH BOY (*Comfortably*): I'd enjoy sleeping in the sun.

9TH BOY: But don't you want to holler? And shout? And yell?

4TH BOY: I'll croak. That's yelling for a frog.

3RD GIRL: Don't you want to run around?

4TH BOY: I'll hop.

4TH GIRL: But — what *use* would you be?

4TH BOY (*Unconcerned*): Use? No use. I'd just be a Do-Nothing Frog.

8TH BOY: Wouldn't you do *anything* useful?

4TH BOY: Oh, I might catch a few flies.

2ND GIRL: What would you do with the flies after you caught them?

4TH BOY: I'd eat them.

GIRLS: Ick!

4TH BOY (*Loftily*): Frogs don't think so.

5TH GIRL: Why do you want to be a frog? Frogs are ugly!

4TH BOY: Not to other frogs. Anyhow, maybe frogs think *people* are ugly!

I'll be a frog that hops and croaks,
And catches flies before they land on folks.

SHOPKEEPER (*Stepping forward*): See here, my young friend, don't you think you're being a little difficult? All these other boys and girls are planning a future that will make the world a better place, but *you* —

4TH BOY: The world would be a better place without flies.

SHOPKEEPER: Oh, come, come! Catching flies is surely not a full-time career.

4TH BOY: For a Do-Nothing Frog, it is.

SHOPKEEPER: But you'll be putting some other hardworking frog out of business!

4TH BOY (*Suddenly perturbed*): Oh, my! I wouldn't want to do that! I *like* frogs! I like all animals. That's why I wanted to be one.

SHOPKEEPER: You don't have to *be* an animal because you like them. And I really don't think the world would be a better place if you just hopped and croaked and sat in the sun all day.

4TH BOY: *And* caught flies.

SHOPKEEPER (*Firmly*): It still isn't enough. It may be the best a *frog* can do, but it isn't enough for a boy.

4TH BOY: But animals are so nice! I'd like to live with animals.

SHOPKEEPER: Live with animals all you like. *I* don't mind. But when you grow up, the world will look to you to make it a better place.

4TH BOY (*In amazement*): The whole *world?* All looking at *me?*

SHOPKEEPER: In a way, yes.

4TH BOY (*Impressed*): Wow!

SHOPKEEPER: Now, wouldn't you like to take a look around my shop? You may find just the right future.

4TH BOY: Well, all right. But I did so much want to be a Do-

Nothing Frog! (*He goes to counter and looks through articles.*)

SHOPKEEPER (*Shaking his head*): A very sad case! The whole world waiting, and *he* wants to be a Do-Nothing Frog!

6TH GIRL: You mustn't worry about just one boy.

SHOPKEEPER: Somebody must. It might as well be me.

2ND GIRL: *We* think your shop is a great idea, don't we, everybody?

ALL: Yes!

2ND GIRL: And it's good to know just what our futures are, isn't it?

ALL: Yes!

1ST GIRL: And you have our promises, Mr. Shopkeeper, sir. We all promise to make the world a better place when we grow up. We'll give the world *care*.

3RD BOY: And safety.

5TH BOY: And exciting sports.

2ND GIRL: And entertainment.

3RD GIRL: And beauty.

4TH GIRL: And good education.

6TH BOY: And thoughtful service.

7TH BOY: And better transportation.

8TH BOY: And good food. (4TH BOY *comes downstage carrying a hat.*)

4TH BOY: And animals!

ALL: *Animals?*

4TH BOY: Yes! I know what *I'm* going to do!

ALL: What?

4TH BOY (*Triumphantly*): Be a keeper in a zoo! (*He plops hat labeled "Zoo" on his head.*)

ALL (*Pleased*):

He'll be a keeper at the zoo!
That's an excellent thing to do!

4TH BOY: But I still bet frogs have fun!

ALL: Thank you, Mr. Shopkeeper! (SHOPKEEPER *bows*)

Now we know
The futures that are waiting for us while we grow.
There's a lot to learn and a lot to do,

4TH BOY (*Stepping forward*): If you want to be the keeper of the City Zoo. (*Steps back*)

ALL:

And when anyone asks, "Now let me see,
What did you say you were going to be?"
Not a Do-Nothing Frog is what we'll say.

4TH BOY (*Stepping forward again*): Cr-r-roak-k-k!

ALL: But a Better-World Maker in every way! (*Curtain*)

THE END

PINK PARASOL

by Helen Louise Miller

Characters

SALLY MARSHALL
MRS. MARSHALL
SALLY RANDOLPH
MRS. RANDOLPH
CURTIS RANDOLPH
DORA RANDOLPH
MARY LOU RANDOLPH
CLAYTON RANDOLPH
A FEDERAL SOLDIER

SCENE 1

SETTING: *A corner of a garden.*

AT RISE: MRS. MARSHALL *and her daughter* SALLY *enter left. Both are carrying armloads or baskets of flowers.*

SALLY: Oh Mother, please couldn't I have my birthday presents before we take the flowers to the cemetery?

MOTHER: What makes you think there'll be any presents this year?

SALLY: Oh, I know there'll be presents. You and Brother Don have been whispering together for days; and last week I saw a big package with a foreign postmark in the hall. I'll bet that was from Daddy.

MOTHER: Maybe you're right. But a soldier's daughter should be more interested in paying tribute to the soldiers of yesterday than she is in her own birthday presents . . . particularly if she happens to be born on Memorial Day.

SALLY: I know you're right, Mother, but I just love birthdays—especially my own. Maybe I am a little pig, but I can't get my mind off those presents.

MOTHER (*Smiling*): Well, after all, your tenth birthday comes only once in a lifetime, so I tell you what we'll do. We'll compromise.

SALLY: Com . . . pro . . . what's that?

MOTHER: I'll give you one of your presents now. Then we'll take the flowers out to the cemetery, stay for the services, and have the rest of the presents after awhile.

SALLY: Will there be speeches and everything same as last year?

MOTHER: Even more so. This year the Governor of the State is the guest of honor at our Memorial Day program.

SALLY: Oh dear! The speeches are so long and dry! *Must* we go?

MOTHER: Why, Sally Marshall! Memorial Day is one of our greatest National Holidays. But I suppose to you, Memorial Day means only one thing.

SALLY: My birthday!

MOTHER: Exactly. Very well. Do you want your present now?

SALLY: Oh, yes . . . please.

MOTHER (*Pointing to package on table*): Then there it is.

SALLY: Oh, I'm so excited. Is it from you? (*Begins to open package.*)

MOTHER: No . . . not from me.

SALLY: From Don?

MOTHER: No.

SALLY: Not from Daddy?

MOTHER: No.

SALLY: Then who in the world could have sent this? And what do you suppose it could be?

MOTHER: It's from someone you have never seen.

SALLY (*Opening parcel and holding up an old-fashioned pink parasol*): A parasol! (*With disappointment*) But...but...it's not a new one. It looks terribly old and faded.

MOTHER: That's not surprising when I tell you that the person who gave it to you lived here in this house and played in this garden about ninety years ago. The parasol itself is eighty years old.

SALLY: Why, Mother! What a strange present! Tell me . . . who really did send it to me?

MOTHER: To tell the truth . . . I did. But I want you to consider it a gift from one of your ancestors...your great-great-great Aunt Sally Randolph. You were named for her, and just eighty years ago today she received this parasol, here in this garden, as her tenth birthday present.

SALLY: It sounds like a fairy story.

MOTHER: But it is a true story. Let's sit down a few minutes and I'll tell you all about the pink parasol and explain why I have given it to you. (MOTHER *and* SALLY *sit on bench outside curtains which slowly close after they are seated.*)

SALLY: I always love your stories, Mother, and it's a special treat to hear one about my birthday present.

MOTHER: When Sally Randolph was a little girl, she must have been a great deal like you, and I guess her mother had as much trouble as I do, keeping her birthday presents a surprise. Sally's tenth birthday occurred during the Civil War.

SALLY: And was she disappointed about not having a birthday party on account of the war?

MOTHER: No, I guess she wasn't very much disappointed about a birthday party, for her three cousins lived close by, and every time they got together it was as good as a party. At the beginning of my story, Mrs. Randolph was sitting in the garden lengthening one of Sally's skirts and watching the children play. She was happy because it was her little girl's birthday; but she was also sad because her only son, Clayton, was in the war, and she hadn't heard from him for some time. She was also nervous and worried because this town had been captured by the Yankees and Northern soldiers were in command. A Federal Major and his staff were quartered in this very house. But although Mrs. Randolph had her troubles, she was not too despondent to enjoy the children and their fun.

CURTAIN

* * *

SCENE 2

SETTING: *Same garden scene, during the Civil War.*

AT RISE: MRS. RANDOLPH *is sewing as she sits on the garden bench watching the four children playing and singing Rig-a-jig-jig, or any other singing game.*

MRS. RANDOLPH: You children had best sit down in the shade and cool off. It's too soon after dinner for such a romp.

SALLY: That will help us work up an appetite for supper.

CURTIS: I guess Aunty won't want us to work up too big an appetite. Mother says she is always thankful when she gets us filled up at one meal, but before she turns around, it's time for the next.

MRS. RANDOLPH: Feeding the family was never a problem to any of us before this dreadful war.

SALLY: Anyhow, we did manage a birthday cake and that's a real treat these days.

DORA: A birthday cake is always a treat, and you're a lucky girl, Cousin Sally, to get so many presents.

MRS. RANDOLPH: Indeed, she is. And be sure to thank your mother for the scent bottle and the lace mitts. Sally shall write her a note the first thing in the morning.

MARY LOU: Oh, Aunt Harriet, won't you let Sally drive home with us this evening to spend a few days? Then she could thank Mother herself and wouldn't need to write a note.

SALLY: Oh, could I, Mother? Please.

MRS. RANDOLPH: That would be very nice, Mary Lou, but I don't like the notion of having Sally away from home just now.

DORA: But Rose Hill isn't "away from home." Really it isn't. Sally is as much at home over there as she is here.

MRS. RANDOLPH: I know. But you children just don't understand. Somehow I can't bear to have Sally out of my sight since your Uncle Leigh and Clayton are gone.

CURTIS: I understand, Aunt Harriet. Mother is the same way. She says she's like an old mother hen when we children aren't right under her wing. And I'm sure if it hadn't been Sally's birthday, she wouldn't have wanted us all to leave today.

SALLY: Oh, this hateful old war! I'm getting plenty sick and tired of it! It spoils all our fun. No parties! No visiting! No barbecues! Nothing but made-over clothes and doing without things! I declare I just hate war and battles and uniforms and soldiers!

DORA: So do I!

MARY LOU: Me, too. There better not be any nasty old wars when I grow up. I don't want to marry a soldier who's always tearin' off to war some place. I want my husband to stay at home with me.

MRS. RANDOLPH: And I hope that's the sort of husband you'll have, my dear. Nobody likes war . . . not even the men . . . and least of all the women. But don't let me hear you talking about hating soldiers. Remember . . . our fathers and husbands and brothers are all soldiers these days.

MARY LOU: Oh, I know they are, Aunt Harriet, and I don't really hate them . . . not our own boys anyhow. But oh dear! I do wish the whole thing would be over.

CURTIS: Well, I don't — not till I'm old enough to get into it.

MRS. RANDOLPH: Curtis Randolph! Don't you ever let me hear you talk like that again. What would your mother say?

CURTIS: Oh, I'm sorry, Aunt Harriet! I know how worried you are about Clayton and Uncle Leigh, but confound it! Clayton's only two or three years older than I am, and he's right there in all the excitement . . . and here I am sitting at home learning Latin verbs from old Dr. Foster and helping Uncle Zeke hoe a turnip patch.

MRS. RANDOLPH: And I suppose you call that doing nothing at all. But I daresay boys are all alike. That's exactly the way Clayton talked before he left. It seemed such a great adventure to him. I wonder how he feels about it now. . . . (*Sighs*) Just a year . . . and it seems a lifetime.

SALLY: Don't talk about it any more, Mother. It just makes you feel worse. But I know you keep thinking about my party last year when Clayton wore his uniform for the first time. He looked so handsome! And we were all so proud of him!

MRS. RANDOLPH: Yes indeed! And we're still mighty proud of him! But he was too young. He didn't realize the seriousness of what he was going into. Why, he even talked of coming back in a year with another birthday present for you . . . and now, poor lad, his own home is occupied by the enemy. And goodness knows where he is today.

CURTIS: Don't worry about Clayton, Aunt Harriet. You can be sure that wherever he is, he's able to look out for himself.

MARY LOU (*In excitement*): Look, look, Aunt Harriet. Somebody's coming up the drive. Look how funny he's walking.

DORA: It looks like a tramp . . . maybe we better go inside.

CURTIS: Fraidy cat! Why should you be afraid of a tramp? A fine soldier you'd make!

SALLY (*Almost screaming*): Look! Mother! Mother! Look! Don't you see who it is? It's not a tramp . . . it's —

MRS. RANDOLPH: Clayton! It's your brother, Clayton! (*Starts running toward the wings.* CLAYTON *appears dressed in the remnants of a dirty, bedraggled uniform. He carries a brown paper-wrapped parcel. He walks with a halting step and almost leans on his mother as he embraces her.*)

MRS. RANDOLPH: Clayton! Clayton! My boy! You're home again! Oh, My son! What's happened to you? Are you hurt?

CLAYTON: No, no, Mother. Just tired. Now don't be so upset. This shouldn't be such a shock to you! I told you I'd be home for Sally's birthday.

SALLY: Clayton! Clayton! You did come after all. I can hardly believe it! We were just talking about last year and how you promised you'd be here today.

CURTIS AND THE OTHERS: Hello, Clayton. Welcome home! Well, isn't this a surprise? etc., etc. (*During the greetings, they all move center stage.*)

MRS. RANDOLPH: Here, dear, sit down. You must be nearly dead. Oh, you poor boy. Look at those shoes! How far have you walked? Are you hungry? When did you eat last?

CLAYTON: One question at a time, Mother. (*Sits down*) Ah-ah! (*Sighs*) That's more like it...and as for eating, just let me show you what I could do to some of Aunt Bessie's biscuits and a plate of fried chicken!

MRS. RANDOLPH: I won't promise you fried chicken, but I'll find something for you to eat at once. You sit right here and rest and I'll bring you something right away.

CLAYTON (*Catching hold of her skirt to stop her and attempting to rise*): No . . . no . . . Don't wait on me as if I were visiting royalty. I'll rest here a minute and then we'll go up to the house. Hungry as I am, I wouldn't want to eat before I clean up a bit.

SALLY: Oh, but Clayton . . . you can't. You can't go up to the house.

CLAYTON: I can't go up to the house? And why not? (*Silence*) Why not? What has happened to the house? It hasn't been burned. I could see it as I came up the river road, and I can tell you that was a relief. I've passed so many places that are in ruins. It gave me fresh courage when I saw the roof and chimney tops of Locust Hall.

CURTIS: Well, you see, Clayton. . . . Confound it, man, hasn't anyone told you? The Yankees are in charge here. As a matter of fact, Major Henderson of Massachusetts has your old room. His whole staff is quartered at Locust Hall. To tell the truth, you're not safe here, Cousin Clayton. We'll have to think of a way to hide you.

CLAYTON: A Yankee Officer in my room! Why, the nerve! Mother, I'll have the whole tribe of 'em out of here by nightfall.

MRS. RANDOLPH: Hush, hush, Clayton. You must rest. You're hardly fit to stand up . . . let alone get into an argument with a parcel of Yankees. Curtis is right. We'll get you something to eat and try to think of a plan to keep you here a few days till you're stronger. Fortunately, the house is empty just now. I'm fairly sure that all of the men have gone into the village.

CURTIS: Suppose I stand guard down by the entrance to the drive, and send the girls up to the house to get Clayton some food and be ready to sound the alarm if anyone comes back by the other road. That will give you and Clayton and Sally a little time to visit in peace and quiet.

CLAYTON: Curt, you've grown up while I've been away. His suggestions are good, mother. We'll do as he says.

CURTIS: Right. Then, I'm off for the driveway. If you hear me whistle three times, somebody's coming . . . so get under cover. (*Exit* CURTIS.)

DORA: Mary Lou and I will run up to the house. She can bring you the food and I'll stand guard up in the cupola. From there I can see in every direction.

MRS. RANDOLPH: Don't even tell Aunt Bessie that he's here, Mary Lou. Just ask her to fix a tray with some sandwiches and milk and cake and anything else that she happens to have. Bring it down here as fast as you can.

MARY LOU: I will, Aunt Harriet. Oh, Clayton, I'm so glad you're here.

DORA: Come on, Mary Lou. Clayton will like us a lot better if we can bring him some food. (*Girls exit.*)

SALLY: Oh, Clayton, it seems like a dream to have you home again.

CLAYTON: And it's like a dream to be here with you and Mother . . . but not exactly the kind of dream I'd like it to be.

MRS. RANDOLPH: But where on earth did you come from? And where have you been that we haven't heard from you? I've been worried sick.

CLAYTON: Sorry, Mother. It's a secret. The kind I can't talk about, so let's not waste time on that now. Something tells me I won't be here very long so let's make the most of Sally's birthday.

MRS. RANDOLPH: Clayton — you don't mean that your business is so secret and so dangerous that it would mean death if you were to be caught here.

CLAYTON: Nonsense, of course not. It's just . . . well, just a little errand I'm doing for a friend of mine. Now don't bother your head about military affairs. This is a family party . . . not a court of inquiry. Look here, Sally, didn't I tell you I was going to bring you a present?

SALLY: You sure did, Clay . . . but I know you haven't had any time for presents.

CLAYTON: The mischief, I haven't. What do you call this? (*Holds up package.*) Here's as fine a present as any little girl could expect in the whole state of Georgia. . . . Quick now, open it up and see what it is. The wrappings aren't very fancy, but I think you'll like what's inside.

MRS. RANDOLPH: The same old generous spirit! The war hasn't taken that out of you.

SALLY (*Opening package and disclosing pink parasol identical with the one the other* SALLY *had*): Oh, Clayton, where did you get it? It's darling! Look at the dear little ruffles and the lovely handle. And it's my favorite color. I declare you're the best brother in the world. Isn't it beautiful, Mother?

MRS. RANDOLPH: It certainly is. It looks like a big pink rose turned inside out.

SALLY: I'll carry it to church on Sunday. All the girls will be green with envy.

MRS. RANDOLPH: That's not a Christian spirit, Sally.

CLAYTON: But just like a girl, Mother. Never saw one yet that wouldn't put her vanity ahead of her soul . . . that is all except Mrs. Randolph and she is three-fourths angel to start with.

MRS. RANDOLPH (*Laughing*): Well, Mrs. Randolph's children

don't show any signs of sprouting wings, although she does have the best son in the whole Confederate army. But seriously, Clayton, I'm afraid you're running a frightful risk to come here.

SALLY: I'd never get over it if anything should happen to you on account of my birthday.

CLAYTON: Nothing is going to happen to me, so get that idea out of your bonnet. I bear a charmed life. (*Sound of whistle off-stage.*) Uh-Oh! I missed my guess that time. That's Curt's signal. I'll have to clear out of here in short order. (MARY LOU *enters with a tray of food. She is almost breathless.*)

MARY LOU: Mercy me! I thought I'd never get here with this tray. That whistle of Curt's most scared the wits out of me! But here's your lunch, Clayton, safe and sound.

MRS. RANDOLPH: He'll have no time for it now. We'll have to risk taking him up to the house. We'll manage to find a hiding place for him.

SALLY: Then we'll have to hurry. Come on, Clayton. You can hide in my room and I'll smuggle your meals in to you.

MARY LOU: Then this evening we'll try to sneak you out of the house and take you home with us.

MRS. RANDOLPH: We can hide you in the bottom of the wagon . . . (*Enter* DORA, *also breathless and excited.*) For mercy's sake, Dora, what is it? You look as if you had seen a ghost.

DORA: Oh, Aunt Harriet, Major Henderson is on his way to the house by the short cut. I just caught sight of him as he rounded the big bend in the road above the bridge. What on earth shall we do?

CLAYTON (*With a short laugh*): Looks as if we're surrounded, eh? Well, one thing's certain. We'll not try to reach the house ahead of him. We'd never make it.

MRS. RANDOLPH: Oh, Clayton, Clayton! We won't let them take you. We'll find a way to hide you.

CLAYTON: I'm not exactly worried, Mother . . . not yet. I've been in some pretty tight places before. (*Whistle is repeated.*) By George! There's our sentinel giving us another warning. They must be closing in on me. Look, Mother. I don't want to frighten you, but it is important for me to escape. Not just to save my own skin, but because of information I'm carrying back to our lines. If only we could stall them off till dusk, I'd follow your plan for getting to Rose Hill and then leave from there in the morning. If only I could disappear for a while, become invisible or something.

MRS. RANDOLPH (*Seizing skirt she had been sewing on*): Here, here, son. Try this. Quick. Put it on.

CLAYTON: Hey! Wait a minute. What are you trying to do? I can't escape in this thing.

DORA (*Helping to force* CLAYTON *into the skirt*): Oh, Aunt Harriet, that's a wonderful idea. We'll be able to hide him in plain sight of the enemy.

MRS. RANDOLPH: There! It's a little short, but you'll have to draw your feet up under you.

SALLY (*Half laughing*): But, Mother, look at the top of him!

MRS. RANDOLPH: Sh! Don't argue. Turn that chair around so the back of it faces this way. Now, Clay, dear, sit over there, and the girls will arrange your skirts for you. (DORA *and* MARY LOU *pull the full skirt around so that it fluffs out around the legs of the chair.*) That's good. Now here, we'll drape my shawl around his shoulders. There! Oh dear! If we only had a hat. Something must be done about his head.

DORA: I'll try to run up to the house and get a bonnet.

MARY LOU: There's not enough time. (*Rising*) He looks wonderful from the back . . . all but the head.

SALLY: That's easily remedied. When a lady sits in the garden in the sun, she should have a parasol to prevent freckles. (*Opens parasol and puts it into* CLAYTON'S *hand, so that his head and part of his shoulders are concealed.*) There, Mother, how's that? I declare, he looks for all the world like Aunt Millicent.

MRS. RANDOLPH: That's a good name for him . . . and don't you forget it.

DORA: Oh, my goodness, what shall we do with this tray of food?

SALLY: We'll have a tea party. There's no reason why Aunt Millicent should not enjoy a bite to eat with us.

MRS. RANDOLPH: That's right. Try to act as natural as possible. I'll do most of the talking. (*Sound of whistling.*)

MARY LOU: That's Curt. He's letting us know we should be on our guard. How do we look, Aunt Harriet? (*The two girls,* DORA *and* MARY LOU, *are seated on either side of the disguised* AUNT MILLICENT. SALLY *leans over the arm of her brother's chair.*)

MRS. RANDOLPH: Like a very informal garden party. Pass the sandwiches, Sally, and make believe it is a *real* party.

CURTIS (*As he enters with young* NORTHERN SOLDIER): I tell you, sir, no strangers have showed up here in a blue moon. Aunt Harriet, this is one of the river guards. He has had word that one of our men was seen in the village and he had an idea he might have headed this way.

MRS. RANDOLPH: Good afternoon, Sir. You are welcome to look around. But we lead very quiet lives here now and company is quite scarce as you can well imagine.

SOLDIER: Thank you, Ma'am. I'm sorry to trouble you. But we have been given strict orders to let no one through our lines. I must make a thorough search and then report to Major Henderson.

MRS. RANDOLPH: You'll find him up at the house. My niece happened to see him arriving when she brought the refreshments down from the kitchen a few moments ago.

SOLDIER (*Smiling*): Refreshments! Ah, that sounds like a party.

MRS. RANDOLPH: A very simple one, Sir. My daughter's tenth birthday.

SALLY: Perhaps the gentleman would enjoy a piece of birthday cake, Mother.

MRS. RANDOLPH: I hope there is some left on that plate. These youngsters are hearty eaters, and Cousin Millicent herself has a sweet tooth.

SALLY: Try some of my birthday cake, Sir. It's made from a wartime recipe, but I think you'll find it palatable.

SOLDIER: Thank you, child. I never can resist fresh cake and there's something about a birthday cake that is doubly tempting. (*Helps himself to a piece of cake.*) Are all these folks residents of this place, Ma'am?

MRS. RANDOLPH: Oh, no, indeed. Just my daughter and I are living here now. The others are my nieces, my young nephew and Cousin Millicent. You'll have to excuse her, Sir, she has an especial aversion to you gentlemen from the North and avoids exchanging words with them whenever possible. Besides, she is a trifle deaf. Poor Cousin Millicent, it is hard for her to accept changes at her age.

SOLDIER (*Munching cake*): Well, I'm sure I have no intentions of disturbing her or you either, Ma'am. Now, I shall have to pursue my search and make my report. Thank you for your kindness.

CURTIS: I'll be glad to show you the way to the house, Sir.

SOLDIER: No thanks, lad. I'll just follow the path and do a little poking around. No doubt Major Henderson will order a searching party when I make my report. We can't be too careful.

MRS. RANDOLPH: Then good day to you, Sir.

SOLDIER: Good day to you, Ma'am, and I hope your little girl and her friends enjoy the birthday spread as much as I enjoyed that cake. (*The group remains frozen to the spot watching the soldier as he exits. Then all relax with a sigh.*)

CLAYTON: Is it safe for Cousin Millicent to turn around?

SALLY (*Looking after the soldier*): Not yet; he might change his mind and come back. Just go on eating for a few minutes.

MARY LOU: Aunt Harriet, you should go on the stage. Why, you're a real actress. I could never have thought of all that on the spur of the moment.

MRS. RANDOLPH: I really do believe we managed to pull the wool over his eyes. Oh, my, now that he's gone, my knees feel as weak as water. I think I'll have to sit down.

SALLY: Oh, Mother, you were wonderful.

CURTIS: Indeed, you were, Aunt Harriet. The wind was knocked clear out of my sails when I saw this festive little group on the lawn, eating birthday cake as calm as you please. For a minute, I couldn't imagine what you had done with Clayton. How about it, old fellow? How does it feel to sit under a sun shade and wear a skirt? I think it's safe for you to come out now and be yourself for a few minutes.

CLAYTON: I feel as if I had a new lease on life, thanks to all of you. For a few minutes there I believed the jig was up and it would have been too, if it hadn't been for my quick thinking mother with her talent for dressmaking.

SALLY: And my parasol. I think that is the thing that really saved you, Clayton.

DORA: I think so, too. Without that, he could never have passed for Aunt Millicent.

MARY LOU (*Laughing*): Who has a sweet tooth and is a trifle deaf.

CURTIS: Good old Aunt Millicent. But enough of this, Clayton, we'll have to get you out of here. Get out of those frills and furbelows and make a dash for the carriage shed. The wagon's out there and we'll stow you away in the bottom so we can make a quick getaway. The coast will be clear for a few minutes while that bloodhound is up there making that report.

CLAYTON (*Getting out of his makeshift costume*): You're developing into a strategist for sure.

MRS. RANDOLPH: I'll go out to the carriage shed with you and see if I can make you comfortable with a blanket or a robe. Mary Lou, put the rest of that food in a napkin and bring it along. He'll probably need it.

CLAYTON: Indeed, I will. Well, goodbye, girls. Be good! And don't be surprised if your Aunt Millicent pops in again one of these days for a little chat over the teacups.

GIRLS: Goodbye, Clayton. Take care of yourself. Be sure to write to us, etc., etc.

CLAYTON: Goodbye, Sis . . . and take the best of care of this parasol. I might need it again in a hurry.

SALLY: Oh, I will, I will. It's my dearest possession now that it has saved your life. Goodbye, Clayton, and hurry home.

MRS. RANDOLPH: We'll have to hurry these farewells. Come, dear, you and Curtis, run on ahead and I'll follow as fast as my age and dignity permit. (*Exit* CURTIS, CLAYTON, *with* MRS. RANDOLPH *following.*)

DORA: Sally, this was the most exciting birthday party I ever attended.

MARY LOU (*Tying up the sandwiches and cake in a napkin*): With the most unexpected guests and the most startling surprises.

SALLY (*Opening her pink parasol and twirling it over her shoulder*): And with the most ravishing parasol in the state of Georgia from the bravest brother in the world!

CURTAIN

* * *

SCENE 3

SETTING: *Front of drawn curtains.*

AT RISE: SALLY *and her* MOTHER *are sitting on bench in front of curtains.*

MOTHER: So you see, Sally, your old-fashioned parasol has quite a romantic history.

SALLY: I should say so, and one that I am very proud of. That other Sally and I have other things in common besides a parasol. Her father was a soldier and so is mine.

MOTHER: And both of you have seen something of the griefs and sorrows of war . . . enough to make you hate and fear it all your lives long.

SALLY: I'm glad you told me that story, Mother, and I'm glad you gave me the pink parasol. I always thought of Civil War days as something in a history book. The battles and the people never seemed real to me; but now they do. There were people on both sides . . . just like you and me . . . a little girl and her mother . . . waiting for our menfolks to come home again.

MOTHER: Now you have the idea, Sally, and you also have the idea of Memorial Day. The day when the women of the North and South honor our dear ones who fought and died for what they believed was right. (*Sound of band music in the distance.*) And now would you like to have the rest of your birthday presents?

SALLY: Not till after we come home, Mother. I think I'd rather celebrate the thirtieth of May, first as Memorial Day and second, as my birthday. Come on, Mother, let's go to the cemetery and listen to all the speeches. (*Both rise.*) And don't you think the other Sally would be mighty happy if I carried her pink parasol?

MOTHER: I'm sure she would be, Sally, very happy and very proud of the namesake who honors her memory across the years. (*As the band music increases to a climax,* MRS. MARSHALL *and* SALLY *make their exit.*)

THE END

COLUMBUS SAILS THE SEA

by Lindsey Barbee

Characters
COLUMBUS
GIANNINI
ISABELLA
SAILORS
INDIANS
TWO COURTIERS

SCENE 1

SETTING: *A dock.*

AT RISE: *Before an old sailor, sits* COLUMBUS, *a wide-eyed, serious boy, hanging on each word of his companion, while the* SAILOR, *inspired by the eager interest of the boy, grows more excited in his narrative and emphasizes his words with many vigorous gestures.*

SAILOR:
And so, you see, my boy, the world is flat,
So flat that merchant ships come suddenly
Upon the very edge; and down they go
Into an ugly, dark, and boiling sea.

COLUMBUS:
Does anyone come back to tell the tale,
To prove that such a thing could ever be?

SAILOR: They tell their tales. Sometimes it is a bird,
A monstrous bird, that drags the little ship:
Sometimes it is a serpent; and again,
A fiery demon with huge, clutching hands
That close and open, close again, and crush
And hurl all things that lie across the path.

COLUMBUS:
But, Giannini, I cannot believe

Such fairy stories, for I know full well
That in their very sailing, there is proof
The world is round, not flat.

SAILOR:

Come, come, my boy,
Such talk is foolish, and why should you think
The world is round?

COLUMBUS:

Look, Giannini, look — (*He points.*)
That vessel out at sea! It is the prow
That disappears, and then the ship itself,
And finally the masts. Does that not prove?
The world is round?

SAILOR:

The world is flat, I say.
What puts this fancy in your head, Columbus?

COLUMBUS:

It is no fancy, and some day you'll watch
My ships departing.

SAILOR:

Oh, you dream too much.

COLUMBUS:

But one must dream if ever dreams come true.
For I have read the many wondrous tales
Of Marco Polo, of his Indian land,
Its camels, silks and spices — where one learns
The ways and manners of another world.
Some day, oh Giannini, I shall reach
Those shining cities and those golden ports —
The far-off, wonder land of India.

CURTAIN

* * *

SCENE 2

SETTING: *Throne room of Queen Isabella.*

AT RISE: QUEEN ISABELLA, *in court robes, is seated on a throne.*

On one side stands a courtier. Another courtier, entering, bows before her.

1ST COURTIER:
Columbus stands outside, Your Majesty,
And he would speak with you; nay, he implores
An audience.

ISABELLA:
Who is this man, Columbus?

1ST COURTIER:
He has been here before; he begs that you
Will hear him for a moment. He will speak
Most briefly.

ISABELLA:
But I say, who is the man?

1ST COURTIER:
Columbus, dreamer, yet a man of deeds.
Twice has he sought the presence of the Queen.
Once while the Moorish war was raging, then
Again when Spain was occupied elsewhere.
At present, he is on his way to France
Where interest in his venture is assured.

ISABELLA:
To France, you say?

1ST COURTIER:
Should not Your Majesty
Bestow the honor of an interview.

ISABELLA:
Then bring him in and I shall hear what scheme
He has to offer. Should it prove to be
For Spain's enrichment, I shall see that France
Will profit not. So bring him in, forthwith.
(*The* COURTIER *bows and withdraws*)

2ND COURTIER:
He seeks to find a way to India
By sailing west.
(1ST COURTIER *enters followed by* COLUMBUS.)

1ST COURTIER:
Columbus waits, my Queen.
(COLUMBUS *advances to throne and kneels.*)

ISABELLA:

You have been most insistent in requests
For royal interviews. Will you explain
What special mission brings you to our court?

COLUMBUS
(*Rising as she gives the sign*):

Your Majesty, I know within my soul
That India lies westward. I would find
A shorter, quicker route.

ISABELLA:

And why should you
Believe that such a route is possible?

COLUMBUS:

Because, Your Majesty, I know — *I know;*
And why I cannot tell save that my faith
In this, my dream, is steadfast like a star
Forever pointing through its golden path,
Fulfillment.

ISABELLA:

What has this to do with us?
With Spain? Why do you tell us of the dream?

COLUMBUS:

Because from you I seek my help, because
I must have ships and men and gold to sail
To India; and my success would mean
Spain's everlasting glory and renown,
Spain's fame and strength throughout the world, Spain's share
Of gorgeous blue and white and yellow silks,
Of priceless rubies, pearls and diamonds.

ISABELLA:

Your words paint pretty pictures, yet we know
That dreams lack substance, and we cannot risk
Our ships, our men in venture.

COLUMBUS:

But I pledge
Success for Spain. Oh, grant me what I ask.

ISABELLA:

The country's coffers have been emptied since
Our wars have been such costly ones; I fear
I cannot listen to your plea. (*Pauses*) And yet

I wish within my heart it were not so.
Like you, Columbus, I have faith and hope.

COLUMBUS:
I thank you for those words, Your Majesty,
For even if you cannot grant my wish,
I know that you believe — and wish me well.
(*He bows, and turns to leave the room.*)

ISABELLA:
But tarry! I have thought of one sure way
To raise the money for your ships and men.
My jewels! I shall sell them — and the sum
Obtained will be most adequate, I trust,
To start the undertaking. Later on,
Perhaps we may give more substantial aid.

COLUMBUS:
Your Majesty, I am bereft of words.
I only hope that you will understand
The boundless measure of my gratitude.

ISABELLA:
Like you, Columbus, I have faith and hope.

CURTAIN

* * *

SCENE 3

SETTING: *The rounding part of a vessel with its ropes and sails.*

AT RISE: COLUMBUS *stands against the rail, in his hands a map unrolled. Close by is a sailor.*

1ST SAILOR:
For sixty dark and dreary days we've sailed
Along the treacherous sea. No sight of land —
No hope of land. The sailors mutiny.
They long for home, they dread each waking morn,
They feel that you have led them on a phantom quest.

COLUMBUS:

And yet, perchance, another day may bring
Some sign, some token that the land is near,
The end of all our wanderings — the end
Of all uncertainty, of all our fears.

1ST SAILOR:

So often have they heard these words, they scorn
To hear them once again. They must have proof
That they are nearing land.

COLUMBUS:

And have you told
That to the first who sights the land will go
A gold and velvet coat?

1ST SAILOR:

But even so,
They quarrel, they are sullen, and, alas,
They lose their zest, their spirit and their strength.

COLUMBUS:

But still, my soul is dauntless, unafraid,
I have the faith to know that we shall win;
I still have courage to sail on and on.

1ST SAILOR

(*Suddenly*): Look there! A bird! (*Excitedly*) A bird would not be far
From land.

COLUMBUS:

Our prayers are granted. 'Tis a sign
That we are almost at our sailing's end. (2ND SAILOR *appears in great excitement, holding a branch with berries.*)

2ND SAILOR:

Behold what we have found! 'Twas floating near
The ship — a branch with berries. This must mean
That there is land close by — perhaps *our* land.

COLUMBUS:

Our land, indeed; and now we all unite
In effort to sail on and on and on!

CURTAIN

* * *

Scene 4

Setting: *A landing place in the New World.*

At Rise: Columbus, *bearing the flag of Spain on a standard, advances, while the* Sailors *follow. At one side lurk one or two* Indians. *The* Sailors *are excited, and look from side to side, admiring and wondering.*

1st Sailor:

There never has been sky so blue and clear,
Nor trees so green nor flowers so many-colored,
It is a golden land — a beauteous land.

2nd Sailor:

Worth all fear and foreboding on the sea —
A land in which to rest, to live, to die. (Columbus *does not seem to hear. His eyes gaze into distance; his voice is calm and commanding.*)

Columbus:

I claim this country in the name of Spain!

THE END

THE MAGIC SPELL

by Esther Cooper

Characters

TEENA
HER MOTHER
BETTY
JIMMY
MRS. LANE
JENNY

SETTING: *A small, simply-furnished room.*

AT RISE: TEENA, *a little witch, is standing in the center of the stage with her mother, a taller and older witch.*

TEENA: Look, Mother! This is the playroom where Jimmy and Betty have their good times!

MOTHER (*Warningly*): Shh-h-h, Teena! Not so loud!

TEENA: I've always wanted to see how little boys and girls live! I'm sure they have much more fun than witches like us. Oh, thank you, Mother, for letting me come here!

MOTHER: But we must go now, Teena, we really must! Tonight is Halloween, and there is much to be done.

TEENA: Oh, please let me stay a little longer! They're going to have a Halloween party. I heard them talking about it. All the children will be wearing costumes and nobody will know I'm a *real* witch!

MOTHER (*Anxiously*): Oh, Teena, I don't think you should! Witches aren't supposed to be seen.

TEENA: I won't let them see me. I promise. Please, Mother, just this once!

MOTHER: Very well. But do be careful, dear. I'll come back for you before the Witching Hour.

TEENA (*Happily*): Oh, thank you! (MOTHER *kisses* TEENA *and goes out.* TEENA *looks at toys on the table. Suddenly, she hears voices outside and runs to hide behind the armchair. Enter* JIMMY *and* BETTY, *children about ten.* JIMMY *is carrying a pumpkin jack-o-lantern.*)

JIMMY: I think this is a pretty fine jack-o-lantern, even if I did make it, myself.

BETTY (*Admiringly*): Yes, it has a wonderful face. And, oh, Jimmy, the party will be more wonderful still! (JIMMY *places jack-o-lantern on table and sits in chair at left, while* BETTY *takes chair at right.*)

JIMMY: Did you see all the decorations and prizes we're going to have at the party?

BETTY: And the pretty table with the favors and candles and big, grinning pumpkin-face?

JIMMY: Just think, Betty! It will be our very first party!

BETTY: Orphans never have parties of their own, I guess. We wouldn't have had this one if Mrs. Lane hadn't planned it for us and bought our costumes.

JIMMY: She's awfully nice, isn't she? (*Wistfully*) I bet our own mother was good and sweet, just like her.

BETTY: Remember the day she came to the Home and said she wanted to take a brother and sister to her house for a visit?

JIMMY: And we were so scared she wouldn't choose us!

BETTY: I shook in my shoes, I was so afraid she wouldn't! But she did, Jimmy — and haven't we had fun?

JIMMY: Yes, but —

BETTY: But what?

JIMMY: Don't you wish we could stay here with Mrs. Lane always?

BETTY: Yes, I do. Mrs. Lane has been so good to us that I feel as if she sort of belonged to us.

JIMMY: So do I. She's like a real mother, isn't she?

BETTY: We'll be pretty lonesome without her when we go back to the Home. Do you s'pose she'll come to see us often?

JIMMY: I hope so! (*They are silent for a moment.*)

BETTY (*Suddenly*): Jimmy!

JIMMY: Yes?

BETTY: Do you think — do you s'pose she'd *adopt* us?

JIMMY: Oh, we couldn't ask her to do that!

BETTY: No, I guess we couldn't, but — (*Warningly*) Sh-h-h-h! I think she's coming! (*Enter* MRS. LANE, *a pretty young woman.*

JIMMY *rises as she enters and stands until she seats herself in the chair at center.*)

MRS. LANE: Jenny said you were in the playroom. Are you all ready for the party?

JIMMY: Oh, yes, indeed! And I made another pumpkin-face! (*Points to it.*)

MRS. LANE (*Admiring it*): It's a very lovely one, Jimmy.

BETTY: We were just talking about the party. How pretty it's going to be and how —

JIMMY: How nice of you to plan it for us!

BETTY: You've been so good to us, Mrs. Lane.

JIMMY: And we never will forget you — never!

MRS. LANE: Thank you, my dears. It was lonely in this house before you came. But now it is a happy place. And I am glad to hear you say you are happy here, because — (*Enter* JENNY, *the maid. She is carrying a tray which holds a teacup, saucer, napkin, spoon, and sugar-bowl.*) I thought I'd have a cup of tea before the party began. Put it here, Jenny. (*Motions to table.* JENNY *puts tray on table, pours tea, and drops sugar into cup.*)

JENNY: Is that all, ma'am?

MRS. LANE: Yes, thank you, Jenny. (JENNY *goes out. As* MRS. LANE *begins to speak again,* TEENA *rises slowly from her hiding place behind the armchair. They do not see her. She leans over the table and passes her hands across the teacup, her lips moving.*) This is your first party, and I want you to have a very good time. There will be games and favors and stunts and prizes for everyone. Ice cream too. (*The children clap their hands in delight.*) When the guests arrive, you must meet them at the door and tell them how glad you are to see them. You won't know them, of course, because they'll be masked. But you can make them feel welcome just the same. (TEENA *hides again.*)

JIMMY: Shall we go in and look for them now?

BETTY: It must be almost time. (MRS. LANE *picks up the teacup and sips some of the tea. Then she replaces it on the saucer.*)

MRS. LANE: Before you go, there's something I want to tell you. You said you were happy here — and I am happy, too. So I'm going to ask you to stay with me and be my very own children.

JIMMY (*Astonished*): You mean you want to — adopt us?

BETTY: Really and truly?

MRS. LANE (*Rising*): Yes, really and truly! (*They run to her.*)

JIMMY: Oh, Mrs. Lane, it would be grand!

BETTY: Oh, I could cry — I'm so happy! (*They hug* MRS. LANE *happily. Enter* JENNY.)

JENNY: The children are coming, ma'am.

MRS. LANE: We'll come at once. (JENNY *leaves.*) Put on your masks when we reach the living-room. (*Laughs.*) You're my own boy and girl, now, and must do as I say. (*They go out. In a moment* TEENA'S MOTHER *steals in and looks about.*)

MOTHER (*Softly*): Teena? Teena, where are you?

TEENA (*Rising merrily*): Here I am, Mother! I was hiding.

MOTHER: Come, dear, It's time for our Witching Flight. Did anyone see you here?

TEENA: Oh, no, Mother! But I had a wonderful time! I saw two little orphan children, and heard them wishing they could be adopted by the lady who lives here — and, Mother, I made her adopt them!

MOTHER: You did? How could you do that?

TEENA: I said a magic spell over her teacup, Mother — and it worked! It really worked! I think I'm a very good little witch, don't you, Mother?

MOTHER (*Smiling, as she puts her arm about* TEENA): Yes, dear. You're a very good little witch.

THE END

THE WITCH'S PUMPKIN

by Esther Cooper

Characters
BETSY, *a little girl*
ANNE, *her friend*
CINDY, *the Witch*

SETTING: *A room in* BETSY'S *home.*

AT RISE: BETSY *is sitting in the chair behind the table, making a jack-o-lantern from a small pumpkin. It is almost completed and she works busily.*

ANNE (*Outside*): Betsy! Oh, Betsy!

BETSY (*Looking up*): Here I am, Anne. Come on in! (*Enter* ANNE. *She is about* BETSY'S *age and is wearing a gay Halloween costume.*)

ANNE (*Anxiously*): It's getting late, Betsy, and I think we'd better hurry if we don't want to be — (*Stops and stares at* BETSY.) Why aren't you *ready!* It's nearly eight!

BETSY: I — I'm not going, Anne.

ANNE: Not going? Why, what do you *mean?* It's going to be the best Halloween party the school ever had! Everybody in our class will be there, and the gym is all decorated and everything. Why, we're going to have cider — and bob for apples — and eat ice cream and — oh, Betsy, you *must* be joking! (*She sits down in one of the chairs nearby.*)

BETSY: No, Anne, I'm not joking. I — I just can't go.

ANNE: But *why?*

BETSY: I just can't go — that's all.

ANNE: But you must have some reason. (*She waits a moment, but there is no answer, so she speaks again.*) Betsy — is it because— you have no costume?

BETSY: Yes, it is — if you must know! (*Pleadingly*) But please don't tell the others.

ANNE: You know I won't. But they're sure to wonder why you aren't there.

BETSY: Just tell them I couldn't come.

ANNE: Oh, Betsy, I'm so sorry you're going to miss the party. It's sure to be *such* a nice one!

BETSY: I know — I'm sorry, too. I could — just *cry* — I want to go so much. But Mother couldn't buy a costume for me this year — or even the material to make one. You know we've not had very much money, Anne, since Dad died.

ANNE: Why didn't you tell me? I'm sure my mother could have found something for you to wear?

BETSY: Mother doesn't like me to ask favors. Never mind, Anne. You go on to the party. You can tell me about it afterward.

ANNE: Oh, it's going to be so exciting. Jane Livingstone is coming. I heard her say so. She's so new here I haven't had a chance to get acquainted with her yet — but she seems awfully nice. Most rich girls are a little snooty sometimes — but Jane isn't!

BETSY: No, she's sweet.

ANNE: She gave me one of her new books to read. I'd have brought it along for you, if I'd known you weren't going. It's just full of the best stories! There's one about making your wishes come true on Halloween. Seeing that jack-o-lantern made me think of it.

BETSY: What has a jack-o-lantern to do with wishes?

ANNE: The stories says that if you write a note on a jack-o-lantern and tell your wish, and then put the lantern outside on Halloween, some good witch will find it and make your wish come true.

BETSY: Why, that would be fun! I'd like to try it, myself — only, of course, there aren't any witches, really — good or bad.

ANNE: There might be. How do we know? Just because we never saw one —

BETSY: I know what wish I'd make!

ANNE: What, Betsy?

BETSY: I'd wish to go to the party! (*Laughs*) Just as Cinderella wished to go to the ball.

ANNE: Wish for a costume. Then you *know* you can go!

BETSY: Yes, wouldn't that be fun?

ANNE: Go on, Betsy — do it! Write your wish on the jack-o-lantern and put it out on the steps.

BETSY: Oh, Anne, that's silly! You know there aren't any witches!

ANNE: Do it, anyway! I sort of believe in magic, myself.

BETSY: Besides, unless the witch came right away, it would be too late to go to the party.

ANNE: Here, let me do it. (*Takes a pencil and begins to write on the pumpkin*) "To a Good Witch — Please bring me a Halloween costume so I can go to the class party. This is my wish. Betsy."

BETSY: Oh, Anne, this is *ridiculous!* (*Laughs*)

ANNE: It's worth trying, anyway. (*She goes to the door, taking the pumpkin.*) I'll put it on the steps. (*Goes out.*)

BETSY (*Calling after her*): Anne, you'd better be going to that party instead of writing notes to witches! You'll be late — and there's no use in waiting for a witch to come in here!

ANNE (*Coming back*): Well, we've tried, anyway. I think I'll have plenty of time to get to the party — where's the clock?

BETSY: In the hall. Wait, I'll see what time it is. (*Goes to the other door.*) It's a quarter to eight.

ANNE: Then I still have fifteen minutes. I'll wait a little while. It must be lonely for you — staying here by yourself.

BETSY: It is — a little. But I'm sure the evenings are much harder for Mother. She works until so late — and she's always so tired. (*There is a knock at the door.*)

ANNE: What's that?

BETSY: Sounded like somebody at the door.

ANNE: Goodness, you don't suppose — !

BETSY (*Laughing*): Oh, no! It's probably Mrs. Carter — one of our neighbors. She's always running over to look after me when Mother's gone. (*Calling*) Come in, Mrs. Carter! (*Enter* CINDY, *the witch, carrying a broom and a package.*)

CINDY (*Laughing*): It isn't Mrs. Carter. It's Cindy — the witch!

BETSY: Witch! (*She utters a startled cry and clings to* ANNE.)

ANNE: You — you read the note on the pumpkin?

CINDY: Yes, I saw it as I came up the steps.

BETSY: Then you must be a good witch. I mean — the note was meant for a good witch.

CINDY: I try to be good. I brought you a costume so you could go to the party. I hope it fits you.

BETSY: A costume?

ANNE: Oh, Betsy, try it on quick! Maybe you can go to the party after all!

BETSY (*Opening package*): Oh, thank you very much. (*Holds up the costume.*) What a pretty one! I'm sure it will fit me, too!

ANNE: Put it on quick!

CINDY: Yes, we mustn't be late.

BETSY: Are you — going with us?

CINDY: Of course. I love parties.

BETSY: But — but — suppose they find out you're a witch?

CINDY: I *want* them to think I'm a witch.

BETSY: But —

CINDY (*Laughing*): Don't look so worried. I'm a very good witch. And, anyway, it's all a joke.

ANNE: What's a joke?

CINDY: My pretending to be a witch — when I'm really not. (*She takes off mask.*)

ANNE: Jane!

BETSY: Jane Livingstone!

ANNE: And we thought you really *were* a witch!

BETSY (*Confused*): I know there aren't any — but after the note, and everything —

ANNE: And then you coming in with a costume —

JANE: Well, you see, it was like this — Betsy's mother is helping my mother with a party tonight, at our house. So I talked to her about the school party and found out why Betsy wasn't going. I had a costume I'd hardly worn, so I asked if I might bring it over here for you.

ANNE: Oh, that was *sweet* of you!

JANE: I didn't want Betsy to miss the party.

BETSY: Oh, thank you — thank you *very* much! I'm *so* glad I can go, too!

JANE: Dad will take us to the school in our car. He's outside now, waiting for us.

ANNE: Betsy, *do* get dressed!

BETSY: I will. It won't take me a moment — but I'm so excited, I hardly know what I'm doing! Because I'm sure I'll be the only person there whose costume was brought to her by a Good Witch! (*They laugh as the curtain closes.*)

THE END

GOBLIN PARADE

by Beulah Folmsbee

Characters

JANITOR, *one of the tallest boys in the class*
BOY
GOBLINS
SCARECROW
CAT
BAT
WITCH *on a Broom*
HARRY
JACK

SETTING: *A schoolroom.*

AT RISE: THE JANITOR *enters wearily, dragging his broom.*

JANITOR: Bless my soul, but I'm tired! I've swept and dusted every room in the schoolhouse—except this. My back is nearly broken! Well, this is the last room, and thank goodness nothing is going on here. No play or anything like that, thank goodness. Plays are a terrible lot of bother. Why, last year the eighth-graders put on a play and I thought I'd *never* get the room clean again. (*Leans on broom and looks about.*) But as I say, nothing's going on here, thank goodness. I believe I'll sit down and rest my old bones before I begin. (*Sits in chair, broom between his knees.*) I believe I need forty winks. (*Yawns.*) Yes, that's just what I need — forty winks. After that I'll sweep and dust the room, put out the lights, lock the schoolhouse door and go home to bed. (*Longer and louder yawn.*) My, but I'm glad all the teachers and children have gone home. No one to pester me about anything. No sir, not a soul. Ho-o-o-o-o hum-m-m-mm! (*Makes himself as comfortable as he can and falls asleep.*)

BOY (*Rising from his seat in front row of the audience*): Mr. Janitor! Mr. Janitor! (JANITOR *shifts uneasily and mutters in his sleep.* BOY *calls louder and comes nearer.*) Mr. Janitor! But you're mistaken! We haven't gone home. We're all right here, you see.

JANITOR (*Nearly awake now*): What's that? I could swear I heard someone pestering me. Oh, well, probably I'm dreaming. This chair isn't as comfortable as it might be. (*Settles down again.*)

BOY (*Coming to* JANITOR *and shaking him by shoulder*): No, no! You're *not* dreaming! Wake up! Wake up and see for yourself!

JANITOR (*Clutching broom, jumps up in alarm*): What's that? Well, bless my soul, where did you come from? (*Sees audience; his mouth drops open in surprise.*) And where did all of *you* come from? (*Scratches head in bewilderment.*)

BOY: Why, don't you know? You must have forgotten! It's the play, you know.

JANITOR (*In disgust*): Play? Did you say *play?*

BOY: Yes, don't you remember? There's going to be a play here today. We've been rehearsing it for ever so long.

JANITOR (*Looking around the stage wonderingly*): What kind of play?

BOY: A Halloween play of course. Everything's all ready. (*Goes to exit at left, and turns, waiting for* JANITOR *to follow.*)

JANITOR (*Still at centre, groans comically*): Just my luck! A Halloween play! They're the *worst* kind to clean up after. (*More cheerful.*) But, bless my soul, there isn't a sign of anything around here. No scenery, or anything like that. (*With hand at his mouth so* BOY *won't hear, he speaks in loud whisper to audience.*) Not much of a play, I'd say. Why, whoever heard of a play without scenery and things? (*Leaning on broom and beginning to enjoy his conversation with the audience.*) Let's see now, there ought to be a cornfield, or something like that, with the sun shining on it, maybe. Or a moon — why yes, certainly, that's it! There ought to be a moon for a Halloween play. And a scarecrow, maybe; and black cats, and bats, and owls, and a witch and things. Oh my, no, (*In growing disdain*) this is going to be no kind of a play at all. No kind of a play at all!

BOY (*Still at exit where he has been trying to get the* JANITOR'S *attention*): Pssst! Psssssst! Mr. Janitor! Come off the stage.

The play's going to begin. If you don't come off, *you'll* be in it!

JANITOR (*Shrugging his shoulders*): All right, all right, I'm coming. But bless my soul and body, it can't be much of a play! Mind you (*Appealing to audience*) not a stick of furniture even, except this chair. . . .

BOY: Pssssst! Hurry, hurry, and please bring that chair with you.

JANITOR (*Triumphantly*): There! Just what I said! Now they're not even going to have a chair for a body to sit on. (*To audience again*) I'm sorry for you, I am. I could put on a better play myself. (*Music is heard off stage.*)

BOY: There! It's beginning! Will you *please* come off?

JANITOR (*Grabs chair and broom and goes out stumbling over broom in his hurry, and muttering as he goes*): Never heard of such a thing! No kind of a play at all, I say; no kind of a play at all! (JANITOR *goes off left, and* BOY *returns to his seat in front row.*)

BOY (*As he sits down*): There! Now it can begin. (*Music grows louder, a sprightly goblin-like music, and* THE GOBLINS *enter, hopping along in time with it. Two of them carry a step-ladder which they place near the back wall at left; two more carry a huge orange-colored sun which they hang on the wall, after which the other* GOBLINS *remove the ladder from the stage. From right and left other* GOBLINS *enter, carrying two corn shocks which they set up at right and left a few feet from the back wall. Two or three more* GOBLINS *enter prancing along with a huge jack-o-lantern which they place near one of the corn shocks being careful to keep the uncut side toward the audience so that it will look like a pumpkin growing in the field. Other* GOBLINS *lead in the* SCARECROW *who walks very stiffly and has to be straightened out and steadied as he is placed in center near the back. All during the setting of the stage, the* GOBLINS *have moved in a sprightly manner, the music still accompanying their movements, and as each bit of stage setting is accomplished they point to it with satisfacion and with a gesture as if to say "How's that?" When all is in readiness, they join hands in a grotesque kind of dance and start out, half to the right, half to the left. When they are nearly out, the music breaks in a comical way as* SCARECROW *starts to slump and fall over. The last goblin on each side rushes back; with some difficulty they prop the* SCARECROW *up again.* GOBLINS *go out. This action can be curtailed or expanded with many comic effects depending upon the skill of the young players.*)

HARRY (*Shouting off stage and running on*): Here it is! This is the place. Farmer Brown's field. I saw a fine one growing here.

JACK (*Entering directly after* HARRY): This is Farmer Brown's field all right. That's his funny old hat on the scarecrow; and I guess that red thing round its neck must be Mrs. Brown's petticoat!

HARRY: Don't be bothering about any old scarecrows. You've got to find a good pumpkin for your jack-o-lantern if you want to be in the parade tonight. (*Sees pumpkin.*) Hi! Look there!

JACK: Where?

HARRY: There! (*Pointing to pumpkin and running to it as if to pull it from the vines*) I told you I'd seen a jim-dandy. Why, that's the biggest one I've seen anywhere.

JACK (*Rushing to stop him*): Harry! Wait a minute, don't pick it! I've just remembered something.

HARRY (*On his knees with hands on pumpkin*): What? What is it?

JACK: It's a jim-dandy all right, but . . .

HARRY: But what? Here I go and find you a pumpkin — better than any of the rest of us have — and now you look as if you didn't even want it!

JACK: Oh, I *want* it all right enough. It would make the best lantern in the whole parade. . . .

HARRY: You mean it will if you get busy and make it into one. You won't have any lantern at all if you don't get started pretty soon!

JACK (*Uncomfortably, looking in all directions*): Yes . . . but . . . do you think . . . It's such a nice one . . .

HARRY (*Exploding*): Well, isn't that what you want?

JACK: Yes, but Harry . . . you know the County Fair they're going to have next week?

HARRY: Of course, I know. My dad's going to be one of the judges, and I'm going to help put ribbons on the winners.

JACK: That's just it! I heard *my* dad say that Farmer Brown is going to try for first prize for pumpkins this year; he almost won it last year, but there was one just a little better than his . . .

HARRY (*Whistling*): Phe-e-e-e-w! You mean you think this is for the Fair?

JACK: Yes. That's what I'm afraid of. If only we could find Farmer Brown; or if there was another pumpkin around somewhere. I know he would let us have it if we asked him. You see I couldn't take this one without asking because . . . well, my dad said the reason Farmer Brown didn't get that first prize last year is because some of his best pumpkins were taken by boys. So, you see . . .

HARRY: Sure; I don't want to take any prize pumpkins for jack-o-lanterns; but, shucks, Jack, what did you have to wait till today for, anyway? You should have started days ago to look for your pumpkin. My lantern's been ready for almost a week.

JACK: I know it. (*Miserably*) And I wouldn't miss the parade for anything. They're going to have all kinds of things this year, I've heard.

HARRY: Yes, and then we're all going down to the edge of the pond and have a big fire, and a corn roast, and tell ghost stories and everything! Boy, I can hardly wait! Well, I'd help you look some more, but I've got to go up in our attic for some old clothes, and my false face and things. What are you going to do?

JACK: I . . . I think I'll just wait a while and see if I can find Farmer Brown. I know he comes this way with his cows, and it must be nearly four o'clock now.

HARRY: Four o'clock! Say, I've got to hurry. I'm going to get my things ready so I can get dressed right after supper. Whooopee! Wait till you see how I'm going to look! This is going to be the best parade we've ever had. Don't forget we're all going to meet at the corner. So long! It gets dark early, too! Whe-e-e-e-e! (*He goes jumping and running off left.* JACK *walks slowly over and watches* HARRY*; comes back, looking around for some other pumpkin, shakes his head, and kneels by the pumpkin, running his hands over its smooth sides.*)

JACK: Boy, what a beauty! Wouldn't I like to make my lantern out of you! (*Takes knife from pocket, opens it and feels edge.*) I'd just stick this in, cut all around the top . . . (*Takes hold of stem and goes through motions of cutting, but is careful not to really come anywhere near the pumpkin with his knife.*) Then I'd scoop out the inside and cut the eyes and nose and . . . oh, well, what's the use of talking. I'll sit back here for a little while and wait for Farmer Brown to come by with his cows. (*Sits almost hidden by corn shock at left with his back to the audience and facing the* SCARECROW.) Shucks! Why couldn't *you* be some help and tell me whether Farmer Brown has gone by? But then, of course, you're really not good for anything except to scare the crows away. (*Drowsily*) Hmmmmmm! It would be funny if you *could* see and talk. I bet you'd see a lot of things in a field like this. In the daytime all the bugs, and grasshoppers and things (*Growing more drowsy*) and at night, when everything is quiet, and dark . . . just a moon maybe, or some stars; and little animals, maybe, coming out of their holes, and . . . and . . . (*His head goes down upon his knees. He is asleep.* SCARECROW *comes to life, stretches stiffly, goes to* BOY *and makes sure he is asleep. Beckons off stage each side. Goblin music, a little more sombre than before, is heard. Again* GOBLINS *enter, take down the sun, bring in a huge yellow moon and hang it up on the opposite side of the back wall. The* SCARECROW, *removing ladder as before, directs them to the sleeping boy, cautioning them to be quiet.*)

SCARECROW (*Moving away from boy and motioning* GOBLINS *to follow; music stops*): Know what that is? (GOBLINS *shake heads.*) It's a boy! You know, one of the earth people. (GOBLINS *draw back in fright.*) Oh, *he* won't hurt you! He's really pretty good—for a boy! He wanted like everything to take that pumpkin over there for some kind of a — what-do-you-call-it — that they carry in parades. It seems that people dress themselves up in all sorts of queer things, though between you and me, they're a queer looking lot just as they are! They go parading up and down the street making queer noises, tapping on windows — all sorts of things. *He* wanted this pumpkin to carry in the parade, but he wouldn't take it without asking Farmer Brown. I could have told him it would be all right because Farmer Brown went by with the cows just before those boys came here. I heard him say he didn't care if boys took pumpkins now because the best ones were all packed and ready for the Fair. (GOBLINS *whisper together, then one of them goes to* SCARECROW *and whispers in his ear.*) Did you say parade? A Goblin parade? (GOBLINS *nod delightedly.*) That's a good idea. I wonder I didn't think of it myself! Yes sir, that's *just* what we'll do. Go find old Owl and tell him to call everybody together. (GOBLINS *run out,* SCARECROW *jerks back to his place, stifling his laughter.*) Haw Haw Haw! You'll see a parade after all; and afterwards, you'll think you've been dreaming!

OWL (*Whose voice always sounds from off stage*): Whoooooo — Wooooooo — Whoooo!

CAT (*Entering importantly*): Who indeed?
I'm the cat
The big black cat!
Miaoww, Miaoww, Miaow-w-w-w!
(*Prowling about in circle as he repeats.*)

BAT (*Entering with a rush from the other side*):
And I'm the Bat
As black as your hat,
Whir-r-r, Whir-r-r, Whir-r-r!
(*Sweeping about in circles*)

OWL: Whoooo — Who-o-o-o — Who-o-o-o-o.

SCARECROW: Who, me?
Why, I'm the scarecrow made of straw
Nothing poetic,
In fact quite pathetic
(*Offstage a crow cries "'Caw Caw Caw'"*)
Funny, I never *thought* of that!
Haw, haw, haw-w-w-w!
(*Jerking with laughter,* SCARECROW *begins to fall over.*) Oh, help, help! Straighten me up somebody! I'm not used to laughing so hard. (GOBLINS *enter and prop* SCARECROW *up again.*) Thank you, thank you kindly. And see here, why wouldn't it be a good idea to take that pumpkin and make one of those what-do-you-call it — you know; what they carry in parades. (*He goes through motions of cutting out top, and making jack-o-lantern, and pretends he is holding it up as he makes a terrible face.* GOBLINS *nod with delight and tiptoe over to pumpkin, carry it off to corner, and sit around it at work.*) What a surprise *that'll* be when he wakes up! Haw! haw! haw! Ouch, there I go again. Help me somebody! (CAT *and* BAT *help the* SCARECROW *to straighten up again.*)

OWL: Who-o-o-o Who-o-o-o Who-o-o-o-o!

WITCH (*Entering astride her broom and galloping to centre*):
I'm the funny old witch

That rides on a broom,
And I'll ride and I'll ride
Till the day of my doom!

(WITCH *rides madly in a circle in center,* CAT *prowls in a circle at right.* BAT *sweeps in a circle at left, all making characteristic cries, while* SCARECROW *keeps time. All engage in a grotesque kind of dance in which the* GOBLINS *join, two of them carrying the completed jack-o-lantern, and leading the others around the stage in a parade.*)

OWL: Who-o-o-o-o-o-o! (*In a warning voice this time*) Who-o-o-o-o-o!

SCARECROW (*Peering into distance*): Boys coming this way! Girls too! Quick, everybody, hide! Parade's over! (*All except the* GOBLINS *run off; they bring Jack-o-lantern to* SCARECROW *offering it to him*) No, no, put it over there, right where it was! And hurry! (GOBLINS *place pumpkin in its original position, but with the cut-out face toward the audience, and steal off, looking back over their shoulders at it in admiration. As they go,* JACK *starts to waken as* SCARECROW *is jerking himself back into his original position. As* JACK *jumps up in amazement, he sees the last jerk of the* SCARECROW'S *arms as he becomes once more just a straw man.*)

JACK (*Rubbing his eyes and looking about*): I've been asleep! Of course, I *must* have been asleep and it was all a dream, but . . . but . . . I was *sure* I saw him move his arm just then. (*Sees jack-o-lantern*). And if it was a *dream,* where did this come from? (*He runs to lantern and takes it up*) Wow! What a beauty! (*Voices of boys and girls off stage calling for* JACK.)

HARRY (*Offstage*): Jack! Jack! Where are you? The parade's all over and we're going to the cornroast. Jack!

JACK: I'm here! I'm coming too! Harry, wait for me. I'm coming, (*He starts to go and then turns toward* SCARECROW.) and I've got a lantern, too, thanks to you. A jim-dandy of a lantern and that was the best parade I ever saw! A witch, and everything! Thanks! (*Running off*) Harry, look! Look at my lantern! (*When all is quiet,* GOBLINS *enter and remove all traces of the play — the moon, corn stacks, and scarecrow. If any lights have been used for sun or moon effects, these are now turned off and the stage is as it was in the beginning. Music which has been playing as the* GOBLINS *clear the stage stops and boy in the front row begins to applaud. As other children join in the applause, the* JANITOR *pokes his head cautiously in, and seeing the stage empty comes on looking about.*)

JANITOR: It it all over? Ho, hummmmmm! I've been down in the basement having a snooze. Bless my soul, I don't believe a thing has happened here. Everything looks just as it did when that boy shooed me off. (*Sees audience.*) What! Are you still here? Well, I *told* you you couldn't have a play without — oh, *you* know, scenery — a cornfield, a moon and witches and things! Well, as there's to be no play, I'll get at my work! Ho hummm! Good-bye children. (*He starts to sweep the floor making the dust fly as the curtain falls.*)

THE END

THE MAGIC JACK-O-LANTERN

by Helen Littler Howard

Characters

GOBLINS:
- TRAPPY, *who is always playing tricks on others*
- FLAPPY, *who has enormous ears*
- NAPPY, *who never is fully awake*
- (*And as many more as you care to have*)

ELVES:
- MICKY
- NICKY, *and others if you want them.*

A WITCH

SETTING: *Any spot where elves and goblins might meet on Halloween.*

TIME: *Just before the Halloween Jamboree.*

AT RISE: FLAPPY *comes on the stage carrying a large jack-o-lantern.*

FLAPPY: Halloween at last! I do wish I could think of a way to get that beautiful scarlet leaf from Trappy. He is always playing tricks on others so I wouldn't feel mean if I could trick him once. If I had that leaf to wear in my cap at the Halloween Jamboree no one would notice my ears. Here comes my friend the Witch. Maybe she could tell me a thing or two. (OLD WITCH *comes hobbling in on a broomstick.*)

FLAPPY: Hi, Witch. You are just in time to help me.

WITCH: Greetings, Flappy. A fine Halloween night to be sure. What can I do for you? A magic potion perhaps?

FLAPPY: Perhaps. Trappy has a magnificent scarlet leaf which I hanker to wear to the Jamboree tonight so that no one would notice my ears. He won't lend it, sell it, or trade it. He sets so many traps for others that I wouldn't feel mean about tricking him out of it.

WITCH: Let me see! How about a magic jack-o-lantern?

FLAPPY: But I haven't a magic jack-o-lantern.

WITCH: You have a jack-o-lantern and I can tell you how to make it magic.

FLAPPY: Can you? Oh, please do.

WITCH: Come close so I can whisper the secret to you. . . . I wouldn't want anyone else to hear. (FLAPPY *comes close to the* WITCH *and she whispers something in his ear.*)

FLAPPY: The very thing! I do thank you with all my heart.

WITCH: Good luck. (*Goes off stage.*)

FLAPPY: I'll wear the leaf to the Jamboree, and then no one will notice my ears! (*Enter* TRAPPY, NAPPY *and other Goblins.*)

FLAPPY: Hi, fellows. All ready for the Jamboree? I see you are wearing your scarlet leaf, Trappy. I wish I had one to stick in my cap so that no one would notice my ears.

TRAPPY: I won't give it to you, sell it to you, nor trade it.

NAPPY (*Yawning*): Who said something about a raid?

TRAPPY: No, no, Nappy. Wake up. I said I wouldn't trade my leaf for anything Flappy has.

FLAPPY: That's too bad you won't consider a trade. I thought you might like my magic jack-o-lantern.

TRAPPY: *Magic* jack-o-lantern! What's magic about it? It looks like any other jack-o-lantern to me.

NAPPY: Looks like any other jack-o-lantern to me! Looks just like mine. (*Others laugh.*)

FLAPPY: It is a magic jack-o-lantern though.

TRAPPY: What can it do?

FLAPPY: I'll show you. Trappy, I'll take off the lid and blow out the light, and you put your leaf inside. (*Does so.*) Now I'll wager that I can get the leaf and I won't touch the jack-o-lantern.

TRAPPY: Agreed! If you can get the leaf without touching the lantern I'll give it to you. (GOBLINS *gather around.*)

FLAPPY (*Walks slowly around the jack-o-lantern three times*): Adaca Cadabra . . . Adaca Cadabra, *etc.* Now take off the lid, Trappy. (TRAPPY *does so.*) And I take the leaf. (*Does so without touching the lantern.*)

TRAPPY: Here, give me my leaf.

NAPPY: The leaf!

FLAPPY: It's mine. I said I'd wager that I could get the leaf without touching the lantern and I did. (GOBLINS *laugh.*)

NAPPY: I guess that's right. You won it all right. (GOBLINS *go off stage leaving* TRAPPY *and* NAPPY.)

TRAPPY: Well, I lost my leaf, but it was a good trick. I wish I had a lantern so I could play it on some of the elves when they come. Let me use yours, Nappy.

NAPPY: I want to lay the brick . . . I mean play the joke. It's my lantern, but I'll give you whatever I get. Here come the elves, and look, one of them has a scarlet robin's feather in his cap. I'll get it for you.

TRAPPY: Do you think you know how, Nappy? Were you awake all of the time so you know how it goes?

NAPPY: Of course I was . . . I can remember it exactly . . . I think. (ELVES *enter.* MICKY *is wearing a cap with a red feather in it.*)

MICKY: Hi, Goblins! Can you tell us where the Jamboree is to be?

TRAPPY: Over there in the forest under the biggest oak tree.

NAPPY: That's a fine feather you have in your cap, Micky. How would you like to borrow it . . . I mean lend it to Trappy.

MICKY: I really wouldn't part with it. It's a special feather.

NICKY: The Queen gave it to him. She put it in his cap with her own hands.

NAPPY: Maybe you would like to trade it for my magic jack-o-lantern . . .

MICKY: *Magic* jack-o-lantern! It looks like any other pumpkin face to me. What's magic about it?

NAPPY: Here, you show me . . . I mean I'll show you.

TRAPPY (*Aside*): Are you sure you can do it, Nappy?

NAPPY: Now you meave it to le . . . I mean me. Now I'll take off the lid and you put the feather inside. (*They do so.*) Now, I'll bet that you can't get the feather unless I touch the lantern.

MICKY: That I can't get the feather unless you touch the lantern! I'll wager my feather against your lantern that I can.

NAPPY (*Greatly excited*): I'll go around the lantern like this . . . (*Goes around three times saying "Adaca Cadabra" . . .*) Now take off the lid, Mickey. (MICKY *does so and also takes the feather.*)

MICKY: There I took the feather and you didn't touch the lantern . . . (*Takes lantern*) so the lantern and feather are both mine.

You must be touched by the moonlight, Nappy. (ELVES *go off laughing.*)

TRAPPY (*Rolling about in delight*): That was worth losing my leaf!

NAPPY: Now, what did I say wrong! I can't touch the feather unless you — no, no . . . You can't touch the lantern until I . . . Oh, how does it go!

TRAPPY: Never mind, Nappy. I guess the tables were turned on us that time . . .

NAPPY: And I lost my beautiful lack-o-jantern!

TRAPPY: Maybe you'll learn to keep awake after this. Hi ho for the Halloween Jamboree! (*They go off laughing.*)

THE END

THE MAGIC PUMPKIN

by Lee Kingman

Characters

WANDA
GILDA
THE MINSTREL
MRS. FITCH
TONY
MOTHER
TOMMY
WILLIE
LONNY
MARY
MILLIE
FIRST GUARD
SECOND GUARD
CAPTAIN OF THE GUARD
THE KING
JACKO

SETTING: *A bench by the wayside on a bright fall morning.*

AT RISE: WANDA *and* GILDA *are sitting on the bench when the* MINSTREL *comes in left, weeping into a tremendous white handkerchief.*

MINSTREL: Hello.
WANDA *and* GILDA: Hello.
MINSTREL (*Sniffing*): Is it a nice day?
GILDA: Certainly. Can't you see that it is?
MINSTREL: I haven't looked.
WANDA: What's the matter? Have you a piece of something in your eye?
MINSTREL (*Crossly*): Of course I haven't. Just use your head and you'd know why I'm crying.
GILDA: I don't see why.

MINSTREL: Well, what day is it today?

WANDA: It's the end of October.

MINSTREL: There . . . you see. It's Halloween.

GILDA: What's Halloween?

MINSTREL: My dear child! What's Halloween! But I suppose you may call it All Saints' Eve. It's one and the same. Good to some and evil to others. (*Sighing*) It was evil to me!

WANDA: Why, what happened?

MINSTREL: It's so sad that I wrote a song about it . . . only I'm a monotone, so I'll have to recite it instead. Sit down, now, and I'll say it to you . . . with gestures. (*They settle on the bench, and he bows to them, takes a deep breath and begins.*)

MINSTREL:

I am a homeless wanderer.
This is my tale of woe.
I have no home, I have no friends,
I have no place to go.

I used to live in splendor,
In a large and gilded nook,
In the palace of our royal king . . .
I was the pastry cook.

Boo-hoo, I was the cook.

The king was kind and gentle,
And he had a little boy . . .
His only son, named Jacko,
Who was his pride and joy.

Now Jacko, though he was a prince,
Was quite a little brat.
And he had a nasty habit
Of blowing up like that. (MINSTREL *puffs up his cheeks.*)

Boo-hoo. He used to blow 'em up like that.

It happened several years ago,
Upon an All Saints' Eve,
That Jacko puffed his cheeks up
And his nurse got in a peeve.

The nurse was old and fussy.
She didn't wait to yell
But placed on little Jacko
An old and magic spell.

Boo-hoo. A wicked, magic spell.

GILDA: Don't stop!
WANDA: Do go on.
GILDA: We want to know what happened!
MINSTREL: Well . . .
Jacko gave one feeble scream
And vanished in thin air. . . .
He became in just one second
The boy who wasn't there.
WANDA: Oh!
GILDA: You can't stop there!
MINSTREL: Oh yes, I can. You try and make up a song sometime. It's hard work.
WANDA: But what happened . . . who did it?
MINSTREL: It was the nurse. She turned him into a pumpkin seed . . . and lost the seed. She was very careless.
GILDA: It is sad.
WANDA: But what happened to you . . . what makes you so sad?
MINSTREL: Because the king had been very fond of just one thing . . . he ate it for breakfast and dinner and supper . . . pumpkin pie. And I was the only one who could make it the way he liked it. But, of course, after that, he couldn't bear to eat pumpkin pie . . . so he fired me. And that's the reason I'm out of work . . . pumpkin pie is the only thing I can cook.
WANDA: I'm very sorry.
MINSTREL: Thank you. So now you see, every Halloween I go out looking for pumpkins . . . just in case Jacko should have grown up to be one. There's a ghost of a chance I might find him.
GILDA: Was he a very bad boy?
MINSTREL: No. Do you have a brother?
WANDA: Yes. Tony.
MINSTREL: Does he like to tease? And play noisy games?
WANDA: Yes.

MINSTREL: Then Jacko was like Tony. Not bad. Just a boy. (*He gets up.*) Well, I'm on my way. Just remember. It's Halloween.

WANDA: I hope you find him. (MINSTREL *goes out right.*)

GILDA: So that's why the king never comes out of the castle any more.

WANDA: And that's why no one is allowed to make pumpkin pies.

GILDA: And the penalty for eating a pumpkin is death.

WANDA: Poor little boy! I wonder what it would be like to be turned into a pumpkin seed.

MRS. FITCH (*Entering, left*): Good morning, dearies. Could an old lady rest her bones a minute on your bench?

GILDA: There's not very much room for three.

WANDA: I guess you can take my place. (*She gets up.*)

MRS. FITCH (*Sitting down slowly*): Thank you, dear. This is a very exciting day and I don't want to be too tired to enjoy it.

TONY (*Strolling in from right*): Heigho!

GILDA: What's exciting about today?

WANDA: Just because it's Halloween?

TONY: Nothing's happened yet.

MRS. FITCH: Does anything ever happen in broad daylight? No, no. A picket-fence and a gatepost are a picket-fence and a gatepost in broad daylight. But at night . . . you can't quite tell what they are, can you?

TONY: No, you can't.

GILDA: They do look different.

MRS. FITCH: There you are. A perfectly ordinary day can turn into a most extraordinary night. You just wait and see.

WANDA (*Thoughtfully*): But you have to see for yourself, don't you?

MRS. FITCH: Yes. (*Getting up*) Thank you for the rest, lovey. I'm off to find me a black cat and a cup of tea. (*To* WANDA) Here's a present for you. (*She pulls out a handful of brown stones.*) You can choose one . . . any one.

WANDA: What are they?

MRS. FITCH: Take one and take care of it and you shall see. (WANDA *chooses one and the children look at it as* MRS. FITCH *hobbles out right.*)

GILDA: It's nothing but an old brown stone.

TONY: Old Mrs. Fitch
Is a witch!

WANDA: Is she!

GILDA: Of course she is. I wouldn't keep anything she gave me.

WANDA: But she had so many of them.

MOTHER (*Coming in from right*): Aren't you children hungry? I've been waiting lunch for you.

TONY: We're coming.

GILDA: We've been talking to people. Do you know why the king never comes out of the castle any more? (TONY, GILDA *and* MOTHER *exit, right.*)

WANDA (*Speaking to the stone*): I wonder what you are. You aren't very clean and you look very old. (*She drops it onto the ground.*) There. (*She puts her foot over it.*) I'll bury you anyway. You aren't exactly what I'd call a present. What a funny day this is!

CURTAIN

* * *

SCENE 2

SETTING: *The same roadway. The same bench. But it is dusk, and where* WANDA *buried the stone is a tremendous pumpkin.*

AT RISE: *A group of children hurry in from left.*

TOMMY: Here it is!

WILLIE: Look at it!

LONNY: It's so huge!

MARY: It glows . . . like a star!

MILLIE: We could see it from way across the meadow!

WILLIE: What is it!

TOMMY: It's a pumpkin.

LONNY: But no one is allowed to grow pumpkins.

MARY: I thought it must at least be the moon sitting down! (*The children walk around the pumpkin, looking at it.* TONY *and* WANDA *and* GILDA *and* MOTHER *enter, from right.*)

TONY: What's all the excitement?

GILDA: Maybe someone's seen a ghost.

WANDA: Look . . . look at the pumpkin!

GILDA: Isn't it huge!

TONY (*Stretching up one arm*): Why, it's taller than I am!

MOTHER: I wonder how it got there.

WANDA: It's right where I buried the stone!

MOTHER: What stone?

WANDA: An old woman came by this morning and sat on our bench. And when she left, she pulled a handful of old brown stones out of her pocket. . . .

TONY: And she gave one to Wanda.

GILDA: And we told her to throw it away. (*Two gentlemen of the King's Guard come in from left.*)

WANDA: But I didn't throw it away. . . . I buried it.

MOTHER: But that wasn't a stone, child. That was a seed.

FIRST GUARD: What ho! It is a pumpkin.

SECOND GUARD: Planting a pumpkin is high treason and not to be tolerated. Rule 46. (*The children shrink away, and* WANDA *puts her arms around* MOTHER *and hides her face.*)

FIRST GUARD: Who is responsible for this deed? (THE MINSTREL *enters from right, still dabbing his eyes with the handkerchief.*)

SECOND GUARD: Come, come. Speak up. (*No one speaks.*)

FIRST GUARD (*To* WANDA): Didn't I hear you say you buried something? (WANDA *nods miserably.*)

GILDA: It was just an old stone. (MRS. FITCH *enters from the left and stands in the background.*)

FIRST GUARD (*To his fellow officer*): Call the captain of the guard. We ought to make an arrest.

MOTHER: But the child didn't know it was a pumpkin seed.

SECOND GUARD: Oh, so you admit it was a pumpkin seed. (*He blows his whistle.* THE MINSTREL *enters a bit further and then steps way forward.*)

MINSTREL (*To* WANDA): Now, now, my dear.

WANDA (*Looking up and seeing* MRS. FITCH): There she is! She's the one who gave it to me!

MINSTREL: Where?

WANDA: Over there!

MINSTREL: That's the nurse! That's Jacko's old nurse! (MRS. FITCH *turns and hobbles quickly out left.*) Arrest that woman!

(FIRST GUARD *rushes out left, blowing his whistle.* SECOND GUARD *rushes out right, blowing his whistle.*)

MOTHER: Whatever shall we do! My poor Wanda.

MINSTREL: Does anyone have a pocket-knife?

TOMMY: I have one!

MINSTREL: Thank you.

WANDA: You aren't going to cut up the pumpkin?

MINSTREL: Most certainly. It just might be the right one.

WANDA: But she had a whole handful of seeds! There were so many of them!

MINSTREL (*Shrugging his shoulders*): Well, if we don't try it, where are we? (*He thrusts the knife into the pumpkin. Enter the King from right, very fat and puffing. Behind him is the* CAPTAIN OF THE GUARD *and the* SECOND GUARD.)

CAPTAIN: Stop!

KING: Stop!

CAPTAIN: Don't you know that cutting a pumpkin is a crime punishable by death.

MINSTREL (*Pulling out the knife*): Yes. (*He bows to the* KING.) Your Majesty, I don't know if you remember me or not. I used to be chief cook in your kitchen.

CAPTAIN: Your Majesty, this man is obviously insane!

KING: Wait a minute . . . wait a minute! Go ahead. . . .

MINSTREL: If I have Your Majesty's permission, I would like to cut open this pumpkin.

KING: And why do you wish to cut open this pumpkin?

MINSTREL: I want to see if there's anything in it. I have a feeling that His Royal Highness, Prince Jacko, might be inside.

KING: Well!

CAPTAIN: Your Majesty, if you'll just let me take him away.

KING: No. You may open the pumpkin. But remember, if my son is not inside, you will be put to death tomorrow morning.

MINSTREL (*Shudders*): Well, fate is fate, I suppose. (*He goes up to the pumpkin and cuts two large holes for eyes, another for a nose and a large one for a mouth. For a moment, nothing happens. Then as he steps back,* JACKO *crawls out of the mouth.*)

KING: Jacko! (*Everyone cheers.*)

JACKO (*Blinking*): Hello.

KING: Well, well, well. Let me look at you!

JACKO (*Shaking himself*): I'm certainly glad to be out of there.

KING: Thanks to my cook, my boy. (FIRST GUARD *comes in from left, and seeing the* CAPTAIN, *salutes.*)

FIRST GUARD: We have captured the nurse. What shall we do with her, sir?

CAPTAIN: What do you wish, Your Majesty?

KING: Put her in a dungeon and have someone make faces at her for a few days.

JACKO: Like this. (*He blows up his cheeks.*)

KING (*Severely*): That will do, Jacko. Remember what happened the last time you did that.

WANDA: Look at the pumpkin! (*The pumpkin has lit up and the face cut by the* MINSTREL *glows out.*)

MINSTREL: I knew it was a magic pumpkin!

KING (*To* MINSTREL): Cook, will you come back and be chef in my kitchen?

MINSTREL (*Kneeling*): Your Majesty, nothing would please me more.

KING (*Touching him on the shoulder*): I make you Lord Sir Bottle-Washer Cook, Thirty-Fifth Lord of the Realm.

MINSTREL: Your Majesty, I am deeply touched. (*Still kneeling*) But may I ask one favor?

KING: Gladly, my lord.

MINSTREL: After all, I was only the one who opened the pumpkin. I feel that the little lady who planted the seed should also have some reward. (*He beckons to* WANDA, *who comes forward.*) Your Majesty, may I present Wanda? (WANDA *curtsies.*)

KING: How do you do, Wanda. I suppose the traditional reward is half of the Kingdom and the hand of the fair princess. However, I don't think you'd know what to do with half of my kingdom, would you?

WANDA: No, your Majesty.

KING: And as you are a girl, I couldn't very well give you the hand of the fair princess even if I had a daughter. All I have is Jacko, and I don't know as you'd want him.

WANDA (*As* JACKO *makes a face at her*): I . . . don't think so.

KING: Then suppose we solve it by making you the fair princess. Ladies and Gentlemen, I give you Princess Wanda.

TOMMY: Three cheers for Princess Wanda! (*They cheer.*)

KING (*To* WANDA): You can live at home or in the castle or do anything you please. The castle isn't steam-heated.

WANDA (*Curtseying*): You are very kind, Your Majesty.

KING: And one more thing. From now on, every year on this day, the people of my kingdom shall celebrate Halloween, the day when my son was returned to me. (*To* WANDA) What would be a good way to celebrate?

WANDA (*Thinking a moment*): I think every one ought to cut out a face on a pumpkin and put a candle in it, and call it a Jack-o-lantern.

THE END

WONDERS OF STORYBOOK LAND

by Alice D'Arcy

Characters

BILLY, *12-year-old boy*
BETTY, *10-year-old girl*
LITTLE RED RIDING HOOD
WHITE RABBIT
ALICE-IN-WONDERLAND
CAPTAIN HOOK
SMEE
PETER PAN
LOST BOY
SNOW WHITE
HAPPY
SLEEPY
PINOCCHIO
TIGER LILY
RAGGEDY ANN
RAGGEDY ANDY
BLUE FAIRY
CINDERELLA
LITTLE LAME PRINCE

SCENE 1

SETTING: *Living-room of the Robertson home.*

AT RISE: BETTY *and* BILLY ROBERTSON *are sitting by the living-room table.* BETTY *is sewing, and* BILLY *is thumbing the pages of a book.*

BILLY (*Tossing book aside*): It's no use. (*Sighs.*)
BETTY (*Looking up from sewing*): What's the matter, Billy?
BILLY: I was trying to find a game.
BETTY: What kind of game did you want?
BILLY: Something new and different. Something with adventure — that's it!

BETTY (*Laying sewing aside*): I know! I have just the game!

BILLY: A game that two of us can play?

BETTY: Of course. Any number of people can play — even one can play it alone.

BILLY: Tell me more about it.

BETTY: It is very simple — it is the game of Make Believe.

BILLY: Are you *fooling,* Betty? Do you expect me —

BETTY: Now, wait a minute, Billy — you have heard of imagination, haven't you?

BILLY: Who hasn't? But if you think I am going to sit around imagining things you're mistaken. (*Rises and starts off stage.*)

BETTY: Won't you play with me just once?

BILLY (*Returning to chair*): Oh, well, all right — but if I don't like it I won't stay.

BETTY: But you *will* — I know you will.

BILLY: Well, how does it begin?

BETTY: First you decide what you want to wish.

BILLY: That's not hard. I wish I had an airplane, a new bicycle and a — say, maybe I'd settle for a million dollars and then I could buy anything I want.

BETTY: No, Billy, that isn't it, exactly. Let me explain.

BILLY: Never mind. I might have known there was a catch. You name your wish.

BETTY: All right — but promise you won't laugh. I think we should wish —

BILLY: Go ahead —

BETTY: Wish that we could make a trip to Storybook Land!

BILLY: Of all the —

BETTY: Wouldn't you like to see the folks we read about in books?

BILLY: Sure, only it sounds crazy to me — Storybook Land!

BETTY: It isn't, Billy, really it isn't. I've been there many times. All you have to do is — close your eyes, make a wish, open them, and you'll see. Are you ready?

BILLY: Sure.

BETTY (*Very slowly*): Close your eyes — (*Both children place hands over eyes*) make a wish — (*Pause*) wish *hard,* Billy — open them — (*Before they open eyes the curtain falls.*)

* * *

SCENE 2

SETTING: *Storybook Land.*

AT RISE: BETTY *and* BILLY *are standing in the middle of the stage with their hands still over their eyes.*

BETTY: Open them — take a look — see what happens.

BILLY (*As both children remove hands from eyes*): Nothing will happen — I can tell you that. (*Looks around*) But — but — something *has* happened. Look, Betty!

BETTY: What a pretty cottage!

BILLY: Where *are* we? That's what I'd like to know.

BETTY (*Hesitatingly*): Well — we wished to be in Storybook Land — maybe this is it.

BILLY: I wonder who lives in the cottage. Let's knock on the door. (*Goes toward cottage, but door opens before he reaches it and out steps* LITTLE RED RIDING HOOD *with a basket on her arm.*)

LITTLE RED RIDING HOOD: Good morning. Were you looking for someone?

BETTY: Why, Little Red Riding Hood! How exciting!

BILLY: We were — that is —

LITTLE RED RIDING HOOD: Goodness, little boy, you seem to be a bit mixed up. (*Smiles.*)

BETTY: What we would like to know is — would you please tell us where we are?

LITTLE RED RIDING HOOD: You are in Storybook Land; didn't you know?

BILLY: You are just like your pictures.

LITTLE RED RIDING HOOD: And what is so strange about that? You look like your pictures, too.

BILLY: It's all so funny.

BETTY: Where are you going, Little Red Riding Hood?

LITTLE RED RIDING HOOD: Through the woods to Grandmother's house. I must hurry, too. Mother wishes me to return before long.

BETTY: Please, please be careful, won't you?

BILLY: I don't think you'd better go.

LITTLE RED RIDING HOOD: Of course, I must. Grandmother is not well and this delicious butter and cake will help her (*Points *to basket*). Goodbye, I'll see you later. (*Walks off left of stage waving goodbye.*)

BILLY: We certainly hope so. Goodbye.

BETTY: Goodbye, Little Red Riding Hood. (*After her departure,* BETTY *and* BILLY *look about them cautiously.*)

BILLY: Well, what next, do you suppose?

BETTY (*Placing finger to lips*): Sh-h-h! I think I hear footsteps.

BILLY (*Whispering*): So do I. (*Sound of footsteps in distance gradually becoming louder. Enter* WHITE RABBIT.)

WHITE RABBIT (*Walks hurriedly looking to left and right. Pauses abruptly and speaks*): Where *can* I have left them? (*Shakes head and reaches into waistcoat pocket, pulls out very large cardboard watch, looks at it and continues to walk up and down stage hurriedly.*) My ears and whiskers, I'll be late again! What can I do?

BETTY: You are the White Rabbit, aren't you? Is there anything we can do to help?

WHITE RABBIT (*Comes to a stop; looks curiously at* BETTY *and* BILLY): Young lady, speak when you are spoken to.

BILLY: I must say, Mr. White Rabbit, you are very rude.

WHITE RABBIT: What you say makes no difference to me, young man, and if I weren't in such a hurry — (*Glances at watch again, raises it to ear and shakes it*) My ears and whiskers! I must be off! (*With tiny running steps leaves stage at left.* BETTY *and* BILLY *start after him.*)

BETTY: Oh, please don't leave!

BILLY: We came all the way to Storybook Land to see you. (ALICE IN WONDERLAND *enters right as* WHITE RABBIT *disappears.*)

ALICE: Have you seen him? Did he pass this way? I *must* find him. I have his white gloves. (*Holds up her hands on which she has placed gloves.*)

BETTY (*Walking toward* ALICE): How *nice* to see you here!

BILLY: Alice in Wonderland! And you look just like — oh, oh — I better not say *that* again — Little Red Riding Hood didn't seem to like it.

ALICE: The White Rabbit — do you know what became of him?

BETTY (*Nodding in direction of* WHITE RABBIT): He went that way. If you hurry, you will find him.

ALICE (*Hurriedly leaving*): Thank you — thank you so much!

BILLY: This place gets crazier every minute!

BETTY: Why, Billy, everything is perfectly natural — that is, for Storybook Land.

BILLY: I'm glad *you* think so. (*Voices offstage, loud and quarrelsome.* BETTY *and* BILLY, *frightened, look questioningly at each other and run toward tree for shelter.*)

CAPTAIN HOOK: But I tell you, Smee, he must be here!

SMEE: No, Hook, you are wrong.

HOOK (*Enraged*): Who are you to tell me I'm wrong? I've a good mind to make you walk the plank.

BETTY (*In a small voice*): Oh, Billy, I *do* wish we hadn't come.

BILLY (*Unsteadily*): J-j-just l-like a g-girl — always s-scared.

BETTY: I'm not — (*Enter* CAPTAIN HOOK *with large strides.* SMEE *follows.*)

BILLY: Sh-h-h! Don't let them see us.

HOOK (*Paces up and down stage, talking loudly, slowly, and with emphasis*): Peter Pan! I'll conquer him if it's the last thing I do. A fight to the finish — that is what it shall be! What's that? Did I hear you say something, Smee?

SMEE: Not me — not me — I didn't say a word, honestly I didn't!

HOOK (*Steps to front of stage with swagger and in sing-song voice recites*):

I am Captain Hook, yo-ho
A brave and haughty sailor.
Many men I've sent below
Beware, beware this sailor!
For if you do not satisfy,
You are surely doomed to die —

(*A loud ticking sound is heard and* HOOK *stares ahead in terror.*)

HOOK: The crocodile! The *crocodile!* Quick, Smee, let us be off! (*Leave hurriedly. As* HOOK *leaves left,* PETER PAN *and one of the* LOST BOYS *enter right.*)

PETER PAN (*Clapping hands with glee*): You see, I fooled him again. (*Folds arms in front of chest and stands astride.*) I am a very remarkable fellow!

LOST BOY: Ever since that crocodile tasted his arm, he follows Hook around to devour the rest of him.

PETER PAN: Lucky for Hook the crocodile swallowed that alarm clock!

LOST BOY: And lucky for you that you can fool Hook with your ticking! (BETTY *and* BILLY *come quickly from behind tree.*)

BILLY: Quick, Peter Pan! You better leave here. The terrible Captain Hook is searching for you.

BETTY: Oh, please Peter Pan — we love you so, and we don't want anything to happen to you.

PETER PAN: Ho-ho! You talk as if the great Peter Pan were a coward. (*Struts across stage.*) *I* am a very remarkable fellow. What have *I* to fear from Hook? I will meet him in fair fight and that will be the end of Hook. (*Turns to* LOST BOY *and then starts offstage right.*) Come, we will end Hook's search for us.

BETTY: But Captain Hook went —

BILLY (*Clasping hand over* BETTY's *mouth*): Sh-h-h! Don't tell him. Hook may kill him.

BETTY: Oh, I'm so glad you stopped me. I never thought of that. (*Enter* LITTLE RED RIDING HOOD, *left.*)

LITTLE RED RIDING HOOD: Have you enjoyed yourselves in Storybook Land?

BILLY (*Surprised*): Didn't the wolf get you?

LITTLE RED RIDING HOOD: Oh, my no! Just as he was about to eat me up, woodchoppers heard my screams and saved me.

BETTY: But your poor Grandmother!

LITTLE RED RIDING HOOD: She's all right, too. I'll tell you all about it sometime, but I must hurry into the house now.

BILLY: But won't you stay and play with us for a little while?

LITTLE RED RIDING HOOD: Oh, I musn't because I am having a garden party for all the little folks of Storybook Land and they will be here any minute now. (*Enters house.*)

BETTY: We certainly visited Storybook Land at a good time. Everything seems to be happening today.

BILLY (*Looking off stage right*): Will you look at who is coming? (*Enter* SNOW WHITE *followed by* HAPPY. SLEEPY *trails behind.*)

SNOW WHITE: For goodness sake, Sleepy, can't you stay awake even long enough to go to Little Red Riding Hood's party? (SLEEPY *rubs eyes, stretches, yawns and goes back to rubbing eyes again.*)

HAPPY: It's no use, Snow White; might as well let him sleep. He always does, you know.

SNOW WHITE (*Smiling*): I suppose you are right, Happy. Would you, then, like to take him over to the foot of that tree and let him make himself as comfortable as possible?

HAPPY: Certainly, Snow White, it would be a pleasure. (HAPPY *leads* SLEEPY *to tree.* SLEEPY *yawns again, stretches and falls off to sleep.*)

BILLY (*Walking toward* SNOW WHITE): Pardon us, Snow White, we didn't mean to intrude. I am Billy, and this is my sister, Betty.

SNOW WHITE: I am very glad to know you, and I am sure Happy is, too.

HAPPY (*With broad grin*): Of course, I am. I'm always happy. Say, tell me — are you — (HAPPY *is interrupted by the entrance of* WHITE RABBIT *and* ALICE.)

WHITE RABBIT (*Pulling on white gloves*): But it *is* your fault, I say!

ALICE (*Following* WHITE RABBIT *across stage and tugging at waistcoat*): I gave you the gloves as soon as I found them, didn't I?

WHITE RABBIT: What right did you have to find them?

ALICE: That's a stupid question!

WHITE RABBIT (*Abruptly facing* ALICE *and wagging finger in front of her nose*): Stupid! Stupid, you say? You listen to me, young lady — and listen carefully —

BILLY: My goodness! If that isn't the funniest sight I ever saw — a white rabbit scolding.

WHITE RABBIT (*Brushes past* ALICE *and stands in front of* BILLY, *again wagging finger*): This, young man —

BILLY (*Clasping* WHITE RABBIT'S *finger*): Take it easy, Mr. White Rabbit. After all, we think it was very kind of Alice-in-Wonderland to go to all the trouble of searching for you so that she might return your gloves.

BETTY: It certainly was. And you should be ashamed of yourself for acting in such a manner!

WHITE RABBIT (*Scratching ear with gloved hand*): Do you really think so?

BILLY: Of course we do! (WHITE RABBIT *hangs head, scrapes floor with right foot and finally breaks into loud sobbing.*)

BETTY (*Alarmed*): Oh, *please* don't do that!

BILLY: What's the matter now?

WHITE RABBIT (*Between sobs*): I've been such a *bad,* bad rabbit. (BETTY *and* BILLY *comfort* WHITE RABBIT *while* ALICE *walks over to tree, looks curiously at* SLEEPY. SNOW WHITE *and* HAPPY *follow her and in pantomime explain that he can't be awakened.* SLEEPY *yawns, stretches and goes to sleep again.*)

BETTY: There, there White Rabbit. Do you feel better now? (*Enter* PINOCCHIO *excitedly.*)

PINOCCHIO: Has the party begun yet? Am I late? Look at the present I brought. I'll bet it is the biggest one Red Riding Hood will get! (*Displays large package.*)

SNOW WHITE (*Dips into pocket and takes out small package.* ALICE *does likewise*): I hope you and I didn't bring the same thing.

PINOCCHIO: This is heavy. Where shall we pile the presents?

HAPPY (*Taking present from inside his jacket*): I suggest we put them over near Sleepy. (*As* BETTY *and* BILLY *watch, others arrange presents. Enter from left and right* TIGER LILY, RAGGEDY ANN, RAGGEDY ANDY, BLUE FAIRY, CINDERELLA, LITTLE LAME PRINCE, *and place gifts at foot of tree.*)

BETTY: My, Bill, Little Red Riding Hood will certainly be pleased!

WHITE RABBIT: I am having my present delivered. I hope it arrives in time.

RAGGEDY ANDY: What is it, Mr. White Rabbit?

RAGGEDY ANN: Please tell us, won't you?

WHITE RABBIT: Will everybody promise not to tell Little Red Riding Hood?

ALL: Of course, we won't tell.

WHITE RABBIT (*Stretching out arms*): Well then, it was a *big* birthday cake and on it was written — but wait until you see it — you'll all be surprised.

CINDERELLA: Little Red Riding Hood will be more surprised than anyone.

BLUE FAIRY: I wonder if she knows we are here.

ALICE: Let's sing the "Happy Birthday Song" and then she will surely know.

PINOCCHIO (*Excitedly*): And do I love to sing! (*Begins ahead of rest*)

Happy Birthday to you
Happy —

(BLUE FAIRY *places restraining hand on* PINOCCHIO'S *shoulder.*)

BLUE FAIRY: Pinocchio, Pinocchio! (*Shakes her head sadly.*) Haven't I taught you any manners? Wait for the others. (PINOCCHIO *hangs head in shame, but joyfully raises it as all sing.*)

ALL: Happy Birthday to you,
Happy Birthday to you,

Happy Birthday, dear Riding Hood,
Happy Birthday to you.
(*As last line of song is sung,* LITTLE RED RIDING HOOD *steps out of cottage door.*)

LITTLE RED RIDING HOOD: Welcome, most welcome, good friends! I am so glad you were all able to come to my party.

ALL: We are very happy to be here, Little Red Riding Hood.

BETTY: Billy and I really shouldn't — (HOOK'S *voice is heard offstage left and he enters shortly.*)

HOOK: I tell you, Smee, we are *not* running away. We are not running away from Peter Pan. (*Walks hurriedly across stage to center, with* SMEE *following. Stops abruptly, faces* SMEE *pointing iron claw at him.*) Do you understand me, Smee?

SMEE (*Doubtfully*): But if we aren't running away what are we doing? (*Characters on stage whisper excitedly to one another, then quietly seek hiding places.*)

HOOK: If Peter Pan *thinks* I am running away he will be sure to follow me here and then — (*With grimacing gestures*)
Yo-ho, yo-ho I'll have you know
I'm a mean and wicked sailor
It's to the bottom of the sea you'll go
Should you displease this sailor!
I'm captain of the pirate band
The wickedest on sea or land!
(*Enter left* PETER PAN *and* LOST BOY.)

PETER PAN: So there you are, Hook! At last I've caught up with you! And now for the fight to the finish! (*Draws sword from side.* HOOK *steps up to* PETER PAN *and draws sword, too. Other characters cautiously step forward.* LITTLE LAME PRINCE *excitedly throws cap into air.*)

LITTLE LAME PRINCE: Oh, what I wouldn't give to join in the sport! (TIGER LILY *rushes to side* of PETER PAN.)

TIGER LILY: Peter Pan! Peter Pan! Do you wish me to go for my Indian Braves? (PETER PAN *and* HOOK *continue crossing swords, with* PETER *playing dramatically to audience, bowing, etc., in between times.*)

PETER PAN: For shame, Tiger Lily! Never let it be said that Peter Pan is a coward! (*Suddenly from crowd steps* RAGGEDY ANN *with* RAGGEDY ANDY *by the hand. She claps her hands together to get the attention of* PETER *and* HOOK *and wags finger as she speaks.*)

RAGGEDY ANN: You two should be *ashamed* of yourselves, spoiling dear Little Red Riding Hood's party. (*Points to large heart pinned on dress.*) My candy heart tells me it is wrong to quarrel, isn't it, folks of Storybook Land?

ALL: It certainly is! (*Peter Pan and* HOOK *stop and look at each other.*)

PETER PAN: Is it possible we could be wrong?

HOOK: Everyone else seems to think so.

PETER PAN: I, Peter Pan, a most remarkable fellow?

HOOK: And I, Hook, the boldest, badest, wickedest pirate on the seven seas?

RAGGEDY ANN: Yes — you are wrong — very wrong.

PETER PAN (*Scratches head*): And anyway, Hook, I've been thinking — if I kill you, I'll miss you. Yes, sir, miss you very much.

HOOK: I would miss you, too, Peter Pan — (*Sadly*) as much as you would miss me. (*Starts to break down, ending with sobs which become wails*) Oh, somebody do something — somebody stop us before it is too late!

PINOCCHIO (*Excitedly*): The Blue Fairy will make you be good. She always sees that I do the right thing — at least when she is around.

BLUE FAIRY: Yes, Peter Pan and Captain Hook. I suggest that you shake hands and then we can get on with this party.

LITTLE RED RIDING HOOD: Please do. Mother will be so disappointed if the party is spoiled. She did so want it to be a nice one.

BETTY: Oh, goodness — goodness!

RAGGEDY ANDY: What is the matter, little girl?

BETTY: When Little Red Riding Hood mentioned her mother I suddenly remembered that our mother would be looking for us — we've been away so long!

BILLY: That's right. She may be worried about us this very minute. Make up you two before we leave.

PETER PAN: What else can we do, Hook? We're not *really* selfish, you know.

ALL: Of course not!

HOOK: All right, Peter Pan. We'll put our swords over by the tree. (PETER *and* HOOK *place swords at foot of tree.*)

LITTLE RED RIDING HOOD: Oh, thank you — thank you so much! Now we can go on with the party.

BILLY: Sorry, we can't stay, but we'll come back another day.

ALL: Yes, do.

BILLY: Gosh, Betty, how are we going to get home?

BETTY: Why, just the way we came, of course. Close your eyes — make a wish — (BETTY *and* BILLY *place hands over eyes and* PINOCCHIO *does likewise.* BLUE FAIRY, *alarmed, interrupts proceedings.*)

BLUE FAIRY: Pinocchio! What are you doing now? Don't you want to stay for the party?

PINOCCHIO (*Quickly removing hands from eyes*): Of course I do. I only wanted to see what would happen if I made a wish!

BILLY (*Smiling*): Well, you better try it some other time. Let's start again, Betty.

BETTY: Yes, Billy. Goodbye everybody. We certainly enjoyed our trip to Storybook Land.

ALL: Goodbye, we were glad to have you visit us.

BETTY: This time when we open our eyes, Billy, we'll be right in our own living room again — so close your eyes — (*They place hands over eyes*) make a wish — (*Curtain slowly — commences to fall*) open them — (*Curtain falls as folks of Storybook Land wave goodbye.*)

THE END

OFF THE SHELF

by Mildred Hark and Noel McQueen

Characters

MISS POETRY
MR. DICTIONARY
MR. HISTORY BOOK
MISS GRAMMAR
MR. ARITHMETIC
MR. NONSENSE BOOK
MISS STORY BOOK
MR. BIOGRAPHY

TIME: *Late evening.*

SETTING: *A reading room in a public library.*

AT RISE: *A low moaning sound is heard but there is no sign of anyone on the stage. A little voice* (MISS POETRY) *says*: "Oh, dear me. Oh, dear me. I wish somebody would help me!" MR. DICTIONARY *comes from between the stacks of books at left. On a large placard made to look like the front cover of a book and hung from around his neck is printed*: "Universal Unabridged Dictionary."

MR. DICTIONARY (*As he enters*): Do my ears deceive me, or did I hear someone call?

MISS POETRY (*A little head pops up from behind the top of the library table.* MISS POETRY *can be curled up on the chair "at rise" so she is not seen*): Is that you, Mr. Dictionary?

MR. DICTIONARY (*Crossing over*): Why, Miss Poetry, what are you doing on that chair?

MISS POETRY: A little girl left me here this afternoon — face down. Then another one came in and sat on me. Hard! I think my back is broken. Help me, Mr. Dictionary! (MR. DICTIONARY *pulls at* MISS POETRY. *Finally, with* MR. DIC-

TIONARY'S *help, she gets to her feet.* MISS POETRY'S *front cover has "Collected Poems" printed on it. She is sniffling.*)

MISS POETRY:

I'm sorry to sniffle
And moan and cry;
But when I tell you my story —
You'll understand why.

MR. DICTIONARY (*A little pompously*): Now, Miss Poetry, it isn't necessary for you to make rhymes every minute. Just state facts. Do you feel better?

MISS POETRY: I — I guess so. (*Feeling her back.*) Maybe my back isn't broken after all. Only strained. Oh, why do the children treat me so carelessly?

MR. DICTIONARY: Tst — tst. A most regrettable state of affairs. I am grieved.

MISS POETRY: Oh, Mr. Dictionary, please don't use all of your big words now. I'm too nervous.

MR. DICTIONARY: But I like big words. I'm full of them.

MISS POETRY: Well, I like only pretty words. Rosy dawns and blue skies and perfumed flowers.

MR. DICTIONARY: I have those words, also. Any word you can think of I have right inside me. But let's not quarrel at a time like this. We've got to do something. The children treat me carelessly, too.

MISS POETRY: They do?

MR. DICTIONARY: Certainly they do — and what's more they don't use me enough. Why, think of the things they could learn from me — what's a "yak"? I'll tell them. What does "concatenation" mean? They can find out if they look in me — (MR. HISTORY BOOK *comes in from right, walking slowly and stretching his arms. He is covered with dust and on his front cover is printed: "History — Ancient and Modern."*)

MR. HISTORY BOOK: What's going on in here?

MR. DICTIONARY: Oh, hello, Mr. History Book.

MR. HISTORY BOOK: I thought I heard someone. You woke me up. (*He is still stretching.*)

MISS POETRY: Oh, I'm sorry.

MR. HISTORY BOOK: Never mind. It'll probably do me good to stretch out. I've been on that shelf so long! (*He blows dust off his shoulders.*) Look at that. Dust!

MISS POETRY: My, a lot of it!

MR. DICTIONARY: Why, you're literally covered with dust.

MR. HISTORY BOOK (*Still blowing*): Of course I am. I look a sight. No one ever takes me off the shelf.

MISS POETRY: Never?

MR. HISTORY BOOK: Well, hardly ever. The last time a little boy took me off the shelf, he squeezed me back in between a lot of other fat history books where I didn't belong. Now, I feel all flattened out like a pancake.

MISS POETRY: I think it's a shame. No one ever opens you and—why, you're exciting. So many wonderful things have happened in history!

MR. HISTORY BOOK: That's true, but the little boy said I was as dry as dust — and now, look! I'm covered with it. (*He blows off more dust.*)

MR. DICTIONARY: Perhaps he felt you were dry because you're full of dates. You know — the Pilgrims landed in 1620 — George Washington crossed the Delaware in —

MISS POETRY: Oh, but that's what makes History so interesting! You aren't held down to the present or any one time — why, you can go into all the times there are. It's wonderful!

MR. HISTORY BOOK: Of course it is. If the children would really read me, they'd be interested, too. (MISS GRAMMAR *and* MR. ARITHMETIC *come in from right.* MISS GRAMMAR *has "English Grammar" printed on her front cover and* MR. ARITHMETIC *has "Arithmetic" on his.*)

MR. DICTIONARY: Why, Miss Grammar —

MR. HISTORY BOOK: And Mr. Arithmetic!

MISS POETRY: Where did you come from?

MR. ARITHMETIC: We jumped off the textbook shelf.

MISS GRAMMAR: Yes. In Aisle Six.

MR. ARITHMETIC: We heard you talking and wondered what was going on.

MR. DICTIONARY: Well, you might say we were holding an indignation meeting.

MISS POETRY: The children treat us carelessly.

MR. HISTORY BOOK: They don't appreciate us.

MISS GRAMMAR: They certainly don't appreciate me. They refuse to learn to conjugate a verb and they cannot tell the subject from the object.

MR. ARITHMETIC: Some little boys like me well enough, but even they don't realize how fascinating arithmetic is. Why, there's romance in numbers. Just between you and I —

MISS GRAMAR: Mr. Arithmetic, never say "between you and I." That's horrible grammar. Between you and *me*.

MR. ARITHMETIC: Look, Miss Grammar, you can't expect me to know about things like that. Numbers are my specialty. 7 x 8 is 56; 9 x 12 is 108 —

MR. HISTORY BOOK: Stop it, you two. If we're really going to have a meeting, let's organize. Let's do something!

MISS POETRY: I second the motion. I'll represent the poetry books! (*A* NONSENSE BOOK *comes tumbling in. He has "Nonsense, Wit and Humour" on his front cover. He runs up behind* MR. DICTIONARY *and pulls his hair.*)

MR. NONSENSE BOOK: Surprise!

MR. DICTIONARY: Stop that! Who is it?

MISS POETRY: It's Mr. Nonsense Book.

MR. NONSENSE BOOK: In person. Chuck full of wit and humour! May I join your meeting?

MR. DICTIONARY: If you think you can behave yourself.

MR. HISTORY BOOK: You're so flighty, and we're here to discuss a serious question —

MR. NONSENSE BOOK:

I'll be as serious as I can be —
Just watch me now and see!
(*He jumps up on the library table and tumbles about.*)

MR. DICTIONARY (*Angrily*): If you cannot conduct yourself with dignity —

MR. NONSENSE BOOK (*Laughing*): Mr. Dictionary looks worried. That must be because he's so *over burdened* with words.

MR. ARITHMETIC (*Laughing*): That was funny.

MR. DICTIONARY (*Aggrieved*): Stop laughing!

MR. NONSENSE BOOK (*Innocently*): But you're supposed to laugh at jokes.

MR. DICTIONARY: Humph, you call what he said about me a joke?

MISS POETRY: Well, what was it then, Mr. Dictionary?

MR. DICTIONARY: It was a pun — and a pun is the lowest form of wit. (*He looks sternly at* MR. NONSENSE BOOK.)

MR. NONSENSE BOOK (*Jumping off the table*): Now, now, Mr. Dictionary, my wit is of the highest quality, but I'm sorry if I offended you and I'll be good. I do really want to help.

MR. DICTIONARY: Help? How can you help?

MR. NONSENSE BOOK: Oh, lots of ways and you needn't high-hat me. The children need to read me, too. I show them how to play games and how to have fun — and I develop their senses of humour — that's important. (MISS STORY BOOK *enters. She has "Famous Stories for Children" printed on her front cover. She looks tattered and worn.*)

MR. HISTORY BOOK: Why, hello, Miss Story Book.

MISS STORY BOOK: Oh, I'm so glad you're all here. I've been having nightmares.

MR. DICTIONARY: Nightmares?

MISS POETRY: Nightmares? (*Shaking her head.*) How can that be? You're full of such *nice* stories!

MISS STORY BOOK: I know, but I haven't felt well at all lately. A little girl liked one of my pictures and she tore it out and took it home with her.

MISS GRAMMAR: How awful!

MISS STORY BOOK: And somebody else scribbled on me — until the next person who borrows me won't be able to read me at all. I'm a wreck, I tell you!

MR. ARITHMETIC: But won't the librarian fix you up?

MISS STORY BOOK: I guess so, but she hasn't gotten around to it yet. I—I feel so sad. I try to give the children pleasure and—

MR. HISTORY BOOK: Well, it seems Miss Story Book is treated just as badly as the rest of us. Let's not delay another minute. Let's get down to business.

MISS POETRY: That's what I say — and we need somebody to run our meeting. We can't just all talk at once.

MISS GRAMMAR: What about Mr. Dictionary?

MR. DICTIONARY: Why, I'll be very happy to take charge. I'll just sit at the end of the table here, (*He seats himself.*) and you can all group yourselves around me. (*The others take seats at the other end and along the upstage side.*) Now, let me see. We've got to begin this meeting properly. How does this sound? It is indeed a strange concatenation of circumstances that brings us all together —

MISS POETRY: Please, Mr. Dictionary, don't use your big words. We haven't time.

OTHERS (*All talking at once*): No, no, who cares about all that? We've got to do something! We've got to make the children appreciate us. Rebel, that's what we'll have to do. The rebellion of the books!

MR. DICTIONARY: Stop it! Order! Order! (*Shouting louder*) May I have order, please? I can't run this meeting unless I can have order — (MR. BIOGRAPHY *enters. His front cover has "Lives of Great Men" printed on it. He comes in hurriedly.*)

MR. BIOGRAPHY: Wait for me — wait for me — I want to attend your meeting —

MR. DICTIONARY: Why, surely, Mr. Biography...

MR. BIOGRAPHY: I'm very important — lives of great men make fine reading for children. In fact —

"Lives of great men all remind us
We can make our lives sublime,
And, departing, leave behind us
Footprints on the sands of time."

MISS POETRY: Shame on you, Mr. Biography. You're stealing my stuff — that's poetry.

MR. BIOGRAPHY: But it's true, isn't it?

MISS POETRY: Yes, but Mr. Longfellow wrote it and it's one of my poems. I have a very fine collection.

MR. DICTIONARY: Well, never mind that now. Sit down, Mr. Biography — sit down — we'll begin again — and please, everyone, see if you can be more quiet and speak in turn. (*Looking around.*) Now, where's Mr. Nonsense Book? (MR. NONSENSE BOOK *has wandered over to the librarian's desk and now comes skipping back with a ruler in his hand.*)

MR. NONSENSE BOOK: Here I am — and I brought you this. (*He hands* MR. DICTIONARY *the ruler.*)

MR. DICTIONARY: What's this for?

MR. NONSENSE BOOK: Well, if you're going to rule, you'll need a ruler. (*The others laugh and* MR. DICTIONARY *makes a face.*)

MR. DICTIONARY: Oh, you and your puns. But thank you, anyway. (*He raps the table with the ruler.*) Meeting come to order. Meeting come to order, please! (NONSENSE BOOK *scurries to his seat and they are all quiet for a moment.*) Now, Miss Poetry, you've been very badly treated. Suppose you tell us what you think we ought to do.

MISS POETRY (*Rising at her place*): We ought to revolt, that's what I say —

MR. HISTORY BOOK: Well, I don't know. Revolutions have

worked, but I think education would be better. If we could educate the children.

MISS STORY BOOK (*Rising*): Excuse me, but neither one will work. The children have got to love us — all of us. If they just realized that we're all their friends. That we'll help them.

MISS GRAMMAR: Yes, that's it.

MR. ARITHMETIC: I think she's got something there. There's no use our rebelling — we've got to stage a campaign — sell the children on us —

MR. BIOGRAPHY: Make the children know what they're missing if they don't read us —

MISS POETRY: And teach them to take care of us, too, so when they've finished reading us, we'll still be whole and other people can enjoy us.

MR. DICTIONARY: Good — good — I think we're accomplishing something. What have you to say, Mr. Nonsense Book? (*Looking around for him.*) Has he disappeared again? (MR. NONSENSE BOOK *has wandered over to the librarian's desk again. He looks up when he hears his name called.*)

MR. NONSENSE BOOK (*Running over with a calendar in his hand*): Listen, I've got a wonderful idea! Do you know what week this is?

MR. DICTIONARY: No, and we don't care —

MR. NONSENSE BOOK: But you should. This is Book Week.

MR. BIOGRAPHY: It's what?

MR. NONSENSE BOOK: Book Week. The librarian has drawn a big red mark on her calendar — why, this is the perfect time for our campaign. Book Week! Let's show the children the way to knowledge and happiness and fun. Read books, we'll tell them! (*They are all rising excitedly.*)

MISS POETRY: Yes. Yes!

ALL: Read books — read books!

MR. DICTIONARY (*Spiritedly*):

Read books, we'll tell the children,
And see what you will see —
And if there's a word you can't make out —
Just come and ask of me.
I'm full of many many words,
All listed, A to Z —
Your reading will be much more fun

If you make friends with me!
(*He finishes with a little dance step.*)

MR. NONSENSE BOOK: Splendid, Mr. Dictionary — splendid! I didn't think you had it in you. Let's all tell the boys and girls what we think. (*He steps forward a little.*)

Oh, boys and girls, please read us —
You'll like us very well;
We've many a stirring message —
And many a tale to tell!
As for me, I'm full of nonsense —
You'll laugh and chuckle with glee;
But you'll develop a sense of humour—
If you keep on reading me!
(*He tumbles about to end his little rhyme.*)

MISS POETRY (*Stepping forward*): I want to tell them how to take care of us so we won't wear out.

Don't break my back, dear children —
Please take this gentle hint —
And do not turn my corners down,
Or scribble on my print.
Take care of me and treat me well —
I'm full of verse and rhyme,
And pretty words that make you sing —
And lofty thoughts sublime!

ALL: Hooray for Miss Poetry. Hooray! (*They all clap.* MR. HISTORY BOOK *steps forward.*)

MR. HISTORY BOOK:

I'm Mr. History, as good as a mystery —
If you read me all the way through;
So don't let me stay upon the shelf —
I can do a great deal for you.
Oh, history is exciting —
It tells a thousand stories;
There's romance and adventure —
The past and all its glories!
(*They all laugh and applaud.*)

MR. DICTIONARY: How about you, Miss Grammar? What have you got to say to the children?

MISS GRAMMAR (*Skipping forward*):

Please don't neglect me, boys and girls,

I am a grammar book —
But really very interesting,
If you'll just take a look.
For verbs and nouns and adjectives
Are lots of fun, you know —
And if you'll learn to use them —
They'll help you talk — just so!

ALL: Hooray — hooray for Miss Grammar! Read the textbooks, too — that's what we say! Come on, Mr. Arithmetic — you next!

MR. ARITHMETIC:
Oh, six and six are twelve,
And four times two is eight;
Numbers are not hard to learn —
If you'll just concentrate.
Arithmetic is like a game,
You'll have a lot of pleasure —
And if you read me carefully —
You'll learn to count and measure.

MR. BIOGRAPHY (*Stepping forward*):
Lives of great men all remind us
We can make our lives sublime —

MISS POETRY (*Shaking her finger at him*): Now, now, Mr. Biography —

MR. BIOGRAPHY: All right, I'll make up my own verse.
Oh, I tell of great men —
Of wise men and bright;
Of men we all admire
Who helped to make things right.
But when these men were little boys —
Like you — and you — and you — (*Pointing*)
They were really very human —
They did the things you do!

MISS STORY BOOK (*Skipping forward*):
Please don't tear my pictures out,
And take them home with you —
Because lots of other children
Like to read me, too.
My stories take you everywhere —
I'm full of fun and joy;
I try to be a faithful friend

To every girl and boy!

(*She steps back and all the characters form a half circle at stage center and join hands, except* MR. NONSENSE BOOK *who has again wandered away to the librarian's desk.*)

ALL (*Looking out at audience*): We're all your friends — your friends and helpers! (MR. NONSENSE BOOK *now comes running back and breaks the circle. He is excited and carries several large white posters. These must be of stiff cardboard.*)

MR. NONSENSE BOOK: Look — look what else I found on the librarian's desk! She made them, I guess, for Book Week! (*He holds up several posters excitedly, and you see the printing on some of them. Each character takes one. There are eight posters and the printing is as follows*: (1) *Joy in Books.* (2) *Knowledge in Books.* (3) *Fun in Books.* (4) *Beauty in Books.* (5) *Treat Your Books Well.* (6) *Books Are Friends.* (7) *Books Are Helpers.* (8) *Take Care of Your Books. After each one has a poster, he or she holds it high and faces the audience.*)

ALL (*Holding their posters up, smiling and shaking their heads gaily*):

Oh, books are friends
Who bring you cheer;
We're good companions
All the year!
We bring you joy
And truth and light;
We help you all
To grow up bright!

(*Quick curtain*)

THE END

MR. LONGFELLOW OBSERVES BOOK WEEK

by Edna G. Moore

Characters

HENRY WADSWORTH LONGFELLOW, *the poet*
ALICE, EDITH, ALLEGRA — *the three little daughters of the poet*

Characters from books which have won the Newberry medal.

JOSEPH, *a Polish boy.* (From the "Trumpeter of Cracow," by Kelly.)
HITTY, *a wooden doll.* (From "Hitty," by Field.)
SMOKY, *a cow horse.* (From "Young Fu," by Lewis.)
DR. HUGH DOOLITTLE. (From "Dr. Doolittle," by Lofting.)
YOUNGER BROTHER, *an Indian boy.* (From "Waterless Mountain," by Armer.)
DANIEL BOONE. (From "Daniel Boone," by Daugherty.)
LUCINDA. (From "Roller Skates," by Sawyer.)

SETTING: MR. LONGFELLOW'S *study in his home.*

AT RISE: MR. LONGFELLOW *is seated in an armchair, writing at a sloping desk. Sound of rustling and whispering offstage. Then a rush of footsteps and three little girls enter from different directions and throw themselves into his lap and on the arms of his chair.*

ALICE: It's five o'clock, Father.
EDITH: It's the Children's Hour.
ALLEGRA: Put away your writing — it's our time.
LONGFELLOW: Blue-eyed banditti! How did you get in here?
ALLEGRA: So we're bandits, are we? Yes, we're bandits — come to steal your time. What are you going to do with us?
LONGFELLOW: Do you think such an old mustache as I am is not a match for you all? All of you, grave Alice (*Pats her*) —

laughing Allegra (*Points at her*) — and Edith with the golden hair. (*Pulls a ringlet of* EDITH'S. *He tries to rise, but they crowd him back in his chair, with their arms around him. Still struggling.*) I'll put you down in the dungeon, in the round tower of my heart.

ALLEGRA: And we'll put you down in your armchair and hold you there for a ransom.

LONGFELLOW: I give up. (*Sinks back in his chair.*) What must I pay you three wicked highwaymen? What must I pay to be free?

THE THREE GIRLS (*Joining hands and dancing around him in a circle, chanting*): A ransom! A ransom! A ransom!

LONGFELLOW: Tell me the worst. What must I pay?

ALL THREE (*Together*): A story, Father, a story!

LONGFELLOW: I knew it! I knew it! It is always a story, isn't it? Well, I'll tell you a story, my children. You, Alice, draw up a chair and sit there.

ALLEGRA (*Teasingly*): Remember, Alice —

"There was a little girl,
Who had a little curl
Right in the middle of her forehead.
When she was good
She was very good, indeed,
But when she was bad, she was horrid."

LONGFELLOW: I'd better write a poem about you, young lady. Sit there on my right, where I can keep an eye on you. And you, Edith, here. I will tell you a story of books now unborn — a story of the future.

ALLEGRA: What do you mean, Father — books not yet born?

LONGFELLOW: Listen and you shall hear. Do you not know that books are born every year? In the brain of some man or woman, an idea grows and grows. A hand writes it down, the printing presses stamp it on paper; then it is bound into a book, to charm and delight thousands of people.

ALICE: The way you make poems, Father!

EDITH: Some books you have to study and learn from — those don't delight you!

LONGFELLOW: I'm talking about those you read for pleasure, but I'm sure if you bent your golden head more often over your school books, even they might give you pleasure. You call this the Children's Hour, and it is the Children's Hour for you three alone, you three and me. Can you imagine the same thing grown bigger — a week instead of an hour? A big public room, instead of my study? Hundreds of children and thousands of books? So it shall be some day, my darlings. So it shall be, I feel sure.

Wait. Be very quiet. I have an idea. I shall not tell you a fairy tale today. Instead I shall call upon the fairies to come here in the person of books unborn. You will not live to read these books but you will get a preview of them today — the books the boys and girls of the future will read. Be very quiet — behind my chair! (*The three little girls scamper to hide behind his chair, but keep peeping around it. A trumpet blast is heard. Enter a boy in a Polish costume, who blows a few notes on his horn. He turns and bows low to* LONGFELLOW.)

JOSEPH, *the Polish boy*: I am the trumpeter of Cracow. Yes, I'm a Polish boy, and my country and my people have known things, which, please God, America may never know. These notes I sound, the music of the Heynal, mean a great deal to me and to my people. From the church tower in Cracow, they were sounded every day, from the four sides of the tower, East, West, North and South. I, Joseph, learned from my father to play the Heynal, and it is good that I did, for I was able to save from brutal men the famous crystal which had been entrusted to my father's family for safekeeping. But you wouldn't know about that, Mr. Longfellow. Let me salute you again. (*Blows his trumpet, bows low and steps to one side as a patter of light footsteps is heard. A doll-like person enters.*)

HITTY: I am Hitty. I'm a doll, yes, but a famous one. Miss Rachel Field saw me in a store window in New York City and liked my looks so well she put me in a book, and got a medal for doing it —

JOSEPH (*Stepping forward*): I forgot to say that my author, Mr. Eric Kelly, got a medal for the book he wrote about me. Here it is. (*Shows a medal hanging around his neck. Steps aside.*)

HITTY: It's just like mine, though I'm not a bit like you. I'm a wooden doll. A pedlar made me out of a piece of mountain ash wood, which is supposed to be lucky — but what I've been through in my first hundred years! I suppose that's how I'm lucky — I'm still here, starting my second hundred. I've been shipwrecked; I've been lost in India. I've belonged to the Van Rensselaers of Washington Square and spent a night with the Dooley family in the slums. Charles Dickens, the famous author, once picked me up when I was carelessly dropped and — (*Gallop of horse is heard offstage and there enters a horse with a large medal around his neck.*)

SMOKY: I'm Smoky, the cow horse. You wouldn't know about the likes of me, Mr. Longfellow. I belong out where the West begins, and you belong to the East. I belong to the West where the coyotes call and the rattlesnakes coil by the trail — and have they fangs! We're all rough and tough out there, but very genui-i-ne.

"You're some cow horse," said Clint, the cowboy of the Rocking R Ranch to me. And I was his horse, a one-man horse, until something happened to turn me into the Cougar, the bucking broncho, that no man could ride. Am I bragging? Well, I'll stop right there, but there's plenty more I could say. Will you faint if I stand here by you, sister? (*Walks over and stands by* HITTY.)

HITTY: I never fainted in my whole hundred years, not even when the South Sea savages took me for their idol. Who's this? (*Enter a Chinese boy.*)

YOUNG FU: Lay down your hearts. It is only Young Fu, from Chungking, deep in the center of China. Honorable and respected sir, I greet you. (*Bows low.*) Once I would have been afraid of you, for I thought all such as you were foreign devils — when I first came as a country boy to the vast and mysterious city of Chungking. I learned much going around the steep and narrow streets as errand boy for my master, Tang, the coppersmith. I learned about bandits and about the military men who are cruel and dangerous. But mostly I learned that life is good for a young man who uses his brain and his hands.

JOSEPH: Come over here and stand by me. We're both from countries far away. (*Enter a man in a tall hat and long-tailed coat. He has a large nose.*)

DR. DOOLITTLE: I heard you saying something about one hundred years old. If you think one hundred years is old, you should have seen my parrot, Polynesia. She was one hundred and eighty-two, or maybe it was one hundred and eighty-three — she wasn't quite sure. A wise old bird she was! If it hadn't been for her, I'd never have gotten to Africa that time. I'm John Doolittle, M.D. (*To* SMOKY) I say, were you ever sick?

SMOKY: Was I ever sick? Just nearly beaten to death!

DR. DOOLITTLE: I'm a handy man with animals, you know. Yes, they sent for me to come to Africa, when the monkeys got sick. Nearly got caught in the kingdom of the Jollikinki. But those clever monkeys! They took hold of each other's hands and feet and tails and made a bridge across a steep gorge, over which I escaped with the king's men at my coattails. (*To* HITTY) You've traveled a lot I take it — did you ever see a Pushmi-pullyu?

SMOKY (*Scornfully*): A what? Never heard of it!

DR. DOOLITTLE: The rarest animal in the African jungle! The only two-headed beast in the world — a head at each end! And the monkeys gave me one! (*To* LONGFELLOW) Beg pardon, sir. I'm John Doolittle, M.D. And I'd like to bring my Pushmi-pullyu to show you some day. Bless my soul, who's this?

YOUNGER BROTHER: Once I rode my Pinto pony to the wide waters of the Western Sea. I wanted to follow the Sun-bearer to where he hangs the sun on a turquoise peg in the turquoise walls of the Turquoise Lady's house. There I filled a wicker jar with sea water to take back to my uncle, who is a great medicine man. He has taught me all the legends and songs, so I can be a medicine man, too.

YOUNG FU: And so you got put in a book, too?

DR. DOOLITTLE: Yes, we all got put into books, as far as we are concerned; but as far as you are concerned, Mr. Longfellow, we are not yet born. It is all rather confusing, what?

YOUNGER BROTHER: Here's someone else.

DANIEL BOONE: Daniel Boone, pioneer and backwoodsman. Many books have been written about me. It is a wonder you haven't made a poem about me, Mr. Longfellow, the way you did about the Indians. (*Casts a look at* YOUNGER BROTHER.) All the things I did, hunting, and trapping, fighting Indians, chopping down trees, exploring — it would make a grand poem. I represent today a new book about me for young people, by James Daugherty, a good exciting one. They like it. And here we are, Mr. Longfellow. The fairies sent us to show you what the books for the boys and girls of the future will be like.

HITTY: There will be many more of us. My fairy said we are only char — char — char —

DR. DOOLITTLE: Characteristic, you mean. That's too big a word for a doll.

HITTY (*Hurrying on*): My fairy said we were to tell you about Book Week, in the future, when boys and girls get together to celebrate books for children — with storytelling, plays and exhibits of good books — a whole week of celebration. (*A girl enters, circling around on roller skates.*)

LUCINDA: Am I late? I stopped to watch a soft fluffy cloud change its shape. The sun was behind it, making it rosy. It changed into my friend, Mr. Gilligan, the handsomest hansom cab driver in New York City. His face is very pink. (*Swoops around again in a half-circle.*) I'm nearly always late, even though I go around on skates instead of hoofing it, because I have so many friends to talk to. There's the old rags-and-bottle man. Once I rode in his cart, but no one knows it, especially my Aunt Emily. There's Tony Coppini, the Italian boy, who keeps his father's fruit stand. There's a new bambino every year in the basement where the Coppinis live. It's getting crowded. Mr. Night Owl, my reporter friend, says I'd be like my Aunt Emily, who's awfully interfering, only I'm so friendly and interested and like people so well. (*Skates around again in a wide swoop.*)

ALLEGRA (*She steps out into full view*): I want skates like those! (*The book characters look around in amazement and fright at her voice, for they can't see her. They vanish.*)

LONGFELLOW: You have scared them away, Allegra. They didn't know anything about you. They were sent to show themselves to me. Never mind. (*Takes her on his lap.*) You've seen them — the books the boys and girls of the future will be reading — and you've heard about their Book Week. Nice idea, isn't it, to celebrate books for boys and girls? In fact, I think we have had an advance celebration, ourselves, today, don't you think so, daughters?

EDITH: Oh, Father, they sounded wonderful!

LONGFELLOW (*He pushes them off his lap and off the arms of his chair*): And now our Children's Hour is over for today, and I must get to work.

THE THREE GIRLS (*Running off the stage*): Thank you, Father, thank you.

THE END

HUBBUB ON THE BOOKSHELF

by Alice Woster

Characters

EIGHT YOUNG BOOKWORMS, *identical in size, appearance, and actions*
ONE OLD BOOKWORM, *like the others but wearing a white beard*

SETTING: *An old bookshelf in an attic*

AT RISE: *The stage is empty. The* EIGHT BOOKWORMS *enter, walking just alike. They pause and all look at the books. Then they look at one another.*

1ST BOOKWORM: It is true!
2ND BOOKWORM: Books and books and books!
3RD BOOKWORM: A paradise for bookworms!
4TH BOOKWORM: And no sign of inhabitants!
5TH BOOKWORM: That spider told us the truth!
6TH BOOKWORM: The place is ours!
7TH BOOKWORM: Our long journey has not been in vain!
8TH BOOKWORM: We will never be hungry again!
ALL: Let us eat! (*They start for the books. The* OLD BOOKWORM *steps out of the Encyclopedia, and stares at them in amazement. They look at him, disappointed.*) Oh!
OLD BOOKWORM: As I live and wiggle, these are creatures of my own kind! (*Stretches out arms.*) Welcome, friends, welcome! (*They are silent.*) What is the matter? I am a Bookworm, too, just like yourselves. Are you not glad to see me?
YOUNG BOOKWORMS (*Looking at each other in dismay*): We are lost! The place is already inhabited!
1ST YOUNG BOOKWORM: No, we are not glad to see you, because we had hoped this place was not inhabited. We are a band of colonists. We and all our people have been driven from our former home. An old spider told us of this shelf of books in the attic, and we traveled here, hoping to form a colony and send for our families. Now we have no place to go.

2ND: And we are so hungry!

ALL: We are so hungry!

OLD BOOKWORM: But, my dear friends, this place is not inhabited! I am the only inhabitant! There is plenty of room for you.

ALL: Hooray! (*They shake one another's hands.*)

3RD (*To* OLD BOOKWORM): How does it happen that you live here all alone?

OLD BOOKWORM: I do not know. I grew up here and cannot remember any other life. There is a rumor that I was kidnapped in infancy by a gypsy moth.

ALL: How sad!

OLD BOOKWORM: I have been very lonely. It is true that the crickets and centipedes have been kind to me, but all my life I have wished for the companionship of my own people. That is why I am so happy to welcome you. There is nothing I would rather see than a thriving community of bookworms on this old bookshelf.

ALL: Then we are happy, too. (*They file by the* OLD BOOKWORM, *and one by one, shake his hand, then form group on opposite side of bookshelf.*)

OLD BOOKWORM: But now tell me how you were driven from your homes.

4TH: It was a dreadful disaster that happened to us. Perhaps you do not know, but the household below is a dangerous world for insects to live in. There is constant danger from vacuum cleaners, dusters, mops and spray-guns.

OLD BOOKWORM: How horrible!

5TH: Yes, many of our people have been wiped out by such weapons. But we thought we were safe. We lived in an old box of stationery which belonged to the cook of the household.

ALL (*Sadly*): An old box of stationery — it was our happy home.

6TH: Always we have lived there, at peace with the world, and bothering no one.

OLD BOOKWORM: Then what was the great disaster which came upon you?

7TH: The cook decided to write a letter.

OLD BOOKWORM: Oh, no!

8TH: Yes, she did. And we hadn't ever done a thing to her.

OLD BOOKWORM: Well, my friends, it is safe up here in the attic. These old books have long been forgotten. The children who once owned and read them have grown into men and women and gone into the big world. You may settle here in security, and live a life of peace.

ALL: Hooray!

OLD BOOKWORM: Let us hastily organize the colony, so that you may send for your families. I am very anxious for them to arrive.

1ST: So are we. But first we have to eat.

ALL: Yes, let's eat. (*They start for books.*)

OLD BOOKWORM: Wait! (*They stop.*) I shall be very happy to prepare a lunch for you.

2ND: Oh, that's not necessary. Here are many big books. We'll just help ourselves.

OLD BOOKWORM: Oh, no! You mustn't do that!

3RD: Why not?

OLD BOOKWORM: If you have always lived in a box of blank stationery, you are accustomed to a very plain diet. There is some rich fare in these books. It is all wholesome, of course, but too much of one thing is apt to upset you.

4TH: Oh, that's foolishness.

ALL: That's foolishness.

OLD BOOKWORM: I assure you, it is not foolishness. I have lived here all my life, and I know.

5TH: We're perfectly able to choose for ourselves.

ALL: Yes, we're perfectly able to choose for ourselves.

OLD BOOKWORM (*Worried*): If you won't let me help you choose your food, at least let us have the meeting and organize the colony before you eat.

6TH: Oh, no. We are too hungry.

7TH: It will take us only a few moments to eat; then we will organize the colony.

8TH: Anyway, the meeting won't amount to much, because we are all agreed on our future. We always agree on everything.

ALL: We always agree on everything.

1ST: And after we have eaten, we will be better able to make plans.

OLD BOOKWORM (*Solemnly*): I doubt that. I seriously doubt it. I warn you, you are doing this against my advice.

2ND: We will see you in a little bit. Let's eat.

ALL: Let's eat! (*They duck into the books, through little flaps at bottom of each book. Seven* BOOKWORMS *go into the first seven books, leaving only Arithmetic unoccupied. One* YOUNG BOOKWORM *lingers behind.*)

YOUNG BOOKWORM (*Who has remained, pulling scrap of blank paper from his pocket*) : I still have a bit of stationery left. We brought some to eat on the way. I'll finish this first, and then try one of the books. (*He sits and commences eating.*)

OLD BOOKWORM (*Absently*) : Suit yourself. (*He paces the floor, shaking head anxiously.*) I'm afraid there is going to be trouble.

YOUNG BOOKWORM (*Between bites*) : Why do you worry so?

OLD BOOKWORM : Your families are waiting in a dangerous place. Think what a serious matter it will be if they do not soon hear from you.

YOUNG BOOKWORM : We'll send a message right away. Everything is going to be all right, now that we have found food.

OLD BOOKWORM : I don't know. Maybe everything will be all wrong.

YOUNG BOOKWORM : Don't you think you're making too much of this? We can digest your big books!

OLD BOOKWORM : Oh, I'm sure you can digest them all right. Too well, probably. But you should have let me choose a balanced diet for you. Too much of one thing is bad — very bad.

YOUNG BOOKWORM : Do you really believe there is a difference in books? A book is a book!

OLD BOOKWORM : Oh, no, my young friend. Too many people think that, but it is not so.

YOUNG BOOKWORM : All right, then tell me which of those is the best one. I will sample it pretty soon.

OLD BOOKWORM : Well, now, I cannot say that any one of them is best. They are all very good. There is the Encyclopedia — I am very fond of that. Especially at dinner time. It is a little heavy for breakfast. I like something lighter at breakfast: this book of Fairy Tales, for instance. Here's American History — that's very good! Etiquette — King Arthur and His Knights — Book of Poems — Travel Stories — Arithmetic — they are all very good books. I would advise you to try some of each, for you will enjoy them all. Besides, it will likely save you a lot of trouble.

YOUNG BOOKWORM : You have your mind set on trouble, haven't you? Wait till my friends come out of the books, and you'll see your worries were for nothing. They'll be just the same as they were before.

OLD BOOKWORM: That, my young friend, is impossible.

YOUNG BOOKWORM: Look — here comes one now.

OLD BOOKWORM: Yes, out of the book of Etiquette. We shall see, now. We shall see! (GIRL BOOKWORM *comes out of book of Etiquette. She carries a lorgnette, which she peers through in a very affected manner. She trains the lorgnette on the two bookworms, and stares haughtily at them.*)

YOUNG BOOKWORM: For goodness' sake!

OLD BOOKWORM (*Groaning*): It is just as I feared!

MISS ETIQUETTE (*We will call her this from now on to distinguish her from the others*): How do you do? (*In gushing voice*) I'm so *very* happy to see you again! (*She extends her hand, raised high to the* OLD BOOKWORM, *who resignedly shakes it.*) I *hope* you are in good health?

YOUNG BOOKWORM: My goodness!

MISS ETIQUETTE: (*Walking toward* YOUNG BOOKWORM, *and using lorgnette*): I beg your pardon for intruding, but why don't you rise when a lady enters the room?

YOUNG BOOKWORM: What for? (*Reluctantly gets up. Happens to glance at books.*) Oh, look! Someone else is coming out!

OLD BOOKWORM: Yes, from the Book of Fairy Tales. (*The book of Fairy Tales opens and out comes another* GIRL BOOKWORM. *She wears a Red Riding Hood cape and carries a basket.*)

YOUNG BOOKWORM: For goodness' sake!

RED RIDING HOOD: Just see the nice cake I am taking to Grandmother! (*Lifts napkin in basket.*) Which is the way to Grandmother's house? That way? (*Hippety-hops gaily across stage to left, singing loudly, and looks out.*) Or that way? (*Hippety-hops right, and looks off stage.*)

MISS ETIQUETTE: Please stop that giddy skipping, child. Don't you know children should be seen and not heard? Come here and curtsy to me.

RED RIDING HOOD: Why?

MISS ETIQUETTE: Little girls should always curtsy to ladies. And I am a lady-bug. (*The Encyclopedia opens and out comes a* BOY BOOKWORM, *wearing an academic cap and horn-rimmed spectacles. We will call him* MR. WISE.)

MR. WISE (*Impressively*): A photo-heliograph is an instrument for photographing the sun.

RED RIDING HOOD (*Giggles*): Who cares?

MISS ETIQUETTE: My dear child, that is very rude.

RED RIDING HOOD (*Hippety-hops across stage to* MR. WISE): See my nice cake for Grandmother?

MR. WISE (*Looking at cake*): It is manifestly a culinary achievement.

RED RIDING HOOD: Oh, no, it's a cake! (OLD BOOKWORM *is shaking his head in dismay. The occupant of the Book of Poems now comes out. He is dreamy in manner; gazes into space and gestures gracefully.*)

POET:

What a lovely, pretty thing
Are bunnies blooming in the spring!

YOUNG BOOKWORM: My goodness! . . . What are bunnies?

POET (*Airily*): I don't know.

MR. WISE (*Sternly*): "Bunny" is a pet name for rabbit, a burrowing rodent. But bunnies do not bloom, in the spring or any other time. Your talk does not make sense.

POET: Well, anyway, it rhymes.

RED RIDING HOOD: Yes, and I like it. (*She skips over to* POET.) Say it again.

POET (*With gestures*):

What a lovely, pretty thing
Are bunnies blooming in the spring.

MR. WISE: I *don't* like it.

MISS ETIQUETTE: I do not wish to be overly critical, but I don't like it, either.

RED RIDING HOOD: I like it. (*To* POET) Say it again.

MR. WISE: No, don't say it again.

OLD BOOKWORM: Wait. Let's not have an argument.

MISS ETIQUETTE: No, arguments are very rude.

RED RIDING HOOD: Look, here comes somebody else. (BOY BOOKWORM *comes from American History book. He wears a three-sided colonial hat, and carries a small hatchet.*)

HISTORIAN: Then George said, "Father, I cannot tell a lie!"

YOUNG BOOKWORM: For goodness' sake!

HISTORIAN (*Going toward* RED RIDING HOOD): "I did it with my little hatchet!" (*He raises hatchet to illustrate.* RED RIDING HOOD *shrieks and scurries across stage.*)

RED RIDING HOOD: Ooooh! He must be an ogre! I'm afraid!

(*Hides face in hands. From the book of King Arthur and His Knights steps a* Boy Bookworm, *wearing armored helmet and a girdle with sword. He sees* Red Riding Hood.)

Knight: Forsooth! A damsel in distress! (*Draws sword; strides to her.*) Fair damsel, tell me wherefore thou makest this sorrow, and, by my faith, will I avenge thee!

Red Riding Hood (*Pointing at* Historian): An ogre!

Knight (*Striding toward* Historian): If thou hast in truth distressed that damsel, make ready to defend thyself!

Historian (*Brandishing hatchet*): Defend your own self! As John Paul Jones said, "I have not yet begun to fight!"

Mr. Wise: Such unwarranted belligerency is incomprehensible!

Poet (*Shaking finger at* Knight *and* Historian):

An angry look or wrathful word
Is better never seen or heard!

(*The Travel Stories book opens and out comes its occupant. He wears a hat and carries a suitcase.*)

Traveler (*Sets suitcase down and clasps hands in rapture*): Ah! The Alps of Switzerland! The fjords of Norway! The pyramids of Egypt! The Great Wall of China! The Canals of Venice!

Miss Etiquette: Please remove your hat in the presence of ladies.

Traveler (*Takes off hat and gazes thoughtfully at it*): In India the men wear turbans. In Mexico, they wear sombreros. A Turkish man wears a fez, and a Scotchman, a tam-o'-shanter. (*Puts hat back on head.*)

Red Riding Hood: My grandmother wears a lace cap.

Poet:

It isn't your hat, nor the name of your hatter;
But what's in the head underneath which doth matter!

Mr. Wise (*To* Poet): For once I am in total accordance with your sentiment.

Old Bookworm: My friends, it troubles me greatly to see you carry on in this manner.

Young Bookworm: Me, too! I don't know what's got into all of you. I think I'll leave. I'm going to eat, now.

Red Riding Hood: Then do try some Fairy Tales. You'll love them.

Miss Etiquette: If you will allow me to suggest, try a bit of Etiquette.

TRAVELER: Oh, no. Try a little travel.

HISTORIAN: I say you will do better to go into the History of the United States. As Daniel Webster said, "I was born an American, I live an American, and I shall die an American."

KNIGHT: If thou wilt take thy repast at the Round Table of King Arthur, thou wilt surely find it to thy liking.

MR. WISE: I feel confident that you will appreciate the superlative quality of the all-inclusive Encyclopedia.

POET:

You cannot do better; you'll likely do worse
To choose anything but a volume of verse.

YOUNG BOOKWORM: No, I don't want to be like any of you. There's a book at the end that none of you tried — I think I'll sample that. (*Squints up at book.*) What's the name of it?

OLD BOOKWORM: That's Arithmetic, my boy. It's a good book — pretty solid stuff, of course, but wholesome and beneficial. It can't possibly hurt you. But hurry back because we must have our meeting.

YOUNG BOOKWORM: Yes, we must have it right away. You start it now, and I'll be right back and help you. (*Goes into Arithmetic book.*)

OLD BOOKWORM: The meeting will come to order. Please sit in a group over there. (*The seven* BOOKWORMS *sit in group.*) My friends, I do not have any desire to exercise authority over you, but I am taking it upon myself to call this meeting and to preside until you have elected your government. I am very anxious for you to establish your colony, for I shall not rest until your families are here, safely settled in their new homes.

POET:

Though one may gad the whole world round,
Home is the best place ever found.

TRAVELER: Home! Ah, to an Eskimo home means an igloo. To an Indian, it is a wigwam. But a Swiss mountaineer, thinking of home, fondly pictures a rock cabin.

MISS ETIQUETTE: Yes, indeed, we must have immediate consideration for our dear families.

KNIGHT (*Jumps up*): By my faith, we must tarry not, but make haste to deliver that noble company.

HISTORIAN (*Rising*): As Patrick Henry said, "Why stand we here idle?"

RED RIDING HOOD: We must hurry, because I don't want anything to happen to my dear grandma.

MR. WISE: We must employ all expedition.

OLD BOOKWORM: I am glad you all agree. Let us quickly form a government.

MR. WISE: A government is an established system of administration of public affairs.

OLD BOOKWORM: Yes. What kind of a government do you want?

RED RIDING HOOD: I think it would be nice to have a lovely queen, as the fairies do.

KNIGHT: Or perchance a noble king, like good King Arthur.

MR. WISE: That is a monarchy.

POET (*Rising*):

For me, I don't see any call
To have a government at all.
Let's be as free as little breezes:
Everyone do as he pleases.

MR. WISE: That is anarchy.

HISTORIAN: As Abraham Lincoln said, I am for government of the people, by the people, for the people.

MR. WISE: That is democracy.

OLD BOOKWORM (*Anxiously*): Perhaps we can better decide upon a form of government if we first decide what we wish it to do for us.

MISS ETIQUETTE: I think the chief purpose of our colony should be to teach everyone good manners.

KNIGHT: I fain would have a goodly company of brave knights, to protect ladies and young damsels, and to slay all dragons, serpents and giants in the countryside.

TRAVELER: I think it would be jolly to live in tree houses as the South Sea Islanders do, have ice-skating matches like those in Holland, and to ride on elephants as people do in India.

MR. WISE: My opinion is that we should devote ourselves profoundly to the acquisition of knowledge.

RED RIDING HOOD: I think every one of us should have a pair of seven league boots, a goose that lays golden eggs, and a fairy godmother.

POET:

Such magic gifts might prove a curse.
But I think we should have free verse.

HISTORIAN: I say our only objective should be independence. Let's have a Boston Tea Party, and throw tea in the ocean.

MR. WISE: That is a ridiculous idea.

HISTORIAN (*Brandishing hatchet*): Oh, is that so? It was good enough for George Washington, and, as Colonel Henry Lee said, George Washington was "first in war, first in peace, and first in the hearts of his countrymen." That's the way the United States began. Why shouldn't we start out in the same way?

MR. WISE: In the first place, we haven't any tea. In the second place, we haven't any ocean.

RED RIDING HOOD: My grandma loves tea.

TRAVELER: Yes, and the poor people of Asia work very hard picking tea leaves and sending them over here. It would be a shame to throw away the product of their labor.

HISTORIAN: People of Asia! Hmf! You'd better stop your gadding about, and take some interest in the people of the United States.

MR. WISE (*To* HISTORIAN): Yes, and you'd better travel up through your history book about a century and three-quarters, and find out what the people of the United States do nowadays. They don't throw tea away now.

MISS ETIQUETTE (*To* MR. WISE): No, but they do try to have a few manners — at least cultured people do — and they don't deliberately make insulting remarks.

MR. WISE: My dear lady, let me point out that individuals who have really good manners don't display them incessantly.

MISS ETIQUETTE: Why, the idea! The very idea! I've never heard such rudeness! Oh, I've never been so insulted in my life!

KNIGHT (*Drawing sword and going toward* MR. WISE): Fie on thee! Why dost thou besiege this lady?

MR. WISE: Now, now, Mr. Knight! Melodrama is uncalled for.

KNIGHT: Say what ye list, I care not, but do not besiege this lady or I will smite off thy head.

MISS ETIQUETTE: Oh, don't you think that would be going a little too far? It wouldn't be polite.

RED RIDING HOOD: No, it wouldn't be polite at all. He acts as bad as an ogre. I don't think we ought to have a company of knights in our colony. If they all ran around acting like he does, it would scare me to death. They would be worse than a wolf.

POET:

Yes, his noise distracts my mind so much,
I cannot think of rhymes — of rhymes — of rhymes —of — oh, dear!
Just see what he's done! I cannot make rhymes any more!

TRAVELER: That's something to be thankful for!

POET:

Oh, is that so?
I suppose you think you're awfully smart,
Because you can't appreciate art!

TRAVELER: Oh, I appreciate art, all right! Take Shakespeare, for instance — he lived in England, you know, at Stratford-On-Avon. I love *art*. But I don't care for your rhymes.

OLD BOOKWORM: Please, please! Don't waste your time in idle bickering. Let us concentrate on forming our colony. We must agree or we are lost! Won't you try to unite?

MISS ETIQUETTE: Really, I don't see how you can expect anyone to get along with persons who are so uncouth!

MR. WISE: And so ignorant!

TRAVELER: So narrow!

POET: So prosaic!

HISTORIAN: So unpatriotic!

KNIGHT: So lacking in gallantry!

OLD BOOKWORM (*In despair*): Isn't there anything that will persuade you to cooperate?

MISS ETIQUETTE (*Nose in air*): I don't seem to feel very cooperative.

MR. WISE: Nor do I.

TRAVELER: Nor I.

POET: Nor I.

HISTORIAN: Nor I.

KNIGHT: Nor I.

RED RIDING HOOD: Nor I.

OLD BOOKWORM: It is just as I feared from the first! Our hopes are lost! (*He sinks down, overcome with grief, and puts his head in his hands.*)

RED RIDING HOOD (*Pointing at Arithmetic book*): Look! He's coming out.

OLD BOOKWORM (*Shaking head*): He is a nice young bookworm, and Arithmetic is sound, substantial stuff, but I fear nothing can help us now.

YOUNG BOOKWORM (*Steps out of Arithmetic. He has an old hat pulled low over his eyes, and a dark handkerchief tied over nose and mouth. He is pointing a gun — an insect spray-gun — at the group*): Stick 'em up! (*All stand stupidly and stare at him in amazement.*) Stick 'em up, or I'll shoot! Reach for the skies, and make it snappy! (*Everyone slowly raises arms.*) That's better. (*He pulls handkerchief from nose and mouth. Sternly*) Now, what's going on here?

OLD BOOKWORM: Why, our meeting! Have you forgotten? Our meeting to form a government!

GANGSTER (*Laughing harshly*): Oh, yes, the meeting. But don't bother about forming a government — *I'm* your government from now on. All you have to do is just what I tell you.

POET:

What strange caprice, what ugly whim,
What madness has got into him?

OLD BOOKWORM: I can't imagine! I always had the highest regard for Arithmetic. I can't see how it could have affected him this way.

RED RIDING HOOD: Maybe he has been enchanted by a wicked witch!

KNIGHT: Truly must there be a loathly dragon within that book!

MISS ETIQUETTE: It sounds to me like plain, everyday selfishness!

MR. WISE: It is undoubtedly caused by lack of learning.

GANGSTER: Silence! I'll have no more of that chatter!

OLD BOOKWORM: My boy, why do you act this way?

GANGSTER: Silence, I said! Obey when I tell you something! From now on you are all my slaves! (*All gasp.*)

MR. WISE: This is incomprehensible!

HISTORIAN (*Angrily*): Say! Don't you know what the Constitution of the United States says? Amendment Thirteen says: There shall be no slavery within the United States.

KNIGHT: I, for one, will never pay thee tribute!

TRAVELER: You ought to see what's happened in Europe and Asia because of a few gangsters like you.

MISS ETIQUETTE: If you want me to do anything, you'll have to say "please!"

RED RIDING HOOD: If you start telling me what to do, I'll scream for some woodcutters!

POET:

I wished to be a little breeze,
Free to do just what I please.
But *you* — false-hearted desperado —
You want to be a big tornado!

HISTORIAN: As Patrick Henry said, "Give me liberty or give me death!"

KNIGHT (*Brandishing sword*): Let us encounter him!

GANGSTER (*Sneering*): You don't dare! One shot of this gun and you'll be goners.

KNIGHT: Thou boasteth greatly, and speaketh proud words, but I fear not! I will fight thee to the utmost! (*Advances.*)

MR. WISE: No; stop! Your courage is inspiring, but a sword hasn't a chance against a gun.

RED RIDING HOOD: Please don't, Sir Knight. You might get hurt.

TRAVELER: One of us hasn't any chance alone. We must form a plan.

HISTORIAN: Yes, as Benjamin Franklin said, "We must all hang together, or we will hang separately."

MR. WISE: Let us — excuse my slang, won't you? — let us go into a huddle. (*All seven put their heads together and whisper, while the* OLD BOOKWORM *and the* GANGSTER *watch.*)

GANGSTER: Pooh! As if you could think of anything!

OLD BOOKWORM (*Sorrowfully*): My boy, I cannot understand what has caused this terrible change in you. Surely Arithmetic could not have done it. It is a dreadful mystery.

GANGSTER: Silence! (*The huddle breaks up, with the seven nodding at one another.*)

TRAVELER (*To* GANGSTER, *in discouraged voice*): Well, Mr. Gangster, I guess you've got us.

GANGSTER: Of course I've got you! No doubt about that.

MR. WISE: Defeat is very humiliating, but (*Shrugs*) what can we do?

GANGSTER: Nothing — I told you that!

POET (*Very humbly*):

Since I'm obliged to be your slave,
I'll try my hardest to behave.

GANGSTER: If you don't, it'll be too bad for you. . . . Well! I'm glad you all had sense enough to give up. (*All nod, sadly.*)

RED RIDING HOOD: Oh, yoo-hoo, Grandma! Come right in! (*She waves happily at someone apparently behind the gangster. The* GANGSTER *whirls around to see who is behind him, and in a twinkling the seven other* BOOKWORMS *are upon him. The gun is knocked from his hand, and the* POET *gleefully picks it up.*)

POET (*Points gun at* GANGSTER):

You should have thought a little faster;
Now who's the slave, and who's the master?
(*The* GANGSTER *cowers.*)

HISTORIAN (*Exultantly*): As Commodore Perry said, "We have met the enemy and he is ours!"

MR. WISE: Yes, he's ours, all right. But now, what are we going to do with him?

MISS ETIQUETTE: He should be made to apologize to each of us!

RED RIDING HOOD: I think he ought to be turned into a donkey and be forced to pull a heavy load for a year and a day.

TRAVELER: He should be exiled to Siberia or Iceland or the Sahara Desert.

HISTORIAN: I would have him confined in stocks.

KNIGHT: Right willingly would I smite off his head.

OLD BOOKWORM: Wait — please wait a few moments before you choose a punishment for him. I cannot understand how this could have happened. Let me go into the Arithmetic book and see if I can find any clue to this mystery. (*He goes into Arithmetic book.*)

MR. WISE: All right, we'll wait a little while, but eventually this hoodlum is going to get what's coming to him.

HISTORIAN: Absolutely! As Calvin Coolidge said, "There is no right to strike against the public safety by anybody, anywhere, anytime."

POET:

He must be convinced, and without much delay,
What all hoodlums learn: that crime does not pay!

TRAVELER: Just see him tremble! A bully is always a coward at heart.

RED RIDING HOOD: And he used to be a real nice fellow.

KNIGHT: Yea, he was of noble and gentle nature.

MISS ETIQUETTE: It certainly is peculiar how he changed, isn't it? I cannot imagine what caused it.

MR. WISE: No, I am anxious to find out.

OLD BOOKWORM (*Coming out*): All my life I have lived here, and never before have I discovered *that!* It is astounding!

ALL: What's astounding?

OLD BOOKWORM: It is astounding! Do you know, some mischievous youngster who once owned that Arithmetic book hid a volume of Trashy Stories in the middle of it!

ALL: Oh, Oh, Oh!

OLD BOOKWORM (*To* GANGSTER): That was what you ate, wasn't it?

GANGSTER (*Sullenly*): Well, what if it was?

OLD BOOKWORM (*To others*): He happened to get into the very worst part, and he has obviously swallowed every word of it!

ALL: Oh, oh, oh!

OLD BOOKWORM (*To* GANGSTER): Didn't you?

GANGSTER: Is it any of your business?

OLD BOOKWORM: Poor boy! He probably has bad indigestion. (*In kindly voice*) Tell me, my boy, does your stomach hurt?

GANGSTER (*Suddenly breaking down and moaning, and holding hands on stomach*): Oh, yes, it does! It hurts awfully! Owoooooh!

MISS ETIQUETTE: No wonder, after filling up on trash!

GANGSTER: Owooooh! My stomach! Owoooooooh!

RED RIDING HOOD: The poor fellow! What can we do for him?

MR. WISE: He needs something to counteract the poison.

TRAVELER: Maybe a little poetry would be good for him. It is soothing.

ALL: Oh, yes, a little poetry!

RED RIDING HOOD: And a little travel. It improves one's taste.

ALL: Oh, yes, a little travel!

HISTORIAN: A bit of King Arthur's Knights would be invigorating.

ALL: Oh, yes, a bit of King Arthur!

MR. WISE: A little etiquette would be beneficial.

ALL: Oh, yes, a little etiquette. (*The* OLD BOOKWORM *is smiling and nodding approval.*)

POET:

Let me suggest that, the way things look,
He needs a little of every book.

ALL: Yes, a little of every book!

OLD BOOKWORM: I believe you have found the right solution.

MISS ETIQUETTE: Come on, you would-be gangster. We will soon make a good citizen of you. You may begin on the Encyclopedia. (GANGSTER, *still holding stomach, and doubled over, goes into Encyclopedia.*) And it might be a good idea if we all vary our diet a bit.

ALL: It would be a good idea!

OLD BOOKWORM: Now I know that you will have no trouble forming a successful colony.

MR. WISE: No, let's do that right away. And our first official act must be to put a danger sign on that Trashy Stories book. It is very dangerous.

ALL (*Shaking heads solemnly*): It is very dangerous.

OLD BOOKWORM: Have you decided what kind of a government you want?

ALL (*Loudly*): A democracy!

OLD BOOKWORM: Very well. (*Raps.*) The meeting will come to order, and the first business will be election of officers.

THE END

THE BOOK HOSPITAL

by Jean Brabham McKinney

Characters

DR. LIBRARIAN
NURSE MARY
ROBINSON CRUSOE
HEIDI
TOM SAWYER
CINDERELLA
KING ARTHUR
PAUL BUNYAN

SETTING: *The book hospital. There are two or three cots and several chairs for patients.*

BEFORE RISE: *Loud moans and groans are heard from behind curtain. Then a hospital bell is heard and a voice calls, "Calling Dr. Librarian! Calling Dr. Librarian!"* DR. LIBRARIAN *comes onto apron of stage, walking briskly. Behind her, pushing a hospital cart, is* NURSE MARY. *On the cart are large containers labeled "Glue," "Shellac," and "Mending Tape," rolls of binding tape, a large bottle labeled "Pain Pills," etc.* DR. LIBRARIAN *opens the curtain wide enough to enter through the center, and marches on stage followed by* NURSE MARY. *Loud moans and cries of "Oh, doctor," "Please help me," etc., are heard, then the curtain rises.*

AT RISE: HEIDI, TOM SAWYER, CINDERELLA, KING ARTHUR, *and* PAUL BUNYAN *are seated on chairs.* ROBINSON CRUSOE *is lying down on one of the cots. Each book character wears a cardboard cover representing a book.* DR. LIBRARIAN *goes to* ROBINSON CRUSOE'*s cot and takes his pulse.* NURSE MARY *places a thermometer in* HEIDI'*s mouth.*

ROBINSON CRUSOE: Oh, doctor, I have never suffered so much. There I was, brand new and standing dressed in my beautiful book cover, just waiting for some child to check me out, when along came a little boy who jerked me from the shelf. I heard myself go, "Creak, creak, creak!" Then I felt limp, and knew my spine was broken. I haven't been able to stand up since then. Oh, oh, oh!

DR. LIBRARIAN (*Soothingly*): Yes, you are a very sick man, Robinson Crusoe. I'll give you some pills to ease your pain. Nurse Mary, the pain pills, please. (NURSE MARY *goes to the cart and gets the bottle marked "Pain Pills," takes two pills from it, and brings them to* DR. LIBRARIAN *with a glass of water.*) Now, take these, Crusoe. (*They hold* ROBINSON CRUSOE*'s head up from the pillow for him to swallow the pills and water.*) These will make you feel better. The nurse will give you two of these every hour, and tomorrow we'll get you ready for surgery at the bindery. You'll be good as new then.

ROBINSON CRUSOE: Thank you! Thank you! (*Drowsily*) I feel better already — I think I'll just go to sleep. (*He closes his eyes and turns his head on the pillow.* NURSE MARY *and* DR. LIBRARIAN *pull up the blanket from the foot of the bed and tuck it around* ROBINSON CRUSOE. NURSE MARY *then takes the thermometer from* HEIDI*'s mouth.*)

DR. LIBRARIAN: Good morning, Heidi. (*Reads thermometer*) Hmmm — quite a bit of fever. (HEIDI *coughs miserably.*) How did you catch such a terrible cold?

HEIDI: I'm used to the Swiss Alps, and cold weather doesn't usually bother me. But oh, I was so mistreated by a careless little girl. (HEIDI *coughs and cries.*)

NURSE MARY: There, there, tell us about it.

HEIDI: One bitterly cold day the little girl checked me out of the library and took me home with her. Just as she was going up the steps to her nice warm house, she dropped me. She didn't even notice me, and I lay on the steps all night while the snow and rain came down. Now I'm all faded and out of shape. (*Cries*)

DR. LIBRARIAN: You did get a soaking. You're still limp. We'll get you dry and dose this cold first. Nurse Mary, she must have plenty of aspirin and juices.

NURSE MARY: Yes, Dr. Librarian.

DR. LIBRARIAN: Now don't fret, Heidi. In a few days you'll be well enough to go to the bindery and select a new cover for yourself.

HEIDI (*Greatly cheered*): Oh, Dr. Librarian, I'd like a red cover this time with my name in big gold letters.

DR. LIBRARIAN: I think that could be arranged.

NURSE MARY (*In a stage whisper*): Dr. Librarian, that's Tom Sawyer over there. Isn't his breathing dreadful? It sounds as though he were playing the accordion.

DR. LIBRARIAN (*Goes to* TOM SAWYER): Hello, Tom. How are you?

TOM SAWYER (*Breathing loudly*): I'm in a dreadful state. Every time I breathe, I feel as though my lungs were glued together. (NURSE MARY *takes* TOM SAWYER'*s pulse while* DR. LIBRARIAN *listens to his chest with her stethoscope.*)

DR. LIBRARIAN: Stand up, Tom, and let me take a look between your covers. (TOM SAWYER *stands obediently. He is still breathing heavily while* DR. LIBRARIAN *and* NURSE MARY *stand on each side of him and take a look between his book covers.*) Ah ha, I see the trouble. Nurse Mary, bring me a pair of pliers.

TOM SAWYER (*Frightened*): Dr. Librarian, what are you going to do?

DR. LIBRARIAN: Your wheezing has been caused by a wad of chewing gum that a child stuck inside you.

TOM SAWYER: Oh, what will these children do next! (*Piteously*) Will it hurt to pull it out?

DR. LIBRARIAN: A little, but it won't take long. (*She pulls a long rubbery substance out while* TOM SAWYER *gives a loud yelp.*) There now, Tom. You'll be all right. Fortunately, no pages are torn. Nurse Mary, bring the alcohol and cotton. (NURSE MARY *goes to the hospital cart and brings cotton and alcohol.* DR. LIBRARIAN *gives the spot beneath* TOM SAWYER'*s cover a dab.* TOM *is now breathing normally.*)

TOM SAWYER: Thank you, Dr. Librarian. I feel ever so much better.

DR. LIBRARIAN: Stay here in the hospital for a few days and then you may return to your place on the shelf. (*To* NURSE MARY *in a stage whisper*) Who's that dirty little ragamuffin over there?

NURSE MARY: Oh, Dr. Librarian, that's Cinderella.

DR. LIBRARIAN: Cinderella! Oh, Cinderella, you were the prettiest book in the library! What happened to you?

CINDERELLA: Two children, not one, but two, with the dirtiest hands you've ever seen, came and leafed through my pages and smudged my cover.

DR. LIBRARIAN: Evidently one was eating chocolate. Your whole cover is streaked.

NURSE MARY: I'll get the sponge and that new cleaning fluid. (*She goes to the cart and returns with a large bottle and sponge. They both work vigorously on* CINDERELLA'*s book cover.*)

DR. LIBRARIAN: Now, you look much better. Nurse Mary will use art gum and cleaner on your pages later today.

CINDERELLA: Thank you, Dr. Librarian.

NURSE MARY (*Going ahead to next patient*): Why, King Arthur, let's straighten that crown. You look a bit bedraggled to be a king.

KING ARTHUR: I don't even feel like a king. Who ever heard of a king who was chewed up by a puppy? I'm really dog-eared.

DR. LIBRARIAN: That is a dreadful thing to happen to a king. But don't worry, King Arthur. Nurse, bring me a roll of that binding tape and some scissors. (NURSE MARY *brings tape and scissors and she and* DR. LIBRARIAN *quickly repair the ragged corners of the book cover.*) Now, you look much better.

KING ARTHUR: I feel much better, too. Thank you, Dr. Librarian.

DR. LIBRARIAN (*To next patient*): Why, Paul Bunyan! You look as big and strapping as ever. What are you doing here?

PAUL BUNYAN (*Moaning*): I'm afraid I have internal injuries. I feel torn inside.

DR. LIBRARIAN: Let us take a look. (PAUL BUNYAN *stands painfully while* DR. LIBRARIAN *and* NURSE MARY *look between the covers.*) You *are* torn inside. Two of your pages are ripped in two. Get the mending tape, Nurse Mary. (NURSE MARY *brings mending tape from cart and they quickly repair the pages.*) Now sit back down and be quiet until you're entirely healed. Then you may return to the library.

PAUL BUNYAN (*Grumbling*): A big outdoor fellow like me having to be in the hospital with torn pages! Isn't that something! (*Sits obediently.* NURSE MARY *and* DR. LIBRARIAN *walk downstage away from the patients.*)

DR. LIBRARIAN: I try hard to show the boys and girls who come to the library what a treasure they have on the shelves and what exciting adventures books can offer them.

NURSE MARY: If only the children would take care of their books!

DR. LIBRARIAN: I've spoken to the children about that, too. I'm sure that when our patients are back in circulation, the children will take better care of them.

NURSE MARY: In the meantime, I'll do my best to make our patients comfortable.

DR. LIBRARIAN: I'll be back tomorrow. Goodbye, children. (DR. LIBRARIAN *exits while* NURSE MARY *crosses stage to hospital cart. Curtain.*)

THE END

I'LL SHARE MY FARE

by Helen Littler Howard

Characters

FARMER
BUTCHER
STOREKEEPER
BAKER
BASKETWEAVER
GLORIA, *her little girl*

SETTING: *Marketplace. There are three booths.*

TIME: *Day before Thanksgiving.*

AT RISE: *The* BUTCHER, *the* STOREKEEPER *and the* BAKER *are in their booths quietly arranging their wares. The* FARMER *comes riding in on a hobbyhorse carrying a basket. He comes from the left side of the stage, rides once around and pauses near the* BUTCHER'S *booth.*

FARMER:
God is good.
He gave me food.
I'll share my fare
In gratitude.
(*Trots his pony up to* BUTCHER'S *booth.*)
Good day, Butcher.

BUTCHER: Good day, friend Farmer. What have you in your basket?

FARMER: I've had a fine year. I have more than enough food for my family and my animals for the winter. So I've brought you a turkey for your Thanksgiving dinner.
God is good.
He gave me food.
I'll share my fare
In gratitude.
(*Gives* BUTCHER *the turkey in basket.*)

BUTCHER (*Looks in basket*): Oh, what a fine turkey! A Thanksgiving feast for my family. Thank you, friend Farmer.

FARMER: You are welcome. Happy Thanksgiving to you. (*Rides away.*)

BUTCHER: How thankful I am to have this fine turkey! I'll share my good fortune with my friend the Storekeeper. I'll give him the goose I was going to have for Thanksgiving. (*He puts goose in the basket and takes it to the* STOREKEEPER'S *booth.*) Good day, friend Storekeeper.

STOREKEEPER: Good day, friend Butcher.

BUTCHER: I've just had good fortune. My friend the Farmer just brought me a fine fat turkey for our Thanksgiving dinner. So I've brought you the goose I was going to have.

The Farmer is good.
He gave me food.
I'll share my fare
In gratitude.

(*The* BUTCHER *gives the* STOREKEEPER *the basket.*)

STOREKEEPER (*Looking in basket*): Oh, thank you. What a fine Thanksgiving dinner this goose will make. (BUTCHER *goes back to his booth.*)

STOREKEEPER: Now that I have this fine fat goose for our Thanksgiving dinner I'll take my friend the Baker this chicken for his dinner. (*Puts chicken in basket and goes to* BAKER'S *booth*) Good day, friend Baker.

BAKER: Good day to you, friend Storekeeper.

STOREKEEPER: My neighbor, the Butcher, just brought me a fine, fat goose for Thanksgiving. So I thought I'd bring you this chicken for your dinner.

The Butcher is good.
He gave me food.
I'll share my fare
In gratitude.

(*Gives* BAKER *the basket.*)

BAKER: Oh, thank you! I'm so glad to have a chicken for my family for Thanksgiving. (STOREKEEPER *goes back to his booth. Enter* THE BASKETWEAVER *and* GLORIA.)

BAKER: Here comes my friend the Basketweaver with her little girl. I'll just put this meat pie I had made for our Thanksgiving dinner into this basket and give it to them.

BASKETWEAVER: Good day, friend Baker.

BAKER: Good day. I made this meat pie for our Thanksgiving dinner, but my friend, the Storekeeper, gave me a plump chicken. Would you like to have this meat pie for yourselves?

The Storekeeper is good.
He gave me food.
I'll share my fare
In gratitude.

BASKETWEAVER (*Taking basket*): Oh, thank you very much. How glad I am to have a fine meat pie to share with my little girl for Thanksgiving.

BASKETWEAVER *and* GLORIA:

The Baker is good.
He gave us food.
We'll share our fare
In gratitude.

(BASKETWEAVER *and* GLORIA *go off stage carrying the basket happily between them.*)

THE END

THANKS TO SAMMY SCARECROW

by Helen Littler Howard

Characters

SAMMY SCARECROW
MARI ELLEN
SANDY SQUIRREL
WALLY

TIME: *Thanksgiving Day.*

SETTING: *In a corn field.*

AT RISE: *On left stage center is* SAMMY SCARECROW. *He is quite dilapidated and hangs on to crossed sticks in a haphazard way.* SANDY SQUIRREL *is scurrying about the corn shock.*

SAMMY (*Sadly*):
Today is Thanksgiving,
But what need of living,
The crows have all flown away.

No more come they thieving,
And I am left grieving,
I'm useless this Thanksgiving Day.

That's a bit of poetry I made up. I have time for all sorts of thinking since I'm not looking after the corn any longer. This is a sad Thanksgiving Day for me. Nothing to be thankful for, I say. Nobody cares about a scarecrow when the corn is safely shocked. When one isn't busy doing something useful he can't be thankful.

SANDY (*Comes to* SCARECROW): You're useful to me, old Sammy!

SAMMY: You're a thief, Sandy, and I don't call it being useful to help you in your stealing. I want to protect, not to harm.

SANDY: You won't tell on me, will you, Sammy? You can't because it's against the rules to talk when anybody is near. I'm sorry for you, Sammy. You do look a bit worse for the wear. But I can't stay and talk. My Thanksgiving dinner is ready. I'll be back for dessert. (*Frisks off stage right.*)

SAMMY: Oh hum! I suppose I may as well take another nap. (*Pretends to go to sleep. Enter* WALLY *and* MARI ELLEN, *who is carrying a gaily decorated basket.*)

WALLY: What a surprise we have for Thanksgiving dinner!

MARI ELLEN: I'm glad we hid the nuts until Thanksgiving Day. Only this morning mother said it wouldn't seem like a Thanksgiving dinner without a basket of nuts. I could hardly keep from telling her.

WALLY: I'm glad you didn't. Secrets and surprises are lots of fun when you keep them secrets and surprises. (*Children go to the corn shock.* WALLY *kneels down and begins searching among the corn stalks.*) There must be a whole basketful here.

MARI ELLEN (*Kneels beside him*): There should be. We spent a half day gathering them. There were so few this year.

WALLY: I can't find any! That's queer.

MARI ELLEN (*Stands up and looks around*): Are you sure this is the right corn shock?

WALLY (*Stands too*): Yes. Don't you remember. It was the one nearest Sammy Scarecrow.

MARI ELLEN: Yes, I do remember. We chose it especially so Sammy could keep an eye on them.

WALLY: Much good it did. They aren't here.

MARI ELLEN (*Kneels again*): Let me look. No, I can't find any either. Can't blame Sammy, though. Poor fellow, one of his eyes is washed away by the rain and the other one is blurred.

WALLY: Maybe it was on the other side of the shock we hid them. (*Goes behind shock.*)

MARI ELLEN (*Goes to* SCARECROW): Now if Sammy could talk perhaps he could tell us what happened to those nuts. Couldn't you, Sammy? (SCARECROW *nods head*) Look, Wally, he's nodding his head.

WALLY (*Comes from behind corn shock*): Who's nodding whose head?

MARI ELLEN: Sammy Scarecrow. I said perhaps he could tell us where the nuts are and he nodded his head.

WALLY (*Comes to* SCARECROW): It was only the wind blowing his head about.

MARI ELLEN: Well, maybe. (*Examines* SCARECROW.) His neck is awfully wobbly. He's wobbly all over. Poor Sammy! He was so handsome when we put him out here. Now look at him. The wind and rain have made a bundle of rags of him.

WALLY (*Returns to corn shock*): Well, mooning about the old fellow won't help find those nuts.

MARI ELLEN: But I feel sorry for him. He spent his whole life guarding the corn, and now he's lonely and unhappy, and it's Thanksgiving Day!

WALLY: Well, how can we thank a scarecrow?

MARI ELLEN: We could take him home with us and fix him up. Then we could use him again next summer.

WALLY: Yes, we could. I'm sure the old fellow would like that. We could keep him in the barn.

MARI ELLEN: And I could mend his coat and paint eyes so he could see better.

WALLY: And I could find him another hat and some better shoes.

MARI ELLEN: Oh, Wally, let's do it! Let's show him we're thankful for what he's done for us!

WALLY: All right. But it doesn't make up for our lost surprise. We can't put him in our basket and put him on the table and say, "Surprise!"

MARI ELLEN: No, that would be a joke rather than a surprise.

WALLY: And jokes don't belong to Thanksgiving. That's Halloween. I do wish we could find those nuts! (*Begins looking again.*)

MARI ELLEN: I'm going to take him down. He must be tired hanging on to those crossed sticks. (*Begins to loosen* SCARECROW.)

WALLY: No use looking any more. There aren't any nuts there. I suppose we may as well go. (*Comes back to* SCARECROW.)

MARI ELLEN: Let's take Sammy with us.

WALLY: I guess we may as well make somebody thankful. (*As the children begin to loosen* SAMMY, SANDY SQUIRREL *peeps around the corn shock.*)

MARI ELLEN: Look, Wally, there's a squirrel.

WALLY: Sure enough. I'll bet he's the thief. He stole our nuts. Where do you suppose he put them?

MARI ELLEN: If Sammy could talk, I'm sure he could tell us. Couldn't you, Sammy? (SCARECROW *nods head.*)

WALLY: Say, it's funny that whenever you ask a question the wind blows Sammy's head up and down. (SQUIRREL *goes back behind corn shock.*)

MARI ELLEN: There, the squirrel's gone. He saw us.

WALLY: Come on. Let's take Sammy down. You take that side of him. . . . Look out, he's falling. (SCARECROW *tumbles down and nuts roll about him.*)

MARI ELLEN: See. He did know. The squirrel hid the nuts in his pockets. Look! His pockets are full of nuts!

WALLY: Sure enough. Sammy was guarding them for us. I'm glad you insisted that we take him along. (*Children gather up scattered nuts and put them in the basket.*)

MARI ELLEN: Sammy can carry the rest of them in his pockets and we'll help him along. How thankful we are to him for helping us and how thankful he'll be for our care. (*Children help* SAMMY *to his feet. He brightens up and looks happy. He tries to hold up his head which wobbles over now and then.*)

WALLY: We'll have nuts for our Thanksgiving dinner after all. Thanks to Sammy Scarecrow! (*They go out stage left.*)

SANDY (*Comes to center of stage and looks after them.*):

There goes my dessert!
Today is Thanksgiving.
Sammy's glad he is living.
His friends are taking him away!

Because of my thieving
The children were grieving,
But now they are thankful and gay!

THE END

MR. THANKS HAS HIS DAY

by Lee Kingman

Characters

MR. THANKS
POLICEMAN
GRANNY
BOY
GIRL
2ND GIRL
2ND POLICEMAN
MAYOR
MAN
WOMAN
2ND BOY

SCENE 1

SETTING: *A city street facing a park.*

AT RISE: MR. THANKS *is sleeping on a park bench. He wakes up and stretches hard.*

MR. THANKS: Oh, my! (*Opens one eye.*) Another day begun. (*Opens other eye.*) The sun can't wait for us to sleep, but wants us up like him, instead of snoozing soundly on in bed. (*Looks around him.*) In bed? I suppose you'd call it that. A place to stretch out and a pedlar's pack to make a pillow. It could be worse. (*Shakes head sadly.*) But it could be better, too.

POLICEMAN (*Coming in from right, swinging his stick*): Well, well. Just getting up?

MR. THANKS (*Pulling his pack toward him*): Oh, no! I just sat down here to rest a moment.

POLICEMAN (*Seeing pack*): Oh — you don't need to worry. We don't mind your sleeping in the park if you're a pedlar. As long as you have a legitimate occupation, it's all right. We only arrest tramps — people with nothing to do. This is a city where no one can remain idle. All tramps and vagabonds, therefore, have to be speedily eliminated.

MR. THANKS: Oh, I have a lot to do. In fact, I lead a very busy life. (*Advancing a step and starting to open his pack*) I sell things!

POLICEMAN (*Backing off*): I'll take your word for it. Although I don't think I've ever seen you in the city before. Do we have your name on the pedlar's records?

MR. THANKS: Oh, I think so. My name is Thanks. Mr. Thanks.

POLICEMAN: Thanks? I don't seem to remember the name.

MR. THANKS: You're not the only one. It's such an odd name, nobody ever remembers it. I don't like it at all.

POLICEMAN: If you don't like it, why don't you change it?

MR. THANKS (*Joyfully*): What a wonderful idea! Only — what can I change it to?

POLICEMAN: Well, take a name that means something. There are plenty of names to choose from.

MR. THANKS: Yes. There's Mr. Storm or Mr. Moon or Mr. Port or Mrs. Housekeeper. But Mr. Thanks — whoever heard of a Thanks?

POLICEMAN: I'm sorry. I never did.

MR. THANKS: If it were just a nice-sounding name, I wouldn't care what it meant. But I don't want to pick one out for me because then I'd never forgive myself if I didn't like it all the rest of my days. I'd give anything in my pack to anyone who gave me a good name.

POLICEMAN (*Brightening*): You would?

MR. THANKS (*Opening his pack wide*): Sure.

POLICEMAN (*Leaning over to look inside*): Mmmm. Rubbers and hairpins and ribbons and laces and needles and pins and hair-ribbons and a sack of flour and shoes and a scarf. That's a nice looking warm scarf there. That would keep my neck warm while I'm walking around the city in the winter. I'd like that.

MR. THANKS: Take it and welcome. But what about a name for me?

POLICEMAN: Oh — Mr. Weaver. How about that?

MR. THANKS: Weaver? Oh, that's wonderful! (*Gives him the scarf.*)

POLICEMAN: This is fine. Well, I hope you enjoy your name, Mr. Weaver. Good day.

MR. THANKS (*As* POLICEMAN *walks off*): Good day. (*Leans over to tie up pack again.*) Mr. Weaver. What a lovely sounding name and all mine. (*Picks up pack and starts along.*)

Oh, my name is Mr. Weaver,
I'm as busy as a beaver.
I can sell you a knick or a knack.
If you want anything at all
From a beehive to a ball,
You'll find it in my pack.
Just a knick or a knack in my pack —
For, I'm as busy as a beaver
And my name is Mr. Weaver.

GRANNY (*Looking out from a doorway*): Mr. Weaver? You're just the man I'm looking for.

MR. THANKS (*Putting down his pack and starting to open it*): Yes, ma'am. I have here —

GRANNY: Oh, I don't want to buy anything new. But I have a lovely woven shawl that the moths got into, and I wonder if you could weave me a strip for a new edge to it.

MR. THANKS: I'm sorry, but I'm not a weaver.

GRANNY: But you said your name was Weaver.

MR. THANKS (*Shaking his head sadly*): I guess that isn't such a good name after all. It's making me out to be something I'm not. You see, I'm looking for a name. A good name that means something, because Thanks — that's my real name — doesn't mean anything to anybody.

GRANNY: It is odd, isn't it?

MR. THANKS: So the policeman suggested Weaver. I don't want to pick out a name because I'd never forgive myself if I didn't like it all the rest of my days, but I'll give you anything in my pack if you'll tell me a good name. (*Opens pack.*)

GRANNY (*Poking through pack*): Rubbers and hairpins and ribbons and laces and needles and pins and hair-ribbons and a sack of flour and shoes. (*Holds up shoes.*) That's a lovely pair of shoes and I've needed a new pair for a long time and haven't had money to buy them.

MR. THANKS: Take them and welcome. But what about a name for me?

GRANNY: Why, Mr. Shoemaker, of course. (*Turns away, holding up shoes and admiring them.*) I hope you enjoy your name, Mr. Shoemaker. Good day. (*Exits through doorway.*)

MR. THANKS: Good day. (*Shouldering his pack*)
Shoemaker, Shoemaker, that's my name,
And I can sell you anything
From a box to a ball,
From a doily to a doll,
Or a ramrod fit for a king!

BOY (*Running in*): Did you say you were a shoemaker?

MR. THANKS (*Proudly*): That's my name.

BOY (*Taking a pair of shoes from the little girl with him*): Would you like to buy some shoes? They've got real leather in them and you could probably sell them again.

MR. THANKS: Don't you wear them?

BOY: No, I don't like to wear shoes. Besides (*With a sigh*) I've got to sell them so my sister and I can buy some bread to eat.

MR. THANKS (*Sorrowfully*): Well — I'm not a shoemaker — even though that was my name.

BOY (*Turning away sadly*): Oh!

MR. THANKS: But I tell you what we'll do. (*Reaches in pack.*) You'll need those shoes in the winter, but if you'll tell me a good name — one that I'll like all the rest of my days — I'll give you a sack of flour, and you can trade it with Mr. Baker for a loaf of bread.

BOY (*Looking at flour longingly*): Well — let's see. . . .

GIRL (*Pushing hair out of eyes*): You could be Mr. Miller.

MR. THANKS: That's a fine idea. (*Reaches in pack*). Here's a hair-ribbon to keep your hair out of your eyes. Take it and welcome.

GIRL (*Holding it up*): My — it's beautiful.

BOY: The flour will save our lives, Mr. Miller. (*Walks away with girl.*) Good day.

MR. THANKS (*Swinging pack over back joyfully, starts off left.*)
Ah, my name is Mr. Miller,
And my life is like a thriller.
I can sell you anything
From a box to a ball,
From a doily to a doll,
Or a ramrod fit for a king.
(*Exits.*)

CURTAIN

* * *

SCENE 2

SETTING: *Same as Scene* 1, *sometime later. There is a bench at left.*

AT RISE: *Enter* MR. THANKS, *dragging his feet and pulling an empty pack behind him.*

MR. THANKS (*Sitting down wearily on bench*): I ask you now — is this fair? I've traded off every single thing in my pack for names — just names — and not one of them proved to be a good one. Rubbers and hairpins and ribbons and laces and needles and pins and balls and boxes and dolls and doilies and hair-ribbons and shoes and a sack of flour and a scarf — all gone for nothing. And now I have nothing left to sell and no money to buy with. (*Puts his head in his hands.*) I haven't even got a name — except Thanks.

BOY (*Coming in right, holding little girl by the hand*): Look! There's the pedlar who gave us the sack of flour.

GIRL: And the hair-ribbon. Hello.

MR. THANKS (*Not looking up*): Hello.

BOY: Do you live in the park?

MR. THANKS: I didn't before, but it looks as if I were going to now.

GIRL: We live under the oak tree down by the pond — in the summer, that is. It's very nice.

MR. THANKS: I'm sure it is. Lots of fresh air — if you like it.

BOY: The only difficulty is not letting the policemen know you're here.

GIRL: They're awfully snoopy.

BOY (*Looking up*): Quick — here comes one now!

GIRL (*Pulling at* MR. THANKS' *hand*): Hurry! Run and hide!

MR. THANKS (*Gently removing her hand and pushing her away*): No. You run along. I'm just a nameless person, so I don't exist. (BOY *and* GIRL *run to left and hide.*)

2ND POLICEMAN (*Walking up and swinging stick*): And what, may I ask, are you doing?

MR. THANKS: This is my home. I live here.

2ND POLICEMAN: Oh, you do. And what may I ask is your occupation?

MR. THANKS: I used to be a pedlar. I could sell you anything at all — but as of this evening, I am unemployed. I have nothing more to sell and no money to buy anything new.

2ND POLICEMAN (*Pulling out notebook*): And what, may I ask, is your name?

MR. THANKS: You may well ask, but I'm sure I can't tell you. It might be Weaver or Shoemaker or Miller or Porter or Cook or Baker or Bank — but it isn't.

2ND POLICEMAN: With all those names, you're a suspicious character. You'd better come with me!

MR. THANKS: I suppose I couldn't convince you that I haven't any name at all.

2ND POLICEMAN: You most certainly could not. (*Grabbing him by the collar and pushing him off right stage*) There's only one place for idlers — the Mayor likes to make an example of them.

BOY (*Crawling out of his hiding place*): He's arrested the pedlar!

GIRL: And he was such a kind pedlar. He never did anyone harm!

BOY: The Mayor will probably sentence him to ten years of hard labor.

GIRL: He was so nice to everyone — giving things like that. I wish we could do something for him.

BOY: What could we do? He'll be tried first thing in the morning.

GIRL: There must be some way we can help him —

BOY: I think I know what we can do. Come on — we've got a lot of work to do before sunrise. (*They run off.*)

CURTAIN

* * *

SCENE 3

SETTING: *The park bench, where the* MAYOR *likes to hold court. The next morning.*

AT RISE: *At one side, the two* POLICEMEN *are holding the* PEDLAR. *The* MAYOR *makes a gesture and the* POLICEMEN *bring the prisoner over to the bench.*

MAYOR: And with what is this man charged?

POLICEMAN: He is a loiterer. We found him idling in the park.

MAYOR (*Horrified*): Idling! Loitering! That's one thing we never allow in this city.

MR. THANKS: Yes, sir.

MAYOR: Let me see — that calls for a good stiff sentence. Ten to twelve years at hard labor, I believe. It's just a question of whether salt mines or rock piles would be worse for you.

BOY (*Running in right, followed by all the people to whom the* PEDLAR *gave things in exchange for names*): There they are! There's the pedlar.

GIRL (*Running up boldly, but stopping to curtsy to the* MAYOR): Mr. Mayor, you're making an awful mistake — the pedlar is a very kind man.

GRANNY (*Stepping forward*): Yes — he's a good man — he gave me a new pair of shoes I needed badly.

MAN: He gave me some nails so I could fix the roof of my house, and the rain won't come in any more.

WOMAN: He gave me a ball that kept my baby happy all afternoon.

2ND BOY: He gave me a fishhook, and I caught enough fish for supper.

2ND GIRL: He gave me some crayons so I could finish some drawings.

GIRL: He gave me a hair-ribbon, and it makes me feel lovely to wear it.

BOY: He gave me a sack of flour — and my sister and I traded it for some bread to eat.

POLICEMAN: He gave me a scarf to keep me warm in the winter.

MAYOR (*Turning to* PEDLAR): But why were you giving things away instead of selling them?

MR. THANKS: I was trying to find a good name and they all gave me names in exchange. But none of them was right.

MAYOR: What's wrong with your own name?

MR. THANKS: Everyone but me has a useful name that means something. My name doesn't mean anything at all. It's Thanks.

MAYOR: Thanks?

EVERYONE: Thanks?

MR. THANKS: Yes, Thanks.

MAYOR (*Thoughtfully*): In consideration of all your kindnesses, which seem to have helped so many people, I think we would be doing you an injustice to sentence you to hard labor.

EVERYONE: Oh, yes indeed.
Oh, yes.
Think of what he's done for us.

MAYOR: In fact, I think we should give you something and make the name Thanks a name to be proud of.

MR. THANKS: That's very kind of you, sir.

MAYOR: Not at all. But —I must say your name is very hard to do anything with. What can we make it mean?

BOY: Please, sir. I have an idea.

MAYOR: Go ahead, my boy.

BOY: Well, I've noticed that whenever anyone does something for us or gives us anything, we always want to express our appreciation, and we sometimes don't know what to say. We could say, "Thanks."

MAYOR (*Beaming*): Indeed, we could. Why, thanks, my boy.

MR. THANKS (*Beaming*): Oh, yes — why — my thanks to all of you.

EVERYONE: Our thanks to you, Mr. Thanks.
Thanks yourself.

MAYOR: In fact, if I may make a slight suggestion, thanking people is something we should do a lot more of every day. But in honor of Mr. Thanks and in appreciation of all the kindnesses that people do for us, I think we ought to have one special day every year in celebration of all good things. We can call it Thanksgiving.

EVERYONE: Thanksgiving! What a wonderful idea!
A celebration!
Another way of showing Thanks!
Speech, speech, Mr. Thanks!

MR. THANKS: I can only say that I'll never again be ashamed of my name. It makes me very proud to be a useful person — Mr. Thanks.

THE END

JONATHAN'S THANKSGIVING

by Alice Very

Characters

THANKFUL, *a little girl*
DEBORAH, *her sister*
MOTHER, *a Pilgrim*
JONATHAN, *a little boy*
FATHER, *a Pilgrim*
JOSHUA, *his son*
TOWN CRIER
OPATUCK, *an Indian squaw*
PAPOOSE (*a large mama doll will serve*)
GOODY SPRY, *a neighbor*
PRUDENCE, *a girl*
PUNKAPOAG, *Indian chief*

SCENE 1

SETTING: *Kitchen of Pilgrim home. Outer door right back. Fireplace left back. Window right. Inner door left. Furnishings in style of period, if possible.*

AT RISE: MOTHER *spinning.* DEBORAH *sewing pieces.* THANKFUL *studying horn book.* JONATHAN *whittling arrows.*

THANKFUL: Mother, I can say my ABC's. Now I can read!
DEBORAH: Oh no, Thankful, not yet. You must learn a good deal more before you can read.
THANKFUL (*Eagerly*) : But I can learn soon, can't I, Mother?
MOTHER: Yes, Thankful, soon you will know your whole horn book.
THANKFUL (*Looking at large Bible*) : Then may I read the Bible, Mother?
MOTHER: Yes, but you must take great care of the Book. It came all the way from England, in a ship.

DEBORAH: I remember. It was the *Mayflower,* and we came with it.

THANKFUL: Did I come with it?

MOTHER: No, you were not born then.

DEBORAH: I was born in England, so I am English.

THANKFUL: But what am I, Mother?

MOTHER: You were born in the New World, so you are —

DEBORAH (*Interrupting*): She is an Indian.

MOTHER (*Smiling*): No, you are an American.

THANKFUL: That's why I was named Thankful, wasn't it?

JONATHAN: I'd rather be an Indian.

DEBORAH: What do you want to be an Indian for, Jonathan?

JONATHAN: So I can go hunting with my bow and arrows I made. See. (*Showing bow and arrow*) They're just like the Indian boys'. Heap big chief! Wa-wa-wa! (*Stamping and clatter outside. Enter* FATHER *with sickle and* JOSHUA *with ears of corn.*)

FATHER: Well, Mother, the harvest is in.

JOSHUA (*Happily*): There was so much we could hardly get it all in the corn crib.

MOTHER: The Lord be praised! We shall have plenty to eat this year.

JOSHUA: We shan't be hungry the way we were last winter. (*Pauses*) Jonathan, do you remember how we used to hunt for acorns?

JONATHAN: Yes, and how good they tasted when we were so hungry.

DEBORAH: And now we can parch corn over the fire. (*Rubbing corn from ears into spider*)

FATHER: This is a good land. Look you, children, do well so you may keep it. (*Hangs up sickle. A bell rings offstage. A knock at the door.* JONATHAN *opens. Enter* TOWN CRIER *with bell and roll of paper with seal.*)

TOWN CRIER (*Reads*): Hear ye, good people. The Governor has sent me to all the town of Plymouth to proclaim Thursday, the last of November, a day of Thanksgiving. Ye shall gather together to feast and make merry and give thanks to God for His plentiful blessings. (*Goes out, ringing.*)

CHILDREN (*Joyfully, dancing around their mother*): A feast! Hurrah!

JOSHUA: Will I eat my fill!

JONATHAN: I can eat more than you.

DEBORAH: Let's make ready now.

THANKFUL: I want to help.

MOTHER (*Sighing*): Cornbread and beans will scarce make a feast.

FATHER: There is meat enough in the woods. I'll take my musket and go a-hunting. (*Takes musket from over fireplace.*)

JONATHAN: O Father, let me go with you and Joshua.

JOSHUA: What could you do!

JONATHAN (*Showing bow and arrows*): I can shoot a bear with my bow and arrows.

DEBORAH: Bear meat's too tough.

THANKFUL (*Frightened*): O Jonathan don't go near any bears!

JONATHAN (*Boasting*): I'm not afraid of bears. (*Hesitantly*) Besides, Father will be there.

MOTHER: But what about the Indians?

FATHER: I hear the tribe left for their winter camp down the Cape. Let him come with us; he can help carry home the game. (JONATHAN *and* JOSHUA *fill their pockets with parched corn and go out with* FATHER.)

MOTHER: Oh, if I could only make the mince pies we had in England!

DEBORAH: You have the fine flour Goody Spry gave you.

MOTHER: But what to put in them?

DEBORAH: Just wait. I'll bring you somewhat. (*Runs out*)

THANKFUL: What is it, Debby? (*Runs after* DEBORAH. MOTHER *tends fire.* DEBORAH *and* THANKFUL *come in again, carrying a large pumpkin.*)

DEBORAH: See our big pumpkin! Let's put this in the pies.

MOTHER: A pumpkin! Still, with eggs and honey, maybe — (*Puts pumpkin on table.*)

THANKFUL: It looks as if it were all made of gold.

DEBORAH: I wish it were.

THANKFUL: Then we'd be rich.

MOTHER: We must be content with what we have. (*A knock at the door.*)

MOTHER: Come in! (*Enter* OPATUCK *with* PAPOOSE. OPATUCK *walks slowly leaning on stick.*)

OPATUCK: Pray, mistress, food for papoose. (MOTHER *helps* OPATUCK *to chair.*)

MOTHER (*To* DEBORAH *and* THANKFUL): Run, fetch bread and milk. (*They hurry to inner door, return with loaf, knife, and jug.*)

MOTHER (*Sympathetically*): Why, poor woman, how is it you are not with your people?

OPATUCK: Opatuck hurt foot. No walk fast with papoose. Left behind.

MOTHER: Stay here till they return. You're welcome to share with us what little we have. (*Cuts bread, pours milk into mug and gives it to* OPATUCK.)

OPATUCK: You kind mistress. Opatuck work for you.

DEBORAH: Isn't the baby uncomfortable tied to that board?

THANKFUL: She can have my cradle. (DEBORAH *and* THANKFUL *pull up cradle.*)

MOTHER: Will you let us put your baby in the cradle? My little girl is too big for it.

OPATUCK: Yes, yes, fine bed. (*They put* PAPOOSE *in cradle.*)

THANKFUL: Now you are my poppet. (DEBOBAH *and* THANKFUL *rock cradle.* PAPOOSE *cries.*)

OPATUCK: Papoose no like too much rock. (*Singing to Indian tune.*)

CURTAIN

* * *

SCENE 2

SETTING: *The same, a little later.*

AT RISE: MOTHER *is busy at fireplace.* DEBORAH, THANKFUL, *and* OPATUCK *enter with baskets.*

DEBORAH: See the wild grapes and cranberries I found for our Thanksgiving. (*Puts basket on table.*)

THANKFUL: I got red leaves to make the house pretty. (*Puts leaves in jar on table.*)

OPATUCK: Opatuck know roots make good smell in pies. (*Takes basket into inner door.*)

MOTHER: Now if we but had the meat Father is bringing. (*Looking at hour glass*) What can be keeping them so long? (DEBORAH *and* THANKFUL *look out of window.*)

DEBORAH: I don't see them, but here come Goody Spry and Prudence.

MOTHER: So early? And we not ready yet! (*A knock. Enter* GOODY SPRY *and* PRUDENCE, *carrying hamper.*)

GOODY SPRY: A fine day to you, good wife. Have ye heard the news? Prudence, your respects. (PRUDENCE *curtsies.*)

MOTHER: Pray, sit down. What is the news?

GOODY SPRY (*Sitting*): You haven't heard? But what are those scarlet leaves?

MOTHER: They are to deck the house for the feast.

GOODY SPRY: Such colors do not befit a godly house.

MOTHER: Thanksgiving is a day for joy, not dumps, Goody.

GOODY SPRY: No matter, I have brought you some dainties for the feast. Prudence, unpack the hamper.

PRUDENCE: Yes, ma'am. (*Curtsies.*)

DEBORAH: Prudence, we have somewhat for you. (PRUDENCE, DERORAH, *and* THANKFUL *carry hamper out inner door.*)

GOODY SPRY: Is your man at home?

MOTHER: Not yet. (OPATUCK *comes in from inner door with kettle.*)

GOODY SPRY (*Taken back*): Bless us! Who is this?

OPATUCK: Me Opatuck. (*Hangs kettle over fire.*)

MOTHER: My hand maid.

GOODY SPRY: What a start she gave me! The Indians are on the warpath again. 'Tis said they are creeping through the woods over Loon Pond way. (DEBORAH, THANKFUL, *and* PRUDENCE *rush in.*)

DEBORAH: Oh Mother! Father and the boys are in the woods!

THANKFUL (*Frightened*): The Indians may hurt them!

OPATUCK: Indians no hurt good white man. (*Goes out inner door. A noise outside.*)

CHILDREN: Hark! What was that?

GOODY SPRY: There they are now! (MOTHER *stands in front of* CHILDREN. *Enter* FATHER *and* JOSHUA. CHILDREN *rush to hug them.*)

CHILDREN: Father!

JOSHUA: Guess what we brought.

GOODY SPRY: What have you — a deer?

FATHER: We saw a fine deer —

GOODY SPRY: Good! I am fond of deer.

JOSHUA: A big one, leaping like this — (*Bounding across room.*)

GOODY SPRY: The bigger, the better.

FATHER: I took aim — (*Holding musket*) fired —

GOODY SPRY: Ah, and the deer —

JOSHUA: Leaped over the brook (*Jumping over stool.*) and away —

FATHER: Out of sight.

GOODY SPRY: You hit him?

FATHER: No, I missed him.

GOODY SPRY (*Disappointed*): What, no meat!

FATHER: Jonathan has your meat. (*Enter* JONATHAN *with a large turkey.*)

CHILDREN: What is that?

FATHER: A wild turkey.

JONATHAN (*Proudly*): I shot it.

JOSHUA: He shot it all himself.

JONATHAN: With my bow and arrows. (*Gives turkey to* MOTHER.)

THANKFUL: We have something, too.

JOSHUA: Something to eat?

JONATHAN: I'm hungry. (DEBORAH *and* THANKFUL *bring* PAPOOSE.)

FATHER: What is this?

THANKFUL: Our new baby.

DEBORAH: It is an Indian baby. (*A war whoop offstage.* PUNKAPOAG *bursts in door with tomahawk and seizes* FATHER *by hair.*)

PUNKAPOAG: You catch papoose, squaw. (*Raises tomahawk.* OPATUCK *runs in and seizes arm.*)

OPATUCK: No, no, Punkapoag, paleface no catch papoose. You leave Opatuck big swamp — no can go.

PUNKAPOAG: Chief lose Opatuck, go back, find.

OPATUCK: White squaw good, all safe.

JONATHAN (*Going to him*): Hullo, Chief!

PUNKAPOAG (*Pleased to see him*): How, master Jonathan!

FATHER (*Surprised*): You know this man?

JONATHAN: He's my friend. He showed me how to make bows and arrows.

PUNKAPOAG: Good hunter, catch plenty meat.

FATHER: Indians, will you be our friends and feast with us?

CHILDREN (*Pleading*): Yes, come to our Thanksgiving feast.

OPATUCK: We come (*To* PUNKAPOAG) — all right?

PUNKAPOAG: All right. (FATHER *shakes hands with* PUNKAPOAG.)

MOTHER: We'll roast the turkey.

OPATUCK: Make him good — mmh!

DEBORAH: We'll have pumpkin pies —

THANKFUL: And cranberry sauce —

JOSHUA: And chestnuts —

JONATHAN: And corn —

PUNKAPOAG: Chief bring plenty deer meat —

PRUDENCE (*To* GOODY SPRY): Debby gave me this necklace of cranberries. Will you give me leave to wear it?

GOODY SPRY: Well, since it is Thanksgiving Day —

PRUDENCE: Thank you, ma'am. (*Curtsies.*)

FATHER (*Quietly*): This is Thanksgiving Day. So let us thank Him Who brought us over the wide sea and gave us this good and fruitful land and made friends of our foes, so we may live at peace.

THE END

THE HOLLY HANGS HIGH

by Lindsey Barbee

Characters

MARILYN TAYLOR
LOIS TAYLOR, *a younger sister*
JACK TAYLOR
HANNAH, *a maid*
GEORGE JARVIS, *a forest ranger*
TOM MEREDITH
ROSE MEREDITH

SETTING: *Main room in the* TAYLOR *mountain home.*

TIME: *Late afternoon.*

AT RISE: JACK *is sprawled in the large chair.* LOIS *is on the fireside bench.* MARILYN *is at the telephone.*

MARILYN (*At telephone*): But—Mother! It's Christmas Eve— and the tree is ready — Why, you and Dad must make it — I can't understand why — yes, of course it's snowing, but —

JACK: Here — let me take it. (*Crosses to desk.*)

MARILYN: Jack wants to talk with you — Goodbye — oh goodbye — And oh, do find a way — please — (*Crosses to* LOIS) Oh dear, oh dear!

JACK: Why, Mother, what's this about being snowbound? — The roads aren't clear? — That's pretty strange for it isn't that big a storm — Well try again. — It's Christmas Eve in case you've forgotten — We'll be looking for you. (*Hangs up.*)

LOIS (*Mournfully*): It's just like Jo in "Little Women."

JACK: What do you mean — just like Jo?

LOIS: Why, she said, "It won't be Christmas without any presents." And we say, "It won't be Christmas without Mother and Father."

JACK (*In telephone chair*): For the life of me I can't see why any storm would block the road to this cabin.

MARILYN: This isn't so far from the city and the clubhouse has a snowplough.

LOIS: Is there anybody at the clubhouse?

MARILYN: The manager is always there, and people often come for winter sports.

JACK: Well, you're to blame for the whole thing, Marilyn.

MARILYN: I don't like your tone.

JACK: If you hadn't begged Mother and Father to spend Christmas at our mountain cabin, there wouldn't have been any of this mess.

MARILYN: If the storm hadn't come —

JACK: But you might have known that Christmas is the time for storms.

MARILYN: If Mother hadn't waited for the guests —

JACK: And if we had sense enough to wait for Mother and Father —

MARILYN: But we had the chance to come up earlier and to arrange things.

JACK: That was your idea, too.

LOIS (*At window*): The wind's howling — and there are big clouds of snow —

JACK: Just the same, the roads shouldn't be blocked. (*Turns*) I'll call the clubhouse and see what I can find out. (*Takes receiver*) Clubhouse? — Hi, Mr. Parker, this is Jack Taylor — We're up for Christmas — came this morning — Nothing splendid about it — Mother and Father were to follow this afternoon but they've telephoned that the road is skiddy and that they can't make it tonight — Now what do you know about the roads? — Oh, all right — So-long. (*Hangs up receiver.*) I might as well have kept quiet.

MARILYN: Why?

JACK: He doesn't seem to know any more than I know. Acted funny.

LOIS: How did he act funny?

JACK: Didn't seem to want to talk about it.

MARILYN (*Clasping her hands*): Then the storm is bad — and they won't get here.

JACK: Stop acting like a tragedy queen.

MARILYN: Stop being so hateful.

LOIS: Stop quarreling. It isn't right to quarrel on Christmas Eve. (*Comes back to bench.*)

JACK: And you wanted a surprise Christmas, Marilyn. Plenty of surprises.

MARILYN: What if I did?

JACK: You're getting them all right.

MARILYN: Maybe I'll get another.

JACK: What?

MARILYN: Mother and Dad may get here.

JACK: Not tonight. Maybe tomorrow.

MARILYN: Then there's Rose —

JACK: And Tom.

MARILYN: Oh they just must come!

LOIS: Mother expected them to arrive just in time to bring them up here.

JACK: What's the use in getting excited over a girl you've never seen?

MARILYN: She's the daughter of Mother's school friend — and you've been just as excited over her brother, Tom.

LOIS: And it will be such fun to show them the cabin.

JACK: It looks as if we can show each other the cabin.

MARILYN: You're a crabby old thing.

JACK: And you're the world's prize idiot.

LOIS: You're dreadful — both of you.

MARILYN: I'm disappointed.

JACK: And I'm thinking just what a lark it would have been to stay at home.

LOIS (*Weeping a little*): The tree looks so lovely.

JACK: Silly to trim it so soon.

LOIS: We wanted to surprise everybody.

JACK: One too many surprises, I'd say. (*Crosses to right*) I'm going for a walk.

MARILYN: In all this storm?

JACK: Maybe I'll calm down if I tramp around for a while.

MARILYN: Please don't go far.

JACK: I'll be back for dinner — and I'll tell Hannah to have a corking one. (*Goes off*)

LOIS (*Wiping her eyes*): Oh, dear — oh, dear!

MARILYN: Do hush, Lois. (*In a moment* HANNAH *enters from right.*)

HANNAH: An' jus' why is Mr. Jack goin' out in all this storm?

LOIS: He's dreadfully upset because the folks can't get through to us.

HANNAH: The barometer's goin' down all the time.

MARILYN: I'm frightened.

HANNAH: An' I'm scared — an' I've been scared ever since that snow began. (*Pauses and smooths down her apron*) It's jus' as if somethin's about to happen.

MARILYN: Don't say that.

HANNAH: It's sort of second sight I'm havin' — maybe it's a sixth sense.

MARILYN: Sixth sense isn't so important as common sense.

HANNAH: You jus' can't tell what'll happen on a day like this.

LOIS (*Again at window*): It looks a little clearer — over there.

HANNAH (*Following*): No, Miss Lois. It's darker if anythin'. (*There's a sharp rap at the door at left*)

LOIS: Oh!

HANNAH: I'll go, Miss Marilyn. (*Crosses to left*) Who's there?

VOICE: Forest ranger.

MARILYN: Open the door, Hannah. (*As* HANNAH *opens the door*) Why, George Jarvis!

GEORGE: Hello, Marilyn. Hello, Lois.

MARILYN: Come on in. (HANNAH *goes out right*)

GEORGE: For just a minute. (*Steps inside*) I was passing by and saw a car in your shed.

MARILYN: Our garage man drove us up this morning and then went on to the clubhouse.

GEORGE: Jack here?

MARILYN: He's just gone for a tramp.

GEORGE: Great idea to spend Christmas here.

MARILYN: We thought it would be wonderful, but now, Mother and Father can't get here until tomorrow.

GEORGE: Why?

MARILYN: The roads are so bad.

GEORGE: Oh, come now. This snow isn't heavy enough to block the roads.

MARILYN: They've just telephoned.

GEORGE: Don't understand it.

MARILYN: Anyway, it's hard luck.

GEORGE: Don't want to scare you, but I might as well say there's been a young fellow around these parts breaking into cabins and staging a few stickups.

LOIS: Oh — how — dreadful!

GEORGE: When I saw your car I decided to stop and leave a warning.

MARILYN: That's good of you, but I'm pretty sure that no tramp would try to hold up four people.

GEORGE: I guess you're right.

MARILYN: Thanks a lot, just the same.

GEORGE (*Turning*): I'm on my way to the city.

MARILYN: How do you like the ranger life?

GEORGE: It's great!

MARILYN: Any chance for a girl ranger?

GEORGE: Why not?

MARILYN: I'll apply — right away.

GEORGE: And I'll pull for you. (*As he goes out*) Goodbye. (HANNAH *enters at right*)

HANNAH: There's a pot of hot chocolate all ready for you children. How about it?

LOIS (*Clapping her hands*): Super.

HANNAH: You need something to cheer you up. (*Goes out right*)

MARILYN (*Mournfully*): We planned to have such a lovely evening — presents all around the tree —

LOIS: And the bunch of holly looks so lovely above the mantel.

MARILYN: The house is warm and cozy, isn't it?

LOIS: Shall we take the screen from around the tree?

MARILYN: Oh, I can't bear to do it without all the others! (*Pauses, then adds emphatically*) No — we won't. (HANNAH *enters from right carrying a tray with a pot of chocolate and two cups and saucers*)

HANNAH: Here you are — and maybe it will help things along. (*Places tray on table*)

MARILYN (*Sitting by table*): Everything looks brighter already. (LOIS *sits on fireside bench. While* MARILYN *pours the chocolate,* HANNAH *crosses to desk and straightens chair. As she turns to push the hassock to its proper position, she speaks in a lowered tone.*)

HANNAH: Don't move, Miss Marilyn — and you, too, Miss Lois —and pretend you don't know what I'm saying — for there's a strange fellow looking in the window. (*Whereupon, there is a sharp tap on the window although no face is visible. No one turns. Again the tap.*)

MARILYN (*In a whisper*): It's the tramp.

HANNAH (*Also in a whisper*): What tramp?

MARILYN: Someone who's been breaking into houses and holding up people.

HANNAH: Good gracious!

MARILYN: Go into the kitchen right away and see that every door is locked. Stand near.

HANNAH (*Grimly*): I'll stand near with a poker. (*Goes out right. Another sharp tap, but* MARILYN'S *face is averted and* LOIS *is motionless. In a moment there is a knock on the door, a rattling of the knob, and then silence.*)

LOIS (*Whispering*): Has he gone?

MARILYN (*Rushing to window, cup in hand*): Yes. (*Pauses*) He must have gone around the house.

LOIS: Funny way for a tramp to act.

MARILYN: I think so, too. (*Comes back to table and deposits her cup*)

LOIS: Oh, we hadn't planned for all this. (*Places her cup on table and goes to window*)

MARILYN (*Following her*): It certainly doesn't seem like Christmas Eve.

LOIS: Anyway, the mist is going.

MARILYN: I believe it is. (*As* HANNAH *enters from right*) Why, Hannah, what's the matter? (*For* HANNAH *is auite out of breath, a bit disheveled, and stands with her back against the door.*)

HANNAH: I've got him, Miss Marilyn, I've got him.

MARILYN: Got — the — tramp? (MARILYN *and* LOIS *rush to center*)

HANNAN: Sure.

LOIS: Where, Hannah — where?

HANNAH: Out in the little porch by the side of the kitchen.

MARILYN: How did you manage it?

HANNAH: Followed him 'round the house until I saw him go on the porch — an' then — quick as lightnin' — I locked the door.

LOIS: Hannah, you're wonderful.

HANNAH: He's poundin' that door, an' yellin' to beat the band.

MARILYN: Oh, I wish that Jack would come!

HANNAH: I'm goin' right back to the kitchen, an' if he manages to get out I'll use the poker.

MARILYN: If you need us, Hannah, just yell. (HANNAH *goes out*) Wouldn't you think that Jack would be tired of tramping around? (*Goes back to window*)

LOIS: He ought to be right here with us.

MARILYN: Look! There he is.

LOIS: Somebody's with him.

MARILYN (*Peering*): A girl.

LOIS: And she's almost blown off her feet.

MARILYN: Oh-h-h! Who can it be? (*Opens door and cries*) Jack!

JACK (*Appearing at door*): I came across this girl — right out here — and she's just about all done in. (*With* MARILYN'S *help, he guides the girl to the big chair.* LOIS *closes the door*)

MARILYN: Here, Lois, take off her boots — and her hat — and Jack, help her off with her coat. (*As they act accordingly*) There! (*They busy themselves with the stranger who seems stunned and a bit uncomprehending. Finally she murmurs, "I'm cold." And in the meantime,* LOIS *has carried the hat, coat and boots off right.*)

JACK: Then come over here to the fire. (*The girl moves slowly to the bench where she seats herself.* LOIS *comes in from right*)

MARILYN: That's better.

JACK: I found her stumbling along that upper road and she's sort of dazed — doesn't seem to know what's happened.

MARILYN: Were you waiting for someone? (*The girl looks at her blankly, then nods her head*) For whom? (*But there is no answer*)

JACK: Well, what are we going to do about her?

MARILYN: Keep her, of course.

JACK: But it seems pretty queer for her to be wandering around in this storm.

MARILYN: It's queer for you to be wandering around. (*As* LOIS *begins to weep*) Lois! What's the matter now?

LOIS: It doesn't seem like Christmas Eve.

MARILYN: Of course it doesn't.

LOIS: This funny acting girl and the tramp on the porch—and—

JACK: Tramp?

MARILYN: Some fellow tried to get into the house, and Hannah locked him on the back porch.

JACK: How do you know he's a tramp?

MARILYN: The forest ranger —

LOIS (*Eagerly*): George Jarvis —

MARILYN: Came by to warn us about a tramp who's breaking into cabins and holding up people.

THE GIRL (*Suddenly*): Oh! Oh!

MARILYN: Have you remembered anything?

THE GIRL (*Dazed*): My brother was with me.

MARILYN (*Soothingly*): Now think very hard and tell us just where he was — when you were separated from him.

THE GIRL (*In a whisper*): My brother!

JACK: That fellow's pounding like a steam engine. (*Crosses to right*) I'll settle our friend on the porch.

MARILYN: Oh, Jack, please be careful.

JACK: No tramp would be out in this snow storm.

LOIS: He knocked at the window — and at the door — and —

JACK: Then I know he's not a tramp. You girls have done something else that's silly. (*Goes out*)

THE GIRL: Was — was — he — hurt?

MARILYN: The tramp? Of course not. (*Suddenly*) Don't you think you ought to be quiet? (*Pause*) Can't you even tell us your name? (*The girl snakes her head, walks back to the chair, and leans her head against the back*)

LOIS: We can't do much until you tell us something about yourself. (*Sits on hassock. Before she can answer,* JACK *appears at right*)

JACK: That fellow is no more a tramp than I am. He saw you people through the window and just wanted to come in. (MARILYN *crosses to him*)

THE GIRL (*Smiling*): Let — him — come — in.

MARILYN: Maybe it's her brother.

JACK (*Turning his head*): This way. (TOM, *a pleasant-looking young man, enters.*)

TOM: First time I've ever been taken for a tramp. (*Crosses to the girl*) What's the matter?

THE GIRL: Nothing's the matter. I've been play acting. (*Crosses to* MARILYN *and slips an arm through hers*) Forgive me, for I expected to see Tom here — and didn't know just what to do.

JACK: Tom?

TOM: I came on ahead, hoping to give you people a surprise.

JACK: You gave it all right.

TOM: And Rose was to follow.

MARILYN: Rose? (*Pauses*) Rose?

TOM: She was to pretend that the snow had blinded her —

JACK: And then what?

TOM: We were to throw a super surprise stunt. (*And right here, the girl becomes* ROSE)

ROSE: We're your guests, Tom and Rose Meredith.

LOIS: Oh, it can't be so! (*Comes to other side of* ROSE)

ROSE: You see, your mother and father thought it would be a joke and surprise all rolled into one if we'd come on ahead of them.

TOM: If I'd drop in sort of informal like — and —

JACK: You dropped all right.

TOM: Get acquainted.

JACK: Instead, you were locked up all because somebody had told the girls about a tramp.

ROSE: I was to come along and pretend that I was lost.

TOM: And then your mother and father were to happen in and tell you just who we are.

ROSE: But everything got a little mixed up.

MARILYN: Rose! Where are Mother and Father?

ROSE: At the clubhouse, of course.

TOM: I thought you'd guess.

JACK: And all that story about not reaching us until tomorrow wasn't so?

ROSE: Their arrival was to be a surprise.

LOIS: Oh — how — wonderful!

TOM: Even if it didn't work out, it's been a surprise all right. (*The telephone rings*)

MARILYN: Let me take it. (*Crosses*) Oh — Mother! Tom and Rose are here — and it's been a perfectly thrilling surprise. Yes — they told us you were at the clubhouse — why, you must have been there when you telephoned us the first time — Oh, hurry — hurry. (*Hangs up receiver*) They're starting right now.

JACK: Then let's get this screen away. (*With* TOM's *help, the screen is placed at the side, and a beautiful Christmas tree is revealed with packages around the base*)

ROSE: Oh — how — lovely!

TOM: Christmas in the mountains! It's swell.

MARILYN: Put on the lights, Jack. (JACK *touches a switch and the tree is ablaze with lights*)

ROSE: Just like fairyland.

LOIS (*Clapping her hands*): Look at our presents.

TOM: There's a real snow storm.

JACK: The fire is jolly and bright.

ROSE: The tree is sparkling.

MARILYN (*Laughing as she points to the holly*): And the holly hangs high! (*There is the sound of a motor horn close by. They all rush to left and throw open the door*)

LOIS (*Ecstatically*): Mother! Father!

THE END

MERRY, MERRY, MERRY

by Gladys Hasty Carroll

Characters

MOTHER
RAYMOND
HALLIE
EVELYN
RALPH
GRANDMOTHER
GRANDFATHER
DORIS
CHORUS OF YOUNG PEOPLE (*6 or more*)
SYLVIA
PETER
GORDON
MYRTLE
JACK
CHRISTMAS FAIRY
CHRISTMAS ELVES (*Several boys and girls*)
SANTY

SETTING: *Family livingroom on Christmas Eve; outside door on left of stage; upstairs door on right.*

AT RISE: MOTHER *sits in rocking chair holding little daughter and sings "Away in a Manger." Four stockings hang from the mantel in center. Three sons are finishing decorating Christmas tree.*

MOTHER: There, doesn't that look fine? Aren't we going to have a *lovely* Christmas?

RAYMOND: *Except* that Dad won't be here!

MOTHER: Well you know we weren't going to keep thinking and talking about that! We're pretty lucky that Dad isn't so terribly sick any more. There'll be a good turkey dinner for him at the hospital, and he'll want us to have a good time at home.

HALLIE: But we'll surely go to see him in the afternoon and take him his presents, won't we?

MOTHER: Oh, he'll get his presents all right. We'll take care of that.

EVELYN: I've got a present for him, one I made myself, with paints.

RALPH: Yes, and got more paint on yourself than you did on the paper, I bet!

HALLIE: If she spilled any more than you fellows did on the porch floor when you tried to paint the blind —

MOTHER: There, now, that'll do, boys. Ralph and Raymond were doing the best they could to keep the house looking as it would if Dad were here, and Evie's picture is very pretty indeed.... To hear you boys talk anybody'd think that you didn't think the world of one another — as I know very well you do....Now, (*Putting* EVIE *down and wrapping a white shawl around her*) off to bed with you! All four!

RAYMOND: What — Ralph and I, too?

RALPH (*Disappointed*): Aw-w-w!

MOTHER: Yes, all of you. The sooner you get to sleep tonight the sooner it'll be morning.

EVIE: Do you s'pose Santy'll really come this very night? I wish I could see him!

HALLIE (*Laughing, wagging his finger at her*): Oh, *no!*

MOTHER: Why, Evie! Nobody's ever supposed to see Santa Claus! Why, if he should get here, and find you in this room by any chance, I suppose he'd go right back up the chimney and not leave a single thing in the stockings.

HALLIE (*Serious now*): No! Would he, honest?

MOTHER: At least, that's what they always told me when *I* was a little girl, and I never took any chance on it. I shouldn't advise you to.

HALLIE (*Taking* EVIE'S *hand*): Don't worry. We won't.

MOTHER: You boys take good care of Baby. I'll be up later to make sure she's tucked in. And if I run out for a few minutes by and by, Grandma and Grandpa'll be right here.

EVIE: Hallie'll tuck me in. He's a good tucker — almost as good as Daddy....But, oh, I *do* wish my daddy were home!

MOTHER (*Laughing*): Always back to the same refrain! Why don't you sing a different tune? Sing "Good St. Nick." (*Chil-

dren go off singing. MOTHER *goes about busily picking up things while humming to herself.* GRANDMOTHER *comes in.*)

MOTHER: Here you are! In good season, too. Oh, it's nice to see you.

GRANDMOTHER (*Cheerily*): Well, it's as fine a Christmas Eve as I've ever seen. Just a little skim of snow over everything and the sky dark blue, and the stars bright. We heard two or three groups of Christmas carollers as we rode over. Singing always sounds fine in the night air — especially in the winter time. (*Door opens to let in* GRANDFATHER, *carrying basket.*)

GRANDMOTHER: There, listen! Hear them, Althea? (*Voices sing "O Little Town" off stage, as* GRANDFATHER *holds door open.*)

MOTHER: Yes. It's lovely. But somehow I can't settle down to listen tonight. I'm so anxious to get to the hospital and see how Horace is. If he's still gaining as he was yesterday, maybe — well, it won't be long before he's home. . . . Hello, Father! You going to help Mother hold the fort for me tonight?

GRANDFATHER: Yes. Sure. No bogeymen'll get in while we're here. But you bundle up! It's cold out, now I tell you! (*Gives* GRANDMOTHER *packages.*)

GRANDMOTHER: Yes, and go right ahead, Althea. We've got a few things for the children we'll be putting on the tree. And don't you worry a bit about anything here. If a chick or a child stirs, we'll know it!

MOTHER (*Now with her coat and hat on.*): I know you will. Of course. It's so good of you — (*Starts out and then puts her head back in.*) But listen especially for Evie, will you? She's walked twice in her sleep the last two weeks. I think she's lonesome for her father, and goes looking for him.

GRANDFATHER: We'll listen for them all! Now you clear out of here, and have your visit with Horace. (*She goes, laughing.*) Anybody'd think we hadn't brought up four of our own and got them a good deal farther along than hers are. And no bones broken, either! Though I'm not saying there hadn't ought to have been, sometimes. We spoiled our young ones, Hattie. That's why they order us around now the way they do. And they're spoiling theirs just the same!

GRANDMOTHER (*Laughing*): Well, of course parents are the *only* ones who spoil the children. Grandparents don't have a thing to do with it, Eben, do they? Here's a doll. And here's a drum.

And here's a top. (*She names each toy as she picks it up out of the basket. Sound of singing "Deck the Hall" offstage grows louder. Enter at least six young people. Men carry baskets heaped with presents.*)

GRANDFATHER (*Peering around*): Who's that? Am I seeing quadruple, or is it Santa Claus himself?

CHORUS: No, we're not Santa Claus!

GRANDMOTHER: Some of them look to me like our own children, Eben, but I don't see enough of them lately to be sure. Besides, they're all dressed up so fancy!

DORIS (*Hugging her mother*): Oh, Mother, dear, we *mean* to get home oftener! But when a girl works in an office, all the time she has is nights — and you folks go to bed so *early!* By the time Jack and I get our supper dishes washed, you're sound asleep!

GRANDMOTHER (*Smiling*): Well, I suppose that excuse does as well as any. But how does it happen you're here now?

SYLVIA: Oh, we had to stop by and leave a few things for Althea's children. We've been shopping all afternoon. (*Goes to her father and hugs him.*) I know just how they'll miss Horace, because I remember how we felt that time Father was down East and didn't get back for Christmas. Why, I *really* thought I was going to *die!*

PETER: So, because of *their* sad recollections, *we* dragged up a flight of fourteen steps — I counted them! — the biggest load of Christmas being delivered anywhere in this town tonight, I bet!

GORDON: And I know building on a rock is according to the Bible, but why did Horace and Althea have to pick such a high one? If you ask me, I'd say it was probably climbing that flight of stairs that put Horace where he's been the last two weeks! I'd kind of like to lie down in a nice, comfortable bed myself right now! (*Young men put down baskets.* PETER *starts putting presents on and around tree, with grandparents helping.*)

DORIS: But — instead of that — you're taking us all to a country dance at Cranberry Meadows, aren't you?

GORDON: Well — I *was!*

MYRTLE: Oh, you *are!*

GORDON: Well — if I thought I could dance when I got there —

JACK: If you can't dance with Myrtle, you know who can! Choose your partners for a Lady of the Lake! (GRANDFATHER *pulls out a jew's harp and they dance a few turns, and dancing, go off, calling back good-night and merry Christmas.*)

PETER (*Following*): Tell Althea we'll drop around again in the morning — help liven up the day for the kids.

GRANDMOTHER: Yes, I'll tell her. And you all have a good time tonight. You won't be young but once — (*Voices singing "Deck the Hall" come back, growing fainter.*)

GRANDFATHER: No, they won't be young but once, and who'd want to be? Who'd want to be young any time except when they *were* young? Way young folks do now is nothing to the times they had when we were growing up, do you say so, Hattie?

GRANDMOTHER: No, Eben. No, I feel just the same as you do about that.

GRANDFATHER: Take the dancing: Of course, this new-fangled dancing is nothing but jump and jerk. And what they were doing here just now was all gone by as long ago as I can remember — all out of date. Now *we* learned some *pretty* steps! Remember that — what was it? — Varsoviana? (*He sings it and they do it together. A polka would do as well.*)

GRANDMOTHER: There, I hadn't thought of that for years, 'til you spoke. (*They sit down, she with folded hands, he with his pipe.*) You remember, Eben, the night they serenaded us?...

GRANDFATHER (*Nods, slowly*): Yeah . . . and I was thinking of the day every summer when we used to meet, all the families around, with horses and carriages, at Flat Rocks, and drive on down to the beach...

GRANDMOTHER (*Smiling*): Singing!... We'd always be singing. ...Oh, — I promised Althea I'd see to Evie — (*Hurries out softly, with two boxes.* GRANDFATHER, *humming, winds clock, fixes pipe, looks out window.*)

GRANDMOTHER (*Returning*): Yes, they're all sound asleep. (*They sit again.*)...That row of stockings, Eben, reminds me of how they used to hang under our mantelpiece, Christmas Eve years ago. Just the same number. Only ours were for three girls and one boy.

GRANDFATHER (*Nodding*): Yeah. (*Chuckles.*) Remember the night Peter put tin pans beside the stove for Santa Claus to stumble over? So we'd be sure to hear him when he came?

GRANDMOTHER: And we did all right. Something happened, just before daylight. I can hear that crash now....

GRANDFATHER: But when Pete got to the kitchen, all he found were the pans strewed over the floor. No other signs of Santy —

GRANDMOTHER: But the stockings were full!

GRANDFATHER: Yes. Yes, the stockings were always full at our house as long as they were hung.... We've managed pretty well, Hattie.

GRANDMOTHER: Yes, I think so, Eben... I think we managed pretty well.... And I know God has been good....

GRANDFATHER: Do you remember?

GRANDMOTHER: I was just thinking the same....

GRANDFATHER: Seems to me as though...

GRANDMOTHER: Yes.... Yes, 'twas, Eben.... (*They fall asleep. Voices sing softly outside — "Hark the Herald Angels." Silence, and enter two boys in guard uniforms with silver spears, standing one on each side of the door. Then enter the* CHRISTMAS FAIRY *in white and silver, with a bit of red, looking all about. She sees the grandparents, runs on tiptoe from one to the other, touching them with her wand, then she runs back to the door and calls.*)

FAIRY: Come in, come in!
It is safe, — quite safe!
Two sleep here, but they are grown,
And I have touched them with my wand!
They will not wake until we go!
Until we go! Until we go!
Come in now!
Come in, come in!
(*Enter the* CHRISTMAS ELVES, *all in green and gold, marching like soldiers. They stand saluting before the* FAIRY.)

FAIRY:
Look at this tree!
Already 'tis laden —

ELVES (*In chorus*): Laden? *How* laden!

FAIRY:
So forget now the tree!
It has no need of thee —

LITTLEST ELF (*Throwing out his chest*):
What? No need of *me?*

FAIRY (*Laughing*):
Not even of *thee!*...

But there are the stockings,
Four in a row. Three boys, I trow,
And *one* little girl —

GIRL ELF: The girl is mine. *I* claim the girl. I know all about girls. They like *dolls!*

FAIRY: You are right about girls. You know about girls. They like dolls —

BIGGEST BOY ELF: Dolls — pfui! We'll take the boys. We know about boys. Boys like *balls!*

OTHER BOY ELVES (*In turn*): And *knives*... and *drums*... and *harmonicas* —

FAIRY: But now — what do they *all* like?

ELVES (*In chorus*): We know what they all like!... *candy*... *oranges*... and *nuts!* (*They run two to a stocking and hold the tops open.*) But where's the bag? Where's Santy, with his wonderful, magical Santy's bag, — full of such wonderful, magical things?

FAIRY (*Running to door*):
Sa-anty! Sa-anty!
Two sleep here but they are grown,
And I have touched them with my wand, —
They will not wake until we go!
Sa-anty! Come in!
(FAIRY *runs back to stand with the tree as her background, her silver wand raised. Voices sing softly outside, "O, Little Town." Then silence, and* SANTY *enters. He is a little man in a red suit — no beard — dragging a bag almost as big as he is, and full.*)

ELVES (*Chanting with bright faces*):
Oh, merry, merry, merry!
Merry Sir!
Merry, merry, merry —

SANTY (*Stopping in middle of room and saluting sharply*): *Merry!*

ELVES (*Saluting*): *Merry!*

FAIRY (*Softly*): Merry, merry Christmas, Santy dear!

SANTY (*Gruffly, with a wave of his hand*): What have we *here?* Stockings?

FAIRY (*Laughing*):
You seem surprised!
Is it because there are so many?

Or because there are not more?
Certain it is you've seen *stockings* before —
On Christmas Eves!

SANTY (*Gruffly*):
A million, more or less!
A quadrillion, I should guess!
Even a decillion, maybe —
And — what *is* more than that, my lady?

FAIRY (*Laughing*): I don't know!

ELVES (*To each other.*): What *they* don't know, isn't so!... Come on, Santy, open up! We need toys! We need toys —

FAIRY: For one little girl —

OTHER ELVES: And three bigger boys!

SANTY (*Dragging bag over*): Well! Well! Help yourselves! As much as you take out at the top, more will come in at the bottom!

FAIRY (*Softly*): Oh, yes, it's a magic bag!

ELVES (*Dipping, running, chanting*): Magic bag, magic bag, magic bag, magic bag! Magic bag — (*Door opens, and enter* EVIE, *dressed in a pink nightgown, hands out ahead of her, moving very slowly. She walks slowly.*)

EVIE (*In monotone*): *Daddy! Daddy! Daddy!* (*Complete cessation of activity;* SANTY, FAIRY, *and* ELVES *keep position as they were.* EVIE *proceeding around the room, in and out among them.*) *Daddy! Daddy! Daddy!* (*Finally touches* GRANDFATHER'S *knee, climbs up there, and lays her head against him.*) Oh, Daddy, I do like sitting in your lap. Let me sleep tonight in your lap, Daddy. (*His arms close around and settle her comfortably, but otherwise he does not stir.*)

SANTY (*Softly, to* FAIRY): Has your wand touched her?

FAIRY:
You know I never touch children,
And if I did, my wand would never make them sleep!...
Still this one sleeps —

SANTY: And any minute she may wake! Be quick now, elves! Be quick!

FAIRY (*Softly*): She's such a lovely little girl —

GIRL ELF: Give her the best!

BOY ELVES (*Sighing*): Yes, the best! The very best! She's just a girl — only a little girl — but such a lovely, *lovely* little girl!

(*As they run back and forth from bag to* EVIE'S *stocking, chanting this, the door opens again. All movement stops.* HALLIE *enters, looks around in amazement; then in alarm.*)

HALLIE: Oh, boy! Oh, boy, oh, boy, oh boy! And she's here! Of course she'd have to come down here! (*Drives fist into palm of hand and makes grimace of hard thinking; then looks around.*) Why the dickens doesn't Grandpa wake up? Why doesn't *somebody* wake up? I knew Evie walked in her sleep, but I didn't s'pose *everybody*.... Why, maybe they've all turned to salt like Lot's wife. (*Crosses and gingerly pokes biggest* ELF. *Whispering*) Hey! Hey, you fellers!

SANTY (*Loudly and sternly*): Hands off there, boy!

HALLIE (*Startled, putting hands in pocket*): Oh, oh — I — I just wanted to see if he were real.

SANTY: Curiosity kills cats!...What are you here for? What's the matter with this family, anyway? Didn't your mother and father ever teach you that the place for children on Christmas Eve is *bed?* And for them, too! (*Points at grandparents.*) If you think you can play tricks on Santy —

HALLIE (*Teeth chattering*): But — but — (*Bursts out*) Don't you say anything against my father and mother! They're the best parents in the world, and they've told us everything they ought to — but my father's sick in the hospital! And my mother's gone to visit him! And they can't help it if Evie walks in her sleep, can they? And she can't help it either. It's all *my* fault. — I was supposed to tend to her. But I dropped off, and she — oh, Santy, you wouldn't take back her presents, would you? Mother said maybe you would if any child came around. But Evie isn't really here! I mean her mind isn't! Nor her eyes! She hasn't seen you; and she doesn't know a thing about it all; She's sound asleep, Santy, honest! *Just* as if she were in her bed!

GIRL ELF (*Beginning slowly and reluctantly to take* EVIE'S *gifts*): Oh! We *forgot!* But it *is* the rule! If a child gets up—and comes downstairs ——on Christmas Eve —

SANTY (*Saluting*): Put her presents back. There is something in what the boy says. After all, the child sleeps.

ELVES (*Saluting happily*):

Merry, merry, merry.
Put her presents back!

There is something in what he says!
After all, she sleeps.

GIRL ELF (*Finishing, turning, pointing*): But what about *him?* He does not sleep.

BOY ELVES (*Pointing and chanting*):
What about him? He does not sleep.

SANTY: Yes, what about you? *You* do not sleep!

HALLIE (*Soberly*): No, I'm awake all right. I *guess.* (*He pinches himself.*) Yes, sir. I'm awake. I certainly am. And I see you all plain as day. A Christmas Fairy, and seven elves and — and Santy himself! Oh-h-h-h, boy! But I thought you'd be a lot *bigger* than this, Santy!

SANTY: Hm. What made you think people could paint good pictures of somebody nobody else ever saw? I can look a lot of different ways. Well, now, what have *you* got to say for *yourself?* Anything you say will be held against you. Any reason why I shouldn't take what's in your stocking?

HALLIE (*Slowly*): No. I guess not. No. You'll have to take my presents back, all right.

ELVES: We've got to take his back; got to take his back, got to take his back all right. The *knife*... and the *candy*... and the *harmonica* —

FAIRY (*Gently*):
Poor boy!
If you say you're sorry,
Sorry you came and found us here, —
I think if you say you're *very* sorry
And now will know better another year —

HALLIE (*Hands in pocket*): No, I can't say that. I'll never know better. Evie's my sister and I look out for her. Always have; always will. And I can't say I'm sorry, because I'm not. If I hadn't come, she'd have lost *her* presents instead — and without even seeing you either! (*Looking around, grinning*) Anyway, *I've* sure *seen* you! Nothing can change that! And, honest, it's *almost* worth it to me! You know, seeing Santy, and you elves, to say nothing of the Christmas Fairy, — and oh, boy, is she a queen! This is just about the biggest thing that has ever happened to me!

SANTY (*Grimly*): Well, if that's the way you feel about it! Do your duty, men.

ELVES (*Saluting sadly*) : Our duty, Sir!

CHRISTMAS FAIRY:

Oh, Santy, dear Santy,
He's a very pretty boy!
And the words he says fall sweetly on my ear!
Oh, don't you think he's right —
And don't you think we *might* —
I mean, after all, no other children need to hear
What we have done —
If we should do it —
And I don't think that you would rue it —
Oh, Santy, Santy, dear!
He's such a brave, good, honest, *pretty* boy!

SANTY (*Grinning*) : Pretty is a fighting word to you, eh, Hallie?

HALLIE (*Stoutly*) : Not when a fairy says it.

SANTY: Oh! Oh, I see. Makes a difference, eh? Well, now, let me think. What's this you say about your father being in the hospital and your mother being away? Who are *they?*

HALLIE: Grandpa and Grandma.

SANTY: Oh. Oh, I see.... Hm....

EVIE: Daddy...Daddy...Daddy... (FAIRY *wipes a sympathetic tear.* GIRL ELF *sniffs.*)

LITTLEST ELF: Oh-h-h, — boo — hoo — hoo — hoo!

SANTY (*Quickly, clearing his throat*) : There; there; none of that, now! I know just how you feel. Hallie, promise you'll never tell what you've seen tonight?

HALLIE: Promise! Cross my heart!

SANTY: Men! Fill up that stocking again! (*Salutes*) *Merry!*

ELVES (*Saluting*) : *Merry!* (*And chanting*)

He knows how we feel! He knows about boys!
Fill up the stocking, fill up the stocking,
Fill up the stocking for Hallie!

SANTY (*As they finish*) : All right. All right. Off we go now. Seems early, but it'll be daybreak before we know it, and we've got a lot to do yet — (*Tugging at bag*)

FAIRY (*Sings to tune of "Good Morning to You," while* ELVES *dance in circle around.*) :

Merry Christmas, dear Evie!
Merry Christmas, brave Hal!
To all that you love,

Blessings from above.
Merry Christmas, dear Evie!
Merry Christmas, brave Hal!
(*She goes off, looking back and smiling, waving her wand.* ELVES *follow, dancing.*)

SANTY (*At door*): Well, young fellow, good night and good luck! After this, you won't believe all you see in pictures, will you? And don't believe all you see with your own eyes either. Because —I'm not Santa *Claus.* I'm just Santy, his right-hand man! Santa Claus *is* a big man, *just as you thought!* (*Saluting.*) *Merry!*

HALLIE (*Dazed, saluting.*): Merry — (SANTY *exits, followed by guards.* HALLIE *stands, still dazed in middle of floor, rubbing his eyes. Voices outside sing softly "Silent Night." Enter* MOTHER *and* FATHER. *Voices continue very softly.*)

MOTHER: Why — Hallie!

FATHER: What's this mean, old fellow? How'd you get down here?

HALLIE (*Running to him*): *Dad!*

EVIE (*Waking quickly*): Daddy! Daddy! (*Also running to him*)

GRANDPARENTS (*Waking*): Why — why —

GRANDFATHER: Horace Webster, that's never you, standing on your feet in your own house just two weeks after —

MOTHER: Oh, but he's gained so fast, Father! The doctor's been saying for a week he *might,* and tonight he said he *could* come home for Christmas! Isn't it wonderful? We didn't tell any of you, because at the last minute something — but here he is! Good as new, except for resting! Of course we've got to take good care of him! (*Tucks him up in a big chair.*)

FATHER: Yes, save some of the cotton around that tree to wrap me in! (*Whistles, sitting with* EVIE *on his knee and* HALLIE *on the arm of the chair.*) Hey! What a loaded tree! (*Looking around*) And — by the Great Horn Spoon — if Santa Claus hasn't been here already!

HALLIE: No, Dad. Not Santa Claus himself — (*Claps hand wildly over his mouth.*)

FATHER: Why, yes, he has, too! Look at that, Evie! Do you see what I see?

EVIE: Oooooh! (*Runs, gets doll, conspicuous at top of stocking, and runs back to her father.*)

MOTHER: Why, what in the *world,* Mother — and how did the children get down here?

GRANDMOTHER (*Fidgeting*): Well — well — you know you *said* Evie was walking in her sleep lately!

GRANDFATHER: Yes, here we were sitting, talking over old times and first thing we knew,—well—well, here she was! That's all!

HALLIE: And I came down after her! That's all!

GRANDMOTHER (*Relieved*): Yes, that's all!

MOTHER: I'm not so sure it's *quite* all. I rather *suspect* a trick somewhere — (*Enter* RAYMOND *and* RALPH *in cowboy clothes.*)

RALPH: Who said something about *Dad?*

RAYMOND: Oh, boy, am I seeing things?

HALLIE: Seeing *Dad!*

EVIE: Daddy!

FATHER: Come here, you two hard-riding, rope-swinging, spur-booted cowboys! (*They stride over, grinning.*)

MOTHER: Well, where in the world did those outfits come from?

RAYMOND: Good Old St. Nick, I guess —

RALPH: We found them on the foot of our bed!

HALLIE: Why, he never went up—(*Claps hand again over mouth.* RAYMOND *and* RALPH *lean on back of* FATHER'S *chair and sing cowboy song.*)

HALLIE: Oh, boy, aren't they *beauts!*

GRANDMOTHER: There's another one of 'em on the tree, Hallie—looks about your size.

HALLIE: Oh, boy. (*Runs toward tree, comes back with it, putting it on. Off-stage voice sings "Deck the Halls." Door opens and young people troop in.*)

SYLVIA: We had to stop. We're dying of curiosity. *Why* all the lights?

PETER (*Sees* FATHER *and shakes hands cordially.*): Well, Horace, old man! I'm not exactly surprised. Kind of suspected it all along. But it sure makes Christmas in this house!

DORIS: Doesn't it!

SYLVIA: Oh, Althea, I'm so happy for you! (*Jingle of bells outside. Knock on door.*)

ALTHEA: Who in the world, — honestly, seems as if *anything* could happen tonight! (*One of young men opens door to lady in furs.*)

LADY: Good-evening. I hope you will forgive me for calling so late. But you see, your happiness is reaching out a long way. Even I heard of it, and wished I might share it. I spoke to my husband, and though he is a very busy man, he said he would drive me over.... And if you like, he, too, will join you —

MOTHER (*Gently*): And you, — will you tell us your name? Of course I should know it, but —

LADY (*Shaking her head*): No, you would have no way. My name is familiar to few. But my husband — my husband is — Santa Claus!

EVIE (*Sliding off her father's knee*): Ooooh,—*Mrs.* Santa Claus!

LADY (*Smiling*): Yes, dear. Merry Christmas!

HALLIE: You say — you say, Sir — I mean, Ma'am — *he's* out here?

LADY (*Turning*): Santa! Will you come in? (*Offstage — "Jingle Bells."*)

SANTA (*Outside*): *Whoa, Dasher! Whoa, Dancer!* Stand, *Prancer* and *Vixen!* (*Another jingle of bells and he enters.*) Hello, hello, everybody! Well, I guess you're having quite a party here tonight. How do, Mr. Webster, how do. Glad to know you're home again... Well, youngsters, it's Christmas already for you, I guess, — how'd you like to have me strip your tree for you?

RAYMOND *and* RALPH: Gee, that would be swell!

HALLIE: Oh, boy! What a night!

EVIE (*Curtseying*): That would be *very* good of you, Santa!

SANTA: Would, hey? (*Chucks her under chin.*) Well, let's see: Stockings first, eh? (*He brings* EVIE'S *first, then the boys'. Boys speak low to* FATHER. SANTA *marches toward tree.*)

FATHER: Just a minute, Santa Claus. My boys here have a suggestion to make. Who's your spokesman, boys?

HALLIE (*Prodded by other two*): Well, Santa Claus, it's like this. Seems to us we've already had about the best Christmas any kids could have. And of course a lot of the things on the tree there, folks got for us because they thought we wouldn't have Dad. But now we've got *him*. So —

RAYMOND: So seems as if you'd better give most of what's on the tree to other kids in the neighborhood. That is, we're willing, if the aunts and uncles, and grandpa and grandma are —

CHORUS: Oh, it's all right with us if it's what *you* want!

RALPH: You know their names, of course, Santa Claus. And they're *all* darned nice kids around here, honest!

SANTA CLAUS (*Nodding*): I'll bet they are. They are if the Websters are any sample, that's sure. You know, we hear pretty well of these children of yours up at the North Pole, Mrs. Webster!

ALTHEA (*Gently*): I'm glad of that.

MRS. SANTA CLAUS: Yes. I said it was the particular happiness of this family which brought us here tonight. But it was your unselfishness, too. These qualities have great appeal for us — especially this year!

SANTA CLAUS: All right. All right now. Here we go! (*With the help of the grown-ups he strips tree.*)

SANTA CLAUS (*Finishing*): There we are! I guess that's all! And what a tree it was! Now, Mrs., we've got to be getting right back up North —

LADY: Yes. Yes, we must get started on our next year's work. We always have a good deal to do ourselves, although as we get older, of course we have more and more help from the young folks of *our* neighborhood. . . . *You* know what I mean, Hallie?

HALLIE (*Grinning*): You bet!

LADY: Good-night, everyone, and Merry Christmas!

CHORUS: Good-night! Merry Christmas!

SANTA (*In door, soberly.*): You know, you're mighty lucky people to be living this year in a part of the world where you can have a Christmas like this! Nothing but stars above your chimney, nothing but snowflakes falling on your roofs. Laden tree, turkey in the oven, —

MOTHER: And being together, Santa Claus. That's best of all.

SANTA: Yes, that's right. Being together. With love in your hearts. That's what the world needs right now. Love for *all* men. If only America can keep it —

HALLIE: America's going to keep it, Santa Claus!

SANTA CLAUS: Hm, I shouldn't wonder. I shouldn't wonder if it will — if you say so! . . . You know, I wish you folks would sing your national hymn. I'd like to hear that tonight. I'd like to have it lingering on the air as I ride away from a world I can't visit for another year —

BOYS: We will, Santa Claus! (*Group sings it.*)

SANTA CLAUS (*With a wave*): Oh, that's fine! *Fine!* Thank you! Good-night, all!

HALLIE (*Saluting*): *Merry!*

SANTA CLAUS (*Smiling, saluting*): *Merry!*

ALL (*Turning to audience*): Merry, merry, merry — Christmas!

THE END

THE FIRST NEW ENGLAND CHRISTMAS TREE

by Ella Stratton Colbo

Characters

MISTRESS HARCUS, *mother*
JAMIE, *her crippled son*
CYNTHIA, *her little daughter*
GEORGE, *her oldest son*
WILLIAM, *her second son*
NEIGHBOR WARREN
CAPTAIN HARCUS
ELDER HOPKINS
VILLAGERS

SCENE 1

TIME: *Early Colonial Days. Two weeks before Christmas.*

SETTING: *Room in the Harcus cottage. There must be two doors and a window. Table, chairs and rocker.*

AT RISE: MISTRESS HARCUS *is discovered peering anxiously out of window.* JAMIE *is seated in rocker with a shawl over his legs and knees.*

JAMIE (*Anxiously*): Is the storm bad, Mother? Can you see them? Are they coming?

MOTHER (*Slowly*): No — they are not yet in sight. I wish I had not let little Cynthia go with them, but she begged so hard, and both George and William promised to mind her carefully. The morning looked bright and fair. I had no thought that it might be cold and stormy by nightfall.

JAMIE: Don't worry, Mother. They will be here soon, now that Neighbor Warren has gone to meet them.

MOTHER (*Turning from window with determined cheerfulness*): Yes. It was kind of Neighbor Warren to offer to go. If little

Cynthia is tired, he can swing her up in his strong arms and carry her easily. It is but eight miles to the mill, and the trail is fairly good. They would have had to travel slowly both ways, taking the corn and carrying home the sack of ground meal. I am sure there is no need to worry. Tomorrow I will make a nice big bowl of Indian pudding with the fresh corn meal.

JAMIE (*With satisfaction*): I can't wait to feast on that good Indian pudding. Could we have some for Christmas too? And while we are waiting for them, tell me more about Christmas in Merrie England when you were a little girl. Tell me more about the beautiful Christmas boughs the English people have in their homes.

MOTHER (*Laughing*): Oh, Jamie, I have told you of them so often! I'd think you'd be *tired* of Christmas boughs by this time!

JAMIE (*Earnestly*): I'd *never* tire of the Christmas boughs, never! Tell me again what you tied to the boughs to make them beautiful.

MOTHER: Oh, there were sweetmeats, and small toys, and bright paper flowers, and lighted candles — but best of all I liked the little golden Wishing Nuts that we always found on our Christmas bough at home.

JAMIE: *Wishing Nuts?* You never told me of *those* before. What were *they* like?

MOTHER: My grandmother was from Germany. It was she who made the little golden Wishing Nuts and tied them to the Christmas Bough — one for each of us. She took the nutmeats carefully from English Walnuts and saved the empty shells. On a slip of paper she wrote a wish for the future for each of us. Then she placed it between two halves of the shell, and glued them together carefully with a loop of bright ribbon in the top to fasten them to the bough. Next she gilded them with golden paint. The wishes were read aloud for every one to hear. I will never forget how happy and proud I was one Christmas when my wish read "May your new baby doll behave as well as you have all year."

JAMIE (*Wistfully*): How I wish *we* might have a lovely Christmas Bough, *just once*. I shut my eyes and imagine how beautiful it would look with the gay paper flowers, and the little golden Wishing Nuts tied to the dark evergreen — and the tiny lighted candles shining and twinkling like so many bright stars!

MOTHER: I wish so too, Jamie. But you know the Elders do not approve of making merry at Christmas. They would be very angry if anyone decorated a Christmas Bough.

JAMIE (*Sadly*): I know. But Mother dear, how could you *bear* to leave England, with all its fun and feasting at Christmas time? (*There is a sound of stamping feet, and voices outside.* MOTHER *hurries to open the door. Enter* NEIGHBOR WARREN *carrying little* CYNTHIA. *He is followed by* GEORGE *and* WILLIAM *carrying a sack of cornmeal.*)

NEIGHBOR WARREN (*Heartily as he sets* CYNTHIA *carefully on her feet on the floor*): Greetings, Widow Harcus. Here's your little girl — all safe and sound. And you'd never guess where I *found* her! In the trunk of a big hollow tree — all cozy and warm — snug as a bug in a rug!

MOTHER (*With great surprise as she unwraps* CYNTHIA'S *scarf and removes her hood and cloak*): In the trunk of a hollow tree! How came she there?

NEIGHBOR WARREN: That's where she was! When your two smart lads here (*Putting a hand on each of the boys' shoulders*) found that the storm was getting so bad there was danger of losing their way, they saw the huge hollow tree along the trail with its opening almost as large as a small doorway, and just popped her in where she was safe from the wind and cold. Then they both stood guard until they heard me calling. When I got there she was having a nice little nap for herself!

MOTHER: Oh, I do not know how to thank you, good Sir. I am so happy to have them all home again — safe from the storm. Will you not bide awhile with us for a cup of hot soup, after your cold journey?

NEIGHBOR WARREN: It was nothing, Widow Harcus, nothing. Little enough to do for a friend and neighbor. But I had best be getting home myself. Mistress Warren is no doubt waiting anxiously for word that your two lads are back safely with little Cynthia and the ground meal you needed so badly. Good night to you all! (*Exits as they all chorus together — "Good night, Neighbor Warren, and thank you kindly!"*)

MOTHER: Come now, boys, off with your things and help Jamie to the table. We will have a bit of hot supper now, while you tell us of the day's adventures.

CURTAIN

* * *

Scene 2

Setting: *The same.*

Time: *Later that same evening.*

At Rise: George *and* William *are discovered seated at table talking.*

William: Feels good to be inside out of the storm, doesn't it?

George: It does that! Warm and full of supper! I was afraid for awhile we might not get little Cynthia home safely.

William: When we were out there in the storm, not knowing which way to turn, I kept thinking of Father, lost at sea. It was just about this time of year, three years ago, that he bade us goodbye in Boston and set sail on the cruise that he hoped would make his fortune.

George: Aye! and just such a wild stormy night as this, Brother, that we were coming back home on the stage coach when the accident happened that crippled poor Jamie. How sad Father would feel if he knew Jamie had not walked in the three years since he left.

William: Wouldn't it be wonderful if he should come home for Christmas? I keep hoping that he *will* come, even though the whole village has long since given up all hope for the safe return of the crew of the good ship *Gallant.*

George: And did you notice how the neighbors have begun to call mother "the *Widow* Harcus"? I like it not!

William: No more do I! I can see how it grieves her. But hush, here she comes now. (*Enter* Mistress Harcus.)

Mother: Boys, now that Cynthia and Jamie are safely in bed, there is something I wish to talk to you about.

William: Yes, Mother. We were waiting to talk to you too—about Christmas.

George: It's only a fortnight till Christmas Eve.

Mother: Just a fortnight — but that will be time enough to carry out my plans if you will both help me.

William: What plans, Mother?

Mother: I have made up my mind to give little Cynthia and poor Jamie a real Christmas. The happy kind I used to have when I was a child in England. They have so little pleasure, and Jamie is possessed with longing to have a Christmas Bough as we did then. It may even be that the joy of having something he wants so badly would make him stronger, so that he might walk again.

WILLIAM: Little Cynthia chattered of Christmas on the way to the mill. She remembers that Father promised her a doll when he returned — but where would *we* get decorations, or a doll?

MOTHER: I have planned that too. I will journey to Boston by the next stage and find what I can in the stores there. Some sweetmeats, a small doll, a bit of bright paper, some English walnuts and a tiny vial of gilt paint for the Wishing Nuts. It would take naught else to make them very happy.

GEORGE (*Soberly*): But, Mother, what will happen should the Elders hear of it. You know how stern they are about such things. Any merry-making seems to them very wicked. At one of the last meetings they read aloud the law which says "Whosoever shall be found observing any such day as Christmas, or the like, either by forbearing labor, or by feasting, or in any other way, shall be fined five shillings." Think of the disgrace if we were discovered.

MOTHER: I have thought of it — but I feel that we must take the risk to make Jamie and Cynthia happy. If we carry out our plans carefully enough, no one need ever know of it but ourselves.

WILLIAM. On our way to the mill, I saw a beautiful little spruce tree growing close beside the trail. It is not far. George and I can cut it when we go to gather firewood. Some night while the village sleeps we can drag it home and hide it in the woodshed until Christmas eve.

GEORGE: We can make the window dark by nailing a blanket across the inside so that anyone who might chance to pass by, will not dream but what we are all asleep in bed as we should be, instead of wickedly decorating a Christmas Bough!

MOTHER: Then it is all settled. We three will do what we can to make this Christmas a happy memory for your little sister and poor Jamie. I have a feeling that your father would wish it this way. It is late now. Hasten to bed — for you must be up at dawn to lay in a good supply of firewood before the snow gets too deep. I have faith that your father will return to us some day, and that he will be very proud of you both, when he does come.

WILLIAM *and* GEORGE (*Rising*): Good night, Mother dear. (*Start to leave room.*)

CURTAIN

* * *

SCENE 3

SETTING: *The same.*

TIME: *Christmas Eve.*

AT RISE: *A small, partly decorated spruce stands in one corner of the room. A blanket is fastened across the window.* MISTRESS HARCUS, WILLIAM *and* GEORGE *are discovered busily putting the finishing touches on the tree. A small doll is tied to the tree in plain sight.*

WILLIAM: How *excited* Cynthia will be!

GEORGE: Jamie will *love* it! Just think — a whole *Christmas tree,* instead of just a *Christmas Bough!*

MOTHER (*Removing cover from box and taking out several silver paper stars*): And how fortunate I was to find the tinsel paper to make these stars! We will put the biggest one on the very tip of the tree and let the others shine among the branches.

WILLIAM: Give them to me. (*Reaches out to take them*) George and I will place the stars while you tie on the Wishing Nuts. Then our Christmas tree will be ready. Just think, Mother! The *first Christmas tree in New England!* How I wish we could show it to the whole village, instead of keeping it only for ourselves!

GEORGE (*Practically*): You know well we cannot do that! We would be in a pretty peck of trouble if we did!

MOTHER (*Busily tying on the Wishing Nuts, each with a white plainly marked name tag*) : The good Elders do not mean to be unkind. They only do what they think is right.

GEORGE: Methinks they have forgotten what it is like to be young and happy!

WILLIAM: And methinks they *never knew,* or they would not have forgotten! Nothing as beautiful as our Christmas tree could be wicked.

MOTHER: It does not seem wicked to me. I have not worked with such a light heart these many weary months. (*Steps back*) There! It is all finished. Now we will waken Cynthia and Jamie.

WILLIAM: They will be sleepy-eyed at first, but this will soon open their eyes wide!

MOTHER: Light a taper at the hearth, William, and hold it to the six little candles, so that they will be shining when Cynthia and Jamie first see the tree. I have placed this pail of water near it. Watch the candles very carefully, and put them out at once with the wet cloth if there seems any danger of their burning the branches. Come with me, George, to help Jamie. I will carry in little Cynthia. (*Exit* MOTHER *and* GEORGE. WILLIAM *carefully lights the candles and steps back to admire tree. Reënter* MOTHER *and* GEORGE *with* CYNTHIA *and* JAMIE, *who are both rubbing their eyes sleepily with their fists.*)

GEORGE: Look, Cynthia! Little sister, look! Look, Jamie! It is Christmas Eve. We have a Christmas Bough of our own! Isn't it beautiful?

CYNTHIA *and* JAMIE (*Exclaiming joyously*) : Beautiful! Beautiful!

MOTHER: Hush, dears. We must enjoy it *very* quietly. No one in the village must know we have it. The Elders would be very angry with us.

CYNTHIA (*Lowering voice and pointing at tree*) : The little doll on that branch, Mother. Is it mine?

MOTHER: Yes, dear, it is yours. Get it for her, George. (GEORGE *removes doll and places it in her hands. She hugs it rapturously, then sits down and begins to rock it.*)

JAMIE (*Softly*) : It is even more beautiful than I had dreamed, Mother. I did not know about the stars!

MOTHER: The stars are on the tree because of a legend that was written down by the Monks in a Sicilian monastery in the middle ages.

WILLIAM: Tell us the legend about the stars, Mother.

MOTHER: "It was on the first Christmas Eve of all, that Holy Night when our Lord was born. All the creatures came to worship in Bethlehem, and the trees did likewise. None of the other trees came as far as the least among them, a small spruce tree like this one. It was so weary it could hardly stand, and the other trees, with their fragrant blossoms, and great trunks and leafy boughs all but covered up the small stranger. But the stars saw, and took pity on it, and lo, a rain of them fell down from Heaven, and the bright Christmas Star alighted on the tip-top of the little spruce, and all the rest on its branches. And the Child in the Manger saw the beautiful star-lighted little spruce, and blessed it with a smile."

JAMIE: That is the loveliest story of all, Mother. No wonder *our* little spruce tree holds its stars so proudly.

WILLIAM: Is it time to take off the Wishing Nuts, mother? May we do that now?

MOTHER: Yes, it is time. I tied them on the lower branches so Cynthia could reach them. See if you can find one for each of us, Cynthia. When you have found one bring it to me and I will tell you whose name it bears.

GEORGE: Hurry, sister! I want to know my wish for the future!

CYNTHIA (*Running to tree, removes one of the Wishing Nuts and brings it to her mother*): Whose wish is *this,* Mother?

MOTHER: It is for you, yourself, little daughter. Press it apart, and we will read your wish. (CYNTHIA *opens nut and removes folded slip of paper.* MOTHER *reads from it.*) "May your new little dolly be a good child like her new little mother."

CYNTHIA (*Laughing delightedly*): Oh, she will be! I'm sure she will! She is much too pretty to ever be naughty! (*Runs back to tree and brings another nut to* MOTHER) Is this one for George?

MOTHER: No, this one is for William. Take it to him.

WILLIAM (*Opens nut, removes slip of paper and reads aloud*): "May you grow up to be as wise and just a man as good Governor Bradford for whom you were named." (*Smiles at* MOTHER.)

CYNTHIA: *I* think he is as wise as Governor Bradford right now! It was William who thought of putting me into the hollow tree to keep warm. (*Runs to tree*) This time I will find *your* wish, George. (*Removes another nut and takes it to* MOTHER.)

MOTHER (*Looking at name tag*) : Yes, George, now you will know your wish. (*Hands it to him.*)

GEORGE (*Opens it and reads*) : "May your father soon know how bravely and well you have carried on in his place." (*Quietly*) Thank you, Mother. I *have* tried to think each day what he would wish me to do. (CYNTHIA *removes another nut from the tree and gives it to her* MOTHER.)

MOTHER (*In pleased surprise*) : Why, this one has *my* name on it! Who could have fixed a Wishing Nut for me? (*Opens it and reads*) "May this coming year see the safe return of Captain David Harcus and the good ship *Gallant*."

WILLIAM: George and I made it for you, Mother. We know it's what you want most of all.

MOTHER: It is indeed. I have faith that another Christmas will find us reunited.

JAMIE: Now, Cynthia, do try to find a wish for me!

CYNTHIA (*Searching through tree branches*) : Here it is Jamie. It must be yours. All the rest of us have one. (*Gives it to him.*)

JAMIE (*Opens nut and reads slip of paper*) : "May it please the good Lord to make you well and strong, Jamie Boy, so that you may run about and play with the others." (*Speaking to* MOTHER) I do feel stronger already. Each day I will try to walk a little.

CYNTHIA: I'm sorry there are no more little golden Wishing Nuts for me to find.

MOTHER: But there *is one more,* Cynthia. I made one for your father too. When you find it we will put it away, and let him open it when he does return. Then he will know we thought of him this Christmas Eve. (*As* CYNTHIA *searches through the branches for her father's Wishing Nut, the others sit quietly admiring the tree. Suddenly she spies it and cries out*) Oh, I see it! *Here* it is! (*Begins to remove it from the tree. Suddenly in the stillness there sounds the tramp of many feet outside — a light tapping on the window, a loud rapping on the door, the mingling of excited voices. Someone outside calls loudly — "Mistress Harcus! Mistress Harcus! Make haste to unbolt your door!" All except* JAMIE *spring to their feet in terrified alarm.*)

GEORGE (*In stricken tones*) : We are discovered! How *could* they have found out?

WILLIAM: Don't unbolt the door, Mother. I will put out the candles. We will make no sound and go quietly to bed and pretend to be asleep. (CYNTHIA *begins to sob softly.*)

MOTHER (*Bravely*): No. We have had our happy Christmas Eve. They cannot take that from us. I will unbolt the door, and we will take our punishment together. (*Loud rapping is renewed. Voice calls urgently — "Mistress Harcus! Mistress Harcus! Awaken! Awaken! Let us in!" She goes slowly to the door and opens it wide. Enter* CAPTAIN DAVID HARCUS, *followed by* NEIGHBOR WARREN, ELDER HOPKINS, *and excited* VILLAGERS *who crowd into the room after him.* WILLIAM *and* GEORGE *step close to their* MOTHER'S *side.* CYNTHIA *clings to her skirts.*)

CAPTAIN HARCUS (*Shouts*): Ahoy, my hearties! (*Seizes his wife's hand and places one arm across* GEORGE'S *shoulders.*)

MISTRESS HARCUS: Oh, David! David! I *knew* you would come back to us!

NEIGHBOR WARREN: This afternoon the stage driver brought the news that the *Gallant* had been sighted off shore.

CAPTAIN HARCUS: Aye! When the *Gallant* finally docked in Boston Harbor the Stage had already gone — so I started home afoot.

ELDER HOPKINS: We knew he would waste no time in getting home to his family, so we waited at the edge of the village to meet him, to help him awaken you, and to share in your happy surprise. (*Suddenly notices decorated tree. Points to it and speaks very sternly*) But what is *this* foolishness? Mistress Harcus, it would seem that you were *not* sleeping quietly as we had supposed, but were wickedly disobeying the laws of the Colony!

MISTRESS HARCUS (*Falteringly*): We — It was but —

GEORGE (*Interrupting*): The fault was mine. I cut the spruce. I wanted —

WILLIAM (*Interrupting*): It is not so! The fault was *entirely mine.* I thought to please little Cynthia with the decorated tree.

JAMIE (*Suddenly stands up — takes a few steps forward to center of stage and interrupts dramatically*): No! No! Do not blame any of them. The fault is *entirely mine.* I kept asking for a Christmas Bough like they have in each home in Merrie England. Is it not beautiful? Nothing so beautiful could be wicked. It is not Mother's fault. She did it all for me, I tell you! To bring me happiness, because I cannot run about and play with the others.

NEIGHBOR WARREN: The boy is right, Elder Hopkins. What can be wicked about bringing happiness to a wee girl and a crippled lad?

VILLAGERS (*In chorus*): What indeed! He is right! (ELDER HOPKINS *nods and smiles at* CYNTHIA *as she steps out beside* JAMIE.)

CYNTHIA: Look, Father, my new dolly — and here is *your* golden Wishing Nut. Open it quickly. Mother wrote the wish inside just for you. (*Hands it to her* FATHER) Read it to us.

CAPTAIN HARCUS (*Opens the nut and removes slip of paper and reads aloud*): "David, I would like to hear you sing again 'Oh Little Town of Bethlehem' as you did long ago when you were a choir boy in England." (*There is a moment of silence. The whole group looks expectantly at* CAPTAIN HARCUS. *He clears his throat loudly and speaks to them*) It is my good wife's first request in three years — and a fitting one it is for Christmas Eve. I *will* sing it for *her* — and for *you* my good neighbors. (*Steps over beside the little Christmas tree — faces audience and sings "Oh, Little Town of Bethlehem."*)

THE END

THE LITTLE CAKE

by E. Clayton McCarty

Characters

SONIA
MARIA
MOTHER
OLD MAN
NATALIA
SECOND GIRL
THIRD GIRL
THE CAPTAIN
OTHER GIRLS
CAROLERS

SETTING: *It is Christmas Eve in a little medieval kingdom. All the day, peasants and rich townsmen have been collecting at the Duke's castle, for there is to be a feast in the great hall tonight, and the king will grace it with his presence. But we are in a comfortable room of a wealthy villager's house.*

AT RISE: *Outside sleigh bells jingle, men call cheery greetings to one another, and the music of carols sounds sometimes close at hand and sometimes softened by distance. Inside* SONIA, *haughty, with a disdainful curl to her lip, stands in the window. Her* MOTHER *sews at the table.* MARIA, *a child of twelve, packs a huge basket of food near the fireplace.*

SONIA: Hurry, Mother. Gregory just drove by with his sleigh full of mistletoe. (*The music becomes louder. There is a definite march rhythm to the Christmas song as the footsteps of the* CAROLERS *beat time. The sleigh bells die away.*)

MARIA: Here come the carolers. (*She runs to the window.*)

MOTHER: Maria, finish packing your basket.

MARIA: May I watch them pass?

SONIA: There isn't time. Mother, hurry. (MARIA *comes slowly back to the fireplace where she works. The song grows louder until the melody drowns all voices within, and then the music begins to fade as the singers pass beyond the house.*)

MARIA: Are they going to the castle?

SONIA (*With a short laugh*): The mayor's daughter expects to sit at the King's right hand. She can ill afford to equal the gift I shall present to the poor tonight.

MOTHER: Aye, and neither can we. You will have us in the poorhouse with your offering. Who told you about the mayor's daughter?

SONIA: Natalia. She told me the mayor vowed I should never win over his daughter.

MARIA: I wish I might lay a gift for the poor upon the King's table tonight.

SONIA (*Laughing*): What have you to give?

MARIA: Nothing.

SONIA: Nothing! (*Laughs.*) A gift fit for a king indeed!

MOTHER: Sonia, stop teasing the child. Now, Maria, finish your work and stop that dreaming. You have nothing to take. Your mother left me little enough for your keep. No gift can come out of that.

MARIA: I would like to give something — no matter how small. There would be lights and music — and offerings of silver and gifts of crystal and gold. And I would place mine when no one looked — and see the King give them to the poor — even mine.

SONIA: There is another beggar in the lane.

MOTHER: Leave the window, Sonia. He may see you and come asking for something.

SONIA: There are more this year than ever before.

MOTHER: Aye, they flock like flies to honey.

MARIA: It is because they want to share in the feast our King gives to the poor.

SONIA: One of them stopped me this afternoon by the church. I thought I should never get away. His eyes seemed to burn through me — as if he wanted to take the very rings from my fingers.

MOTHER: The King's men should scourge such vermin from the highway. Come, Sonia. Your dress is ready. Hurry into it or we shall be late. See that the basket is packed when we return, Maria. (*They leave. Music is again heard in the distance. A sleigh jingles past, and someone calls out cheerily.* MARIA *looks wistfully at the snowy world outside. As she turns away from the window a knock is heard. She opens the door. An* OLD MAN *stands there. He is bent with age and clutches a huge cloak tightly about him. From the depths of his hood a lean, hawk-like face looks forth.*)

MARIA: Oh!

OLD MAN: I am cold. May I warm myself at your fire?

MARIA (*Doubtfully*): Yes — yes. I don't think they'd mind. (*The* OLD MAN *comes down to the fire.*) Here is a stool.

OLD MAN: Thank you. Why are there so many people in the town tonight?

MARIA: They all go to the King's feast for the poor.

OLD MAN: Are you going?

MARIA: I must stay here to mind the fire. But Sonia and Aunty will go. Everyone will have such fun with the music and lights and food, and it will be warm and beautiful. The King will be there to give to the poor all the gifts which we lay upon his table. Listen, you can hear the music now. And he who brings the greatest offering will sit at the King's right hand and be honored in all the land throughout the new year.

OLD MAN: And why is that honor given? (*He asks the question almost too casually.*)

MARIA: Our King is good. He does not wish the poor to want for food, and he rewards those who care for them.

OLD MAN: And all are welcome to his feast?

MARIA: Yes.

OLD MAN: Even one like me?

MARIA: Yes. And the King will give you gifts with his own hands. I wish I could be there to see Sonia sit at his right.

OLD MAN: Has the King chosen her?

MARIA: No. But none can bring a richer gift than hers. It is a casket of jewels — a fortune. And the King will be pleased because she loved the poor so much.

OLD MAN: Aye, she must love the poor to bring so rich a thing. (*The* MOTHER *comes back from the hall.*)

MOTHER: Maria, have you finished? (*Notices* OLD MAN.) What are you doing here?

OLD MAN: I was cold. I came to warm myself at your fire.

MOTHER: Maria, did you let him in?

MARIA: I didn't think you'd mind —

MOTHER: We are too busy to bother with you today, old man, so I'm afraid you'll have to go.

MARIA: But he isn't warm yet.

OLD MAN: It is cold outside.

MOTHER: They will take care of such as you at the castle. (OLD MAN *stands, looks her in the eye.*)

OLD MAN (*Slowly*): All through the mountains they talk of the hospitality of this town on Christmas Eve.

MOTHER: Plenty will be given you at the King's feast. Open the door, Maria. (CAROLERS *are heard approaching.*)

OLD MAN (*Going*): All this day I have looked for someone with compassion in his heart — someone who gave not for vanity but for the love in his heart. It is cold outside, mother, and your fire is large enough to warm one more.

MOTHER: Hold your tongue and be gone.

OLD MAN: Mother, when you turn me away you turn away your King. He himself has said it. It is in his proclamation in the public square. Read it. (*His eyes burn into hers. For a moment she draws back, but she recovers herself and turns to the child.*)

MOTHER: Maria, you haven't packed the sausages. Come, child. Close the door when you leave, old man.

OLD MAN: A house is much better with the blessing of those who cross its threshold — even though they be beggars. (*Leaves and calls back over shoulder.*) Take care lest a beggar's curse bring ill fortune in the new year. (CAROLERS *pass near the house and the music rings loudly in the frosty air. On the heels of the singers come* NATALIA *and several other girls, richly dressed and bubbling with excitement. They knock.*)

MOTHER: Maria! Open the door.

MARIA: Yes, Aunty. (*She opens it. The* GIRLS *enter talking.*)

MOTHER: Natalia, you're early.

NATALIA: Didn't you hear them singing? They are already beginning.

SECOND GIRL: Did that beggar come from here?

THIRD GIRL: Only an hour ago he was on our doorstep muttering curses against those "whose giving is a lie." (*Laughs.*) Lena sent him packing fast enough.

NATALIA: I don't like him. The light of the devil is in his eyes. He frightens me.

SECOND GIRL: Where is Sonia? (*She warms her hands at the fire.*)

MOTHER: Maria, child, fetch Sonia. (MARIA *leaves.* MOTHER *inspects basket on table.*) Oh that child! Where are the puddings? And the sausages? She has forgotten them.

NATALIA: She has been dreaming again perhaps. (*Crosses to window.*)

MOTHER: I'll teach her to — (MARIA *enters.*) So there you are. Where are the puddings and sausages? And where is Sonia? I thought I told you to fetch her.

MARIA: She will be here soon.

MOTHER: Find those puddings.

MARIA: They are on the table, aunty. I haven't had time to pack them yet. (*Crosses to fireplace and carries puddings to basket.*)

MOTHER: Then hurry. And don't let me catch you dreaming again.

NATALIA: All the poor in the village are hurrying to the feast.

SECOND GIRL: They are hoping for a sight of the King.

THIRD GIRL: Or to fill their stomachs.

SECOND GIRL: Give them the leavings from the Duke's table, and let them see the King descend from his carriage, and they are satisfied to live another year in filth and rags.

THIRD GIRL: Does Sonia have her gift?

MOTHER: Aye, and a grand one.

NATALIA (*Sits*): Is it better than that of the mayor's daughter?

MOTHER: Aye. (*Sharply*) Maria!

MARIA (*Starts*): Yes?

MOTHER: We are late now. Finish packing that basket. What are you dreaming about?

NATALIA (*Laughs*): Dreaming she would make the best gift to the poor and be chosen to sit at the King's right hand.

MARIA (*Confused, sits on stool*): I can't help it.

NATALIA (*Scoffs*): What gift will you give to the poor, child?

THIRD GIRL: Nothing less than a king's ransom, I'm sure.

SECOND GIRL: You cannot give anything worthy to the poor. And the King would choose only the richest and most beautiful to sit beside him.

MOTHER (*Harshly*): Leave off dreaming, child. You cannot even go to the feast. You have no gift.

MARIA: I could give the little cake Sonia dropped in the ashes, the one you said I might have for my dinner. (ALL *laugh.*) I know it isn't grand enough for the King to notice —

NATALIA: Hardly.

MARIA: But I would like to make a gift to the poor, and that is all I have. (SECOND GIRL *goes up to window.*)

MOTHER: You won't have that if you make us late. Is that basket packed? (THIRD GIRL *crosses to table.*)

MARIA: Yes. And may I have the little sausage that is broken?

MOTHER: No. Bring the basket here. And go tell Sonia to hurry. (SONIA *enters.*)

NATALIA (*Jumps up*): Here she comes. Sonia, did you hear the news? (SONIA *crosses to* MOTHER. NATALIA *crosses to* SONIA.)

SONIA (*Crossly*): Mother, is my hair all right? What news?

MOTHER: Yes.

NATALIA: You can't sit beside the King.

SONIA (*Shrilly*): What?

NATALIA: Maria here has a gift better than yours. She will be chosen this Christmas.

SONIA (*Laughs*): Oh, she will, eh?

SECOND GIRL (*Crosses*): She will give to the poor a basket of jewels.

MOTHER: Leave off teasing the child. She'll be believing you in a minute, and then I'll never get any work out of her. (*Carries basket off.*)

MARIA: No. I know they're laughing at me. I don't want to sit with the grand people —

SECOND GIRL: Such humility. She is a princess at least.

MARIA: I am not good enough — nor rich enough —

SONIA: With a mountain of gold?

MARIA: I only want to give something to the poor — my little cake —

THIRD GIRL: Make way for the princess to give her little cake to the poor.

MARIA: But I didn't mean to —

MOTHER (*Calling from hall*): Are you teasing that child again?

SONIA: No, Mother. (*In a moment the* OLD MAN *enters and stands watching them gravely. They suddenly discover him and gather in a group plainly afraid of him.*) Who is that?

NATALIA: It's that old beggar I saw in the public square this morning.

SECOND GIRL: He was asking everyone for alms.

THIRD GIRL: Probably he heard of Maria's little ash-covered cake.

NATALIA: Send him away. He frightens me.

SONIA (*Crossly*): What do you want?

OLD MAN: A little morsel of food. I am hungry.

SONIA: We haven't any.

OLD MAN: Just a little. Just one bit out of the basket you are taking to the feast.

SONIA: Go to the castle. We have no time to bother with you.

OLD MAN: And a moment to warm myself at your fire. It is cold tonight.

SONIA: No.

MARIA: I will give him my little cake.

NATALIA: Let Maria give him her cake.

SONIA: We have nothing for you. Go.

OLD MAN: Just a moment to warm myself at your fire.

SONIA: Go.

NATALIA: Hurry, old man.

MARIA: Give him my cake.

SONIA: No.

OLD MAN (*Mumbles*): Even as you do it unto the least of these—

SONIA: What are you mumbling?

OLD MAN: When rich folk cannot spare a crust then the land is poor indeed. (SONIA *follows him across center, but suddenly the* OLD MAN *turns. She shrinks back, afraid of something she sees in his eyes.*)

SONIA: Go. This moment!

OLD MAN (*Fiercely*): Give, if you will, only when you are rewarded for giving. But I say to you he who gives in such a way shall not reap the benefit of that giving, and on his house shall be the blight of the beggar's curse. (*The* OLD MAN *leaves muttering. There is a momentary silence.*)

NATALIA: I don't like the look in his eye. He's a vicious old man.

THIRD GIRL: Of all the times for something like that to happen!

MOTHER (*Coming to door*): Hurry, Sonia. We'll be late.

SONIA (*Upset*): Where is my cloak? I'm all upset. (NATALIA *runs up to window.*)

MOTHER: Maria!

MARIA: Yes?

MOTHER: Fetch Sonia's cloak. (*Crosses to* SONIA. MARIA *obeys.*)

NATALIA: Hurry. (*Everybody is talking at once.*)

MOTHER: Smooth your hair.

MARIA: Here is your cloak.

SONIA: Help me.

SECOND GIRL: Hurry.

THIRD GIRL: The mayor just drove to the hall.

NATALIA: Hurry, before the King arrives.

SONIA: I shall look a sight to sit beside the King. Where is my gift?

MARIA: Here. (*Brings it from table.*)

MOTHER: Now, we're ready. Maria, don't let the fire go out.

MARIA: I won't.

MOTHER: And mind you, don't leave this house to watch the dancing as you did last year. (*There comes the sound of far-away carols.*)

MARIA: May I just peep through the window?

MOTHER: No.

SECOND GIRL: Hurry! We'll miss something.

MARIA: Will you take my little cake to give to the poor?

MOTHER: No.

SONIA: I would look fine giving a cake to the King.

THIRD GIRL: They're starting. (*All leave.* MARIA *stands at window listening to song. She cries quietly. The* OLD MAN *enters softly. The music is not so loud now, but it continues with brief pauses until the end of the play.*)

OLD MAN: Do you want to go with them?

MARIA (*Answering before she thinks*): Yes. (*Gasps*) Oh!

OLD MAN: They are gone now. May I warm myself at your fire?

MARIA: Yes — yes. How did you get in? I didn't see you come.

OLD MAN: Why are you here alone?

MARIA: They have all gone to the Christmas feast.

OLD MAN: Didn't you want to go?

MARIA: Yes. Listen, they are singing again. (*The music becomes louder.* MARIA *goes to the window.*)

OLD MAN: It is very pretty.

MARIA: Yes. And there are lights, and food — little round sausages — and puddings — and spice cakes —. The King will be there.

OLD MAN (*To himself*): The King.

MARIA: And Sonia will sit at his right.

OLD MAN: But surely there are other gifts. Why does your cousin sit by the King?

MARIA: No gift can be grander than hers. A whole casket of jewels. They will shine. Oh, I want to see them.

OLD MAN: Why don't you go?

MARIA (*Turns away*): I must stay here — to keep the house warm.

OLD MAN: But surely everyone must take a gift to the poor on Christmas Eve. The King would wish it. Why are you not there with yours?

MARIA: I have nothing but my little cake.

OLD MAN: Cake?

MARIA: The one Sonia dropped in the ashes — and they gave it to me for my supper. No one wants it — not even the poor.

OLD MAN: How do you know?

MARIA: I couldn't lay my cake beside all the jewels and bright new gold pieces. (*Crosses down center.*) No one would let me do that.

OLD MAN: But the King wants everyone to make a gift to the poor, no matter how small.

MARIA: But I must stay here to keep the fire. They will beat me if I don't.

OLD MAN: I will keep it for you until you come back. Go, child.

MARIA: I'm afraid.

OLD MAN: Go quickly. The King would want everyone at his feast. Go long enough to lay your cake on the table.

MARIA: If I only dared.

OLD MAN: I promise you the fire will be blazing when you come back.

MARIA: I'll go. (*Crosses right.*)

OLD MAN: Child.

MARIA: Yes?

OLD MAN: I am hungry. May I have something to eat while you are gone?

MARIA: Oh! — Oh!

OLD MAN: Just a crust of bread.

MARIA: They won't let me. There is nothing but my supper — my little cake.

OLD MAN: I am hungry.

MARIA: But I cannot give it to the poor if I let you eat it.

OLD MAN: I have traveled all day without food.

MARIA: I will get it for you. (*Gives it to him.*) There will be so many gifts. They won't miss my little cake. (*She looks wistfully toward the window as the singing becomes louder.*)

OLD MAN (*Takes it*): Don't you want to sit beside the King?

MARIA: Only the giver of the richest gift may do that.

OLD MAN: But sometimes the richest gift does not come from the heart.

MARIA: The King won't know that. You are hungry. Eat my little cake.

OLD MAN: No. Listen! They are singing. (*Crosses to window and back.*) Run, child. And when the King comes, give him your little cake.

MARIA (*Hesitates*): But —

OLD MAN: Hurry. And child, a gift that comes from the heart the King will know above all others, though it be only a little cake.

MARIA: No. I could not take it to the King when you are hungry. Please eat it.

OLD MAN: You are good, child. (*There is a noise outside. The* CAPTAIN, *a huge man resplendent in scarlet and gold strides into the room. His glance darts restlessly about.*)

CAPTAIN: Your majesty! (*The* OLD MAN *stands and seems to grow in height until his stature equals that of his aide.*)

OLD MAN: What is it, Captain?

MARIA (*Realizing*): Oh!

CAPTAIN: Your majesty, everyone is assembled at the castle and they await you.

KING: Thank you, Captain. (*He throws off the beggar's cloak and reveals the King's robes beneath.*) We shall take this girl with us. Tonight she is to sit beside me.

MARIA: Your majesty, I have nothing to give.

KING: The gift you offered to your King came truly from the heart. Your little cake is worth more than all the gold and silver in my kingdom.

MARIA: But your majesty, my aunt and Sonia would not like it.

KING: One of my men shall tend your fire, child. All day I have wandered among the people of this town and all have turned me away — but you showed kindness to a beggar and your King is grateful. Call my carriage, Captain.

CAPTAIN: Yes, sire. (*Steps to door.*)

KING: We must go to the Christmas Eve feast. Come.

MARIA: Oh! And I will see the lights and hear the music — (*The* KING *throws his cape around her and leads her to the door. The music rises to a triumphal chorus as the curtain falls.*)

THE END

CHRISTMAS COMES TO HAMELIN

by Grace Evelyn Mills

Characters

THE STRANGER
MAYOR
THE TOYMAN
DOLLS, *who walk and dance*
MISS JENKINS
CITIZENS

CHILDREN AT THE ORPHANAGE

ROSEMARY	RALPH
ELSIE	ALICE
JOE	SUE
IRMA	FRED
BETTY	PEGGY
ANN	ALMA
ANGELINE	BOB
NANCY	HUGHIE
RUTH	PETE
DICK	JOHN
ANDY	

SCENE 1

SETTING: *Town Hall of Hamelin.*

AT RISE: *People of Hamelin are sitting, or standing about the Town Hall. At the table sits* THE MAYOR, *with a large book open before him, in which he apparently makes notations with his pen. Everyone seems very serious; a couple of gentlemen look over his shoulder; a clerk, perhaps, hands him notes across the table.* A STRANGER *enters hesitantly.*

STRANGER: Pardon me, my good people. I trust I am not intruding. (*The people move back suspiciously, as if to make room for him.* THE MAYOR *lays down his pen.*) I am a stranger in your village; I met no one, and came hither. May I ask why you are gathered here with such sad faces?

1st Citizen: We are met because of a sad anniversary.

Stranger (*Leans on his staff to listen. People eye him very suspiciously*): Anniversary? Anniversary of what? And what a strange town it is, anyway; do you know, I have not seen a child since I entered it.

2nd Citizen: *That* is the reason for our sad anniversary.

Stranger: You speak in riddles.

3rd Citizen: Have you not heard what happened in Hamelin?

Mayor: Methought all the world knew our tragedy. Tell him; make short work of the story; and then, Sir, we shall appreciate it if you do not tarry here.

Stranger: Nay, do not tell me, my friends, if the telling is indeed so painful as I see by your countenances it is. (*They gather about; several start to speak at once — "Strange that you have not heard"—"From what land do you come?" "Surely you are from a far country indeed—"*) Yes, I am from a far country. Never have I seen so many sad faces.

4th Citizen: We have reason to be sad. It is a long story, and one we thought the whole world knew. Once upon a time, Hamelin was visited with a plague of rats. There were rats everywhere. No one was safe from them. They drove us, literally, out of house and home. Rats threatened our peace, our security, our very lives. We knew that steps must be taken—

5th Citizen (*Interrupting*): So we went to the Mayor. We told him something must be done. He was a well-meaning man, but a weak one. He did not know what to do, any more than we did. As the meeting was still in progress, in came the Piper.

Stranger: The Piper?

6th Citizen: Aye. The Piper. He made a bargain with us. He said he would rid our town of rats, for a thousand guilders.

Stranger: A fair offer, I should think, since the rats were so bad.

7th Citizen: Aye, but he did the thing so easily. He simply stepped to the door, blew three notes on that outlandish horn of his, and out came the rats—'twas no effort on his part, the scoundrel!

8th Citizen: They came out of every house, and barn and shed in Hamelin. An army of rats followed the Piper—followed as he piped through our streets, straight to the river brink. And then, the stupid rats fell in, and were drowned in the swift Weser. It was all a part of the spell he'd put upon them.

STRANGER: And then, I suppose, you paid him?

1ST CITIZEN: Nay! Then we did not pay him anything; and bitterly must we regret it. (*Voice among the mothers, "Aye, bitterly."*) The thing had been so easily done; we needed the money for other things; it had been a bad year, and the rats had played havoc. We people of Hamelin pride ourselves on our thrift, and on our ability to drive a bargain.

9TH CITIZEN: But here was a fellow who would not be bargained with. It was a thousand guilders or nothing —

10TH CITIZEN: And we refused to listen to his threat. More fools we! He played again—(*Here he pauses, as if overcome; others bury their faces in their hands, or gaze stonily away.*) And our children, our dear, innocent children—followed just as the rats had done.

STRANGER: The same?

11TH CITIZEN: Nay — for they were not drowned. We feared they would be. We were rooted to our places. We could not move to help our little ones. But the villain turned aside at the river — they turned too. Up the mountainside they went, the Piper leading them forever from us—

12TH CITIZEN: And a door in the mountainside opened to receive them. He went in—our children followed; the door closed, and we have never seen them since. They are lost to us forever.

STRANGER: A terrible calamity, truly.

MAYOR: All joy went from us, along with the children. You can see, perhaps, Sir, why we like not strangers. Ever since that fatal day, we have been suspicious of strangers in our midst.

STRANGER: No need, good Sir, to feel at all suspicious about me. I am but a poor countryman, and my heart aches for you—since you say that joy has gone from you forever.

13TH CITIZEN: Every year, we meet several times to commemorate the occasion. They left on the twenty-second of July—

STRANGER: This then, is not the anniversary?

13TH CITIZEN: No, this is the half-yearly commemoration of the sad event. You see, we endeavor to keep things exactly as the children liked to have them—in case they should come back, you know.

ANOTHER: But they do not come! They do not come!

14TH CITIZEN: All is exactly as they would like it to be. Down by the stream, the grapevine swings are allowed to grow; the teeter-totters, the rope swings, the trapezes, the playhouse, are all kept in perfect condition. The toymaker keeps a fresh supply of toys always on hand.

3RD CITIZEN: And every year, he makes more marvelous toys!

4TH CITIZEN: At last, he has even achieved dolls that walk, dolls that talk, dolls that dance, and dolls that sing.

5TH CITIZEN: Nowhere in all the world are there such toys as ours.

7TH CITIZEN: He made them life-size—he thought if they looked like children, it might comfort the mothers.

8TH CITIZEN: But what is a mechanical doll, to one who has had a real child to love?

9TH CITIZEN: It is a comfort to our bereaved hearts to know that if they should come back, at any season of the year, they will find things as they most wish to have them; the finest berries are left unpicked, the nuts are left ungathered in the Fall; the cookie jars are always full; thick new mittens await their hands, skates are kept bright—all is in readiness for their return.

STRANGER: May I see those dolls that walk and talk and sing?

MAYOR: Stay and see them if you like; the toymaker will bring them in—he won't mind. Call him, will you, somebody? (*Someone goes out and returns immediately with a little bent man in spectacles and apron and whiskers.*)

TOYMAKER: Something's gone wrong with Belinda. (*He scratches his head in perplexity.*)

10TH CITIZEN: That's the talking doll, sir. This gentleman (*Turns to* TOYMAKER.) wants to see the dolls.

TOYMAN: Just a minute. If one of you gentlemen will help me, I'll be glad to bring them in. Sorry about Belinda. Something's wrong with her works. (*He goes off, followed by a couple of men who will assist him.*)

STRANGER: Who's that funny old lady over there? (*The "funny old lady" sits up straight and tall, all during this, with glasses and a bonnet on, a book on her lap, and a ruler or pointer held stiff and upright in her hand. She appears not to notice the others, but relaxes to watch the dolls presently*)

11TH CITIZEN: S-sh. That's the schoolmistress. She's not quite right here (*Touches head.*) since the children went away. We never knew how much she loved the children, until it happened. Every day she opens the schoolhouse door as usual—no one has the heart to tell her not to; we continue to pay her her salary just as if she were really teaching—(*A citizen near him lays a hand on his arm, saying, "Here's the Toyman." There is the whirr of toys being wound; it may be a loud mechanical toy, or a couple of eggbeaters beating rapidly offstage; the* WALKING DOLLS *walk across the stage, very stiffly. They enter from the direction the* TOYMAN *went in, walk across stage, where a citizen gently turns each in turn to the audience, and they stop, looking expressionlessly straight ahead; last of all comes the* TOYMAN *towing the* DANCING DOLL, *who is limp and graceless. The* TOYMAN *winds and the doll goes into her specialty dance —stiffly at first—then like a person, as of course, she is; at the end, she goes stiff and wobbly and collapses. The* TOYMAN *helps her off, winding her up just enough so she can make it; there is a whirr as each of the remaining dolls is wound up by a citizen; they go off, stiffly the way they came.*)

5TH CITIZEN: Do they not look real?

STRANGER: Indeed they do! What about the singing doll?

MAYOR: I'd rather not embarrass the toyman. He is very sensitive, and feels to blame for Belinda's trouble. It is a beautiful doll—a work of art—but some of her delicate mechanism has become broken, apparently.

TOYMAN (*Reappearing*): Here she is! Here's Belinda! (*Citizens cry "She works!"* BELINDA *is brought in; she is wound up; there is a different whirr—the kind of whirr a mechanical toy makes when the spring is released. The* TOYMAN *looks troubled. Shakes head, and produces from his apron pocket an oil can. He applies it, and winds again. This time* BELINDA *opens her mouth, and crumples up in a heap on the floor.*)

TOYMAN: Oh, my poor Belinda! Help me, someone. (*Two men support* BELINDA *between them and take her out. The* TOYMAN *follows, looking unhappy.*)

STRANGER: What a pity there are no children to enjoy them!

9TH CITIZEN: Do we not know it?

1ST CITIZEN: Would we not give our lives, if our children could see them?

STRANGER: If not your children—why not others?

MAYOR: Sir! You speak like a madman. No other children will ever be welcomed here! We will have no children but our own!

STRANGER: My friends, listen to me. As I passed through a town not far from here, I visited an orphanage; a cold, bleak, cheerless place, with a cold and cheerless woman in charge of it. I did a few tricks, told some old jokes, played a few games with those unfortunate children. My friends, you have no children; think, I beseech you, of the far more desolate state of those children who have no parents. Friends—do not nourish your own sorrow forever. Think of those more afflicted than you—

2ND CITIZEN: I knew it was a mistake to be cordial to you!

STRANGER: You are selfish—

3RD CITIZEN: Who are you to call us selfish?

ANOTHER: Aye—who indeed?

STRANGER: Who I am, makes no difference. I shall go, for I like not your dreary town. Through greed, you lost your children; through selfishness, you destroy your souls. You say yourselves, that joy has gone from you. Your hearts are hard. You are not willing to give these other little ones the joy that belongs to childhood. Until you think of others, you will never know peace.

4TH CITIZEN: Away with this rude stranger!

1ST CITIZEN: Soft! We dare not hurry him urgently away—we did that once—to our sorrow!

STRANGER: I go, of my own accord. Friends, yonder is the spire of a great cathedral. Go there to make your decision. Go there—and may the spirit of the Christmas season enter into your hearts. (*He goes.*)

11TH CITIZEN: What manner of man is this? (*They look strangely at one another.*)

12TH CITIZEN: Something about him awakens an old thought—old words I had almost forgotten—"I was a stranger, and ye took me not in—"

7TH CITIZEN: We need decide nothing rashly; but this I know. Another Christmas approaches. Too long it has been an empty day. Can we face another childless festival? (*Cries of "no" as curtain closes.*)

* * *

Scene 2

SETTING: *The Orphanage.*

AT RISE: *A group of children of all ages are grouped about a big girl,* ROSEMARY. *She is telling them a story.*

ROSEMARY:
"And I heard him exclaim, as he drove out of sight,
Merry Christmas to all, and to all a good night."

ELSIE: I never saw Santa Claus.

JOE: Nor I.

ROSEMARY: Some day, p'raps you will.

IRMA: Not here. Miss Jenkins doesn't approve of him.

BETTY: I guess he doesn't come to orphan asylums.

ANN: Tell us about when you were little, Rosemary, and had parents and a home and everything.

ANGELINE: What was it your mother called you?

ROSEMARY: She called me "Bunny." We lived in a little white house. And we did have the grandest time at Christmas.

NANCY: Tell us again about the Christmas cookies.

ROSEMARY: My mother had special cutters she used only at Christmas—

RUTH: I like to hear about the pink ones best. I had some once. A lady sent them to me. In a box.

ROSEMARY: My Daddy had made those cutters himself, so there weren't any like them in the whole world. There was a bird, and a squirrel and a fish and an elephant. They had red candy eyes—my mother let me put the eyes in. And we'd have gifts, all done up so beautiful; and we'd sing carols and have a tree—

DICK: So'll we have a tree. And sing carols. We always do.

ROSEMARY: Yes—I'm glad. You can look at the tree and imagine you're home. There'll be a good dinner, too—chicken maybe—and ice-cream. And toys. The rich children always send us the toys they don't want any more—

RALPH: Aw! I'd like a toy just for me!

ELSIE: Why, Rosemary, you're crying!

ROSEMARY: Oh, no. It's just a cold—and remembering. (*Wipes eyes.*) It isn't the tree and the lights and the cookies and the gifts that make Christmas—it's being loved by one's very own people.

RUTH: I had an aunt once.

JOE: I never had any.

ANOTHER: Nor I.

ANOTHER: Nor I.

ALICE: Oh, I had a doll once. I guess I was too little to appreciate it.

ROSEMARY: If you're very good, perhaps some day you'll be adopted like Ginny was.

SUE: But Ginny could sing and play the piano, and she had curls —I don't believe anyone would want just a plain child like me.

ELSIE: Well, there's Beth: She plays a violin.

FRED: It's the girls that get adopted, every time. I guess no one wants a boy. The only time I ever saw Miss Jenkins smile was the time she read somewhere that a small boy is a noise with dirt on it. Gosh, I can't remember all the things she thinks are important—table manners, and clean shoes, and scrubbed nails, and slick hair—

ROSEMARY: Mothers aren't cross about those things. Mine wasn't. If they scold, they don't really mean it. It's just that they want us to make a good impression on the neighbors.

IRMA: Say "'Twas the night before Christmas," Rosemary. Won't you please?

ROSEMARY: "'Twas the night before Christmas—"

MISS JENKINS (*Offstage*): Rosemary!

ROSEMARY: Yes'm — Here I am, Miss Jenkins. (*Children stand up.*)

MISS JENKINS (*Entering*): Rosemary! What are you doing?

ROSEMARY: N—nothing, Miss Jenkins. Just amusing the children. (*The children wiggle back from* MISS JENKINS *and are quiet.*)

MISS JENKINS: I should prefer to have you do something useful. I shall send the rest in, and you may practice for the Christmas exercises until supper time.

ROSEMARY: Yes, Miss Jenkins.

MISS JENKINS: I am particularly anxious for you to make a good impression on the trustees, and be a credit to my training. I hope you will be orderly, well-mannered, quiet, and intelligent. Otherwise, perhaps they will not provide such a good Christmas for you ever again. (*Other children enter; they creep past* MISS JENKINS *as she leaves the stage. As she goes, more than one child makes a face behind her retreating back.*)

ROSEMARY: Well—that's fun, practising for Christmas, I mean. First, let's hear your Scripture Verses. (*They repeat in concert, the part of Luke, beginning "And there were in the same country, shepherds, keeping watch over their flocks by night—"* Now let's hear Ann's solo. She doesn't really need to rehearse, but I do love to hear it.

ANN: All right. (*Sings "Silent Night."*)

HUGHIE: Bet Ann'll get adopted!

ROSEMARY: Let's sing a carol. What will it be?

RUTH: "Good King Wenceslas." (*They sing one stanza.*)

PEGGY: I'd like to sit on someone's lap.

ROSEMARY: Come on.

PEGGY (*Looks disparagingly at* ROSEMARY'S *lap, but slides over*): I'd like a lady with a great big lap.

ALMA: Once *I* sat on a lady's lap.

BOB: I'd like the kind of mother that could make cookies.

BETTY: And sew doll clothes.

HUGHIE: I choose the kind that comes upstairs and tucks you in bed.

JOHN: Fathers are nice, too.

IRMA: You never did finish the story, Rosemary.

ROSEMARY: Where was I? 'Twas the night—

MISS JENKINS (*Entering*): Attention! (*They stand, the little ones tumbling off* ROSEMARY'S *lap.*)

MISS JENKINS: I have news for you. (*Children steal wondering looks at one another.*) All the citizens of Hamelin will be here tomorrow. If they like you, there is a chance that you may be adopted. Watch your manners. Stay clean! Don't make any noise! Be seen and not heard! Remember, nobody ever adopts a naughty child. (*Exit.*)

PETE: Gosh!

JOHN: All the people of Hamelin? That doesn't seem sensible to me. There's something wrong.

ROSEMARY: Why, that's the town that hasn't any children—

ANDY: Aw, they'll never even look at a guy like me. They'll want the little cute kind. I know.

SUE: You can't tell. Somebody might even like a boy. Oh, Rosemary, isn't it exciting?

RUTH (*A tall, lanky child*): I wish I was little and cuddly!

ROSEMARY: Don't you worry! If the whole town comes—who can tell what might happen. Perhaps lots of you will be adopted!

SEVERAL: Oh, goody! (*They join hands in a circle, and dance around the stage, singing.*)

CHILDREN:

We're going to be adop — ted
We're going to be adop — ted —

BETTY: I made up a poem, all by myself. It goes like this —

No more cereal in thick dishes,
No more lonely little wishes,
No Miss Jenkins — cross old thing!
We shall dance — and we shall sing.
(*They gallop about the stage, singing.*)
We want moth–ers
We want moth–ers
We want —

MISS JENKINS (*Heard offstage as curtain closes*): Cease this unseemly noise!

* * *

SCENE 3

SETTING: *The Orphanage.*

AT RISE: *The orphans are seated very decorously about the same room, with hands folded.* MISS JENKINS, *showing signs that her composure is not what it might be, reads from a list.* ROSEMARY, *trying to conceal her excitement, answers sedately, but it is evident that she is bursting — and the orphans occasionally bounce in their chairs with suppressed happiness. They have hard work keeping sober faces, and when* MISS JENKINS' *eyes are on the list they nudge one another, and clap hands noiselessly.*

MISS JENKINS (*Consulting list*): These people are most unreasonable — Here's one — wanted, one little girl with front teeth missing.

ROSEMARY: There's Sue — and May, too. P'raps we'd better send both of 'em to interview the lady.

MISS JENKINS: Sue! May! Go at once to the reception room. Do not loiter — (*Reads*) Three boys. Ages preferably five, seven, and nine. Boys with healthy appetites preferred. Hmf! (*Three boys arise as one: "That's us, Miss Jenkins." They go.* MISS JENKINS *continues to read*) Wanted: One small girl who likes kittens. One girl who likes to play with biscuit dough.

ROSEMARY: Oh — I know! Ruthie and Alma!

MISS JENKINS: Hurry along, you two. Let us get this silly matter over with. Mercy! "One small boy afraid of the dark"! Not one parent has asked for anything sensible! Dick, you may go. (*He runs out, looking gleefully back over his shoulder.*) One child who likes doll-clothes —

BETTY: O — oh! May I go try out for that one, Miss Jenkins?

MISS JENKINS: As well you as any other! I never heard of anything so preposterous! Not one person has asked for a *useful* child! (*Reads*) Two little girls who look like sisters. One should be plump.

ROSEMARY: That'd be Irma and Alice, Miss Jenkins. They're always together.

MISS JENKINS: Hush! (*The little girls sneak out fast.*) Two small children the size to cuddle. Cuddle, indeed! Nobody ever cuddled *me.*

ROSEMARY: P'raps that's what's the matter—

MISS JENKINS: Are you being impertinent?

ROSEMARY: Oh, no, Miss Jenkins! (*Hastily*) Don't you think Hugh and Peggy —

VOICE (*Offstage*): Are there any more, Miss Jenkins? We're so delighted so far — (*Kind motherly soul enters*)

MISS JENKINS: It certainly doesn't take much to please some people! (*The lady disregards the tone.*)

LADY: I think you're wonderful, Miss Jenkins, to pick exactly the child each of us most wanted — (MISS JENKINS *smiles and tries to look as if she'd done it herself.* ROSEMARY *opens her mouth in some amazement. The other parents come on, each with the child or children of their choice. They touch their new children hungrily, lovingly, and one or two wipe their eyes.*)

SUE: And you don't mind my front teeth?

NEW MOTHER: No, indeed! There's just one thing nicer than a little girl with no front teeth — and that's two of 'em! (*She squeezes both little girls to her.*)

PEGGY: Are you sure I'm not too big to be a lap-sitter.

MOTHER: No, indeed. You're exactly the right size.

PETE: To think anybody'd pick me up! Gosh!

JOHN: Where's Rosemary?

ALICE: Yes, where's Rosemary gone?

PEGGY: I want Rosemary!

IRMA: She mothered us when we hadn't any mothers —

ELSIE: I don't want any mother unless Rosemary has one too —

OTHERS: Nor I!

A MOTHER: There, there. Rosemary won't be forgotten. She may go exactly where she likes.

ROSEMARY (*Entering*): Oh, what do you think? The Toyman has given me a job! A real, sure-enough job! To tend the dolls, and take care of the toys, for always!

TOYMAN: I want to show my dolls.

A FATHER: Did — did you get Belinda to working? Does she sing?

TOYMAN: Yes, sirree! Nobody can beat me when it comes to tinkering. Just needed a bit of overhauling, that was all. (*Toys are brought in, same way as before. The orphans applaud. Last of all,* BELINDA *is brought in. Her song is "Santa Claus is Coming to Town" or some such classic. She starts — and goes over one note again and again, as a phonograph record does when it is cracked. More winding: another false start.* THE TOYMAN *is perturbed.*) Funny thing. Where's that oil can? (*Someone hands it to him. He works back of* BELINDA*; there is a whirr, we see his winding motion, and this time her song is sung to a successful conclusion.* THE TOYMAN *approves; the orphans applaud.*)

AN ORPHAN: I never was so happy in all my life!

ROSEMARY: Let's sing our carols! (*They stand and sing.*)

1ST CITIZEN: We have found Christmas.

2ND CITIZEN: We have found happiness.

3RD CITIZEN: We have found peace. (*They sing, "Joy to the World" as the curtain closes.*)

THE END

HAPPY CHRISTMAS TO ALL

by Jeannette Covert Nolan

Characters

DR. CLEMENT CLARKE MOORE
MRS. MOORE, *his wife*
EMILY, *Mrs. Moore's cousin*
THE MOORE CHILDREN, *two small boys and a girl of eight*

SCENE 1

TIME: *Six o'clock in the evening of December 24, 1822.*

SETTING: *The library of Dr. Moore's comfortable home in Chelsea, New York.*

AT RISE: DR. MOORE *is seated at his desk. He is a handsome man in early middle age. Books are piled in front of him. He turns the pages, and writes, scratching diligently with his quill pen. From outside can be heard the jingle of sleigh-bells and bursts of carols from passing singers. From door at left,* MRS. MOORE *enters. She is a youthful, pretty woman. She is carrying a tall red candle which she sets on the sill of the rear window.*

MRS. MOORE: Clement?

DR. MOORE (*Without glancing up*): Yes, my dear?

MRS. MOORE: I am sorry to disturb you. But something has occurred. Something rather dreadful. I don't see how I could have done so! It was the confusion, I suppose. So much to think about. Straightening the parlors, readying the spare bedroom for Cousin Emily, preparing the children's gifts and the sweetmeats. (*She pauses.*) Clement, you're not listening! *Clement!*

DR. MOORE (*Glancing guiltily at her*): Eh? Yes, my dear?

MRS. MOORE: I declare, you haven't heard a word I've said!

DR. MOORE: Ah, but I have. You said you were confused, you had neglected the parlors, straightened the sweetmeats and prepared the children's gifts for Emily.

MRS. MOORE (*Exasperated, yet smiling in spite of herself*) : Nothing of the kind. You were not listening. I'm talking about the *turkey*.

DR. MOORE: Turkey, eh? What turkey?

MRS. MOORE: The Christmas turkey. For tomorrow.

DR. MOORE (*Nodding*) : Ah, yes, of course. I prefer chestnut stuffing, a bit of sage, a hint of garlic — but *just* a hint — and a minimum of spices. I have never fancied a spicy stuffing for roast fowl —

MRS. MOORE (*Advancing, and leaning over the desk*) : Clement, do come out of those dusty old books for once. There will be no dressing at all. There is no turkey.

DR. MOORE (*Half-rising, and in shocked voice, as if the gravity of the situation has finally been borne upon him*) : No turkey! For Christmas! My dear, why ever *not?*

MRS. MOORE: Simply because I've forgotten it — as I've been trying to tell you.

DR. MOORE (*Sinking back into his chair*) : But this is terrible! Something must be done about this!

MRS. MOORE: Exactly.

DR. MOORE: Without a turkey, it would scarcely be Christmas!

MRS. MOORE: I agree.

DR. MOORE: The children would be disappointed —

MRS. MOORE: And you, too, Clement. You are very fond of turkey.

DR. MOORE: I am, indeed. (*Thoughtfully*) Well, how can we solve the problem?

MRS. MOORE: Actually, there *is* no problem.

DR. MOORE: Eh? What do you mean?

MRS. MOORE: I mean, you must go to the market and purchase a turkey.

DR. MOORE (*Frowning*) : At this hour?

MRS. MOORE: The shops will not have closed.

DR. MOORE (*Shuffling the papers on his desk*) : If I were not so — so occupied —

MRS. MOORE: But you will have to put your writing aside, anyway, tonight, won't you?

DR. MOORE: Yes, I daresay. But —

MRS. MOORE: Get your coat and your hat, Clement. And do hurry.

DR. MOORE (*Obviously reluctant*): It is quite cold, snowing —

MRS. MOORE: But you never mind a little snow.

DR. MOORE (*Gazing at the fire, and seeming to have an inspiration*): I would go, and gladly. But I've lost my *shoes.* (*He stretches forth his feet, on which are felt slippers.*) See, wife? (*Gently, yet with a note of triumph*) You would scarcely expect me to venture outdoors in *these?*

MRS. MOORE (*Laughing at him*): Oh, Clement, Clement, you are only making excuses. You haven't lost your shoes. Where are they?

DR. MOORE (*Solemnly*): I have no idea.

MRS. MOORE (*Circling his chair, and bending down*): I have! They are here. Just where you took them off. Just where you take them off every evening when you come home from your classes. (*She holds up the shoes.*)

DR. MOORE (*Shaking his head*): Astonishing! (*He sighs, and gets to his feet.*) Well, I suppose — (*He reaches for the shoes, steps out of the slippers and puts on the shoes. He is smiling ruefully.*) I have never before bought a turkey, you know.

MRS. MOORE: High time you had the experience! (*She runs out door at left, returning with* DR. MOORE'S *overcoat and black stovepipe hat.*) Here you are! And I advise you to wear your muffler. (*She produces black woolen muffler from pocket of coat.*) And your gloves, Clement. (*She helps him don all these wraps, tying the muffler over the hat and knotting it under his chin.*) Now you will be snug. (*She pats him on the back and gives him a little push toward the door in rear wall.*)

DR. MOORE (*Pausing, and looking at her and then at his desk*): I hope no one from the Seminary spies me. None of my students. They might think it comical. Dr. Moore, professor of Hebrew and classical languages at the General Theological Seminary — and strolling about on Christmas Eve with a plucked turkey on his shoulder!

MRS. MOORE: Nonsense!

DR. MOORE: I doubt if my father would have consented to such an indignity. He was a gentleman and a scholar, the Protestant Episcopal bishop of New York.

MRS. MOORE (*Edging him toward the door*): Yes, yes, I know.

DR. MOORE: My father officiated at the inauguration of President George Washington and at the death of Alexander Hamilton.

He had a position to maintain, and he always maintained it.

MRS. MOORE (*Impatiently*): Clement, you hesitate because you are merely lazy. Let us just forget about the turkey. Have off your things; go back to your books. There is some salt cod in the house. I shall cook that for our dinner tomorrow.

DR. MOORE (*Horrified*): Salt cod!

MRS. MOORE: And very good, too. I like salt cod. So wholesome.

DR. MOORE (*Shuddering*): My dear! (*He bustles out, slamming door behind him.* MRS. MOORE *smiles, shrugs, hums softly to herself as she straightens a chair or two and then exits through left door. Stage is empty only a moment, then a* SMALL BOY *enters through rear door. He carries a covered basket. He moves to center stage, whistles once, mysteriously. Immediately a* SECOND SMALL BOY *and a* LITTLE GIRL *appear on threshold of left door.*)

GIRL: Oh, Bud, did you get it? (*She closes door furtively.*)

FIRST BOY: No need to be so careful. I passed Father on the street. But he didn't recognize me in the darkness.

GIRL (*Crossing to basket, lifting lid and peering in*): What a sweet, cunning one!

SECOND BOY: Here, let me look. (*He peers into basket.*) Yes, it's just right. Who gave it to you, Bud?

FIRST BOY: Mrs. De Paul.

GIRL: As usual!

SECOND BOY: What did you tell Mrs. De Paul?

FIRST BOY: That we wanted a fine Christmas present for Father.

GIRL: As usual! And what did she say?

FIRST BOY: She laughed and said she didn't think Father *could* be so very surprised.

GIRL: Because you have the same present for him every Christmas!

SECOND BOY: Oh, not *every* Christmas.

GIRL: Every Christmas for the last three years.

SECOND BOY: Well, Father always *is* surprised, though.

GIRL: Perhaps he only acts surprised.

FIRST BOY (*Crestfallen and indignant*): What's the matter? Are you sorry we planned on this? Is it all a mistake? Shall I take the present back to Mrs. De Paul?

SECOND BOY: No, no! Why, what else could we get *now?*

FIRST BOY: But if it isn't a surprise —

GIRL (*Less critically, and smiling down into the basket*): Well, I suppose we mustn't bother. And it *is* so sweet! But — (*Slowly*) —next year we'll begin very early, and we'll plan something quite different and original.

FIRST BOY: Sh — sh! Who's coming? Father? (*He snatches up basket, clamps on lid and hastens through left door, reëntering almost instantly, as someone knocks on rear door.*) No, it isn't Father. (*He flings open door.*) It's —

THE CHILDREN (*In a joyful chorus*): Cousin Emily!

EMILY (*Entering*): So it is. (*She is attractive. Her arms are laden with packages.*) Merry Christmas, my darlings!

SECOND BOY: I'll call Mother. (*Scampering to left door, he shouts*): Mother! Cousin Emily's here.

FIRST BOY (*Politely*): May I relieve you of your burden?

EMILY (*Chuckling*): Thank you, no. My trinkets I shall stow away, myself. They're secrets.

MRS. MOORE (*Entering and embracing* EMILY): Dear Emily! Now we shall have the best of holidays.

EMILY (*As* FIRST BOY *assists her with her wraps*): A charming welcome!

MRS. MOORE: Children, what's in that basket in the hall?

FIRST BOY: Father's surprise. It's — (*He whispers in* EMILY'S *ear.*)

EMILY: What, again? Mrs. De Paul must have an endless supply. I'd think your yard would be swarming by this time!

FIRST BOY: No, we keep them only until they grow large. Then we take them out to the farm.

EMILY: And at the farm you're starting a colony, are you?

SECOND BOY (*Anxiously*): Cousin Emily, we're rather afraid Father won't be surprised.

EMILY: Oh, certainly he will be! Delighted also. But where is your father?

MRS. MOORE: At the market.

EMILY: Dr. Moore, the distinguished professor, at market?

MRS. MOORE: He hated to go, but I insisted. And he should be returning any minute. (*Laughing, she glances out window.*) Yes, here he is! (*Enter* DR. MOORE, *his hat powdered with snow, a turkey over his shoulder. There is a general buzz of greetings.*)

DR. MOORE (*Shaking hands with* EMILY): Emily, behold in me a much abused man.

EMILY: Doing the family marketing?

DR. MOORE: I had to. (*Muttering*) Salt cod!

MRS. MOORE (*Inspecting turkey*): I must say you did well, Clement. A beautiful bird!

FIRST BOY (*Gesturing to his brother and sister*): Shall we?

GIRL: Yes. Father, we have a gift for you. If you and Mother and Cousin Emily will sit down — (*She rushes offstage, comes back with basket, which she deposits in front of* DR. MOORE.)

DR. MOORE: For me? Well, how nice! (*He stoops.*)

GIRL: Wait, though! Father, do you suspect what's in the basket?

DR. MOORE: No. I can't imagine. Fruit? Candies? A holly wreath? (*He taps his forehead, as if in deep thought.*) But I seem to catch a tiny, scratching sound! Can it be something alive?

SECOND BOY (*Excitedly*): Yes! Alive!

DR. MOORE: Can it be — (*He removes lid.*) Well, *well!* A black kitten! Of all the splendid Christmas tokens! *Just* what I've been wishing for!

SECOND BOY: Honestly, Father?

FIRST BOY: We chose a black one, to match your clothes, sir.

GIRL: We gave you one last year, you know. And for several years.

DR. MOORE: The very reason I didn't anticipate receiving one this year.

SECOND BOY: There, do you see! He *is* surprised! (*Still anxiously*) You haven't got tired of black kittens, Father?

DR. MOORE: I *never* get tired of them! (*He sets the kitten on his lap, and strokes it.*)

GIRL: Just the same, *next* year — (*She nods wisely to herself.*)

EMILY: That looks like a superior kitten. May I have a closer acquaintance? (*She takes the kitten from* DR. MOORE, *who rises, fumbles in pocket of his coat, and crosses to his desk.*)

DR. MOORE: And now I have a trifling surprise for you children.

FIRST BOY: Not our presents, sir? We don't get them until tomorrow morning. (*The children all lift eager faces.*)

DR. MOORE: No. This is a little something. (*He pauses, as if embarrassed.*) Well, I wrote something for you.

SECOND BOY (*Flatly*): Oh! Like — the books you're always writing?

DR. MOORE: Not exactly, no. (*He sits, and spreads before him a crumpled bit of paper.*) Verses. Rhymes.

MRS. MOORE (*Amazed*): Rhymes? Why, Clement!

DR. MOORE: I know it's a most extraordinary thing for me to do. But as I was walking along the streets, as I stood in the market — somehow, rhymes suggested themselves to me. About Christmas. So I jotted them down. I haven't yet finished. Would you care to — to —

MRS. MOORE: Oh, do read them, Clement.

DR. MOORE:

" 'Twas the night before Christmas, when all through the house
Not a creature was stirring, not even a mouse;"

(*Beginning timidly, he gains assurance, reading first ten lines of "A Visit from St. Nicholas."*)

GIRL (*Interrupting enthusiastically*): But, father, this isn't a bit like the things you write! It's — it's good!

MRS. MOORE: Extremely good, Clement!

DR. MOORE (*Beaming over his spectacles*): Oh, it's nothing, really.

EMILY: Nothing? A poem! I shall want a copy, Clement.

DR. MOORE (*Alarmed*): No, no! I should be distressed if anyone ever knew I was so — so foolish. (*He has picked up his pen and is writing rapidly.*) It just spins out in the strangest manner! Well, shall I continue reading?

CHORUS: Yes! Yes, do read!

DR. MOORE:

"Away to the window I flew like a flash,
Tore open the shutters and threw up the sash..."

(*As he reads, the lights dim and the curtain falls.*)

* * *

SCENE 2

TIME: *Evening, December 24, 1823.*

SETTING: *The library, as it was in previous scene, except for minor changes which show the passage of a year's time.*

AT RISE: DR. MOORE *is seated in armchair before the fireplace, has slippered feet on footstool. He is reading a newspaper.* MRS. MOORE *sits in another chair, a large bowl in her lap, the con-*

tents of which she stirs with a pewter spoon. Occasionally, and rather apprehensively, she looks at DR. MOORE.

DR. MOORE: Where are the children, my dear?

MRS. MOORE: Upstairs. Very busy with their Christmas tasks.

DR. MOORE: I daresay I shall have the customary offering of a black kitten from Mrs. De Paul's never-failing cattery?

MRS. MOORE: Probably. The youngsters give you kittens because they themselves fairly dote on kittens.

DR. MOORE (*Smiling*): Well, that's an excellent rule for the selection of gifts. And is Emily coming?

MRS. MOORE: I — I think she is.

DR. MOORE: Good! There is never much alteration in our scheme of life, from season to season, is there? I prefer it so. Peace, serenity, nothing to upset routine. And this year the turkey was bought on schedule, and I'll not be forced to parade with it in the public streets.

MRS. MOORE: I'm mixing the stuffing according to your taste.

DR. MOORE: Ah! (*He beams, and resumes his scanning of the newspaper. Suddenly he rattles the pages, stares incredulously.*) Do my eyes deceive me? No! It is! It really is! That ridiculous poem of mine, those silly whimsical verses I wrote last Christmas! About St. Nick! That drivel — it's printed here, in the *Troy Sentinel,* in type, where everybody can see! (*He kicks over the footstool and rises, clutching the newspaper. Much agitated, he paces around the room.*) Oh, this is terrible! A disgrace! And who can have done it? Well, why don't you say something? (*He stops.*) You did it! You sent my verses to the *Sentinel!*

MRS. MOORE: No! No, I didn't!

DR. MOORE: But who else — (*Pausing*) — Emily! Emily, of course!

MRS. MOORE: Clement, I am so sorry —

DR. MOORE: Your Cousin Emily! Knowing how I felt, my own poor opinion of them, Emily deliberately sent them to the paper!

MRS. MOORE: No, Clement. Please be calm. It wasn't like that. Not quite. Emily did make a copy of your poem; she read it to a few friends, and they repeated it to a few of their friends; and soon she had a request from the editor of the *Sentinel* for permission to print it —

DR. MOORE (*Furiously*): A request which she complied with! (*As* MRS. MOORE *nods sadly*) Emily is a meddling woman!

MRS. MOORE: She did not intend to annoy you, Clement.

DR. MOORE: Annoy? She has ruined me! (*He paces, muttering.*)

MRS. MOORE: Oh, no! In her letter last month, Emily told me —

DR. MOORE: So you knew it would be in the paper?

MRS. MOORE: Well, yes, I knew. But I — I hoped you wouldn't notice.

DR. MOORE: Indeed? Everybody will notice. Hundreds of people, thousands. And they will all think that Clement Moore, professor at the Theological Seminary, has turned imbecile!

MRS. MOORE (*Rising, speaking decisively*): I am rather sure they'll not think that. Instead, they'll read the verses with interest and admiration. You should not be ashamed of the poem, Clement. You should be proud. It is lovely, a picture in words. Perhaps it will be reprinted — often. Perhaps it will be read ten years from now — twenty years. You've witten all these books. (*She gestures toward the desk.*) Possibly not one of them will live so long or be so popular as the little poem you dashed off just for our children.

DR. MOORE: I can't believe that! (*Pausing in his pacing, he looks at her.*) Are you — are you *weeping?*

MRS. MOORE (*Dabbing at her eyes*): Only — only a bit. Forgive me.

DR. MOORE: But you mustn't weep at all! Why should you?

MRS. MOORE: Well, our Christmas is — is spoiled —

DR. MOORE (*Remorsefully*): My dear! How badly I'm behaving! (*He goes quickly to her and takes her hand.*) I'm the one to apologize, and I do. (*Slowly.*) The printing, against my wishes, of the poem is merely a minor incident; I have exaggerated its importance. What matters is that we, under this roof, shall be happy together on Christmas Eve.

MRS. MOORE: Oh, Clement, —

DR. MOORE: Dry your tears, my dear. (*As she obeys, he is looking into the bowl which is on the desk.*) Is there spice in the stuffing? Not too much, I trust.

MRS. MOORE: Won't you sample it?

DR. MOORE (*Glad that her attention has been distracted*): Yes, I will. (*He dips the pewter spoon into the bowl and nibbles.*) Umm! Delicate and delicious! (*They are smiling at each other as the rear door opens, and* EMILY *enters.*) Ah, good evening, Emily!

EMILY (*After embracing* MRS. MOORE *and walking shyly toward* DR. MOORE): Are you angry with me, Clement?

DR. MOORE: No. No, I have been somewhat startled, I admit. But not angry. (*He glances at* MRS. MOORE.) Would you say that I displayed anger?

MRS. MOORE (*Stoutly*): Certainly not! (*As she helps* EMILY *off with her wraps, voices are heard offstage, and the* THREE CHILDREN *troop in, left door. They are carrying a covered basket which they deposit at* DR. MOORE'S *feet.*)

CHILDREN: Surprise! Surprise for Father!

MRS. MOORE: But you haven't greeted Cousin Emily, children.

CHILDREN (*In chorus*): How do you do, Cousin Emily! Surprise for Father —

DR. MOORE: Well, well, what can this be? (*Gazing at the basket.*) Candies? Fruit? A holly wreath?

CHILDREN: No, no!

DR. MOORE: Not a black kitten?

FIRST BOY: No, sir!

GIRL: We said it would be a different present this year. It is!

SECOND BOY (*Dancing about with excitement*): Different! Very different. Oh, you never could guess!

DR. MOORE (*In an aside to* MRS. MOORE): If it isn't a black kitten, then I'm truly mystified. (*He stoops.*) But surely I catch a tiny, scratching sound. Something alive?

SECOND BOY: Yes, alive!

DR. MOORE (*Lifting basket cover*): 'Pon my soul! A *white* kitten!

CHILDREN: Surprise, surprise!

GIRL: Would you ever have guessed?

DR. MOORE: Never, never. And I've been wishing for a white kitten.

GIRL (*As* CHILDREN *demonstrate elation at their success*): Father, do you remember the poem you read to us last Christmas Eve?

DR. MOORE: Yes, I remember.

GIRL: Such a nice poem. Read it again tonight.

FIRST BOY: But he said it was a "trifle," and maybe he doesn't have the poem any more.

DR. MOORE: As it happens, I've been providentially supplied with a copy of that poem. (*He glances at* EMILY, *who smiles.*)

GIRL: Then you *will* read it, Father?

MRS. MOORE: You get into your nightgowns, children. Father will read to all of us before the fire. (*Exit* CHILDREN *and* MRS. MOORE.)

DR. MOORE (*Wandering to the window.*): A beautiful night, Emily. The snow is like a thick, soft veil over the world.

EMILY: Yes. My dear Clement, you see how it's going to be with that poem of yours, don't you? Everyone who encounters it will remember it. *A Visit from St. Nicholas* will make you famous

DR. MOORE: Oh, no! The rhymes have no literary merit.

EMILY: But they have such appeal!

DR. MOORE: They seemed just to come to me — out of the air.

EMILY: I think I recognize your St. Nick, though. Isn't he Van Kroyt, the butcher here in Chelsea?

DR. MOORE: Perhaps. I bought the turkey in Van Kroyt's shop. I was watching him. (*Looking thoughtful*) "His eyes—how they twinkled! his dimples, how merry!"

EMILY (*Also quoting*): "His cheeks were like roses, his nose like a cherry!" Yes, that's Mr. Van Kroyt. But what prompted you to invent the reindeer?

DR. MOORE: Reindeer? I suppose I *did* invent them.

EMILY: Of course, you did. No one ever before described St. Nick's mode of travel. "Now, Dasher! now, Dancer! now, Prancer and Vixen!"

DR. MOORE: "On, Comet! on, Cupid! on, Donner and Blitzen!" (*He sighs.*) Well, as I've told you, Emily, the circumstances of my composing the poem were odd, to say the least. I can't explain it.

EMILY: Perhaps inspiration can never be explained, Clement. (*Door opens;* MRS. MOORE *enters with* CHILDREN.)

GIRL: Here we are, Father! (*All settle down around the hearth.* DR. MOORE *takes up newspaper and begins to read.*)

DR. MOORE:

" 'Twas the night before Christmas, when all through the house
Not a creature was stirring, not even a mouse —"

(*He continues; lights dim and curtain slowly falls.*)

THE END

NO ROOM AT THE INN

by Emma L. Patterson

Characters

THE INNKEEPER
TWO TRAVELERS (*Men*)
THE BOY, *servant to innkeeper, about ten years old*
JOSEPH
MARY
FOUR SHEPHERDS
SERVANT TO BALTHAZAR
BALTHAZAR, *a young man* }
MELCHIOR, *a middle-aged man* } *the Three Wise Men*
CASPAR, *an old man* }
SERVANTS *and* GUESTS *at the Inn*

TIME: *Eve and early morning of the first Christmas.*

PLACE: *The inn yard at Bethlehem.*

SCENE 1

SETTING: *A section of the inn yard.*

AT RISE: *It is late afternoon. There is a red cast in the sky more intensified at left. People entering the courtyard from the highway are framed in a red glow. Throughout the scene there is activity — servants coming from the inn with pitchers or jars to draw water from the well, people walking between the stable and the inn. If the stage is shallow, this activity should be omitted in order not to cause confusion. The* INNKEEPER *is seated on the bench beside the door.* TWO TRAVELERS *enter through left gate. The* INNKEEPER *rises and advances toward them. They meet at center.*

FIRST TRAVELER: Are you the keeper of this inn?

INNKEEPER: I am, sirs. How may I serve you?

SECOND TRAVELER: We wish lodging for the night.

INNKEEPER (*Rubbing his hands*): How many are there of your party?

FIRST TRAVELER: We are traveling alone.

INNKEEPER (*Hesitantly*): Oh, I see. And you left your pack animals outside?

FIRST TRAVELER: We have no pack animals, no baggage.

SECOND TRAVELER: The very simplest accommodations will do for us. We are not wealthy.

INNKEEPER: Gentlemen, I am sorry, but I haven't a bed left. People have been pouring into town all day, registering to be taxed, you know.

SECOND TRAVELER: Yes, that is what brings us. We have come quite a distance.

INNKEEPER: Yes? Well, you will have to try somewhere else for lodging.

FIRST TRAVELER: Is there another inn here in Bethlehem?

INNKEEPER (*Walks back to bench*): No, but you will doubtless find some place. Perhaps you have acquaintances who live here.

SECOND TRAVELER: No, we are strangers.

INNKEEPER: Oh, too bad. (*Sits on bench.*) Well, good evening, gentlemen, and good luck to you in finding a place. (THE TRAVELERS *hesitate an instant, then turn and go out by left gate.* INNKEEPER *claps his hands and calls*) Boy, where are you? Come here, boy. (BOY *enters at center gate.*)

BOY: Yes, master?

INNKEEPER: Come here, you lazy oaf. Why do you loiter in the stables when there is so much work to do?

BOY: Why, master, you told me to feed the horse of the guest who just arrived.

INNKEEPER: Umph! You took too long about it.

BOY: I am finished now, master. What shall I do next?

INNKEEPER: Go stand outside the entrance gate. If any wayfarers come past and wish to enter, tell them there is no more room in the inn.

BOY: But, master, have you forgotten? There is still a room vacant, a fine large one, the best in the house.

INNKEEPER: Silence, fool! Of course I know that, but I am not so stupid as to rent that to any common traveler for a few farthings when if I but wait an hour some man of wealth is sure to come along and give me a good price for it.

BOY: Yes, master.

INNKEEPER: Go, now. Stand outside the gate and note the travelers carefully. If they come on foot or with only a pack mule, tell them there is no room. But if you see a man on horseback with a retinue of servants, send for me at once. We will have room for him!

BOY: Yes, master.

INNKEEPER: There! Someone approaches now, a couple of peasants. See, he is lifting her down from the donkey. Go and meet them. Tell them there is no room. (THE BOY *runs off stage left. The* INNKEEPER *sits on the bench beside the door, folding his hands on his stomach.* JOSEPH *and* MARY *enter left. She is leaning heavily upon his arm.* THE BOY *runs in after them and circling around in front of them, bars the way so that they are forced to halt.*)

BOY: I tell you, sir, it is no use to come in here. There is no room. (JOSEPH *leads* MARY *to the well-curb and she sits down, leaning back wearily.* THE BOY *crosses to right.*) I told them what you said, master, but they would come in. The lady is very tired.

INNKEEPER: Humph! Lady, is it? Woman is good enough for her. Just a peasant woman. (JOSEPH *crosses to right and stands before* INNKEEPER.)

JOSEPH: Is there not some small place somewhere that you could give us for the night? My wife is too exhausted to go further.

INNKEEPER (*With an extravagant show of patience*): The boy told you there was no room. Why, then, must you persist in intruding? Do you expect *me* to move out and sleep in the mire of this courtyard in order to give you a place? Move on, now, and don't annoy me further. (JOSEPH *turns away reluctantly.*)

BOY (*To* INNKEEPER): There is a vacant cattle stall. Perhaps we could —

INNKEEPER: Be quiet boy. We will need that for the horses of the late-comers.

JOSEPH: But you have no room for late-comers. So you have said.

BOY: Horses can be picketed anywhere, master.

INNKEEPER: But these people would not wish to be lodged with the beasts.

JOSEPH: Indeed we would be very glad even of such a place.

BOY: I will put down some fresh sweet hay for a bed.

INNKEEPER (*Reluctantly*): Very well. The price will be the same as for the stabling of a beast — of two beasts.

BOY (*Capering toward the exit*): This way, sir. I will make it ready for you. (JOSEPH *goes to the well-curb and helps* MARY *up. Exeunt* BOY, MARY *and* JOSEPH.)

INNKEEPER: See that you get back here promptly. I am going in to my supper. (*Exit* INNKEEPER *right.*)

CURTAIN

* * *

SCENE 2

TIME: *Six hours later. It is after midnight.*

AT RISE: *The* INNKEEPER *is seated on the bench.* THE BOY *enters at rear.*

BOY: Oh, master, the most wonderful thing has happened. A baby has been born, a little boy.

INNKEEPER: A baby born! Where?

BOY: In the stable.

INNKEEPER: Umph! A wonderful thing indeed. One more added to the already too numerous population of the poor and ignorant.

BOY: But this baby seems different. When I look at him, it makes me feel — well, I can't describe it. You come and see him, master.

INNKEEPER: *I?* I go to look at a peasant child born in my stables? (*He gives a short scornful laugh.*)

BOY: I can stay here in the courtyard and keep watch for travelers.

INNKEEPER: Travelers! There are none abroad tonight. Here it is past midnight and my best room still vacant. In all my life I never had such bad luck at this season.

BOY: Someone may stop even yet. It is a good night for traveling, starlit and mild.

INNKEEPER: Yes, I never knew it to be so light at midnight.

BOY: That one star seems to hang right over the stable. (*Enter* FOUR SHEPHERDS *left. They pause and look about them, then cross to center.*)

INNKEEPER (*Brusquely*): Well, what is your business, shepherds?

FIRST SHEPHERD: Sir, could you tell me? Has there been a child born at this inn tonight?

BOY (*Eagerly*): Yes, there has. A wonderful baby! He is in a manger in our stable. Shall I show you —? (*He runs toward rear exit.*)

INNKEEPER: Stay here, boy. (THE SHEPHERDS *draw together at center and talk among themselves.*)

SECOND SHEPHERD: This must be the place.

THIRD SHEPHERD: It is as they said — lying in a manger.

FOURTH SHEPHERD (*To* INNKEEPER): May we go and see the child?

INNKEEPER: A fine lot of shepherds you are, leaving your sheep in the middle of the night to look at a baby. I manage my business day and night and even so can scarcely make a living.

THIRD SHEPHERD: There are more important things than business.

INNKEEPER: Well, move on. Don't clutter up the courtyard. (*Exeunt* SHEPHERDS.)

BOY: How do you suppose they knew about the baby?

INNKEEPER: They are probably relatives or friends of the couple. It is the same class of people. I don't like to have such common trash making free about the place. It gives people wrong ideas about the sort of guests I keep.

BOY: Why, master, shepherds are very fine people. I know one named —

INNKEEPER: On second thought, perhaps you had better go to the stables and keep an eye on those shepherds. See that they don't hide some lambs under their cloaks on the way out.

BOY: Yes, master! (*He turns and starts toward rear gate. Stops at center and gazes out through left gate.*) Master! Master! There is a camel caravan at the gate. (INNKEEPER *leaps up and starts through left gate.*)

INNKEEPER: Horses too! Arabian horses and servants galore. (*There is the sound of hoofs in the dust and of men calling.*) Ah, my chance has come. Now if I only had three or four vacant rooms. Oh such wealth! Such magnificence!

BOY: They are stopping. Some are dismounting. Shall I go out and greet them?

INNKEEPER: No, I will attend to this. You go into the stables and send those shepherds away. (*Exit* THE BOY. *Enter left* THE SERVANT OF BALTHAZAR. *He stands very erect just inside the gate, bows, then folds his arms.* INNKEEPER *advances and bows.*)

INNKEEPER: A good evening to you, sir. My humble dwelling is at your disposal.

SERVANT (*In a deliberate, expressionless tone as though speaking in a tongue foreign to him.*): Is there a newborn babe in this place?

INNKEEPER: A newborn babe? Why — why — yes, there is — but — it is not — (SERVANT *bows and goes out left.* INNKEEPER *stares after him, puzzled. He paces across the courtyard muttering.*) Newborn babe! What do they want of a newborn babe? There must be some mistake. (*Enter* SERVANT OF BALTHAZAR *left. He takes up his previous stand by the gate. Enter* THE THREE WISE MEN *each bearing a small coffer. They cross to center.* INNKEEPER *bows very low.*)

MELCHIOR: Where is the child?

INNKEEPER (*With many bows indicates rear gate*): This way, my lords. (THE WISE MEN *walk out rear.* SERVANT *crosses and takes up position beside rear gate, arms folded.* INNKEEPER *starts to follow* WISE MEN *but comes face to face with* SERVANT *who has the attitude of standing guard.* INNKEEPER *halts, crosses back to bench, turns and goes back to face* SERVANT.)

INNKEEPER: This child is no person of importance. His parents are ordinary peasants. They came here begging a place to stay only this afternoon. If I had not taken pity on them and allowed them in, the child might have been born right by the roadside. Oh no, your masters must have made a mistake.

SERVANT: My master is a prince of India. The other two are Oriental nobles. Their wisdom is great and infallible. They do not make mistakes.

INNKEEPER: But what do they want of this child?

SERVANT: There is for him a great destiny. They have read it in the stars. They wish to do him homage. They bring him gifts.

INNKEEPER (*Shrugs his shoulders*): All this sounds foolish to me. But then I am not a sage, only a simple businessman —

and speaking of business, these gentlemen will wish to stay overnight here, won't they?

SERVANT: I will ask my master when he returns.

INNKEEPER: But surely they would not think of starting on at this hour. Shall I have beds prepared?

SERVANT: I will ask my master when he returns. (*Enter* THE SHEPHERDS. *They start toward gate at left.*)

INNKEEPER: Well, my men, did you find the child for whom you were searching?

SECOND SHEPHERD: Yes.

INNKEEPER: Is he a very remarkable babe, unusual in any way? (THE SHEPHERDS *look at each other. They speak a few words in an undertone.*)

FIRST SHEPHERD: He appears like any other child.

INNKEEPER (*To* SERVANT): You see? (*To* SHEPHERDS) And why did you wish to see the child? How did you hear about him? (*Again the* SHEPHERDS *confer with each other.*)

THIRD SHEPHERD: While we watched our flocks we were told of it.

INNKEEPER: Ah, by someone who had been here and seen him perhaps?

FOURTH SHEPHERD: Perhaps. (*Exeunt* THE SHEPHERDS *left.*)

INNKEEPER: You see, it is just the ordinary story of a very ordinary birth. It is remarkable how rapidly news gets around among the lower classes. I'm afraid your masters will have to seek further — tomorrow. (*Enter* THE THREE WISE MEN *rear.* SERVANT *approaches* BALTHAZAR *and murmurs something in a foreign tongue.* BALTHAZAR *looks sharply at* THE INNKEEPER.)

BALTHAZAR: Is it true that you have a vacant room in your inn?

INNKEEPER: Yes, my lord, it is at your service, a fine large room. I have held it for you at great expense and inconvenience.

BALTHAZAR: Then why must this family whom we have just left be lodged on a bed of straw in a cattle stall?

INNKEEPER: But — but — my lord, I did not realize — I would have gladly — A boy, one of my servants, took them there. I did not know — (*His stammerings fade off into silence.*)

MELCHIOR: Innkeeper, this night you are host to a king. Your finest room, if hung with the rarest of our tapestries, would have been but a poor setting for his glory. And you entertained him — in a manger. (INNKEEPER *falls to his knees.*)

CASPAR: Friends, your words of reproof are useless and worse than useless. It were better to leave this man in his ignorance. Come, let us journey on. (THE THREE WISE MEN *turn left to depart.*)

INNKEEPER: Masters! Masters! Stay but a few moments and I will even now show homage to this king. I will prepare the room with my own hands and myself lift him from the straw to a bed of down.

CASPAR: Do not disturb the child. All has taken place as it was destined to do since the beginning of time.

INNKEEPER: But a king lying in a stable!

BALTHAZAR: That is of no consequence to him. Yours is the loss, not his. Had you shown kindness to these humble people last evening, you would have been lauded and revered through all the ages to the end of time. You chose otherwise.

INNKEEPER: But, my lords, I have none of your great learning. How was I to recognize royalty in such a guise?

MELCHIOR: It is not a question of learning. The shepherds knew him and so did your little errand boy. Those who have saved room for him in their hearts shall see him and know him. The rest shall go blind to their graves.

BALTHAZAR: You had no room for him in your heart or in your house, no room for anything but yourself, comfort for yourself, money for yourself. Is it not true?

INNKEEPER (*With bowed head*): It is true. My heart is as empty as that vacant room.

CASPAR: Do not despair, innkeeper. You were thoughtless and selfish, but it is not too late for you to do this king a service yet.

INNKEEPER: What is it, my lord? Only tell me and it shall be done.

CASPAR: It is this. Say nothing to anyone of our visit. Help the parents to escape with the child in secrecy from the country. Herod is seeking him to kill him.

MELCHIOR: The shepherds are pledged to silence. If you say nothing, the child is safe.

INNKEEPER: I shall keep silence, my lords.

CASPAR: It is well. Let us depart. (*Exeunt left* THREE WISE MEN *and* SERVANT. INNKEEPER *rises from his knees, goes to bench and sits lost in thought. Enter* THE BOY *from rear.*) Come here, lad. Those Oriental princes who were just here told me about the babe, who he is. I think I should like to see him.

BOY: Oh master, I am so glad! Come, I will show you.

INNKEEPER: Just a minute, son. You started once to tell me how it made you feel to look upon this child, but I would not hear it. Now I am ready to listen.

BOY: Well, master, it is a hard thing to describe. I forget about myself and my heart seems to swell within me. And I feel that the only important thing in life is being friendly and kind.

INNKEEPER: I need that. Yes, I need to see him. But I have no gift to take him.

BOY: You need no gift, master.

INNKEEPER: But those eastern princes carried in rich coffers.

BOY: Yes, and, master, one box was heaped with gleaming gold.

INNKEEPER: But out of their great wealth those gifts were nothing. Their real service to him was in finding him and in recognizing him as king.

BOY: That is true, and we can do that also.

INNKEEPER: It will be easier for you than for me. All my life I have assumed that kings could be recognized by their fine raiment.

BOY: I will help you, master.

INNKEEPER: Good! With your help I shall succeed. And my gift will be the empty room, the room that was too good for a king.

BOY: How do you mean, master?

INNKEEPER: I shall never rent that room again. Hereafter it will be free each night to the one who needs it most.

BOY: He will like that gift the best of any you could make.

INNKEEPER: Come, lad. Morning will soon break. Lead me to the king. (INNKEEPER *rises and takes the hand of* THE BOY *who leads him to rear gate.*)

THE END

CHRISTMAS HOUSE

by Helen E. Waite and Elbert M. Hoppenstedt

Characters

MARGERY, *a girl about 14*
CLIFFORD, *her brother, her senior by a year or two*
MRS. MARSTENS, *their mother*
MARY, TOM, NANCY, ALICE, MARTIN — *school friends of* CLIFFORD'S
HENRY DU BOIS, *a visitor to Christmas House*
KAY, *his daughter, and* MARGERY'S *school friend*

TIME: *Christmas Eve. The present.*

SETTING: *The Marstens living room.*

AT RISE: CLIFFORD *is busy with a partially decorated Christmas tree, and* MARGERY *is seated on the arm of an easy chair, swinging one foot and pretending to read a magazine, but taking side-glances at her brother, who carefully keeps his back toward her as he lifts ornaments from box on nearby table. He is whistling. After a minute, during which she increases the tempo of her foot-swinging,* MARGERY *speaks with sarcasm.*

MARGERY: What a truly charming picture you and the tree do make! To see you take up each piece so tenderly—(*She makes a mincing little gesture her brother does not see.*)

CLIFFORD (*With a grunt*): Well, you can't treat a Christmas tree ornament the way you would a football.

MARGERY (*In mock surprise*): Oh, *do* you know how to treat a football? Do boys in this funny two-by-four town actually know about football? (CLIFFORD *wisely maintains silence, although he involuntarily squares his shoulders, and his head gives a quick jerk.* MARGERY *laughs annoyingly and continues with irritating lightness*) But it *is* so delightful to watch you— every bit of tinsel adjusted with care, every ball hung with love —

CLIFFORD: Someone has to do it. Mother's much too busy, and I haven't noticed *you* bothering to hang up love anywhere —

MARGERY (*Airily*): Not my line. Mrs. Simmons, the housekeeper, always did that.

CLIFFORD: Nice household Cousin Janice must have had, if the housekeeper was the only person who dealt out love. That explains several things about you. (*He has finished the tree and now turns on tree lights.*)

MARGERY (*Springing up and stamping her foot*): Clifford Marstens, you know perfectly well I only meant that Mrs. Simmons was the person who decorated our Christmas trees! Cousin Janice was the dearest, sweetest person! *Everybody* was always *happy* in her house — we didn't even hear anything sad or horrid — (*She suddenly chokes and dabs at her eyes.*) I wish — I just wish —

CLIFFORD (*Extending hand*): Shake. So do I.

MARGERY (*Stiffening*): Oh, indeed! And just what do *you* wish?

CLIFFORD: If Cousin Janice was the "dearest, sweetest" person, and she had a habit of making everybody happy. I wish she had bequeathed a little of her disposition to you! (*Slowly and seriously*) Look here, Marge! I know everything about this place *must* be queer and different after the way you lived with Cousin Janice! This house must be funny and old-fashioned and shabby when you remember her grand city apartment; and I know you think Heddonville is in the backwoods, but it really isn't! And believe it or not, there are lots of nice people here, even though they don't own private yachts and have winter homes in California, and look down their noses at the rest of the world! I know we do everything different from the way you've done it most of your life! But now that you've come back to live with Mums and me, can't you be a sport, and try to like us?

MARGERY (*Wrinkling her nose and speaking scornfully*): "Mums"! Whenever you say that it always reminds me of peppermint candy.

CLIFFORD (*Clenching his hands*): I asked if you couldn't be a sport?

MARGERY: Is there any good reason why I should be?

CLIFFORD: To make it easier for Mum... for Mother, for one thing.

MARGERY (*Tossing head*): You'll have to find a better reason than that, my dear brother! My mother gave me away when I was a year old. And I thank her for it. She gave me to a person who could teach me to appreciate *nice* things, and *nice* society. Cousin Janice taught me to be a lady —

CLIFFORD: Maybe she did, but if so, it didn't take!

MARGERY (*Her voice trembling*): And now, because dear Cousin Janice is dead, I must come back to live with my mother and brother, who know absolutely *nothing* of the *sensitive* side of life, and who live in a run-down old cubby-hole of a place called Christmas House in a back-of-nowhere country town, and my mother — well, I find my mother *takes in tourists!* (*Utter scorn shows in her voice.*) Tourists! Oh! If any of my friends at Highwood School ever discovered *that*—why, I'd freeze stiff and die of shame!

CLIFFORD (*Hotly*): You should be proud of Mums instead of talking like that. All the time Cousin Janice was turning you into an insufferable spoiled brat, Mums was going over some pretty rough sledding. But she's been gritting her teeth and working, and building up a reputation for courage and friendship. Christmas House isn't anything to look down your nose at. You'd better stick out your chest and be *proud* of it! Some pretty fine people have stayed here, let me tell you, Marge. The Governor of the State, and the Dean of Vassar —

MARGERY: You will admit, I suppose, that celebrities do not drop in every day? And meantime, I'm supposed to associate with country rustics. Why Cousin Janice didn't leave me the money to stay on at Highwood School I just don't see.

CLIFFORD: I wish she had, for Pete's sake!

MARGERY (*Stamping foot*): If *you* are a sample of boys here—! You haven't one shred of sympathy with my plight! You are the most unfeeling... (*She is interrupted by the sound of a bell.*) That's the President of the United States coming to spend Christmas with us, I suppose? (*Sounds of gay voices and laughter off-stage, then, before she is seen,* MRS. MARSTENS *is heard saying: "They're in here, I think. Yes, come right on in!" She leads in a group of boys and girls clad in heavy wraps.)*

MRS. MARSTENS (*To* MARGERY *and* CLIFFORD): Yes, I imagined you would have finished with the tree. Just in time, too. (*To group*) Girls and boys, have you all met my daughter, Margery? Margery, here are some of Heddonville's nicest young people. (*There is a chorus of "Hello's" and "How-dee-do's," to which* MARGERY *responds with a cool inclination of her head, and a rather stilted "Good evening."*)

TOM: We stopped in to take you carolling with us.

NANCY: We've been looking forward to knowing you ever since we heard you were coming to live at Christmas House!

ALICE: If your voice is anything like Cliff's, you'll be a grand asset tonight!

MARTIN: Hey! Stop talking and let 'em get into their things!

MARY: Better make it your wooliest, Margery — going out tonight is like joining a Byrd expedition!

CLIFFORD: Give us three minutes and we'll be with you — (*He starts toward door when* MARGERY'S *cool voice stops him.*)

MARGERY: Only bring woolies for one, Cliff. *I* do not happen to be going. (*There is a chorus of protest and disappointment.* MARGERY *strolls over to the couch, drops upon it, tilts her head and smiles blandly upon the group.*)

MRS. MARSTENS: Perhaps you haven't understood, dear. It's a custom here in Heddonville, as it is in many other places, for the young people to go about the town singing carols on Christmas Eve, especially to the sick or shut-in. Sometimes they are invited in, and given cakes or other goodies. And when they have finished their rounds they hold a little Christmas feast at one of the houses.

MARTIN: I'm to have the honor this year. And boy, are the things good to smell! I can't guarantee the taste — my mother wouldn't let me at 'em.

ALICE (*Coaxingly*): We do have such fun! Please come!

MARGERY: Thank you. It sounds very quaint, and I suppose you country people do enjoy it, but I'm not interested. (*Group stare at one another first in bewilderment, and then, as comprehension dawns, some look hurt, and others angry.*)

MARY: So — that's how the wind blows!

NANCY (*In a small voice*): Cliff — are — are you coming with us? (CLIFFORD *shakes his head, muttering in the negative.*)

MARGERY: Please don't let me keep you from enjoying yourself. (CLIFFORD *gives her a withering look, but does not speak.*)

TOM: We'd — we'd better get going, I guess. Sorry to have disturbed you, Mrs. Marstens. So long — Cliff! Merry Christmas! (*Others echo "Merry Christmas" rather dejectedly, and trail off-stage.* MRS. MARSTENS *escorts them to door.*)

CLIFFORD: So *that's* what *you* call being a lady?

MARGERY (*Rocking back and forth in glee*): Oh, if the girls at Highwood ever heard that I'd been invited to go carol-singing to the shut-ins, in the hope I'd be invited in and rewarded with cakes, they'd simply shriek themselves sick! (MRS. MARSTENS *has returned and, seating herself, looks at* MARGERY *gravely. Her voice is grave, too.*)

MRS. MARSTENS: I wonder, Margery, if you have any idea how unspeakably rude you were just now?

MARGERY (*Frightened, but defiant*): I don't care —

MRS. MARSTENS: Yes, we realize that. Oh, Margery, when your father died, our affairs were in such a desperate state that I thought I'd have to send you and Cliff to a Children's Home. I was so glad when Cousin Janice came and offered to take you as her own child. I was sure you would have every advantage in her home. Well, perhaps you did, but if so, you didn't use them. You are all sunshine when everything is soft and easy for you, but you have no courage to face new ways, and no intelligence to see friendliness and generosity and worthwhileness in anybody outside your own narrow circle. Because Cousin Janice died and you were forced to leave her lovely home and your fashionable school, you are miserable and angry and hurt, and you haven't learned how to do anything except hurt back. You've hurt Clifford and myself every day for a month. You may have been a delightful girl with Cousin Janice or at Highwood, Margery, but here you certainly are a failure. (MARGERY *straightens and puts out her hand quickly. She stares at her mother in bewilderment.* CLIFFORD, *glancing at the two, starts quietly for the door. His mother stops him.*) I want you to hear this too, Clifford. I had intended to tell you both on Margery's birthday in January, but I've decided to tell you tonight. Margery, Cousin Janice expected you to be unhappy and strange here in Heddonville so she left me the money to provide for your education at Highwood School — in case you really wanted to continue there. But first, *I* wanted you to know what living with your own mother and brother would be like. I had wanted to claim you for so long — I was so sure we'd be happy. (*Sadly*) It hasn't turned out that way. Perhaps it will be best to send you back to Highwood after this Christmas vacation —

MARGERY (*Springing up excitedly*): Mother! You — you mean I *can* go back to Highwood School? I can go back to the city?

MRS. MARSTENS: Yes, if you can honestly say you wish to go — that you want to leave your own family, just when we're together again after thirteen years. Try to think carefully, my dear.

MARGERY (*Hugging mother*): I don't have to think! — I *know.* (*This is a different* MARGERY *from the girl we have seen so far in the scene. This* MARGERY *is all sparkling eagerness and laughter.*) Oh, Cousin Janice was a dear to fix things like that, and you're a dear to let me go! (*She dances joyously about room.*) Oh, I must write Peg and Joyce and Kay that I'm coming — (*Even while she talks she is dancing toward the door. There is a moment of silence after her exit.*)

CLIFFORD: You needn't try to smile, Mums. I know exactly how you feel. Well, I guess that finishes us with Margery — (*Bell peals again, twice.*)

MRS. MARSTENS: Will you answer that for me, Cliff? (CLIFFORD *nods, leaves stage. A moment later we hear his voice saying, "Yes, sir, I'm sure you may. This way, please." Enter* CLIFFORD *with* HENRY DU BOIS *and* KAY. The newcomers are *simply but expensively dressed in out-of-door clothing.*)

CLIFFORD: Mother, this gentleman wishes to know if he and his daughter may spend Christmas with us?

MRS. MARSTENS (*Coming forward*): You will be very welcome.

DU BOIS (*Bowing slightly*): Thank you, Mrs. Marstens. My name is Du Bois — Henry Du Bois. And (*Indicating* KAY) this is my daughter, Kay. It was she who was attracted by the name of your house, and begged to stop here.

MRS. MARSTENS (*Smiling at* KAY) I'm very glad. I hope you will have a joyous Christmas in Christmas House.

KAY: I — I know we will. It makes me feel as if it's the kind of house where wishes came true!

MRS. MARSTENS: Well, I know one person whose wish did come true in Christmas House tonight. Maybe it's a good omen! If you'll come with me I'll show you your rooms.

CURTAIN

* * *

SCENE 2

SETTING: *Same room perhaps an hour later.*

AT RISE: CLIFFORD *is rearranging logs.* MARGERY *enters, full of enthusiasm.*

MARGERY: Cliff, look! I just had the duckiest idea for my letters telling the girls I'm coming back to Highwood! See, it's a sketch of Santa Claus leading me up to the Highwood gate!

CLIFFORD: What a marvelous present for the school!

MARGERY (*Furious*): You certainly do have a talent for making obnoxious remarks!

CLIFFORD (*Guilelessly*): So glad you like them. (*At that moment, unseen by either,* KAY *appears. She hesitates, seems about to withdraw, and then takes a step forward.*)

KAY: May — may I come in? (*The sound of her voice causes both* CLIFFORD *and* MARGERY *to jump.* MARGERY, *who has stood with her back toward the door, wheels about.* KAY *takes another step into the room, and, recognizing each other, the girls give simultaneous cries.*)

MARGERY: Kay Du Bois! But when — why —

KAY: It *is* — it really *is* Margery Marstens! I thought of you when we saw the name Marstens on your sign, but I never dreamed of finding you —

MARGERY (*Wincing*): No, you wouldn't have, would you?

KAY (*Coming over and slipping arm around* MARGERY): You look as though you were in a haze, Marge, and I don't wonder!

But you see Daddy and I decided to have a little Christmas adventure just by ourselves, so we left the city early this morning, and rode and rode. We weren't aiming for a special place, but when I saw this lovely old house, and the name "Christmas House" I begged Daddy to stop. And I'm so glad we did. I've always wished I'd have a chance to see you alone — away from the rest of that silly Highwood crowd, I mean, and see if you weren't a real human being! (*She laughs a little shakily*) Maybe this'll sound queer to you, Marge, but — I always thought you had the makings of a lovely friend! (MARGERY *clutches the sketches tightly against her breast. She tries to speak, but her lips open and shut without a sound.* CLIFFORD *comes to the rescue.*)

CLIFFORD: Won't you sit down, Kay? Was that what Marge called you? (*He pulls easy chair toward the tree.*) I'm Margery's brother, Clifford. She'll recover her breath in a minute or two. It never deserts her for long! Tell me, do you think there are enough lights on this side of the tree?

KAY (*Who has taken the offered chair*): Perhaps — you might move that ball — the one on the second branch from the top — yes, that one (*As* CLIFFORD *touches it*), move it so it catches the light from the red bulb. Oh! It's a lovely tree! I've always wanted to help decorate one. Wasn't it fun? (*She looks questioningly at* MARGERY, *who is uncertain and embarrassed.*)

MARGERY: Why, I — I —

CLIFFORD (*With merciful promptness*): Marge stood by and gave me expert encouragement and advice.

KAY: How could you keep your hands off, Marge? Oh, aren't you the lucky girl? Your cousin's apartment was wonderful, of course, and so was she, but somehow it never seemed like a home! Besides, I don't know how you ever endured being away from your mother and brother!

MARGERY (*Who has settled herself on the couch, speaking hurriedly*): You're a rather lucky girl yourself, Kay: Your father's such a marvelous singer — he's Henry Du Bois, the opera star, Cliff. (CLIFFORD *nods*) And you have those beautiful rooms at the Hotel Viking, and that darling old French governess, and a car of your own —

KAY: Well, I'd give them all up in a minute, just like that— (*She snaps her fingers.*) all except Daddy, of course! — if we could have a tiny house all to ourselves, and stay in one spot!

You *can't* know how horrid it is to be famous, and having reporters spying on you! Oh, the Hotel Viking's well enough, and I'm always glad when Daddy sings for the season at the Belvedere Opera. But I've lived in twenty-six different hotels, and gone to school in twenty-one different places! And I hate cities and hotels anyway. Oh — don't tell Daddy I said that! (*She laughs unsteadily.*) I wouldn't have him different for the world! (MARGERY *stares unbelievingly, but* CLIFFORD *tactfully changes the subject.*)

CLIFFORD: So you like our Christmas House, do you?

KAY: I love it.

MARGERY: How did you happen to find it?

KAY: Christmas in a hotel is horrid. And Daddy's just getting over a cold, so he had no engagements to sing tonight or tomorrow. I coaxed him until he said we'd drive into the country and see if we could find a little place which we could pretend was our home that we were coming back to for Christmas. We started early this morning, and somehow I couldn't find anything that seemed just right. I'm afraid Daddy was beginning to be discouraged when—we found this! I saw the tree through the window, and I simply couldn't resist! (*She pauses, holds her hands out toward tree.*) Maybe you won't believe it, but this is the first Christmas tree I've been close to — in a real home — since I was a little girl!

MARGERY (*Surprised and shocked*): It — *is?*

KAY (*Nodding*): It really is. We've always spent Christmas in hotels, or else with my grandmother. She doesn't believe "in decking one's house like a Roman carnival" just because it's Christmas time. She says the ridiculous way in which most people behave during the Christmas holidays is idiotic.

CLIFFORD: *I* must be hopelessly foolish! (*Enter* MRS. MARSTENS *and* DU BOIS. KAY *springs up and darts to her father.*)

KAY (*Excitedly*): Daddy — Daddy, this is a nicer Christmas adventure than we planned! Guess who I found here? Margery Marstens —

DU BOIS (*Politely*): Margery Marstens —?

KAY: Don't you remember I told you about Marge last month, Daddy? She's the girl I said was so lucky, even though the cousin she lived with had died, because she had a chance to get away from the city and that priggish Highwood School, and come up to the country to her own mother and brother?

DU BOIS (*Heartily*): I *do* remember. Kay and I both envied you, Miss Margery. Congratulations on your escape from that smug city. The best Kay and I can do is to run away over Christmas!

KAY: Daddy — finding Marge and her family like this will make it a special celebration. Couldn't we — couldn't we go up to our rooms and plan some special Christmas surprises?

DU BOIS: I think it might be possible.

MRS. MARSTENS: Oh, no! You mustn't think—

DU BOIS: I've found, Mrs. Marstens, that it's best not to interfere with Kay's surprises. So, if you will excuse us! (DU BOIS *and* KAY *make exit.*)

CLIFFORD (*Looking after them*): Poor kid! Did you ever see anyone so sort of *hungry* for Christmas?

MARGERY (*Chokingly*): And when I think of all good times *I've* had — why, Merry Christmas was something I just took for granted!

CLIFFORD: Here too!

MARGERY: I never dreamed — she was always so gay — the girls all envied her — (*She slowly tears her sketches in four pieces which flutter to the floor.*) I guess she's right about the girls at school, too.

MRS. MARSTENS (*Looking from her son to her daughter in a puzzled way*): My dears, what is it you're talking about?

MARGERY: Kay. She's been cheated out of so many things. Even Christmas trees. Her grandmother doesn't believe in turning her house into a Roman carnival just because it's Christmas!

MRS. MARSTENS: Poor woman.

CLIFFORD: Let's show her what Christmas really can be like — take her into the family — share our things with her —

MARGERY: I'll give her the necklace I had for Moth — for Mums. You won't mind, will you, Mums? I — I think — I have another present for you.

MRS. MARSTENS: Of course I won't mind, dear.

MARGERY (*Falteringly*): This — this other present — it isn't — well, it isn't much good just now, but perhaps — perhaps it will improve. You see, Mums, I'm going to give you — well, I'm going to give you a daughter! A daughter who's going to stick by you and Cliff and Christmas House, and try — try to be a — sport! (*And as she looks up into her mother's face, the curtain falls.*)

THE END

THE CRYSTAL FLASK

by Karin Asbrand

Characters

PRINCESS LILITA
THE KING
THE QUEEN
CARA, *a Lady-in-waiting*
FIRST FAIRY GODMOTHER
SECOND FAIRY GODMOTHER
PRINCE SIGWALD
A NURSE

SETTING: *A room in the Palace*

TIME: *Once Upon a Time.*

AT RISE: *The* KING *and* QUEEN *are seated on their thrones in center of stage. The* NURSE *stands in foreground, holding the* BABY PRINCESS LILITA. *A* FAIRY GODMOTHER *stands on either side of them. There is gay music playing off stage.*

1ST GODMOTHER: It has been a royal christening indeed.

THE KING (*With satisfaction*): Aye, so it has. Tables loaded high with good things to eat and drink so that none should go hungry. And I have hired bands of musicians to play, that all my guests might sing and dance and make merry.

2ND GODMOTHER: For such a beautiful Princess it is none too much.

THE QUEEN: Aye, she is fair to look upon, I grant you.

1ST GODMOTHER (*Takes silver flask from her pocket*): I have a gift to give my godchild. This silver flask. 'Tis filled with laughter. So keep it lightly corked that her laughter may bubble over and stay by her always. (*Hands flask to the* KING.)

THE KING (*Rises as he accepts it, and bows*): In behalf of the little Princess, I thank you

2ND GODMOTHER: I, too, have a gift, this crystal flask. A flask of tears, Lilita's tears which she must some day shed.

THE QUEEN (*In alarm*): Tears? Nay, she must not know the meaning of tears or sadness. We'll keep it tightly corked.

THE KING: Or better still we'll hide the flask where she can never find it.

2ND GODMOTHER (*Sagely*): There is no joy but is better for having known some sadness. But be that as it may. The gift is hers. Do with it as you will. (*She hands flask to the* QUEEN.)

THE QUEEN (*Holds it up and looks at it*): 'Tis beautiful, indeed. and yet, I like it not. We'll hide it. Of that you may be sure.

1ST GODMOTHER (*Bends over to kiss* BABY'S *forehead*): And so farewell, and may your merry laughter ring clear throughout the palace halls for many a long day.

2ND GODMOTHER (*Kisses Baby*): I, too, bid you farewell. Some day you'll find that even tears will bless your day and bring you happiness. (*The two* GODMOTHERS *go out.*)

THE QUEEN (*Crossly*): Even tears will bring her happiness, forsooth. We'll hide this flask of tears upon the highest shelf, and none but you and I shall ever know where it can be found.

THE KING: Quite right, my dear. We'll hide it now before a single tear escapes. (*They rise, and go out together, followed by the* NURSE *with the* BABY.)

CURTAIN

* * *

SCENE 2

SETTING: *The same, sixteen years later.*

AT RISE: *The* NURSE *and* MAID-IN-WAITING *stand in center of stage.*

NURSE (*Yawns*): My time hangs heavy on my hands now that the Princess is grown up.

MAID-IN-WAITING (*Looks around, cautiously*): Where is Lilita now?

NURSE: I left her playing about in the garden.

MAID-IN-WAITING: I am getting very tired of hearing the Princess laugh. It seems to me she does nothing but laugh.

NURSE (*Crossly*): Well, there is nothing we can do about it. It's true she does nothing but laugh. She laughs when she has to go to bed, when she eats, even when she falls and skins her royal knees she laughs. She has always laughed at everybody and everything.

MAID-IN-WAITING: Even in church she laughs, and the Queen has to put the stopper on the silver flask very tightly. People are beginning to think the Princess queer.

NURSE: I wish I knew where they had hidden that crystal flask. I would get it and pull out the stopper. It would be a relief to see the Princess cry for a change. Wouldn't it, Cara?

MAID-IN-WAITING: You would be severely punished, so let her laugh.

NURSE (*Shrugs her shoulders*): Who cares? I love the Princess very much, but her feelings are all bottled up. One needs to cry every once in a while.

MAID-IN-WAITING (*Moves closer to her companion*): If you won't tell anyone, I'll tell you a little secret.

NURSE (*Eagerly*): Of course I won't tell. Tell me, Cara dear.

MAID-IN-WAITING (*Mysteriously*): I know where the crystal flask is hidden.

NURSE (*In great surprise*): You do?

MAID-IN-WAITING: Yes. I do. I was the one who climbed up on the ladder and hid it on the day of the christening. But I would never dare tell anyone. The King said that if I did tell I would have my head chopped off.

NURSE: The King tells that to everyone, but he has never chopped off a head yet.

MAID-IN-WAITING: Hush. Here comes the Princess now. (*Enter right, the* PRINCESS LILITA. *She stands and laughs merrily at the two standing looking at her.*)

NURSE: Well, what is so funny about us? Can you tell us that?

MAID-IN-WAITING (*Looks down at her clothes*): Is my petticoat hanging? Is anything wrong?

PRINCESS: Oh, don't mind me. You know that I'm always laughing. I just can't help myself. Sometimes I wish I could stop, but I never can except when my royal mother puts the stopper on the silver flask very tightly, and then I always feel like a mummy. Then I have no feelings at all. (*Laughs again, so she almost chokes*) Isn't that funny? (*As the other two do not laugh*) No, I suppose it isn't funny, but I've got to laugh just the same. I wish I could find the crystal flask that my other Godmother gave to me. I would be so happy if I could cry just once.

MAID-IN-WAITING (*Goes to her*): I know where the crystal flask is hidden, Princess Lilita. I should know. I hid it.

PRINCESS: And you've kept it from me all these years?

MAID-IN-WAITING (*Shrugs her shoulders*): What else could I do? Your royal father has quite a temper when he is crossed, you know.

PRINCESS: Please tell me where it is. I will reward you well.

MAID-IN-WAITING: You will probably get my head. But I'll tell you because I am getting so tired of hearing you laugh myself. Come, we will get a ladder. You shall have your crystal flask. (*Exeunt* PRINCESS LILITA, MAID-IN-WAITING, *and* NURSE, *right just as the* KING *and* QUEEN *enter left.*)

THE KING (*With a sigh*): For all our care I don't believe our little Lilita is happy.

THE QUEEN (*As they take their places on their thrones*): Why shouldn't she be happy? She never cries.

THE KING: But perhaps a few tears never really hurt anyone, my dear. Perhaps we had better take the crystal flask from its hiding place and give it to her. (*Shakes his head, sadly*) To think she has never shed a tear in all her life.

THE QUEEN (*Brusquely*): And she never shall shed one, if I can help it. (*Enter right,* PRINCESS LILITA, *holding the crystal flask in her hand, and crying into her handkerchief. There is no stopper on the flask. She is closely followed by the* MAID-IN-WAITING *and the* NURSE *who are trying their best to console her, one on either side of her.*)

THE KING (*In alarm*): What has happened? (*Runs down to the* PRINCESS.)

THE QUEEN (*Hurries over to her and takes her in her arms*): What has happened to my precious child? (*Sees the flask*) The crystal flask! Who has done this terrible thing?

MAID-IN-WAITING: She climbed up on the ladder and brought it down herself, but when she was halfway down she took the stopper out and dropped it.

NURSE: And her pet dog, who was playing about below, took it in his mouth and ran with it down the palace corridor into the garden.

MAID-IN-WAITING: And none of us can find it.

PRINCESS (*Who has been constantly wailing*): And now I cannot stop crying.

THE QUEEN (*Puts her hand over the top of bottle, but the* PRINCESS *does not stop crying*): No other stopper will do except the right one.

THE KING: We must find it at once. Post notices all over my kingdom. I'll offer a big reward to anyone who finds the stopper to the crystal flask. (*Darkly*) And as for you, my disobedient wenches, unless the stopper is found within a week, you shall both be severely punished.

PRINCESS (*Still crying*): Don't punish them. Punish me. Then I will have something to cry about.

CURTAIN

* * *

SCENE 3

SETTING: *The same, one week later.*

AT RISE: *The* KING *and* QUEEN *are sitting on their throne, thoughtfully staring into space, their chins resting on their cupped hands.*

THE KING: A whole week has now gone by, and nowhere can the stopper to the crystal flask be found.

THE QUEEN: The Princess will drown in her own tears unless someone can find it, and that right soon.

THE KING: The gardeners have dug up the whole garden, but the dog did not bury it there, for it cannot be found.

THE QUEEN: Ah, lackaday, and woe is me! I who had thought to keep my precious Princess happy all the days of her life, can do nothing for her now.

THE KING: Let him who finds the stopper to the flask ask of me anything his heart desires and I will give it to him. (*Enter* PRINCE SIGWALD.)

PRINCE SIGWALD (*Bowing low before the* KING *and* QUEEN): I am your neighbor, Prince Sigwald, your majesties, come to pay my respects to a good and mighty ruler and his Queen.

THE KING (*Stroking his chin, thoughtfully*): Sigwald! Sigwald! Have I ever met you before, young man?

PRINCE: Aye, when as a lad I came with my parents to the Princess Lilita's christening. (*He takes from a pocket the stopper to the crystal flask.*) Sire, is this mayhap what you have been seeking?

THE QUEEN (*Overjoyed*): It is, indeed. It is the stopper to the crystal flask.

THE KING: Where did you find it, young man?

PRINCE: What matters it, your majesty, where I found it, as long as it is found? But, if you would know, one day when I was riding through your land a week ago, my horse did stumble, and there, beneath his hoof, I found this stopper to the crystal flask.

THE KING (*Claps his hands twice*): I will send for the Princess so that we may check her tears, and bring happiness into her life again. (*Enter right,* MAID-IN-WAITING.)

MAID-IN-WAITING: Didst call for me, your majesty?

THE KING: Aye, that I did. Take the stopper to the crystal flask which this good Prince has found and put it tightly on. Then bring the Princess in to me.

MAID-IN-WAITING (*As the* PRINCE *hands her the stopper*): Aye, that I will, and quickly. (*Hurries out, right*)

THE KING: And now, Prince Sigwald, as to your reward, ask of me what you will. It shall be yours.

PRINCE: I ask no other reward, your Majesty, than the hand of the Princess Lilita in marriage.

THE KING (*Joyfully*): It shall be yours. To join our two great countries has been my fondest dream. (*Enter right,* PRINCESS LILITA.)

PRINCESS (*Curtsies to the* KING *and* QUEEN, *then to the* PRINCE): Didst send for me, your majesty?

THE KING (*Goes down and takes her hand, and lays it in that of the* PRINCE): Prince Sigwald, here is your reward to prove that I am a man of honor, the hand of the Princess Lilita in marriage. (*To* LILITA) My dear, it is a pleasure to see you smile again.

PRINCESS: I feel so light-hearted and gay. And yet I think my tears have washed my troubles all away.

THE QUEEN: And now we must hide that awful flask again where she can never find it.

PRINCE: Nay, give it in my keeping. For there is no joy but what is greater for a tear or two.

THE QUEEN (*Wonderingly*): 'Tis so the fairy godmother said.

PRINCE: Aye, side by side we'll keep the flasks, the silver flask of laughter, and the crystal one of tears. For unless she knows how to weep once in a while, she cannot understand her subjects. And she will understand her subjects better if she can weep with them, if needs must be, and then she'll be a better queen. I'll take good care that her tears be few.

THE KING: Well said, O wise and noble Prince. So may you rule together, wisely and well, for many years.

THE END

Adapted from the story "The Laughing Princess," by the Author.

LITTLE HERO OF HOLLAND

by Karin Asbrand

Characters

HANS, GRETCHEN, HILDA, LUDWIG, JULIANA, JACOB, KATRINKA, CARL, BETJE, PETER — *children of Holland*

JAN, *the burgomaster's son*

FLOWER FAIRIES, *4 Tulips and 4 Hyacinths*

TIPSEY, TOPSEY — *Imps of the Dyke*

SCENE 1

SETTING: *The banks of the Zuyder Zee, Holland.*

AT RISE: HILDA, LUDWIG, JULIANA, JACOB, KATRINKA, CARL, *and* BETJE *come out on the stage, each carrying a pail and scrub brush, singing to the tune of "Ach, du lieber Augustine," doing the step, brush hop in time to the music.*

HILDA:

Holland is a country that everybody likes
Because so many flowers grow beside its fertile dykes,
Because the little children look so very clean and sweet,
Because we scrub inside and out to keep it nice and neat.

JULIANA:

So every morning early when birds begin to sing
We take our little pails in hand and scrub like anything.

We scour the cobblestones and streets; we scrub our houses, too, (*All wink*)
And if you happened very close then maybe we'd scrub you. (*Point brushes at audience.*)

LUDWIG: Well, let's go. Tomorrow is the Sabbath and we must certainly make this place shine.

JACOB (*Cheerfully*): It isn't our job exactly, but if you girls want to go on the picnic with us I suppose we will have to lend a hand. (*They all get down on their knees and make motions of scrubbing.*)

ALL (*Singing to the tune of "East Side, West Side"*):
Scrub, scrub, scrub, scrub,
In the pail or tub.
Now Holland will shine so brightly
As we gaily scrub.
Early in the morning
We'll be on our way
To scrub all the streets and houses
So they'll shine today.

(*After song is finished they jump up and run to left where they leave their pails and brushes. Enter* GRETCHEN *and* HANS, *hand in hand.* GRETCHEN *carries a basket covered with a white napkin.*)

GRETCHEN: Oh, how nice everything looks.

HANS: Yes, even if I had nothing to do with it, it doesn't look bad.

GRETCHEN: I'm glad to see that you boys are working, too, for a change.

LUDWIG: Of course. That is why it looks so good.

GRETCHEN: It's too bad you don't pitch in more often.

JACOB: Why should we? What do we have women for anyway?

KATRINKA: You are lazy like the men already. And we women have to wait on you.

JACOB: But certainly. That is what women were put into the world for, to wait on the men.

CARL: Besides, you have nothing else to do all day.

JULIANA: Not much. Only cleaning and scrubbing and cooking and darning and patching and sewing, *and* tending the peat for the fire, *and* milking the cows, *and* bathing the baby, and a few odd little things like that plus extras thrown in like seeing that you men are comfortable.

KATRINKA (*With a big sigh*): I wish I had been born a boy.

BETJE (*Helpfully*): Maybe when you grow a little bigger you will grow into a boy.

CARL: You are what you are and you'll be what you'll be. I think girls are very nice, especially you, my Betje.

BETJE (*Curtsies to him, demurely*): Oh, thank you. I think you are nice, too, Carl.

LUDWIG: You two think that because Betje has no brothers and Carl has no sisters.

CARL: Ah, but you forget. I have a new baby sister. Didn't you see the little pink cushion hanging on my door?

LUDWIG: Sure, I did. But she isn't old enough to count yet.

HANS: I haven't a sister, but for a cousin Gretchen isn't too bad a girl.

GRETCHEN: That is a compliment coming from you, Hans.

HANS: When she grows up she is going to marry me. Her father has already promised it.

GRETCHEN: And I suppose I will have nothing at all to say. But you are a good scout. I could do worse, I guess. (*Enter* JAN *and* PETER, *their arms filled with tulips.*)

JAN: The boats have come in all loaded with tulips and the market-place is full.

PETER: We are taking these to church for Tulip Sunday.

KATRINKA: What lovely ones! How is your father today, Jan?

JAN: He's better, thank you. But still very angry with that stupid cook.

GRETCHEN: What stupid cook, Jan?

JAN: Oh, haven't you heard? My father got a new cook, an American. He found a pile of my father's tulip bulbs in a basket in the cellar, and cooked and creamed them for onions. His prize tulips they were, too. My father nearly died of apoplexy.

PETER: It was a costly dinner.

JAN: Yes, and most unpalatable, too.

HANS: We must hurry, Gretchen, if I am to get you to Tante Anna's in time for dinner.

HILDA: What's your hurry? Where are you going anyway?

JULIANA: We haven't played all day long. Can't you stop and play a while?

GRETCHEN: Oh, no. My Tante Anna is expecting me. I must bring her this basket of cakes my mother baked for her.

HANS: Yes, let us be on our way to Tante Anna's.

LUDWIG (*To the other children*): And we will go and play on the canal boats.

KATRINKA: Take care you do not run into the Imps of the Dyke, Hans and Gretchen.

HANS: Pooh. Don't frighten Gretchen. Tipsey and Topsey are nothing but myths.

JAN (*Seriously*): Oh, I don't know. I think there are really imps that live along the dykes and cause all the trouble when the dykes break.

JACOB: Ach, such silly fairy tales. You must not believe everything you hear.

LUDWIG: People in fairy tales are quite harmless.

GRETCHEN: I'll run all the way. I am glad I am going to stay all night at my Tante Anna's.

HANS: I am not though. I have to come back all alone. (*Laughs.*) But I am afraid of nothing.

BETJE: Here's for a jolly good time. Let's go. (*Children all join hands, and skip around in a circle.*)

ALL (*Singing to tune of "Solomon Levi"*):

Oh, we are jolly Dutch children and we've plenty of things to do
But we can always spare the time to sing and play for you.
For there is nothing helps so much when things seem to go wrong
As looking at the brightest side and singing a jolly song.
Here is to Holland, tra la la la la la la.
Here is to Holland, tra la la la la la la.
Oh, we are jolly Dutch children, and we've plenty to do all day,
But we can always find time to laugh and sing and play.

(*They all skip out left holding hands, except* HANS *and* GRETCHEN, *who start slowly toward right.*)

GRETCHEN: I wish you were going to stay all night, too, Hans. (*Wistfully*) I shall miss you. Will you miss me a little, too?

HANS: Well, perhaps a little.

GRETCHEN (*As they stop for a moment and look at the dyke*): Look, Peter. The water looks so calm, and yet it can be so dangerous. Can't it?

HANS: Only if the dyke should break, little silly. It would drown the whole town.

GRETCHEN: How awful that would be! But the dyke is really quite safe. Nothing ever happens.

HANS (*Shrugs his shoulders*): Safe enough, I guess. I can't remember anything happening, so I guess nothing will.

GRETCHEN: If anything does, I hope they will remember to take care of my little duck, Tina. She is so small she could never swim away herself.

HANS: Neither could anyone else. The water would gobble her up, and you and me and everybody. The water would be so crazy wild if it ever got away from the dyke.

GRETCHEN (*In an awed voice*): Let's hurry away from it, Hans. I want to get to Tante Anna's quickly.

HANS (*Laughs at her*): You are a little 'fraidy-cat, my Gretchen. You can't ever get away from the dykes as long as you live in Holland. But don't worry. (*Puts a protecting arm around her.*) After all, you are a girl. But I won't let anything happen to you while you are with me.

GRETCHEN: It's funny. I am never afraid of anything when I am with you, Hans. You are so big and strong. I am glad you are my cousin. (HANS *and* GRETCHEN *go out right.*)

CURTAIN

* * *

SCENE 2

SETTING: *The same. That evening.*

AT RISE: HANS *saunters in holding in his hands a toy windmill.*

HANS (*Talks to his windmill*): You will have to keep me company, little windmill, until I reach home. I am glad that my Uncle Benjamin made you for me. (*Stops short and looks at the dyke.*) Oh, my goodness! Oh, MY GOODNESS! What shall we do, little windmill? There is a leak in the dyke. Only a small leak, it is true, but a small leak will soon become a big leak. It is getting late, and perhaps nobody but me will pass this way before morning. (*Sets windmill down on the ground, kneels down and puts his finger into the hole.*) It is just big enough for my finger. I guess we will have to stay here, little windmill, until someone comes or else the hole will get bigger and bigger until the whole dyke breaks down. (*Settles himself into a more comfortable position, and lays his free hand on the windmill.*) Stay by me, little windmill. (*Chimes or bells ring off-stage. Soft music is heard.*) I am getting very sleepy. Is that music we hear, little windmill? Whatever shall I do to keep awake? My hand is quite numb. Pretty soon the whole of me will be numb. I only hope I can keep my finger in the hole in the dyke. (*He sleeps.* FLOWER FAIRIES *waltz in.*)

FLOWER FAIRIES (*Singing to the tune of "Daisy Bell"*):

Flower fairies,
  Here by the Zuyder Zee,
Tend the flowers
  Lovely as they can be.
Oh, there is nothing sweeter,
  That you must all agree,
Than sweet tulips on Holland's ships
  Down by the Zuyder Zee.
Flower season
  When lovely blossoms grow
Is the very nicest
  Time that you'll ever know.
Oh, there is nothing sweeter
  In all the world to see
Than flower time, sweet flower time
  Down by the Zuyder Zee.

HANS (*As he opens his eyes*): You are very pretty. You are the fairies that all the children talk about. Or maybe I am dreaming.

FIRST FLOWER GIRL: Yes, we are only dreams, Hans. But we are staying here to keep you company while you are here holding the dyke. (*Enter* TIPSEY *and* TOPSEY.)

TIPSEY AND TOPSEY (*Step brush hopping to the tune of "Ach, du Lieber Augustine" as they sing*):

Ach, du lieber Hans, now we'll all have some fun, fun, fun,
  For the sun is sinking and this day is done.
You stopped the trickle, but Dutch dykes are fickle,

The Zuyder Zee will break down and drown everyone.
(*They turn cartwheels around the stage.*)

SECOND FLOWER FAIRY: Oh, dear, what did you have to come around for, you old trouble-makers?

THIRD FLOWER FAIRY: Don't worry, Hans. They are only bad dreams. Nightmares, you know.

FOURTH FLOWER FAIRY: We will watch out so they can't hurt you.

FIFTH FLOWER FAIRY: After all, you are only dreaming anyway because your hand and your body are getting numb from the cold water.

SIXTH FLOWER FAIRY: We will try to make your dream as pleasant as we can.

TIPSEY: Ha, ha. You can't as long as we are here. We will do our best to make him miserable. (*Makes a face at* HANS.)

TOPSEY: You bet we will. (*Tickles* HANS.)

SEVENTH FLOWER FAIRY: But why? What have you got against him?

TIPSEY: He is interfering with our fun. We made that hole in the dyke so that it would get bigger and bigger and drown everybody.

TOPSEY: Besides, we like to see people miserable.

HANS: Well, I fooled you. The hole isn't going to get any bigger.

TIPSEY: Pooh. You won't stay there long. We'll see to that. (*Goes to push him, but* FIRST FLOWER FAIRY *gets in his way.*)

TOPSEY: What a silly little boy he is!

HANS: I certainly shall stay here or the whole dyke will give way. When your country is in danger you must do your best to save it.

TIPSEY: You can't save it. The dyke will give way anyhow. (*Shrugs his shoulders.*) Heaps of fun it would be, too.

HANS (*Sighs*): Ouch, my hand hurts; it is so cold.

TOPSEY: Certainly it is cold. You don't think we would warm the water for you, do you?

TIPSEY (*Coaxingly*): Come along now, remove your finger and come and dance and sing with us.

HANS (*Pushes with his free hand*): Go away and leave me alone. Go away, and let me have my nice dreams.

TOPSEY: Don't be silly, Hans. Let the old dyke go. It would be such fun to see the water pouring out over the town.

HANS: What cute ideas of fun you have!

TIPSEY: We have lots of cute little ideas like that.

SECOND FLOWER FAIRY: Leave him alone. You have pestered him enough.

THIRD FLOWER FAIRY: Can't you see how uncomfortable he is?

TOPSEY: Certainly we can. And we mean to make him more uncomfortable.

TIPSEY (*Tries to pull* HANS *away by the leg*): Come on. Try being naughty once, and see what fun it is. There is no fun in being good all the time.

HANS: That's what *you* think. I am often naughty, and I don't think it's fun. You make people you love feel sorry, and you get punished and everything. Oh, dear, why doesn't someone come?

FOURTH FLOWER FAIRY (*Sadly*): I wish we could get help, but we are only dreams. Maybe if one of us could go to some friend of yours —

FIFTH FLOWER FAIRY: That's an idea! (*Claps her hands.*) I'll go. I'll go to little Katrinka in a dream, and tell her to come to you. (*She runs out.*)

TOPSEY (*In alarm*): Hurry, Tipsey. We haven't much time if that meddler succeeds in reaching Katrinka.

SIXTH FLOWER FAIRY (*Severely*): She will. The good fairies succeed. Why don't you both turn over a new leaf and join our ranks instead?

TOPSEY: No, thanks. Somebody has to create mischief. We like to push children off the quays into the water, and to make holes in dykes. And we like to make wars, and make people hate each other, too.

FIRST FLOWER FAIRY: Maybe if we recite some poetry for you the time will go faster. (*She recites.*)

Bring little flowers that bloom all day
Make a dull corner more cheerful and gay.

SECOND FLOWER FAIRY:

Tulips and hyacinths bloom everywhere
Making dark places more cheerful and fair.

TIPSEY (*Covers his ears with his hands*): Oh! Oh! I don't like it.

THIRD FLOWER FAIRY:

Pick them and place them in your bright bouquet
To gladden the table on Tulip Day.

FOURTH FLOWER FAIRY:
Sweet is the message and brimful of joy
That each flower brings to each small girl and boy.

FIFTH FLOWER FAIRY:
Wherever you are, we want you to know
Of the beauty that blooms where the flowers grow.

SIXTH FLOWER FAIRY:
Gentle and pure as a Dutch maiden's prayer
And the thoughts of the flowers that breathe everywhere.

SEVENTH FLOWER FAIRY:
Give the best that you have, as the flowers do,
And the best will always come back to you.

EIGHTH FLOWER FAIRY:
The fragrance of flowers is round and about
Trying to put the bad dreams to rout.

TOPSEY: But that is something you cannot do. We are here, and here we stay.

TIPSEY: The dyke belongs to us. We live here.

HANS: Go away.

TOPSEY: *You* go away.

HANS: Try and make me. (*Bright light shines on* HANS.)

TOPSEY: See, how the moon shines, Hans. Be sensible. Pretty soon you won't be able to feel anything at all.

TIPSEY: Stop bothering about a lot of people who don't mean anything to you.

HANS: Everybody means something to me. I won't let the dyke break. (*Shuts his eyes and prays, as* FLOWER FAIRIES *hum very softly.*) Father, I cannot fold my hands, but Thou Art One who understands. I know Thou wilt listen anyway. Help save Thy people from danger, I pray. Give me the strength to hold on tight. Please, send some help ere morning light. (*As he has been praying,* TIPSEY *and* TOPSEY *go, cowering, towards boulder, and hide behind it. The stage becomes very brightly lighted.*)

TIPSEY (*Peeks from behind boulder*): It is the dawn.

TOPSEY: Yes, he has won, and we must go back into the Zuyder Zee.

FIRST FLOWER FAIRY: Good always conquers evil. See, someone is coming with help. Be of good cheer, Hans. (*They all run off stage, as the Dutch children, led by* JAN *and* KATRINKA, *carrying lanterns, enter left.*)

KATRINKA: It is true. My dream was right. Oh, Hans, Hans, how brave you are. I had a dream that you were here, so I woke everybody up, and here we are.

JAN (*Putting down his lantern*): And not a moment too soon, I should think. (*Kneels down beside* HANS, *and takes a plug from his pocket.*) See, I have brought some plugs to fit into the hole. I hope one of them fits. The men are on their way with help for us. (*Gently withdraws* HANS' *hand, and quickly inserts plug.*) Yes, it fits. But he has fainted, poor little fellow.

HANS (*Opens one eye*): No, I haven't. Only my hand hurts rather badly.

JAN: Of course it does. Why shouldn't it? Spending the night in the icy water.

HILDA: Weren't you scared, Hans?

HANS: Now that I think of it, I was scared to death. I am glad that you are all here now. But I had some very pretty dreams to keep me company.

JACOB: If it were not for you we would all be fighting for our lives at this very moment. We might even be dead. (*Bows low to him.*) I for one am very proud to know you, little hero of Holland.

HILDA (*Curtsies*): And so am I.

JAN: So are we all.

HANS: When your country and those you love are in danger you forget everything except that you must do something to save them. It is easy then to be brave.

JAN (*Fervently*): Of such stuff as you are heroes made.

THE END

RUMPELSTILTSKEN

by Helen Cotts Bennett

Characters

KING
JONATHAN, *a huntsman*
RICHARD, *a huntsman*
PETER, *a huntsman*
MILLER, *owner of the mill*
MARILYN, *his daughter*
RUMPELSTILTSKEN, *a dwarf*
MESSENGER
SERVANT

SCENE 1

SETTING: *The King's courtroom.*

AT RISE: KING *is seated on throne, reading scroll in hand, as* HUNTSMEN *enter and bow low before him.*

KING (*Jovially, rolling up scroll*): So — you have returned from your hunting, my men. What luck did you have?
JONATHAN: Indeed the hunting was not as good as usual.
RICHARD: The deer were scarce.
JONATHAN: Wild game, in general, was not in evidence.
PETER (*Eagerly*): 'Tis true, but (*Pause*) we interrupted our hunting, Your Majesty, to bring you news of great importance.
KING (*Surprised*): News, you say? What kind of news?
JONATHAN: It happened this way, Your Majesty. One night we chanced to come upon an old mill at the edge of the forest, and in the mill lived an old Miller with his beautiful daughter.
KING (*Musing*): Mmmmmm, a beautiful daughter —
JONATHAN: Yes, Your Majesty. We found this maiden to be of great charm —
PETER (*Interrupting*): And she was also very accomplished.

KING: Accomplished, you say —

RICHARD (*Nodding head*): Oh, indeed.

JONATHAN (*Leaning head toward* KING, *confidentially*): The maiden spins gold out of straw!

KING (*Astonished*): Gold out of straw? (*Disgusted*) Impossible! (*Eagerly*) Did you see her?

JONATHAN (*Hesitating*): No — not exactly, but her father boasted that she has spun it many times.

RICHARD: Yes, he has seen her.

KING (*Flustered*): Well — where is she? Where can I find her? A maiden with such accomplishments must not be neglected!

JONATHAN (*Happily*): That is what we thought, Your Majesty, so —

PETER (*Delightedly*): We brought the Miller and his daughter to court with us.

KING (*Pleased*): You did? Well, bring them to me at once.

JONATHAN (*Bows, goes to door, calls out*): The king wishes to see you. (MILLER *and* DAUGHTER *enter.*)

MILLER (*Bowing low before* KING): Your Majesty, this is a great honor for a poor old miller.

KING (*Friendly*): The story these men tell me about you and your daughter interests me greatly. Is your daughter really as clever as you say?

MILLER (*Swells with pride*): Indeed and even more so! She has many accomplishments!

KING: There is only one in which I am interested.

MILLER: And which one is that?

KING: The claim that your daughter can spin gold out of straw.

MILLER (*Chagrined*): Indeed, did I say that?

KING: You did!

MILLER (*Visibly perturbed*): Perhaps — perhaps — ah —

KING (*Matter-of-fact-like*): I have decided to find out if this story is true, so I will have a spinning wheel and a pile of straw placed in the next room —

MARILYN (*Interrupting*): But, Your Majesty, I know not how to spin straw into gold. It was just an idle boast.my father made.

KING: We shall see. Come with me. (MARILYN *follows* KING *to door of next room.*) Now, here is the room. When I return, see that all the straw has been spun and that gold is heaped in its place. If you value your life, you will spin it quickly and well.

MARILYN (*Tearfully*): But, my King —

MILLER: Perhaps I was a bit hasty in —

KING: I have reasons to believe you were not. Come, we will leave your daughter to her work.

CURTAIN

* * *

SCENE 2

SETTING: *Room in palace.*

AT RISE: MARILYN *is sitting alone, weeping.*

MARILYN (*Sorrowfully*): How can anyone spin straw into gold? I know not how! When the King returns, he will surely put me to death. What can I do? What can I do?

DWARF (*Hopping into room, bells jingling on his shoes*): Good morning, good morning, my pretty maiden. Why are you so unhappy?

MARILYN: The King has commanded me to spin this straw into gold and I know not how.

DWARF: Hmmm! A sorry state of affairs.

MARILYN: Indeed you are right. My life is in danger!

DWARF (*Business-like*): Pretty maiden, what will you give me if I spin the straw for you.

MARILYN (*Surprised*): You? Can you spin straw into gold?

DWARF: Indeed. I have spun it many times.

MARILYN (*Excited*): Oh, I will give you anything — I'll — I'll give you this necklace I'm wearing.

DWARF (*Looking at necklace*): Hmmm! A pretty necklace it is. Very well, let me sit at the spinning wheel.

MARILYN (*Eagerly*): Do you think you can spin it?

DWARF: Of course. (*Starts to spin.*)
Round about, Round about,
Lo and behold!

Reel away, Reel away
Straw into gold.
(*Blows gold colored bits of paper through tube, so it covers pile of straw.*)

MARILYN: Oh, the straw is changing. It is beautiful.

DWARF:

Round about, Round about,
Lo and behold.

Reel away, Reel away,
Straw into gold!
(*Blows more papers through, onto pile.*)

MARILYN: It is really gold!

DWARF: Yes, pretty maiden, the straw has turned, just as I promised it would.

MARILYN: Oh, little dwarf, you have saved my life! (*Hands him necklace.*) Here is my necklace for your pay.

DWARF (*Skips around*:) It has been a pleasure! Now I must leave. Good-bye! (*Exits.*)

MARILYN: Goodbye, little dwarf. (*Pause*) Now, I must call the King. (*Calls off stage*) King! King — Come quickly!

KING (*Entering*): You have finished so soon?

MARILYN (*Proudly*): Yes, yes, Your Majesty. Here is the pile of gold.

KING (*Jovially*): An excellent task well performed.

MARILYN: Then it pleases Your Majesty, and I may go home?

KING: Indeed, you are all that of which your father has boasted, but as for going home — indeed not, my child. You must spin some more.

MARILYN (*Alarmed*): But my King —

KING (*Walking to another pile of straw*): Now in this other corner, I have placed another pile of straw, higher and larger than the first. See that you spin it well.

MARILYN: But, my King —

KING (*Interrupting*): Do not use your strength in idle chatter, my child; spin, spin, and then spin some more.

MARILYN: But King I have already spun this large pile for you. Is not that enough to prove my worth?

KING (*Doubtfully*): You are afraid of this final test?

MARILYN: Oh no!

KING: Then to your work, and remember this. If you spin this well, I will make you Queen of all the land. A poor miller's daughter, a queen. That should make your fingers fly. (*Leaving room*) Ha, ha, ha! A poor miller's daughter a queen.

MARILYN: I hope the dwarf is still in the palace. (*Calls softly*) Dwarf, little dwarf, where are you? (*Looks around corners in room*) Please little dwarf, come and help me once more. (*Pause*) Oh, he doesn't answer. He's gone. Now, what will I do? I will try to spin it myself. I'll say the same words:
Round about, Round about,
Lo and behold.

Reel away, Reel away,
Straw into gold.

It is no use. The straw will not lose its dull, ugly color. What will I do?

DWARF (*Tumbles into room, bells on shoes jingling*): Ha, ha, ha! You could never change that pile to gold. You haven't the magic I have.

MARILYN (*Happy to see him*): Oh, little dwarf, I called you, but when you didn't answer I thought you had gone away.

DWARF (*Hopping about*): You called me just in time. In another minute I would have been far away. (*Stops. Looks at her.*) Hmmmm. I see you are troubled again.

MARILYN: Indeed. The King has given me this last pile of straw and I can do nothing with it.

DWARF: Is he never satisfied?

MARILYN: He will not ask me again, if I can only change this last bit of straw.

DWARF: Ah, and he will make you his Queen. I heard him say so.

MARILYN: Yes, that's true. Please help me once more.

DWARF (*Hopping around*): Very well, but what will you give me?

MARILYN: I'm sorry, I have nothing. I've already given you my necklace.

DWARF: Then I'm sorry I cannot help you. I always get paid for my work.

MARILYN (*Pleading*): But the King will put me to death.

DWARF (*Stops dancing*): Let me think! (*Pause*) Ah, I have it. Will you promise to give me anything I ask?

MARILYN: Yes, anything!

DWARF: Then promise to give me the first child you have, when you become Queen.

MARILYN (*Surprised*): My first child?

DWARF: Yes. I'm a lonely little fellow. I wish to have company.

MARILYN: Very well. I'll agree to anything — anything — if you'll only spin the gold.

DWARF: Remember, a bargain is a bargain! Your first child shall belong to me! (*Sits at spinning wheel and spins*)

Round about, Round about,
Lo and behold.

Reel away, Reel away
Straw into gold!

CURTAIN

* * *

SCENE 3

SETTING: *The* QUEEN'S *room.*

TIME: *Two years later.*

SERVANT: The King has been playing with the little Prince all morning.

MARILYN: It is time for the Prince to have his nap. Will you take him to his room. I will be there shortly.

SERVANT (*Bowing*): Yes, Your Highness. I will go to him at once.

DWARF (*Tumbling in, bells jingling*): Ha, ha, ha! Here I am again.

MARILYN (*Startled*): Why — why — who are you?

DWARF (*Haughtily*): Have you forgotten me so quickly? Remember it was I who made you a queen, by spinning the straw into gold.

MARILYN: Oh, of course, I didn't recognize you.

DWARF (*Disgusted*): Queens have poor memories. (*Brightly*) I have come for my pay.

MARILYN: Your pay?

DWARF (*Disgusted again*): Indeed, you have not forgotten that, too, have you? Your first child was to be given to me.

MARILYN (*Alarmed*): Oh, little dwarf, I had forgotten our bargain. Please do not take the little Prince from us.

DWARF (*Firmly*): A bargain is a bargain!

MARILYN (*Pleading*): I know, but I will give you money, lots of it, or — or — land, acres and acres of it, if you will take it, and forget about the child.

DWARF (*Firmly*): No, a bargain is a bargain!

MARILYN (*Sorrowfully*): But, little dwarf, when the King finds that I have tricked him, he will put me to death. Please help me. My life is in your hands.

DWARF (*Softening*): But you promised —

MARILYN (*Urgently*): Yes, yes, I know, but now I am so distressed.

DWARF (*Briskly*): Very well, your pleadings have softened my heart. I will give you one more chance. In three days I will return to this room. If you can tell me my name at that time, you may keep the Prince. If not, I will take him home with me to the forest. It will not be an easy one to guess. Remember, just three days you shall have, and no more. Good day! (*Tumbles out of room.*)

CURTAIN

* * *

SCENE 4

SETTING: QUEEN'S *room.*

TIME: *Three days later.*

SERVANT: Why are you so sad, my lady?

MARILYN (*Sorrowfully*): Today the little dwarf returns. If I cannot tell him his name, he will take the little Prince home with him.

SERVANT (*Hopefully*): But you have sent messengers all over the land to learn new names. Surely one of them will bring the right one back.

MARILYN (*Shaking head*): No, I'm afraid not. Most of the messengers have already returned. They learned not a single new or different one.

SERVANT (*Brightly*): Here comes a messenger now.

MESSENGER (*Enters, bows low*): My Queen.

MARILYN (*Anxiously*): What news? Have you learned a new name?

MESSENGER (*Excitedly*): Yes, I have. Yesterday as I was climbing a high hill, I saw a hut. Before the hut burned a fire, and round about the fire, a funny little dwarf was dancing on one leg singing:

"Merrily the feast I'll make
Today I'll brew, tomorrow bake,
Merrily I'll dance and sing,
For next day will a stranger bring,
Little does my lady dream,
Rumpelstiltsken is my name."

MARILYN (*Thoughtfully*): Rumpelstiltsken!

MESSENGER: Yes, the name is very unusual and it belongs to a little dwarf.

MARILYN (*Excitedly*): You are right. That must be the name we are seeking. My good man, you shall be well rewarded for this.

MESSENGER (*Bows*): Thank you, my Queen.

MARILYN (*Anxiously*): Now leave me alone. The dwarf will soon be here. (MESSENGER *and* SERVANT *bow and leave room.*)

DWARF (*Dancing in*): Ha, ha, ha! Today is the day!

MARILYN (*Slyly*): You seem very happy today, little dwarf.

DWARF (*Dancing around*): Today is the day. By nightfall, I will have your little Prince safely in my hut in the midst of the great forest.

MARILYN: That is, if I cannot guess your name.

DWARF: You will never guess it, I am certain!

MARILYN: We shall see. (*Sweetly*) Is your name John?

DWARF (*Laughing*): Ha, ha, ha! No, Madam, it is not! (*Dances around room.*)

MARILYN (*Thoughtfully*): Is it Tom?

DWARF (*Turning somersaults*): Ha, ha, ha, ha! No, Madam, it is not!

MARILYN (*Saucily*): Could your name be Timothy?

DWARF (*Doubled over, holding his sides*): Ho, ho, ho! 'Scuse me, Madam, for holding my sides. But your guesses make me laugh so hard. Indeed my name is not Timothy. (*Suddenly sober*) You have just one more guess.

MARILYN (*Slowly*): I wonder — could your name possibly be — Rumpelstiltsken?

DWARF (*Surprised*): Rumpelstiltsken? (*Angrily*) How did you know? The witches must have told you! The witches!

MARILYN (*Eagerly*): Then it is your name!

DWARF (*Stamping around*): You knew it all the time. You cheated me! I will still be lonely.

MARILYN (*Gratefully*): No, I only wanted to keep the little Prince. And now, because a bargain is a bargain, and you are so lonely, how would you like to come and live with us?

DWARF (*Surprised*): You mean, this beautiful palace will be my home?

MARILYN: Yes, and you can play with the little Prince every day.

DWARF (*Joyfully*): Then I'll never be lonely again!

MARILYN (*Happily*): One kindness deserves another. You helped me when I needed it, and now I will return the favor.

DWARF (*Tumbling and singing*): And we'll all live happily together forever after!

THE END

11 copies

SLEEPING BEAUTY

by Helen Cotts Bennett

Characters

THE KING
THE QUEEN
THE SEVEN FAIRIES
WICKED FAIRY
THE PRINCESS
SPINNING WOMAN
GUARD
PRINCE
THREE HUNTERS

SETTING: *In the King's Palace.*

TIME: *Once Upon a Time.*

AT RISE: SEVEN FAIRIES *are grouped together talking.*

1ST FAIRY: The King has commanded us to appear at his royal palace today —

3RD FAIRY: And no one seems to know the reason!

2ND FAIRY: The messenger said we were to be here at high noon.

3RD FAIRY: It is past that time now.

1ST FAIRY (*Counting*): Let me see, we are all here, aren't we?

4TH FAIRY: Yes, all except one —

1ST FAIRY: Which one is missing?

4TH FAIRY: Don't you remember? The Wicked Fairy isn't here—the one who brings everyone such bad luck!

5TH FAIRY: Surely you would not expect the King to summon *her,* too.

6TH FAIRY: *She* might bring disaster to the entire household!

5TH FAIRY: Furthermore, she never associates with us!

4TH FAIRY (*Laughing*): At least, not if she can help it.

1ST FAIRY (*Seriously*): The King must have outstanding news for us —

GOOD FAIRY: Or perhaps an event of great importance has taken place. (*Trumpets blow.*)

ROYAL GUARD (*Calls out*): The King and Queen and Princess Mary!

FAIRIES (*To each other, surprised*): Princess Mary! (KING *and* QUEEN *enter pushing perambulator, elaborately adorned with ribbons and bows.* FAIRIES *bow low.*)

KING: Good Fairies, I know you must wonder why you have been summoned to the royal palace.

1ST FAIRY: Indeed, Your Majesty, it has caused us great speculation.

KING (*Smiles*): As you can see, since your last visit, we have been honored with a new little Princess. Princess Mary!

FAIRIES (*Nod at each other happily*): Princess Mary.

KING: We thought it most fitting and proper that you fairies should be the godmothers to the little child —

QUEEN: And so we have invited you to the christening which will be held today.

GOOD FAIRY: We are highly honored, Your Majesties!

2ND FAIRY: Not knowing that this was to be a christening we did not bring our usual presents —

GOOD FAIRY: But it is within the power of each fairy to bestow, with her magic wand, a *priceless* gift upon the little Princess.

1ST FAIRY: May we render our gifts now?

KING: Indeed, it will make the Queen and myself very happy. (*Both go to throne at back of stage and sit. Baby buggy remains in center of stage.*)

1ST FAIRY (*Raising her wand over carriage*): Princess Mary, I bestow upon you, great beauty — you shall grow up to be the fairest person in all the world.

2ND FAIRY (*Raising wand*): Princess Mary, I bestow upon you a disposition as sweet as that of an angel.

3RD FAIRY (*Raising wand*): Princess Mary, I bestow upon you a great singing voice.

4TH FAIRY: Princess Mary, I bestow upon you the gift of good health and a joyful spirit.

5TH FAIRY: Princess Mary, you shall be gracious and kind, and help others less fortunate than yourself.

6TH FAIRY: Princess Mary, you shall have great wealth and comforts throughout your life. (*Commotion off stage.* WICKED FAIRY *hobbles in.*)

WICKED FAIRY (*Stamping her foot*): So, I am not good enough to be invited to the christening, eh? Because I am no longer young and beautiful you would not have me, eh? Well, the newly born Princess shall suffer for this!

KING (*Rising to his feet*): A thousand pardons for this mistake, Wicked Fairy. We had no idea you were still living.

QUEEN: No one has heard from you for over fifty years — not since you shut yourself away in the old stone tower.

WICKED FAIRY (*Still raging*): That is no excuse! You could have sent a messenger to find out! I have been slighted! But do not forget — I, too, can bestow a gift upon the little Princess!

KING (*Tearfully*): Please, do not cast a wicked spell over the little child.

WICKED FAIRY: It will be worse than that! (*Goes to cradle, raises wand*) Little Princess, when you become full grown, you shall *pierce* your hand while spinning, and you shall *die* of the wound!

QUEEN (*Anxiously*): Please, please take back your wicked gift!

KING (*Pleading*): I will give you my land, my kingdom, anything!

WICKED FAIRY (*Firmly*): My word is spoken! It shall be! (*Laughing*) Ha, ha, ha! The little Princess shall suffer for your mistake! Ha, ha, ha! (*Exits*)

QUEEN (*Tearfully*): Oh, what can we do? Our child has been cursed!

KING (*Hopelessly*): What *can* we do?

GOOD FAIRY (*Stepping forward*): Do not grieve too greatly, my King and Queen, as yet, I have not bestowed *my* gift upon the little Princess.

KING (*Pleading*): Then take away this *terrible* curse, I beseech you!

GOOD FAIRY: Unfortunately, I have not the power to change entirely the ill fortune just wished upon the Princess. The Princess will indeed pierce her finger with a spindle, but she will not die. Instead, she will sink into a deep sleep, that will last one hundred years. At the end of that time, a Prince shall come and awaken her.

QUEEN (*Alarmed*): A sleep that will last one hundred years?

KING: Thank you, good Fairy, you have done your best to undo this terrible deed. However, I believe I have a plan that will succeed entirely.

QUEEN: And what is that?

KING (*Standing, as if giving proclamation*): Henceforth and forever after, I forbid all persons in my kingdom to spin, or have spinning wheels in their homes. If my command is disregarded, all offending persons will meet with instant death!

QUEEN (*Brightening*): That is a *fine* plan! If there are no spinning wheels, the Princess cannot pierce her finger on one.

GOOD FAIRY (*Shaking head*): Good King and Queen, I hope that this will prove true, but alas, a Fairy's gift has never yet been washed away by royal commands!

CURTAIN

* * *

SCENE 2

SETTING: *A tower-room in the palace, fifteen years later.*

AT RISE: SPINNING WOMAN *is busy at a spinning wheel.* THE PRINCESS *enters.*

SPINNER (*Stands up, bows*): Welcome to my little room, beautiful Princess.

PRINCESS: Thank you!

SPINNER: How did you find it — it is in the very top of the castle tower?

PRINCESS: I was wandering through the castle today, and I found a winding stair. It led me to this room.

SPINNER: So that's it. Let me look at you. I haven't seen you since you were a tiny baby.

PRINCESS: I am very much of a young lady now.

SPINNER: So you are, and you have grown to be most beautiful.

PRINCESS: Thank you. (*Pause*) What a strange wheel you are working. I have not seen any like it before.

SPINNER: This is a spinning wheel, my pretty child.

PRINCESS: It is a very odd contraption. What makes the wheel go around?

SPINNER: The lever here at the bottom. See I work it with my foot.

PRINCESS: How charming. Do let me try to work it.

SPINNER: Oh, Princess, never, never! A pretty princess like you should never labor with spinning wheels.

PRINCESS: Oh, please, just once.

SPINNER: It would be better if you just sat on that stool and talked with me.

PRINCESS: But I want to learn to spin. You could grant me no greater favor than that.

SPINNER (*Laughing*): Very well, then, if it means so much to you. Here sit at the wheel.

PRINCESS: Oh, this will be such fun.

SPINNER: Now, take this spindle. (*Hands spindle to her*)

PRINCESS (*Takes it, drops it*): Oh, oh, I have pierced my finger.

SPINNER: Never mind. I often do that. It is nothing.

PRINCESS (*Raising hand to forehead*): But — but I feel as though I were going to faint.

SPINNER (*Excitedly*): I will fetch you some water.

PRINCESS: Hurry. Please hurry.

SPINNER (*With glass of water in hand*): Here is the water. Princess! Princess! Wake up. What can be the matter with you? Princess!

KING (*Entering*): Is this the room? (*To* GUARD)

GUARD (*Entering also*): Yes, I saw her climbing the stairs. She must be here.

KING (*To* SPINNER *who has run to him*): Have you seen the Princess? I have searched for her everywhere.

SPINNER: She is here, Your Majesty, but she suddenly fell in a swoon.

KING (*Kneeling beside* PRINCESS): Princess, speak to me! (*Pause*) Woman, what has happened?

SPINNER: I was sitting here spinning when —

KING (*Angrily*): Spinning? I commanded every spinning wheel be destroyed. You have disobeyed!

GOOD FAIRY (*Entering*): So, the cruel fairy's wish has come to pass. The Princess has fallen into a deep sleep.

KING: Yes, good fairy, it has happened. Can't you do something?

GOOD FAIRY: I am afraid I can do nothing. The Princess will sleep one hundred years. Nothing can prevent it.

KING (*In despair*): But a hundred years — by that time everyone in this palace will be dead and gone. When my poor Princess awakens, she will be entirely alone.

GOOD FAIRY: That is the only thing I *can* arrange. See, I have my magic wand. I will go through this palace touching all living things — the kitchen maids, the page boys, the footmen, even the horses in the stables. They, too, shall sleep through the hundred years, and all shall awaken when she does.

KING: That is a good plan, my fairy. Please start with me.

GOOD FAIRY (*Touching him*): Very well. There.

KING (*Yawns, falls asleep on floor*): I — am — so — sleepy.

SPINNER: Touch me, good Fairy.

GOOD FAIRY (*Touching her*): There — and now you, Guard — there. (*Both yawn, fall asleep.*)

GOOD FAIRY (*Goes to door, looks back*): Pleasant dreams, everyone! (*Softly*)

CURTAIN

* * *

SCENE 3

SETTING: *In a forest, one hundred years later.*

AT RISE: PRINCE *and* THREE HUNTERS *wander on stage. They are tired.*

PRINCE: We have come a long way. Let us stop and rest for awhile.

1ST HUNTER (*Sitting*): Yes. Our hunting has taken us farther in the woods than we have ever come before.

2ND HUNTER: It has been many years since I passed this way.

3RD HUNTER: And I. The last time I was but a boy. A long time that is, indeed.

PRINCE: Look, do my eyes, perchance, see a castle on the top of that hill, there in the distance?

1ST HUNTER: Yes, indeed. 'Tis said that is the castle of some fairy.

3RD HUNTER: Or a monster — no one knows.

PRINCE (*Surprised*): What? Has no man paid the castle a visit to find out?

1ST HUNTER (*Shaking head*): No one has been there for many a year. There is a forest about the castle that is so thick and thorny, a man could not get through.

3RD HUNTER: One would not know a castle were there, did the top not show above the trees.

PRINCE: Truly, it is a castle of mystery. I should like to explore it.

1ST HUNTER: Prince, more than fifty years ago I heard my father say that there was in that castle the most beautiful princess ever seen. She was supposed to be under the spell of some fairy, and was to sleep for a hundred years. Then she was to be awakened by a Prince, who was later to marry her.

PRINCE: And does no one know if the story be true?

1ST HUNTER: No one knows for no one has been able to reach the castle to explore it.

PRINCE: Good. Then it will be an exciting adventure for us. Come, we will see what this castle of mystery contains!

CURTAIN

* * *

SCENE 4

SETTING: *Same as scene two. The tower room, a few days later.*

AT RISE: *Men are entering room cautiously, looking around.*

1ST HUNTER: Prince, let us go no further. This castle is haunted, there is no doubt about it.

PRINCE: Yes, it is all very strange, I will agree. But we have fared well, so far.

1ST HUNTER: 'Tis true, but there is always a time when one's luck fails.

PRINCE: Nonsense. You told me the forest around this castle

was so thick and thorny a man couldn't get through. We had no trouble.

1ST HUNTER: I can't understand it. Other men have tried before us, and they could never gain entrance to this place, but for us, the trees and bushes seemed to part to let us pass.

2ND HUNTER (*Afraid*): It is magic, that's what —

3RD HUNTER: And the courtyard, filled with the bodies of men and animals — The guards sitting there with their muskets on their shoulders. Bah — it gives me the shivers!

1ST HUNTER: And now, look at this room. It is the same as the others. Filled with dead people!

PRINCE: But they are not dead. Haven't you noticed?

1ST HUNTER: Not dead? Then what are they?

PRINCE: They are sleeping! Look, they all have rosy cheeks, and red lips. They are far from dead.

2ND HUNTER: It's just what I told you — it's magic! Let's get out of here.

3RD HUNTER: We can tell by their clothing and dress they haven't stirred for a century or more.

1ST HUNTER: Prince —

PRINCE: Yes?

1ST HUNTER: Look who sleeps on yonder cot?

PRINCE: A sleeping beauty she is, if ever my eyes beheld one.

1ST HUNTER: There is a guard at her feet —

2ND HUNTER: And this must be the King — he has a crown on his head.

PRINCE: Then *she* must be the princess — the King's daughter, no doubt. But what could have caused this strange affair. (*Goes toward her.*)

1ST HUNTER (*Alarmed*): Prince, stay away from her! Do not touch her!

PRINCE: Why?

1ST HUNTER: You, too, might come under the sleeping spell.

PRINCE (*Looks at her*): I am not afraid. I will see if I can awaken her.

2ND HUNTER: Prince, I implore you — do not touch these sleeping people.

PRINCE: I cannot leave this beauty now. I have fallen quite in love with her.

1ST HUNTER (*Anxiously*): Prince, have you gone out of your mind?

PRINCE: I am going to take her hand. There. (*Takes it*) She is warm and very much alive.

2ND HUNTER (*Alarmed*): She moved her hand. I saw her. Let us flee for our lives.

1ST HUNTER: Yes, she might be a witch.

PRINCE: Nonsense! A witch could not be so fair. Go if you must, but I shall stay.

1ST HUNTER (*To others*): Let us wait outside the door. (*All go to door*)

2ND HUNTER (*Looks back*): Prince, you are so foolhardy. (HUNTERS *exit*)

PRINCE: I will shake her gently. (*Softly*) Princess, Princess, awaken! (PRINCESS *yawns, and makes sounds of awakening.*)

PRINCE: You are really coming to life. Open your eyes.

PRINCESS (*Yawns. Opens eyes*): O — how — sleepy — I — am! (*Slowly*)

KING (*Awakes and yawns. Sees the* PRINCE): Why, you must be the Prince. I thought you would never get here.

PRINCE: Have you been sleeping long?

KING: Oh, a hundred years or more.

GUARD (*Yawning*): Oh, hum! What a long sleep for a guard. I must be about my duties. (*He goes out.*)

KING (*To* PRINCE): You have shown great bravery to come here and rescue us from the curse of the Wicked Fairy. To reward you for your courage, you may have anything within my power.

PRINCE: There is just one thing I desire, Your Majesty.

KING (*Jovially*): Yes, yes, I know — the hand of my daughter in marriage. Well, it shall be granted, and with her goes my entire kingdom for you to rule.

PRINCE (*Happily*): Thank you, sir! And I'm sure we'll live happily together forever after! (*Curtain falls.*)

THE END

THE LION AND THE MOUSE

by Rowena Bennett

SETTING: *A woodsy place. At the right, a net is caught in the bushes.*

AT RISE: *Enter* LION, *left.*

LION (*Looking about*):
Oh for a nap in the jungle shade!
Much too long on the plains I've stayed.
Fine is my coat, but it's furry and hot,
And I'd like to be where the sun is not.
(*He finds a comfortable couch of grass center, back*)
Here is a grassy bed for me
With a vine overhead for a canopy.
(*He settles himself comfortably, paws stretched out in front of him.*)
Oh, let him tremble and let him weep
Who dares disturb the lion in sleep!
(*He yawns and closes his eyes. The* MOUSE *enters.*)

MOUSE (*Dancing about stage on tiptoe*):
When a mousey starts a-dancing through the wildwood on her toes,
When a mousey goes a-prancing, in her childhood, no one knows
That she passes through the grasses, for so quietly she goes!
When a mousey starts a-dancing and a-prancing on her toes.
(*As she dances she circles nearer and nearer to the* LION *without seeing him.*)
When a mousey starts a-leaping
She disturbs no one who's sleeping,
For she does the high jump nightly
And she practices it lightly.
Till she's really very spritely
In her dancing and her leaping
And disturbs no one who's sleeping.

(*As she chants the last two lines she runs right across the* LION'S *paw.*)

LION (*Angrily*): What? What's that?

MOUSE (*Terrified*): Help! Help! (*She tries to run away but he holds her back with his paw.*)

LION (*Fiercely*):

Who dares disturb this kingly beast
Shall turn into a kingly feast...

MOUSE (*Pleadingly*):

No! Spare me, spare me, monarch royal!
I did not mean to be disloyal
Or disrespectful to your highness
I'm truly noted for my shyness
And never would have been so bold
As to come near, had I been told
That you were sleeping in the jungle.
I really didn't mean to bungle.
I didn't see your outstretched paw...

LION: Well then, it's surely time you saw it now.... (*He lifts it threateningly*)

MOUSE (*Shrinking and trembling*):

I pray you do not strike me
If you but knew me you would like me.
Oh save my life! And when I'm braver
Someday I shall return the favor.

LION (*Now holding on to her with both paws*):

Ha, ha! Ho, ho! My what a joke!
I never knew a mouse who spoke
Of saving lions. That's absurd—
The funniest thing I ever heard.
(*He roars with laughter*)

MOUSE (*Hurt*):

My promise does not call for mirth.
Strange things may happen on this earth.
My mother taught me from my birth
That even mice may be of worth...

LION:

Well, I shall lift my giant paws
And free you. But it's not because
I think you'll ever be of use
To one like me....I've no excuse

For letting such a silly go
Except that you're so small, you know,
And I am much too tender hearted.
(*He releases her.*)
There! Run along. It's time we parted.

MOUSE (*Rushing off stage in a hurry*):
O thank you, thank you, gracious king!
Your kindness is a noble thing
As sure as there is sun and shade
Within this wood, you'll be repaid.
(*Exit* MOUSE.)

LION (*Yawning and stretching*):
I guess I'd better move along (*He rises*)
The thrush begins its evensong,
The sunlight wanes. The shadows throng.
It will be time for hunting soon
I hope there'll be a hunter's moon.
(*He starts off stage, right, but gets caught in the net.*)
Oh, what is this? I'm in a tangle.
(*He rolls over and gets more tangled*)
I'm going to choke. I'm going to strangle.
I must be caught within a net,
A dreadful trap that men have set.
(*He roars as he struggles.*)
The more I pull the tighter yet
These knotted strings and meshes get.
(*Enter* MOUSE *cautiously*)

MOUSE:
Oh did I hear the lion roaring
As though in pain? Or was he snoring?

LION (*Moaning*):
Take care. Take care, O, don't come near,
You foolish mouse! There's danger here.
I'm caught within a trapper's net
And there's not been a lion yet
Who could outwit the trapper man...

MOUSE:
Well, then, perhaps a mousie can.
(*She runs forward and examines the net.*)
Ah, well and good, it's made of rope...

LION: And how can that fact give me hope?

MOUSE:

Because a rope will break with gnawing,
And my sharp teeth are made for sawing.
Now stop your struggling and your pawing...
(*She settles herself to gnaw the rope.*)

LION:

Can it be possible a mouse
Can free me from this prison-house
Of rope and string and knotted cord
Without the scissors or a sword?
(*He sighs.*)
Oh no, there are too many ropes
For you to gnaw, I have no hopes...
In all this time you've gnawed but one.
The men will come before you're done.

MOUSE (*Holding up the severed rope proudly*):

One rope's enough, when it's a drawstring (*She pulls it out.*)
Let's see you do a little paw spring
(*She unwraps the whole net easily, now.*)

LION (*Leaping to freedom*):

See! I am free, quite free at last.
The rope no longer holds me fast;
And I no longer shall despise
Another creature for his size.

LION *and* MOUSE (*Taking hands and dancing off stage together*):

Oh do not judge your friends in haste!
A kindness never goes to waste.

THE END

THE THREE WISHES

by Cora Burlingame

Characters

MRS. KEHOE, *a widow,* 30
TERRY KEHOE, *her son,* 6
MAGGIE KEHOE, *her daughter,* 10
PATRICK, *a truck driver,* 20
MRS. MCGINNIS, *a neighbor,* 40
COL. MOORE, *a thoroughbred horse breeder*
MIKE MCGINNIS, 16
JILL MCGINNIS, 11
A JEWELER

SETTING: *A room furnished simply as a combination kitchen, dining-room and living-room.*

AT RISE: MRS. KEHOE *watches the door leading into the yard, as she puts the finishing touches on a small print dress. She disappears at left with it and returns immediately without it. She takes out of a box a cake covered with white icing, into which ten small pink candles are stuck, admires it, replaces it in the box and hides it behind a pile of towels. Taking one of the towels, she goes to the door.*

MRS. KEHOE: Maggie! Terry!

VOICES: Coming, Mother! Coming!

MRS. KEHOE (*Standing in the door, smiling, looking out*): It's a very fine pair of children I have, if I do say it myself, as shouldn't. (*Raising her voice*) Are you two feeding the pigs or cutting up highjacks this fine morning with not a bite in your mouths since last night's supper?

TERRY (*Running, laughing, up to his mother*): I let Maggie pour the swill because it's her birthday and she didn't spill so very much because she's so old!

MRS. KEHOE (*Laughing with him*): Come wash your hands and to your breakfast! (*She throws the towel to him*) It's like your father you are — God rest his soul — as if you were two peas in one pod. He would see spilling good swill as a joke if some one else did it! (*She peers into the yard.*) But what is Maggie doing on her knees on the dew-wet green? (TERRY *goes just outside the door.*)

TERRY (*Calling*): 'Scuse me for reminding you where you are, Mother. But it's surely not green but blue-grass she's kneeling on. She's talking to five violets she found. (*He appears, drying his hands on the towel.*)

MRS. KEHOE (*Frowning and smiling at the same time*): Maggie! Do you choose to eat burnt porridge on your birthday?

MAGGIE (*Appearing with five violets and some leaves lying in her outstretched hand*) Mother, yesterday a girl at school spoke a piece about fairies painting flowers. She said if you brought the violets or whatever they were on, very kindly into the house, they would stay on them, even though you couldn't see them. (*She transfers the flowers from her own to her mother's hands, using great caution.*) Please put them on the table while I wash my hands.

TERRY (*Laying the towel over her shoulder*): And if they do come into the house? What's the good of things you can't see? (*She goes just outside the door.*)

MAGGIE (*Calling from outside the door*): They might give me my three birthday wishes. They're supposed to bring good luck into whatever house they enter.

MRS. KEHOE (*Going to the table, lays the violets beside* MAGGIE'S *bowl*): Three birthday wishes. . . . My! My! (*She ladles cereal into three bowls, shakes up a bottle of milk and places it with glasses on the table. The children go to table.*) Mind you keep your thoughts on thankfulness, while we say grace, Maggie, and not on birthday gifts!

MAGGIE (*Demurely*): Yes, Mother. (*They stand behind their chairs and say a silent grace.*)

ALL THREE (*Aloud*): And especially do we thank Thee, Our Father, in the name of Thy Son, that we were brought safely out of our war-torn native land. Amen. (*They seat themselves.* MAGGIE, *turning her head and covering her mouth with her hand, makes some slight movements.*)

MRS. KEHOE: Maggie, put more milk on your porridge if it is too hot. But start eating it!

TERRY (*Attacking his porridge with a will*): She spit over her little finger and made a wish.

MRS. KEHOE (*Pouring a glass of milk for* MAGGIE): Will you grieve me on your birthday by starving yourself, my daughter?

MAGGIE: The girls at school say if you spit only a teeny drop over your little finger and make a wish, it will come true. I spit a teeny drop and wished for the three things I want for my birthday.

TERRY (*Takes up the saltcellar, shakes it and places it on the table. Grinning at his mother*): Empty.

MRS. KEHOE (*Snatching it up before* TERRY *can rise to his feet, she fills it from a box she takes off the kitchen cabinet*): I'm that excited by wearing earrings and my new dress on a morning of a weekday!

MAGGIE (*Laying down her spoon*): What is salt, Mother?

MRS. KEHOE: Ask your brother, who is eating too fast. (*She smiles at* TERRY.) You take up your spoon and let him lay his down for a minute to tell us what salt is. He knows everything.

TERRY (*Laying down his spoon*): I know what salt is. It's what makes porridge taste like nothing if you don't put it in! (*They all laugh.*) And Mother, I know more than Maggie does about St. Patrick! She got a double A in school yesterday for the best theme on St. Patrick, but she didn't know he drove the snakes out of Ireland.

MAGGIE (*Taking up her spoon, plays with her porridge*): I did know about that, Mother. But I didn't put it in my theme because I believe St. Patrick was too kind to drown things in the sea — even snakes. I think he must have changed them to birds! And I wanted to write the nicest things I could believe about St. Patrick, so good luck would come to both of us on our birthdays. Maybe even in Heaven he has three wishes.

MRS. KEHOE (*Laying down her spoon and leaning over the table*): Maggie, you speak of three birthday wishes. What could they be?

TERRY (*Laughing*): A bundle of switches for one thing!

MRS. KEHOE: Hush Terry! Let your sister tell what her three birthday wishes are. (*There is the sound of a truck stopping near the house.*)

MAGGIE (*With assurance*): I have long thought I should have on my tenth birthday a string of coral and a bowl of goldfish. And since I have lived in Kentucky, I have wanted to go to Hiring Fair. (*A whistle sounds outside the house.*)

TERRY (*Springing to his feet*): 'Scuse me, Mother! It's Patrick! (*He runs out.*)

MRS. KEHOE (*Rising from the table she looks distractedly about*): My lace! Help me find my lace, Maggie! Patrick has come to take my year's making of lace to the Mountain Home Industries' Booth at the Hiring Fair! I do not know where I put it! (*They look under tables, chairs, and behind the crayon picture.*)

MAGGIE (*Lying flat on her stomach in front of the cot, drags a small basket, filled with lace, from under it*): Here it is, Mother. (*She jumps up and hangs the basket on her mother's arm.*)

PATRICK (*Appearing at the door*): You are to go with your lace to the Hiring Fair, Mrs. Kehoe, according to what I'm told by Colonel Moore!

MRS. KEHOE (*Looking about distractedly*): But the dishes!

MAGGIE (*Taking her mother's hat and cape out of a closet*): Let them be!

PATRICK (*Holding up three long green tickets*): Maggie will come along and Terry, if he will keep his legs out of the gears. Col. Moore is treating all of his tenants to lunch and there are coupons for the merry-go-round, the roller-coaster, rides on the camel and what-not!

MAGGIE (*Closing the window, taking the porridge pot off the stove and laying a cloth over the soiled dishes on the breakfast table*): I'll get my coat and Terry's sweater.

MRS. KEHOE (*Turning around and around in one spot*): We . . . the three of us . . . to the Hiring Fair?

PATRICK (*Grinning toward* MAGGIE, *he drops the tickets into* MRS. KEHOE'S *basket*): If you didn't plan on goin' to the Hiring Fair why did you dress up in your best bib and tucker this Saturday morning, Mrs. Kehoe?

MRS. KEHOE (*After feeling the bow on her hair and her earrings, she smoothes her new print dress*): Maggie wanted me to dress up in my best because it's her birthday.

MAGGIE (*Placing her mother's hat on her head and hanging her cloak over her arm*): I thought we might be going to the Fair.

TERRY (*Running up to the door*): What are you all waiting for?

MAGGIE: Nothing. (*To* TERRY) Take your sweater and be sure you don't lose it. (PATRICK *takes the basket off* MRS. KEHOE'S *arm. He leads her out the door.* MAGGIE *stands with her hand on the knob.*) I'll close the door. (*She waits till they are a little way off. She fills a glass of water and places the violets in it.*) If you should be here, Little Painters, stay awake till I get back and I'll show you something you maybe never saw before. (*She steps out of the door and closes it behind her. Sound of the truck's engine starting.*)

CURTAIN

* * *

SCENE 2

SETTING: *A portion of the Hiring Fair, showing a jeweler's stall and The Mountain Home Industries' Booth almost stripped of merchandise.*

AT RISE: *A jeweler is rearranging the necklaces, bracelets, etc., in his stall. Children run talking and laughing across the stage from left to right. Sounds of horns, whistles, hawking and the music of a merry-go-round.* MRS. MCGINNIS *limps along holding on to* MRS. KEHOE.

MRS. MCGINNIS: I'm that footsore! Walkin' around in shoes all day is not what I'm used to.

MRS. KEHOE: It's been a grand day and 'tis surely a pity it's not just beginning instead of ending. (*She points toward a cord strung across The Mountain Home Industries' Booth to which one lace collar is pinned.*) And what grand luck I have had! All my lace sold but the littlest, cheapest piece!

MRS. MCGINNIS (*Standing first on one foot and then on the other*): It's been a grand day for them that have young feet. Now if I could take off my shoes . . . U-u-u--m! (*Sound of small drums and tin horns come nearer.*)

MRS. KEHOE (*Placing her basket on the counter of The Mountain Home Industries' Booth, she kneels and begins to untie the laces of* MRS. MCGINNIS'S *oxfords*): Why not take off your shoes? Surely a Fair is a place to enjoy yourself! And you with your feet covered with the handsome wool stockings you knit yourself! Sure if I had them, I'd take off my shoes, if only to show them off!

MRS. MCGINNIS (*Jumping back and pulling her friend to her feet*): Here comes Col. Moore! I'll pay my respects to him standing in my shoes if I fall in my tracks!

COL. MOORE (*Entering from right, followed by children carrying flags and noise-makers. He stops, and they gather about him*): Children, I came to the Fair to see the grand sights just as you did. And the grandest thing I see is you girls and boys enjoying yourselves. It happens to be my birthday. All anyone can say about me is that I raise thoroughbred horses. But this is St. Patrick's birthday, also. Who knows how he spent his time?

MIKE: He chased the snakes out of Ireland! (*His face grows red, and he ducks behind his mother when everyone begins to laugh.*)

COL. MOORE (*Smiling*): Thank you, Mike! That's what they say about St. Patrick. Who knows what else he did? (*All the children look at* MAGGIE.)

JILL: Maggie Kehoe got a double A at Friday exercise, yesterday, for a theme she wrote on St. Patrick!

COL. MOORE (*Lifting a wooden stool out of the jeweler's booth, he places it in the center of the road*): Come, Maggie, mount this stool and tell us what won you your double A in yesterday's exercises.

MRS. KEHOE (*Shaking her head vigorously at* MAGGIE): Likely she will forget, Col. Moore! Likely she has by now forgotten!

TERRY (*Nervously fluttering the small American flag he carries*): She read it off a paper in school yesterday.

JILL: Maggie doesn't have her paper with her, Col. Moore. Teacher pinned it on the wall because it was the best!

MAGGIE (*Smiling up at* COL. MOORE): I remember what I wrote, at least the most of it.

COL. MOORE: Grand! (*He leads* MAGGIE *to the stool and lifts her onto it.*) We are all your friends, here, Maggie. Look each of us in the eye and begin.

MAGGIE (*Smiling at her mother, she begins counting on her fin-*

gers. Appearing to make a mistake, she shakes her head and begins counting over again): About fifteen hundred and seventy-five years ago, a man-child was baptized *Souchet.* (*She turns, still smiling, to* COL. MOORE) I might be a little wrong about the years because arithmetic is my hard subject.

MRS. MCGINNIS (*Anxiously*): The colonel is expectin' you to speak of St. Patrick, Maggie!

JILL (*Tugging at her mother's arm*): Let her begin as she wills, Mother.

MAGGIE (*Smiling serenely, her eyes fixed on* COL MOORE): He must have been a fine, strong lad because, in Gaul, where they baptized him, the word *souchet* meant a little tree. (*She turns to smile at her mother.*) When this Souchet was as old as Terry and myself put together, he was stolen from Gaul and taken to Ireland. But he didn't grieve for long. He began to love the Irish. But the more he loved them, the more he was troubled because the Irish knew nothing about the true and only God. (*She unbuttons her coat and pushes back her curls.*) Seven years, he served his masters. When he was free he went out into the world to learn how he could bring God to the Irish. That was his job. Three times seven years he worked at it. At the end of the time, he had parts of the Bible, preachers and churches in Ireland. The Irish were so very thankful for the preachers, the churches, the Bible and God that they called Souchet *Peter civicus* which is a way of saying he was the father of the country. Only they shortened his long name to Patrick.

MRS. MCGINNIS (*In admiration*): What the child doesn't know about St. Patrick!

MAGGIE: Thank you. (*She starts to jump down from the stool, but stops.*) Oh! I almost forgot to say that Patrick lived to be one hundred and twenty years old, and since he spent all his time doing good, they made him a saint on earth, after he had been one in Heaven a very long time.

COL. MOORE (*Lifting* MAGGIE *from the stool, he takes her by the hand*): I am sure you will all agree that Maggie deserves a pretty for the grand account of St. Patrick she has given us. (*He leads her to the jeweler's stall.*) Look the pretties over. Choose what you will and it is yours, Maggie.

MAGGIE (*Smiling up at* COL. MOORE *without so much as a glance at the jewelry*): I don't have to look the pretties over, Col. Moore. I know what I will have.

COL. MOORE (*Smiling down at her*): What is it you will have, Maggie?

MAGGIE (*With her eyes still fixed on his face*): I have long believed I would have a string of coral beads by the time I was ten.

COL. MOORE (*To the jeweler*): Coral beads it is! (*He takes the necklace the jeweler hands him and fastens it around* MAGGIE'S *neck.*) There you are and God bless you, Maggie!

MAGGIE (*Curtsying prettily*): Thank you, Col. Moore!

MRS. KEHOE: Thank you, Col. Moore. (*She fans herself with her hat.*) When will I begin knowing something about my own children!

COL. MOORE (*Peering down the road*): I see the camels are coming. Let's all ride! (*He goes offstage followed by all the children except the little girls who are gathered around* MAGGIE *to look at her corals.*)

MRS. KEHOE (*Dropping to her knees, she finishes unlacing* MRS. MCGINNIS'S *oxfords*): There! Kick them off and enjoy yourself for the rest of the day.

MRS. MCGINNIS (*Pulling off her shoes, she ties the laces together and hangs them over her arm. She points to the lace collar pinned to the cord stretched across the Mountain Home Indusdustries' Booth*): That collar would look grand on the neck of my dress.

MRS. KEHOE (*Unpinning the collar and laying it around her friend's throat*): It makes the dress look grand. Have it for the cost of the thread. You're welcome to the work.

MRS. MCGINNIS (*Twisting her head to look admiringly at the collar*): Did the thread cost but a penny, I could not pay for it. I gave my man my last copper to buy a goat. (*She takes the collar from around her neck and holds it out.*)

MRS. KEHOE (*Refusing to take the collar*): Have it as a gift! Take it, woman, and welcome!

MRS. MCGINNIS: I'll not have so much work as a gift! But I have something in my basket I got at a drawing I have no use for! Will you trade — sight unseen?

MRS. KEHOE: I will do no trading for a bit of lace! Have the collar as a gift or leave it! Shame on me for speaking of the price of the thread — me that have had such good luck this day selling more than I dreamed and all!

MRS. MCGINNIS: I will leave the collar if you will not agree Maggie shall have what is in my basket — not counting my shoes — as a birthday gift. It's under the flag.

MRS. KEHOE: Maggie! (*The little girls except* MAGGIE *run off stage.*) Take what you find in Mrs. McGinnis's basket — not counting the shoes — and be thankful! Look under the flag.

MAGGIE (*Lifting out of* MRS. MCGINNIS's *basket, with both hands, a bowl of goldfish. She speaks softly*): Fairy castle. Seashells. White sand and green waterweed. Five goldfish . . . O-o-oh!

THE END

THE SALT IN THE SEA

by Mildred Colbert

Characters

THE MERCHANT, *who really is the* MILLER *and the* PEDDLER
GILES, *a poor man*
MARGO, *his wife*
JOAN, *his daughter*
GODFREY, *his son*
HUMPHRY, *Giles' rich brother*
TWO SERVANTS
CAPTAIN *of a ship*
ROGER, *the mate*
EVAN, GUY, JULES — *sailors.*
DWARFS
CLERK

SCENE 1

TIME: *Afternoon, long ago.*

SETTING: *Humphry's store room.*

AT RISE: HUMPHRY, *wearing the rich garments of a prosperous man, strides back and forth impatiently as he calls out the list of supplies he is counting to a* CLERK, *a timid old man who keeps his nearsighted eyes close to the scroll upon which he is writing with a long quill. After he writes what* HUMPHRY *dictates, he repeats the words he has written.*

HUMPHRY: Ten bags of meal.
CLERK (*Writes on the scroll then repeats*): Ten bags of meal.
HUMPHRY: Six kegs of sprats.

CLERK (*Repeats as before*): Six kegs of sprats.

HUMPHRY: Eight fine hams.

CLERK (*Repeating*): Eight fine hams.

HUMPHRY: Four — (*A* SERVANT *enters.*)

SERVANT: Begging your pardon, sir.

HUMPHRY: I do not wish to be interrupted.

SERVANT: Your brother, sir. (*Pause.*) Your brother, Giles.

HUMPHRY: Well?

SERVANT: He wants to see you, sir.

HUMPHRY: I am busy. I have no time to see him. (*He turns to the* CLERK *and continues as the* SERVANT *goes out.*) Four casks of malt. (HUMPHRY *strides about angrily;* CLERK *writes busily. Before the* CLERK *repeats what he has written the* SERVANT *reënters.*)

SERVANT: I crave your pardon, my master, but he will not go away.

HUMPHRY: Who, dolt?

SERVANT: Your brother, Giles, sir.

HUMPHRY: A plague on him. Show him in. (SERVANT *goes out.* GILES *wearing a faded cape over well-worn clothes enters. He carries in his hand a cap with a long stiff feather in it.*)

GILES: I give you a good day, Brother.

HUMPHRY: Never mind the day. What do you want?

GILES: Why act so strange and proud, Humphry? Don't you remember —

HUMPHRY: No one helps me.

GILES: Since early morning I have been trying to find work.

HUMPHRY: Well, what has that to do with me?

GILES: There is no work anywhere.

HUMPHRY: I always find plenty to do.

GILES: You do not understand!

HUMPHRY: Oh, yes, I do.

GILES: But I must have work to be able to buy food for my family.

HUMPHRY: I still do not see what that has to do with me.

GILES: We have no food in our house. Yesterday we ate our last bit of meal. (GILES *seats himself on a chair and buries his head in his hands.*)

HUMPHRY: Ahem, ahem. (*Rubs his hands together and coughs again.*) Ahem, well?

GILES (*Rouses himself; looks surprisedly at* HUMPHRY *and goes to him pleadingly*) : Surely with all you have, you could give us enough to keep us until I get work again. You must help me Humphry!

HUMPHRY: Help you? Why should I help you? Poor folks are always wanting things.

GILES: I will pay you back, Humphry. Do you not remember when your children were small and you had no food, and we div—

HUMPHRY: Enough, enough, I say. (*He snatches up a ham and tosses it to* GILES.) Here, take this. Go now, and do not let me see your face again!

GILES: Thanks, Humphry. (GILES *takes the ham and hurries out.*)

HUMPHRY (*As he walks impatiently about*) : Always asking for things! Always asking for things! (*He frowns, snaps his fingers to the* CLERK *who takes up his quill again hastily and they proceed.*) Let's get on with this. Four casks of —

CURTAIN

* * *

SCENE 2

TIME: *Later the same day.*

SETTING: *The stage is arranged for two scenes. Behind the curtain is the workshop of the* DWARFS. *One* DWARF *is sewing on a coat,* ANOTHER *is polishing a golden pitcher, a* THIRD *is drinking from a silver cup,* SEVERAL OTHERS *are busily engaged in making various articles. Near the right front of the stage, partly concealed by a drape, stands an old mill. In front of the curtain is the forest.*

AT RISE: GILES *is hurrying home through the forest with the ham carefully wrapped in his cloak. He meets a man with a sack of meal on his back going in the opposite direction. The stranger wears the dusty clothes of a* MILLER. GILES *doffs his hat pleasantly to the stranger.*

GILES: I give you good day, stranger.

MILLER: A good day to you. (GILES *pauses; the* STRANGER *puts down his sack of meal as he continues.*) I am a poor miller. a stranger in this part of the kingdom, good sir, trying to sell meal. Would you like to buy some?

GILES: I am sorry, miller, but I have no gold to pay you with.

MILLER: You carry a heavy package, friend. Do you have something to sell, too?

GILES: No, I have a fine ham. See, I will show it to you. (*He unwraps the ham and shows it to the* MILLER.) Did you ever smell a more savory ham? Come close and smell it.

MILLER (*Smells the ham*): You are right, my friend. It has a marvelous smell. What are you going to do with it?

GILES: Eat it, and it please you.

MILLER: I would not *eat* it if *I* were you. I know of a place where you can get almost anything you wish for a ham like that.

GILES: No, really?

MILLER: Truly.

GILES: Where?

MILLER: In the land of dwarfs.

GILES: In the land of dwarfs?

MILLER: Aye, that is the place.

GILES: But *I* could never get there.

MILLER: Oh, yes, you could.

GILES: If I did get there, could I get back?

MILLER: Just as easily as you got there.

GILES: Do you know how to get there?

MILLER: Aye.

GILES: Would you tell me how to get there and back?

MILLER (*Thinks*): Promise me that you will trade the ham for nothing but the old mill that stands behind the door.

GILES: Oh, but I want gold. They say that the dwarfs have great chests full of gold.

MILLER: They do have great heaps of gold, but that one old mill is worth more than all the gold they have.

GILES: Why?

MILLER: Their gold is fairy gold. Once you got it away, you would find that it was only yellow clay.

GILES: What would I do with an old mill?

MILLER: You could sell the mill for real gold. (*Walks a few steps.*) I have it. I need another mill, and I will buy it from you.

GILES: What would you give me for the mill?

MILLER (*He pulls a small bag of gold from his pocket. He takes out a handful and shows it to* GILES) : I will give you this whole sack of gold for the mill.

GILES (*Excitedly*) : It is a bargain. Tell me how to get there, and I will get the mill for you.

MILLER: Very well. Do what I tell you and you will be in the land of dwarfs.

GILES: Hurry, tell me; I want to go.

MILLER: Mark well what I say. Walk three steps to the east.

GILES: Walk three steps to the east.

MILLER: Walk three steps to the west.

GILES: Walk three steps to the west.

MILLER: Hop around a magic circle.

GILES: Hop around a magic circle.

MILLER: Spin on your heel.

GILES: Spin on your heel.

MILLER: Now say, "Little friends, let me in."

GILES: Little friends, let me in.

MILLER: Exactly right.

GILES: I know *that* now, miller. Tell me how to get back again.

MILLER: Do the charm backwards. Spin on your heel; hop around a magic circle; walk three steps west; walk three steps east; then you will be home again.

GILES: I shall remember. Thanks I give you miller. (*To himself.*) It is sort of foolishness, but it will not hurt to try. I'll do it and see what happens. (GILES *begins to repeat the charm. As he does so the* MILLER *steals away and just as* GILES *says, "Little friends, etc." the curtain parts quietly behind him disclosing the* Dwarfs *at work. When* GILES *turns to speak to the* MILLER, *he finds himself in the land of the dwarfs.*) Walk three steps to the east. (*He walks three steps east.*) Walk three steps west. (*He walks three steps to the west.*) Hop around a magic circle. (*He hops around a magic circle.*) Spin on my heel. (*He spins on his heel.*) What do I say? — Oh, yes, I remember, "Little friends, let me in." (*He turns to speak to the* MILLER. *The* DWARFS *sniff the air avidly.*)

DWARFS: Ham! (*They sniff, rub their eyes, look at each other in surprise, and sniff again.*) Ham! (*They leave their work and close in on* GILES.)

1st Dwarf: Brothers, I smell ham!

2nd Dwarf: That mortal has it.

3rd Dwarf: See the bundle he has under his arm.

4th Dwarf (*Approaching* Giles *cautiously*): It is a ham; is it not?

Giles: Aye. (*Unwraps the ham.*) See!

Dwarfs (*Capering gleefully around* Giles *chanting*): A ham, a ham, it is a ham! A ham, a ham, it is a *ham.*

1st Dwarf (*Runs back to his work bench and returns with a coat he has been making*): Give me the ham and I will give you this coat.

Giles (*While he pretends to examine the cloak carefully,* Giles *looks around the room until he locates the mill.*): It is too small, and besides, I do not need a cloak. No, you must offer me something else for the ham.

2nd Dwarf (*Bringing a golden vase from his work bench*): You may have this golden vase for the ham.

Giles: I have no use for a golden vase. (*Pointing to the old mill*) How about the old mill over there? I need a mill.

2nd Dwarf (*As he backs away*): Oh, no. We could not trade that.

3rd Dwarf (*Approaching* Giles *with a silver jug and cup*): Here is a silver jug. It will always be full of nice sweet milk.

Giles (*To himself*): I wonder if I should take this jug. My children could always have milk if I did.

3rd Dwarf (*Pouring milk into the cup*): See. It is never empty. (*He pours milk into the cup again.*)

Giles (*To himself*): I promised the stranger to trade for the mill. I will keep my promise. (*To the* Dwarf.) No, I do not want the jug. If I cannot have the mill, I will not trade with you at all. (*He uncovers the ham and smells it. The* Dwarfs *sniff and draw together as they consult hurriedly.*) I shall take it home. It will make a fine dinner. (*He wraps the ham and starts spinning on his heel.*)

1st Dwarf (*He rushes over to the mill and takes it to* Giles): Here, take it. We must have the ham.

Giles: Fine! Here is the ham.

Dwarfs (*Singing and dancing about*): It is our ham, our very own ham! (Giles *wraps the mill in his cloak and starts to spin on his heel when one of the* Dwarfs, *who has not been dancing skips over to* GILES *and catches him by the cloak.* GILES *stoops to hear what the* DWARF *whispers to him. The* DWARF *skips back to the other dwarfs and dances.* GILES *partly uncovers the mill, looks at it with surprise before he wraps it close in his cloak again. As the curtain closes,* GILES *is spinning on his heel, hopping around the magic circle, etc., on his way home again.*)

CURTAIN

* * *

SCENE 3

TIME: *Later the same day*

SETTING: *The kitchen in the house of* GILES.

AT RISE: *On a bench in front of the bare crudely made table, right front, sits* MARGO *with her arms around* JOAN. GODFREY *sits on a stool left side, near a Welsh cupboard, right elbow on knee, head on hand, looking dejectedly at the floor. Their clothes are faded and worn.* JOAN *has been crying.*

JOAN: Mother, I am hungry. When will father come?

MARGO: I do not know,... soon, I hope.

JOAN: Wouldn't a bowl of bread and milk taste good, Mother?

MARGO: Hush, child.

JOAN: I would like even one little crust of bread.

GODFREY (*Raising his head*): Can you not see how hard it is for Mother when you talk that way? (*He rises.*) Father should be back anytime now. Maybe he will bring something for us. (*Pause.*) He has been gone such a long time. (*He walks towards the fireplace.*)

MARGO: I am afraid he has found no work, or he would be back by this time.

GODFREY (*Turns and listens*): Listen! (*A sound is heard, left door.*) There is father. (FATHER *enters briskly with something wrapped carefully in his long cloak. He smiles as he greets everyone.)*

GILES: Greetings, my dear ones, see what I have for you!

JOAN AND GODFREY: Father, what have you? (*They rush to* GILES *and throw their arms about him. He pauses, waiting for* MARGO *to greet him.* MARGO *looks steadily at him with no sign of welcome.)*

MARGO (*Stands*): Where have you been this long time?

GILES: You could never guess, Margo. I have been to the Land of Dwarfs.

MARGO: The Land of Dwarfs!

GILES: Aye, see what I have brought back. (*He unwraps the mill and places it on the table.* MARGO *moves to the table to examine the mill. The children stand behind the table eagerly examining the mill.)*

MARGO: An old thing; ready to fall to pieces. What did you get that for? We have nothing to grind in it.

GILES: But, Margo —

MARGO: You foolish man, why did you not bring us something to eat? Throw it away! (*She puts her apron before her face and begins to cry silently.)*

GILES: Wait, Margo; I shall not throw it away. It is a magic mill. The dwarf told me so. It will give us anything we want.

GODFREY: What do we turn it with? I want to see it work.

JOAN: What is a mill for, Godfrey?

GILES: Wait, children.

MARGO (*Seating herself on the stool*): I have waited so long. (*She continues to cry softly.* GILES *moves the mill from the table to the wide shelf of the Welsh cupboard. He faces the children.)*

GILES: O, Mill, give us food. (*A little tinkling tune comes from the mill; a door in front of the mill flies open and a jug of milk and a fine oat cake slide out upon the shelf.* GILES *stoops and whispers to the mill. The door shuts and the tune stops.)*

GODFREY (*As the door of the mill opens*): Mother, look!

JOAN (*A little frightened, runs to* MARGO *and takes her by the hand*): Mother! Look, look at the mill! (MARGO *continues to cry in her apron.)*

GILES (*Takes up the oat cake and goes to* MARGO. *He shakes her shoulder gently*): Look, Margo! Did you ever see a finer oat cake?

MARGO (*Wiping her tears away*): Where did you get that cake? (*She feels the cake.*) It's just baked.

GILES: The mill gave it to us. See the jug of milk Godfrey has. (GODFREY *has taken down two mugs and is busily pouring milk for* JOAN *and himself.*)

MARGO: I can't believe it, Giles. I can't believe it.

GILES: Very well, watch. (*He goes to the mill; the children stop drinking long enough to watch him.*) Give us a cheese, O, Mill. (*The little tinkling tune begins as the door flies open and a cheese slides out of the mill.* GILES *stoops and whispers to the mill. The door closes and the tune stops.*)

GILES: Come, good wife, let us eat. We have a feast fit for a king. (*As* GILES, MARGO, *and* GODFREY *eat,* JOAN *steals over to the mill and whispers to it. The door flies open and the tune begins. Those at the table turn and watch her. Out of the mill roll gaily colored little cakes.* JOAN *tries to gather them before they drop on the floor but she soon has more than she can hold.*)

JOAN: Stop, you mill! (*The mill keeps on sending out little cakes.*) Stop, oh, please stop! Father!

GILES (*Hastening to the mill to whisper to it*): You must never do that again, Joan. The mill will not stop unless I say the magic word to it.

JOAN: What is the magic word?

GILES: Only the owner of the mill can know it. If I told you, it would not be a magic word any longer. The dwarf whispered it to me when I got the mill.

MARGO: Truly a strange mill. Come, children, let us eat Joan's little cakes.

CURTAIN

* * *

SCENE 4

TIME: *One week later.*

SETTING: *The same as Scene 1.*

AT RISE: MARGO, *richly arrayed, is arranging bright yarns seated near the table.* GILES, *also richly dressed, as are* JOAN *and* GOD-

FREY, *is sitting by the fireplace smoking a long stemmed pipe.* GODFREY *is tying the tail of a kite, and* JOAN *is sitting on the stool sewing with a very long thread.*

MARGO: No one can say that we are hungry and cold any more, my good man.

GILES (*Nods and smiles*): True, true, good wife.

MARGO: What was the hatter's Anna asking you this afternoon, Joan?

JOAN: She said she would give me a big red apple if I would tell her where you got our new kettles.

MARGO: What did you say?

JOAN: I said Father got them for us.

GILES: Good. What did she say then?

JOAN: She crossed herself and said some strange words as she went away.

GILES: That was right, Joan. I do get the things for you. Don't tell how I do it. No one needs to know. The man who told me how to get to the Land of Dwarfs met me in the wood today. He wanted to buy the mill from me.

MARGO: O, Giles, you are not going to sell the mill, are you?

GILES: That would be a very foolish thing to do. I told him that we would not part with the mill. He offered me so much gold for it that he must have known the secret, too.

MARGO: Your brother was surely surprised at your good fortune when he came to see you yesterday. Did you tell him where we got our riches?

GILES: No, and I am not going to tell anyone, not even my own brother. If our neighbors knew where we got our riches they might steal the mill. (*Pause.*) Before Humphry left, I gave him a ham!

MARGO: Did you? (*They laugh.*)

GILES: Aye, I gave him a ham. (*A knock is heard.* GILES *opens the door and the* MILLER, *disguised as a peddler, comes in with a pack on his back. He takes off his hat and bows, looking furtively about as he does so.*)

PEDDLER: I give you good evening, kind sir, and good evening to you, mistress.

GILES and MARGO: A good evening to you, stranger.

PEDDLER: Would you like to buy some beautiful silver? (*He*

reaches into his pack and takes out a silver basket.) Hand wrought and of the purest metal. What will you trade for it?

GILES: We have nothing that we want to trade.

PEDDLER (*Looks around the room*): Mayhap you would like to exchange yon old mill for something new. I have other things to barter. (*He reaches into his pack and brings out a new mill.*) Here is a nice new mill; I will give it to you for that old mill yonder. It is much better looking, and, what is more, it will last longer.

GILES: No, I do not wish to trade the mill. A good night to you, sir. (GILES *opens the door. The* PEDDLER *puts his pack on his back and hurriedly departs.*)

PEDDLER: A good night to you, sir; and a good night to you, fair lady.

MARGO: Giles, I don't like that man.

GILES: He's all right, Margo. He is just a poor man trying to earn an honest living.

MARGO: You may be right, but I still do not like the way he looked around the room. Come, children, time for bed.

GILES: I'll bring in a bundle of faggots to make fire with tomorrow morning. (MARGO *and the children go out right door;* GILES *goes out back door for the faggots. The* PEDDLER *sneaks back through the left door.*)

PEDDLER: This is the mill. He would not trade it. I have made no mistake. (*He takes the mill and hurries out the left door.* GILES *returns, rear door.*)

GILES (*Dropping an arm load of faggots by the fireplace*): I shall put the mill away and bar the door. (*He goes toward the mill, pauses, rubs his eyes, and looks at the place where the mill had stood.*) It is gone! Margo! It is gone! Margo! Margo!

MARGO (*Rushing in*): What can be the matter, Giles?

GILES: Did you take the mill?

MARGO: No, of course not. (*She looks to the place where the mill had stood.*) It is gone! Our mill is gone! Joan, Godfrey! Come here, quickly! (*Enter* JOAN *and* GODFREY, *right.*)

GILES: Joan, Godfrey, did you take the mill?

JOAN and GODFREY: No, Father.

GILES: It cannot be gone. Look behind the cupboard. Maybe someone has hidden it from us. (*They look every place.*) It is gone. Someone took the mill while I was getting the faggots.

MARGO: Our mill, our precious mill. (*She puts her head down on the table and sobs.* GILES *snatches up cap and cloak and rushes toward the right door.*)

GILES: I am going out to find the mill!

GODFREY (*Snatches up hat and cloak and follows his father*): Wait, Father, I am going with you! (JOAN *falls on her knees by her mother, puts her head in her mother's lap and weeps as the curtain closes.*)

* * *

SCENE 5

TIME: *Two days later than Scene IV, late afternoon.*

SETTING: *Deck of a ship before the captain's quarters.*

AT RISE: EVAN *and* JULES, *sail makers, sit on a chest, right back, mending a sail.* GUY, *a cabin boy, sits left back, tying ropes.* ROGER, *the mate, stands near the rail steadily scanning the shore, left front. The* CAPTAIN *of the ship paces back and forth across the front. The sound of a chanty is heard off stage, before the curtain rises, continues softly a few moments.*

CAPTAIN: Where can that merchant with the salt be? My men are ready to hoist the sails. Do you see him coming, Roger?

ROGER (*Salutes captain*): Nobody comes, sir.

CAPTAIN: He knows that I must get my load and be away before the turn of the tide. (*The* CAPTAIN *paces back and forth impatiently;* ROGER *turns to scan the shore again; the* SAILORS *whisper as they work.*)

ROGER (*Saluting captain*): Sir, I saw a small boat putting out from the shore.

CAPTAIN: Look well, mate; make sure who it is. It is about time he comes, the lubber. (*He paces across the deck.*) He promised me to have the salt here by midday, and it is almost sunset now.

ROGER (*Saluting*): He is coming, sir, the merchant.

CAPTAIN: Stand by, men, to cast off! (*Several* SAILORS *enter right.* ROGER *exits left.*)

MERCHANT (*Off stage left*): Ship ahoy!

ROGER (*Off stage*): Ahoy! (*Enter left.*) The merchant is below, sir.

CAPTAIN: Help him up the ladder. (*Exit* ROGER *and* JULES, *left.* CAPTAIN *speaks to the men.*) Man the capstan to heave the anchor! (*Exit right all sailors except* EVAN *and* GUY. *Enter* ROGER *with* JULES *carrying the mill, right. The* MERCHANT, *who was the* MILLER *and the* PEDDLER, *rushes in ahead of* ROGER *excitedly.*)

MERCHANT: Cast off! Cast off, Captain!

CAPTAIN: Where is the salt? We cannot sail without ballast.

MERCHANT: I have the salt.

CAPTAIN: Where?

MERCHANT (*Rushing over to* JULES *who holds the mill and unwrapping it*): Here, in the mill! All the salt we want.

CAPTAIN: Are you a wizard that salt should come from a mill? Stop this foolishness, man. Where is the salt?

MERCHANT: In this mill, I say. This old mill will quickly fill your ship with fine, white salt. Cast off, Captain, cast off! They may miss the mill and come after me. I travelled a night and a day to get here. We must get away quickly.

CAPTAIN: Heave the anchor, men. (CAPTAIN, ROGER *and* SAILORS *go off right and left. The anchor chanty is heard off stage.*)

MERCHANT (*To* JULES *holding the mill*): Take the mill down to the hold, and I shall come and start it. (*Exit* JULES *right with the mill.* MERCHANT *follows.*)

EVAN: Did you see the rats leaving the ship just before mid-day?

GUY: No, did you, Evan?

EVAN: Aye, I did, Guy. It is a bad sign, my friend, when rats leave a ship. If I had not given my word to the captain to go with him on this trip I would take my bag and go right now. It is not seemly, my lad, that one little mill should fill a big ship with salt. (*The tinkling tune of the mill is heard off stage.*)

GUY: Whence comes that strange tune, Evan? Hist, here comes the captain.

CAPTAIN (*Enters from right talking to himself*): It is a magic mill; as soon as he said, "Give me salt, O, Mill," the salt began to pour out. We should have a full load in no time. (*He rubs his hands together as he paces back and forth. He looks left.*) Ah, we are beyond the headlands now; no one can catch us. (*Enter* MERCHANT *smiling. Sound of mill continues. It does so to the end but is very faint after it is submerged in the sea.*)

MERCHANT: The mill is grinding out salt so fast that the men have trouble keeping sacks ready to store it in.

CAPTAIN: Fine, friend, fine.

MERCHANT: I had much trouble getting that mill. The dwarfs knew me; but luckily I found a poor man who got it for me. In some way he learned the secret of the mill, and he would not sell the mill to me.

CAPTAIN: How did you get it then?

MERCHANT: I disguised myself as a peddler and located the mill, then I watched my chance and stole it. (*Both laugh.*) Now we shall be rich, Captain; we shall be rich.

CAPTAIN: You are a clever fellow, my friend. Sit down and let us drink a mug of ale together. Boy, (*To* GUY) bring a jug of ale and two mugs. (*Exit* GUY *into captain's quarters.*)

ROGER (*Enters hurriedly from right*): Your pardon, sir. Every hold is full of salt. Our ship cannot carry more, sir. (*The* MERCHANT *hurries out.*)

CAPTAIN: Make it strong, Evan; we shall need all our sails before we finish this trip. (*Reënter* GUY *with the ale. He pours a drink for the* CAPTAIN; CAPTAIN *drinks.*) Pour one for the merchant — a fine fellow, the merchant. (GUY *pours a drink and sets the jug and mug down on the sea chest.*)

MERCHANT (*Entering from the right excitedly*): Captain, oh, Captain, what shall we do?

CAPTAIN: About what, my good man, about what?

MERCHANT (*Wringing his hands*): About the mill. It will not stop grinding salt!

CAPTAIN: Why?

MERCHANT: I do not know the magic word to stop the mill.

CAPTAIN: Blockhead! Why didn't you get the word?

MERCHANT: You can't steal a word. I thought I could guess what it was. I couldn't. The mill still grinds.

JULES (*Runs in from the left*): Salt pours out on the deck. (*To the* CAPTAIN.) Come, help us, sir.

CAPTAIN (*To* MERCHANT): Simpleton! Am I to lose my ship because you cannot think of one word?

MERCHANT: I am trying to find it. (*He snaps his fingers hopelessly as he walks about muttering to himself.*)

CAPTAIN (*To* JULES): Heave the salt overboard. I follow you! (JULES *leaves, right, followed by the* CAPTAIN *and* ROGER.)

GUY (*To* EVAN): Had we better take the small boat and try for land, Evan?

EVAN: Not yet; we will wait for the captain.

MERCHANT (*To himself*): I was so long getting the mill, and now that I have it, I cannot stop it. All my salt is being spoiled. The magic word, I will try again. Stop! Quit! Do not grind. That is enough! Cease! No, no, these will not do! I have tried them all. (*The sound of the mill has suddenly become very faint; the* CAPTAIN *enters left.*)

CAPTAIN: Come, quickly. (EVAN *and* GUY *drop their work and start toward the* CAPTAIN.) We leave the ship.

MERCHANT (*Desperately*): Wait, I may yet find the word!

CAPTAIN: Too late now. We threw the mill overboard. All is lost.

MERCHANT (*With a sob*): Not my mill?

CAPTAIN: Go, men, help man the small boats. (*Exit men.*)

ROGER (*Entering*): The ship is lost. The water washes over the deck!

CAPTAIN: There is too much salt! To the boats! (*They rush off as the curtain falls.*)

THE END

10 copies

CINDERELLA

by Alice D'Arcy

Characters

FIRST SISTER.
SECOND SISTER.
CINDERELLA.
FAIRY GODMOTHER.
PRINCE.
TRUMPETERS (2).
ATTENDANTS (6).
DANCERS. (*Optional — using the Two Sisters, Prince, Cinderella, and six attendants with four more female characters would suffice, but if stage permits, the more dancers the larger effect will be produced by ballroom scene.*)

SCENE 1

SETTING: *By the fireplace.*

AT RISE: CINDERELLA, *ragged and with a smudge of soot on her face, is sweeping in front of the fireplace. She places broom in corner and sits on box gazing into fire.*

CINDERELLA: Tonight is the night. (*Sighs and cups head in her hands.*) If only *I* were going to the ball. (*Enter* SISTERS *in new gowns.* FIRST SISTER *holds piece of lace in hand;* SECOND SISTER *a piece of ribbon.*)

FIRST SISTER: Will you look at the little goose! (*Snickers.*) Ella sit by the cinders. Have you nothing else to do?

SECOND SISTER: Why, my dear sister, of *course* she has nothing else to do — (*Clips words*) she is too stupid!

CINDERELLA (*Rising*): How *lovely* your gowns are! If only I —

FIRST SISTER: Come now — stop talking idle words —

SECOND SISTER: Help us dress. Here. (*Hands her ribbon.*) Tie this on my neck — not there, you simpleton!

CINDERELLA: Oh, I'm sorry. I was thinking —

SECOND SISTER: We'll do the thinking around here. (*Shoves* CINDERELLA.) I'll fix my own ribbon. Go help your sister pin that ruffle on her sleeve.

CINDERELLA (*Perplexed*): Ruffle on her sleeve? Why I didn't know —

FIRST SISTER (*Haughtily*): Of *course* you didn't know. How would you know anything about the latest fashions? (CINDERELLA *hastily adjusts ruffle while other sister ties bow.*)

CINDERELLA: My, how beautiful you look! What lovely gowns! (*Sisters parade back and forth smoothing folds, admiring selves, etc.*)

SECOND SISTER: Well, Sister, I think we might as well be off.

FIRST SISTER: Yes, we must not be late, for who knows — the Prince may choose one of us as his dancing partner for the evening. (*Claps hands.*) Cinderella! Our capes. (CINDERELLA *takes capes from chair and places them on shoulders of sisters.*)

SECOND SISTER: What an honor to be chosen the Prince's partner! (*Sisters start off stage.* CINDERELLA *follows quickly tugging at skirt of* SECOND SISTER.)

CINDERELLA: Please wait! May I not go too?

FIRST SISTER (*Laughs harshly*): And what, may I ask, would you wear?

SECOND SISTER (*Angrily*): Do you want to disgrace us?

CINDERELLA (*Pleadingly*): No one would have to know I am your sister, and there is a whole trunkful of old gowns in the attic. I am sure I could find *something* among them.

SECOND SISTER: Such nonsense! Why you are only plain Cinderella. Come, Sister. (*They flounce off stage.*)

CINDERELLA: Oh, dear — oh, dear. (*Begins to sob.*) Why must I be so plain? (*Covers face in hands, walks over to box by fireplace and sits down, continues sobbing.*) If only I could go to *one* ball! (CINDERELLA *gazes into fire as* FAIRY GODMOTHER *enters softly.*)

FAIRY GODMOTHER (*With cracking voice*): Well, my poor little child!

CINDERELLA (*Looks up startled*): You frightened me. I don't remember ever seeing you before.

FAIRY GODMOTHER: But I have seen you many times. I am your Fairy Godmother.

CINDERELLA: Fairy Godmother! How wonderful!

FAIRY GODMOTHER: I have never come to you before, but tonight you need me.

CINDERELLA (*Rising quickly*): You mean you will stay with me so that I won't be lonely?

FAIRY GODMOTHER: You sweet child, I will do more than that for you. I will see that you get to the ball.

CINDERELLA: But how did you know I longed —

FAIRY GODMOTHER: Fairies know everything. But hurry now. We have no time to lose.

CINDERELLA (*Excitedly*): Just tell me what you want me to do.

FAIRY GODMOTHER: Have you a pumpkin?

CINDERELLA: Why, yes, right here in the cupboard. (*Starts toward cupboard, but turns back.*) Oh, I forgot. My sisters wish me to make a pumpkin pie for dinner tomorrow night.

FAIRY GODMOTHER: Bring it here. I shall return it. (CINDERELLA *gives pumpkin to* FAIRY GODMOTHER.) Thank you. Now four white mice. (CINDERELLA *walks to side of fireplace and picks up cage through which can be seen four toy mice.*) The pumpkin I shall change into a splendid carriage to carry you to the ball; the mice into handsome horses. No one at the ball shall arrive in greater splendor!

CINDERELLA: Oh, how kind you are, dear Fairy Godmother. (*Suddenly gasps and raises hand to lips.*) Oh-h-h, I cannot go to the ball after all.

FAIRY GODMOTHER: And why, pray tell me?

CINDERELLA: I have nothing but my sisters' old gowns from which to choose. Not one of them could be worn in such a beautiful carriage.

FAIRY GODMOTHER: A lovely gown you shall wear — all shimmering white and silver, and a silver covering for your hair.

CINDERELLA: But how?

FAIRY GODMOTHER: I shall use my magic spell, and you will turn into the loveliest creature on earth. *But you must promise me one thing.*

CINDERELLA: Anything, Fairy Godmother — *anything.*

FAIRY GODMOTHER: You must leave the ball before the stroke of twelve — or you will become Cinderella again, your coach will become a pumpkin, and your grand horses nothing more than the mice I now hold.

CINDERELLA (*Eagerly*): Before the stroke of twelve. I'll remember, I'll surely remember!

FAIRY GODMOTHER: Very well, then. Now hold this pumpkin so that I may have one hand free. (CINDERELLA *takes pumpkin.*)
My spell I cast over you — (*Curtain slowly falls.*)
Kala wala woo,
My spell over you
One is for the carriage
With horses so fine —

CURTAIN

* * *

SCENE 2

SETTING: *The hall.*

AT RISE: *Music is heard and a dance is just ending. When the music stops, the guests stand about in groups, and await the arrival of the* PRINCE. *In the center of the stage and to the rear stands the royal throne in all its splendor. Before it, a few of the guests move to and fro, conversing. Standing near the front of the stage are* CINDERELLA'S *sisters. They are glancing through the gathering.*

FIRST SISTER (*In audible whisper*): I see no one among the ladies in finer fashion than we.

SECOND SISTER: I am *sure* that one of us must be chosen as the Prince's dancing partner.

GENTLEMAN (*Heard above the others*): Where can his Royal Highness be? I *do* hope he does not disappoint us.

SECOND GENTLEMAN: Have no fear. The Prince is ever thoughtful. (*Trumpet sound is heard in distance; gradually becomes louder.*)

FIRST SISTER: The Prince must be on his way here now. (*Enter* TRUMPETERS, *cross to middle of stage, march to rear of stage and take places on either side of throne. Enter four* ATTENDANTS *before* PRINCE, *two following.* PRINCE *ascends throne and* ATTENDANTS *take places on either side.*)

SECOND SISTER: Isn't he *handsome?* (*As* PRINCE *reaches throne, he turns and faces court in regal manner. They pay homage to him and he is seated.*)

PRINCE (*With dignified wave of hand*): Let the dancing continue. As is the custom of the realm, I shall select a dancing partner from among the fairest of this fair land. (*Music starts and the dancing begins. But a few bars are played when the* PRINCE *arises quickly from the throne.*) Stop! Stop, I say. (*Music ceases.* PRINCE *claps hands in command.*) Page! Quickly bring me that lovely maiden I behold standing in the outer court. Be quick, be quick, I say, else she may slip away. (PRINCE *is seated resting elbow on knee and chin in hand while other hand drums on arm of throne impatiently. The guests show their surprise by whispered conversation among them. The* PAGE *slips out to obey command and in a brief moment returns alone.*)

PAGE: The beautiful lady begs Your Highness to continue with the ball. She desires no more than to stand on the threshold and watch.

PRINCE: An humble maiden, I would say! I did not know that such existed in my land — and as beautiful as she is modest! (*Rises from throne.*)

GENTLEMAN: Do you wish me to fetch her, Your Majesty?

PRINCE: Your thoughtfulness is most commendable, but I shall escort her to the ballroom myself. (*As* PRINCE *leaves ballroom several dancers crowd to entrance to watch proceeding, but quickly disperse as* PRINCE *and* CINDERELLA *return. Exclamations at* CINDERELLA'S *beauty can be heard.*)

LADY: What a gorgeous gown!

GENTLEMAN: The loveliest lady here! No wonder the Prince waited!

FIRST SISTER (*Vexed*): Where do you suppose *she* came from? Someone *would* spoil our chances!

SECOND SISTER: Such luck! Probably from a neighboring kingdom. We'll soon know.

PRINCE (*Waves hand*): Let us be gay — return to your dancing! (*Music starts and dancing continues with other guests paying more attention to* PRINCE *and* CINDERELLA *than to dancing. After several minutes a gong strikes twelve and* CINDERELLA, *suddenly remembering* GODMOTHER'S *warning, hastily leaves room.*)

PRINCE (*Music ceases*): After her — do not let her get away! Why, I do not even know the lovely creature's name. (*Several court attendants follow* CINDERELLA *but quickly return.*)

FIRST ATTENDANT: She is nowhere in sight.

SECOND: She is as swift as the deer.

THIRD (*Producing glass slipper*): Your Highness, as she fled she lost this glass slipper — I thought perhaps —

PRINCE (*Taking slipper in hand*): A glass slipper! What a dainty foot she must have! Tomorrow, I will search the entire realm for the maiden who can wear this slipper, and to her I shall offer my heart, hand and kingdom!

TRUMPETERS (*Step to front of stage and after three blasts on trumpets announce*): Hear ye! Hear ye! His Royal Highness has proclaimed, and let it be known to all in this land —

CURTAIN

* * *

SCENE 3

SETTING: *Same as Scene 1.*

AT RISE: CINDERELLA *is busily sweeping in front of the fireplace.* FIRST SISTER *is hobbling about room in shoes which are entirely too small;* SECOND SISTER *is seated on chair with feet wrapped in cloth.*

FIRST SISTER (*Standing on one foot and hopping*): Oh-h-h! I can't bear it — the pain is too great! (*Kicks shoes off and sits down on chair stretching feet and wiggling toes.*)

SECOND SISTER (*Crossly*): Anyone would know that you cannot make your feet smaller by forcing them in shoes two sizes too small.

FIRST SISTER (*Snapping words*): Why, the idea! They are not small — well, maybe just a little bit. Anyway, who told you that feet could be reduced by binding them? It seems to me —

SECOND SISTER (*Removing cloth from feet*): I suppose we have both been rather foolish. I don't see where anything will do much good now.

CINDERELLA (*Stops sweeping and rests hands on broom*): Dear sisters, why should you wish to make your feet smaller all of a sudden? Have they not served you well all these years?

SECOND SISTER: Don't you *ever* know what is going on in this world?

FIRST SISTER (*Wearily and with wave of hand*): Tell her, tell her. At least it will make conversation until he gets here.

SECOND SISTER: Last night at the ball — (*Stops suddenly and appears to be perplexed*) — that's strange!

FIRST SISTER: What is strange? What are you talking about?

SECOND SISTER: Cinderella, now that I think of it, you have asked no questions about the ball. How did that happen?

CINDERELLA (*Begins to sweep again and answers guardedly*): I — I — was waiting for you to mention it.

FIRST SISTER: If that isn't just like the stupid goose! (*Rises, still in stocking feet, and goes to doorway as if searching for someone.*)

SECOND SISTER: Anyway the Prince, after keeping everyone in suspense for hours, chose as his partner a beautiful lady —

FIRST SISTER (*Glancing back from doorway and interrupting*): From a neighboring kingdom —

CINDERELLA: What makes you say she was from a neighboring kingdom?

SECOND SISTER: I will *not* finish my story if you two are going to persist in your interruptions.

CINDERELLA: Oh, please — please go on —

SECOND SISTER: To make it short, his dancing partner left the ball unexpectedly, and as she was running — heaven knows why! —she lost one of her glass slippers. It was a very small one —

CINDERELLA (*Excitedly*): Then the *Prince* must have found the slipper!

FIRST SISTER (*Hurriedly returning from window*): He is here! His Majesty just turned around the bend!

SECOND SISTER: Mercy me — so soon!

CINDERELLA: You mean the Prince is coming *here* to our humble dwelling?

FIRST SISTER: Of course. He is visiting every house in the land to find the owner of the glass slipper.

SECOND SISTER: And to offer her his hand in marriage!

CINDERELLA (*Bewildered*): Oh-h-h-h!

FIRST SISTER: Well, don't stand there acting the simpleton that you are. Help us tidy this room. Oh, *goodness,* why didn't we change our gowns?

SECOND SISTER: I *told* you we should not have stayed so late. (*Both sisters begin to run about frantically straightening furniture, etc.*)

CINDERELLA: I think I heard a knock on the door. Shall I answer it?

SECOND SISTER: Of course, and then leave the room. What could the Prince possibly want of *you?*

FIRST SISTER: No! Allow her to stay — the contrast will be all in our favor. (CINDERELLA *opens door and* PRINCE *and* ATTENDANT *enter.*)

ATTENDANT: His Majesty begs that you forgive his intrusion, but he is most desirous of finding the owner of this glass slipper. (*Holds slipper in front of him.*)

FIRST SISTER: It is a great pleasure to entertain His Royal Highness. (*Both sisters bow before* PRINCE. CINDERELLA *finds her place in the corner by the fireplace.*)

ATTENDANT (*To* SECOND SISTER): May I fit your foot?

SECOND SISTER: By all means. (*Giggles while slipper is being fitted.*) I'm certain it will go on! (*Tries to force the slipper on her foot.*)

PRINCE: You are mistaken. It will not fit. (SECOND SISTER *looks very much disappointed as* FIRST SISTER *brushes past her and extends her foot for fitting.*)

PRINCE (*Nodding head sadly*): I have searched everywhere, but in vain. (*Looks about room and discovers* CINDERELLA.) What ho! Who is this creature who sits by the fire?

CINDERELLA (*Rises and bows before the* PRINCE): Please, Your Majesty, I am only Cinderella.

PRINCE: Only Cinderella — but I would still have you try the slipper.

CINDERELLA: If it pleases His Royal Highness. (ATTENDANT *steps forward, but* PRINCE *takes slipper from him.*)

PRINCE: It will be my pleasure this time. (FIRST SISTER *nudges* SECOND SISTER; *when* CINDERELLA *easily slips foot into slipper, sisters look at each other in surprise.*)

PRINCE (*Joyfully*) : At last, I have come to the end of my quest! (*Off stage is heard the voice of the* FAIRY GODMOTHER.)

FAIRY GODMOTHER: Cinderella! Cinderella!

CINDERELLA (*Distressed, leaves*) : Forgive me, Prince, but someone to whom I owe a great deal is calling.

FIRST SISTER: Can you imagine! Such rudeness!

SECOND SISTER: What can you expect?

PRINCE: I am certain Cinderella had a very good reason for her actions. Let us not judge her before she returns.

SECOND SISTER: As His Royal Highness wishes.

PRINCE (*In jubilant manner to* ATTENDANT) : Prepare the best coach at the palace! Order the most excellent food. Have the servants in their finest array! For today is the day I shall take home with me a bride — one who will be the sweetest princess ever known.

FIRST SISTER: But surely His Majesty is joking!

PRINCE (*Angrily*) : And why should I be joking?

FIRST SISTER: You can not mean Cinderella!

PRINCE (*Striding across stage*) : Most certainly I do — and who are *you* to question?

SECOND SISTER (*Alarmed*) : Please forgive my sister for her thoughts. You cannot blame her entirely. After all, Cinderella is nothing but a little drudge. Why, His Majesty has but to look at her clothes —

PRINCE: Enough! Enough, I say. What care I for her appearance? She is kind and thoughtful. (PRINCE *stops speaking abruptly as if suddenly realizing something, and then seizes* ATTENDANT *by arm*) You think Cinderella will accept *me?* It is true I have everything to offer her, but maybe she will prefer the simple life.

FIRST SISTER: She would be a bigger goose than I thought —

PRINCE: Hush! I will have no more of such talk!

FIRST SISTER (*Claps hand over mouth*) : I didn't mean anything against dear Cinderella. We love her, do we not, my sister?

SECOND SISTER: Most certainly we do!

PRINCE: Why did you not allow her to attend the ball with you last evening?

SECOND SISTER (*Wiping eyes with handkerchief*) : B-b-believe me, most gracious Prince, she was *ashamed* of us, her very own sisters.

FIRST SISTER: She absolutely refused to go with us.

PRINCE: You mean she did not attend the ball then?

FIRST SISTER: Oh, no!

SECOND SISTER: Indeed not!

PRINCE (*Disturbed, walks up and down stage for a few minutes*): That's strange — most incredibly strange! The slipper fits her as if it were made for her.

ATTENDANT: Anything I can do for His Royal Highness?

PRINCE: Yes — yes, there is. Bring the girl to me. (ATTENDANT *goes to door right;* PRINCE *sits down.*) I cannot believe Cinderella is anything but the sweet, lovely maiden I picture her. (*Shakes head.*)

FIRST SISTER: That is only because you do not know her as we do.

SECOND SISTER: Why, if you only knew —

ATTENDANT (*Returns to place before* PRINCE): Cinderella approaches, Oh Prince! (CINDERELLA *enters. She is dressed in same gown she wore at the ball.* PRINCE *rises and drops to knee at her feet.*)

PRINCE (*Joyfully*): How right I was! Cinderella, will you return to my castle to take your place at my side on the royal throne? Everything I have is yours, and I offer you my heart forever.

CINDERELLA (*Clasping hands*): Oh, my Prince Charming! Gladly will I go with you. Even my loveliest dreams were never as beautiful as this. (PRINCE *rises and takes* CINDERELLA'S *hand. Sisters look at each other and begin to rush around to pack things.*)

FIRST SISTER: It won't take a minute for us to get ready, Your Majesty.

PRINCE: And where are you going?

SECOND SISTER: Why, with dear Cinderella, of course.

PRINCE: Oh, no you're not. I do know though that Cinderella is so kind and forgiving that she will want you to visit her once in a while. That you may do.

CINDERELLA: You are so kind!

PRINCE (*To* ATTENDANT): Lead the way. I cannot wait to spread the good news over the land! My Cinderella! (PRINCE *and* CINDERELLA *start to leave as curtain falls.*)

THE END

THE FLOATING STONE

by C. W. Foulk and Doris P. Buck

Characters

FIRST COURT LADY
SECOND COURT LADY
THIRD COURT LADY
THE PRINCESS
THE SHEPHERD
THE KING
THE HERALD
THE PRINCE OF ARNA
THE ROYAL WIZARD
THE PRINCE OF TRIPOTA

SCENE 1

SETTING: *A King's court.*

AT RISE: TWO COURT LADIES *are deep in gossip.*

FIRST LADY: I must say I'm enjoying my visit at your court, but there's one thing I can't understand.

SECOND LADY: What is that?

FIRST LADY: Your Princess is beautiful, so kind, so sweet —

SECOND LADY: She is, indeed.

FIRST LADY: Why doesn't some prince marry her?

SECOND LADY (*Putting her fingers on her lips*): Hush! (*The* LADIES *draw close to each other.*)

FIRST LADY (*Whispering*): What's the matter?

SECOND LADY: The King won't hear of it. Don't say *marry!* He won't let the word be spoken.

FIRST LADY: Why?

SECOND LADY: He must want to keep her all to himself. He's so rude to visiting princes that they go home.

FIRST LADY: Poor Princess, what does she do?

SECOND LADY: I don't believe she minds.

FIRST LADY: Indeed!

SECOND LADY: You see, she's in love with a shepherd, and though he never can hope to win her, at least she doesn't have to marry anyone else. (*The* THIRD COURT LADY *enters.*)

THIRD LADY: Have you heard the news?

SECOND LADY: What news?

THIRD LADY: You haven't heard yet! Why, everyone in court is laughing about it!

FIRST AND SECOND LADIES: Tell us.

THIRD LADY: The King, the King. . . . (*She giggles.*)

FIRST AND SECOND LADIES: What *is* it?

THIRD LADY: He says the Princess can be married.

FIRST LADY: When?

SECOND LADY (*Almost at the same time*): To whom?

THIRD LADY: To the man who can make a stone float in the air!

FIRST LADY (*Slowly*): Make a stone *float* in the air!

THIRD LADY: That's his way of keeping the Princess by his side forever.

FIRST LADY: Poor Princess, she'll die an old maid. (*The* LADIES *go out.*)

CURTAIN

* * *

SCENE 2

SETTING: *Same as Scene* 1.

AT RISE: *The* PRINCESS *and the* SHEPHERD *enter from the right.*

PRINCESS: Now there is some hope.

SHEPHERD: Is there? I'd do anything in the world to win you, but no man can make a stone float in the air.

PRINCESS: Are you sure?

SHEPHERD: Perhaps if I studied magic for years and years, I could learn.

PRINCESS: Magic! (*Scornfully*) Hocus pocus! Father used to keep a magician at court till we found how he did his tricks.

SHEPHERD: Then how can I ever make that stone float in the air?

PRINCESS (*Taking a paper from a little bag she carries*): Here is a paper my father gave me. He said it would help.

SHEPHERD (*Eagerly*): Let me see. Why, I can't even read it!

PRINCESS (*Over his shoulder*): It looks like writing only it isn't.

SHEPHERD: We're no better off than we were before.

PRINCESS: Oh, why did my father do this to me?

SHEPHERD: Your father loves you, Princess. This must have a meaning and I shall find out what it is.

PRINCESS: It looks like writing done the wrong way round —

SHEPHERD: As if you saw it in a mirror . . . mirror. . . . I've heard of mirror writing. Maybe this is it. Let's look at it in a glass.

PRINCESS: Here is one. (*She produces a mirror from her bag.*)

SHEPHERD (*Holding the paper in front of the glass*): Look. The King's message. "Try Science." What's Science?

PRINCESS (*Speaking at the same time*): Who's Science?

SHEPHERD (*Unfolding the paper*): There's more. (*Reads*) . .
"He who by Science would be led
Must learn to look inside his head."

PRINCESS: What does that mean?

SHEPHERD: I don't know, but I'm going to find out and win your hand. (*They go out together.*)

CURTAIN

* * *

SCENE 3

SETTING: *The same.*

AT RISE: *The* KING *and all his court enter. The* KING *and the* PRINCESS *sit on thrones.*

KING: Daughter, this is the day when young men may ask for your hand. All they have to do is to make a stone — a very small stone — float in the air. I am certain that anyone who really loves you should have no difficulty at all.

PRINCESS (*Softly*): If only my shepherd comes in time!

HERALD: A stranger is at the gate, Your Highness.

KING: Announce him.

HERALD: His Royal Highness, the Prince of Arna. (*With a flourish the* HERALD *steps aside and the* PRINCE *enters with the* ROYAL WIZARD.)

KING (*Advancing to meet him*): Welcome, Your Royal Highness. Have you come to ask for my daughter's hand?

PRINCE OF ARNA: I have. I have learned from the stars that she is to be my wife. The Royal Wizard has told me.

KING: Indeed.

PRINCE OF ARNA (*Nudging the* WIZARD *with his foot*): Speak up. You did say so, didn't you?

WIZARD: It is so written in the stars.

KING (*Very solemnly*): Bring in the stone. (*The* HERALD *goes out, and returns with the stone, which he carries on a small table covered with silver cloth. He deposits it with the utmost ceremony in front of the thrones.*)

WIZARD (*Advancing to the table*):

Dark stars and bright stars,
Red stars and white stars.

KING: The Prince has to do it himself.

PRINCE OF ARNA: I'm not sure I remember all the words in the spell. Some of them were quite long.

PRINCESS (*Eagerly*): Perhaps you'd rather not try, Prince.

SECOND LADY: Poor girl, she's still hoping her shepherd will win her.

PRINCE OF ARNA:

Red stars and white stars,
Something, something and bright stars.

(*As the* PRINCE *is speaking, he lifts the silver cloth. The* LADIES *titter as he gets mixed up.* PRINCE *looks closely at stone.*) I think it moved a little.

PRINCESS (*Positively*): I'm sure it didn't. It didn't move the tiniest bit. I was watching.

PRINCE OF ARNA (*To the* WIZARD): You wretch. You've been fooling me. This Princess doesn't want to marry me. You and your stars! I'll make you pay for this! (*Exit, pushing the* WIZARD *in front of him.*)

PRINCESS (*Covering the stone again*): Oh father, how glad I am I didn't have to marry such a silly prince! I hope my shepherd comes in time.

HERALD: Another man is at the gate, Your Highness.

KING: Announce him.

HERALD: The Prince of Tripota. (*The* PRINCE *enters, self-important and rather fussy.*)

PRINCE OF TRIPOTA: I have come to move mountains to win the lady. (*He bows with a great flourish to the* PRINCESS.)

KING: Oh, no, not mountains, just a very small stone. I don't even ask to have it float in the air a long while, half a minute will be enough.

PRINCE OF TRIPOTA: Most beautiful lady, I have studied magic since I was a child. I can make dewdrops into diamonds.

KING: I'd like to see some of those diamonds.

PRINCE OF TRIPOTA: Unfortunately I left them all in my own country. But everyone there says I am a very great magician. They have said it since I was a little boy. Show me the stone and I shall make it float.

PRINCESS (*Lifting the cloth*): It is on the table, Your Highness.

PRINCE OF TRIPOTA: That tiny thing — a trifle. Watch me keep it in the air.

PRINCESS (*Aside*): Oh, I hope not.

PRINCE OF TRIPOTA (*Making gestures*): Vir Luro Arcadeyevna. Abacadabra. (*He drops his handkerchief over the pebble.*) When I lift this handkerchief, the stone will rise into the air. (*He pulls the handkerchief away, and his face falls.*)

FIRST LADY: It's still on the table.

SECOND LADY: I knew it would be.

THIRD LADY: And he thought he was a magician.

PRINCE OF TRIPOTA: But they all told me I was a great magician, ever since I was a little, little boy — and that stone hasn't moved at all.

KING: It doesn't pay to believe everything that's told you. Good-bye, Prince.

PRINCE OF TRIPOTA: If I can't do it, nobody can. (*The* PRINCE *goes out.*)

PRINCESS: Poor fellow, he really believed the stories he told about himself. (*She replaces the silver cloth.*)

KING: Neither of these foolish Princes has won you. I'm glad, for I'd hate to have you marry a fool. You'll be much better off with me.

PRINCESS: I had hoped that someone else would come.

FIRST LADY: It's very late.

KING: Take the stone away.

PRINCESS: Father, let us wait a little while longer. (*She hangs on his arm, pleading.*)

KING: As you wish, child, but the sun is down now. No one is likely to come.

HERALD: A man is at the gate, Your Highness.

KING: Announce him.

HERALD: I can't. He hasn't any title. He's just a shepherd.

SHEPHERD (*Bursting in*): I can do it! I can do it! I've just seen how. Where's the stone?

KING: Don't be too sure, shepherd. Two Princes thought they could make that stone float, but failed.

SHEPHERD: Let me try, Your Majesty. You said that anyone who made the stone float would win the Princess.

KING: There lies the stone. (*The* PRINCESS *uncovers it.*)

THIRD LADY: Where did a shepherd learn magic spells?

SHEPHERD: This is not magic, Your Ladyship. It is Science.

THIRD LADY: Science! What's Science? Where do you find it?

SHEPHERD (*Smiling at the King, who smiles back*): He who by Science would be led, Must learn to look inside his head.

KING: Did you?

SHEPHERD: Yes, Your Majesty. Watch. (*He takes a mortar and pestle which he has brought in a bundle tied to his crook, and grinds the pebble.*)

FIRST LADY: He's grinding up the stone. Its quite fine powder now.

SHEPHERD: Of course. Powder can stay up in the air half a minute, can't it? Look, Your Majesty, the stone is ready to float. (*He pours the dust into his hand, holds his hand in front of his lips, and blows the dust into the air.*)

KING: Take my daughter, shepherd. (*He joins their hands.*) I kept her only till I was sure she married a man who could use his brain.

THE END

JACK AND JILL

By Helen L. Freudenberger

Characters

JACK, *small boy of about eleven. Dressed in play suit with large tie.*

JILL, *slightly smaller than* JACK. *Dressed in print dress and large white apron, which she takes off to play in.*

MOTHER, *taller girl, dressed in long, full skirt and apron. Made up severely. May wear wig or dust cap if desired.*

FAIRY, *graceful, slender girl who can do a simple dance. Wears the traditional fairy costume with wings, etc. White dress.*

ELVES, *three small boys of about the same height and who march together in simple design.*

TIME: *The morning of the eventful tumble.*

SETTING: *A door-yard before a rather large plain brown cottage painted on the background. A door and window in the house actually open off stage. Flowers made of crepe paper or real potted plants are set in beds along the house to give a cheery home-like atmosphere. A walk of flat stones leads from the door to the right of the stage and off right. A carpet of green paper matting may be used to give the appearance of grass.*

AT RISE: JACK *and* JILL *are playing, making mud pies, near the walk.*

JACK: Here, Jill, let me do that stirring. You'll get mud on your nice clean dress.

JILL: No, I won't get it on me, Jack. Besides, I'm not as messy as you are; and if you get mud on yourself, Mother will scold you something awful.

JACK: Not any worse than she would you. Isn't this a nice mud pie? Anyway, I'd rather she would punish me than you.

JILL: Well, I wouldn't. Come on, let's not make mud pies any more. Let's play Tag. (*They play, running about noisily on the stage.*)

MOTHER (*Thrusts her head out of the window*): Here, here! What's this? (*The children stop.*) Why aren't you after that water? Answer me? Why aren't you getting the pail filled? You lazy children; I've a mind. . . .

JACK: It's my fault, Mother. I. . . .

JILL: No, it's my fault. I wanted to play.

MOTHER: I've told you not to interrupt me. Now go fetch that water and then I'll punish you for having been naughty. Hurry now, because I need the water for the lentils!

JACK: Please, where's the pail?

MOTHER: Don't ask such silly questions. Where it always is, of course. It's by the back door. (JACK *goes off left.*) Such stupid children I never thought I'd have. And you're dirty, too. Why. . . . (JACK *reenters, left, carrying very large wooden pail.*) Now hurry there; don't go slow!

JILL (*Who has been cowering back, runs to* JACK): Here, let me help you.

MOTHER: No you don't, Miss Priss! You'll go to the kitchen and keep the lentils from scorching.

JILL: Please, Mother; the pail's too heavy for him.

MOTHER: Don't sass me. Now march. To your work, both of you. And don't sing, because I want to sleep. (*She roughly pushes* JILL *off left, then enters through door of house.* JACK *goes off right, slowly. After a second, both* JACK *and* JILL *come tiptoeing onto the stage and bump into each other, center, because they are watching the window.*)

JILL: Oh!

JACK: Jill, I came back for you. Did she beat you?

JILL: No, but she said she would when she woke up.

JACK: Maybe you'd better go back and watch the lentils. She'd be awful mad if they scorched.

JILL (*Tossing her head*): Let her be mad then. I'm going with you to carry the water.

JACK: I can get along all right.

JILL: No, I'm going to help you carry it. It's too heavy for you to carry alone.

JACK: We'd better hurry, then, before she wakes up. (*They hurry off right, carrying pail between them.*)

CURTAIN

* * *

Scene 2

Setting: *The same.*

At Rise: Fairy *enters right doing a sprightly dance. She pauses center stage.*

Fairy:

This is my birthday
And I must make it a mirth-day
Because I'm now a real fairy
And my wings are so airy
I must make everyone gay.

(*Does a few more steps.*) Jack and Jill are sad, did you see them? They are the best and kindest children in the village. I shall have to reward them. I must make them happy. But how? (*A noise of marching feet off right. Enter* Elves.)

Elves: Ha.

1st Elf: Ha.

2nd Elf: Ha.

3rd Elf: Ha, ha!

Fairy: Who are you?

Elves:

We are the elves of the well on the hill;
We don't like Jack and we don't like Jill.
We came out of our caves,
Like so many knaves,
To do what harm we could.

Fairy: Why do you want to do harm? There's so much good you can do!

Elves:

They riled our well,
And now we tell,
That those who disturb us
Will not long perturb us;
Though they are small,
They all must fall!

Fairy: Oh, you mean things.

1st Elf: We aren't mean; we're just looking out for ourselves.

3rd Elf: They riled our water. They yelled down our well. And they disturb us.

2ND ELF: And we must punish them.

ELVES:

Though we're not churlish
Still we're not girlish.
We know our work
And may not shirk.
Do our duty we must,
Though earth turn to dust.

FAIRY: But surely they didn't mean to disturb you. They probably didn't know that it was your water.

1ST ELF: But they knew it was someone's water.

2ND ELF: And they shouldn't have disturbed it without permission anyway. So we shall teach them a lesson they'll not forget.

3RD ELF:

Ha, ha! We'll get them yet.
A lesson they'll learn
When we finish our turn.

FAIRY: What are you going to do to them?

ELVES:

They climbed our hill
Now let them spill
All the water
So their Mother will spank them for their fall
And then they will bawl!
(*They march in formation and exit right.*)

FAIRY (*Goes center*): Oh, those mean elves! What will I do to help poor Jack and Jill! I can't stop those mean elves; and they'll make Jack and Jill late so their Mother will beat them. Oh, what can I do? (*She sinks to the floor and buries her head in her hands. After a second, she rises happily.*) But I've forgotten that I'm now a real grown-up fairy! I can do something! I'll not let them hurt the children! (*Noise off right. Screams of* JACK *and* JILL.) Oh, I'm too late.

MOTHER (*Thrusts head out of window*): What was that noise? (*She cannot see the* FAIRY.) I'll bet those children are up to something again. Yes, that Jill had to go along after the water . . . and they've fallen down and spilled it! Just wait till I get to them. I'll teach them to disobey me! (*She disappears from the window.*)

FAIRY: I can stop her from being so cruel to them.

Hi lee, hi lo,
Now fast, not slow,
Drop your frown from your face
And smile apace,
Be kind and good
As a Mother should.
Hi lee, hi lo.

(*Does light steps down right as* MOTHER *enters from door of house. Waves wand, then stands in corner.*)

MOTHER: Well, I'll fix those two. I'll . . . Why, I feel so strange. I wonder what's the matter. (*Passes hand over face; begins smiling.*) Where are Jack and Jill? Now I remember; they fell. Oh, are they hurt? (*Exits right, calling*) Jack, Jill! (*Enter* ELVES *marching.*)

ELVES:

Ha! Ha! Ha!
Those children fell,
As we did tell,
And now we watch with glee
To see them across their mother's knee.
Then them she'll spank,
And their ears she'll yank,
Because they spilled the water.

3RD ELF: How they'll cry and cry!

1ST ELF: They'll be sorry they riled our well.

2ND ELF: We are doing our duty when we punish them.

ELVES:

Let's go turn the milk
And rot the silk
And fill the garden with weeds.
For we must show
That they can grow
As well as plants she needs.

1ST ELF: No, let's wait till she punishes them. It'll be fun. (*Enter* MOTHER, JACK *and* JILL *right, arm in arm.*)

MOTHER: So Jack fell down first?

JILL: Yes, and broke his crown.

MOTHER: His crown? Broke?

JACK: Aw, I just hit my head real hard. And then Jill came tumbling after!

JILL: And I'm glad I did, too. It was so much quicker. I got to you much sooner than if I'd had to walk down that steep hill.

MOTHER: There, there, dear. I know that you like to be with your brother. I'll not ever separate you again. And I won't ever be mean to you again, nor beat you. Here, let's all peel these apples to eat.

ELVES (*Coming forward*):

What's wrong with the woman, has she lost her mind?
To punish them has she declined?
We must do something!

FAIRY (*Enters right*): No, you'll not do anything!

ELVES: What! You back again?

FAIRY: Yes, and for always. I am the spirit of Kindness, and I've just become a real grown-up fairy. This is my birthday, and I shall celebrate it by making Jack and Jill happy.

Away, away, bad elves!
You belong on shelves.
So hi lee, hi lo,
Away you go.
Back to your well
Where you shall dwell.
No more be mean,
But always gleam
On those who come for water.
Hi lee, hi lo,
Away you go.

(*She drives them off right. Trips over to the* MOTHER *and* JACK *and* JILL; *touches them with her wand.*) Now they are gone. They will not trouble you any more.

MOTHER: Who are you? Who will not trouble us any more?

FAIRY: I am the Spirit of Kindness. I have just removed the spell of the Well-Elves from you. They were the cause of your misfortunes, dear lady. But they will not trouble you again. You will always be happy.

JILL: What lovely wings you have!

FAIRY: I have two of them, because brothers and sisters should never quarrel or fight. And they are pure white because little boys and girls should never disobey their mothers. And they are light and graceful because I love my mother, as you should love yours, too.

JACK AND JILL: Oh, we do! She's so nice now!

MOTHER: I'm so glad you're here. Won't you stay with us always?

FAIRY: No, you are happy now. I must go and find others that are not happy, and make them so. So goodbye, Jack and Jill. Goodbye, dear lady. I'm glad that you are now good to Jack and Jill. Goodbye, goodbye. . . . (*Dances off right.*)

MOTHER: She's such a good fairy. And to think, you were almost killed!

JACK: But we weren't, Mother.

JILL: May we help you, Mother?

MOTHER: Yes, you may play with Jack while I fix the lentils.

JACK AND JILL: Let us help you!

MOTHER: Of course, dears, if you want to. (*Takes a step forward.*) And to think, this happiness is all because of the spirit of Kindness! (JACK *and* JILL *run up and embrace her.*)

THE END

BROOM MARKET DAY

by Lida Lisle Molloy

Characters

TOBIAS CROWDER *or* GRANTHER, *who tries out ancient spells on his brooms*
MARGIT CROWDER, *who keeps house for her grandfather*
PARSON WITTLEBY, *who wants a hearth broom and buys a hobby-horse broom*
NICHOLAS WORTHY, *who wants a hobby-horse and buys a hearth broom*
DAME DICKENS, *who wants a "riding" broom and buys a scare-crow*
DAME WORTHY, *who wants a little time to worry in peace*
ELDER SNOW, *who likes a good witch hunt*
DAME SNOW, *who knows a witch when she sees one*
TOWN CRIER

SETTING: *The broom maker's cottage on Broom Market Day.*

AT RISE: GRANTHER *is seated on a stool stitching on the last broom.* MARGIT *briskly dusts mugs and plates, standing on tip-toe to reach them. As she works she chants.*

MARGIT:

Broom market day! Broom market day!
Come one! Come all!
From hearth and stall!
Come, buy our brooms today.

GRANTHER (*Repeating*): "Lover's knot, sailor's knot..."

MARGIT (*Brushing up hearth*): If you are not away before the buyers come, Granther, it will be the same as always.

GRANTHER (*Scratching head*): What comes next?

MARGIT: Dame Pennyroyal will say her husband is ailing again and you will pick out the finest broom and (*Demonstrating*) give it to her with a bow. "Not a farthing! Not a farthing, good

Mistress!" (*Shakes finger at* GRANTHER) And you with no linen fit for wearing on the Sabbath.

GRANTHER (*Sadly*): I've forgotten the spell for the witch's broom.

MARGIT: Spell? (*Sits down on hearth suddenly and stares at* GRANTHER) Witch's broom?

GRANTHER: There are spells to be woven into the making of every sort of broom, my child. I've not told you before since you are only a lass and need never learn the secrets of the trade. Ours came from the first Crowder, master broom maker for King Arthur in the days of the great Merlin.

MARGIT (*Severely*): This is the seventeenth century, Granther. What would Parson Wittleby say?

GRANTHER: What, indeed! He could preach a year of sermons on this one broom. (*Repeating*)

Wood of yew
  Twisted and torn,
Straw of midnight
  Cut in moon's dark,
Stitched with thread
  From blind man's shroud.

Tie with lover's knot!
Tie with sailor's knot!
Tie . . .

There! I've forgotten the rest.

MARGIT (*Touching brooms timidly*): What will the spells *do* to the brooms, Granther?

GRANTHER: Eh? Spells? Mark you, for six generations no Crowder has used the spells to make selling brooms but 'tis said if a person buys a magic broom 'twill serve only the work and not the master.

MARGIT (*With scarecrow broom*): Then the scarecrow broom can only frighten birds from the fields.

GRANTHER: So 'tis said.

MARGIT (*Picking up hearth broom*): And the hearth broom...

GRANTHER (*Chuckling*): Can never beat the scullery maid.

MARGIT: Suppose the spells work, Granther? (*Shivering*) Suppose Parson Wittleby bought the witch's broom?

GRANTHER: Fiddle-dee-dee! What spell would dare work on the Parson.

MARGIT: But, Granther, if it did work—if someone were whisked away on the witch's broom the town council would h-hang you.

GRANTHER: Hang?...Hangman's knot!... (*Sets to work on the broom*)...The last knot of the spell. Thank you, my child. (*Sets finished broom on floor*) Done! I'll warrant no stouter flying broom ever was made by a Crowder.

MARGIT (*Picks up broom gingerly*): There's a look of mischief about it. It's not to be trusted, Granther. (*Carries it to alcove*) Now! Stay out of sight.

TOWN CRIER (*Far away*): Seven o' the clock and a fair-r-r morning!

MARGIT (*Returns with coat, broad-brimmed hat and white parcel*): Into your walking coat, Granther.

GRANTHER (*Putting on coat*): Hadn't I best stay and help with the broom selling, Margit?

MARGIT: So you may give away your summer's work? (*Gives him white parcel*) Here's bread and cheese for your eating.

GRANTHER (*Starting toward door*): Thank you, my child.

MARGIT (*Looking around at the brooms*): They'll not do any mischief, will they, Granther?

GRANTHER (*Heartily*): Not a mischief among them, I'll warrant. Spells, like men, get old and worn out. You'll have a nice quiet day, as always, with a bit of gossip for spice. (*At door, chuckling*) Ah, but 'twould be a fine sight!

MARGIT: A fine sight, Granther?

GRANTHER: Parson on the witch's broom, his coat tails flying (*Gesturing*) behind. (*Exit* TOBIAS CROWDER.)

MARGIT: Granther! (MARGIT *turns back and begins to straighten room. Puts brooms of one kind together, making a small verse as she does so.*)

Hobbyhorse brooms for school boys' riding,
Strong hearth brooms for housewives' tidying,
Scarecrow brooms of willow switches,
Spell-made brooms...

(*The witch's broom falls down with a terrific thump.* MARGIT *jumps.*)

for night-borne witches.

(*Picks up broom and puts it back in alcove.*) Stay there, Broom. Don't you dare get Granther into trouble.

TOWN CRIER (*Far away*): Broom market day at the Crowders! Broom market day!

PARSON WITTLEBY (*Entering*): Mistress Margit.

MARGIT (*Curtsey*): Parson Wittleby.

PARSON WITTLEBY: I want a hearth broom for my study. (*The witch's broom falls down and* MARGIT *scuttles to put it back. She keeps glancing at the alcove apprehensively.* PARSON *looks over all the brooms and selects one of the hobbyhorse variety.*) The price of this one, Mistress Margit?

MARGIT: One pence, your reverence. (*Shows him real hearth broom.*) Here is a better broom, Parson Wittleby. It is stronger and costs but a penny more.

PARSON WITTLEBY: "A penny saved is a penny earned."

MARGIT: This will outlast the other two times over.

PARSON WITTLEBY: Margit Crowder, you are exhibiting a marked stubbornness of mind. It is unbecoming in one of your tender years.

MARGIT: I know, Parson Wittleby, but...

PARSON WITTLEBY: The one penny broom, *if you please,* Mistress Margit. (*Gives her coin.*)

MARGIT (*Putting penny in pocket*): Thank you, your reverence. (*The brush of the* PARSON'S *broom begins to wriggle about on the floor.*)

PARSON WITTLEBY: Whoa! Whoa, there! (*Finds himself astride the broom.*) Ahem! Odd! Very odd, indeed! (*The broom leads the* PARSON *about the room. Finally, he is prancing like a school boy*) Giddap! Giddap, Dobbin! (*Strikes at broom with imaginary whip.*) Faster, my good horse! Faster! (*Exit.*)

MARGIT (*Running to the door*): Parson Wittleby! (*Turns, weeping, to fireplace. Sits on the three-legged stool.*) O Granther, they work. The spells work! (*Enter* NICHOLAS WORTHY. *He tiptoes toward* MARGIT *and tickles her with broom straw.*)

MARGIT (*Jumps*): Nicholas Worthy, what do you mean by spying like that?

NICHOLAS (*Hopping on one foot*): You wouldn't have minded if you hadn't been crying.

MARGIT: Why aren't you home tending the cows like a proper boy?

NICHOLAS (*Hopping and looking at brooms*): Who wants to be a proper boy? (*Chants*)

Everybody works but Nicholas
And he plays 'round all day.

MARGIT: Well, what do you want, Nicholas Worthy?

NICHOLAS: A hobby-horse broom. (*Holds out hand with several coins in it.*) Elder Snow gave me a six-pence and three pennies for finding his purse with the gold sovereigns in it.

MARGIT: That's a great deal of money, Nicholas. Why don't you go to Dame Goody's shop and buy a fine kerchief for your mother?

NICHOLAS: Because, Margit Crowder, I want a hobby-horse broom. (*Picks up hearth broom.*) Here, this one. (*Gives* MARGIT *coins. Broom begins to act strangely. It refuses to move when* NICHOLAS *tries to ride it*) This clumsy broom. (*Tries tugging and pulling*) I can't even move it, Margit.

MARGIT (*Takes broom and begins to sweep hearth*): Push it like this, Nicholas. So-o-o. Very gently or you will raise a dust. (NICHOLAS *takes over, sweeping in silence.*)

NICHOLAS (*Happily*): This is good fun — more fun than hobby-horse riding. (*Picks up straws and looks at* MARGIT *severely*) What an untidy housekeeper. See! Three broom straws and a thimbleful of ashes on the hearth. (*Continues sweeping toward door.* MARGIT *follows after, clapping hands silently*) I wonder if mother has swept the keeping room? (*Exit* NICHOLAS *sweeping*) I so hope she hasn't. (MARGET *stands at door, laughing.*)

TOWN CRIER (*Far away*): Oyez, mesdames. A broom for every fancy at Crowder's today. (*The witch's broom falls.* MARGIT *runs to put it back.*)

MARGIT: O you witch of a broom!

DAME DICKENS (*Entering*): Were you speaking to me, Mistress?

MARGIT (*Curtsey*): No, indeed, Dame Dickens.

DAME DICKENS: 'Tis no matter. I've been called worse. Well, Miss, I want a broom for (*Lowers voice*) night work.

MARGIT (*Sympathetically*): What a pity, Dame. So ever busy you must sweep at night!

DAME DICKENS: Who said anything about *sweeping* at night? (*Picks up large scarecrow broom*) Here. I'll take this.

MARGIT (*Substituting a hearth broom*): Let me show you a better one, Dame Dickens.

DAME DICKENS (*Snapping*): I've a good eye for a broom, Mistress Margit. This one is strong. It will stand a deal of hard riding.

MARGIT (*Puzzled*) Riding? If it's riding that you want, Dame, here are the hobby-horse brooms for children.

DAME DICKENS: Hobby-horse brooms! (*Sputters*) It's enough to make a body give up the business what with the sleep one loses. (*Puts scarecrow broom under arm*) This is the broom I want.

MARGIT: It costs a sixpence, Mistress Dickens.

DAME DICKENS: Worth a silver shilling to Dickens any day. (*Gives* MARGIT *money. Broom begins to twist and turn, brush toward the ceiling*) Upon my word, I've never seen a broom so lively before sundown. (*Puts own hat on broom. Broom jerks along toward door*) A shawl, now, would set you up in grand style. Come along, my hearty.

MARGIT: Please take back the shilling, Dame. (*Exit* DAME DICKENS) It's a s-scarecrow broom. (*Weeping*) Granther, see what your spells have done. (*Enter* DAME WORTHY.)

DAME WORTHY (*Giving* MARGIT *a handkerchief*): Wipe your eyes, child.

MARGIT (*Sobbing*): D-do you w-want a b-broom, Dame Worthy?

DAME WORTHY (*Sitting*): After my worrying's done, Margit.

MARGIT: Is anything wrong?

DAME WORTHY: Nicholas.

MARGIT: Nicholas?

DAME WORTHY: A boy as afraid of honest work as a scalped man of an Indian, suddenly takes to sweeping and tidying. It must be a spell of sickness. (*Witch broom falls down*) That, my child, is as tempting a broom as ever I saw.

MARGIT (*Putting it back*): It's not for sale, Dame Worthy.

DAME WORTHY (*Sighing*): I don't know that I'd forgive myself if Nicholas sickened with a *sweeping* fever. (*Broom thumps down again.* DAME WORTHY *picks it up*) A lifetime of wear in that, I'll warrant. (*Tries it out. Broom flies around the room*) My! my! A light broom for all its weight. Worth a sixpence if it's worth a penny. (*Gives* MARGIT *money. Coin drops on floor.*)

MARGIT: Please, Dame Worthy, it can't be sold. It's a prankish broom truly, and not to be trusted.

DAME WORTHY (*Broom held horizontally in hands*): I've always had a mind for traveling, Margit. To Providence, perhaps, or

New Amsterdam village. (*Broom tugs toward door*) Flying would be pleasant, wouldn't it? Very pleasant, indeed! (*Exit* DAME WORTHY *and witch's broom.*)

MARGIT (*At doorway*): Oh-h-h! (*Reenter* PARSON WITTLEBY.)

PARSON WITTLEBY: Ah! you have noticed it, too.

MARGIT: Y-yes, Parson Wittleby.

PARSON WITTLEBY (*Looking up at door*): I don't know when I've seen so large a bird. Very interesting. Very. It may, indeed, be the fabulous auk. (*Turning into room*) I'll not trouble you long, Mistress Margit. I just came back for more of the — er — exercising brooms.

MARGIT: How many, Parson?

PARSON: One for each of my sons — (*Counting on fingers*) — Isaiah, Jeremiah, Lamentations, Ezekiel, Daniel, Hosea, Joel, Amos, Obadiah, Jonah, Micah....Eleven and an extra one for myself. Twelve in all.

MARGIT (*Picking up brooms*): Yes, your reverence. Twelve.

PARSON (*At door*): Of course, it may only be a great eagle. (*Enter* ELDER SNOW *and* DAME SNOW, *breathlessly.*)

ELDER SNOW (*Waggling his finger toward sky*): Witchcraft, that's what it is!

PARSON: Witchcraft?

DAME SNOW: Dame Worthy, up there cavorting with the swallows. (MARGIT *drops brooms.* DAME SNOW *turns and glares.*)

PARSON: Dame Worthy? (*Polishes spectacles and looks again*) Really?

MARGIT: Let me explain, Parson Wittleby.

DAME SNOW: Explain? What is there to explain about riding on a broom. (*Shrilly*) In broad daylight, too. She should at least have had the decency to stay at home until midnight.

PARSON (*Sadly*): This must come to trial.

ELDER SNOW: At once! (*Severely*) Ordinance seventeen of the village council: "Any person or persons seen riding a broom after nightfall, with or without a black cat for companions, shall be known as a witch and shall, forthwith, be punished by ducking, hanging or such measures as the selectmen shall devise..."

DAME SNOW (*At door*): She is turning back. The witch!

MARGIT: Dame Worthy is not a witch. She is a good, kind woman.

PARSON: Leave these matters to your elders, my child.

DAME SNOW (*Still looking up*): Giddy as a swallow, I do declare. (*Bumping and thumping outside.* DAME WORTHY *enters with flushed face and untidy hair. She drags broom in and stands it by door. Straightens cap.*)

DAME WORTHY: A good day to you, neighbors.

DAME SNOW: Hmmmph!

MARGIT (*Running to her*): Oh, Dame Worthy, why did you come back?

DAME WORTHY: The broom didn't want to but I was very firm. Susannah's braids, you know. They weren't down when I left this morning and she's very touchy about combing.

MARGIT: Dame Worthy, they're going to bring you to trial.

DAME WORTHY: Trial?

PARSON WITTLEBY: You have brought the grave charge of witching against yourself.

DAME WORTHY (*Sits down suddenly on stool*): Witching? (*Enter* DAME DICKENS. *Scarecrow now has carrot nose, corn silk hair and wears a shawl.*)

DAME DICKENS: Witching, eh? (*Thumps scarecrow against wall.*) Mind your manners, Hepzibah. (*Turning*) What's this talk about witching?

DAME WORTHY: My broom sailed away with me, Mistress Dickens. (*Weakly*) I must be a witch.

DAME DICKENS: So, Dame Worthy, you're a witch. How would you set about giving Elder Snow chilblains in December?

DAME WORTHY (*Sympathetically*): Are you troubled with chilblains, Elder Snow? Tsk! Tsk! Turpentine mixed with a little good lard is a fine remedy.

DAME DICKENS: What spell would you use to mildew Dame Snow's fine madeira linen, Witch Worthy?

DAME SNOW: You! The tablecloth on the bayberry bush, last midsummer night!

DAME DICKENS: La! La! Mistress, you could never prove it. (*To* PARSON) Parson, no Witches' Union in New England would take her (*Pointing to* DAME WORTHY) as apprentice.

ELDER SNOW: Mistress Dickens, she was seen riding a broom in broad daylight.

MARGIT: Daylight? (*Firmly*) Then she isn't a witch.

PARSON WITTLEBY: Explain yourself, Margit Crowder. This is a serious matter.

MARGIT: The town ordinance says: "Any person or persons seen riding a broom after nightfall..." Dear Mistress Worthy can't be a witch.

DAME SNOW (*Flouncing out*): Well, I never! (*Exit*)

ELDER SNOW (*Stalking out*): I shall have the ordinance amended. At once. (*Exit.*)

PARSON WITTLEBY: You are not a witch, Dame Worthy?

DAME WORTHY: I — I don't believe so.

PARSON WITTLEBY: Then if you must ride (*Softly*) — an exercising broom is the thing!

MARGIT: Your brooms, Parson Wittleby.

PARSON WITTLEBY: Ah, yes the brooms. (*Starts toward exit.*)

MARGIT: Twelve pence, Parson Wittleby.

PARSON WITTLEBY: Ah, yes, twelve pence. (*Pays* MARGIT) Good day to you, Mistresses. (*Bows. Exit.*)

DAME WORTHY: Thank you, my child. Thank you, Dame Dickens.

DAME DICKENS: La! Haven't had so much fun since I mildewed Gossip Snow's tablecloth last summer. (*Looks out door.*) A fine black crow, Hepzibah. Get along with you. (*Catches up scarecrow*) Margit Crowder, save all the scarecrow brooms for me. (*Exit. From without*) I've decided to give up witching. (*Puts head around door*) A body loses so much sleep.

DAME WORTHY (*Goes to witch's broom*): I can never take it home, Margit. 'Twould turn me into a gadabout if not a witch. (*Sighing*) But I shall always remember how peaceful — how free it was up there above the tree tops, with the wind and the sun and the swallows for company. (*Enter* NICHOLAS WORTHY, *breathless. He carries his broom.*)

NICHOLAS: Mother.

DAME WORTHY: Yes, Nicholas.

NICHOLAS WORTHY: Such fun! I've swept the hearth. I've swept the dooryard and the path to the milk house. What may I sweep now?

DAME WORTHY: With ten children about I think (*Laughing*) you might start on the hearth again.

NICHOLAS: How nice to have ten children in the house, mother. I and my broom will never be done tidying.

DAME WORTHY: You may be ill, Nicholas, but (*Patting his head*) I shall not look for a remedy. (*Bowing*) A good day to you, Margit.

MARGIT: A very good day to you both. (*Exit* DAME WORTHY *and* NICHOLAS.)

TOWN CRIER (*Far away*): Have you bought your Crowder broom, Mistress? There's none like them. (*Still further away*) None like them.

MARGIT (*To witch's broom*): None like you, indeed, you wicked broom! (*Shaking it*) Try to put Granther in jail, will you? Try to witch good Dame Worthy? (*Crossing to fireplace*) I know what I'll do with you. I'll burn you. I'll let you boil the kettle for Granther's tea. (*Puts broom against the fireplace. Bustles about filling kettle on hob. As she returns to fireplace she trips over witch's broom. Other brooms tumble over. She sits there, astonished, holding kettle high in air when* GRANTHER *re-enters.*)

GRANTHER: Well, my child, I can see you've had a nice quiet broom market day.

TOWN CRIER (*Very far away*): Broom market day! Broom market day!... (GRANTHER *and* MARGIT *look at each other and laugh.*)

THE END

JENNY-BY-THE-DAY

by Lida Lisle Molloy

Characters

MARGERY DAW, *wife of Jack Daw and mistress of the Jack Daw Inn*
DILLY } *the Daw twins*
DALLY }
JENNY-BY-THE-DAY
THE KING'S TRUMPETER
THE KING'S HERALD
THE MAN *who is also* THE KING

SETTING: *The Jack Daw Inn*

AT RISE: MARGERY DAW *is shaking cloth at the open door. Ashes strew the hearth. Woodpile is askew. There is a large bowl, spoon and several crocks and jars on trestle table.*

MARGERY DAW (*Squinting at sun*): Lawkamercy! Sun's noon-high and the plum duff not yet in the boiling pot. (*Calling*) Dilly, cease pulling the cat's tail. Dally, you were sent to pick gooseberries, not to fall napping under the bush. Into the kitchen, both of you. (*Bustles inside, laying cloth away in chest. Brings pitcher from chest to table. Pretends to put various ingredients in large bowl*) Barley meal, three measures... good yellow butter . . . whitethorn honey . . . a ladle of milk. (*Sound of howling, from offstage*) Mercy on me! It's a lone woman I am with the Jack Daw Inn on my hands, besides Dilly and Dally Daw, a donkey that balks and a cow that won't give cream on a Sunday. (*Enter* DILLY *leading a howling* DALLY *by the ear*) What's the matter now?

DALLY (*Wailing*): Mother.

MARGERY DAW: Dilly Daw, that's your own twin brother's ear. (DILLY *drops hands and looks virtuous.* DALLY *snuffles and wipes his eyes.*)

DILLY: He was napping again, Dally was, right after you told us to come in.

MARGERY DAW (*Severely*): Where are the gooseberries, Master Daw?

DALLY (*Mumbling*): The gooseberries?

MARGARET DAW: The gooseberries for tarts I sent you to pick.

DILLY (*Calmly*): I ate them.

MARGERY DAW: Dilly, Dally, if your father weren't sailing the seven seas...

DILLY: There was only a handful. (*Smugly*) Dally is a lazy-bones.

MARGERY DAW (*Sharply*): To work now and no nonsense. Dally, put a faggot under the pudding pot. Dilly, fetch the duff bag. (DALLY *lazily moves to fireplace, picks up faggot, throws it down, takes another. Yawns prodigiously. Crawls to fire and pokes at it with his stick.*)

DILLY: I'm hungry.

MARGERY DAW (*Pretending to shape pudding in bowl*): The pudding bag, if you please.

DILLY: I'm hungry and I shall have a bowl of pease porridge or I will scream down the roof.

MARGERY DAW (*Throwing up her floury hands*): Get on with your porridge, pepper pot. I'll fetch the bag myself. (DILLY *scampers to fireplace, lifts lid of kettle sitting in ashes and sniffs. Sound of hoofbeats, without.* MARGERY *tries to listen.* DILLY *takes ladle and dips it into kettle, brings it to her mouth with loud smacking noises.*) Dilly, hush your noise. (*Hoofbeats grow louder.*)

DILLY (*Skipping to chest for bowl*):

Pease porridge hot, pease porridge cold,
Pease porridge in the pot nine days old.
Some like it hot, some like it cold,
Some like it in the pot nine... (*Trumpet, without.*)

TRUMPETER (*Without*): The King's Herald! Make way for His Majesty's Herald. (*Enter* TRUMPETER *and* HERALD *with proclamation.*)

MARGERY DAW (*Straightening cap*): Lawkamercy!

TRUMPETER: Are you one Margery Daw, mistress of Jack Daw Inn?

MARGERY DAW (*Bobbing her head*): I am.

TRUMPETER: Word is abroad that you make plum duff fit for the King.

MARGERY DAW: Jack Daw himself says there is never a cook on the seven seas can match my boiled pudding. (*Sits down, suddenly, on three-legged stool*) The King! Mercy o' me, duff for the King!

TRUMPETER: Silence, woman, while the royal Herald reads the royal proclamation. (*Trumpet*) His Exalted Excellency, Third Lord of the Audience Chamber, the Kings' Herald. (DALLY *inches over to mother's stool.* DILLY *wanders over to listen.*)

HERALD (*Unrolls proclamation*): Know ye, Good Peoples, that our Sovereign the King, having suffered most grievous sorrow through the death of his daughter, the Princess Ellin, doth travel about the land seeking ease of mind. If there be any among you who can amuse the King or add to his pleasure, let him do so with hearty good will. Signed. The Lord High Chancellor. (*Pushes down spectacles and looks at* MARGERY DAW) Duff is His Majesty's favorite pudding. There is talk — only talk, mind you — that the Royal Party will drive by Jack Daw Inn so that His Majesty may sample your plum duff. On the other hand, he has been advised to see the two-headed calf down Donnybrooke way.

DILLY (*Holding up one leg, begins to hop around in front of* TRUMPETER *and* HERALD):
Duff is duff
And good enough,
But a two-headed calf
Would make me laugh. (*Stops before* HERALD)
If I were a king I would go to see the two-headed calf.

MARGERY DAW: Dilly!

HERALD (*Motioning* TRUMPETER *to leave*): Madam (*Coldly*), if His Most Gracious Majesty deigns to stop at this Inn, I beg you to keep this (*Sputtering*) giddy jackanapes out of sight. (*Turns quickly, then exits.*) I shall definitely recommend His Majesty's departure to Donnybrooke. (DILLY *hops to the door.*)

MARGERY DAW (*Fanning herself with frying pan from fireplace*): Mercy o' me! It's a lone woman I am with the duff not yet aboiling and the King himself practically on my doorstep! (*Enter* JENNY-BY-THE-DAY, *neat and friendly.*)

JENNY: Good morrow, Mistress. (*Curtsey*) Have you a good heart?

MARGERY DAW (*Claps frying pan back on hook*): And if I have a kind heart or if I haven't, Miss! (*Rises, briskly.*)

DILLY (*Hopping in front of* JENNY): What's your name?

JENNY: Jenny-by-the-day, if you please, Mother says I am only to work for a person with a kind heart.

MARGERY DAW (*Settling her skirts*): Dally, blow on the fire and set the kettle to boiling. (DALLY *yawns, dawdles and scatters ashes.* MARGERY *gets pudding bag and string from chest.*)

DILLY (*Still hopping*): Why are you Jenny-by-the-Day?

JENNY (*Keeping an eye on* DALLY'S *work*): I am the oldest and two rooms are a very tight fit for ten. Besides Nora is eight and quite old enough to bib the babies and tuck their porridge into them. (DALLY *tips the pot and water spills*) No! No! (JENNY *crosses to fireplace, kneeling beside* DALLY) First, the ashes away from the coals. Then a gentle blowing like a breeze. (*Blows on coals*) Then — twigs to feed the flame. Now... (*Fans fire with apron*) Mother says there's never a man with a hand light enough for laying a cottage fire. Dally, five faggots, dry and seasoned. (*Stacks faggots under pot, rises and straightens kettle on crane*) The kettle will be boiling in a twinkle.

DILLY (*Hopping to fireplace*): I am going to be a sailor like my father. What are you working for, Jenny?

DALLY (*Under his breath*): A girl sailor!

JENNY (*Standing very straight*): For two pennies a day.

MARGERY DAW (*Tying pudding bag at table*): Tuppence, is it? That's a great deal of money, Miss-Small-Pint-of-Milk.

JENNY: It will take a great deal of money for Jamie's doublet and the small twin's christening robe.

MARGERY DAW: Well, out with it. What can you do for a tuppence a day? (DALLY *saunters left, throwing a small twig in air and catching it. Sits on floor under casement window and yawns himself to sleep.*)

JENNY (*Anxiously*): I am always the first to find the speckled hen's egg when she hides her nest.

MARGERY DAW: Lackamercy! There'll be no egg hunting this day with what's likely to take place. See if the pot's boiling. (DILLY *hops to kettle. Lifts lid and burns herself*) Mind your fingers if you don't want to get burned, Mistress Dilly. (MARGERY *puts bag in kettle.* JENNY *looks at crying* DILLY'S *fingers. Draws her to table and puts butter on the burn*) Listen well, Jenny.

JENNY (*Curtsey*) : Yes, Mistress.

MARGERY DAW : I must go to the milk house and skim the crocks. There's some will want clabber and some cream with their duff. (*Takes ladle from fireplace*) You are to sweep the floor, polish the cups and plates, scour the table and keep the kettle boiling. You understand?

JENNY : Yes, Mistress, I understand about puddings. Mother makes them every day because with ten of us she needs something filling.

MARGERY DAW : Work well and there will be tuppence for you. If not... (*To* DILLY *who is tickling* DALLY *with a straw*) Dilly, mind you no hindering. (JENNY *begins taking cups and plates from mantel.* MARGERY *stops at door to shake finger at* JENNY.) The kettle, Jenny. Nothing must go amiss with the duff today. (JENNY *puts plates and cups on table and runs back to look in pot.*)

DILLY : You were nice about my finger, Jenny. It doesn't burn at all any more. I think I shall sweep for you.

JENNY (*Polishing cups*) : Take the broom then and begin. Sister Norah has been sweeping the hearth twice a day since she was old enough to hold the broom stick. (DILLY *grabs broom and begins to push it about violently in the center of the room.*)

DILLY : Why, there is nothing at all to sweeping.

JENNY (*Coughing because of the dust*) : Tsk! tsk! a great girl like you raising a whirlwind! Here, let me show you. (*Goes right. Begins to sweep gently, swiftly*) So. Softly that you do not lift the dust. Now... (DILLY *tries again*) Good, Dilly Daw. Very good. With a little practice you will do as well as Norah.

DILLY : Norah is a silly. I am going to be a sailor and shall never have to sweep and clean.

JENNY : What kind of a sailor would that be! When my father was young and brave and a seaman in His Majesty's service, he scrubbed the decks every day till they shone like a fine lady's mirror. (DALLY *begins to watch* JENNY *with interest.*)

DILLY (*Nearing door*) : He did?

JENNY (*Putting back cups and plates*) : He did, indeed! (*Bends over fire*) Now (*With glance at* DALLY) if there were only a man about to fetch more faggots and lay the pile straight.

DALLY (*Jumping up*) : I am here, Jenny.

JENNY: So you are, Dally Daw. Do you think you could...?

DALLY: Oh, yes, Jenny, and I shall be very quick about it. I'll not dally at all. (*Runs out.*)

DILLY (*Taking swipe at* DALLY *with broom she sights spider*): Look! A fat, silly spider. What fun! (*Holds up broom as if to sweep web away.*)

JENNY: Poor Master Spider! (DILLY *turns in astonishment*) He will be very sad.

DILLY: Sad, Jenny? (JENNY *begins scrubbing table with brush.*)

JENNY: He is a fine spider but no one ever lets him finish his work. (*Crosses to door*) See how pretty his web is. Mother says there is nothing in the world so pretty as spider's lace unless it is the soft gray of a mouse.

DILLY (*Disappointed*) : Then I can't sweep it away?

JENNY (*Back at table*) : What he needs is a new home — say in the cow's stall — where he can make lace all day long and no one will bother him.

DILLY: I'll find a place, Jenny. A funny, secret place. (*Exit* DILLY.)

JENNY: Oh, Master Spider... (*Chanting*)
We'll carry you there on your spinning thread
And leave you to fashion your lacy bed.
(*Re-enter* DALLY *with faggots. Piles them neatly, right, fireplace.*) Very good, Dally. Brother Jamie could have done no better.

DALLY (*Running out*) : I'm going to help Dilly find a house for the spider.

JENNY (*Putting away scrub brush*) : See that it is a fine house, Dally. (*Looking about her*) First, to gather apple blossoms and then — water for the pudding pot. (*Crosses left and begins to break branches through open casement window. Chanting*)
Master Spider,
Your web will be so silken a thing
'Twould make a coverlid fit for the King. (MAN *appears at door.*)

MAN (*Looking in*) : Good morrow, the Inn.

JENNY (*Turning in surprise*) : Oh-h! (*Curtsey*) Pray you come in, sir. But mind the spider, please, sir. Your plume might brush him away.

MAN (*Doffs hat and bows to spider*): Sir Spider, by your leave! Who am I to disturb so industrious a worker. (*Enters*) And would you be Mistress Margery Daw of plum-duff fame?

JENNY: Not I, sir. Mistress Margery is skimming cream for the plum duff in the buttery.

MAN: Ah! The plum duff!

JENNY: I'm Jenny-by-the-day.

MAN: Jenny-by-the-day? You should be a Jenny-at-play, child.

JENNY: Oh, no, sir! There's Jamie's doublet and the small twin's christening robe and if I work hard I shall earn tuppence today. (*Holds out apple blossoms*) Would you care to hold the flowers, sir, while I fetch a pitcher for them? (*Runs for flower holder.*)

MAN (*Sighing*): It has been a long time — a very long time, indeed, since a small maid gave me flowers to hold.

JENNY (*Returning with pitcher*): Mother says there is nothing makes a room so gay as apple blossoms. (*Puts pitcher and flowers on table*) What was her name? The little girl who gave you flowers to hold?

MAN (*Sitting on bench*): Ellin. Her name was Ellin.

JENNY: Ellin? What a lovely name! Quite lovely enough for a princess...

MAN (*Smiling*): Yes, Jenny, quite lovely enough for a princess.

MARGERY DAW (*Appearing in doorway with huge crock under her arm*): Lawkamercy! (*Sniffs*) The pudding! (*Rushes to fireplace, thumping crock on the table in passing.* JENNY *follows*) Chattering of princesses while the pot boils dry. (*Lid clatters to floor*) I should thump your empty head with a cooking ladle.

JENNY: That I should be so neglectful, Mistress. (*Leans over toward* MARGERY) Thump it, please. Hard. (TWINS *appear in the doorway and stand gaping.*)

MARGERY DAW (*Lifts up pudding bag with long fork*): Stuck to the pot and spoiled it is!

JENNY (*Crying*): You need not pay me the tuppence, Mistress.

MARGERY DAW: Tuppence! Indeed you'll get no tuppence but will that fetch me my pudding so firm and round and speckled with plums and the King himself coming to eat a slice?

JENNY (*Awed*): The King? Oh Mistress Daw, I will work every day for a score of years to pay you back.

MAN (*Clearly*): Mistress Daw!

MARGERY DAW: Your pardon, sir. You can see I have had an upsetting. What will you have? There's cold pease porridge or cold pie of fat hare with parsnips. But no duff what with a daft maid burning the pudding.

MAN: I came for a taste of the pudding but I think I would like the daft little maid instead.

MARGERY DAW: Humph!

DILLY (*Left, begins to jump up and down, chanting*):
See-saw, Margery Daw,
Jenny shall have a new master...

MAN: Jenny-by-the-Day, (JENNY *goes to him*) would you come to live at my house?

JENNY: To work, sir?

MAN: To work at being a happy child.

MARGERY DAW (*In disapproval*): Weladay!

JENNY (*Primly*): What would be my duties, sir?

MAN: Playing at ball in the garden, rolling a ribboned hoop down long corridors and watching the swallows from every high window.

JENNY: It sounds very pleasant, sir, but would that be work? And what are the wages, sir? There's Jamie's doublet and the small twin's christening robe, you know.

MAN (*Smiling*): What would you say to a bright, shining penny?

DILLY (*Giggling*):
She shall have but a penny a day (DALLY *tries to stop her*)
Because she can't work any faster.

MARGERY DAW (*Grumbles as she clatters around fireplace*): Half-penny's more like it!

JENNY: A penny will do very well, sir. (*Sadly*) I can never ask for tuppence again after letting the pudding burn.

MAN (*Holding out his hand*): Is it a bargain then?

JENNY: A bargain, sir, (*Curtsey*) if it pleases my mother.

MAN (*Rising and bowing*): Let us go at once, my lady, and inquire her pleasure.

JENNY: Good day to you, Mistress Daw. I shall pay for the pudding out of my penny a day. (*Skipping toward door*) Goodbye, Dilly. Goodbye, Dally. You will see Master Spider to his new home, won't you?

DILLY *and* DALLY (*Unhappily*): Yes, Jenny.

MAN (*Crossing left to door*): Shall we arrive in time for tea, Jenny?

JENNY: Proper time, sir. There will be plum duff, if it please you, sir, but a very thin slice. You see, there are ten of us in Woodcutter's Lane. (*Exit* JENNY, *humming gaily.*)

MAN: Mistress Daw, if two strange and excited men who call themselves the King's Trumpeter and the King's Herald should come looking for the King, pray tell them that His Majesty has gone to tea in Woodcutter's Lane. (*Sweeping bow. Exit.*)

MARGERY DAW: Lawkamercy! (*Holding onto the fireplace*) Himself! The King!

DILLY (*Sniffling*):

Jenny shall have a new master.
She shall have but a penny a day... (DALLY *shakes her.*)

DALLY: Stop making rhymes about Jenny, I like her.

DILLY: I do too. Jenny is nice. She put butter on my burned finger. (*Pantomime.* CHILDREN *look at spider and then at each other.* DILLY *nods.* DALLY *breaks thread holding spider and carrying it carefully, they leave hand in hand. Sound of hoofbeats.*)

MARGERY DAW (*Crossing to door*): It's a lone woman I am with Jack Daw Inn on my hands, with Dilly and Dally, a donkey that balks (*Hoofbeats grow louder*), a cow that won't give cream of a Sunday and a daft girl that lets the pudding burn.

TRUMPETER (*Without*): Hola, Mistress Daw! Have you seen the King?

MARGERY DAW: Down Woodcutter's Lane he went, Excellencies. (*Hoofbeats. Calling after them*) With Princess Jenny-by-the-Day.

THE END

THE WISE MEN OF GOTHAM

by Ruth Vickery Holmes

Characters

MAYOR OF GOTHAM
DOBBIN, HODGE, PETER — *the leading men of Gotham*
VILLAGERS, *as many as desired, both men and women*
KING'S MESSENGER, *with horn*
KING'S SHERIFF
FIRST *and* SECOND SOLDIERS

NOTE: *During the play, there are many intervals when all the villagers of Gotham talk, all together. The phrases given are to be used, or changed slightly ad libitum. The volume of the sound of all people talking together yet saying different things should ring out with gusto.*

SCENE 1

SETTING: *The market square of Gotham.*

AT RISE: *The villagers of Gotham, with baskets on their arms, and sacks on their shoulders, are moving about, exchanging their wares, and talking ad lib.*

VILLAGERS (*All together*):
Ay, eggs — Fresh eggs — I gathered them this morning.
Look at my apples — Firm and sound for winter.
Who has a shoulder of pork? My wife's been asking for pork.
No pork have I, but fowls I have. Would fowls suit you?
Who wants some apples? (*Etc.*)

HODGE (*Looking off right and pointing*): Look! Look down the road. (*All stop talking, and look.*)

PETER (*Presses through the crowd toward right*): It's Dobbin. Running. Hot foot.

HODGE (*Nods*): And nearly spent. (DOBBIN *enters, staggering and out of breath.*) Quick, Peter, catch his arm. (HODGE *takes* DOBBIN'S *arm, and helps him sit down upon the rim of the well.*)

DOBBIN (*Gasping*): Some water. Then I'll tell you. (PETER *gives* DOBBIN *a bowl of water, and the* VILLAGERS *press around* DOBBIN *as he sips.*)

MAYOR (*Putting his hand on* DOBBIN'S *shoulder*): Take your time, DOBBIN. But tell us when you can. Were you in danger?

DOBBIN (*Nods vigorously*): Ay. So are we all in danger. Everyone in Gotham. In danger of losing all the stores we have for winter. And mayhap, of everything we own —

HODGE (*Pushing away those who are too close*): Stand back, and give the man more chance to breathe. (*Turns to* DOBBIN.) Now, Dobbin, when you can —

DOBBIN (*Stands up*): There's trouble in store for Gotham — (*Points to the hills in rear.*) The King is drawing near, with all his soldiers. He's camping over there, beyond those hills. He's but ten miles away.

MAYOR (*Nods*): But he is pushing northward — to the border. He won't be coming here.

DOBBIN (*Quickly*): But that he will. Tomorrow. Till all his troops are gathered, the army's to be quartered in the neighboring towns.

MAYOR (*Frowning*): And Gotham's to be overrun with troops?

DOBBIN (*Nods*): Ay, the King himself is coming here, with four score men. Gotham's to house them all — to feed them all —

MAYOR (*Much disturbed*): The King himself — and what he likes, he takes. And doesn't pay.

VILLAGERS (*All together*): And all his men are like him.
Four score men — to house and feed for days —
They'll eat up all our food.
And turn us out of our beds.
Ay, we'll like be ruined.

MAYOR (*Holding up his hand*): Silence. Let us think. What can we do?

DOBBIN (*Turning toward the* MAYOR): As I hurried home, I tried to think of something. Else we'll be stripped, and winter'll find us starving.

MAYOR (*Nods*): Ay, ruined we'll be. (*Deep in thought slowly.*) We must turn the King aside. (*Raises his hand, and points to the hills.*) There, where the road is narrow, at the foot of yonder hills, we'll block the road.

DOBBIN (*Approving*): Ay, we can cut some trees if we work fast.

HODGE (*Nods*): And barricade them well.

MAYOR (*Turns to the* VILLAGERS): And it might be — The King might find it easier to turn back whence he came than wait to have the road cleared. Shall we try it?

VILLAGERS (*All together*): Ay, that we will —
Let's go and fell the trees —
Yes, block the road —
And keep the King from Gotham.

MAYOR (*Nodding*): And keep the King from Gotham.

CURTAIN

* * *

SCENE 2

SETTING: *The market square of Gotham the night of the following day.*

AT RISE: THE VILLAGERS *of Gotham are standing around the well, looking off right, tired, anxious, quiet.*

HODGE (*Turning from right, nods*): Our barricade must have held.

PETER (*Nods*): Ay, not a sign has there been of the King all day.

MAYOR (*Raising his hands, and smiling*): Yes, now, my friends, I think that Gotham's safe. 'Twas to good purpose that we blocked the road. Let's all go home, and get some well-earned rest.

DOBBIN (*Pointing off right*): But look — Someone is coming — afoot — and all alone —

VILLAGERS (*All together. Crowding to look off right*):

Afoot — He isn't a soldier
And he's alone. That's good
Alone — then, there's no danger.

THE KING'S MESSENGER (*Enters, and blows his horn*): Ye men of Gotham — Listen well. Listen to this message from your King. (*Pauses, while all* THE VILLAGERS *draw together, and face him*):
His Majesty had it in mind to honor you. Most graciously he planned to come to Gotham town — to accept its hospitality, both for himself, and for his troops. (*Stops and looks carefully at* THE VILLAGERS, *who stand in silence, unmoved.*) But on the way to Gotham he changed his plan —

MAYOR (*Bows*): Then after all, is Gotham *not* to have the honor of welcoming the King?

MESSENGER (*Nods solemnly*): Circumstances compelled his Majesty to change his plan of coming to Gotham — (*Rising his voice, ominously.*) And in his place instead, the King will send his Sheriff.

VILLAGERS (*All together*):
The Sheriff —
The King's Sheriff —
Is not the Sheriff the Executioner?
The Sheriff — The Executioner.

MESSENGER (*Bows right and left*):
His Sheriff, who is, as well, his Executioner.
The Sheriff will come, and with him, his assistants.
They will not have to ride the road.
They'll come as I did, by footpaths through the hills.

VILLAGERS (*All together, muttering*):
The footpaths,
Through the hills,
Do you think by morning?
Ay, the footpaths.

MESSENGER (*Pointing to the hills*): When his Majesty, the King, came to those hills, he found — not a clear road, but piles of trees and brush, blocking the way completely, and so intertwined, they could not be removed.

VILLAGERS (*All together, uneasily*):
Piles of trees?
And brush, all intertwined?
They could not be removed?

MESSENGER (*Nods*): So then, his Majesty summoned his Sheriff and said — these are his words exactly — "We have decided to return to camp. Ourself, and all our men — From Gotham, we'll not accept a welcome as we'd planned—"

VILLAGERS (*All together, nodding to each other*):
So — the King won't come here,
No, nor his men,
Gotham is not to welcome him.

MESSENGER (*Raising his hand and speaking so slowly that each word is emphasized*): "But in our place, go you to Gotham town, and from all of those who live there, whose heads are much too big, and need reducing, go, and *slice off their noses.*"

VILLAGERS (*All together, gasping, and moaning*):
Our noses to be sliced off?
So, our heads are too big, are they?
Better, had we not blocked the road —
Our noses — Oh, our noses.

MAYOR (*Faces the* MESSENGER *courageously*): Is no one to be spared this dreadful sentence?

MESSENGER (*Bows*): Yes, of his graciousness, his Majesty said more —
"Sharp wits" said he, "there are in Gotham town,
And right sharp measures shall be dealt to *them.*
But spare the women, and all the children,
The very old, and those who obviously, are lacking in wit,
And can be classed as fools."
(*Bows right and left, and starts to go out right.*) You've heard the message from your King. Now I'll be off. (MESSENGER *leaves, and* VILLAGERS *turn to each other.*)

VILLAGERS (*All together*): What can we do?
The harshest sentence ever heard of —
Noses — Noses. No, never our noses —
We'll run away before the Sheriff comes —
No — Not our noses.

DOBBIN (*Raising his voice*): Hush, men of Gotham. Hush. I have a plan that may well save us all —

MAYOR (*Raising his hand*): Let Dobbin speak — (*Turns to* DOBBIN.) What, Dobbbin, would you say?

DOBBIN (*Staunchly*): We men of Gotham have but one thing to do — And that will be full easy — Did you mark the part in the King's message — about who will be spared?

MAYOR (*Nods*): Ay — The women — And little children — the very old —

DOBBIN (*Breaking in*): Ay — *And those, who obviously are lacking in wit, and can be classed as fools* — Let's all be fools — All — Everybody in Gotham —

VILLAGERS (*All together, one and all, perceiving* DOBBIN'S *intention*):

We'll all be fools —
We'll all be lacking in wit —
No sense left in all Gotham —
We'll all be fools.

MAYOR (*Nods*): Ay, Dobbin, your plan may save us all. We have the night to make arrangements. (*Raises his hand in resolution.*) All Gotham shall be classed as fools.

VILLAGERS (*Repeat all together, joyously*): All Gotham shall be fools!

CURTAIN

* * *

SCENE 3

SETTING: *The market square of Gotham the next morning at dawn.*

AT RISE: *Gotham seems deserted. Then* THE SHERIFF *enters from right, followed by* FIRST *and* SECOND SOLDIERS, *all with their swords half drawn.*

SHERIFF (*Crossing slowly to left, looks slowly about, then turns to* FIRST SOLDIER): We reached Gotham in good season —

FIRST SOLDIER (*Nods*): Ay, sir, before the sunrise. Dawn is but breaking.

SHERIFF (*Nods*): We'll seize the miscreants before they stir from bed — (*The sound of thumping stones is heard from left.*)

SECOND SOLDIER (*Pointing off left*) : Those sounds, sir. Something seems going on — (DOBBIN *enters from left, pushing and rolling along a large stone, followed by* PETER *and* HODGE, *who, also, are pushing along heavy stones.*)

DOBBIN (*With great excitement*) : Come on — Come, we must hurry.

PETER (*Giving his stone a very vigorous heave*) : Ay, there is no time to spare. We must go help the sun to rise —

HODGE (*Rolling his stone very carefully*) : Ay, the sun won't rise till all our stones are placed —

SHERIFF (*Seizes* HODGE, *and shakes him roughly*) : What's this that's going on? What's this about the sunrise? (FIRST SOLDIER *seizes* DOBBIN, *the* SECOND, PETER.)

DOBBIN (*Turns and faces* SHERIFF) : Oh, sir, you must not stop us. Else the sun won't rise.

SHERIFF (*Angry, yet perplexed*) : What's all this nonsense? What's this about the sunrise?

DOBBIN (*Nods pleasantly*) : Why, sir, it is our duty — to help the sun to rise. Each day at dawn, we push our stones to yonder hill-top. Then (*Triumphantly*) up comes the sun.

HODGE (*Nods*) : Ay, sir, it's been like that for years. All Gotham counts on us to help the sun rise. You must not keep us, or we'll be too late.

SHERIFF (*Letting go his hold on* HODGE) : Ah — You have lost your mind — (*To* SOLDIERS) We need not trouble with him, who has so feeble a wit. But his companions — Are they mad as well?

HODGE (*Stoutly*) : My companions know their duty as well as I do. Each day, as Dobbin just told you, we push our stones to yonder hill-top. Then — up comes the sun.

SHERIFF (*Making a sign to his men, so that* FIRST *and* SECOND SOLDIERS *release* DOBBIN *and* PETER) : Poor, harmless fools. We have no business to carry out with them. We must seek further — (*Nods to* HODGE, DOBBIN, *and* PETER.) See here, good men, just leave those stones alone. As your King's Sheriff, I give my solemn word — The sun will rise without any help from you.

DOBBIN (*Uncertainly*) : Well — If you're sure of that —

SHERIFF (*With decision*) : Entirely sure. There is no doubt whatever about it.

PETER (*Nodding happily*): Then we'll be saved a deal of work.

HODGE (*Turning to* PETER): Then we'll be free to help the others.

SHERIFF (*Sharply*): What others? The men of Gotham?

DOBBIN (*Nods*): Yes, all our friends and neighbors. Everybody in Gotham — They, too, have work to do. We'll go and help them.

SHERIFF (*Beckoning to the* SOLDIERS): And we'll go with you. We have business with the men of Gotham—by the King's command. We'll follow you. Lead on.

CURTAIN

* * *

SCENE 4

SETTING: *An open field near Gotham. A cuckoo is supposedly concealed in the bushes in readiness to fly up and out. A pile of brush is near right center.*

AT RISE: *Complete silence reigns, while* THE VILLAGERS *of Gotham are laying branches to make a fence around the thicket.* DOBBIN, HODGE, *and* PETER *enter from left, followed by the* SHERIFF *and* FIRST *and* SECOND SOLDIERS.

DOBBIN (*Crossing to the brush pile, turns, and whispers*): Quick, Hodge and Peter — We must help build the fence. (*Picks up a branch;* HODGE *and* PETER *also pick up branches, and turn toward fence.*)

SHERIFF (*Looks at* THE VILLAGERS, *who go on working as if unmindful of his presence, then turns to* FIRST SOLDIER): What make you of all this? Whatever are they doing?

DOBBIN (*Going close to* SHERIFF): Hush, sir. (*In a loud, strained whisper.*) Or else, the cuckoo'll hear you.

SHERIFF (*Wondering if he's heard right, but impressed by the silence that continues as* THE VILLAGERS *go on making the fence, he whispers*): Did you say — The *Cuckoo'll* hear me? The Cuckoo? What Cuckoo?

DOBBIN (*Pointing at the thicket, whispers*): The cuckoo, sir, who's resting in that thicket. For years, we men of Gotham have tried to fence him round. But the cuckoo always moves before we finish the fence.

SHERIFF (VILLAGERS *continue working silently.* SHERIFF *mops his brow, helplessly, and turns to* FIRST SOLDIER *again*): Did you ever hear the like?

DOBBIN (*Putting his finger to his lips*): Quiet, sir. The Cuckoo—

SHERIFF (*Pointing to* THE VILLAGERS): Are these the men of Gotham? Are they all here?

DOBBIN (*Nods*): Ay, sir. Though to be sure, I do not see our Mayor.

SHERIFF (*Nods resolutely*): Then no more of this nonsense. (*In loud, firm tones.*) You men of Gotham, at the King's command...

VILLAGERS (*All together. Interrupting him*):

Oh, the cuckoo's gone
The cuckoo's flown away
A-lack a-day — Our cuckoo
Oh, our cuckoo. Where is the cuckoo now?

SHERIFF (*To* SOLDIERS): Has everybody in Gotham lost their wits?

FIRST SOLDIER (*Nods*): Ay. If ever the men of Gotham once had wits, it's plain they've lost them now.

SHERIFF (*Thoughtfully*): But there is still their Mayor. Let's find the Mayor of Gotham.

SECOND SOLDIER (Nods): Ay, let's see the Mayor. There must be some soul in Gotham who is a man of sense.

PETER (*Goes close to* SHERIFF, *and points off right*): Our Mayor is coming now, if you would see him. (MAYOR *enters, staggering under the weight of a door, which he carries on his shoulders.*)

SHERIFF (*Doubtfully*): Are you the Mayor of Gotham?

MAYOR (*Tries to bow*): Yes, at your service. The Mayor of Gotham — (*Door threatens to fall.* MAYOR *raises his voice.*) Oh, give me help, I pray you. My burden seems to have slipped from proper balance.

SHERIFF (*Nods to* SOLDIERS, *who go to the* MAYOR'S *assistance*): Your burden is a strange one to carry on your shoulders. Is it not a door?

MAYOR (*Nods*) : Yes, it is a door. My own front door. My stout, my staunch front door.

SHERIFF (*Looks at* SOLDIERS *helplessly, then turns to* MAYOR) : But why, sir, are you carrying your door about with you?

MAYOR (*Sadly*) : Oh, sir, I always carry my door — Wherever I go — my door goes, too. There is no way to help it — I've so much money at home —

SHERIFF (*Mopping his brow again*) : So — you always carry your door. (*Collects himself, and adds sternly.*) What has your door to do with money?

MAYOR (*Reasonably*) : Where there is money, there is great danger of thieves. Thieves might break down my door, did I not take it with me. But sir, pray tell me this — How can thieves break down a door if it's not there?

SHERIFF (*Puts his hand to his forehead, then looks at* SOLDIERS, *and shakes his head*) : They are all mad. All. Everyone in Gotham —

FIRST SOLDIER (*Nods*) : Ay, sir, our errand is quite hopeless —

SECOND SOLDIER (*Nods*) : There are no *men* in Gotham. All, poor, helpless fools.

SHERIFF (*Turns to* MAYOR, *kindly*) : That's right. Quite right. No thieves can break a door that isn't there. But would it not be easier, when next you leave your home, to leave your door, and take your money with you?

MAYOR (*Drops the door with a crash, and claps his hands*) : Hurrah. Of course. The very thing. I'll leave the door behind. Just carry my *money* with me.

VILLAGERS (*All together, nod and smile*) :
Ah, now our Mayor is free —
He'll carry his door no more —
He'll take his money with him,
Just a small purse of money,
He need not carry the door,
Hurrah, the Mayor is free.

SHERIFF (*To* SOLDIERS) : Come. Back to the King. (*On way out left he pauses, and turns to* SOLDIERS, *who follow him.*)
We'll tell the King what's clear beyond all doubt —
There are no men in Gotham. All, poor, helpless fools.
(SHERIFF *and* SOLDIERS *go off left.* VILLAGERS *throng toward left watching them disappear, then turn to each other laughing.*)

MAYOR (*Holding up his hand*) : You see — There are no *men* in Gotham —

VILLAGERS (*All together, laughing*) :
All — all of us
Everybody in Gotham —
We're all alike —
Poor, helpless fools.

ALL (*In chorus*) :
Poor, helpless fools.

THE END

THE PIED PIPER OF HAMELIN

by Lucy Kennedy

Characters

THE PIPER, *a tall, thin fellow*
OBIE, *a crippled boy of ten who carves wooden cats*
ALDERMAN STEMPERNICKEL, *a fat person*
ALDERMAN BUMPERKOPF, *a still fatter person*
THE MAYOR, *a still fatter person*
KATRINKA, *a woman who is tired of the rats*
WOMEN *of the town*
CHILDREN *of the town*

TIME: *Long ago.*

SETTING: *A street in Hamelin, in front of the Town Hall.*

AT RISE: OBIE, *seated on the Town-Hall steps, is carving a wooden cat, and whistling. The* PIPER *enters and watches him a moment.*

PIPER:
Such care you take!
What is it you make?

OBIE: A wooden cat.

PIPER: A wooden cat?
Now what's the point in that?

OBIE: Well, there are so many rats here, the live cats are scared of them. People buy these for souvenirs — it's kind of a joke!

PIPER:
So you're overrun with rats, who frighten your cats!
And has your town a name, as well as an ill-fame?

OBIE: Why, this is Hamelin town! Everyone who lives here knows that!

PIPER:

Everyone who lives here, true,
Must know the name as well as you.

OBIE (*Looking the stranger up and down*): I guess I haven't seen you around before. (*He whittles some more.*) But if you don't live here, where else? There's the river on that side. (*Pointing left.*) And the mountain on that side. (*Pointing right.*) And no one can live *there,* because the mountain's too high!

PIPER:

In back of the mountain is a beautiful city.
I had to leave it, more's the pity!

OBIE: You mean to tell me there's a town like this back of the mountain?

PIPER:

Oh, it isn't a place like this at all!
For one thing, the houses aren't nearly so tall,
And they're made of mirrors that wink in the sun,
And everyone there has lots of fun,
And in the back yards, where there's a child,
Why lollipop bushes simply grow wild!

OBIE (*Licking his lips*): Any chocolate caramel bushes?

PIPER:

Not bushes, no! *They* grow on a vine,
That all around boys' windows twine!

OBIE: Pretty nice! But what kind of people live there?

PIPER:

They're jolly, laughing, joyous and kind,
And the children there always *want* to mind!

OBIE: Golly, if I'd been you I wouldn't have left *that* place!

PIPER (*With a sigh*):

You see, one day, I was unjust to a neighbor,
And the king there exiled me to labor,
Wandering about the world to teach,
That happiness is lost when we do o'er-reach.
That's why I talk in rhyme like this!
I was a poet there, before I went amiss,
These terrible rhymes grate on my ear
So that I wish sometimes I couldn't hear.

OBIE: Well, they are pretty terrible. But then, when I like someone, *I'm* willing to overlook things!

PIPER:

Thank you, you are very kind,
To overlook my jingles and not mind.
Such was my penance, commanded by the king,
Before I could return there again to sing.

OBIE: Tell me — are there any children there like me — I mean — crippled?

PIPER:

All the children there are straight,
And run about with joyous gait,
And one of the quite most interesting things
Is that every horse has a pair of wings.
And when children are playing in the block
The horses needn't through them walk,
They simply take wing, and over them soar,
And the children keep playing as before.

OBIE: I think I'd like to go there, but (*Shaking his head, sighing*) I have to whittle some cats. My mother sells them, and if we have a good day, we eat — and if we don't — we don't!

PIPER:

But then your neighbors give you food, I guess.
For to feed one more, makes theirs not less.

OBIE: Most of them are as poor as we are. The rats just eat up everything!

PIPER:

Which reminds me: I'm hungry and would like to eat.
I'll ask for my dinner from the first one I meet.

OBIE: Asking and getting are two different things.

PIPER:

Here comes a citizen who looks well-fed,
All dressed in a lovely cloak of red.

OBIE: Oh, that's Alderman Stempernickel! *He* won't give you anything! All he does is sleep. He's too proud to bother. (ALDERMAN STEMPERNICKEL, *looking very important, approaches the Town Hall, wearing his red cloak in quite a regal manner.*)

PIPER (*Simply, confidently*):
I'm hungry, good sir. Could you tell a poor sinner
Where he could come by a good hot dinner?

ALDERMAN (*Pompously*): Out of my way! I'm an *alderman,* and *I* can't be bothered with *you.* (*With a sweeping gesture of his cloak, he goes up the steps, into the Town Hall.*)

PIPER:
Perhaps the man was in a hurry,
Or some thing caused him worry.
Here comes one who jollier looks,
I'll ask if *he* knows any good cooks!

OBIE: Oops!! That's Alderman Bumperkopf! All he likes to do is eat. I don't think he'll help you. (ALDERMAN BUMPERKOPF *approaches Town Hall, looking even more important than* STEMPERNICKEL, *and wearing his fancy green cloak in an even more regal way.*)

PIPER (*Simply*):
I'm hungry, good sir. Could you tell a poor sinner
Where to come by a good hot dinner?

ALDERMAN (*Spluttering, pompous*): What's this? How dare you accost *me?*

PIPER:
Noodles and beef would be very fine,
But even at soup I won't draw the line!

ALDERMAN: Don't bother me! We can't be expected to feed every transient who wanders into Hamelin! Why don't you go back where you came from? (*With a lordly gesture of his hand.*) Out of my way! (*With excessive dignity, he wraps his cloak around him and sails into the Town Hall.*)

OBIE: I tried to tell you!

PIPER:
Back of the mountain in my fair town,
A hungry man is not met with a frown.
To refuse a neighbor is considered a sin.
But here comes someone — I'll ask him!

OBIE: Ooh! That's the Mayor. All he likes to do is count his money. *He* never helps anyone! (*The* MAYOR *approaches, looking very important indeed, and carrying his head mighty high.*)

PIPER (*Simply*):
I'm hungry, good sir. Could you tell a poor sinner
Where he could come by a good hot dinner?

MAYOR: Certainly not! I never help beggars! Go to the Charity League office... they look after those things... after they've investigated you! Out of my way. (*Throwing his cloak over one shoulder in a lordly way, he slowly walks into the Town Hall.*)

PIPER:
Your fellow townsmen seem to me
To be quite cold and crotchety!

OBIE (*Apologetically*): Oh, well, it's just those fellows! They don't understand! (*He takes a bun out of his pocket.*) Here! Take it!

PIPER:
Thank you, child! By your lief! (*Munching.*)
This tastes better than any roast beef!

OBIE: Why, it's only a bun, and kind of worn around the edges. It was my dinner, but if you've traveled so far, you're hungrier than I am.

PIPER:
From a scanty store you helped a neighbor,
And that gives it a very distinctive flavor!
I won't forget that you've been kind,
Those others in there (*Gesturing.*) were simply blind
To their neighbor's hunger, and his need,
So they missed a chance to do a good deed.
But a kindness is something I never forget,
And some day I may discharge this debt.
If you're ever in trouble, you shall see,
Just softly repeat, "Piper, come to me!"
(KATRINKA, *a woman of the town, rushes in.*)

KATRINKA (*Pointing to Town Hall*): Is the Mayor in there?

OBIE: Yes, he is.

KATRINKA: And the Aldermen?

OBIE: Yes, but...

KATRINKA (*Rushing out*): Good! (*Another woman of the town runs in excitedly.*)

WOMAN: Has Katrinka come yet?

OBIE: She went that way. What's the matter?

WOMAN: You'll see! The whole town's coming! (*Voices of a crowd are heard gradually growing louder.*) There! Here they come! (*Three townswomen hurry in excitedly. One carries a broom; one leads a child.*)

1ST WOMAN (*Indignantly*): Why, we can't sit down to our supper but a rat tries to take the food from our plate! (*The* PIPER *moves off to one side, observing and listening.*)

2ND WOMAN (*Angrily*): They're in our cupboards, our cellars, even our beds! They're driving us out of house and home!

3RD WOMAN (*Excitedly*): Would you believe it, when Father went to get his Sunday hat to wear to market this morning, those pesky rats had made a nest in it! (*Two more women come in and join the group. One carries a mop; two children cling to the other's skirts.*)

4TH WOMAN: And our good keg of sardines! Rats in it, mind you!

5TH WOMAN: Last night, their squeaking waked us, and there they were carrying off our candles! (*Two more women run in, their sleeves tucked up, still carrying brooms and mops as though they'd left their work hurriedly. They join the group, talking excitedly.*)

1ST WOMAN (*Shrieking*): Awk! Ouch! Ol, it bit me!

2ND WOMAN (*Brandishing broom*): There he goes! Get him! (*Some of them join in chasing the rat.*)

3RD WOMAN (*Hopelessly*): What's the use of killing one when three more spring up in its place? (KATRINKA *hurries in, with two more women. One carries a cardboard sign on a pole, reading "They (a picture of a large rat) must go!" The other woman has a sign reading "DEFINITELY no more Rats!" They all talk loudly and angrily.* KATRINKA *mounts the steps and motions for silence.*)

KATRINKA: Neighbors! Are we going to stand for being eaten out of house and home?

THE CROWD: No! No!

KATRINKA: It is a question of the rats or us!

THE CROWD: Yes! That's right!

KATRINKA: Is there any one of you who hasn't suffered because of these rodents?

CROWD: No! Not one!

KATRINKA: The men do nothing! They sit and smoke and look wise, and say it can't be helped!

CROWD: Don't depend on them! They do nothing!

KATRINKA: Neighbors, if we are ever to be rid of the rats, it is up to us! We have kept quiet long enough!

CROWD: That's right!

KATRINKA: The Mayor is in there now. (*Gesturing to Town Hall*) He is the one who should do something! What do we pay him for?

CROWD: That's right.

KATRINKA: He makes promises but does nothing. Let him do something to rid us of the rats... or we'll rid of him!

CROWD: We want action! (ALDERMAN BUMPERKOPF *sticks his head out of the door to see what all the noise is about. When he sees the women he comes forward.*)

BUMPERKOPF (*Testily*): Here, here, what's all this noise about? We can't have you women wrangling on the steps of the Town Hall. Run along home, now! We're having a very important meeting! Why, how can you expect us to decide on the food for our annual dinner with all this noise!

KATRINKA: Food for your annual dinner, indeed! What about the rats in the town? Tell the Mayor we want to see him!

BUMPERKOPF: He couldn't possibly be disturbed!

KATRINKA: You tell him to come out here, and be quick!

BUMPERKOPF (*Hesitating*): But — (*Some of the women brandish their brooms at him.*)

KATRINKA: And be quick! (BUMPERKOPF *goes in hurriedly. In a moment* STEMPERNICKEL *comes out.*)

STEMPERNICKEL (*In a suave, conciliatory tone*): My good women, the Mayor is busy right now. As a matter of fact, he's in conference.

KATRINKA: You tell the Mayor to come out here, or we'll go in there. (*Two or three women threaten* STEMPERNICKEL *with their mops, and he goes in hurriedly. The* MAYOR *comes out, and pompously holds up his hand for silence. The* ALDERMEN *peep from behind his gown.*)

MAYOR (*As though to humor them*): Well, well, what's all this fuss about, ladies?

KATRINKA: Mr. Mayor, the rats eat us out of house and home. They're hopping into the cradles nipping at our babies! They even bite you on the street!

1ST WOMAN: They ate our barrel of sugar!

MAYOR (*Unctuously*): Well, well, we'll take the matter under consideration.

KATRINKA: No! You've promised us before and nothing was done. You say "It can't be helped," or "They'll soon go away." But they don't go away. One rat brings in his friends and they set up housekeeping! Things have become so bad we'll soon have to move out and let the rats have the town!

MAYOR: Right now, I have more weighty matters under consideration, but soon —

KATRINKA: We've had enough promises! We want action!

CROWD: That's right! The Mayor should do something! We want action!

MAYOR: My good women, don't you think this rat business is largely imagination? Now, you just all run along back to your kitchens and forget about them. Act as *I* do! You don't see *me* fussing about them! (*He suddenly grabs himself and screeches loudly.*) Ouch! Ouch! Awk! Something's biting me! Why doesn't somebody do something? (*The women beat about with their mops and brooms and chase the rat.*)

1ST WOMAN: He's gone.

KATRINKA: Forget them, indeed! We won't be put off any longer. Something must be done!

MAYOR (*Fussily to* STEMPERNICKEL): Why don't you suggest something! *You're* an alderman! But that's the way! Everything's left to me, as if I hadn't enough to do!

STEMPERNICKEL (*Oilily*): Bumperkopf is your man, your Honor. He's been an alderman a much longer time than I.

BUMPERKOPF: Well... er... I've heard of a fine breed of cats grown in England! They haven't any tails....

KATRINKA: Cats! Might as well suggest Obie's wooden cats. These rats chase the cats! (*The* PIPER *gradually works his way through the crowd and now, at the steps, addresses the* MAYOR.)

PIPER:

Even though they chew the cats,

I can rid you of your rats!

MAYOR: You? And, pray, who are you?

STEMPERNICKEL: Why, he's only a beggar!

BUMPERKOPF: Yes! He stopped me going into Town Hall.

KATRINKA: If he thinks he can rid us of rats, you'd better listen to him. We want something done... *Now!*

MAYOR (*Hating to condescend to the* PIPER): Well, my good fellow, how would you rid us of the rats?

PIPER (*Touching his pipe*):

I'd play a little tune,
A simple little tune.

BUMPERKOPF: I told you, your Honor. Just a faker, trying to get the pennies of the crowd.

PIPER:

A little tune, but a magic tune,
With a charm that comes from behind the moon.
Every creature that hears me play
In spite of himself must do as I say!

MAYOR: You mean to tell me a little tune from that... er... thing... and the rats would do as you willed?

BUMPERKOPF: Not possible!

STEMPERNICKEL: No, else *I'd* have thought of it.

BUMPERKOPF: He is a cuckoo! (OBIE, *crawling through legs and around skirts, is at the steps.*)

OBIE: Please, your Honor, it won't hurt to let him try!

KATRINKA: And remember, you better do *something!*

MAYOR: Well, you have my permission to *try.* Not that I think for a minute...

PIPER:

My tunes cost money, Mr. Mayor.
I'll pipe, but you must pay the player.

MAYOR (*As though stabbed in the back*): Money! What do you mean?

PIPER:

I'll rid you of your rats this very day,
But a thousand pieces of gold is to be my pay.

STEMPERNICKEL: A thousand!

KATRINKA: If he rids us of our rats, it's cheap!

MAYOR: Well... er... but a thousand!

KATRINKA: This is not the time to haggle. We mean to be rid of the rats... or of you!

MAYOR: Well, if he can really do it....

PIPER:

I assure you the rats will be gone,
Before you see another dawn.

MAYOR (*Ungraciously*): Oh, all right....

PIPER:

So be it then. The bargain is made.
A thousand pieces of gold to be paid!

MAYOR: Yes, yes, only rid us of the rats! (*The* PIPER *moves to one side and throws back his dusty cloak, revealing his costume. Slowly, he lifts the pipe to his lips. An eerie tune is heard, as the eyes of the crowd are riveted on him. Suddenly, up the street, there is a queer rustling, which grows louder.*)

OBIE: Look! Look! Look! The rats come out of their holes. (*All turn as the rustling grows louder. There are loud squeaks.*)

KATRINKA (*Excitedly*): Why, they are running down the middle of the street! (*The* PIPER *moves off down the street, but the tune continues.*)

1ST WOMAN: They run toward the river!

2ND WOMAN: They run so fast they can't stop! (*In the distance can be heard splashes.*)

KATRINKA: Look! The piper stands by the river bank, and the rats run into the river!

1ST WOMAN: They'll be drowned!

2ND WOMAN: We'll be rid of the rats!

CROWD: Hurrah! Rid of the rats! Hurrah! Hurrah!

MAYOR (*Smugly*): You see there was nothing to raise all this fuss about. I knew I could get rid of them very quickly once I started to work on it.

STEMPERNICKEL: Right!

BUMPERKOPF: Right! (*The women and children dance about with shouts of joy, some of them join hands and dance in a circle. The* PIPER *enters, works his way through the crowd to the steps.*)

PIPER:

I must be gone and I would like my pay.
Give it to me now, and I'll be on my way.

MAYOR: Pay? Why... er... what are you talking about?

PIPER:

I kept my promise that before another day,
Your million rats would all be gone away.

MAYOR: The rats? Oh, I *guess* they are gone, but...

KATRINKA: Of course they're gone. Didn't we see them all drown?

PIPER:

And now, please, my pay,
I must be on my way.

MAYOR: Oh, of course. (*He reaches under his gown and fishes out some coins from his pocket. He picks them over as though reluctant to part with any, then hands the* PIPER *one.*) Here's a pretty gold piece for your music. Anytime you feel like entertaining the townspeople, come back again.

PIPER:

One gold piece! But the bargain you made,
Was a thousand pieces here to be paid!

MAYOR (*With a forced laugh*): A thousand? Ha! Ha! You joke! (*The crowd murmurs.*)

PIPER:

Nevertheless, that was the bargain!
Pay me now. Enough of this jargon!

MAYOR (*Wheedling*): But a thousand pieces! What would a wandering chap like you do with it. Why, someone would rob you!

PIPER:

Keep to your bargain, or I must teach,
I play another tune for those who overreach!

OBIE: Please your Honor, Mr. Mayor, you *did* promise a thousand pieces, and I'm only a boy, but I know you ought to keep your word!

MAYOR (*Spluttering*): The idea! Such impudence!

KATRINKA: Overrun with rats, a thousand pieces seemed cheap. Keep your bargain!

THE CROWD: Pay him his due!

MAYOR (*Testily*): But the town isn't made of money! We have to have gold to pay for the council dinners! And our wine cellar is almost empty....

BUMPERKOPF: To say nothing of the treasury....

PIPER:

Pay what you owe,
And let me go.

MAYOR: It's perfectly ridiculous to pay all that good money for a little tune!

KATRINKA: You made a bargain. Pay him his money!

MAYOR (*Irritably*): My good woman, will you keep out of things you know nothing about? Why... we'd have to float a bond issue!

OBIE: What's that mean?

1ST WOMAN: I think it means — borrow the money from us!

STEMPERNICKEL: A bond issue! Precisely! (*Rubbing his hands together*) And let *me* handle the money....

MAYOR (*Trying to intimidate* KATRINKA): A super-redeemable, non-recoverable, non-bounce-back-able bond issue! And what would *you* know about that?

KATRINKA: Nothing. But I know a promise is a promise! (*The* MAYOR *and the* ALDERMEN *get in a huddle.*)

MAYOR: Anyhow, who is this fellow? Nobody! If we give him the brushoff... what can he do about it? Nothing!

STEMPERNICKEL: Right!

BUMPERKOPF: Right!

MAYOR (*Righteously to the crowd*): After conferring with my honored colleagues, we feel it our civic duty not to let the fair town of Hamelin be robbed in this manner! (*The crowd murmurs.*)

KATRINKA: It's cheating!

PIPER:

Till now for your town I have done only good.
You keep to your bargain as you should,
If not, you'll find out only too soon,
The piper plays quite a different tune!

MAYOR: You threaten me! Why I'll have you thrown into jail for vagrancy and obstructing traffic! (*The* PIPER *raises his pipe, and plays a different tune. He comes down from the steps, goes slowly off, playing as he goes. At the first note, the children start as if electrified, then with hands outstretched and a happy look on their faces, they start off after the* PIPER. *It is as though they were drawn by a powerful current, yet one to which they are willing to submit. Their mothers start to draw them back, but stand paralyzed with hands outstretched and feet raised, as if for a step, but unable to move.*)

1ST MOTHER: Tina! Tina! Come back!

2ND MOTHER: Greta! Greta! (*But the children move off after the* PIPER. OBIE *stands up and tries to go after them, but he is too slow with his crutches, and before he can manage, the children are gone, and the tune has stopped.*)

STEMPERNICKEL: They go toward the mountain. Well, they'll have to come back, for they can't get around that!

KATRINKA: Look! The side of the mountain opens. They pass inside. Now the mountain closes. They are gone! (*The mothers seem to recover from the spell. They start to wail. One sits down with her apron over her head, another runs toward the mountain, calling, another goes off to her house weeping, etc.*)

KATRINKA (*To* MAYOR): This is your fault! If you'd paid what you rightly owed, he wouldn't have done it!

MOTHERS (*Angrily*): No! That's right! It's his fault!

KATRINKA: He broke his word. We don't want such a mayor! (*The women brandish their mops and brooms at him.*)

MAYOR (*Cowering before the brooms and mops*): But, my good women, I can explain.... You don't understand finance.... (*But the women will not be placated, and the* ALDERMEN, *gathering their gorgeous gowns about their waists take to their heels, followed by the* MAYOR. *He, being fatter, is slower in getting away, and the women chase him and belabor him with their brooms. Exit the* MAYOR, ALDERMEN *and townswomen, running. Only* OBIE *is left. He sits on the steps, weeping. After awhile, he gazes toward the mountain.*)

OBIE: Piper, piper, come to me! (*The* PIPER *comes in very quietly and goes up to* OBIE, *almost before* OBIE *knows it.*)

PIPER:

I was back of the mountain, far away
I heard you crying, I heard you say,
Piper, piper, come to me,
And I am here, as you can see.

OBIE: Please, Piper, I know the mayor was bad, but... you do like *me* a little, don't you?

PIPER:

You have a kind and charitable heart.
I could see that from the start.

OBIE: Then piper... all the mothers are so sad... and piper... I'll never have any children to play with as long as I live.... All my friends, Hans and Greta and Tina and Peter... all, all, gone... and couldn't you... well... maybe... let them come back? (*The* PIPER *lifts his pipe to his lips, but before he plays, he speaks*)

PIPER:

Remember, always, this was my song
Love may even overcome wrong.
When I am gone — stand up! Walk! Be free!
Then from your crutches, carve a figure of me!

(*The* PIPER *plays, moving off softly as* OBIE *looks after him wonderingly. The sound of the pipe recedes in the distance and the murmur of children's voices grows louder.*)

OBIE: What did he mean? Stand up straight? Be free? (OBIE *tries to stand up and, after a trial or two, finds he can. He takes a step or two, and he can walk. He waves his crutches over his head joyously.*)

OBIE: Hurrah! Hurrah! (*The children begin to run in. One carries an enormous lollipop, a foot wide, over his shoulder. Two carry very carefully between them, a vine growing in a pot. Caramels grow on it. The mothers, hearing children's voices come *in joyfully, embrace and kiss them. Soon all the children are back, and they all join together, including* OBIE, *and dance about with gaiety, as the curtain falls.)*

THE END

THE MIXING STICK

by Eleanore Leuser

Characters

MOTHER BROWN
FATHER BROWN
JOHNNY
MARY
FARMER JONES
MRS. JONES
WIDOW POST
BUTCHER
OLD MRS. GOODALL
LAME TOMMY
PEDDLER

SETTING: *An old-fashioned kitchen.*

TIME: *The day before Christmas.*

AT RISE: FATHER *and* MOTHER BROWN *are sitting at an almost empty table.*

MOTHER BROWN: Father, it grieves me sorely that there is so little to eat in the house. It's the day before Christmas, too.

FATHER BROWN: It can't be helped, Mother. It's been a hard winter. The neighbors are no better off than ourselves.

MOTHER BROWN: It's the children I'm thinking about. I wish I had something hot and tasty to give them.

FATHER BROWN: I wouldn't say no to it myself. But there . . . you can't make a rich soup out of a pot of hot water. (*A knock is heard at the door. A cheerful* PEDDLER *enters without waiting to be asked. He is carrying a big mixing stick.*)

PEDDLER: Good evening, goodwife. Good evening, goodman. I couldn't help hearing what you said just now. If you'll give me a pot of boiling water I'll show you what can be done with it.

MOTHER BROWN (*Rising to show him*): There's a pot half full of water on the fire, little man. But I don't understand what good that will be.

PEDDLER (*Cheerily*): Don't you worry, good mother. See this Mixing Stick! (*Holding it up*) It can make the most delicious meal you ever tasted. Just leave it all to my Mixing Stick and me.

FATHER BROWN (*Watching the* PEDDLER *as he starts stirring in the pot*): I've heard of queer things but stirring hot water . . . that's the queerest!

PEDDLER (*To* MOTHER BROWN): You wouldn't have a pinch of salt, would you?

MOTHER BROWN (*Handing him some*): That's about all we do have but you're welcome to it. (JOHNNY *and* MARY *come in from outdoors all bundled up, each holding an onion.*)

JOHNNY: These onions are all we could find, mother. They were far back in the shed.

PEDDLER (*Rubbing his hands*): Onions, you say . . . that's fine, my lad! Just drop them right into the pot. They'll turn into the tastiest dinner you've ever eaten.

MARY (*Looking into the pot*): Onions and water! I don't believe it.

PEDDLER (*As he stirs*): It's all in the magic Mixing Stick, Mary, my girl. Why, when you stir with this stick it makes a dinner fit for a king.

JOHNNY: Could we go and tell the neighbors about it, sir?

MARY: You see, it's the day before Christmas and they don't have much to eat for tomorrow. They'd be so glad to know about a Mixing Stick.

PEDDLER: Run along, both of you and tell the neighbors they're welcome to see what I've got. You might add that if they bring a bit of what they have I'll see to it that the Mixing Stick gives it a good flavor. (*The* CHILDREN *run out. The* PEDDLER *stirs busily.*)

FATHER BROWN (*Stepping up to the pot and sniffing*): You know, Mother, I believe it's beginning to smell good already.

MOTHER BROWN (*To* PEDDLER): I wish you'd tell me where to get a mixing stick like yours, sir. We need it badly around these parts.

PEDDLER (*Mixing and tasting*): The Mixing Stick is only just beginning to work. You'll really want one when it gets busy. But if you like what it makes I'll leave you this stick of mine with the greatest of pleasure. (*The* NEIGHBORS *begin to come in . . . each carrying something.*)

WIDOW POST: Well, Neighbor Brown, the children have been telling me the news about this Mixing Stick . . . so over I come with my potatoes. It's potatoes I've been eating for breakfast and dinner and supper and I'm sick of the sight of them. If your little man with the stick can give them a different taste I'll certainly be thankful. Who wants a meal of potatoes on Christmas Day?

PEDDLER (*Taking the potatoes and putting them into the pot*): Just wait and see what my Mixing Stick can do to a potato. You'll be more than surprised, Widow Post! (*He stirs.* FARMER JONES *and his wife enter. He is carrying some turnips and she, a jar of drippings.*)

FARMER JONES: We've been hearing about the pot of water and the Mixing Stick. We thought to ourselves that something like that is just what we need. So we've brought a few turnips to see what it does to the flavor. Sure, we've boiled turnips in water many a time and thankful we are for them, but they get powerful uninteresting.

MRS. JONES (*Giving a great sigh*): It's not much that we have but some drippings from the pork that was finished. It's been a bad year for us all . . . a bad year!

PEDDLER (*Taking turnips and drippings and putting them into the pot*): Fine . . . Farmer Brown and Mrs. Brown. I'll guarantee to give them a flavor that will make your mouths water. (*He stirs and tastes.*) Um-m! This stick is wonderful! It's getting delicious. (THE BUTCHER *enters with a large bone*)

BUTCHER: What's all this about a magic stick that gives flavors? I'm always willing to try anything new, especially in a time when things are so scarce. I brought this bare bone along. If you can give *that* a flavor, there's more where it came from. Maybe I could even find one with a little meat on it.

PEDDLER (*Taking bone and dropping it into pot*): Mr. Butcher, it's amazing what a Mixing Stick can do with a bone. You'll scarcely believe it. (*Enter* OLD MOTHER GOODALL *with a sprig of parsley.*)

MOTHER GOODALL: The children have been telling me of a magic mixing stick and what it can do. At first I thought I wouldn't be coming. I've only this bit of parsley I've been growing in a little pot in the house. Could you be turning it into something fit for a Christmas dinner?

PEDDLER (*Taking parsley and dropping it into the pot*): Gladly, gladly, Mother Goodall! (*Tasting*) Um-m, the flavor's better already. It's beyond belief what a Mixing Stick can do to it. (JOHNNY *and* MARY *enter, helping* TOMMY *who is lame. He is carrying a few carrots.*)

TOMMY: It's not much that I have, sir . . . just a few carrots. But my mother says if you could put a different flavor to them she'd send you her blessing. We've had carrots in the morning and carrots at noon and carrots at night, for nothing else grew in our garden. It's a wonder we don't turn into carrots ourselves. Yet I can't get around as I ought, to get much of anything else.

PEDDLER (*Taking them and putting them into the pot*): Carrots, is it? Well, now, young sir, it's just the touch the Mixing Stick needs. They'll be wonderful for the flavor.

MOTHER BROWN (*Looking in pot*): Why, the pot is almost full now.

FATHER BROWN (*Sniffing*): It smells better and better.

MRS. JONES: My mouth is beginning to water.

PEDDLER (*Tasting*): It's nearly ready.

JOHNNY (*Looking in pot*): But how will we ever get our onions out? I can't even see them.

WIDOW POST (*Looking in*): It's the same with the potatoes I brought. I doubt if I'd recognize them.

PEDDLER (*Rubbing his hands gleefully*): Well, now that's the trick of my Mixing Stick, good neighbors. You don't get just your own back. Everything is all mixed up together. It tastes better that way and there's lots more of it. A lone sprig of parsley doesn't make a good meal. You don't chew a bone to keep hunger away. Carrots or turnips alone make a poor supper. So put what you have together, stir with the Mixing Stick and when it's done you'll find you have enough for all and a dinner that's good enough for even a Christmas Day. Come, let's taste of it and see. (MOTHER *and* FATHER BROWN *pass bowls around. The* PEDDLER *fills them and all are eating with the appearance of great satisfaction as the curtain falls.*)

THE END

THE MAGIC COOKIE JAR

by Helen Louise Miller

Characters

A PRINCE, *who is a beggar*
A PRINCESS, *who is a kitchen maid*
A BUTLER, *who is a villain*
A COOK, *who is a cook*

SETTING: *A corner of the Royal Kitchen*

AT RISE: *The* HIGH COOK *and the* KITCHEN MAID *are baking cookies. The* COOK *is doing the rolling and cutting while the* KITCHEN MAID *is tending to the ovens.*

COOK (*As she rolls the dough*):
Roly, poly, pudding and pie!
Baking cookies till I die.
Nuts and raisins, sugar and spice —
Roly, poly, mix 'em up nice!

MAID: Why do you say that rhyme every time you roll out a fresh batch of cookies?

COOK: 'Cause it puts a spell on 'em. Keeps 'em from getting too rich, or too crumbly, too hard or too soft.

MAID: Then why can't you say a spell that will keep them from burning when they're in the oven?

COOK: Because that's your job, you wicked girl, and if you let another panful burn, you'll catch it.

MAID (*Ruefully*): Don't I know it? I don't see what's the matter with my nose! I never can smell anything burning until it is too late.

COOK (*Sniffing*): Well, I smell something this very minute. You better fly.

MAID (*Running off stage*): Oh dear, oh dear! In the name of all the fairy godmothers! Don't let those cookies burn.

COOK (*Looking after her and shaking her head in despair*): A worthless child if I ever saw one! Not worth her board and keep! In fact, I don't see why they let her stay in the King's kitchen. (*Shugging her shoulders.*) Well, one good thing, she doesn't eat much. That's a blessing and she does have a sweet disposition. (*Knock at the door.*)

COOK (*Crossly*): Whoever is there, go away! This is baking day and we have no time for visitors.

VOICE: Please, please let me in. I've traveled so far and I'm so hungry.

COOK (*Wiping her hands on her apron and approaching the door*): Indeed, I will not. We have nothing in this house for beggars.

VOICE: But I'm not a beggar. I am a prince.

COOK (*Scoffing*): A likely story! Princes don't come knocking at back doors. Go away, or I'll call the guards. (*As the* COOK *returns to her work table, the* LITTLE MAID *enters left carrying a tray of burned cookies. She is in tears.*)

MAID: Oh dear, oh dear, the cookies have burned again. Now I will be beaten.

COOK: That you will, as soon as the Royal Butler finds out.

MAID: Oh dear, kind, gentle cook, please don't tell him this time. Let's put the cookies in a jar and forget about them.

COOK: I should say not. It was your fault that the cakes burned and you'll have to pay for it.

MAID (*Putting her arm around the* COOK): Please, Cook, the Butler is such a harsh man and I am so afraid of him. Please. Didn't you ever have a little girl like me?

COOK (*Beginning to relent*): Well — yes, I did have a little girl. But she wasn't like you — not one bit. She had a nose and an eye for baking, and she never let the cakes burn.

MAID: But if she *had* let them burn, you wouldn't have turned her over to a wicked old Butler to be beaten and locked up in a dungeon, would you?

COOK: I'm sure I don't know what I would have done. (*Bell rings.*) There's the bell calling me to the royal dining-room. See if you can finish that last batch of cakes.

MAID: And you won't tell the Butler, will you, Cookie?

COOK: Well — not right away. But mind, you be careful of those cakes.

MAID: Oh, I will—I will. (COOK *exits left* MAID *watches her out of sight*) Now's my chance to get rid of these burned cookies. I'll dump them right into this old stone jar and no one will ever know. (*Dumps cookies into stone jar which is standing on a nearby cupboard or shelf among other cookie cans and jars.*) Now, I'm safe till someone eats a cookie out of this particular jar. (*Returns to her work.*) Oh my, oh me! I just love to cook, even if things do burn. I guess I'll never be a really fancy cook. I'll just be a plain, everyday cook and make fried potatoes every night for supper. (*Knock at door, right.*)

MAID: Someone at the door — just when my hands are full of flour, and I'm sure there's a smudge on my nose. (*Calling*) Who's there?

VOICE: Someone who is tired and hungry. Please let me come in.

MAID (*Trying to tidy her dress and hair*): Tired and hungry? Why, this is the very place to come. This is the King's kitchen just running over with good things. Come right in. (*Opens door. A stranger enters wrapped in a long dark cloak and wearing a mask. The* KITCHEN MAID *starts back in terror.*)

MAID (*Screaming*): Help! Help! You're a robber. Take one step further and I'll hit you over the head with this rolling pin. (*Snatches up rolling pin from table and brandishes it in a threatening manner.*)

BEGGAR: Hush! Hush! Put down that weapon. I am not a robber.

MAID: If you were an honest man you would not need to hide your face. Why do you wear a mask?

BEGGAR: Put down that club and I'll tell you.

MAID: It's not a club. It's a rolling pin.

BEGGAR: Anyhow it's a mighty dangerous looking weapon.

MAID: If you swear that you are not a robber, I'll put it down.

BEGGAR: What shall I swear by?

MAID: Swear by your sacred honor and the great horned spoon.

BEGGAR (*Raising his right hand*): Very well. I swear by my sacred honor and the great horned spoon that I am not a robber Now, are you satisfied?

MAID: I guess so. But if you are not a robber, who are you?

BEGGAR: I told you—someone who is tired and very hungry.

MAID: Oh, I know. You are a beggar.

BEGGAR (*In disgust*): No, I am not a beggar. Though I grant you, I must look very much like one.

MAID: If you are not a beggar and not a robber, who are you?

BEGGAR: For goodness sakes, child, what sort of girl are you? Do you think all men are either beggars or robbers?

MAID: No, but you have aroused my curiosity.

BEGGAR: Please find me something to eat, and maybe I can satisfy your curiosity. (*Seats himself at table.*)

MAID: How would you like some cookies and a glass of milk?

BEGGAR: That would just suit me fine. (MAID *gets glass of milk and points out the supply of cookies.*)

MAID: Just help yourself to the cookies. We have any kind you want — sugar cookies, hermits, brownies, sand tarts, ginger snaps, vanilla wafers, macaroons — take your pick.

BEGGAR (*Selecting the stone jar containing the burned cookies*): I'd like to have some out of this jar.

MAID (*Alarmed*): Oh, I wouldn't take those if I were you.

BEGGAR: Why not? Aren't they good?

MAID: Not very . . . You see . . . I burned them.

BEGGAR: But why did you put them in a cookie jar? Who wants to eat burned cookies?

MAID: I know I should not have done it, but I'm always letting the cookies burn and the Royal Butler beats me.

BEGGAR: Why aren't you more careful?

MAID: I don't know. It seems to be my nose. That's the third batch I've burned today just because I couldn't smell them burning. I don't want to be caught again.

BEGGAR: You're a strange sort of child to be a kitchen maid.

MAID: I am afraid I am not a very good one. Maybe I'd do better if I were happier.

BEGGAR: Don't they treat you kindly?

MAID: Oh, no, sir. I never hear a kind word except from the cook. She is better to me than all the rest. I guess she feels sorry for me.

BEGGAR: Did you always live here and work in the kitchen?

MAID (*Doubtfully*): I don't quite remember. Sometimes I can remember playing in a beautiful garden and sleeping in a little gold bed. There was a lovely lady who sang to me and tucked me in bed at night.

BEGGAR: Strange how you came to be a kitchen maid.

MAID: The Royal Butler brought me here. Before he was a butler he used to be a peddler and I used to travel around with him and dance for pennies. When he got this job here, I became a kitchen maid. But he was always cruel to me.

BEGGAR: You should run away if he treats you so badly.

MAID: Where would I go? Here I have a roof over my head and plenty of cookies to eat.

BEGGAR: Why do you bake so many cookies? The place is full of them.

MAID: Oh, we are always baking them for the prince. (*Confidentially*) I call him the "Pig Prince" because he eats so many.

BEGGAR: Have you ever seen him — the prince, I mean?

MAID: Dear me, no. But I hear he is a homely youth and not over-bright.

BEGGAR: Indeed! Who told you that?

MAID: Oh, the Butler and the houseboy. Cook thinks he's wonderful, but that's only because she took care of him when he was a baby.

COOK (*Entering left very much excited*): Child! Child! Good gracious sakes alive! Oh, my stars and shoestrings! There is such excitement in the palace.

MAID: What in the world is the matter?

COOK: The prince is gone. Kidnapped he is. Carried off by two woodsmen and held for ransom.

MAID (*Clapping her hands*): Goody! Goody! Now we won't have to bake any more cookies.

COOK (*Shaking her*): Why, you wicked, wicked girl. I'm sorry I didn't tell the Royal Butler on you. The prince is wise and good. This is a terrible day for our kingdom.

BEGGAR: Where did you hear this news?

COOK: The palace is ringing with it. (*Suddenly remembering her conversation with the* BEGGAR.) And by the way, how did you get in here? Aren't you the fellow who knocked at the door a few minutes ago?

BEGGAR: The very one. The little maid invited me inside and gave me a glass of milk.

COOK: Then out you go, and I'll box her ears for giving away the King's stores.

BEGGAR (*Rising*): I thought you were a woman with a kind heart.

COOK: My heart is kind enough but there is no room in my kitchen for a man who wears a mask.

BEGGAR: Then I will take it off. (*He does so, disclosing himself to be the* PRINCE. *The* COOK *falls to her knees.*)

COOK: Your gracious Highness! (*To* MAID) To your knees, girl. This is our noble Prince!

MAID (*Embarrassed*): Oh, sire, forgive me for calling you a Pig Prince. I'm so ashamed.

BEGGAR: I have no time to be angry. I'm too busy being kidnapped. Rise, both of you, you will have to help me.

MAID: Are you in any danger?

BEGGAR: No, not yet. I overheard the villain plotting with my uncle, the king, to carry me off and murder me in the forest. But I escaped in time. I've been wandering through the hills till I got so hungry for cookies I just had to come home. I thought no one would think of looking for me in our own kitchen.

COOK: How can we help you, Sire?

BEGGAR: It is that Butler who is plotting against me. He and my uncle want to get rid of me and divide the kingdom between them. But I have no actual proof of this. What I need to do is get a confession out of the Butler. We have no time to lose.

MAID (*Picking up cake turner and rolling pin*): These are our only weapons, sir, but we're willing to fight.

BEGGAR: We won't need them. I have a better plan.

MAID: Then tell us. I know I'll make a better detective than a kitchen maid.

BEGGAR: We'll catch him with the magic cookie jar.

MAID: But there isn't such a thing.

BEGGAR: Yes there is — right here on this table. (*Points to jar with burned cookies.*) My mother had this made when I was a little boy. Don't you remember, Cook?

COOK: Land sakes! I had forgotten that!

MAID: But why, why did your mother do such a strange thing?

BEGGAR: Well, you see, I was always so hungry for cookies that I ate more than were good for me. And worse than that, when Cook and Mother refused to give me any more, I used to watch my chance and sneak out here and help myself.

MAID: Why, that was stealing!

BEGGAR: I never thought so, but Mother did, so she had the magic cookie jar made to teach me a lesson.

MAID: I see nothing strange about it. What is the magic?

BEGGAR: Well, I don't know if it is still in working order. But we can try.

MAID: How?

BEGGAR: Reach in and get a cookie.

MAID (*Following his orders*): I have one. Now what?

BEGGAR: Remove the cookie from the jar.

MAID: Why — I can't. I can't. Something is holding fast to my arm. I can't get it out of the jar.

BEGGAR: Of course you can't. That's the magic. When I was a child it used to hold me prisoner till Mother or Cook came and caught me in the act.

MAID: Now that you have seen that your magic is working, make it let go of me.

BEGGAR: Oh, I can't. You have to do that yourself.

MAID (*Struggling*): But I can't. I can't. Please, dear Prince, it's hurting me.

BEGGAR: And it will go right on hurting till you confess what mischief you've been up to during the last 24 hours.

MAID: I haven't been up to any. Ouch! Ouch! It's pinching me!

BEGGAR (*Laughing*): Don't I know it? It used to pinch me too when I tried telling Mother I had been a little angel for the last twenty-four hours. You better make a clean breast of all your crimes.

COOK: Dear me, this old jar reminds me of old times. Do you remember, Your Highness, how it made you confess putting a turtle in the Royal Chancellor's bed?

BEGGAR: I should say I do. Well, little girl, are you going to stay there all day, or are you going to confess your misdeeds?

MAID: Oh dear! I guess I'll have to. You might as well know, Cook, that when your back was turned I hid the burned cookies in this very jar.

COOK: Why, you naughty child!

MAID (*Attempting to release herself*): Say, this magic isn't working. I can't get loose even now.

BEGGAR: That means you haven't told all.

MAID: Oh dear, oh dear. Now cook, you will be cross with me. But I guess I'll have to tell. I filled all the sugar boxes with salt this morning so that all your baking will turn out salt cookies instead of sugar cookies.

COOK: You just wait, young lady, till the Royal Butler catches you this time. I won't lift a finger to save you.

MAID (*Getting her arm out of the jar*): Oh, it is good to be free again. And you can bet your life I'll behave myself in this kitchen from now on. Why, there's no telling what magic is working here. I wouldn't be surprised if the pots and pans and even the rolling pin are enchanted.

BEGGAR: Now that I am sure the magic jar is working, we are ready to catch the Royal Butler. All we need to do is to get him to stick his hand in that jar, and we have him.

MAID: That should be easy. This is his day to inspect the kitchen. He should be coming here any minute now.

COOK: But he doesn't like cookies. Never touches them.

BEGGAR: I'll take care of that. Leave everything to me. Hand me the jar, and I will prepare the bait. (*Throws a handful of gold coins into the magic jar.*) When he catches the glitter of these coins, he will be sure to grab for them. Now, Cook, our trap is set. You may call the butler.

COOK: At once, Your Highness. (*Exit* COOK.)

MAID: Oh, I'm so excited! Do you really think we'll catch him?

BEGGAR: Certainly, if we are patient. Now fill my plate with cookies, and then go about your work as if nothing is happening. I'll adjust my mask. (*Replaces mask.*)

Cook (*To* BUTLER *as they enter left*): I trust everything will meet with your approval. Of course, we have been baking and things are a trifle upset.

BUTLER (*Gruffly*): Don't worry. I'll let you know soon enough if things are not to my liking. (*Catching sight of* KITCHEN MAID) And if that flighty kitchen maid has burned any more cakes, I'll have her thrown into a dungeon. (*Sees* BEGGAR *calmly eating cakes at the table.*) Ho, Ho, Sir, who are you, and what are you doing here?

BEGGAR: Just a poor beggar, sir, who has been given a place at the king's table.

BUTLER: So! And who has the right to give away the king's stores?

MAID (*Bravely*): I said he might sit down for a moment and have a bite to eat. He was so tired and looked so hungry. He has traveled a long way.

BUTLER (*In a rage*): You — you — a serving maid! No better than a beggar yourself! It is not your place to offer food to others. (*Sniffs.*) And what is worse, I smell something burning. Cook, did this miserable girl burn any more cakes?

COOK: Well, I really couldn't say, sir.

BUTLER: Oh, you couldn't! Well, I can. She has burned the cakes and she will be thrown into the dungeon as soon as she has had a good beating. (*He reaches for the* MAID *who runs to* COOK *for protection.*)

MAID: Oh, no, no, no! There are rats in the dungeon and I am so afraid of rats.

BEGGAR (*Mildly*): You seem a harsh sort of fellow.

BUTLER (*Fastening his attention on the* BEGGAR): Oh, I do, do I? Well, you worthless beggar, I'll soon show you just how harsh I can be. There is a law against beggars in this kingdom, and it is especially severe to those who do not show their faces. I am going to have you locked up in the tower this very minute.

BEGGAR (*Pretending to bite on something hard in the cake he is eating. He jumps up, holding his jaw*): Ouch! Say, what kind of cookies do you people bake in this kitchen? Why, I've almost broken my tooth on a stone.

COOK (*Indignantly*): Faith and there are no stones in my cakes!

BUTLER: Serves you right if you've broken your whole jaw. And you'll be glad enough to chew on stones after you've been in the tower for a while on a good round diet of air and water.

MAID (*Inspecting what the* BEGGAR *is holding in his hand*): But — but — it isn't a rock — it's a gold piece!

BEGGAR: Girl, where did you get those cookies?

MAID (*Pointing to magic jar*): Out of that blue jar, sir.

BUTLER: What nonsense is this? (*In surprise*) Why it is a gold piece, and no mistake. Where did this come from? Answer me.

COOK: Out of our oven, sir. We baked 'em this morning.

MAID: She speaks the truth. You see I did burn some cookies and hid them in that stone jar. Then when this beggar came along, I offered him some of the burned cookies and you can see for yourself what happened.

BEGGAR: That must be the magic cookie jar I have heard so much about.

BUTLER: What have you heard about it?

BEGGAR: Oh, I'd be afraid to tell, sir. You'd have me thrown out for a fool and a liar.

BUTLER: Answer me or I'll call the guards.

BEGGAR: In that case, sir, I'll tell you all I know. I have heard tell of a magic cookie jar that turns ordinary sugar cookies into ten-dollar gold pieces, and if the cookies chance to be burned they are changed into twenty-dollar gold pieces. Of course, I never really believed it until now.

COOK (*Opening jar and peering inside*): Faith and I can see something that glitters like gold coins.

BUTLER (*Pushing her away from the jar*): Stand back, woman. Let me look. Why, there is gold in that jar — handfuls of gold — a fortune! (*Reaches in.*)

MAID (*Jumping up and down*): Let me see. Let me see.

BUTLER: Just a minute. My hand seems to be caught.

BEGGAR (*Smiling*): Maybe you were too greedy for the gold.

BUTLER (*Struggling*): Is this a trick? I can't get my hand out of this jar.

BEGGAR (*Shrugging his shoulders*): Think of that! The royal butler can't get his big fist out of the cookie jar.

BUTLER: But when I do, you'll feel the weight of it, you can depend on that.

MAID (*Sticking out her tongue*): Even I am not afraid of you, now!

BUTLER: You let me out of here. I'll call the guards and have you all ground to mincemeat.

COOK: You're such a tough old critter, you wouldn't make mincemeat fit for a decent pie.

BUTLER: You impudent old wretch! I'll have you put in irons.

COOK: Not till you get loose from that jar, you won't.

BUTLER (*To* BEGGAR): *You* have something to do with this, you rogue.

BEGGAR: Easy, easy on the harsh words. You should be more polite to your prince. (*Removes mask.*)

BUTLER (*In amazement*): The Prince! How did you get here?

PRINCE: Aha! You thought I had fallen victim to your evil plans. Well, I fooled you, and now you are going to tell me all about those plans, and this little lady is going to write down everything you say.

MAID: Wait till I get paper and pencil. (*Exits.*)

BUTLER: You can't prove a thing against me. I have always been a faithful servant.

PRINCE: That is what I thought until now. But your story of today will make interesting reading in the courts.

BUTLER: What makes you think I'll talk?

PRINCE: You are not in a very comfortable position, Mr. Butler. After a while, your arm will begin to ache, and your back will begin to ache, and your legs will ache. And in a day or so, the ache will grow beyond all endurance. In fact, if you stay there long enough, you'll die from weakness, hunger, thirst and exhaustion.

BUTLER: You're talking nonsense. I can get free from this jar any time I like.

PRINCE: How?

BUTLER: By calling the guards.

PRINCE: Then I should certainly call them if I were in your place.

BUTLER: I will. (*Shouting*) Guards! Guards! Help! Help! Guards! Guards! (*Silence.*)

BUTLER (*After a pause*): Where are they?

PRINCE: Out looking for me. They think I am kidnapped, and like loyal subjects they have gone to search for me. There is no one to help you.

MAID (*Reentering left*): I am ready to write down his confession.

BUTLER: But I am not ready to make any. I have done nothing to confess. Ouch! Ouch! Oooh! Something's pinching me. Ouch! Ouch!

MAID (*Giggling*): Isn't it awful? That's just the way it pinched me when I told a fib. And it will go right on pinching and pinching. You better confess before you are black and blue.

PRINCE: She knows what she is talking about. You better talk.

BUTLER: Ouch! Ouch! All right. Ouch! What do you want to know?

PRINCE: Your plans for my kidnapping.

BUTLER: They were simple enough. The king and I planned to kill you and divide the kingdom between us.

PRINCE: I thought so. (*To* MAID *now acting as stenographer*) Do you have that down in black and white?

MAID: Every word.

BEGGAR: That's all I want. With this paper, I can force the king to give up his throne, drive this fellow out, and the kingdom will be mine.

COOK: Oh, your Highness, I am so happy for you.

BUTLER: Why can't I get loose from this infernal contraption?

BEGGAR: Probably because you have not told all your secrets.

COOK: Yes, I know he has something else to tell — something about this child here. She is not his daughter. Where did you get this little girl?

BUTLER: I found her on my doorstep when she was a tiny baby and I have cared for her ever since. Ouch! Ouch! Murder! Help! My arm is breaking.

PRINCE: Now maybe you will stop inventing fairy tales.

BUTLER: If you must know, I stole her from the palace garden when she was two years old.

COOK: And kept her for your slave, you villain.

PRINCE: Then she is not a kitchen maid, but a princess.

BUTLER: Your sister, in fact.

PRINCE: My sister. But we had given her up for dead.

MAID: Do you mean I am a really, truly princess?

PRINCE: Of course you are. No wonder you were such a poor kitchen maid. A royal princess seldom has a talent for baking.

COOK: Indeed, I'll be sorry to lose you in my kitchen, even if you did let the cakes burn.

MAID: Then I won't leave you. You must move into the palace with me and be my companion.

COOK: Oh thank you, thank you.

BEGGAR: Oh ho, we have almost forgotten this fellow. What is to be done with him?

COOK: Hanging is almost too good for him.

MAID: Oh, I know — the very thing.

PRINCE: I hope it is something black and awful.

MAID: It is. Let's make him eat every one of those burned cookies — every single one.

BEGGAR: A capital idea.

BUTLER: No, no — anything but that. Spare me. Spare me. Help! Help! (*The three close in around the* BUTLER *and douse his head in the cookie jar as the curtain falls on his futile cries for help.*)

THE END

THE TOWN MOUSE AND HIS COUNTRY COUSIN

by Violet Muse

Characters

MA MOUSE, *the frowsy Country Cousin*
HIS ELEGANCE, *the Honorable Town Mouse*
SQUEAKY MOUSE, *Ma's eldest child, who is very talkative and takes his squeaking seriously*
TEENEY MOUSE, *Ma's baby*
HIS HONOR, *the Mayor of Haughtytown*
MARY, *the Mayor's cantankerous maid-of-all-work*
POUNCER, *the Mayor's cat*
SMELLER, *the Mayor's fox terrier*

SCENE 1

SETTING: *A sunshiny corner of an old barn, back of the corn crib.*

AT RISE: TEENEY *is peering through cracks and holes for probable cats.* SQUEAKY *is industriously sweeping cobwebs down from the walls with corn-husk broom.*

SQUEAKY (*Calling offstage through a knot-hole*): Ma, is His Elegance, the Mayor's Mouse, really coming to see us, his country cousins?

MA (*Calling as she approaches*): Yes, yes, hurry! He's really coming! (MA MOUSE *runs in, fussily.*)

TEENEY (*Dancing up and down*): Eek, eek! His Honor, the Mayor's Mouse! Shall we put on style and take off our aprons, Ma? (MA *nods, and* TEENEY *throws his apron in the corner. Ma seizes a bacon rind and rubs down his fur with it.*) Does he look like me?

MA: Why, I should say not! (*Peering at her baby mouse.*) Well, of course, there may be some resemblance about the nose and eyes, but since he left the country and went into society you would hardly know we belong to the same family. Why, he will probably be wearing a frock coat with fancy white vest, and an opera hat, no doubt!

MICE: Eek, eek! An opera hat!

MA: Of course, for the Mayor's ceremonies! How could he lay cornerstones without an opera hat? And I am sure in his fancy vest he will have *two* gold watches.

TEENEY: *Two* watches — what for?

SQUEAKY (*Giggling and squeaking*): So he will have twice as much time to escape from the cats! (*Merrily the little* MICE *dance about.*)

MA (*Catching and shaking them*): No more of this friskiness, I say! If your honorable cousin wears two watches, it's because it's the style. Enough of the giggling! Wash your paws and whiskers and get ready for dinner.

MICE: O. K., Ma. (*They wash themselves and grease themselves with bacon rinds near a peep hole.*)

MA (*Pointing to the feast on the floor*): Beans and bacon, cheese and corn. But what shall I do for dessert? Squeaky, didn't the hired girl bake those puddings? (*An aeroplane is heard over the barn.*)

SQUEAKY: Eek, eek, Ma, she was too busy. Whiskers Field-Mouse told me she had been threshing in the field all day!

MA (*Wringing her paws*): Oh, what shall I do without pudding for breakfast? Why, the Mayor's Mouse can't eat without pudding for breakfast! Oh, oh! (*A loud knocking, three times repeated, is heard and the* MICE *are frightened.* MA *flings her apron into the corner.*) 'Tis himself, the Honorable Mayor's Mouse! That's his same secret knock. Sh! (*The pounding with walking stick is repeated at the crack.*) Coming, your Honor, coming. (*She pulls open the burlap sacking at the crack and curtseys to the* MAYOR'S MOUSE. *His sleek nose bears Oxford glasses, and he holds aloft his opera hat and swings his cane grandly. In the pockets of his elegant waistcoat dangle two watches.*)

MAYOR'S MOUSE (*Shaking her hand gingerly*): How are you, my good cousin? You will pardon my gloves? It's good to see you after all these years. We often speak of you at the Mayor's house!

MA (*Blushing gratefully and hanging her head*): Go along now, your Honor! I never reckoned you would remember me, but we sure are glad to see you back with hardly a scar on you! Sit down. Just make yourself at home. We didn't go to any extra trouble for you!

MAYOR'S MOUSE (*Sitting on the cushion which* SQUEAKY *brings*): Ah, well if you insist, perhaps I could take a nibble. These plane rides do whet one's appetite, don't you think? Beans, ugh! (*He nibbles one, and pushes it away.*)

MA AND MICE: Plane ride? Plane ride?

MAYOR'S MOUSE: Ah, yes, I travel by that means of locomotion. It saves a mouse's time, don't you think? (*He looks at his two watches with a grand flourish.*)

MA: Yes, it saves a mouse's time! That's what I always told my mice! (SQUEAKY *pushes rinds to the guest.*)

MAYOR'S MOUSE: What? Bacon rinds! (*He yawns.*) Garbage! (*He holds his nose.*) Well, my good cousin, how are times about here?

MA (*Bashfully ducking her head*): Well, I am able to get about, your Elegance. Often we go visiting the Field-Mice. Remember Butch Field-Mouse? The sparrow-hawk caught him just yesterday! Isn't it sad? (*The* MICE *squeak sadly.*) Then sometimes we go down the lane and take a bacon rind to our cousins, the Church-Mice — poor things!

MAYOR'S MOUSE: Ah, yes, poor things! (*Bored.*) Remind me before I go to send them a donation. (SQUEAKY *tries to win his attention by passing him the cheese rinds, which he waves away grandly.*) I never eat anything but Roquefort cheese. (*He jumps up impatiently.*)

MA (*Ashamed*): Well, our food is coarse, but there is always plenty, sir.

MAYOR'S MOUSE (*Pacing about and peering through his glasses*): Upon my word, I do not see how you can stand it. No steam heat — no desserts — and no aeroplanes! Why, you are wasting your time here miserably. A mouse, you know, does not live forever!

MICE: That's right, Ma. We mice must make the most of our time!

MA: I have reached a ripe old age of two years here, and Heaven knows I have done my duty by all eight of my families to raise them as peace-loving citizens. Why, I have fifty children living today, and some two hundred grandchildren! What Town Mouse can say that?

MAYOR'S MOUSE (*Smiling behind his hand*): Ha, quite a record! Your cats and dogs must have taken the sleeping sickness—ha, ha! (*He pulls out his watches.*) Ah, cousin, return with me to town for a visit, and I shall show you life as it should be lived—graceful mice dancing over polished floors with nimble toes, like this! (*He dances mincingly about.*) And you shall hear mice speaking in refined voices, like this! (*He speaks affectedly.*) And all mice wear glazed fur coats, and *two* watches!

MA (*Ashamed*): Aw, do you think I would look all right, your Honor?

MICE (*Blissfully*): You look O.K., Ma. We'll go along!

MA (*Fussily*): About my fur, sir. Perhaps I could have the mice slick it down with bacon rinds! (*The* MICE *start for the rinds.*)

MAYOR'S MOUSE (*Waving his paws*): Don't trouble yourself, my good woman. The odor of bacon would draw the dogs, and we have plenty of pomade for rubbing down our fur, at the Mayor's house.

SQUEAKY: Ma, I want two watches — I want two ... (MA *smothers his squeaking with her paw over his mouth.*)

MAYOR'S MOUSE: Pray, release him, good woman. He shall have two watches. The Mayor is giving a banquet tonight for the councilmen, with an opera party afterward. We will arrive about midnight and do our feasting before the Mayor's return.

TEENEY: Ma, I need some Roquefort cheese! (*His* MA *slaps him.*)

SQUEAKY: Ma, I need two watches! (*She tries to silence him, but he escapes to a knot-hole and safety.*)

MAYOR'S MOUSE: Bless their little hearts! They shall have their Roquefort cheese and two watches.

MA: Squeaky, bring my sunbonnet and shawl! We shall go to the city and live at the Mayor's house in style. Teeney, where did you drag off my umbrella to? And my rubbers?

TEENEY: I'll find them if you'll let me have two watches, Ma! (*She shakes him.*)

MA: Not another squeak out of you! (SQUEAKY *helps her with her sunbonnet.*) Oh, I have forgotten my manners, Squeaky. Run bring His Elegance his gloves and hat first. (*The* MAYOR'S MOUSE *waits grandly, nose in air.*) You must know, cousin, I have taught my children manners, but they have no chances to practice their social graces. That's the reason I want to move to town, so they may have social advantages. (TEENEY *helps* SQUEAKY *bring in the gloves and cane.*)

MAYOR'S MOUSE (*Starting for the crack*): Come, my pilot has started my plane! Follow me, mice! (*All follow him out, shouting*) To the Mayor's house!

CURTAIN

* * *

SCENE 2

SETTING: *The elegant dining room of the* MAYOR OF HAUGHTYTOWN.

AT RISE: *On the table scraps of fancy cakes, candied almonds, and Roquefort cheese reveal the tempting remains of a splendid feast. A plane roars away overhead, and the* COUNTRY COUSIN *enters along with the* MAYOR'S MOUSE. *The* MICE *follow, joyously.* TEENEY *is trying to slick down* MA'S *fur with cleansing cream, now.* SQUEAKY *is enjoying two watches which he dangles from the pockets of a fancy vest.*

MAYOR'S MOUSE (*With a finger to his mouth as he tiptoes to the* MAYOR'S *chair*): Sh! Sh! It isn't good form in town to gnaw before entering a room. The Safety Council for Town Mice considers it more polite to take a cautious look about before announcing one's presence. Sh! All's safe now! Come! (*He pulls out the* MAYOR'S *chair for* MA.) Won't you be seated, Cousin? Try the Mayor's chair!

MA (*Squeaking her fright*): Suppose he comes back and finds me in his chair? (*The* MICE *squeak, terrified.*)

MAYOR'S MOUSE (*Shrugging his shoulders as he glances at his watches*): Compose yourself, my good Cousin. I am a trained listener. Now here is the Mayor's lace napkin. You might tuck it under your chin.

MA (*As she and the* MICE *tuck in their napkins*): Oh, yes, your Honor, I have always warned my children about dripping on their whiskers, haven't I?

MICE: Yes, indeed.

MAYOR'S MOUSE (*Passing her a dish of sweets*): Now, Cousin, try some of these candied almonds. I can't eat them myself unless they are freshly toasted, but perhaps you can digest them!

MA (*Smacking her lips*): Yum-m! These are fine. They certainly do beat hickory nuts! If you can spare some, I'll just slip a few into my pocket for a rainy day. (*She does, and the* MICE *mimic her.*)

MAYOR'S MOUSE (*Stroking his whiskers and raising his brows in horror*): In town we never smack our lips when we eat, and surely you are not going to carry food away from the table! That simply isn't done! (*The* COUNTRY MOUSE *looks ashamed.*) Why don't you move to town for good, where the mice will be raised with social graces? I could use my influence for them, you know! (*He dances affectedly, and the* MICE *attempt to do the same, but step on his tail, ending the dance.*)

SQUEAKY: Yes, Ma, we mice must make the most of our time! (*He jingles his watches.*) Ma, get me an opera hat!

TEENEY: Ma, I need an aeroplane! I need Roquefort cheese! I need —

MAYOR'S MOUSE (*Waving his paws grandly*): Oh, of course, Cousin, I'll buy them an aeroplane, and only Roquefort cheese shall be served! Now, try some of this pecan cake.

MA: Why, land! It's the most elegant food I ever tasted — though I reckon I shouldn't let anyone hear me say that?

MAYOR'S MOUSE: Pray, don't! It would injure my social position terribly with the other mice, you know. They were practically all born with silver spoons in their mouths, as the saying goes. (*A faint barking is heard in the distance, and he freezes in his place, and starts trembling.*)

MA: Upon my honor, I had no idea mice could be so elegant! (*She pays no attention to the barking.*) I wonder now, Cousin, how I could have stood the country now, the eternal beans and bacon, the mouse-trap cheese! No dainties, no steam heat, no aeroplanes to save a mouse's time!

MAYOR'S MOUSE (*Quaking with fear*): Sh! Hush, Cousin! Did you hear a — something? For instance, a dog?

MA (*Simply*): A dog? Upon my honor, dogs do very well at herding the cattle.

MAYOR'S MOUSE (*Looking for a place to hide*): Not this dog! I forgot to mention it, but the Mayor has a rat terrier. I smell him coming! Flee for your lives! (*He runs out the door.*)

MA (*Scampering with her* MICE *behind her, to the shelter of the draperies*): Oh, my poor children! Oh, my two hundred grandchildren! Oh, for my country home! (*A fox terrier,* SMELLER, *races in at the door, sniffing the floor and tracking the* MICE *nearly to their hide-out, barking furiously. Suddenly the* MAYOR'S *voice booms from the living-room.* "Here, Smeller, here, Smeller!" SMELLER *leaves with a whine, importantly wagging his tail.*)

MA (*Coming out of hiding, followed by the others*): My land, but that pup gave me a start! Does he always carry on so?

MAYOR'S MOUSE (*Slyly*): Oh, no! When he has time to carry out his designs he is deadly quiet. Sometimes the Mayor whistles him back just in time!

MA: In time for what?

MAYOR'S MOUSE (*Waving his paws grandly now that he has regained his courage*): Ah, what does that matter! Now, on with the feast! Try some of these after-dinner mints, Cousin — they are so fragrant for a mouse's breath! (*He hears footsteps in the distance, and cringes.*)

MA (*Paying no heed to the footsteps, nibbles the mint daintily*): Delicious! Why, they taste just like the mint bed! (*The* MICE *grab a mint, and sigh happily as they nibble.*) Ah, Cousin, it is so restful here amid all these pleasant smells, so peaceful and comfortable. Why do not all mice come to the city and learn social graces? (*The* MAYOR'S MOUSE *and the others have scampered to hide in the draperies again, and with a wild squeak she follows them, as the* MAYOR *enters the door with* MARY.)

MAYOR: Now, Mary, this is the last time I want this to happen. The next time I have a banquet and you take your night out, you are to clean up the table when you return, understand?

MARY: Yes, sir. For sure I do, sir!

MAYOR: Smeller surely smelled a mouse about the dining room, judging from the barking. Set the traps, Mary, and leave the cat *inside* tonight. That will be enough. Good night!

MARY: Good night, sir. For sure it's the trap I'll be setting! (*She shuffles back into the kitchen.*)

MA (*Darting out of her hiding-place*): Quick, bring my sunbonnet, Squeaky! Teeney, my umbrella!

SQUEAKY (*Shivering his terror*) : O.K., Ma—let's scamper! (*The* MICE *leave to get her wraps.*)

MAYOR'S MOUSE (*Creeping in on tiptoe*) : What, Cousin, going so soon? (*He looks at his two watches.*) We have plenty of time for feasting!

MA : Thanks, Your Elegance, but we must hurry along now. (*She puts on the shawl that* SQUEAKY *brings her.*) Perhaps we can drop in another day, when there is more time!

MAYOR'S MOUSE : But what of the Mice, poor dears! Don't you want them raised in an elegant manner? (*The* MICE *squeak their terror, and* MA *takes their paws as she turns to say good-bye.*)

MA : No, my honored Cousin, I have learned my lesson. The only atmosphere I want them used to is healthy days of sunshine and nights of peace in the country. "Better beans and bacon in peace, than cake and candy in fear." Good-bye!

SQUEAKY (*Quickly returning the two watches*) : Here, Your Elegance! Perhaps you might like these to give a town mouse. In the country we tell time by the sun. Good-bye!

TEENEY (*Placing before the* MAYOR'S MOUSE *the candied almonds from his pocket, and a scrap of Roquefort cheese*) : Good-bye, sir. Your cheese and almonds would be O.K. if one had time to eat them! (*He waves, as* MA *jerks him forward and scampers away with him. The* MAYOR'S MOUSE *stands with his back to the kitchen door, waving sadly.*)

MAYOR'S MOUSE : Bon voyage, Cousin! Happy landing!

MA : Come and see us some time. Good luck with the traps — and the cat! (*She goes off with the* MICE. *The cook appears back of the sad* MAYOR'S MOUSE, *holding the cat, and pointing to the elegant mouse.* POUNCER, *with a great, "Meo-uw!" crouches and springs. The* MAYOR'S MOUSE *is fast caught between the paws of the cat, who is just ready to gobble down the* MAYOR'S MOUSE, *as the curtain falls.*)

THE END

HANS, WHO MADE THE PRINCESS LAUGH

by Elsi Rowland

Characters

HENRIK, *a farmer*
NILS SNEEDORFF, *another farmer*
MARIA, *who sells eggs*
FRU BEEK, *a housewife*
JOHAN KOELLER, *the schoolmaster*
HANS STRUH, *the hero*
PEDER JESSON, *a soldier*
GERTRUDE, *the Palace cook*
A PAGE
THE FAIRY GODMOTHER OF THE PRINCESS
A STREET SWEEPER
PRINCESS DAGMAR
HER ATTENDANT
TOWNSPEOPLE, ETC.
OSCAR, *the dog*

SCENE 1

SETTING: *A market place, a scene of bustle and animation.*

AT RISE: *Everyone is calling his wares at the same time.*

HENRIK: Apples! Grapes! Greens! Watercress!

MARIA: Eggs! Fresh eggs! A krone a dozen! Fine ripe cheeses!

NILS: Pigs for sale! Pigs for sale! As pretty little porkers as you ever saw. (FRU BEEK *stops to examine the pigs.*)

FRU BEEK: Those pigs are nicely fatted, Nils. They should bring a good price.

NILS: I hope to sell one of them, at least, to the cook at the Palace. Every market day she comes out to buy. She will be here soon.

MARIA: She always buys her eggs from me. I have some saved for her, all laid by my good hen, Juliana. (*Enter* HANS *with a basket on his arm. He is a wit-less looking boy, wearing a red wig.*)

HANS: Fesh frish! Fesh frish! (*To* FRU BEEK) Would you like some frish?

FRU BEEK: Let me see what you have.

HANS: I caught them all this morning. This pretty one I'm saving for the Princess. (*They continue in pantomime. A soldier has entered. He stops by the schoolmaster.*)

PEDER (*To* JOHAN KOELLER): Can you direct me to the Palace?

JOHAN (*Not looking up*): The Palace is yonder.

PEDER: How everything has changed!

JOHAN (*Closing his book*): Indeed it has. Nothing is as it used to be.

PEDER: I have been away a long time. Tell me what has happened.

JOHAN: Last year the old King died. His daughter, the Princess Dagmar, was heir to the throne. Since her father's death, she has done nothing but weep, the livelong day.

MARIA (*Who has been listening*): And most of the night, too.

PEDER: But doesn't her grief grow less with time?

JOHAN: On the contrary, it seems to grow more.

NILS: The country is going to rack and ruin while she mops her eyes. But here comes the Palace cook. Now the day's business can begin. (*Enter* GERTRUDE.)

GERTRUDE: Good morning, everyone. What have you to sell today?

HENRIK: Fresh greens, Fru Gertrude. So fresh and tender that they melt in your mouth.

GERTRUDE (*Laughs*): If they melt in my mouth, Henrik, as fast as the truth melts in yours, they will be good indeed. Let me have that bunch. (*Pantomime of buying. Over her shoulder to* MARIA) Have you any eggs, Maria?

MARIA: Yes, indeed. You've no idea how proud Juliana is to lay eggs for the Palace folk. (GERTRUDE *buys the eggs.*)

NILS: Fru Gertrude, will you look at these pretty little pigs? This one, now, most toothsome he would be, roasted and with an apple in his mouth.

GERTRUDE: Let me see him, Nils. Why yes, I think that I must have that little pig. Will you take him around to the kitchen entrance of the Palace?

NILS: With pleasure! (*Exit* NILS *carrying the pig.*)

HANS: Fesh frish! Fesh frish!

GERTRUDE: Come here, boy. What have you? Are they nice and fresh?

HANS: Caught this morning. This pretty one I saved for the Princess. Will you take it to her, please?

GERTRUDE: Alas, boy! The Princess will not look at even the finest food. Great sorrow is upon her and has been for many a day. She weeps all day long, and nothing can cheer her up.

MARIA: The poor, dear Princess!

GERTRUDE: Since her father, the King, died, her grief has never ceased. Day by day she grows thinner and whiter. If she cannot be made to smile soon and forget her grief, she too will die.

MARIA: An evil spell has been put upon her, I do believe.

GERTRUDE: For a week now the Ministers have met. I hear that they have come to a decision and that an important announcement is to be made today.

JOHAN: That will be worth hearing.

GERTRUDE: I must get back to my kitchen. Don't forget my eggs next week, Maria.

MARIA: Never fear, Gertrude. Juliana will not desert you. (*Exit* GERTRUDE. *Enter* NILS.)

HENRIK: Nils, there is news! Gertrude says that a proclamation is to be made today.

NILS: What about?

MARIA: It concerns the Princess.

HENRIK: Here comes the herald now. (*A* PAGE *appears on the balcony above. Everyone stands to listen.*)

PAGE: Hear ye! Hear ye! Hear ye! (*He unrolls a scroll and reads.*) The Ministers of the Court make proclamation. Know ye that for a year and a day the Princess Dagmar has not smiled. She has been stricken with a grievous melancholy which nothing can cure. Being in great fear for the Princess's life, the Ministers of the Court issue the following proclamation. Each morning the Princess will be brought to the balcony. Those of her subjects who believe that they might make her laugh will perform before her. All who fail will be banished from the kingdom. But if there should be one who succeeds in making the Princess smile, that one shall have the Princess's hand in marriage and shall rule as King. (*Exit.*)

HANS: What did he say? What was he talking about?

MARIA: They want someone, Hans, to make the Princess laugh.

HANS: Everyone laughs at me. Perhaps I could do it.

HENRIK: Ha, ha, ha! Long live King Hans!

JOHAN: This puts an idea into *my* head. I believe that I might do it. My friends tell me that I have a flow of very subtle wit.

PEDER: If I were to give an imitation of Sergeant Gomar conducting drill, the Princess would die of laughing.

NILS: I have a very clever dog who does many tricks. It might make the Princess laugh to see him sit up and beg.

JOHAN (*Taking* PEDER'S *arm*): Peder, let us go where we can discuss this at greater length. (*They go out.*)

NILS: I must go and groom my dog and get a ribbon for his collar. An appearance before royalty is not to be taken lightly. (*Exit.*)

MARIA: Come on, Henrik. Let's go round to the kitchen entrance of the Palace and see if we cannot find out more about this from Gertrude. (*Exit, leaving* HANS *alone on the stage. He has been watching the foregoing proceedings with open-mouthed incomprehension.*)

HANS: Now where have they all gone — and who is there to buy my frish? Here comes an old dame now. Fesh frish! Fesh frish! (*Enter an old woman with a goose under her arm.*) Would you like to buy some frish today?

OLD WOMAN: Hist, boy! Are we all alone? Why is the market place deserted?

HANS: I don't know. They never tell me. But they all went.

OLD WOMAN: It is well. Hans, listen to me. I am the Fairy Godmother of the Princess Dagmar. I have come to break the evil spell that is upon her.

HANS: You mean to make her laugh?

OLD WOMAN: Yes, I knew that I should find you here, Hans. You are the one who must save the Princess.

HANS: Save the Princess?

OLD WOMAN: Yes. If you succeed in making her laugh, great good fortune will come to you. For not only will the Princess be freed of her melancholy, but you, as soon as you hear her laugh, will find your wits and will become wise and brave and fit to rule the kingdom.

HANS: I do not know, Fru Fairy Godmother, how I could do that.

OLD WOMAN: Come, boy, sit here and I will tell you. (*He does so and she begins to explain as the curtains close.*)

* * *

SCENE 2

SETTING: *The same as Scene* 1, *the next morning. The booths and stalls have been cleared away. A few benches are at the sides for the spectators.*

AT RISE: *A man is sweeping the square with a broom made of twigs. Enter* HANS *with the goose under his arm.*

SWEEPER: Clear out, fellow! This space is reserved for the contestants who will try to make the Princess laugh this morning.

HANS: I am one of them.

SWEEPER: If you ask me, there are two of you — both geese. But if you are really one of the contestants, go into the Palace and declare yourself. Everything must be done in order.

HANS: Where shall I go?

SWEEPER: In there, through that door. (*Exit* HANS. *Enter* JOHAN, PEDER *and* NILS.)

NILS: Well, here we are.

PEDER: To tell the truth, I am a little nervous. Sergeant Gomar doesn't seem so funny now.

JOHAN: Courage, my boy! Nothing venture, nothing have. (*They exit into the Palace.*)

FRU BEEK (*Entering with* MARIA): It seems that we are the first to arrive.

MARIA: Let's sit here where we can see all that happens. (*They sit on one of the benches.*)

FRU BEEK: How many of them are to try this morning?

MARIA: Three, I think the cook said.

FRU BEEK: I wish them luck. (*The man finishes sweeping and goes out. Enter* HENRIK.)

MARIA: Good morning, Henrik. Have you come to try your luck?

HENRIK: Not I. My luck lies in another direction. (*Reenter the three contestants.*)

NILS: Well, if between us we cannot make the Princess laugh —

HENRIK: That will be the last we shall see of you, Nils. We shall miss you.

NILS: I hope that I have my turn first, I can't stand suspense.

HENRIK: Nils, my boy, this suspense is nothing to the suspense at the end of a rope that may be waiting for you if you fail.

NILS: Oh, keep still, will you? (*Enter* HANS *with his goose.*)

HENRIK: And here is our friend, Hans. Are you going to try to make the Princess laugh?

HANS: Yes, Henrik.

HENRIK: How will you do it, Hans? (HANS *nods his head and wags his finger, but says nothing.*) If you fail, Hans, I think that they will cook you along with the goose. See, here comes the Palace cook now. She is waiting to get her hands on you. (*Enter* GERTRUDE.) Isn't that so, Gertrude? Won't you do Hans up in a nice brown gravy along with his goose if he doesn't make the Princess laugh?

GERTRUDE: For shame, Henrik! Don't tease the boy. (*She sits on one of the benches. Enter the* PAGE *on the balcony.*)

PAGE: Hear ye! Hear ye! Hear ye! (*Everyone faces the balcony.*) At this hour the Princess Dagmar will come forth upon this balcony to view the antics of such of her subjects as believe that they have the wit to break the evil spell of melancholy under which she suffers. The contestants will appear as announced and will perform within view of the Princess. Failure to make the Princess laugh means banishment from the Kingdom. (*He withdraws. The* PRINCESS DAGMAR *appears on the balcony with an attendant, who seats her. She is swathed in black and holds an enormous handkerchief to her eyes. The* PAGE *appears in the square below.*)

PAGE: The first contestant is Nils Sneedorff.

NILS (*Comes forward, quaking. He leads his dog on a leash. He bows.*): Royal Highness, this is my dog, Oscar. Many is the time he has cheered my heart and I hope that he may cheer yours. He will not sit unless he has a chair to sit on, so I have brought his chair along. (*Places chair.*) Sit down, Oscar, and say "How do you do." (*The dog sits on the chair and barks.*) Your Royal Highness, Oscar would be most proud to shake your hands, but he, being only a common dog, could not be so presuming. Instead he will shake hands with the folks here. (OSCAR *goes to the spectators, offering his paw.*) He often takes the baby out for an airing. You can see for yourself that he makes a perfect nursemaid. (OSCAR *wheels a doll carriage across the stage.*) Now, Oscar, if you can make the Princess laugh, how will you feel? (OSCAR *chases his tail and rolls over.*) If she doesn't laugh, how will you feel? (OSCAR *becomes a "dead dog." The audience laughs and applauds. The* PRINCESS *sobs into her handkerchief.*)

PAGE: Hear ye! Hear ye! Hear ye! Nils Sneedorff has tried and failed to make the Princess laugh. Tomorrow he will be taken to the boundaries of the Kingdom and banished from this land. (*Confusion and talking in the crowd.*) Order! Order! Take your places! (*Quiet is restored.*) The next contestant is Peder Jesson of the army. (PEDER *marches in. He goes through a drill, shouting commands, stumbling over his own feet, knocking off his hat with a popgun which he carries, etc. The spectators laugh, but the* PRINCESS *weeps. Her attendant gives her a fresh handkerchief, wringing the tears from the one she has been using and hanging it over the balcony to dry.*)

PAGE: Hear ye! Hear ye! Hear ye! Peder Jesson has tried and failed to make the Princess laugh. With Nils Sneedorff he will be banished from the Kingdom. The last contestant is Johan Koeller, our schoolmaster.

JOHAN (*He stands before the balcony and bows*): Your Royal Highness, ladies and gentlemen! We have assembled here this morning to endeavor to tickle the risibilities of the Princess. I trust I make myself clear. That is, I mean to say, to make her laugh. Since laughter is easily provoked by an exhibition of the incongruous, I shall proceed to give such an exhibition. Do I make myself clear? I mean, I am going to try to be funny. I, Johan Koeller, your schoolmaster, will dance a jig. (JOHAN *has concealed a large inflated balloon in his shirt front, giving the effect of stoutness. The tune for the dance is "Pop Goes the Weasel." He dances stiffly until "Pop" is reached. Then each time there is an accent in the dance also. Suggestions: a shot from* PEDER'S *popgun; as "Pop" is reached, he pricks the balloon in his shirt front with a pin and collapses. The audience laughs, but the* PRINCESS *sobs.*)

PAGE: Hear ye! Hear ye! Hear ye! Johan Koeller has tried and failed to make the Princess laugh. With Nils Sneedorff and Peder Jesson he will be banished from the Kingdom. The contest is now over and none of the contestants has met with success —

HANS: Wait, please! I haven't had my turn.

PAGE: Have you been duly entered as a contestant?

HANS: I don't know.

PRINCESS: Let the boy perform. (*She has stopped weeping and is watching* HANS *with interest.*)

PAGE: Very well, Your Highness. Your name, boy?

HANS: I am Hans Struh. My goose and I know a trick. (*He goes to the center of the stage and speaks to the* PRINCESS.) Royal Princess, will you observe my goose? It is the finest goose in the world. I will show you.

GERTRUDE: Nonsense, Hans. It is old and tough! I can tell. Bring it here. (*He goes to her.*)

HANS (*As she touches the goose*): If you'll come along, then hang on. (*He drags the cook across the stage.*)

GERTRUDE: Help! Help! I can't let go. (HENRIK *seizes her about the waist and is dragged after her.* FRU BEEK *seizes* HENRIK'S *coat tails and joins the procession.* JOHAN *seizes* FRU BEEK *and* MARIA *seizes* JOHAN. PEDER *seizes* MARIA, *and* NILS *and his dog* OSCAR *bring up the rear.* HANS *does a fantastic dance which they must all needs imitate. Finally the* PRINCESS *bursts into a hearty peal of laughter. At the sound,* HANS *drops the goose. The whole procession collapses in a heap.* HANS *snatches off his red wig, revealing himself as a handsome young man. He runs into the Palace and comes out on the balcony, beside the* PRINCESS.)

CURTAIN

(*In a moment the curtains open again. The procession has dissolved and its members have regained their feet.* HANS *and the* PRINCESS *stand on the balcony.*)

ALL: Long live King Hans! Long live Queen Dagmar!

HANS: My faithful subjects, this is indeed a happy day! Not only has our Princess been delivered from the evil spell of her melancholy, but her deliverer has been delivered from the wicked spell of his witlessness. As the first act of my reign over you, I pronounce a pardon for those contestants who this morning tried and failed. (*Cheers.*) And now let there be a holiday and feasting, and may the joy of this day endure forever. (*Cheers. Confetti is thrown. The people in the square form for a folk dance. The Danish dance of greeting is suggested. Upon this dance, the curtain closes.*)

THE END

A PRECEDENT IN PASTRIES

by Elsi Rowland

Characters

JOHN CHUBB, *a baker*
DAME POTHERBY
DAME GREENSMITH
MILLER HODGE
SIMEON HALFPENNY
THOMAS HOOD
WILLIAM DAWSON
THE JUDGE
DAVID COBB
SQUIRE HUMPHREY
COURT CLERK
ATTENDANT
THREE WOMEN
FOUR MEN
SPECTATORS

SETTING: *A courtroom in an English village. The judge's bench is at the back of the stage. The clerk's table is below the bench. The prisoner's dock is at one side of it and the witness stand at the other. On either side of the stage are benches for the spectators.*

AT RISE: *Three women are seated on the benches. They are talking.*

1ST WOMAN: For years he has been cheating us.
2ND WOMAN: But now we have brought him to justice.
3RD WOMAN: The Courts of Law are a great thing. They can decide what's right and what's wrong and no more arguing about it.
1ST WOMAN: It's plenty of arguing I have done with John Chubb about his short weight.
2ND WOMAN: Yes, and much good it has done.

3RD WOMAN: Here come Dame Potherby and Dame Greensmith. (*Enter the two women.*)

DAME POTHERBY: Good morning, neighbors.

1ST WOMAN: Are you going to testify, Dame Potherby?

DAME POTHERBY: Indeed I am! I have brought some buns with me as evidence. I shall tell the judge — (*The rest of her speech is blotted out by the entrance of four men who are talking. They move to the benches and sit down. The women continue to talk in pantomime.*)

1ST MAN: I wonder what John Chubb will have to say for himself.

2ND MAN: I doubt if he ever baked a loaf of bread in his life that was full weight.

3RD MAN: His money chests are not short weight though. I believe he is the richest man in town.

1ST MAN: There's no doubt about that.

3RD WOMAN: Shame on him to rob honest people and to starve their children!

4TH MAN: Well, the case will have a full hearing this day and it may be that John Chubb's money chests will not be filled so quickly after this. (*During these speeches, enough people — men and women — have been coming in to fill the spectators' benches. These characters should be chosen for their ability to pantomime well so that the scene will not lack animation. As soon as they are seated, a trumpet is sounded off-stage. Enter the* COURT CLERK *followed by the* JUDGE. *All of the spectators rise. The* JUDGE *seats himself and the* COURT CLERK *reads the commission authorizing the Court session.*)

COURT CLERK: Hear ye! Hear ye! Hear ye! Attend the opening of this Court of Law where the judge is authorized to administer impartial and even justice and to uphold the laws of the kingdom in the name of his royal Highness, the King of England. (*The spectators are seated.*) The first case is that of John Chubb against the people of this town.

JUDGE: Let the prisoner be brought to the bar. (*Enter a* COURT ATTENDANT *with* JOHN CHUBB *in custody. Whispering among the spectators.*) What is the charge against him?

CLERK: Your Honor, the defendant John Chubb is a baker by trade. He is charged with selling his products short in weight.

JUDGE: Who are the witnesses for the prosecution?

CLERK: Dame Greensmith, Dame Potherby, Miller Hodge and Simeon Halfpenny.

JUDGE: Dame Greensmith, will you take the stand? (*The* CLERK *sits.* DAME GREENSMITH *goes to the witness stand.*) Dame Greensmith, what do you know of Baker Chubb's products?

DAME GREENSMITH: Your Honor, John Chubb has sold bread to me for the past two years. During that time, my children have become thin and pale. Night after night they go to bed crying with hunger. John Chubb's buns, which he sells for six-pence, can be gobbled up in two bites. Unless your Honor can make him give us full weight, I do not know what will become of us. We are the poor people of the town who own no wheat fields.

JUDGE: Have you ever charged the defendant with giving you short weight?

DAME GREENSMITH: Many a time. But he has become angry and told me that if my children were still hungry, they could go out in the fields and eat grass.

JUDGE: Thank you, Dame Greensmith. You may stand down. (*She takes her seat*) Next witness, Dame Potherby. (*She comes forward.*) What is your testimony?

DAME POTHERBY: Your Honor, it is a burning shame! Will you look at this? (*Produces a bun*) This is what John Chubb calls a bun. This is what he sells to the town for six-pence. (*The* JUDGE *takes the bun and examines it.*)

JUDGE: Is this the regular-sized bun?

DAME POTHERBY: It is, your Honor.

JUDGE: I think that there might be three bites in this bun instead of two. However, the proof of the pudding, as they say — (*He begins to eat the bun.*)

DAME POTHERBY: Any decent bun, your Honor, should have four bites in it.

JUDGE: I am inclined to agree with you. (*Chews*) Yes, it can be done in two bites, but three would be more genteel. Have you any further testimony, Dame Potherby?

DAML POTHERBY: I have, your Honor. What John Chubb's buns are made of, only himself knows but I'll wager it's nothing good. I strongly suspect that his flour is mixed with charf.

JUDGE: In Courts of Law, suspicions can not be accepted as evidence. Suspicions are not facts.

DAME POTHERBY: Well, his buns taste as though they were made of straw, your Honor, and that's no suspicion — it's a fact.

JUDGE: Yes, that can be accepted as evidence. I have just eaten a bun.

DAME POTHERBY: You might eat a dozen, your Honor, and still be hungry.

JUDGE: I will take your word for that. I do not care to try the experiment. Thank you, Dame Potherby. That is all. (*She takes her seat.*) Next witness, Miller Hodge. (*He takes the stand.*) Miller Hodge, have you done business with the defendant, John Chubb?

MILLER HODGE: I have, your Honor.

JUDGE: And have your relations with him been satisfactory?

MILLER HODGE: John Chubb is a difficult customer, your Honor.

JUDGE: Why do you say that?

MILLER HODGE: He will not buy my flour, your Honor. He says it is too dear. He is a great one for a bargain, is John Chubb.

JUDGE: Then how do you do business with him?

MILLER HODGE: Well, you see, your Honor, he brings me his wheat to grind.

JUDGE: That is not an unusual practise on the part of the townspeople who raise wheat, is it?

MILLER HODGE: No, your Honor. I do a lot of milling besides my own. The difference is that John Chubb's wheat is ground up chaff and all. His full flour sacks don't weigh six stone. Mine weigh a full eight.

JUDGE: Thank you, Miller Hodge. That will do. (MILLER HODGE *is seated.*) Simeon Halfpenny, will you take the stand? (SIMEON *is a boy of fourteen.*) You have worked for Baker Chubb?

SIMEON: Yes, your Honor.

JUDGE: What do you do in his shop?

SIMEON: At four o'clock in the morning, I open the shop and start the fires going. Then I bring in the sacks of flour. Then I set out the pans. Then the master comes in and he mixes the buns. I stand by and sweep up the flour he spills on the floor and put it back in the sacks.

JUDGE: Go on.

SIMEON: Then I watch the buns while they bake. After the buns are done, I take them out in the little cart to sell. Sometimes I don't sell all the buns and master gives them to me. He says that I can start paying him for them when I finish my apprenticeship. I am not good at figures but master keeps it all in his big books. He says that I owe him forty pounds already. When

I come back to the shop, I wash the pans, rake over the fires, put on the shutters and then go home. Master stays behind to count the money and to do accounts.

JUDGE: Thank you, Simeon. You may stand down.

CLERK (*Rising*): The Court has heard the evidence of the prosecution. It will now hear the case of the defendant.

JUDGE: Who are the witnesses for the defense?

CLERK: John Chubb has no witnesses, your Honor. He will plead his own cause.

JUDGE: Very well. John Chubb, will you take the stand? (*He does so.*) Baker Chubb, you have heard the evidence of the prosecution. Have you anything to say?

JOHN CHUBB: It's all lies, your Honor. My flour is as good as any in this town and my buns are all full weight. (*Gasps from the spectators*)

JUDGE: You saw the bun which Dame Potherby gave to me? Was it one of your buns, Baker Chubb?

JOHN CHUBB: It was, your Honor.

JUDGE: How much do your buns weigh?

JOHN CHUBB: A full pound, your Honor. Not an ounce less.

JUDGE: You testify that the buns all weigh a pound and that they are made of the best flour?

JOHN CHUBB: I do, your Honor.

JUDGE: Is Simeon Halfpenny your only helper?

JOHN CHUBB: Yes, your Honor. I have a fatherly interest in the boy. His name appeals to me.

JUDGE: Do you make a fair profit in your business, Baker Chubb?

JOHN CHUBB: Little or nothing, your Honor. I am so kindhearted that I cannot bear to see any one lack for bread. Last year I must have given away a dozen buns.

JUDGE: Your generosity is very commendable. How much do you weigh, Baker Chubb?

JOHN CHUBB: Why, your Honor, 'twas only this morning I stepped on my scales. I tipped the balance at one hundred and fifty pounds. But why does your Honor want to know?

JUDGE: That will be evident in due time, sir. You may be seated. (*He resumes his place in the prisoner's dock.*) The Court has heard the evidence of the plaintiffs and that of the defendant. This evidence will be weighed carefully. Squire Humphrey, will you go to Baker Chubb's shop next door with Thomas Hood and put one hundred and fifty pounds of his buns into a sack and bring it to the Court.

SQUIRE HUMPHREY: Yes, your Honor. (*He and* THOMAS HOOD *go out.*)

JUDGE: William Dawson and David Cobb, will you go to the anteroom and fetch to the Court the plank and trestle which you will find there. (*Two of the men go out. They return in a moment with the plank and trestle. They place them before the* JUDGE'S *bench.*)

WILLIAM DAWSON: Now what, your Honor.

JUDGE: Now, gentlemen, will you balance the plank upon the trestle so that both ends are equally distant from the floor. (*They do so.*)

DAVID COBB: That's done, your Honor.

JUDGE: That is all, gentlemen. Thank you. (*They take their seats.*) What you see before you is a crude form of scales of justice. From time immemorial, justice has been represented by a blindfolded goddess, holding scales in her outstretched hand. The question to be decided is whether Baker Chubb's buns are short in weight and with the help of our plank and trestle, the case can be settled. (*Enter* SQUIRE HUMPHREY *and* THOMAS HOOD.)

SQUIRE HUMPHREY: Here are the buns, your Honor.

JUDGE: Now, gentlemen, will you bind the sack containing the one hundred and fifty-one-pound buns to one end of the plank. (*One of the spectators produces a piece of rope from his pocket and the men proceed to bind the sack to the plank.*)

THOMAS HOOD: There you are, your Honor.

JUDGE: Baker Chubb, will you mount the other end of the plank? If the one hundred and fifty pounds of your person balances with the one hundred and fifty buns each weighing one pound which are in the sack, your honesty will be proved. If, on the other hand, you are found to outweigh the buns, the charge against you will be upheld.

JOHN CHUBB: Of all the blathering nonsense —

JUDGE: Such expressions may be termed contempt of court, Baker Chubb. You will refrain from giving voice to them.

JOHN CHUBB: I beg your pardon, your Honor, but I might break my neck if I tried to get up there.

JUDGE: There is little danger of that. Gentlemen, will you assist

Baker Chubb to his position. (WILLIAM DAWSON *and* DAVID COBB *seize* JOHN *and hoist him onto the plank.*)

WILLIAM DAWSON: Up with you, Johnny!

DAVID COBB: All aboard! (*The plank comes down with a thud.*)

JOHN CHUBB: Ugh! (*Laughter from the spectators. "That settles it." "I knew he'd fix it." "The Courts of Law are great things," etc.* WILLIAM DAWSON *and* DAVID COBB *help* JOHN *to his feet.*)

JUDGE (*Rapping with his gavel*): Order in the Court. (*The laughter subsides.*)

JOHN CHUBB: All right, your Honor, I confess. I do make my buns short weight and there is chaff in my flour. But it will never happen again if your Honor will be easy with me.

JUDGE: I am glad that you have confessed your dishonesty, John Chubb. But such wrong-doing can not go unpunished. You have robbed the people of this town and have grown rich at their expense. To make amends, you must change your bad practices. Not only must your bread be full weight and of the first quality, but from now on you must put an extra bun into every dozen that you sell. In this town, thirteen will be known as a baker's dozen.

ALL (*Cheers*): Hooray! Thank you, your Honor! Three cheers for our Courts of Law! etc.

THE END

THE THREE AUNTS

by Elsi Rowland

Characters

MAJOR DOMO
NANNETTE, JULIE, MARIANNA — *maids in the castle*
LADY CLOTILDE, LADY MARGUERITE, LADY HELOISE — *ladies-in-waiting*
THE QUEEN
PRINCE BAUDOIN
LORD GERVAIS
LORD PHILLIPE
AUNT GROS BEC (*or Long Nose*)
AUNT BOSSU (*or Hump Back*)
AUNT OEIL ROUGE (*or Red Eye*)
A PAGE

SCENE 1

SETTING: *The throne room of the castle.*

AT RISE: *Enter the* MAJOR DOMO *of the castle followed by three maids with brooms, brushes and other cleaning implements. The light is dim.*

MAJOR DOMO: This room is to be given a thorough turning out and airing.

THE MAIDS: Yes, your Excellency.

MAJOR DOMO: My numerous duties prevent me from supervising the operation. However, the Lady Clotilde will come to inspect your work. Everything must be ready by ten o'clock for the Queen is to hold Court here today.

NANNETTE: You may trust us, your Excellency.

MAJOR DOMO: I wonder! You, Nannette, have a fondness for sweeping dust under the rugs.

NANNETTE: Oh, your Excellency! Maybe once or twice when time ran short, but in the Throne Room — never!

MAJOR DOMO: Nor in any other room, my girl! It is a practice on which the Queen would frown. If she knew that dust was swept under the rugs — well, Nannette, I have known maids to spend some time in the dungeon of the castle for less. I shall leave Julie in charge. Remember, by ten o'clock all must be clean and shining and in order. (*Exits.*)

JULIE: There is no time to lose. Nannette, take this broom and sweep the floor. Marianne, unroll the rug and brush it. (JULIE *takes the cover from the throne and begins to polish it. The two others move about slowly with many pauses for conversation.*)

MARIANNE: Can you tell me why we are doing this?

NANNETTE: Oh, Marianne, don't you know? Prince Baudoin is coming home from his travels. The time has come for him to settle down and to think of choosing a wife. Lady Marguerite and Lady Clotilde were talking about it while I was dusting the Queen's chamber yesterday.

JULIE: Don't you know that you shouldn't listen to the conversation of the Ladies-in-Waiting?

MARIANNE: Oh, pooh! Tell me more, Nannette.

NANNETTE: They said that the Prince is very handsome and very learned, but that he is peculiar in one respect.

MARIANNE: And what is that?

NANNETTE: He is determined to marry the maiden who is the most skilled at spinning and weaving and sewing in the whole kingdom, no matter what her station may be.

MARIANNE: What if she were as homely as could be? Would he care?

NANNETTE: You may be sure he would. Now if he could only see me, he would forget all this nonsense. (*She dances about with the broom.*)

JULIE: You vain girl! Do hurry, Nannette! Lady Clotilde will be here soon. Marianne, please give me those dust covers. (*She takes them and goes out.*)

NANNETTE: Marianne, I have just thought of the best joke to play on Julie! Let's tell Lady Clotilde that Julie can spin and weave and sew better than anyone else in the kingdom. You know Julie can't take a proper stitch. She will be entered in the contest and that is the last we shall see of Julie.

MARIANNE: Nannette, that is a wonderful idea! Here comes the Lady Clotilde and you haven't finished sweeping the floor!

NANETTE: Quick, Marianne! Hold up the corner of the rug while I sweep this dust under it. (*They do so.*)

MARIANNE: Oh, Nannette, what if she looks under?

NANNETTE: Shh! (*Enter* LADY CLOTILDE. *She casts a hasty glance about.*)

LADY CLOTILDE: Everything seems to be in order. Nannette and Marianne, you are dismissed. (*As they leave,* MARIANNE *stumbles over the corner of the rugs, which turns back, disclosing the dust that was swept under it.*) What shiftless practice is this? Which of you is responsible?

NANNETTE (*Stammering*): Oh, my lady! We did not know it was there!

LADY CLOTILDE: Well, who put it there?

NANNETTE: My lady, it must have been Julie.

LADY CLOTILDE: Julie! That is not like her.

NANNETTE: But, my lady, Julie is so distraught. She has her mind so much on how she is to spin and weave and sew for the Prince.

LADY CLOTILDE: For the Prince! And what do you know of the Prince and his interest in spinning and weaving and sewing?

NANNETTE: Julie overheard you telling the Lady Marguerite about it. Julie can spin and weave and sew better than any one else in the kingdom, I do believe. She wants to show the Prince what she can do.

LADY CLOTILDE: Julie will certainly be given a chance to prove her skill. (*Enter* JULIE. *She curtsies.*) Julie, Nannette tells me that you wish to enter the contest in spinning and weaving and sewing for the Prince.

JULIE (*Amazed*): Oh, but, my lady —!

LADY CLOTILDE: Do not hesitate, Julie. Every girl in the country who has such skill, should submit her work.

JULIE: Really, my lady, I can't. What makes you think I can —

LADY CLOTILDE: I will report the matter to the Queen. Come with me, Julie. Nannette and Marianne, take up the dust and then go to the Major Domo. He may have more work for you to do. (*Exit* LADY CLOTILDE *and* JULIE.)

NANNETTE (*Bursts into laughter*): Oh! Oh! Oh! Did you see Julie's face? Not a word could she say for herself.

MARIANNE: Imagine Julie weaving for the royal presses! Why she can't even thread a needle!

CURTAIN

* * *

SCENE 2

SETTING: *A small room in which there is a bench, and a spinning wheel with a chair before it. By the chair is a large basket piled with flax.*

AT RISE: *Stage is empty. Enter* LADY CLOTILDE *and* JULIE.

LADY CLOTILDE: Here you will find everything to prove your skill. Your task is to spin a pound of flax before dawn tomorrow. It is the Queen's intention that the most skillful weaver in the country is to succeed her on the throne as the wife of the Prince.

JULIE (*Curtsying*): Yes, my lady.

LADY CLOTILDE: Much depends upon your success. If you fail, you will spend the rest of your days in the dungeon of the castle.

JULIE: Yes, my lady.

LADY CLOTILDE: I shall leave you now. You will not be interrupted. (*Exits.*)

JULIE: And all I say is, "Yes, my lady." Nannette would not be so tongue-tied. The wife of the Prince, indeed! I am as good as in the castle dungeon already. (*She picks up a bundle of flax and turns it over and over. She seats herself at the spinning wheel and tries first one way and then another.*) No, that can't be the way. (*Finally she drops the flax and hides her face in her hands, weeping. An old woman with a very long nose enters. She watches Julie for a moment.*)

GROS BEC: Julie!

JULIE (*Startled*): Oh!

GROS BEC: Why are you crying?

JULIE: It would do no good for me to tell you.

GROS BEC: Who knows? Maybe I could help you.

JULIE: You can not unless you can spin a pound of flax before dawn. That is the task which the Queen has set for me.

GROS BEC: Why, my dear, nothing could be easier. Dry your eyes and think no more of it.

JULIE: Do you mean that you could do it? Oh, if you only would.

GROS BEC: I could do it with ease. And in payment all that I should require is that you call me Auntie on the happiest day of your life.

JULIE: Is that all! I will do that willingly.

GROS BEC: Sit there and watch me while I spin. (JULIE *sits on the bench.* GROS BEC *spins to the sound of soft music. The lights grow dimmer.* JULIE *falls asleep. Finally the lights go out.* GROS BEC *goes off the stage taking the flax with her and leaving a full spindle behind. Presently the lights come on to disclose* JULIE *still sleeping. She awakes.*)

JULIE: Where am I? Oh, I remember. There was an old woman with a long nose here. She was spinning for me when I fell asleep. (*She gets up.*) It may have been a dream. No, it wasn't! Here is the flax all spun! Oh, how lucky I am! (*Enter* LADY CLOTILDE.)

LADY CLOTILDE: Well, Julie, is your task completed?

JULIE (*Curtsying*): Yes, my lady. (LADY CLOTILDE *inspects the work.*)

LADY CLOTILDE: This is a fine piece of work. The Queen can not help but be pleased. I am glad that you have done so well. You are ready now for your second task. A loom will be brought and you will weave this yarn into fine linen. Tomorrow morning I shall return to inspect your work.

JULIE: Yes, my lady.

LADY CLOTILDE: Weave carefully, Julie. The Queen's eyes can detect the least flaw. (*Exits.*)

JULIE: I have never seen a loom. I wonder what it looks like.

CURTAIN

* * *

Scene 3

Setting: *The same room. Toward dawn.*

At Rise: *The spinning wheel has been removed and a small loom has taken its place. An old woman with a humped back is working at it.* Julie *is asleep.*

Bossu: Warp and woof — warp and woof. Which is more important I cannot decide. Now the work is done and Julie has slept. She is waking up.

Julie: Ho hum! What a dream I have had. I dreamt that I was Queen of the land and that I was walking on a carpet of linen which stretched as far as I could see. Oh, my good Aunt Bossu, is the weaving done?

Bossu: Yes, my child. I am leaving you now, but on the happiest day of your life I shall return.

Julie: Then I shall call you Auntie. I shan't forget my promise.

Bossu: Goodbye till then, Julie. (*Exits.*)

Julie: What if my dream should come true! Surely the Queen will be satisfied with this linen for it is perfect. It is fit for a Prince. I wonder if I am fit to be a Princess? (*She poses.*) My loyal subjects, I have made a decree that no more linen is to be woven in this land. (*She walks across the stage in a regal manner. Enter* Lady Clotilde.)

Lady Clotilde: Julie, are you sleepwalking? Your manner is very strange.

Julie: Oh, a thousand pardons, my lady.

Lady Clotilde: Is the weaving done?

Julie: Yes, my lady. Will you look at it?

Lady Clotilde: Quite perfect, Julie. It might have been woven by the fairies. The Queen is coming this morning to inspect your work, and the Prince is coming with her. I will inform her that everything is ready. (*Exits.*)

Julie: The Prince is coming, and here I am in my old kitchen dress. What will he think of me? If they find out that I have not done this work, I will surely be put in the dungeon. I am afraid. I should like to run away. It is too late. Here they come. (*Enter a* Page.)

Page: Her Majesty, the Queen! His Royal Highness, Prince Baudoin. (*They enter followed by* Lady Clotilde *and* Lady Marguerite. Julie *curtsies.*)

QUEEN: My son, this is the maiden, Julie, who is proving herself so skillful at the arts for which this country is famous. (JULIE *kneels.*) Although she is of humble birth, her skill would bring fresh honor to our name.

BAUDOIN: Rise, Julie. (JULIE *stands.*) She is comely as well. She has a modest and pretty manner. I am not displeased. In suitable garb she would grace a throne. But where is a sample of her handiwork?

LADY CLOTILDE: Here it is, Your Highness. (*They inspect the cloth on the loom.*)

BAUDOIN: I have never seen more perfect linen.

QUEEN: Did I not tell you so, my son?

BAUDOIN: If she passes the final test, our betrothal may be announced.

JULIE: Your Highness, what may the final test be?

QUEEN: You are to sew this linen into shirts for my son. They must be of such perfection of workmanship as to surpass the combined efforts of all the royal seamstresses. Do you think that you can do it?

JULIE: I can but try, Your Majesty.

QUEEN: Tomorrow, dressed as a Princess, you will bring your work to the Throne Room where it will be displayed before all the Court. If it passes the test, your betrothal to the Prince will be announced. If you fail, you will be taken to the castle dungeon where you will spend the rest of your days.

JULIE: Yes, your Majesty. (*Exit the* QUEEN.)

BAUDOIN: Until tomorrow, Julie. (*He follows the* QUEEN *and is followed by the* LADIES-IN-WAITING.)

JULIE: Unless some one comes to help me, my life is over. What are the Prince's measurements? How does he like his shirts cut? I do not know. I have neither scissors nor needle and thread. If I were not imprisoned in this high tower I would run away — back to my father's cottage and spend the rest of my days like the humble one that I am. (*She listens.*) Not a sound. The day is going by. This time no one is coming. (*She sits down and puts her head in her hands. Enter* OEIL ROUGE.)

OEIL ROUGE: Not so, Julie. I am a little late, to be sure, but ready to set to work. Now, my child, calm your fears and rest. Tomorrow your betrothal to the Prince will be announced.

JULIE: But I am afraid.

OEIL ROUGE: Have no fear, Julie. If you will call me Auntie on the happiest day of your life, all will be well. Rest now and sleep until tomorrow.

CURTAIN

* * *

SCENE 4

SETTING: *The Throne Room.*

AT RISE: LADY HELOISE *and* LORDS GERVAIS *and* PHILLIPE *are talking.*

PHILLIPE: A mere nobody!

LADY HELOISE: I hear she was clearing pots and pans in the kitchen a week ago.

GERVAIS: And where does she come from?

PHILLIPE: From the provinces. She was engaged as a kitchen maid.

LADY HELOISE: I wonder if her family will be present at the betrothal. No doubt they are peasants. (*Enter* LADY MARGUERITE.)

LADY MARGUERITE: Gossiping as usual, I see.

LADY HELOISE: And plenty to gossip about, I can tell you.

LADY MARGUERITE: You are never without a subject, Heloise. (*Other Lords and Ladies have been coming in. A* PAGE *appears.*)

PAGE: Her Majesty, the Queen. His Royal Highness, Prince Baudoin. (*They enter. The Lords and Ladies make obeisance. The* QUEEN *seats herself upon the throne. The* PRINCE *stands beside her.*)

QUEEN: My lords and ladies, I wish to announce that a most important decision is impending. A genius has been discovered in the arts of spinning and weaving. This genius is the kitchen maid, Julie. You are all to be judges of the final test — that of sewing. Lady Marguerite, will you conduct the maiden, Julie, to the Throne Room? (LADY MARGUERITE *curtsies and goes out. She returns with* JULIE *who is dressed in court dress and is carrying a shirt of fine linen. She drops on one knee before the throne.)* Rise, Julie. (*She rises.* LADY MARGUERITE *takes the shirt from her and presents it to the* QUEEN *for inspection.*) It is more than could be hoped for. It is perfection!

BAUDOIN: The test is passed. Never before have I had such linen!

COURT (*Gathering around*): Beautiful! Exquisite! Divine! Oh! Ah!

QUEEN: Come forward, Julie. (JULIE *approaches and the* QUEEN *takes her hand.*) My lords and ladies of the Court, I wish to announce the betrothal of my son, Prince Baudoin, to the maiden, Julie. She has proved herself more than worthy of carrying on the tradition of fine handiwork.

COURT (*Bowing*): Honor to the Princess Julie!

QUEEN (*Placing her hand in that of* PRINCE BAUDOIN): Now the royal presses need never lack for the finest linen, for Julie can supply them.

JULIE: I don't know what to say. I am only a simple country girl. (*Enter* AUNT GROS BEC. JULIE *goes forward with outstretched hand.*) Oh, Auntie, I am so glad to see you. (*The Court stares. The ladies raise their eyebrows.*)

LADY HELOISE: What did I tell you! What a charming family she has!

GROS BEC: Julie, my dear, introduce me to the Prince. I hope that he will ask me to live at the castle.

JULIE: Prince Baudoin, this is my Aunt Gros Bec.

BAUDOIN: How do you do?

GROS BEC: I am glad to be here, your Royal Highness. My sisters, Bossu and Oeil Rouge are on the way. We hope to spend the rest of our lives with you.

BAUDOIN: Indeed! My lord Gervais, a chair for our guest. (*A bench is brought in and* GROS BEC *seats herself. Enter* BOSSU *and* OEIL ROUGE.)

BOSSU: Here we are, Julie.

OEIL ROUGE: We came as we promised you we would.

JULIE: I am so glad to see you.

BAUDOIN: And who may your friends be, Julie?

JULIE: Prince Baudoin, they are my aunts — Bossu and Oeil Rouge.

LADY HELOISE (*Aside*): A charming family! I doubt if the Prince can stand this.

BAUDOIN: Will you be seated, ladies?

BOSSU: Thank you, your Royal Highness. Our old bones are weary. We have walked a long way. (*They seat themselves on the bench with* GROS BEC.)

OEIL ROUGE: Sister Gros Bec, it seems to me that Julie is growing to look more like you. Her nose looks longer than it did a year ago.

GROS BEC: I shouldn't wonder. If you can believe it, Prince Baudoin, I looked just like Julie once. But I sat over my spinning for hours and days and my nose gradually grew longer and longer. I can see that Julie's nose has begun to grow. (*The ladies suppress titters.*)

BOSSU: My back used to be as straight as Julie's. But when she has spent as many hours weaving at the loom as I have, she too will have a hump.

BAUDOIN: Heaven forbid! (*He leaves* JULIE'S *side and walks down stage in great agitation.*)

OEIL ROUGE: My eyes were once clear and bright, as Julie's are now. But they have been strained by the fine stitches I have put into my sewing. Soon Julie's will lose their sparkle and will become dull and red.

BAUDOIN (*To himself*): What a bride! Is she to become like these horrors! What can I do?

LADY HELOISE (*Aside*): I think that the Prince is regretting his bargain.

BAUDOIN: I know what I must do, although I regret it with all my heart. I can not have such a bride.

JULIE (*Going to the* PRINCE): Your Royal Highness, I know what you are thinking. Release me from our contract. I wish only to return to my father's home. I am not fit to be a Queen.

BAUDOIN (*Taking her hands*): No, Julie, you must keep our bond. You are sweet and kind and honest and worthy to be a Queen. That you may escape the fate that would be waiting for you, I will forego the delights of your handiwork. Your estimable aunts will supply the palace presses, and you, my dear, will never spend another moment of your life at spinning or weaving or sewing. (*He kisses her hand.*)

COURT: Long live Princess Julie! Long live Prince Baudoin! May they live happily forever!

THE END

HANSEL AND GRETHEL

by Natalie Simonds

Characters

WOODCUTTER
HIS WIFE
HANSEL
GRETHEL
THE WITCH

SCENE 1

SETTING: *The* WOODCUTTER'S *home*

AT RISE: *The* WOODCUTTER'S WIFE *is sitting before the fire. The door opens and the* WOODCUTTER *enters. He stoops under a heavy load of wood and appears very tired. He sets his load near the fireplace and sinks into the nearest chair, his head in his hands.*

WIFE: What luck today?

WOODCUTTER (*His head still bowed, slowly*): No luck. (*Then raising his head*) What are we to do? No one will buy my wood. How can we feed ourselves and the children?

WIFE (*Hesitantly*): I have a plan. It sounds cruel, but it's the only way. Tomorrow when you go to the woods, we must take the children and leave them there. We can give them food and build a fire to keep them warm. Someone will find them there. They will take better care of them than we can.

WOODCUTTER: I wish there were some other way.

WIFE: If we keep them here, we will all starve. We've scarcely enough food for tomorrow. Surely it's kinder to give them that chance than to let them starve slowly.

WOODCUTTER (*Sighing*): Perhaps you're right. (*Rising*) Then come, let us go to bed. We must be up with the sun.

CURTAIN

* * *

SCENE 2

SETTING: *The forest with the* WITCH'S *house at the right.*

AT RISE: HANSEL *and* GRETHEL *enter from left. They are very tired and walk slowly.*

GRETHEL (*Weeping*): Oh, Hans. I'm so tired. We've walked and walked and I just can't go any further. Can't we sit down and rest?

HANSEL (*Comfortingly*): Please don't cry, Grethel. I know you're tired, but soon we'll find some nice people who will take us in and give us food and a warm place to sleep.

GRETHEL (*Through her tears*): But why can't we go home, Hans? You said you would scatter our bread so that we could find our way back and (*Sobbing harder*) we threw away a whole piece of bread and now I'm hungry and the bread is gone.

HANSEL (*Softly*): I know. But the birds ate the bread. (*Cheerfully*) Perhaps they were hungry, too. Hungrier than us maybe. (*At this moment he looks up and sees the* WITCH'S *house.*) Grethel! Look! A house! Such a pretty little house! (*He runs over to it.*) Grethel! Come here! The house is made of candy! Real candy! (GRETHEL *runs quickly to where* HANSEL *is standing. He breaks off a piece of the roof and hands it to her; breaks off another piece and devours it hungrily.*) Isn't it good? (GRETHEL *eats the candy and smiles happily.*)

GRETHEL: Oh, Hans. It's wonderful. A candy house — and all for us! (*They break off piece after piece and eat ravenously. Suddenly* HANSEL *stops. There is a tapping noise from inside the house.*)

HANSEL: Somebody's coming! (*The door opens and the* WITCH *emerges, leaning on her cane.*)

WITCH (*Smiling*): What lovely children! Were you eating my house?

HANSEL: Y-y-yes, we were. (*Politely*) I hope you don't mind. But it's such a lovely tasting house and we're awfully hungry. We've been walking for a long time and we haven't eaten since morning. We're very tired. (*Manfully*) My sister isn't used to walking so much.

WITCH (*Solicitously*): You poor children! You must come in

and warm yourselves by my fire and I'll give you something to eat. I've a place where you can sleep, too.

HANSEL: Oh, thank you. We'd like that.

WITCH: Come ahead. (*She opens the door and motions them inside.* HANSEL *takes* GRETHEL *by the hand and they enter.*)

CURTAIN

* * *

SCENE 3

SETTING: *Inside the* WITCH'S *house.*

AT RISE: HANSEL *and* GRETHEL *are asleep on cots. The* WITCH *is sitting by the fire.*

WITCH (*Rubbing her hands*): What nice children! They'll make a tasty morsel. I should get three good meals out of them. (*Thoughtfully*) The boy *is* a bit thin, but I can fatten him up. I'll eat the girl first. (*Looking towards* GRETHEL) She looks about ready now. (HANSEL *stirs, rubs his eyes and gazes about him. He remembers where he is, looks to see if* GRETHEL *is all right and then rises.*)

HANSEL: Did I sleep long? It's morning, isn't it? I guess I was awfully tired.

WITCH: You were sleeping so soundly I didn't want to wake you. Would you like some breakfast?

HANSEL: Oh, yes! (*Remembering his manners*) If it isn't too much trouble.

WITCH: Of course not, you dear boy. Come with me to the cupboard and we'll see what we can find. (*She takes him by the hand and they go to the cupboard.*)

WITCH (*Opening the door*): Now...what do you see?

HANSEL (*Peering in*): Why, it's so dark, I can't...

WITCH (*Pushing him inside*): In you go! And there you stay until we fatten you up! (*She locks the cupboard.*)

HANSEL (*His voice muffled from inside; banging with his fists on the door*) : Let me out! Let me out!

WITCH (*Chuckling*) : Not yet, my boy, not yet. But soon... when you're nice and fat. (*Going over to* GRETHEL *and shaking her*) Wake up, girl! Wake up, I say. You've work to do.

GRETHEL (*Sleepily*) : What's the matter ? (*She sits up, sees the* WITCH *and is frightened.*) Where is my brother?

WITCH : Your brother is in the cupboard with the rest of the food. You're to get busy and cook so that we can fatten him up. Then we'll see about cooking you. Now (*Giving her a slap*) get about your business!

CURTAIN

* * *

SCENE 4

SETTING: *The same as Scene 3. A few days later.*

AT RISE: *The* WITCH *is sitting in her chair rocking peacefully.* GRETHEL *is busy at the stove.*

WITCH (*Rising*) : We'll see how your brother is getting on. He must be about ready for eating. I'm tired of waiting. If he isn't fat now I'll eat him anyway. (*She goes to the cupboard and knocks at the door.*) Boy, put your finger out and let me see if you're fattening up. (HANSEL *sticks a bone through a hole in the cupboard.*)

WITCH (*Feeling the bone thoughtfully*) : Still pretty bony. I can't see well, but it doesn't *feel* much fatter. I've waited long enough. (*Turning to* GRETHEL) Girl! Climb in the oven and see if it's hot. I'm going to eat your brother today.

GRETHEL: But you can't! He isn't fat yet. (*Pleadingly*) Why don't you wait a couple of days more?

WITCH (*Snapping*) : Don't argue with me. I said today's the day. (*Chuckling*) I'm in the mood for a tender boy, even if he *is* a bit scrawny. (*Smacking her lips*) Today, him! tomorrow, you. Now do as I say! (GRETHEL *doesn't move.*)

WITCH: Climb in the oven, I say. (*Waving her stick*) Or I'll give you a taste of this!

GRETHEL (*Opening the oven*): I don't know how.

WITCH (*Impatiently*): Stupid! I'll show you. (*She goes to the oven and pokes her head in.*)

GRETHEL (*Shoving her in and slamming the door*) Burn up, you old witch! (*She runs to the cupboard, unlocks it and lets* HANSEL *out.*)

HANSEL: What have you done with the witch?

GRETHEL (*Laughing*): I'm cooking her. But let's not stay for dinner. We'll start for home and take something to eat on the way.

HANSEL: I know where she hides her gold! I watched her through the hole in the cupboard while she was counting it. (*He runs over to the chest in the corner and lifts the lid.*) See, Grethel, (*Taking out bags of gold*) bags and bags of gold — and look — jewels! If we can find our way home with this, we'll be rich and father won't have to leave us in the forest again. You can wear pretty dresses like a princess and we can eat candy every day.

GRETHEL (*Wistfully*): Oh, Hans, if we only *could* find our way home....

HANSEL: Don't you worry. We will. Now, fetch me that cloak from the corner and we'll wrap the gold and jewels in it. (GRETHEL *runs happily for the cloak. They are busy emptying the contents of the chest into it as the curtain falls.*)

CURTAIN

* * *

SCENE 5

SETTING: *Same as Scene 1.*

AT RISE: *The* WOODCUTTER *is sitting in a chair staring into the fire.* HANSEL *and* GRETHEL *enter from right and stop short at seeing him. Then* GRETHEL *goes to her father and touches him gently on the shoulder.*

GRETHEL: Father, it's Grethel.

WOODCUTTER (*Starting and looking up*): Grethel! No, it can't be. (*Burying his face in his hands and moaning.*) How could I have been so wicked!

HANSEL (*Going to him*): But we *are* here, father. We're safe.

WOODCUTTER (*Looking up and from one to the other, sees it is really his children and smiles joyfully*): My children! You're safe! Thank Heaven! Thank Heaven! (*He reaches out his arms and embraces them.*)

WOODCUTTER: I'll never let you go again. No matter what happens. Oh my children, can you ever forgive me?

GRETHEL: Of course, father. Everything is all right now.

HANSEL: And father, we're rich!

WOODCUTTER: Rich? What do you mean?

HANSEL: Wait... I'll show you! (*He runs out and returns dragging the bulging knapsack they have made from the cloak. He opens it displaying the jewels and gold. The* WOODCUTTER *stares unbelievingly as* HANSEL *and* GRETHEL *open the bags and pour the gold into his lap.*)

THE END

PETER RABBIT

by Natalie Simonds

Characters

FLOPSY
MOPSY
COTTON-TAIL
PETER
MOTHER RABBIT
FARMER MCGREGOR

SCENE 1

SETTING: *The rabbit-hole.*

AT RISE: MOTHER RABBIT, FLOPSY, MOPSY, COTTON-TAIL *and* PETER *are seated around the breakfast table, just finishing their meal.*

MOTHER RABBIT: Now children, I have to get ready to go into town and do some shopping.

FLOPSY: Can I go too, Mother?

MOPSY: Take me with you.

COTTON-TAIL: I wanna go.

PETER: Me, too.

MOTHER RABBIT: Children! Children! Be quiet! No, I can't take you with me. I have too many errands. But I'll tell you what. . .

CHORUS (*Quickly*): What?

MOTHER RABBIT: If you're very good children, you'll have a surprise for supper. . . .

FLOPSY (*Excitedly*): Red cabbage!

MOPSY (*Stuttering in her eagerness*): R-r-r-radishes!

MOTHER RABBIT (*Laughing*): No. You're both wrong. But if you're good little rabbits and go into the fields to play or gather berries, you may have currant buns tonight.

CHORUS (*Rapturously*): Currant buns! (*They all join hands and dance around the table singing.)* We're going to have currant buns! We're going to have currant buns!

MOTHER RABBIT (*Smiling*): Yes, but only if you're good. You are not under any circumstances to go into Farmer McGregor's garden. Your poor father went in there and that was the last we saw of him. (*She takes a handkerchief from her apron folds and dabs at her eyes.* FLOPSY, MOPSY *and* COTTON-TAIL *gather round their mother trying to comfort her.*)

FLOPSY (*Stroking her cheek*): Don't cry, Mother.

MOPSY (*Pulling at her apron*): Please don't cry.

COTTON-TAIL: We'll be good. Honest we will.

PETER (*Cocking his head to one side with a curious expression*): What happened to Father?

MOTHER RABBIT (*Removing the handkerchief from her eyes for a minute*): I declare, Peter, you're the hopping image of your poor father. Sometimes I think you'll come to the same bad end. Always sticking your ears in someone else's business.

PETER (*Insistently*): But what happened to Father?

MOTHER RABBIT (*Burying her face in her handkerchief again and sobbing loudly*): They put him in a pie, that's what! (*There is a silence and the children look at each other wide-eyed.*)

MOTHER RABBIT (*Dries her eyes; then briskly*): Well, that's over and done with. But you children keep out of Farmer McGregor's garden, and you won't end up on a plate. Now . . . (*Rising*) . . . I'm going to town. (*She goes off right.*)

FLOPSY (*After a moment*): Well, *I'm* going berrying. Who's coming with me?

MOPSY: Me!

COTTON-TAIL: Me, too!

PETER (*With great disgust*): Oh, you two! You always do what Flopsy does.

MOPSY: What of it?

COTTON-TAIL: What are *you* going to do?

FLOPSY: You'd better come with us, Peter Rabbit, and keep out of mischief. (*Haughtily*) Though I daresay I'll have trouble enough watching Mopsy and Cotton-Tail. You're worse than six rabbits.

PETER (*Indignantly*): All right, smarty. Just for that I won't go with you!

FLOPSY (*Bossily*): Well, see that you don't go (*With a sinister note*) . . . you know where.

PETER (*Innocently; he hasn't an idea in the world what she means*): Where?

FLOPSY (*Firmly*): *You* know where. (*Sniffing*) Though I'm sure *I* wouldn't be surprised if you ended up in a pie. (PETER *opens his mouth to utter a withering reply, but* MOTHER RABBIT *comes back into the room. She is wearing her bonnet and cape and carries a market basket.* PETER *is left standing there with his mouth open.*)

MOTHER RABBIT: I'm on my way. Be good children and don't forget what I told you. And Peter . . .

PETER (*Stupidly; he is still thinking*): Huh?

MOTHER RABBIT: Close your mouth! (*She goes off right.*)

CURTAIN

* * *

SCENE 2

SETTING: *Farmer McGregor's garden.*

AT RISE: PETER *is hiding behind the fence watching* FARMER MCGREGOR *pile carrots into a basket. As* FARMER MCGREGOR *picks up the basket and goes off stage,* PETER *sneaks quickly under the fence.*

PETER: Oh boy, oh boy, oh boy! Nobody's around now. *I'm* going to have a party. (*Sniffing*) They can *have* their berries. *I'm* going to have carrots and cabbage and . . . oh boy! RADISHES! (*He gathers a bunch of assorted vegetables, sits down and begins to eat with great relish. Suddenly he cocks his head to one side and listens. His mouth is full, but he picks up a bunch of uneaten vegetables and looks around hurriedly for a hiding-place. He spies the large watering-pot at left and jumps behind it as* FARMER MCGREGOR *enters with rake in hand.*)

FARMER MCGREGOR (*Looking around and pulling at his beard*): Hmmph! That's funny! Could have sworn I heard one of those danged rabbits in here. Well (*Brandishing his rake*), just let them DARE to sneak into my garden and eat my vegetables! I'll fix 'em. Yessir! Like I fixed that last one that got in. (*Chuckles*) Yessir! Sure fixed *him!* (PETER *has poked his head up but seeing* FARMER MCGREGOR *waving the rake, he ducks down again.* FARMER MCGREGOR *starts to leave at right.*)

PETER (*From watering-pot*): KER-CHOO!

FARMER MCGREGOR (*Turning back*): Aha! (*Advances menacingly towards* PETER'S *hiding-place.* PETER *jumps up, takes in the situation and decides to leave. He runs towards the fence.*)

FARMER MCGREGOR (*Waving the rake*): Aha! Caught in the act! Come back here, you rascal. (*He starts toward* PETER, *who is already scrambling under the fence. In his haste he tears his pants, leaving a large piece of them sticking to the fence, and also drops a shoe.*)

FARMER MCGREGOR (*Shaking his fist in* PETER'S *direction*): Stop, thief! Stop, I say! (PETER, *after one quick backward look, runs off stage.*)

CURTAIN

* * *

SCENE 3

SETTING: *Same as Scene* 1.

AT RISE: FLOPSY, MOPSY *and* COTTON-TAIL *are sitting at the table sorting their berries.* MOTHER RABBIT *enters from right.*

MOTHER RABBIT: Hello, children. Were you good rabbits while I was away? (*They all jump up and run to her, pulling at her cape and trying to get a look in her market basket.*)

CHORUS: Oh, yes, Mother! We were *very* good.

FLOPSY: We picked lots of berries!

MOPSY (*Trying to get hold of the market basket*): What did you bring me?

COTTON-TAIL: I wanna currant bun!

MOTHER RABBIT (*Laughing*): All right, children. Let me get my breath. (*She takes off her cape and bonnet, sets down the basket and looks around.*) Where's Peter?

FLOPSY: I don't know. I told him to come with us, but he wouldn't.

MOTHER RABBIT (*Worriedly*): Oh, dear, I do hope he hasn't got into trouble. (*At this moment* PETER *pokes his head in at right, sees that everyone is there and decides to face it. He takes a few cautious steps into the room.*)

MOTHER RABBIT (*Turning*): Oh, there you are, Peter. Well, come in. Don't stand there. (*Relieved*) Thank heavens, you're safe. Come and get washed up for supper. (*Taking a good look*) PETER RABBIT! Look at your pants! And you have only one shoe! Oh, those lovely blue pants I made you. *Look* at them!

PETER (*Looking down dejectedly*): I couldn't help it. I got caught in a fence.

MOTHER RABBIT (*Seeing the light*): A fence? A fence! *What* fence?

PETER (*Nonchalantly*): Oh, just an old green fence.

MOTHER RABBIT (*Sharply*): Peter, have you been in Farmer McGregor's garden?

PETER (*Meekly*): I guess I have. (*Sorrowfully and with growing inspiration*) I ran and ran and I'm awful tired and (*Clutching his stomach*) I don't feel well. (*Starting to cry*) I don't feel well at all.

MOTHER RABBIT (*Looking at him sternly*): That's too bad. Well, stop your crying. I'll fix you up. (*She takes down a large bottle from the shelf, and gets a spoon from the cupboard.*) Come here, Peter.

PETER (*Understanding only too well, he suddenly feels better*): I feel better now. (MOTHER RABBIT *goes over to him and takes him by the ear.*)

PETER (*Crying again*): I feel better. I feel f-i-i-i-n-e. (MOTHER RABBIT *pours out a big spoonful of castor oil and forces it down his throat.* FLOPSY, MOPSY *and* COTTON-TAIL *each take a currant bun from the basket and sit munching contentedly, as the curtain falls.*)

THE END

THE POT OF GOLD

by Claribel N. Spamer

Characters

RED FAIRY
ORANGE FAIRY
YELLOW FAIRY
GREEN FAIRY
BLUE FAIRY
VIOLET FAIRY
RICH MAN
OLD LADY
SUSAN

SCENE 1

SETTING: *Outdoors after a shower.*

AT RISE: *The* RAINBOW FAIRIES *dance onto stage. Each is wearing the color she represents.*

BLUE FAIRY (*Looking around*): We forgot the Pot of Gold.

GREEN FAIRY: So we did! We can't stay here without it. What if someone should find us and no gold at our end?

YELLOW FAIRY (*Stretching leisurely*): Oh relax! No one has ever found us yet.

GREEN FAIRY (*With a worried frown*): But someday someone will. Everyone has heard of the Pot of Gold, and everyone is eager to get it.

RED FAIRY: Well, I don't care if he is. I think as Yellow does — what difference does it make? If anyone finds us and there is no gold to take home, then maybe he'll stay and play with us instead. It'd be fun to have an earth child to play with for a change.

VIOLET FAIRY (*Wistfully*): Yes, it would, wouldn't it?

ORANGE FAIRY: Well, as for me, I'm just glad to be on a visit to

Earth again. I wish the old sun would shine through these showers more often. It's ages since we were here last.

BLUE FAIRY: Green, will you go back with me and get the Pot of Gold?

GREEN FAIRY: Sure. It won't take long, and it will be a load off my mind.

BLUE FAIRY (*Looking at others*): Let's all go.

YELLOW FAIRY: Not me. I'm having too good a time. (*Dances about the stage. Others ignore the* BLUE FAIRY.)

BLUE FAIRY: Well — come on then, Green. (BLUE *and* GREEN FAIRIES *exit.*)

VIOLET FAIRY: People will think the Rainbow is fading if Green and Blue don't hurry back. It's hardly time to fade yet.

ORANGE FAIRY: Oh, they'll be right back. (GREEN *and* BLUE FAIRIES *reënter carrying the Pot of Gold between them.*)

GREEN FAIRY: Here we are. Did anyone come?

YELLOW FAIRY: No, but I think I see someone now. (*Looks off-stage to right. Others also look, shading their eyes with their hands.*)

RED FAIRY: It's a man. He is well dressed. He looks very rich.

BLUE FAIRY: Him! Goodness, *he* mustn't find us!

VIOLET FAIRY: Why not? Don't you think he'd play with us?

BLUE FAIRY: Mercy no! He's not interested in anything but money! All he wants is more and more of it.

GREEN FAIRY: Then our Pot of Gold is not for him. Let's go. (*They start off toward left, except the* RED FAIRY, *who lingers.*)

RED FAIRY: *Maybe* he'd play if we asked him. (ORANGE FAIRY *reaches back and gives her a yank.*)

ORANGE FAIRY: Come on. He wouldn't even notice us. He has no eyes for anything but money. (FAIRIES *exit.* RICH MAN *enters at right.*)

RICH MAN (*Mopping brow*): I must have walked miles. I could have sworn the Rainbow ended right here! But now it seems to be gone. No — there it is. It's way over there now. (*Looks off to left.* OLD LADY *enters from right.*)

OLD LADY: Did you find it? I've been behind you all the way, but I couldn't catch up.

RICH MAN (*Scornfully*): Find what?

OLD LADY: The End of the Rainbow of course. It was here; I saw it. You did too. What did you do with the gold?

RICH MAN: There isn't any gold. You can see for yourself that the Rainbow isn't here.

OLD LADY: But it *was* here. And I bet you found it. I bet you found the gold and have hidden it. I want half of it! I came all this way and I want half.

RICH MAN (*With a sneer*): You! What would an old thing like you do with gold? You don't need any. You're used to having nothing.

OLD LADY (*Angrily shaking her fist at him*): You old miser! You've got everything you need. Yet you want more.

RICH MAN: Well, fighting won't get us anywhere. I'm going on till I find that Rainbow's End. (*Exits at left.* OLD LADY *follows.* FAIRIES *enter at right, carrying Pot of Gold.*)

VIOLET FAIRY (*With satisfaction*): The nicest part about being fairies is the way we can dodge people. We can be practically anywhere we want to be.

RED FAIRY: I bet the Old Lady would play with us. She's not rich and proud.

BLUE FAIRY: I'll call her.

GREEN FAIRY: And then she can have the Pot of Gold. It would be nice for her to have it. (BLUE *starts to follow her, but* ORANGE *holds her back.*)

ORANGE FAIRY: No, don't bring her back. Let her follow the Rich Man. She is poor, it is true, but she is stingy. She wouldn't appreciate the gold any more than he would.

BLUE FAIRY: Are you sure?

YELLOW FAIRY: Yes, Orange is right. I've seen her lots of times when we've been to Earth. She's nothing but a slovenly old woman.

VIOLET FAIRY (*Looking to right*): Here comes somebody else. Shall we move again?

GREEN FAIRY (*Looking up at the sky*): It's nearly time for us to go back to heaven anyhow. The storm has been over quite awhile now.

RED FAIRY (*With disappointment*): Oh not yet! It's a little girl this time.

BLUE FAIRY: It's Susan. She is a nice child. She loves pretty things. She would adore playing with us.

RED FAIRY: Then let's wait for her. Please let's!

GREEN FAIRY: Well, I suppose we could. We aren't in that much of a hurry. What do you say? (*All the* FAIRIES *shout "yes."* SUSAN *enters at right.*)

SUSAN (*Joyfully rushing up to them*): Oh, I've found it! I've found the Rainbow! Aren't you beautiful — every single one of you! Oh how lovely! If I could only stay with you forever!

VIOLET FAIRY (*Bashfully*): Are we really beautiful?

RED FAIRY (*Eagerly*): Will you play with us a little while? You are beautiful too. You're the first earth child we've ever been close to.

SUSAN (*Taking the* RED *and* VIOLET FAIRIES' *hands*): Certainly I'll play with you. What would you like to play?

BLUE FAIRY (*Holding out Pot of Gold to her*): Don't you want the Pot of Gold? You've found the End of the Rainbow.

SUSAN (*Taking the pot*): Pot of Gold?

GREEN FAIRY: That's at the End of the Rainbow. Don't tell me you never heard of it!

SUSAN (*Thoughtfully*): Yes — I guess I have — in stories. Is this really it?

VIOLET FAIRY: Look inside. (SUSAN *looks inside, and lifts out piles of yellow flowers.*)

SUSAN: Dandelions! Marsh marigolds! Buttercups! Aren't they lovely. Are they mine?

ALL THE FAIRIES: All yours.

GREEN FAIRY: Oh goodness, we must go. Come on, Fairies. We must go now. (*Picking up the empty pot, she exits followed by the others.* SUSAN *watches.*)

FAIRIES (*Calling back*): Goodbye, Susan.

SUSAN: Goodbye, Rainbow. Oh dear, they couldn't stay long. But I still have my flowers. (RICH MAN *and* OLD WOMAN *re-enter from left.*)

RICH MAN (*Crossly*): See! We didn't get there on time. All because you stopped to argue with me!

OLD LADY: Hold your tongue. I'm glad we didn't. You've got too much money already.

SUSAN (*Seeing them, and holding out her flowers*): Look what I found. The Pot of Gold!

RICH MAN and OLD LADY (*Excitedly*): Where? Where?

SUSAN: Why — right here!

RICH MAN (*Scoffing*): Dandelions! They're nothing but weeds! You must be crazy! (*Exits in disgust.*)

OLD LADY: Pot of Gold indeed! (*Shaking her head, she exits mumbling.*)

SUSAN: It's a shame they didn't see how pretty they are. They didn't even half look at them. Oh well, Mother will like them anyway. I'll take them home and show them to her. When I tell her I found the Pot of Gold, she'll believe me. (*Exits.*)

THE END

THE TEST

by Loretta Capell Tobey

Characters

THE KING
THE COUNSELOR, *who has a loud voice and pompous manner*
PRINCE RED CAP
PRINCE BLUE CAP
PRINCE GREEN CAP
PRINCE WHITE CAP
EENIE, *page to* PRINCE RED CAP
MEENIE, *page to* PRINCE BLUE CAP
MINEY, *page to* PRINCE GREEN CAP
MO, *page to* PRINCE WHITE CAP
HERALD
LORDS *and* LADIES *of the court (any number)*
HERALDS

SCENE 1

SETTING: *The Throne Room in the Castle.*

AT RISE: *The* KING *is on his throne with his* COUNSELOR *near him.* LORDS *and* LADIES-IN-WAITING, HERALDS *and* PAGES *are grouped around the throne. The* KING *speaks in a quick, rather uncertain manner; the* COUNSELOR *is very pompous and dignified.*

KING: And so, oh, wisest of counselors, I am sure you will agree with me. The choice of a worthy successor to my throne is a very important matter indeed!

COUNSELOR: My king, it is indeed of the greatest importance! But surely any one of your fine sons would make a worthy successor. Four splendid princes!

KING: Aye — four fine sons have I! Each *is* worthy of this honor. But which one, I wonder? (*Thoughtfully*) Prince Red Cap . . . Prince Blue Cap . . . Prince Green Cap . . . Prince White

Cap. . . . Each is honest, kind, and true. Each has a keen intelligence and ready wit! Which would be best?

COUNSELOR: Perhaps a task, oh king! Some trial to determine each prince's courage and honesty?

KING: They have been tested many times, counselor. Each is equally as brave, as kind, as honest, as clever as the other! It is a weighty problem indeed!

COUNSELOR: But how about wisdom? Not wisdom in the great undertakings, doubtless each has this quality, but judgment in the *little* things!

KING (*Attentively*): Ah . . . you interest me, counselor! And what test might you suggest to determine which of my sons has this "best judgment in little things" and so prove himself to be the most worthy successor to my throne?

COUNSELOR (*In deep thought*): Let — me — think — a moment. . . . Ah, I have it!

KING (*Eagerly*): Yes? Yes?

COUNSELOR: Think, oh king! What little things do we use constantly, in everything that we do? With various delicate shades of meanings?

KING (*Bewildered*): What, indeed!

COUNSELOR (*In triumph*): Words, your majesty, words!

KING (*Puzzled*): Words? Words?

COUNSELOR: Yes! Have the princes the judgment to choose exactly the right word for the right place?

KING (*Angrily*): Of course they have! All of them!

COUNSELOR: But wait! Have you ever thought how almost impossible it is to find two words with *exactly* the same meaning?

KING (*Laughing heartily*): Ho, Ho, Ho! Impossible, indeed! What a task that would be! I could name a *dozen,* now!

COUNSELOR: Name them.

KING: Well — er — (*Thinks a moment*) Oh, ho! I have not only *two,* but *three* words with the same meaning!

COUNSELOR (*Patiently*): Name them!

KING (*Triumphantly*): Fog — mist — and haze! Exactly alike! Ho, ho! What a test, what a test!

COUNSELOR: Ah, but majesty, they are not exactly alike! They are only similar. A *haze* is a very thin mist. A *mist* is a very thin fog. A *fog* is much denser than the other two!

KING (*Nonplussed*): Well — er — I always thought — You are

right, of course. Let me think again. Well, how about *vast* and *huge?*

COUNSELOR: Nearly the same again, but the meanings are really quite different. *Vast* is used to describe something that extends for a long distance, such as an ocean or range of mountains. *Huge* is used to describe something of great bulk, like an elephant or large building. You see, it is not so easy!

KING: I see, oh wise one. . . . You are right. (*Convinced at last.*) Of course! The test! I will have the pages summon the princes. (*As the* KING *calls, each* PAGE *comes to the foot of the throne and bows deeply.*) Eenie! Meenie! Miney! Mo! (Mo *is sound asleep!*) Mo! Mo! Wake up that page, somebody! (*The* HERALDS *shake* MO, *who stumbles to the foot of the throne, rubbing his eyes.*) You are to summon your masters, the princes, at once! (*Droll music as the pages depart. The* KING *shakes his head a little doubtfully, then talks to the* COUNSELOR *again.*) I hope this will work, counselor, but it seems too easy. Ah, I have the answer myself! I am sure of it this time!

COUNSELOR: And the words?

KING: My appetite has suggested them! *Luscious* and *delicious.* Exactly alike, or my throne is tottering!

COUNSELOR: It totters, then! For they are different, indeed! One uses the word *luscious* in speaking of something juicy — fruit, for instance. *Delicious* may describe anything exceptionally good to eat.

KING: I give it up. If one of the princes is able to find the words he is deserving of the throne, indeed! And here are the pages with their young majesties. (*Music plays as the* PAGES *and* PRINCES *march in. Each comes to the throne in turn and bows to the* KING.)

RED CAP: Oh, king. . .

BLUE CAP: We are here . . .

GREEN CAP: And await . . .

WHITE CAP: Your pleasure!

KING: My sons, a weighty matter is before us! I must choose from among you a worthy successor to my throne. And so my wise counselor has suggested a test!

PRINCES: A test?

KING: You are all brave princes, and true. All are kind and loyal. This test is to be an unusual one!

PRINCES (*Eagerly*): Yes, yes! What can it be?

KING: It is a test of words!

PRINCES (*Puzzled*): Words?

KING: The counselor will explain.

COUNSELOR: To be a really great king, oh youthful majesties, wisdom is of the utmost importance! Not only wisdom in the great things, but judgment in those so small that they may *seem* unimportant. Many of our words seem so alike in meaning that they are often misused. It is important that the new king should have the judgment and precision to detect these differences in meaning, and so use the words correctly. The test is this. There are many words with *similar* meanings. But you are to find two with *exactly* the same meaning! (*The* PRINCES, *who have been listening attentively, rather puzzled at first, now take it as a joke!*)

PRINCES: Ho, ho! That's easy! I can think of them already! (*Etc., etc.*)

WHITE CAP (*Puzzled*): I don't think it is so easy! I can't think of any!

KING: Wait! It is not so easy! The meaning must be *exact!* And you will have only one hour in which to find the words. You may consult only your own page — no one else! Of course the palace library is at your disposal. Away now, and return within the hour! (*The* PRINCES *go out laughing, all except* PRINCE WHITE CAP, *who is very thoughtful.* MO, *always the awkward one, stumbles and nearly falls as he goes out.*)

CURTAIN

* * *

SCENE 2

SETTING: A *small study near the palace library.*

AT RISE: *Enter* PRINCE RED CAP *and* EENIE. *They are laughing.*

Red Cap: Well, Eenie, my friend, this is one of the simplest things we have had to do in a long time!

Eenie: Ho, ho! You are right, majesty! A fine test, indeed!

Red Cap: No need of books or papers either. We'll just use our wits a moment and settle the thing. Then we'll have a fine game until the hour is up.

Eenie: Good! Then the faster we think, the more time for play! Well, let's think! (*Each sits, chin in hand, thinking. In a moment* Eenie *has an inspiration!*)

Eenie: I have it! How about *surprise* and *astonish?*

Red Cap (*Thoughtfully*): They *do* mean the same, don't they? But wait! I believe *astonish* means much more than *surprise!*

Eenie: You are right, prince. We might be *surprised* if it rained on a sunny day, but if it rained daisies we'd be *astonished!*

Red Cap (*Laughing*): Ha, ha, that's a good one! Well — (*They think hard again.*) How about *obtain* and *receive?*

Eenie: And *acquire.* That means the same thing, too, doesn't it?

Red Cap: We'll surprise them! They'll be astonished! Three alike instead of two!

Eenie (*Doubtfully*): I — don't — know. I've been thinking. I don't believe they *are* exactly alike.

Red Cap: No? How's that?

Eenie: It's this way. If someone hands you something, you *receive* it, but you have to work to *obtain* anything. *Do* something about it, I mean. And if you *acquire* something, you expect to *keep* it!

Red Cap: Yes, I see they *are* different. (*He is tired of so much deep thought.*) Ho, hum! It is not so easy as we thought, is it? Well, let's try again. (*Deep concentration*)

Eenie: I have it!

Red Cap: Sh — not so loud. If you have the right one, the others must not hear! (Eenie *whispers in his ear. He smiles, delightedly.*) Right, this time! And only a few moments of the hour gone! Now we can have our game!

Eenie: Fine! Off we go! (*Exit, laughing. Enter* Prince Blue Cap *and* Meenie. *They are breathless as if from running.*)

Blue Cap: What a fine run! And there is still plenty of time to think of the words.

Meenie: It won't take a minute. Oh, hum! Let's think fast. Then maybe we will have time for a little nap before the hour is up. (*They sit in deep concentration for a moment.*)

BLUE CAP: Let's see. . . . How about *chore* and *task?*

MEENIE: I am sure those are not the same. A *chore* is a light bit of work that is done regularly. A *task* is something harder, something we do because we *have* to! Finding two words with the same meaning is a *task!*

BLUE CAP: But not a hard task, Meenie. It should be easy. Let's try again. Ah, I have it! How about *stop* and *quit?* They mean the same, surely.

MEENIE: No, majesty, I am afraid you are wrong! You might *stop* your work and rest a while, and then go on again. But when you *quit* you would leave it for *good!* Do you see the difference?

BLUE CAP (*Discouraged*): Y — yes. Well — it — isn't — so — easy!

MEENIE: Let's not be discouraged! How about *breeze* and *wind* — and *squall* and *gale?* They seem alike!

BLUE CAP: Now it's my turn to explain the difference! A breeze is only a *little* wind. A squall blows much faster than a wind, and a *gale* blows the fastest of them all!

MEENIE: Oh, well, never mind! I have thought of two others. Listen! *Looking* and *observing!* You can't find any difference in those, can you?

BLUE CAP: Let — me — think. No, those will not do. We could be *looking* at something and not really *observing* it at all! See? (*Pause. Deep concentration.*)

MEENIE (*Jumping up*): Ah!

BLUE CAP: Do you have it?

MEENIE: Sh! Come closer! (*Whispers to the* PRINCE.)

BLUE CAP: Hurrah! At last! Oh! Hum! Such deep thinking has surely made me sleepy! Now for a little nap before the hour is up.

MEENIE (*Looking at clock, which has been moved ahead again*): There's plenty of time. (*They saunter off, yawning and stretching. Enter* PRINCE GREEN CAP *and* MINEY. *They are hurrying.*)

GREEN CAP (*Glancing at clock*): Hurry, Miney! We spent too much time chasing the rabbit. We must think of the words now!

MINEY (*Lazily*): There's no hurry, prince. We have plenty of time! It will only take a minute!

GREEN CAP: Well, let's think hard and fast then. And maybe there will still be time to hunt the rabbit! (*Deep concentration.*)

MINEY: I am so tired, after that chase! Well, now, there's an idea! How about *tired* and *exhausted?* Don't they mean the same, prince?

GREEN CAP: Now you know better than that, Miney! You can be *tired* without being *exhausted.*

MINEY: Y — yes. I suppose so. I am so tired I am just about exhausted. (*They think again*) Well, do *shrub* and *bush* mean the same? I always thought they did.

GREEN CAP: Let — me — think: No, they are not the same. I remember reading that a *bush* grows several stems from the root, while a *shrub* has only *one,* like a little tree.

MINEY: I don't believe there *are* two words alike!

GREEN CAP: There *must* be! Wait! How about *coils* and *spirals?* Aren't they alike?

MINEY: No, you are wrong. I can show you the difference with this wire. (*Demonstrates*) These are *coils.* These are *spirals.* Do you see the difference?

GREEN CAP: I never thought of that before.

GREEN CAP: How about *stupendous* and *tremendous?*

MINEY: And *enormous,* too. They seem to be alike!

GREEN CAP: Let's look them up in the big book to be sure. (*Studies in book a moment*) No, they won't do! *Enormous* means something bigger than normal. *Stupendous* means something so amazing that it would stupefy one. *Tremendous* means something so dreadful that it would make one tremble to see it!

MINEY: Whew! There *is* a difference there!

GREEN CAP: But we must hurry! Time is flying! (*The hands on the clock have been moved.*) We must think fast!

MINEY (*After a moment's thought*): I have a good one!

GREEN CAP (*Eagerly*): Yes?

MINEY: *Prudence* and *wisdom!*

GREEN CAP: They *seem* the same! I believe you have found them! But no, I'm not so sure! (*Thinks a moment*) You see, a *prudent* person is one who *avoids* a difficult situation. A *wise* man knows how to handle it when it comes!

MINEY: We don't seem to be wise enough to handle *this* situation, do we? (*They think again.*)

GREEN CAP: Miney! Miney! I have them at last!

MINEY: Tell me! But don't let anyone hear! (PRINCE *whispers in his ear.*) Right! No chance of going wrong with *those!* (*Looks at clock*) And there's still time left!

GREEN CAP: We will find that rabbit hole! (GREEN CAP *and* MINEY *run out, left. Enter* WHITE CAP *and* MO, *who is lagging far behind. He is staggering under a great load of books which slip and fall as he enters.*)

WHITE CAP: Well, Mo, we have been through the biggest books in the library. There don't seem to be *any* two words with the same meaning! Mo! Mo! Be careful!

MO (*As he picks up the books*): I found a few more books, Prince White Cap. Maybe we can find the words in them!

WHITE CAP: I knew when we started, Mo, that this was going to be a hard thing to do! That's why we hurried straight to the big library to make the most of every minute! But we've hunted *everywhere!* And now the time is nearly up! Words *seem* to mean the same and yet, when we study them a little, we find that they are really different.

MO (*Arranging the new books, busily*): Perhaps, if we hunt through *these,* prince, we might find them. There's still a *little* time!

WHITE CAP: We won't give up until the last minute! Let's see what we can find! (*Both study intently.*)

MO (*Dropping his book in excitement*): Oh, oh! I believe I have it! Look here!

WHITE CAP (*Reading over his shoulder*): Hm — m — m — *elastic* — *pliant* — well — n-no not quite, Mo! Something *pliant* is something that can be bent without breaking. Something *elastic* must spring back to its original shape again. Do you see the difference. I'll show you. (*Demonstrates*) This wire is *pliant.* But this willow branch is *elastic.*

MO (*Nodding his head*): Yes, I see the difference now. Well, I'll see if there is anything else here. How about *acquiesce* and *agree?* I don't believe you can find any fault with *those.*

WHITE CAP (*In excitement*): I believe they do mean the same, Mo!

WHITE CAP: Have we really found the right ones?

MO (*In a discouraged tone as he studies further*): No, Im afraid not. It explains that to *acquiesce* in something means that you agree rather against your will, reluctantly.

WHITE CAP: I see! Against your better judgment. But when you *agree* you do it *willingly.* (*They are both much discouraged*) Mo, the time is nearly up. What can we do? We have no words to report to my father.

Mo (*Turning over the pages, frantically*): I am still hunting, prince. But I have nearly finished the book. Wait! This may do! How about *restive* and *restless?* Surely *they* mean the same!

White Cap: No, they *sound* alike, but the meaning is quite different! One may be *restless* and not be able to help it. One is *restive* in an *obstinate* way! A donkey is often *restive!*

Mo (*Discouraged*): I am afraid there are no more! This is the last page! What can we do?

White Cap: And only two minutes before the hour is up! (*The clock shows this time.*) Read fast, Mo! Read fast! And I will *think.*

Mo (*Nearly overcome with excitement, pointing to bottom of page*): Prince! Prince! Here on the last page! At the very bottom! Look!

White Cap: Why — I — believe — you're — right! At last! But — the time! (*Looks at clock*) Is it too late? No, there's a chance to make it! Come quickly, Mo. We must hurry, hurry! The clock is nearly ready to strike. (*They run off, left.* Mo *tries to carry the big book. It slips from under his arm and he stops to pick it up. He stumbles as he goes.*)

CURTAIN

* * *

Scene 3

Setting: *Same as Scene* 1.

At Rise: *The* King *and his attendants are listening to the chiming of the clock. All of the* Princes *are present except* White Cap. *On the last stroke he rushes in dragging* Mo *behind him.* Mo *drops the book again in his hurry.*

King (*Severely*): You are nearly late, my son.

White Cap: Sorry, Father.

King: Attention, all! Herald, read the proclamation!

HERALD (*Reading from scroll*): We are assembled at this hour to choose a worthy successor to the throne of the king! The counselor will explain the test of the four princes.

COUNSELOR: The test seems a simple one. In reality it is quite difficult. The prince who has discovered two words with exactly the same meaning will become the new king. Princes, are you ready?

PRINCES: We are ready.

WHITE CAP: And I! I am ready, too!

HERALD: Prince Red Cap, as the oldest son, will you speak first? (*As each* PRINCE *has his turn, he comes to the foot of the throne, bows, and speaks loudly and clearly.*)

RED CAP: The words that I have found, oh king, are . . . *tempest* and *hurricane!*

KING (*Smiling*): They seem alike, to be sure. Has he succeeded, counselor?

COUNSELOR (*Shaking his head*): No . . . these have not exactly the same meaning! Both are windstorms, to be sure. But a tempest has heavy rains with the wind, while a hurricane may be only *wind,* without rain. (*The* PRINCE *hangs his head in disappointment.*)

KING (*Kindly*): But not so bad, my son, not so bad! Come, sit here at my feet. (PRINCE *sits at foot of throne.*)

HERALD: Prince Blue Cap, are you ready?

BLUE CAP: I am ready, oh, king! My words are . . . *spurned* and *rejected.* I am sure their meaning is the same!

COUNSELOR: They are similar, but not the same, Prince Blue Cap. *Spurned* means somewhat more than *rejected.* You may *reject* a plan for which you have respect and interest, but if you *spurn* it, you have scorn or contempt for it. I am sure that such a wise prince can see the difference! (PRINCE *shows disappointment.*)

KING: But very near, my son, very near! Come, sit beside your brother. (PRINCE *sits at foot of throne.*)

HERALD: Prince Green Cap, are you ready.

GREEN CAP: I am ready, oh king. My words are *enough* and *sufficient.* I can see no difference in them at all.

COUNSELOR: But there *is* a difference, I fear! Take a very greedy person, for instance. He may have *sufficient* for his needs, but he never thinks that he has *enough,* does he? (*Laughter in the room. The* KING *beckons to the disappointed* PRINCE, *who sits beside his brothers.*)

KING: A very close shade of meaning there. Very close. I am really proud of you, my sons. And now the youngest. Can he have won the test when his elder brothers could not?

MO (*Very much excited*): Yes, yes, yes! We have it!

WHITE CAP: Hush, Mo! Wait!

HERALD: Prince White Cap, are you ready?

WHITE CAP: Yes, I have accomplished the task.

MO (*More and more excited*): Yes, yes, yes, we found the words. At the very end of the book.

WHITE CAP: Sh! Quiet, Mo! . . . The words are . . . *finis* and *end.* They are exactly alike, I believe.

MO (*Quite beside himself*): Yes, yes, they are alike . . . they *are.*

KING: Well, well, well!

COUNSELOR: At last! Exactly alike! *Finis* means *end.* No more . . . no less! The prince has fulfilled the task, oh king. A worthy crown prince, indeed!

KING: The throne is yours, my son. Come and sit beside me.

MO (*Whispering to* WHITE CAP): But how about *me?* I found them for you! (*The* PRINCE *nods, and as he climbs up beside the* KING *he drags* MO *with him. They stand, one on each side of the* KING. MO *fingers his arm holes in pride.*)

KING: Herald, proclaim the new king.

HERALD (*Blowing bugle*): Hail to the king! King White Cap has ascended to the throne! (WHITE CAP *reaches over the* KING'S *head to shake hands with* MO.

THE END

PUSS-IN-BOOTS

by Alice Very

Characters

PUSS-IN-BOOTS
TOM, *the Miller's youngest son, later The Marquis of Carabas*
JACK } *his brothers*
JOE }
DONKEY, *two persons*
HERALDS
GUARDS
LORDS
LADIES
KING
PRINCESS
REAPERS
OGRE
SERVANTS *of Ogre*

SCENE 1

SETTING: *Interior of grist mill.*

AT RISE: PUSS *lies stretched out beside sacks, as if dead.* MOUSE *moves across floor to flour bag.* PUSS *leaps up and pounces on* MOUSE. *Enter* TOM, *shabby and dusty.*

TOM (*Clapping hands*): Attaboy! Smart cat! You always fool them. (PUSS *drags* MOUSE *off. Enter* JACK *and* JOE, *leading* DONKEY *to door.* DONKEY *sticks head and front feet inside, flaps ears.*)
JACK: I'm the biggest, so I get the mill.
JOE: I'm next, so I get the donkey.
TOM: What do I get?
JACK: Oh, you can have the cat. (PUSS *reënters, licking chops.*)

JOE (*To* JACK): Let's be partners. You need my donkey to carry your bags of flour.

TOM: Will you pay me for letting my Puss catch rats in your mill?

JACK: Yes, you can have the rats to eat.

TOM: Is that all?

JOE: You can eat the cat if you like.

PUSS: Meow! (TOM *pets* PUSS.)

JACK (*Singing*):

There was a jolly miller once
Lived on the river Dee;
He worked and sung from morn till night,
No lark more blithe than he.
And this the burden of his song,
Forever used to be —

JOE (*Joining in chorus with* JACK):

I care for nobody, no, not I,
Since nobody cares for me.

TOM: Nobody cares for me, I see.

JACK: Come on, load him up.

JOE: Here goes! (JACK *and* JOE *load sacks of flour on* DONKEY *and lead him away,* JACK *pulling him with rope,* JOE *pushing behind, both whistling tune of "Jolly Miller."*)

TOM (*Sitting on remaining bag and stroking* PUSS): Poor Pussy! What shall we do?

PUSS (*Rubbing against* TOM): Purr, purr! Don't worry, dear master. Just give me a pair of boots and a bag, and I'll show you what I can do.

TOM: A pair of boots! Wait, I have some that will just fit you. (*Takes boots from corner and puts them on* PUSS.) You can have my hat and jacket too, if you like. (*Puts hat and jacket on* PUSS.)

PUSS: Now the bag.

TOM: Here's an empty flour sack. (*Ties sack over* PUSS's *shoulder.*)

PUSS: Who ever saw such a fine Puss-in-Boots! (*Struts out door.* TOM *sits down again, head in hands.*)

TOM: What can a cat do? Still, he's smart. Look at the tricks he plays on rats and mice! (*Sound of hen cackling offstage stops suddenly. Enter* PUSS, *carrying something in his bag.*)

PUSS: Here, master, I've caught a fine fat hen for your supper.

(*Gives bag to* TOM.) Now we won't go hungry—and you won't need to eat me!

TOM (*Looking in bag*): Well, what do you know! You *are* a smart cat! (*Pats* PUSS, *who purrs and rubs against* TOM.)

CURTAIN

* * *

SCENE 2

SETTING: *A grassy meadow. Enter* TOM *and* PUSS-IN-BOOTS.

PUSS: They say the King and the Princess often pass this way to take the air.

TOM: Oh, yes, the Princess! How pretty she is! (*Sighs.*)

PUSS: Perhaps they will come today. Why don't you speak to her?

TOM: Who, me? In these shabby clothes!

PUSS: Well, you might wash in the river. Then at least you wouldn't be so dirty!

TOM: That's a good idea. I'll undress behind this tree. (*Exits behind tree.*)

PUSS: Now watch me sneak up and get his clothes while he's in the water! (*A loud splash offstage.*) There he goes! (PUSS *slips back of tree and returns with* TOM'S *clothes, which he stuffs in the bag, taking out rabbit from bag.*) Now what shall I do with this rabbit? There isn't room for both. (*Sounds of bugles offstage. Enter* HERALDS, *from left, with bugles,* GUARDS *with spears,* LORDS *and* LADIES, *and the* KING *and the* PRINCESS.)

KING (*To* PRINCESS): A lovely day for a walk, my dear.

PRINCESS: Yes, if only there were some company.

KING: Company! What do you call all these people?

PRINCESS: I mean someone to talk to. Pardon me, Sire, but it is dull to be a Princess. (*Yawns behind fan.*)

PUSS-IN-BOOTS (*Taking off hat with a low bow*): Your Majesty, may I present a rabbit from my noble lord, the Marquis of Carabas?

PRINCESS: The Marquis of Carabas!

KING (*Taking rabbit and handing it to a* LORD *to carry*): Tell your master I thank him, and he does me a great deal of pleasure. (*To* PRINCESS) Did you ever hear of this Marquis of Carabas?

PRINCESS: I think so. I'm sure if I saw him I'd know him.

PUSS (*Who has run to river bank*): Help! Help! My Lord the Marquis of Carabas is drowning!

KING (*To* GUARDS): Run, save the noble lord! (GUARDS *drop spears and run back of tree.*)

PRINCESS: Oh, the poor man!

PUSS (*Bowing to* KING): Your Majesty, I am sorry to say, while my master was bathing some thieves ran away with his clothes, and now he has nothing to wear!

KING: What a mean trick! (*To* LORD) Sir, run to my wardrobe and bring a suit of my best clothes for His Lordship. (LORD *runs off.*)

TOM (*Shouting offstage*): Here, what's the meaning of this? Where are my clothes?

GUARD (*Offstage*): Take it easy, sir. You're all right now. (*Reënter* LORD, *puffing and panting, with clothes which he carries behind tree.*)

PRINCESS: I cannot wait to see this noble lord. (*Enter* TOM, *richly dressed.*)

PUSS (*Bowing*): Your Majesty, my Lord the Marquis of Carabas!

TOM (*Taking off hat and bowing*): Your Majesty! How can I thank you?

KING: Be pleased to join us in our walk, Marquis.

PRINCESS: I am so glad you were not drowned.

TOM (*Kissing her hand*): A thousand thanks, Your Highness! (*The* KING *with his party and* TOM *stroll off, left.* PUSS *looks after them, stroking his whiskers and purring. Enter* REAPERS, *right, carrying scythe, sickle, rake, etc.*)

REAPERS (*Singing*):

Shall we show you how the farmer,
Shall we show you how the farmer,
Shall we show you how the farmer
Mows his barley and rye? (*Mowing*)
Look 'tis thus the busy farmer,
Look 'tis thus the busy farmer,
Look 'tis thus the busy farmer
Mows his barley and rye.

PUSS: Well, good people, whose land do you think this is?

FIRST REAPER: This land belongs to a cruel ogre.

SECOND REAPER: He makes us work and slave for him.

FIRST REAPER: He is a powerful magician and can turn himself into all kinds of animals.

SECOND REAPER: They say he turns into a lion sometimes and eats people!

PUSS: All the same, that Ogre has no right to this land. It belongs to my master, the Marquis of Carabas.

REAPERS: Is that so?

PUSS (*Fiercely*): Yes, it is; and if you don't tell the King so when he passes this way you shall be chopped as small as mince meat!

FIRST REAPER: Oh, dear! That's worse than the Ogre!

SECOND REAPER: We'll tell him just what you said.

PUSS: Be sure you say the Marquis of Carabas. (*Enter* KING, PRINCESS, TOM *and* COURTIERS, *left.*)

KING: This is a fine meadow. (*To* REAPERS) To whom does it belong?

REAPERS (*Bowing low*): To our Lord the Marquis of Carabas, Your Majesty.

TOM: You see, Sire, it always yields a good crop every year.

KING: And I suppose yonder castle (*Pointing*) is also yours? Will you lead us thither?

TOM: Why, Sire, I — ah —

PUSS (*Winking at* TOM): I'll go on ahead and make all ready. (*Exits.*)

TOM: I shall be charmed, Sire. (TOM *offers hand to* PRINCESS.)

CURTAIN

* * *

SCENE 3

SETTING: *Hall of* OGRE'S *castle. At head of a heavy table, spread with plenty of food and drink, sits the* OGRE, *in a large armchair. Enter* SERVANT, *followed by* PUSS-IN-BOOTS.

OGRE: Grrumph!

SERVANT (*Bowing*): A cat, sir!

OGRE: What's that? A cat?

PUSS (*Bowing*): If it please you, sir, I could not pass so fine a castle without paying my respects to you, sir.

OGRE: Sit down there. You have heard about me, then?

PUSS: I have heard of your great powers, but I really can't believe all I am told. They say you can even change yourself into an animal, like a lion or an elephant.

OGRE: You don't believe it? Well, you shall see. (*Goes through door back of chair.* PUSS *sticks paw into dish on table and licks paw.* OGRE *reënters in lion's form.*)

OGRE (*Roaring*): Grrrr!

PUSS (*Jumping*): Meow! (PUSS *scrambles up on table, losing boots as he climbs.* OGRE *leaps about hall, roaring, then exits and reënters in his own form.*)

OGRE: I scared you, didn't I?

PUSS (*Getting down off table*): Yes, sir, I must say I was a little bit scared. I see you can turn into a lion; but there is something else they told me that I still can't believe.

OGRE: And what is that?

PUSS: They said that you could turn yourself into a mouse or a rat, but of course you couldn't make yourself as small as that.

OGRE: Oh, I can't can't I? Well, I'll show you! (*Exits as before.* A MOUSE *runs out across floor, as in Act I.* PUSS *leaps on* MOUSE *and makes show of crunching with teeth while hiding* MOUSE *in bag.*)

PUSS: There, that's the last of Mr. Ogre! (*Puts on boots and seats himself in* OGRE'S *chair. Sound of bugles offstage. Enter* SERVANT.)

SERVANT (*Bowing*): His Majesty the King, Her Royal Highness the Princess, and His Lordship the Marquis of Carabas, sir!

PUSS: Very well, I will see them in the shape of a cat. (*Enter* KING, PRINCESS, TOM, LORDS *and* LADIES.)

PUSS (*Rising and bowing*): Welcome to the home of the Marquis of Carabas, Your Majesty!

KING: What a splendid castle you have, my Lord Marquis!

TOM: Yes, Sire. May it please you to sit down and dine with me? (KING, PRINCESS, TOM, LORDS *and* LADIES *sit at table.* PUSS *waits on them, pouring drinks in glasses.*)

PRINCESS: You have a most uncommon cat, sir.

TOM: Yes, and clever as he is handsome, Your Highness.

KING (*Lifting glass*): To your health, my dear Marquis, and may you do me the honor of marrying my daughter!

TOM: Sire, it will make me happy if Her Highness will consent. (*Dropping to one knee before the* PRINCESS.)

PRINCESS: Dear Marquis, I consented the moment I saw you! (*Taking her hand,* TOM *and the* PRINCESS *bow and curtsy to the* KING.)

TOM: And now I have only one more favor to ask of Your Majesty.

KING: What is it, my son?

TOM: That Your Majesty grant knighthood to my faithful servant, Puss-in-Boots.

KING (*Rising*): Come, Puss, kneel down before me. (PUSS *kneels before* KING. *Drawing sword, the* KING *taps* PUSS *on the shoulder.*) Sir Puss, I dub thee Knight!

ALL: Hurrah for Sir Puss-in-Boots! (HERALDS *march in, blowing bugles, and* GUARDS *present arms.* PUSS *bows.*)

THE END

THE THREE SILLIES

by Alice Very

Characters

FARMER MUTTONCHOP
MRS. MUTTONCHOP
LILY LOU, *their daughter*
MR. FUDDYMAN, *her suitor*
JIM, *a farm hand*
JOANN, *a maid*
FARMER JONAS
FARMER HODGE
A CAT (*black*)
A COW
NEIGHBORS

SETTING: *A farmyard.*

AT RISE: *The* BLACK CAT *dozes in the porch. Enter* MR. FUDDYMAN, *dressed in his best.*

FUDDYMAN (*Calling*): Friend Muttonchop, say, are you there?

MUTTONCHOP (*Running from house, with outstretched hands*):
Why, Fuddyman, I do declare!

FUDDYMAN:
I've come here, as I planned with you,
To court your daughter, Lily Lou.
(*Starts to walk under ladder toward* MUTTONCHOP.)

MUTTONCHOP: No, No! Don't take another step!

FUDDYMAN:
What! That's the way your word is kept?
Last night you promised if I had her —

MUTTONCHOP: Yes, but don't walk beneath that ladder.

FUDDYMAN (*Walking around*):
I didn't mean any harm.

MUTTONCHOP:
My daughter must not take alarm.
She's such a timid little creature

We must protect her tender nature. (*Calling*) Oh, Mrs. Muttonchop, come here! (*Enter* MRS. MUTTONCHOP, *all smiles. With a wave of his hand.*) Your future son-in-law, my dear. (*As* MRS. MUTTONCHOP *starts to greet* MR. FUDDYMAN *the* BLACK CAT *crosses the yard.*)

MRS. MUTTONCHOP (*Screaming*): Oh, mercy!

MR. FUDDYMAN: Am I bad as that?

MRS. MUTTONCHOP: No, no, not you — the cat!

MUTTONCHOP: Scat! Scat! (MUTTONCHOP *and* FUDDYMAN *chase* CAT *into barn.*)

CAT: Meow!

MRS. MUTTONCHOP: It's most unlucky!

FUDDYMAN:

I'm perplexed.
What luckless thing shall I see next?
(*Enter* LILY LOU, *plump and red-cheeked.*)

LILY LOU: You called me?

MRS. MUTTONCHOP: Mr. Fuddyman has come to ask for your hand.

LILY LOU: My hand? I thought he wanted me!

FUDDYMAN: And so I do, if you'll agree. (*Giving her a ring.*) This ring may help you to decide.

LILY LOU:

Well, I'll consent to be your bride.
The ring is pretty and you're kind.

FUDDYMAN: Then let us seal it with a kiss. (LILY LOU *starts toward* FUDDYMAN; *stops suddenly with a look of horror.*)

LILY LOU: Oh, dear!

MRS. MUTTONCHOP: My daughter, what's amiss?

FUDDYMAN: Don't tell me you have changed your mind?

LILY LOU:

Oh, no, I only saw the moon
Over my shoulder — Oh, I'll swoon!

FUDDYMAN (*Offering his arm*):

If you'll allow me, I've heard tell,
A pinch of salt will break the spell.

MUTTONCHOP:

A bite of food will cheer her up.
It's nearly time for us to sup.

MRS. MUTTONCHOP:

I'll fry some meat cakes in the spider

And send her for a jug of cider.

MUTTONCHOP:

And while you're busy at your labors,
I'll send our Jim to tell the neighbors.
(*MRS. MUTTONCHOP, LILY LOU, and FUDDYMAN go into house.*)

MUTTONCHOP (*Calling*):

Come, Jim, put on your Sunday shoes,
And tell the neighbors the great news!

JIM (*Shuffling in, carrying axe*):

I've got to feed the ducks and hens,
And shut the chickens in their pens,
And swill the pigs and milk the cow.
I haven't time to bother now.

MUTTONCHOP:

Go, tell the neighbors as I say.
Joann can do your work today.
(*MUTTONCHOP goes into house. JIM hangs axe on nails by chopping block. Enter LILY LOU with cider jug, sits down on stool and starts filling jug from spigot.*)

JIM: What luck! What luck!

LILY LOU: What's lucky, Jim?

JIM: I say, you're lucky getting him.

LILY LOU: Indeed! He's lucky to get me!

JIM: Well, we shall see, we shall see. (*LILY LOU throws cider in jug at JIM, who runs into barn, while she resumes filling jug.*)

LILY LOU (*Gazing at axe*):

Dear me, who put that axe up there?
It might fall down and no one care.
What if we had a little boy,
His father's pride, his mother's joy,
And sent him with the cider jug —
A heavy thing for him to lug —
And just as he was passing under
The axe fell like a clap of thunder!
Oh, dear, oh, dear! Oh, me, oh, my!
It's all so sad it makes me cry! (*Weeping*)

MRS. MUTTONCHOP (*Entering*):

Daughter, what keeps you there so long?
Tell me, has anything gone wrong?

LILY LOU:

Dear mother, if you only knew

The troubles we are coming to!
Our little boy might come some day
And find the axe there in his way,
Then if the axe fell on his head
I'm much afraid he would be dead.

MRS. MUTTONCHOP:
My daughter, you will drive me wild.
That dreadful axe! That darling child!
(*Weeps. Enter* MR. MUTTONCHOP.)

MR. MUTTONCHOP: Where is the cider? What are you doing?

MRS. MUTTONCHOP:
Oh, father, there is trouble brewing.
The axe that hangs there on the wall,
Some day it will be sure to fall
And hit our grandson passing by
And if it does he'll surely die!

MUTTONCHOP:
Alas, alack! Poor boy! Too bad!
How shocking! Oh, how very sad! (*Weeps*)

FUDDYMAN (*Entering*): What's this? I find you all in tears!

LILY LOU (*Pointing*):
There is the cause of all our fears.
The axe you see is going to fall
And kill our boy and grieve us all.

FUDDYMAN:
Is that all? I can plainly see
There are no sillies like you three.
And till I find three worse than you
I'll never marry Lily Lou.

MUTTONCHOP: What, you don't mean to marry Lily?

FUDDYMAN: Not till I find three more as silly.

LILY LOU (*Brightly*):
But how much harder it would be
To find three wiser ones than we!

MUTTONCHOP: She's right. It may not be so bad.

MRS. MUTTONCHOP:
It's settled, then? Oh, I'm so glad!
Then, since you've had the luck to win her,
We'll all go in and have our dinner.

FUDDYMAN: It's not as settled as you think.

MUTTONCHOP (*Looking at cider, which has run over floor*):
That's true.
There's nothing left to drink.

MRS. MUTTONCHOP: We'll all drink milk. (*Calling*) Joann, come here.

JOANN (*Entering with* COW, *which she drives with a long switch*):
Don't call so loud, miss; I can hear.

MRS. MUTTONCHOP: Bring us some milk, please, right away.

JOANN: Cow won't give milk till she has hay.

MRS. MUTTONCHOP: Then give her some.

JOANN: I wish I could.
I've tried and tried, but it's no good.
(*Calling*) Come, bos, come bos! (*Putting cow's foot on ladder*)

COW: Moo-oo-oo-oo!

JOANN:
You see? I don't know what to do.
The more I try, she gets the madder.
She's bound she won't go up the ladder.

FUDDYMAN:
Why not go up yourself instead,
And throw the hay down on her head?

JOANN: Myself? I never thought of it!

FUDDYMAN:
There's *one* that's sillier, I admit.
But tell me where I'll find another?

LILY LOU: Why certainly; it's Jim, her brother. (*Enter* JIM, *in his best clothes, and stocking feet, carrying a pair of large shiny boots. He sets down the boots carefully and tries to make a running broad jump at them.*)

JIM:
Just when a fellow wants to rest
They always tell you to get dressed.

FUDDYMAN: Pray tell me what you aim to do?

JIM: Of course, I'm putting on my shoe.

FUDDYMAN: But tell me why you do it so?

JIM: Why, that's the only way I know.

FUDDYMAN:
If you would only use your head,
You'd put it on your foot instead.

JIM: A pretty trick, if you can do it!

FUDDYMAN: Your head is just as thick as suet! See here! (*Making* JIM *sit on stool and putting his boot on*)

JIM: So that's the way it's done!

FUDDYMAN: That makes another silly one.
(*Sound of shouting offstage*)
But what's that noise outside the gate?

LILY LOU: Our neighbors come to celebrate. (*Enter* NEIGHBORS *in great excitement.*)

FARMER JONAS:
Quick, neighbor, quick! A hoe or rake!
The moon has fallen in the lake!

MUTTONCHOP: It has?

FARMER HODGE:
Come on and see! We caught her!
She's down there underneath the water!

FUDDYMAN:
That's her reflection that you spy.
The moon's still floating in the sky.

FARMER JONAS:
The man is crazy. If you please,
He'll tell us next the moon's green cheese!

FARMER HODGE: Well, so it is. I ought to know.

FARMER JONAS: Why are we waiting, then? Let's go!
(NEIGHBORS *seize hoes and rakes from porch and run out, followed by* JIM, *with the axe.*)

FUDDYMAN:
Did I say three? A town full, rather,
And each one sillier than the other!

LILY LOU:
Remember what you promised me
If you could find a sillier three.

FUDDYMAN:
You win. I'll take you, willy-nilly.
Which proves that I'm the one that's silly.

THE END

A KETTLE OF BRAINS

by Gweneira M. Williams

Characters

NOODLE
CLEM, *his friend.*
THE WISE WOMAN
BETSY

SCENE 1

SETTING: *Glade with trees.*

AT RISE: *Stage is empty. Enter* NOODLE, *grinning, ill at ease, and frightened, propelled by* CLEM, *his friend.*

NOODLE: But I'm afraid.
CLEM (*Pushing him ahead*): You want brains, don't you?
NOODLE (*Grinning*): I need a whole kettleful, I do.
CLEM: Well, then, go to the Wise Woman's hut there and knock at the door. Maybe she knows a way to get you some brains.
NOODLE (*Hanging back*): Aw, Clem, I'm scared.
CLEM: Noodle, don't be more of a fool than you can help, will you? Go on!
NOODLE (*Knocking*): Hello, in there! (*Door creaks open.* WISE WOMAN *appears, comes out to pot on fire. Ignores* NOODLE, *who stands foolishly, mouth open.*)
WISE WOMAN: What do you want, fool?
NOODLE (*Standing on one foot*): Well, well, well—
CLEM: Noodle, you're a fool. (*Exit.*)
NOODLE: It's a fine day isn't it?
WISE WOMAN: Maybe.
NOODLE: Maybe it'll rain, though.
WISE WOMAN: Maybe.
NOODLE (*Gulping*): Or on the other hand, maybe it won't.

WISE WOMAN: Maybe. (*A pause, during which she ignores him. He scratches his head, and twists his hat in his hands, drops it, picks it up, tries again.*)

NOODLE: Well, I can't think of anything else to say about the weather. But, but—

WISE WOMAN: Maybe.

NOODLE (*In a rush*): The crops are getting on fine, aren't they?

WISE WOMAN: Maybe.

NOODLE: The cows are getting fat.

WISE WOMAN: Maybe.

NOODLE: Wise Woman, I thought maybe you could help me.

WISE WOMAN: Maybe.

NOODLE (*Desperately*): I need brains. Do you sell any?

WISE WOMAN: Maybe.

NOODLE: What d'you mean, maybe?

WISE WOMAN: Maybe I have and maybe I haven't. It depends on what kind of brains you want. Do you want a king's brains?

NOODLE (*Mouth falling open*): Ooh, no!

WISE WOMAN: Or a teacher's brains?

NOODLE (*Even more appalled*): Lawkamercy, no!

WISE WOMAN: Or a wizard's brains?

NOODLE: Heavens to Betsy, no!

WISE WOMAN: Well, what kind do you want?

NOODLE: Oh, just ordinary brains. You see, I don't have any at all, at all!

WISE WOMAN: Maybe I can help you.

NOODLE: Maybe, how?

WISE WOMAN (*Striking in kettle*): You'll have to help yourself first.

NOODLE (*Eagerly*): Oh, if I can, I will.

WISE WOMAN (*Paying no attention*): You'll have to bring me the thing you love best.

NOODLE (*Mouth falling open*): How can I do that?

WISE WOMAN: That's not for me to say. But when you bring it here, you must answer a riddle for me, so I'll be sure you can use the brains.

NOODLE (*Appalled*): Oh, gosh to goodness! (*Turns and slouches slowly out.*)

CURTAIN

* * *

SCENE 2

SETTING: *The same. Door of hut is closed.*

AT RISE: *Stage is empty. Enter* NOODLE, *dragging large bag in which something wriggles. He goes over to kettle, peeks inside, shakes head. Then he leaves bag near kettle, while he knocks at hut door.* WISE WOMAN *comes out.*

NOODLE (*Eagerly*): Here it is, Wise Woman.

WISE WOMAN: Here's what?

NOODLE: The thing I love best. (*Points at bag, goes over and touches it.*)

WISE WOMAN: What is it?

NOODLE: My pig! (WISE WOMAN *picks it up, takes it into hut, and reappears.*)

WISE WOMAN: Well, now that you're here, can you answer this riddle?

NOODLE: I'll try!

WISE WOMAN: Tell me, what runs without feet?

NOODLE (*Stupidly*): Maybe—caterpillars?

WISE WOMAN: Idiot! You're not ready for brains! Come back again when you've decided what you love next best! (*Goes into hut, slams door.*)

NOODLE (*Pondering*): What runs without feet? Gosh—I loved my pig best. What do I love best after him? (*Scratches head.*) I know! My hen, my little hen! Wait a minute, hey, wait! Just wait a minute! I'll be back in a jiffy! Wait! (*Rushes out. As soon as he is gone,* WISE WOMAN *comes out of hut, sits down before kettle, stirs it, meanwhile chanting.*)

WISE WOMAN:

Burn, fire, burn,
Burn to a turn,
One thing's sure as sky and fire,
Fools never learn!

(NOODLE *rushes back in, panting, with a small bag.*)

NOODLE: Here it is! Wait, here it is! Gosh, my goodness, heavens to Betsy, wait! Don't sell that kettle of brains! Here it is!

WISE WOMAN: Here's what?

NOODLE: Here's the thing I love best next to my pig!

WISE WOMAN: What is it?

NOODLE: My hen!

WISE WOMAN: Are you ready to answer me another riddle?

NOODLE (*Panting but valiant*): I'll try!

WISE WOMAN: Well, tell me this: what is yellow, and shining, and isn't gold?

NOODLE (*Hopefully*): Cheese, maybe?

WISE WOMAN: Fool! (*Picks up bag with hen in it, goes into hut. Peers out again.*) What do you love next to your hen? (*Slams door.*)

NOODLE (*Sitting down on the boulder, begins to cry*): What'll I do? I've lost the two things I love best! And I still haven't any brains! Whatever will I do now? They were the only two things I loved in the whole world! (*He cries loudly and dismally. Enter* BETSY.)

BETSY: Well, for heaven's sake!

NOODLE (*Between sobs*): Who are you?

BETSY: My name's Betsy. What's the matter with you?

NOOLE: Oh, I wanted some brains—

BETSY: Why?

NOODLE: I don't have any.

BETSY: Well, where did you think you could get some?

NOODLE (*Between sobs*): The Wise Woman in there (*He gestures towards hut*) said she'd give me some if I brought her the things I loved best in the world—(*Bursts out crying again.*)

BETSY: Well, did she?

NOODLE: No-o-o!

BETSY: You poor fool, why not?

NOODLE: I c-c-c-couldn't answer the r-r-r-riddles sh-sh-sh-she asked m-me!

BETSY (*Taking out a handkerchief, going up to him*): There, don't cry. Don't you have anyone to take care of you, silly?

NOODLE: No.

BETSY: No one?

NOODLE (*Crying*): No one!

BETSY: Well, I wouldn't mind taking care of you myself!

NOODLE: Lawkamercy!

BETSY: Well?

NOODLE (*Stammering*): You mean—*marry* me?

BETSY: Well, yes. (*She takes a huge handkerchief out of her pocket and wipes his eyes with it.*)

NOODLE (*Between wipes*): Can you cook?

BETSY: Yes.

NOODLE (*Half heard in handkerchief*): Can you sew?

BETSY: Yes.

NOODLE (*Half smothered*): Can you scrub?

BETSY: Yes, I can. Will you have me? (*She gives his nose a tweak, and he blows it into handkerchief.*)

NOODLE: Well, I guess you'd do as well as anyone else.

BETSY: That's fine.

NOODLE: But, but—

BETSY: But what?

NOODLE (*As he is helped to his feet by* BETSY): What shall I do about the Wise Woman?

BETSY: Let *me* talk to her!

NOODLE: Oh, no, no!

BETSY: Why not?

NOODLE: I'm afraid!

BETSY: I'm not! Don't you need brains?

NOODLE: Well, yes.

BETSY: Come on, then, come on! (*She drags him to the door of the hut, banging on it vigorously.*)

WISE WOMAN (*Opening door*): What do you want, young woman?

BETSY: Brains for my husband here!

WISE WOMAN: Your husband, eh?

BETSY: We're going to be married.

WISE WOMAN: Does he love you the best of anything in the world?

BETSY: Go on, tell her!

NOODLE (*Hanging head*): I reckon I do.

BETSY: There, now give him the brains!

WISE WOMAN: Not so fast, not so fast. He'll have to answer the riddles first.

NOODLE (*His face falling*): Oh, the riddles.

BETSY (*Undaunted*): What are they?

WISE WOMAN: What runs without feet? (NOODLE *stands stupidly, mouth open, until* BETSY *nudges him, whispers something.*)

NOODLE: Well, my goodness, water!

WISE WOMAN: H'm.

BETSY: Give him the next riddle.

WISE WOMAN: What's yellow and shining and isn't gold? (NOODLE *looks desperate until* BETSY *nudges him again and whispers.*)

NOODLE: Well, heavens to Betsy, the sun!

WISE WOMAN: H'm. Here's the third riddle. What has first no legs, then two legs, then four legs? (NOODLE *looks at* BETSY, *who makes swimming motions with her hands. He continues to look blank until she hisses at him.*)

NOODLE: A tadpole!

WISE WOMAN (*Crossly*): That's right. Now go away!

NOODLE: But where is the kettleful of brains?

WISE WOMAN: You already have them.

NOODLE (*Feeling in his pockets*): Where? I don't find them.

WISE WOMAN: In your wife's head, silly. The only cure for a fool is a good wife. And you have one—or will have one. I can't help you any more. Be off with you! Good day! (*She goes into hut, slams the door.*)

NOODLE (*Standing still, scratching his head*): Maybe she's right! (*Turning to* BETSY) You'll marry me, lass? I won't have any brains if you don't!

BETSY: Of course I will! I have brains enough for two anyway! Come on! (*She takes his hand and drags him off stage as the curtain falls.*)

THE END

THE FLAG OF THE UNITED STATES

by Lindsey Barbee

Characters

COMMODORE HOPKINS
JOHN PAUL JONES
CHAIRMAN OF THE CONTINENTAL CONGRESS
CAPTAIN ABRAHAM SWARTOUT
AN OFFICER
ELIZABETH
JANE
PENELOPE
DRUSILLA
MEMBER OF THE CONTINENTAL CONGRESS
CAPTAIN STEPHEN DRIVER
A CIVILIAN
BEARER OF THE FLAG
BUGLER
MEMBERS OF THE SCHOOL COLOR GUARD
OTHER SCHOOL CHILDREN

PROLOGUE

AT RISE: *The stage is clear save for the floating flag upon a standard. The Voice is offstage.*

THE VOICE:

I am the flag of the United States.
The symbol of a nation that has loved
Above all else its freedom, that has fought
Its many battles for the principles
Of justice, freedom, right and equity.

I am the country's glowing Stars and Stripes;
Red for endurance, courage, growth and strength;
White for the purity of high ideals;
Blue for all loyalty and truth and faith.

I am Old Glory — flag for which men die
That right may conquer; flag for which men live
That they may strive for better, higher things.

I am the flag of the United States.

EPISODE 1

Raising of First Navy Ensign
December 3, 1775

AT RISE: *Against a background of ropes, sails, etc., stand* JOHN PAUL JONES *and the* COMMODORE. *The* COMMODORE *holds a flag of thirteen alternate red and white stripes with the British Jack in the upper corner.*

COMMODORE:
Our flagship, *Alfred,* on the Delaware
Gives promise of a long and sturdy life.
It needs the banner of our native land
To mark its voyage, to proclaim the fact
That thirteen colonies have formed a pact,
A pact of independence not suppressed
By edict of an unjust king. This flag,
This Navy Ensign with its thirteen stripes
Of glowing red then white will signify
Our steadfast union, while the corner shows
The symbol of Great Britain, proving that
The colonies still love the mother land.
Here, John Paul Jones, our naval hero, hoist
This flag upon our stern that all the world
May know the Navy Ensign.
JOHN PAUL JONES: Commodore,
It is the proudest moment of my life
To raise this symbol of our hope, our faith,
Our loyalty to the brave land we call
Our own. This flag and I are twins;
In life, in death, we never shall be parted.
As long as we can float, we float together;
If we must sink, we shall go down as one. (*Hoists flag*)

CURTAIN

* * *

Episode 2

Flag Adopted by Congress
June 14, 1777

At Rise: *A small table is placed toward left center, and back of this table stands the chairman of the Continental Congress. Those members of the Congress occupying the first row are visible.*

Chairman:

Until the present time, our flag has borne
The British symbol. On July the fourth,
We signed the document that told the world
Of independence; hence the need to claim
A banner that will truly symbolize
Our union. On this fourteenth day of June
In seventeen seventy-seven, we present
This resolution: (*Reads*)

That the flag of the United States be thirteen stripes alternate red and white, that the union be thirteen stars, white in a blue field representing a new constellation.

You will signify
Your wish regarding its acceptance.
(*Pauses*) Those
In favor will respond the usual way.
(*A chorus of yeas*)
And those opposed? (*Pauses*) The resolution stands.

CURTAIN

Episode 3

The Making of the First American Flag
August 3, 1777

Captain:

The British are assembling on all sides.
We know that an attack is imminent.

Officer:

From Massachusetts come two hundred men
To reinforce our garrison. They bring
The news that Congress has decreed a flag
To signify our union. Thirteen stripes,

First red, then white, against a field of blue,
With thirteen stars of white. I would that we
Could float this flag while we defend our fort.

CAPTAIN:
Why not? Necessity enables us
To act with what we have. (*Takes blue cloak from his arm*)
This cloak of mine
Will furnish what you call the field of blue.
The white shirts of the soldiers are at hand;

OFFICER (*Eagerly*):
And doubtless some wife of a soldier lad
Will find a petticoat of red.

CAPTAIN: Then why
Not make our standard flutter in the breeze
For all our British enemies to see?
'Twill be the first time that the Stars and Stripes
Are fired upon; and it will also be
The making of America's first flag.

CURTAIN

EPISODE 4

The First Official Salute to the Flag
February, 1778

SETTING: Portsmouth, New Hampshire, November 1777.

AT RISE: *To the sound of stately music, four lovely girls are dancing a minuet. As the dance is finished and the music dies away, the four separate.*

ELIZABETH:
No wonder that we want to dance and sing —
Burgoyne has surrendered!

JANE: And our land
Is truly free — a nation.

PENELOPE: Have you heard
That John Paul Jones will take the news to France?
The news of the surrender?

DRUSILLA: Have you heard
That he is made commander of the ship
Called *Ranger?*

ELIZABETH: Oh, it will be wonderful
To know that other ships salute our flag —
The flag of our Republic.

JANE: Listen, girls.
As yet there is no standard flag. I mean
It is decreed but still has not been made
Or fashioned for official use.

PENELOPE: We must
Produce a flag. The *Ranger* must not sail
Without a symbol.

DRUSILLA: Then it is our task
To *make* the flag — of red and white and blue

ELIZABETH (*Eagerly*): My cape — it is the proper shade of red.
(*Catches cape from nearby chair*)

JANE (*To* DRUSILLA): Our panniers are white.

PENELOPE: My gown is blue.

ELIZABETH: Then why not make the flag from what we have?

JANE:
So proud we'll be to know that from the ship
Our flag will fly — the flag that we have made
From our own silken gowns.

DRUSILLA: There is no time
To waste. The ship will leave perchance at dawn
Upon its way to France.

ELIZABETH: Then let's to work.
(*Curtseying*) My cape — my cape of red —

JANE (*Curtseying to* DRUSILLA): Our panniers of white —

PENELOPE: My dear blue gown —
We'll change them all into a flag — a flag
That merits the salute of other ships,
Our flag of red and white and blue.

ELIZABETH (*Suddenly*): Then, haste.

CURTAIN

* * *

EPISODE 5

Final Ruling of Congress
April 14, 1818

AT RISE: *Again the Continental Congress with its small table, its chairman and its first row of members.*

MEMBER (*Rising*):
May I request the reading, Mr. Chairman,
Of that enactment whereby Congress rules
The final placing of the Stars and Stripes.

CHAIRMAN (*Reading*):
Congress enacts that there shall always be
The thirteen stripes that are symbolical
Of thirteen colonies — that each new state
Will mean a star upon a field of blue,
This star to be affixed on July fourth
That follows the admission of the state.

CURTAIN

* * *

EPISODE 6

"Old Glory"
1831

SETTING: *Salem, Massachusetts*

AT RISE: *Again the background of sails, ropes, a large wheel.*

CIVILIAN:
To Captain Stephen Driver and his ship
The citizens of Salem, in respect
And admiration offer this fair flag,
The Stars and Stripes that it may always wave
Through storm and stress as this brave ship begins
Its long and perilous voyage round the world. (*Extends the flag which he holds to* CAPTAIN DRIVER)

CAPTAIN DRIVER (*As he takes the flag*):
I raise the colors. I salute — Old Glory.

CURTAIN

* * *

Episode 7

National Salute to the Flag

At Rise: *To the sound of martial music, the color guard of the school marches in. There is the bearer of the flag, the bugler, and the members of the guard. Orders are given, formations are made, and finally all come to attention with the standard bearer and the bugler in the center, and the various members on either side. After a moment, the flag is lifted high and the members of the guard unite in the oath of allegiance:* "I pledge allegiance to the flag of the United States of America and to the Republic for which it stands: one nation, under God, indivisible, with Liberty and Justice for all."

THE END

NO BRAVER SOLDIER

by J. C. Eleanor Bierling

Characters

THOMAS WHEELER, *a prosperous farmer, dwelling on the outskirts of Concord*
MARGARET WHEELER, *his wife*
BEN, *their son, about* 15
JONATHAN ALLSTON, *a Boston cousin, younger than Ben*
ABEL POMFREY } *minutemen from the neighborhood*
EZRA HAYWARD }
FAITH } *Wheeler's daughters,* 12 *and* 10
ESTHER }
LUBIN FALES, *another neighbor*
SIR FRANCIS MONTFORD } *British Officers*
MAJOR RICHARD CAMPBELL }

TIME: 6:00 *A.M. on the morning of April* 19, 1775.

SETTING: *The kitchen of the Wheeler farm which is situated to the south of Concord on the Lexington-Concord Road.*

AT RISE: THOMAS WHEELER *has just finished his breakfast but remains seated at the table, his attention fixed upon* ABEL POMFREY *and* EZRA HAYWOOD, *who are standing in the doorway.* BEN *and* JONATHAN *are seated opposite to him, dividing their attention between the conversation and the hearty business of consuming porridge.* MARGARET WHEELER *is busy at the dresser, cutting large slices of bacon. She stops occasionally to listen to her husband's words.*

WHEELER (*Laying down knife and fork*): Everything in readiness then, Ezra?

EZRA: Yes, Mr. Wheeler. Our minutemen have been hastening to the North Bridge in Concord these past two hours.

WHEELER: How many have gone up already?

EZRA: Fifteen, thereabouts. From Lincoln and the environs.

WHEELER: There should be more. Didn't Prescott reach all the farms?

EZRA: There'll be more, Mr. Wheeler, don't you worry. They'll be coming in from the back country.

WHEELER: How many, would you say?

EZRA (*In deep thought*): Well er . . . about . . . ten or so. Wouldn't you say that, Abel?

ABEL (*Removing a piece of straw from his mouth*): I reckon ten's about right, Ezra.

WHEELER (*Reflecting and strumming on the table with the fingers of his right hand*): I'll wait for them here, then. They'll pass this way. (*Rises from his chair but remains close to the table.*) You had better get to Concord as fast as you can, boys. I've been there and back this morning. The men are pouring in from Acton, Chelmsford, Bedford and Carlisle. Report to Colonel Barrett at once — he's in command of the militia there — and see that the men obey orders without question.

ABEL: Yes, sir.

EZRA: Yes, Mr. Wheeler. (*They turn to go, but* WHEELER *calls them back.*)

WHEELER: You both have a knowledge of where the stores of our arms and ammunition are hid. Guard that knowledge with your life.

EZRA: I wouldn't let any Britisher get that out of me, Wheeler.

ABEL: Nor me, either.

WHEELER: I am sure of that. But a friendly warning's not amiss. We'll meet at the North Bridge, then. Godspeed! (*As* ABEL *and* EZRA *go off, the door leading into the entryway opens and* FAITH *and* ESTHER *enter.* MR. WHEELER *goes to hearth.*)

FAITH *and* ESTHER (*Together*): Good morning, Father. Good morning, Mother.

MRS. WHEELER (*Who has been moving between dresser and fireplace much occupied with the business of preparing soup in the iron kettle, hanging on the crane*): You are tardy. The sun has been up this half hour.

FAITH: We are sorry, Mother. We were —

BEN (*Interrupting excitedly*): What excitement *you* missed! They should have been here last night, shouldn't they, Jonathan! (JONATHAN *nods and smiles.*)

FAITH (*Advancing with* ESTHER *to the middle of the room*): What happened? Why didn't you wake us then?

BEN (*Loftily*): Girls are no good in an emergency. You would have screamed when Dr. Prescott rode up to the door like a ghost in the moonlight.

FAITH (*Reproachfully*): No, we wouldn't.

BEN: Yes you would, because you're a girl. My, but I'm glad I'm a boy!

ESTHER (*With a show of spirit*): Well, if I were a boy I'd be a better one than you are and I wouldn't plague my sisters.

JONATHAN: Good. There's an answer for you, Ben.

MR. WHEELER (*Having been speaking to* MRS. WHEELER *during this dialogue, now returns to the table*): Quiet! Enough has been said. This is no time for foolish jest. Faith and Esther — come here! (MR. WHEELER *sits down in his chair and draws* ESTHER *to his knee.* FAITH *stands close to him at his left side. The two boys have risen and come over, remaining to the right of him.* MRS. WHEELER, *with an affectionate glance at the group, goes out of the door.*) Daughters, this is a grave and trying time for our country. We have been expecting trouble, and it is now come upon us. Last night Dr. Warren sent a trusted courier, Mr. Paul Revere, from Boston to give us warning that the Regulars are coming. Of course you know that their purpose is to take Mr. Samuel Adams and the Hon. Mr. Hancock prisoners, but I understand that they were foiled. Dr. Prescott tells me that Mr. Revere was able to reach Lexington in time to give the alarm, and Mr. Adams and Mr. Hancock are already making their way to Woburn. That is good news, but the British will now advance upon Concord to seize our stores of ammunition.

BEN: And they will find that they are blocked in their designs. How I wish that I could see their faces when they discover that the cannon and powder have all been removed to places of safety.

MR. WHEELER: You may see more of their faces than you care to before the sun is set.

JONATHAN: I wish it had been my part to ride with Mr. Revere. It is a fine thing to arouse the people to their danger.

MR. WHEELER: You speak a truth there, Jonathan. But it is also a fine thing to offer one's life in protection of our people and that is our part.

JONATHAN (*Wistfully*) : But you said that I could not accompany you, sir.

MR. WHEELER : That is true. While you are my guest you are under my protection. You must abide here. As for Ben, he is older and I fear though I would, I could not keep the lad at home.

BEN (*Laying aside his fun-loving attitude and squaring his shoulders*) : Nay, Father, my place is at your side. And I am a man now and can shoulder a musket as well as any. Have I not trained with the Minutemen these many months and know their oath by heart?

WHEELER : And that oath?

BEN : To hold ourselves in readiness at a minute's warning with arms and ammunition.

WHEELER : Good. (*He sets* ESTHER *down and starts to rise. With a little cry* FAITH *clings to him.*)

FAITH : Oh, Father, do not go. You may be killed.

WHEELER : Hush, Faith. That does not sound like the courageous patriot such as I know you to be. Let us put our faith in God. Ben, bring me the Bible. (*While* BEN *fetches the Bible off the mantel,* FAITH, *hiding her tears in her handkerchief, goes back to the fireplace.* ESTHER *moves quickly to her side to console her.* BEN *places the Bible at his mother's place, so that* MR. WHEELER, *in reading from it, faces the audience. At this point* MRS. WHEELER *reenters the room, carrying a cream bucket and an armful of clean clothes. Seeing that her husband is about to read, she lays these down and, drawing* FAITH *and* ESTHER *to her side, stands near the hearth, an arm about each.* BEN, *holding his father's hat which he has taken from its hook, stands at his father's right hand.* JONATHAN, *who has run to the window anticipating the arrival of the other minutemen, turns toward his uncle and remains standing in respectful attention.* WHEELER *opens the Book and reads from the* 91*st Psalm—verses* 1 *to* 12 *and verse* 16. *As he closes the book, he looks up and sighs deeply. Then, taking the hat from Ben's hand, he turns and faces his wife.*) God guard you all.

MRS. WHEELER : And you, Thomas.

BEN : Mother, I am going, too.

MRS. WHEELER : May God bring you back unharmed, child.

ESTHER : Father, why am I not a man? 'Tis hard to stay at home when I would fight.

JONATHAN: Think how hard it is for me, Esther — nearly grown to man's estate, yet, by my uncle's command, forced to stay here.

MR. WHEELER: You have these loved ones to protect, Jonathan. And that is no small part. Think you that you are capable of it?

JONATHAN: Yes, Uncle. I will guard them with my life.

MR. WHEELER: Spoken like a man. I leave them in your care. And now, Esther, remember, a woman's place is home. Keep *it* and your heart above reproach. The sanctity of our homes and the liberty of our land are the things we are giving our lives for. (*They move quickly to the door. Here* WHEELER *pauses, his gaze fixed on the Ridge yonder.*) Nowhere in sight, Margaret. But I cannot wait. My mind is beset with anxieties for the men at Concord. Should the others pass this way, hurry them on to the Old North Bridge. And now we're off. (MRS. WHEELER *remains at the door until they are out of sight. She stands erect, her lips moving prayerfully.* FAITH *stands at her mother's side, endeavoring to be as courageous. But* ESTHER *and* JONATHAN *kneel on the bench at the window, waving handkerchief and cap.*)

MRS. WHEELER: Come, let us close the door. The air is yet chill at this early hour. Faith, your porringers stand on the hearthstone yet. 'Twill be a mercy if the food is fit to eat.

FAITH: Mother, I could not eat.

MRS. WHEELER: You need the strength for the work that lies before us. Esther, bring the syrup. You may both sit here on the settle before the fire if you like. (FAITH *and* ESTHER *begin on their porridge.*) Now to list the things we have yet to do; butter to churn, this hearth to sweep, wool to card and the soup to finish. Yes, we must have hot soup for the men's return. And hot water for the wounded. Jonathan, that is what you can do now. Draw water and bring in more logs. Pile them here. (*Indicates a place to the left of the fireplace, where some few yet remain.*)

JONATHAN: That I will, Aunt Margaret. (*He goes out.*)

ESTHER (*Anxiously*): Mother, do you fear the Redcoats coming? Will they search our house?

MRS. WHEELER: It is not unlikely. But we have naught to fear. Your father has seen to it that the hidden stores of arms and ammunition are nowhere near. We will treat the British courteously if they come and save ourselves unpleasant treatment in return.

FAITH: Hark! I hear the sound of cartwheels now.

MRS. WHEELER: They will not come in carts, Faith. (*But they listen anxiously as the sound of creaking wagon wheels draws nearer.* MRS. WHEELER *goes to the door and, throwing it open, gasps in astonishment.*) Why Lubin Fales! Why aren't you at Concord?

FALES (*Standing on the steps and gazing at* MRS. WHEELER *sheepishly*): I couldn't, ma'am, till I got these hid.

MRS. WHEELER: These? And what may these be?

FALES: Muskets, ma'am, and powder. Such as were took out of Concord Saturday last.

MRS. WHEELER: But they were in *your* care, Lubin. Why haven't *you* hidden them?

FALES: No, ma'am, I couldn't a-done that. What with Sarie sick abed and a dozen younguns dragging at my heels and the cattle gone astray and —

MRS. WHEELER: Stop! Methinks you are a fool, Lubin, or worse. To bring this load of ammunition over the roads in broad daylight and the British almost upon us. Do you want to be seized and all this lost?

FALES: It's but a few muskets, ma'am, and a handful of powder.

MRS. WHEELER: Everything is precious in the eyes of the militia. Think of our poorly armed men as pitted against the British well-armed troops!

FALES: I couldn't a-left these with Sarie, ma'am, and me gone to the wars.

MRS. WHEELER: But you would bring suspicion upon the house of a good neighbor. And Mr. Wheeler has ever befriended you. (FALES *stands there miserably, twisting his cap in his hands.*) Well! don't stand there gaping. Bring them in. I'm all out of patience with you and have no words to speak my mind. (JONATHAN, *having carried in several logs during this interval and stacked them close to the wall, now looks on in deep concern.* FAITH *and* ESTHER *have been peering around the back of the settle.*) Lend your shoulder to this task, Jonathan, that it may be done the more quickly. Now to find a place for them. (*As* JONATHAN *follows* FALES *out* MRS. WHEELER *goes to the table, deep distress visible in every feature. Suddenly her hand touches the Bible and she rests it there. Then an expression of quiet strength supersedes the look of anxiety. She remains standing thus until* JONATHAN *and* FALES *bring in the few muskets and the powder keg and lay them down; then she turns around.*) I have been over-hasty, Lubin. You must forgive me. Leave these in our care and go to Concord, now. But wait (*As* LUBIN *starts to go*) — take this to Sarah. She has been ailing over-long and this will give her strength. (*Goes to the kettle and dips out hot soup into a pewter jug which she hands to Lubin.*)

FALES: Thank ye, ma'am. She'll be that pleased — and I'll be goin' now. (*Touches his cap and goes out.*)

MRS. WHEELER (*Turning to* JONATHAN): Now, where to hide these!

JONATHAN: That is what I've been trying to figure out, Aunt. Could I hide them in the wood shed, or bury them in the garden?

MRS. WHEELER: Nay, Jonathan. That is the first place they would search. We must think of something better.

ESTHER (*Who has been darting about now discovers open spaces behind the wood pile*): Jonathan, here is a place. The muskets will fit behind these logs nicely. (MRS. WHEELER *and* JONATHAN *exchange a look of relief.* FAITH, *unnoticed, slips out.*)

MRS. WHEELER: It might do, indeed.

ESTHER: And we can pull the settle up close to the logs. See. (*She attempts to shove the settle forward.*)

JONATHAN (*With a show of amusement*): Think you they could not move that if they had a mind to, Esther?

ESTHER (*Taken aback*): Well — (*Claps her hands in delight as a new inspiration comes to her.*) I will feign illness and will lie upon the settle, and no gentleman will dare to move it then.

MRS. WHEELER: Little do you know what gentlemen *will* do in time of war, Esther. Furthermore, I would not permit you to feign illness and act a lie. (ESTHER, *disheartened at her mother's words, walks over to the window and gazes out disconsolately.* MRS. WHEELER *and* JONATHAN *converse in a low tone as they stuff muskets behind the logs. The door opens and* FAITH *enters, burdened with two heavy quilts.*)

FAITH: Could you conceal the muskets under these, Mother?

MRS. WHEELER (*A little impatiently*): Of course not, Faith. But don't look so distressed. Here, pile them on the settle. (FAITH *lays the quilts down, and* JONATHAN *and the two women push the settle around with its back close to the logs, completely concealing the woodpile.*)

ESTHER (*In great agitation*): Jonathan! (*She beckons* JONATHAN *to come to her and, as soon as he reaches her side, directs his attention to the garden. He looks out, then nods in great excitement.*)

JONATHAN: Yes, British officers, two of them. And they are turning in here. (*They gaze at each other in great consternation, then* ESTHER, *with renewed spirit, jumps from the bench and runs across the room to the woodshed. She opens the door and disappears.*)

MRS. WHEELER (*Turning around*): You said British officers, Jonathan?

JONATHAN: Yes, Aunt Margaret. They have dismounted and are coming toward the front door. But have no fear, I will take care of you.

MRS. WHEELER (*Her gaze resting on the keg of powder*): We have forgotten that. Here, Jonathan, help me to lift it on the settle. We will make use of Faith's quilts, after all. But they will see it. (*They place the keg on the settle and cover it with the quilts.*) Now, Faith, be at your churning. Keep your hands busy and make no outcry when the men come in. (*A loud rapping is heard at the front of the house.*)

JONATHAN: Shall I let them in, Aunt Margaret?

MRS. WHEELER: Let them rap again. I must have time to think. (*Glances around suddenly.*) Where is Esther? Where has the child gone? (*The door of the woodshed is pushed open and Esther leans, half-fainting, against it.*)

ESTHER: Mother, come quickly. My foot! The axe —

FAITH: Oh, Esther. (*Puts her hand to her mouth in consternation.*)

JONATHAN: You are hurt. (JONATHAN *and* MRS. WHEELER *rush to her and half carry her to the settle. The blood is visible from a gash in her foot. In the face of an emergency,* FAITH *suddenly becomes as courageous as her mother. Folding one of the quilts over the powder keg to act as a pillow, she then spreads the other across the back and seat, and assists the others in lay-*

ing ESTHER *upon it.* MRS. WHEELER *gently draws off slipper and stocking. Rapping is heard now at kitchen door.*)

MRS. WHEELER: Cold water, Faith — and those cloths — see, lying there. (*Glancing at the others*) Courage. (*In the face of* ESTHER'*s noble act, no signs of nervousness or fear are visible in their faces.* FAITH *remains holding* ESTHER'S *hand, her head high, ready to face a firing squad, if need be.* JONATHAN *hastens to the fireplace and, pulling down an old musket, stands near the dresser, holding it tightly.* MRS. WHEELER *busies herself in the act of bathing the wound.*) Come in. (*The door is thrown open and two officers of the British Army enter.*) How may I serve you, sirs?

MONTFORD: We are under orders, Madam, to search this house.

MRS. WHEELER: The house may be searched. I ask your pardon for not being able to rise. As you see, we are in great distress.

MONTFORD (*Courteously*): An accident, Madam?

MRS. WHEELER: My daughter has cut her foot.

MONTFORD (*Advancing*): Permit me to look at it. I have a knowledge of the science of medicine. (*He waits for her consent and, at her nod, quietly probes the wound.*)

ESTHER (*Wincing, holds her handkerchief to her lips and grips* FAITH'S *hand with her own*): Oh, please, sir!

MONTFORD: The wound is not deep, and no arteries severed. It is a clean cut and should heal quickly.

MRS. WHEELER: The Lord be praised for that. Thank you, sir, for your kindness.

MONTFORD (*Bowing*): It is a pleasure to serve you—(*Looking at* ESTHER) and the young lady is a gallant soldier — an honor to any — (*Pauses, as if searching for words*) army. (JONATHAN'S *hand tightens on the musket and he takes a step forward.*) No offense there, lad. Put up your musket. If the men in the Colonial militia are as brave a force as you, we may have need to look to our guns. (*Turning to* CAMPBELL) Major, search the house. (*Bowing to* MRS. WHEELER) Madam, we will return in a moment. (MRS. WHEELER *indicates to* MAJOR CAMPBELL *the door at the left, and* MONTFORD *goes out the door leading to the shed. There is no word from the others left in the room.* MRS. WHEELER *bandages the foot.* FAITH *tries to make her sister more comfortable.* JONATHAN *retains his position near the dresser.* MONTFORD *returns first and, taking his posi-*

tion near the door leading outside, waits until CAMPBELL *returns.*) Madam, I crave your pardon for disturbing you in this distressing time. Were it not for Major Pitcairn's orders, I would not have troubled you. I thank you for your courtesy and bid you good day.

MRS. WHEELER: Good day, sir. (*The two officers go out. The group in the room relax in utter relief and* MRS. WHEELER, *noticing* JONATHAN'S *face, laughs.*) Jonathan, your face is a picture.

JONATHAN: Had they made any other remark about our Militia or Dr. Warren or Mr. Adams, or advanced to the woodpile, I would have run them through. (*He shows them a long butchering knife he has hidden under the herbs on the dresser, and they all laugh heartily. Laying down his musket, he runs to the door and listens to the retreating hoof beats. Suddenly his face brightens.*) Listen!

FAITH: The Fife and Drum!! (*The strains of "Yankee Doodle" come from afar.*)

JONATHAN: The air the Redcoats taunt us with in Boston. But they'll live to rue the day for that.

MRS. WHEELER: Yankee Doodle — our men — Concord. Through sacrifice, liberty shall come to this land and, with the help of God, we shall be free. (*They all lift their faces reverently as the curtain goes down.*)

THE END

THE HEROINE OF WREN

by Ella Stratton Colbo

Characters

CYNTHIA HALL, *age 12*
GRANDMOTHER HALL
GRANDFATHER HALL
A RIDER
COLONEL DAY
AN ORDERLY

SCENE 1

TIME: *Revolutionary War Days.*

SETTING: *The simple interior of a cottage in the Quaker village of Wren.*

AT RISE: GRANDMOTHER HALL, *in Quaker garb, is discovered tidying the room. She works busily for a moment or so. Sound effect off stage of rapidly running feet. She stops work, listens.* CYNTHIA *bursts into room, crying out excitedly.*

CYNTHIA: Oh, Grandmother, Grandmother, the Redcoats are coming! A rider on horseback is at Neighbor Randall's telling them about it. I was bringing their morning pail of milk to them for Grandfather, and I heard him say we must all leave the village and flee for our lives. Oh, Grandmother, what *shall* we do? I am *so* afraid! (*Begins to sob.*)

GRANDMOTHER (*Coming over to* CYNTHIA *and putting her arm about her*) : I have no doubt the rider will soon be here to tell thy Grandfather all about it, so do thou run to the barn and tell him to come quickly. But first, dry thy tears, Cynthia, like the brave little maid thou art. Thy Grandfather is an old man. Since thy father and his brothers fell at Brandywine he has had naught but trouble, and this will be the worst of all. We must be brave, and try not to make it harder for him.

CYNTHIA (*Earnestly, drying tears*): Oh, I will, Grandmother. I will! Grandfather shall not see me cry.

GRANDMOTHER: That's my own brave little maid. (*Pats* CYNTHIA'S *shoulder*) Now run to call him. There is no time to lose. (*Exit* CYNTHIA. GRANDMOTHER *stands with clasped hands and bowed head, says slowly and bitterly*) War is a *cruel, cruel* thing! (*Sound effect of galloping hoofs outside. Loud knock at door. She goes to open door, admits a man breathless as though from great haste.*)

RIDER (*Urgently*): Mistress Hall? I *must* have speech with thy husband, *at once*.

GRANDMOTHER: He is coming from the barn, Sir. Here he is now. (*Enter* GRANDFATHER *and* CYNTHIA *through back door.*)

RIDER: I am sorry, good Sir, to be the bearer of bad tidings this fine morning, but I am sent to warn all the villagers that they must gather up what food they may, and fly to the hills at once. The Redcoats are less than a day's march to the westward, plundering and pillaging as they come. They are likely to camp in this village tonight. Make ready to leave with all possible haste. Neighbor Randall will stop for you presently, bringing two horses that you may ride. Remember, for safety's sake, you must all be in the hills by nightfall!

GRANDFATHER: Thank you kindly, Sir. We will make ready to leave at once.

RIDER: Now I must hasten to warn the others. (*Exits hurriedly.*)

GRANDMOTHER (*To* GRANDFATHER): I will bring thee the good silver from the chest in the bedroom, and do thou dig a hole in the garden to bury it where the Redcoats will not think to look. Cynthia, child, run to find an old sack to wrap it well. (GRANDMOTHER *exits hurriedly.*)

GRANDFATHER: Yes, Cynthia, lass, thou must lend thy willing hands and quick feet this day to spare thy Grandmother's strength for the sad times ahead. Since our own lads have given their lives for their country, thou art all we have left. Grandmother is old, and I fear that tonight she will look down from the hills to see the sky reddened with the fires of our burning homes.

CYNTHIA: I will do my very best—but oh, Grandfather, even the

Redcoats couldn't be *that* cruel! (*Re-enter* GRANDMOTHER, *carrying parcel wrapped in cloth, hands it to* GRANDFATHER.)

GRANDMOTHER: Here is the silver. I found a sack to wrap it. Do thou hide it quickly.

GRANDFATHER: Don't thee worry. I will find a safe hiding place for thy treasure, and then I will give Old Bess a last good feeding. Mayhap the Redcoats will not harm her if she gives them plenty of her good milk for supper. (*Exits.*)

GRANDMOTHER: We have much to do before Neighbor Randall calls for us. Cynthia lass, run to the kitchen and pack the market basket with the corn cakes, and whatever else is left of yesterday's food. Take all thee can find. We will not dare to light fires to cook our supper tonight. Hurry, child. I will busy myself saving what little we may be able to take with us. (*Exits hurriedly.*)

CYNTHIA (*Speaks aloud to herself*): Burn our home! Harm Old Bess! If the Redcoats only knew how good and kind Grandmother and Grandfather are — how old and helpless — and that no one is left in all this world to care for them, but a little girl, they could not be so cruel and heartless. *I know.* I will write them a note, and ask them to spare this house — this *whole village.* It can do no harm, and it may do some good. (*Seats herself at table, picks up quill pen, dips it in ink well, and begins to write busily. Folds up the sheet of paper. Writes across the outside in large letters—"To the Redcoats." Rises, places letter in her pocket. Leaves room. Enter* GRANDMOTHER, *with two parcels in her hands, and two cloaks over her arm. She places parcels on table.*)

GRANDMOTHER: There—I do not dare to take time for more—besides we could carry little else. (*Calls loudly.*) Cynthia! (GRANDFATHER *enters.*)

GRANDFATHER: Make ready quickly. I can see the villagers beginning to come down the road. (GRANDMOTHER *puts on her hood and cloak. Calls loudly again*) Cynthia! (CYNTHIA *enters with filled market basket covered with white cloth. Places basket on table.* GRANDMOTHER *ties on* CYNTHIA'S *hood and hands her a cloak.*) Come lass, we must start at once. (CYNTHIA *slips into her cloak and picks up basket.* GRANDMOTHER *and* GRANDFATHER *go to front door.* CYNTHIA *starts to follow them, stops, runs to back window and looks out.*)

CYNTHIA: Grandmother, Grandfather! What about the geese? If I open the gate to their pen, they might go to the woods and be safe, too. I simply couldn't *bear* to have anything happen to my pet gander, Nicodemus!

GRANDMOTHER: Run and open the gate to their pen, if it will make thee any happier; but geese are silly things, lass, and they are sure to come back home at nightfall, Redcoats or no Redcoats. Hurry then, and meet us at the front gate. (*They exit to front,* CYNTHIA *to back. In a moment* CYNTHIA *reappears, takes note from her pocket—hastily scribbles a few more lines on bottom of paper, refolds it and places it against candlestick on table, with words "To the Redcoats" visible to audience.*)

GRANDFATHER (*Calling from off stage*): Cynthia, Cynthia! Neighbor Randall is waiting for thee!

CYNTHIA (*Running out of door*): Coming, Grandfather!

CURTAIN

* * *

SCENE 2

SETTING: *The same.*

AT RISE: *Enter* COLONEL DAY, *followed by his orderly.*

COLONEL: I like the looks of this cottage. It shall be my headquarters while we are camped in the village of Wren. Post two guards outside the door. I am both hungry and weary. Give the cook orders to get supper under way immediately. (*Removes sword and places it on table. Notices* CYNTHIA'S *letter*) Ho — what have we here? A message "To the Redcoats," as I live! (*Picks up letter, opens it and reads slowly and loudly*) "Gentlemen: My name is Cynthia Hall. I am twelve years old. I live in this house with my good, kind grandmother and grandfather. It is the only home we have. I beg of you not to burn our home, or harm Old Bess, our cow. We would freeze and starve when the cold winter comes. We need our garden, too, and dear grandmother loves her flowers. Please, sirs, if you have little daughters of your own, think how they would cry if harm came to their homes. We have done you no harm. Have pity on my poor grandparents, and mercy on the village of Wren. Respectfully yours, Mistress Cynthia Hall. P.S. I have just let our geese out of their pens, but they are silly things and will come home at nightfall, Redcoats or no Redcoats. Nicodemus, the gander, is my very own pet. I love him dearly. I could not bear to lose Nicodemus." (COLONEL *laughs heartily*) Ho, ho! Written bravely enough, little Mistress Hall! Methinks my own little Cynthia at home would be as quick to speak up spunkily for her rights if danger threatened. Orderly! Take this command to Captain Flynn, and have him make it known to all the men. Tell him there is to be absolutely no pillage or plunder this night. They are to take only what is needed for one good meal for men and animals—and leave everything else unharmed—*everything,* understand! Tell them I am doing this as a favor to a brave little rebel lass, who asked it in the name of our own little daughters in far-away England. At dawn we will march on, leaving the village as we found it.

ORDERLY (*Saluting*): Very well, Sir. (*Exits.* COLONEL *walks to back window. Looks out, laughs again.*)

COLONEL: Just as she said! Geese *are* silly things! Here they all come, single file, with Nicodemus himself in the lead! I fear the cook will covet those plump fowls for our supper, but they shall spare your pet, I promise you, Mistress Cynthia! (*Seats himself in rocker.*) We will have a good meal, and a good night's rest, and at dawn we will march away, leaving the village of Wren as we found it, like the gentlemen Mistress Cynthia Hall gives us credit for being. (*Rises*) I have business with the cook — about Nicodemus! (Exit.)

CURTAIN

* * *

SCENE 3

SETTING: *The same.*

AT RISE: COLONEL DAY *is discovered seated at table, writing with the quill pen on one of the sheets of paper. Enter* ORDERLY.

ORDERLY: Good morning, Colonel. I have come to report breakfast ready at the cook train.

COLONEL: I will be there presently. Tell me, how have the men observed my order to spare the village?

ORDERLY: Very well, Sir. There was a good bit of muttering among the hot-heads at first but Singing Sam soon fixed that! Hark, Sir! (*They both listen. Off stage several deep voices join in a rollicking chant—*)

VOICES (*Off*):

It has come to pass
That a rebel lass
Is leading his Majesty's men!
For the Colonel's daughter,
From over the water,
We spare the village of Wren!

(COLONEL *nods and smiles with satisfaction. Folds sheet of paper. Addresses it to* MISTRESS CYNTHIA HALL. *Rises, places letter on table against candlestick, where he found* CYNTHIA'S *letter. Exits—*ORDERLY *follows him.*)

CURTAIN

* * *

SCENE 4

SETTING: *The same.*

AT RISE: *Enter* GRANDMOTHER *and* CYNTHIA *very slowly.* CYNTHIA *is helping her to walk. In center of room they stop and look about.*

GRANDMOTHER (*Wonderingly*) : Why, look thee, lass! Nothing is really harmed. Nothing is broken or spoiled! Not a thing! And a good scrubbing with soap and water will make quick work of all these muddy tracks on the floor. We have much to be thankful for, my child. (*Enter* GRANDFATHER.)

GRANDFATHER: The whole village is rejoicing! Nothing has been harmed! Nothing has been taken but food! God hath indeed wrought a miracle for the village of Wren! Our garden is the same as we left it—not even a flower has been trampled. And Old Bess is contentedly chewing her cud in the barn!

GRANDMOTHER: What is this? (*Points to letter.*) It looks like a letter. It is! With Cynthia's name written upon it. (*Picks up letter and hands it to* CYNTHIA.) Read it, child. Read it aloud.

CYNTHIA (*Opens letter and reads*): "To a Brave Little Rebel Lass: You could not have known it when you wrote your note, begging us to spare your grandparents' home and the village of Wren, but I *do* have a little Cynthia of my own in far away England to whom I would wish no harm to come. Therefore, with the compliments of Mistress Cynthia Day, your prayer is granted. My kindest regards, Colonel Day." (*Shouts joyously*) It is indeed a miracle! Grandfather, have you looked for our geese? Is Nicodemus safe? (*Runs to window and looks out, points*) There he is! Walking about all alone. They must have stolen the others after all. (GRANDMOTHER *and* GRANDFATHER *join her at the window.*)

GRANDFATHER: Yes. He is all alone, and the gate is closed again.

GRANDMOTHER: Whatever can that be tied about his neck? It looks like a small sack. It looks heavy. It swings back and forth as he walks. Run outside, lass, and see what it is. Do thou bring it here. (*Exit* CYNTHIA.)

GRANDFATHER: So *that* is the story! It is to our little Cynthia that the whole village of Wren owes its thanks!

GRANDMOTHER: Aye, we may well be proud of our little lass this day. She has served her country bravely and well. But here she comes—(*Enter* CYNTHIA, *laughing.*)

CYNTHIA: Look, look! A whole sackful of coins! And another note from the Redcoats! Listen to this!
Dear Mistress Cynthia:
We have eaten your geese,
But not to be rude!

We were tired and hungry,
We had to have food.

We each leave in payment,
A coin with your pet.
You said we were gentlemen —
We will not forget!

The Redcoats.

GRANDFATHER (*Taking sack and spilling coins out on the table*): A goodly sum, indeed!

GRANDMOTHER: We can buy many, many things with all these coins! The Redcoats *do* have hearts!

CYNTHIA: And *I* have Nicodemus! Oh, I am so happy!

GRANDFATHER (*Placing his hand on* CYNTHIA'S *head*): Thy Grandmother and I are proud of thee, this day, little maid. Thee is a *real heroine!*

THE END

HEARTS OF OAK

by May Emery Hall

Characters

EDMOND ANDROS, *governor of New England*
TIMOTHY MARSHALL, *member of Connecticut Assembly*
LUKE MARSHALL, *his son*
SIMON HUMPHREY, *assemblyman*
BENJAMIN HUMPHREY, *his son*
GOVERNOR'S BODY GUARD
CITIZENS

SCENE 1

SETTING: *Council chamber, Hartford, Connecticut.*

TIME: *Twilight of an October day, 1687.*

AT RISE: *A small group of men enter. As they remove their hats, an expression of grim determination is revealed on every face. So absorbed are they in earnest conversation, all talking and gesturing at once, that at first they fail to notice the two boys,* LUKE *and* BENJAMIN, *who have stealthily crept into the room after them. They are dirty and their clothes are torn. The pair, keeping close together, are plainly trying to escape observation.*

MARSHALL (*Clapping his hands over his ears*): One at a time! One at a time, *please!* (*The din gradually subsides.*)
HUMPHREY: 'Tis difficult to keep one's mouth shut, Timothy, with matters of such importance as we have on hand tonight.
MARSHALL: All the more reason, then, don't you think, to proceed with calmness and order?
HUMPHREY: I suppose so.
MARSHALL: Time is short. The governor may be here any moment now. (*A groan from the company greets the announcement. Two or three make wry faces.*)
HUMPHREY: Whatever induced the king to put that tyrant over

us passes my comprehension. You'd think New York and New Jersey would be enough for him without grabbing all New England.

MARSHALL: Right you are, Simon. Just consider the power that goes with the office! The making of laws, raising of taxes, settling of disputes in courts of his own choice —

HUMPHREY: I know. It looks as if the very word "liberty" were destined to disappear altogether from the English language to make way for such degrading terms as "threats," "punishment," "imprisonment" and such. (*During the foregoing dialogue,* LUKE *and* BENJAMIN, *on hands and knees, have crawled unnoticed to the table and hidden themselves underneath it. They listen in close attention to all that is said.*)

MARSHALL: We must stand firm tonight — every man of us. Are you all with me?

THE COMPANY (*In chorus*): Aye! Aye!

MARSHALL: Even if we have to pay for our daring?

THE COMPANY: Aye! Aye!

MARSHALL: Self-government has gained too good a start in this colony of Connecticut to be snuffed out now. We'll have to remind Andros what he has apparently forgotten — if he ever knew — that nearly fifty years ago our freemen adopted the first written democratic constitution on record. And the liberal royal charter later granted by Charles was in keeping with it. Now to have King James snatch it away —

CITIZEN (*Interrupting uneasily*): Those are brave words, Mr. Marshall, and we are all in agreement with the spirit of them. But seeing that Massachusetts has been coerced into giving up *her* charter —

MARSHALL: You mean, what's to prevent Connecticut's submitting, too?

CITIZEN: Well — yes.

MARSHALL: Stout hearts and the determined will to see that justice is done. Can you think of better weapons?

THE COMPANY (*Deafeningly*): No! No!

MARSHALL: The God-given right to rule ourselves we will never surrender without a struggle! (*The company applaud loudly. The two boys, forgetting themselves, join in, too, and prolong their clapping beyond that of the others. Their hiding-place is therefore discovered by their elders, who turn their surprised attention in the direction of the table.)*

MARSHALL (*Recognizing his son and speaking sternly*): Come here!

HUMPHREY (*Pointing to* BENJAMIN): And you, too. (*The boys, embarrassed and sheepish, get to their feet and approach the two men. The others crowd around curiously.*)

MARSHALL: How did you get in here?

LUKE (*Stumbling*): We — we — just — just — came in.

MARSHALL (*Dryly*): And without taking the trouble, it appears, to ask permission. Don't you know this is no place for striplings? A man's job has got to be done this night. Why, then —

LUKE: Oh, father! Neither Benjamin nor I have ever seen the governor and so —

MARSHALL: Well, that's no reason for pitying yourselves.

LUKE: But he'll have his armed guard with him, won't he?

MARSHALL: In all probability. Still, what is there about soldiers—

HUMPHREY (*Interrupting*): Oh, let the lads stay, Timothy, now that they're here. Why not set them to work straightening out the room? They can at least arrange the benches and light the candles. Yes, and start a fire, too. (*Rubbing his hands together*) This fall dampness goes through one's very bones.

MARSHALL: As you say, Simon. (*Noticing the boys' dishevelled condition for the first time*) But what ever have you been up to? Your clothes are torn and dirty.

LUKE: I know, father. But you see, Benjamin said he could climb higher up in the old oak than I could, and I had to take his dare.

MARSHALL (*Interested in spite of himself*): Well, and who won?

LUKE (*Proudly*): *I* did, of course!

BENJAMIN: He wouldn't have if it hadn't been for a big hollow in the very heart of the tree that we didn't know about. I slipped into it.

HUMPHREY: So! Lucky you got off without a broken neck!

MARSHALL: Lucky, indeed! Now get busy, you two! Quick! (*With alacrity* LUKE *and* BENJAMIN *set about their tasks, first lighting the candles and then placing the benches in parallel rows. They draw the single chair up to the table as if for the governor. After that they busy themselves at the hearth, arranging wood in preparation for a fire. While this work is under way, the older men continue their conversation.*)

HUMPHREY (*Anxiously*): I trust you brought the charter along with you, Timothy.

MARSHALL (*Producing the document from a capacious pocket*): Here it is. (*Holds it up that all may see.*) It may seem to the king and governor a mere scrap of paper to be destroyed and forgotten, but we freemen know that its value is not to be measured in any such belittling fashion. Life, liberty, self-government are all tied up in this parchment — everything, in short, that makes life worth living. We will never give it up!

THE COMPANY (*Lustily*): Never!

LUKE AND BENJAMIN (*After the others*): Never! (*They emphasize the exclamation by noisily banging the bellows on the hearth.*)

CITIZEN: Do you think the governor will really carry out his threat of taking the charter from us, Mr. Marshall?

MARSHALL: Without doubt.

CITIZEN: Here? In this room?

MARSHALL: Where else?

CITIZEN (*Shaking his head*): I fear there'll be trouble, then. Especially if he brings a guard along.

MARSHALL (*Impatiently*): Fear is something we just decided was to be left out of this evening's proceedings.

CITIZEN (*Doubtfully*): I suppose we could hide the charter if we had to.

LUKE (*Shrilly*): Father! I know a good hiding-place!

MARSHALL: Well? Speak out.

LUKE: I'd rather tell you alone. (*Goes to his father and whispers in his ear.*)

MARSHALL: Not such a bad idea, that! (*Voices are heard outside. A deadly silence falls on the group as each man maintains a listening attitude. The next moment the door is thrown open, admitting* GOVERNOR ANDROS *and his guard. All are resplendent in red military uniform trimmed with gold braid. The guardsmen are equipped with swords. The governor's manner is haughty, his bearing that of one used to being obeyed.*)

ANDROS (*Approaching* MARSHALL *as his penetrating gaze falls upon the charter in* MARSHALL'S *hand*): Good evening.

MARSHALL (*Respectfully*): Good evening, your honor. (*Indicating the chair at the table*) Pray be seated, sir.

ANDROS (*Seating himself*): May I ask your name?

MARSHALL: Timothy Marshall, sir.

ANDROS: An accredited member of the Connecticut General Assembly, I take it.

MARSHALL: Its spokesman, as well. May I introduce my fellow citizens? (*Indicating each in turn*) Simon Humphrey, Thomas Carroll, Daniel Foster —

ANDROS (*Interrupting curtly*): That will do. Suppose we get at once to the business in hand. You are all aware, of course, of the errand which brings me hither.

MARSHALL (*With dignity*): We are, your honor.

ANDROS: Acting, then, upon instructions from His Majesty, King James, I demand that you deliver into my hands —

MARSHALL (*Showing irritation*): Is not "demand" a rather strong word, sir, to use in dealing with freemen?

ANDROS (*Irritated in turn*): Indeed! More than ever am I convinced that my royal master knew what he was about in curtailing what you are pleased to call your rights. Methinks the air of this Connecticut colony has gone to your head like new wine.

MARSHALL: Call it what you will, sir, we shall continue to imbibe it — the Connecticut air and the wine of liberty both.

ANDROS (*With increasing anger*): Is that a threat?

MARSHALL: A mere statement of fact, rather.

ANDROS: Nevertheless, a statement that borders close upon sedition.

MARSHALL: I fail to see it in that light, sir. We have been a self-governing body, have been granted in our charter certain rights and have, in every way, tried to be honest, law-abiding citizens —loyal subjects to His Majesty, as well.

ANDROS: Methinks you are seeking a quarrel where no quarrel exists. What is there about your giving up a mere piece of paper that should occasion such an outburst as this you are indulging in?

MARSHALL: The very fact, sir, that our precious charter is no more than a "mere piece of paper" in your opinion shows how little you understand the issue at stake.

ANDROS: I like not the tone of your remarks, Timothy Marshall.

MARSHALL: Still less, if you will pardon me, sir, do I like the substance of yours.

ANDROS (*Half-rising*): Have a care! You are forgetting that I have not only a right to make my demands but also the means of enforcing the same. (*The soldiers of his guard tighten their hold on their swords.*)

MARSHALL: This business is unpleasant enough for all of us, Heaven knows, but we do not intend to surrender our charter.

ANDROS: I will give you five minutes in which to change your mind.

MARSHALL: I do not need *one* minute. Nor do the others.

ANDROS: In that case, you can only blame yourselves if serious trouble ensues. (*Pointing to the charter*) Will you hand me that worthless document or not?

MARSHALL (*Firmly*): I will *not!* (*Draws back, putting the charter behind him.*)

ANDROS (*To the guard*): Close in! Don't let him escape!

MARSHALL (*In a low tone to* HUMPHREY *as the soldiers start to obey*): Out with the candles, Simon! (HUMPHREY, *aided by the other citizens, and* BENJAMIN, *hastily begin blowing out the lights. Noisy confusion follows. In the growing darkness,* LUKE *creeps up behind his father and snatches the charter.*)

LUKE (*In a whisper*): Don't you worry, father! I'll look out for it! (*He surreptiously makes for the door with* BENJAMIN, *apparently unnoticed by the Governor and his guard. Both disappear. The room becomes pitch black as the tumult increases.*)

ANDROS (*His voice shaking with anger*): You'll pay for this! And pay well, you — you — (*The curtain falls.*)

* * *

SCENE 2

SETTING: *Same as Scene 1, two years later, 1689.*

AT RISE: *The company are seated as before.* LUKE *and* BENJAMIN *are absent.*

CITIZEN: I suppose we can look for the boys any minute now.

MARSHALL: Unless one or the other has broken a limb.

HUMPHREY: We shouldn't have allowed them to climb that oak, I suppose, Timothy.

MARSHALL: Perhaps not. But I felt we owed them that much after their discovery.

HUMPHREY: Even so, 'tis a risky business. You remember how Benjamin fell into the treacherous hollow in the first place?

MARSHALL: Shall I ever forget? It was that which provided us with an answer to the governor's demands.

HUMPHREY: *Ex*-governor now, thank Heaven.

MARSHALL: Amen! Ex-king, too. Now that the high-handed James is in exile, perhaps Andros will find out while he languishes in jail, that we Connecticut freemen meant what we said.

HUMPHREY: And that royal favor does not necessarily mean a life job. It is like sitting on a keg of gunpowder which may go off at any minute. How soon will he be shipped to England?

MARSHALL: They say on the first vessel leaving Boston. (*A sound of boyish conversation is heard outside. The door is presently thrown open, admitting* LUKE *and* BENJAMIN. *They have developed greatly in two years, appearing much more mature and manly than in Scene 1.* LUKE *carries a discolored piece of parchment in his hand.*)

LUKE (*Rushing to his father*): Here it is, Father! (*Hands him the parchment.*)

MARSHALL (*Holding it aloft*): The charter of our liberties at last! (*A murmur of approval is heard on all sides. The men draw nearer* MARSHALL *in order to examine the document.*)

HUMPHREY: Not much the worse, I'll be bound, for its long stay in the hollow oak through summer rains and winter snows!

LUKE (*Proudly*): Oh, Benjamin and I knew what we were doing!

BENJAMIN: We couldn't have found a better shelter if we had hunted everywhere!

MARSHALL (*Thoughtfully*): To think that the sturdy old tree which has outwitted a king's agent was nothing but a tiny acorn once! In the same marvellous way does democracy grow — a weak, sprouting thing at first, reaching uncertainly for the right kind of soil and nourishment, but after a time strengthening its fibres to such an extent that even kings cannot tear it asunder.

HUMPHREY: True, Timothy. But, after all, you might say it was an accident which led to our hiding the charter so securely.

MARSHALL (*Shaking his head*): No, not an accident. It was something far bigger than a tree which saved the day for us.

HUMPHREY (*Puzzled*): What, then?

MARSHALL: Hearts of oak!

THE END

A SON OF LIBERTY

by Esther Lipnick

Characters

SARAH ORNE
PAUL REVERE
RACHEL REVERE, *his second wife*
SAMUEL ADAMS
DR. JOSEPH WARREN
PAUL REVERE, JR.
PAUL REVERE, III

SCENE 1

TIME: *Late spring,* 1757.

SETTING: *Room in Paul Revere's home.*

BEFORE RISE: *Horses' hoofs can be heard on the cobblestone walk, and distant drums accompanying the cries of men selling their wares; then comes the ringing of four bells and the street crier announcing "Four o'clock and all is well."*

AT RISE: SARAH ORNE, *breathless, runs in through center door, carrying a straw basket of mayflowers. She is pursued by breathless and laughing* PAUL REVERE. SARAH *seats herself on settee.*

SARAH (*Laughing and still out of breath, as* PAUL *stands looking down at her*): Oh Paul, that's not fair — making a lady look so undignified — and I'm sure that Reverend Ebenezer saw us.

PAUL (*Laughing heartily*): And next Sunday the sermon will run as follows: My good people, take heed that your daughters do not fall into the pit of the devil. You must watch that their actions befit their sex. Last week in the streets of Boston in broad daylight, mind you I said Boston and *in broad daylight,* I saw a young woman pursued by a young swain. Shall we allow such undignified conduct to continue?

SARAH (*Laughing*): Oh, stop that, Paul. It's not right, imitating a clergyman, and besides you asked me here because you had a surprise for me.

PAUL: Surprise? (*Pretends to be puzzled.*) Surprise? Oh, yes, so I have.

SARAH: Oh, Paul, stop teasing — I must know.

PAUL: Hmm — well, you're forgetting something, too. (*Points to flowers.*)

SARAH: Oh, the flowers! I nearly forgot. Fetch some water, quickly, Paul.

PAUL: Well, you stay here a moment, and try to guess what I have for you, while I run out to the barrel for some water. (SARAH *gets up and starts picking out the flowers as* PAUL *exits.*)

SARAH (*To herself*): I wonder what it is — can it be — oh, how I hope it is. I love him so. Oh, would that he'd ask me today. (PAUL *comes in pretending not to have heard the last remark.*)

PAUL: Well, here you are, Sary.

SARAH (*Startled, turns and blushes*): Oh, thank you, Paul. (SARAH *starts to arrange flowers.* PAUL *seats himself in a rocker and watches her work.*)

PAUL: Well, have you guessed what I have for you?

SARAH (*Shyly*): A copperplate? (PAUL *shakes his head.*) Your mother must have roast goose for dinner and wants me to stay.

PAUL: No, but you may stay for dinner.

SARAH: Then is it the locket you promised me?

PAUL: No, all wrong. (*He goes to cabinet and takes a large silver spoon and gives it to Sarah, watching her face.*)

SARAH (*Trying to hide her disappointment*): A spoon! Oh, Paul, how lovely. I'll treasure it — always.

PAUL: Perhaps you will, Sary, when you know its story. My father gave it to me before he died. He told me to give it to my wife, because he hoped she would always cook good meals for me. Father was French, you know, and had a French sense of humor as well as a love of good food.

SARAH (*Looks at him wistfully, holding the spoon closer, a tear in her eye*): Oh, Paul, I'll treasure it, always.

PAUL: Then, Sarah, you will be my wife?

SARAH: Oh, yes, Paul. (*Smiling*) But I'll have to learn to be a good cook.

PAUL (*Smiles*): I'm sure you will — and I'll make you proud. I'll become the best silversmith in the country.

SARAH: Oh, I know you will.

PAUL (*Rather pensively*): But there are other things that I must do, too.

SARAH (*With anxiety*): Paul, you're not going to fight the French and Indians again?

PAUL: No, not that, this time. But I'm going to fight for the same thing I fought for before — so many things have to be fought for.

SARAH (*Completely perplexed, wrinkles her brow*): Paul, sometimes I don't understand you.

PAUL (*Walks over and takes her hand*): Perhaps there are a few things you should know about your future husband. It starts way back in a sunny village in France, Riaucaud, near the great city of Bordeaux. My family, the Revoires, were good people who cultivated their vineyards and tended to their own affairs, but Louis XIV would not let them be. That tyrant denied them the right to worship as they wanted. All the Huguenots were persecuted — and so my father came to Boston to seek freedom.

SARAH: Oh, I'm so glad he did! Just think — I might never have known you.

PAUL (*Smiles at her*): Thank you, Sary. Perhaps now you'll understand why I was so eager to fight the French, to suffer cold and hunger on Lake Champlain.

SARAH: I never knew, before.

PAUL: And that's what I'm going to fight for all my life. I hate tyrants. A man must have liberty — Sary — liberty.

SARAH (*Goes to stand beside him, and echoes softly*): Liberty — (*In the distance bells ring, and the town crier is heard, "Five o'clock and all's well."*)

CURTAIN

* * *

SCENE 2

TIME: *Late afternoon, December* 16, 1773.

SETTING: *Paul Revere's workshop.*

BEFORE RISE: SAM ADAMS' *voice can be heard crying, "Down with the tyrants" and then comes the shouting of the mob,*

"Down with the tyrants." ADAMS *again, "It must be liberty or death." Then the cries of the mob, "Hear ye, hear ye, liberty or death." Then the clanging of bells and the sound of horses' hoofs.*

AT RISE: PAUL REVERE *seated at his bench, writing in his ledger. An unfinished teapot stands beside him.* RACHEL *is seated opposite him knitting. The room shows signs of increasing prosperity.* REVERE'S *engravings hang on the wall, and the display case shows a diversity of objects: teeth, jewelry, copperplates, silverware.*

PAUL (*Talking as he writes*): To Mr. Josiah Gray, artificial fore teeth — to Miss Mary Jane Harmon, silver earrings — to Mr. John Abram, silver teapot—hmmmm . . . (*Taps his fingers as he gazes at what he has written.*)

RACHEL (*Looking up from her knitting and smiling at him as she shakes her head*): I marvel at you, Paul Revere. On such a day you sit calmly writing in your ledger, taking orders, fixing umbrellas —

PAUL (*Gazing up at her*): Umbrellas, did you say, my dear? Will you look out and see if it's still raining?

RACHEL (*Gets up and goes to door, talking as she goes*): That reminds me of little Paul. You shouldn't have sent him out in this rain to look after your horse. He should be here by now.

PAUL: Don't fret, Rachel, he'll be here soon. And you are an angel, dear, to be so good to my children.

RACHEL: Our children, now, Paul. I vowed when I married you that I'd never feel any differently towards them than if they were my own and not Sarah Orne's.

PAUL: Sary Orne — may she rest in peace. She'd be happy if she knew what a mother you are to her children.

RACHEL (*Back at her knitting*): And I must be thankful, too, for such a family and such a husband.

PAUL (*Smiles and goes back to his work*): Tut, tut, my dear girl. . . . To Mr. Benjamin Stafford, copperplate for engraving — to Miss Hannah Snow, book plate.

RACHEL: You're impossible, Paul. Where do you get the patience to sit there and calmly go about your work, when right now under Liberty Tree Sam Adams is rousing an angry mob, and your heart, you know, is really there and not in that colorless ledger.

PAUL (*Looks up at her and there is both admiration and earnestness in his voice.*): I am a fortunate man, my dear, to be married to you — you who are the first woman ever to understand me. But, remember, Rachel, while my heart is feeding the fires of patriotism, my hands must feed my beloved family.

RACHEL (*Rises and goes over to him, kissing his brow.*): You are a good man, Paul Revere. (*At these words, the center door opens, and two rather rain-soaked characters step in, the shorter one,* SAM ADAMS, *first, followed by* DR. JOSEPH WARREN.)

ADAMS (*In his rather gruff voice*): Such domesticity! Nero fiddles while Rome burns. (SAM *goes over and pats* PAUL *on the shoulder good-naturedly. They all laugh heartily.*)

PAUL: Be seated, friends. My wife was just saying something of the sort, too. (*Looks fondly at* RACHEL.)

WARREN: Et tu, Brute.

PAUL: You will excuse me for my lack of knowledge concerning the foreign tongue of Latin, but your meaning is clear. What news, friends?

RACHEL: Excuse me, Paul, but your coats, gentlemen. And surely you'd like a little drink. (*Men take off their coats, which* RACHEL *takes and puts aside.*)

WARREN: Thank you — and a drink would be welcome.

ADAMS: A drink — tonight, perchance, there will be no need for it. (*They all laugh.*) But for the present — a drink, yes, if you please. (RACHEL *exits, right.*)

PAUL: Any news from Hutchinson?

ADAMS: That dog — no, not yet, but what news can we expect except that "The ship shall land." (*Imitates the quivering voice of* GOVERNOR HUTCHINSON.)

WARREN: Poor devil! I wonder what he would do if he knew what consequences such a decision would bring.

PAUL: He probably guesses, and therefore has taken flight from Boston.

ADAMS (*Pacing floor*): Wretched coward — he'll learn he can't tamper with us. Parliament can't tamper with us — with our trade, our lives, our spirits. This is the beginning. They'll all learn.

WARREN: Seems to me they've had a little learning already. Do you not recall the repealing of the Stamp Act and the result of the Quartering Act, and the bloody massacre three years ago? And now, Paul, it looks as though you'll have a subject of another engraving — what will you call it?

ADAMS: The Boston Tea Party.

PAUL: Thank you, gentlemen. You have my work all planned for me. You have left me nothing to do except make the engraving.

ADAMS: Man alive — listen to us jest. Frenzied as I am, I nearly forgot to tell him. (*Looking at* DR. WARREN.)

WARREN: Paul, you have been elected to ride to New York and Philadelphia on the morrow to carry dispatches for the Committee of Correspondence, telling of tonight's work.

PAUL: I am ready, men. My son is at present attending to my horse.

ADAMS (*Pacing the floor, rubbing his hands*): This waiting, waiting — everything must go off as planned.

WARREN (*Opening a little book and reading*): Patience is a virtue.

ADAMS: Patience — bah! (*For a moment* DR. WARREN *is reading to himself from his book,* PAUL *is turning the pages of his ledger, and* SAM ADAMS *paces the floor. Then the door bursts open, and a breathless* PAUL REVERE, JR., *enters.*)

PAUL, JR.: Father! Oh, hello, Mr. Adams, Dr. Warren —

PAUL: What is it, son? Speak!

PAUL, JR.: Word has come. Hutchinson has ordered the tea to be landed. They are clamoring on the streets. (DR. WARREN *and* PAUL REVERE *stand, excited.* SAM ADAMS *is aroused, his face is beaming with satisfaction. The men take their coats.*)

ADAMS: Griffin's Wharf tonight.

WARREN: Griffin's Wharf tonight.

PAUL: Griffin's Wharf. (RACHEL *enters with a tray and cups.*)

WARREN: Thank you, Mrs. Revere, but we cannot drink now.

ADAMS: Boston Harbor will be a teapot tonight, my good woman. (*Exit* ADAMS *and* WARREN. PAUL *turns to his wife.*)

PAUL: I must go now, Rachel. It has come. Paul, is my horse ready?

PAUL, JR.: Yes, father, and I wish I were going with you.

PAUL: Now you are talking like a true son, but you must stay home and take care of mother and the children.

RACHEL: Oh, Paul, you will be careful.

PAUL: I'll be careful, for there must be other nights like this, and other rides. But remember, Rachel, no matter what happens, it's Liberty or Death. (PAUL, JR. *goes to stand near* RACHEL, *who puts her arms around the boy's shoulders.*)

PAUL, JR.: Not death, father, but Liberty.

PAUL: Yes, son, Liberty. (*In the distance the crowd can be heard yelling, "Boston Harbor a teapot tonight," and there is the sound of steps and people running.*)

CURTAIN

* * *

SCENE 3

TIME: *A spring evening,* 1810.

BEFORE RISE: *Horses' hoofs can be heard and the cries, "To arms, the British are coming." — Hoofs again, the cry, "Don't fire until you see the whites of their eyes," then a shot is heard and all is silence.*

SETTING: *Same as Scene* 1.

AT RISE: *A white-haired* PAUL REVERE *is sitting in a rocker, napping, his chin nodding gently on his chest and his mouth slightly open. His grandson,* PAUL REVERE, III, *sits at his feet reading his grandfather's account of his famous ride, and his grandmother,* RACHEL, *sits opposite, knitting.*

PAUL III: "It was a moonlit night . . ." (*His voice drops as he reads to himself and then it rises again*) "when we had got about half way from Lexington to Concord the other two . . ." — who were the other two, grandfather? He's sleeping.

RACHEL: Sh, child. Let him sleep. The other two were William Dawes and Dr. Preston.

PAUL III (*Reading again*): "I kept along, when I had got about 200 yards ahead of them, I saw two officers under a tree. (*Voice drops again and then it rises*) . . . I saw four officers, who rode up to me with their pistols in their hands and said . . ." (*Breaking off*) Did all the redcoats do was curse, Grandma?

RACHEL (*Smiling*): I'm afraid not, Paul. Some were very good soldiers and even married our girls, and some were not so very good.

PAUL III: But not as good as George Washington's soldiers.

RACHEL (*Smiling*) : Not as good as George Washington's soldiers.

PAUL III: "Blank, blank, stop, if you go an inch further you are a dead man. . . ."

PAUL (*Wakes*) : What's this? Who's a dead man?

PAUL III: Grandfather, your story is too hard to read, and besides grandmother doesn't like to hear me curse, and the British soldiers curse in your story. . . .

PAUL (*Laughing his hearty laugh*) : Well, Paul, my man, put the story down and listen to your old grandfather. It was about two o'clock on the Tuesday of April 18, 1775, when my dear friend, Dr. Warren, called for me to set off immediately for Lexington by way of Charlestown. He had already sent William Dawes by way of Roxbury. It wasn't a surprise to me and I was ready.

RACHEL: Ready! Such a mild word. For weeks, Paul, your grandfather had been practically living in the saddle. Why, the Sunday before that midnight ride, he had gone to Lexington to warn his friends Sam Adams and John Hancock that the British were preparing for an attack. Why, it was then that your grandfather arranged with Colonel Conant and some other gentlemen that if the British went by water, the signal would be two lanterns in the North Church Steeple and if by land, one lantern.

PAUL: Your grandmother could tell the story better than I, son. Yes, she is right, and before I left that Tuesday night, I arranged with my friend, Robert Newman, to hang the signal lights.

PAUL III: And your crossing to Charlestown — was it difficult?

PAUL: It was then flood time, and the ship was winding and the moon rising. . . .

RACHEL: And your grandfather took one of your aunt's new woolen petticoats to muffle the sound of the oars.

PAUL (*Chuckling*) : And a very good muffler it proved to be — for Tom Richardson and Josh Bailey rowed me across the river under the very nose of the Somerset, Man-of-War.

PAUL III: Gosh, grandfather, you were brave.

PAUL: No, not brave, just doing my duty. In Charlestown I borrowed Deacon John Larkin's horse and it was about eleven when I set off. At Charlestown Common the road forked, and I took the Cambridge Road.

PAUL III: And when did you see the British soldiers?

PAUL: I had gone about a half mile when I saw two British soldiers lying in wait. Quickly I turned and went back to the fork to take the Medford road. One of the soldiers tried to cut me off by crossing the fields, but fortunately the clay mired his horse, and I escaped.

RACHEL: And it was a very dark and lonely ride with only woods and low stone walls, and a farmhouse here and there. Remember, child, it was your grandfather who awoke his countrymen to the coming danger. It took courage to do it.

PAUL III: Then you are a hero, grandfather.

PAUL: Paul, when you grow up and get ready to marry, I hope you'll find someone who will be as loving and fine as your grandmother and then you'll be a hero in her eyes, too, no matter what you do.

PAUL III: Will I, grandmother?

RACHEL (*Smiles, gently*): Your grandfather says it's so.

PAUL: Now your grandmother is teasing me, but I was telling you a story and I must finish. In Lexington I went to the Clarke house, where Hancock and Adams were staying. There I was met by William Dawes and a little after midnight we set off towards Concord. Dr. Samuel Prescott chanced to meet us and offered to help us spread the alarm. We were halfway to Concord when a party of four Redcoats stopped us. Dawes escaped and so did Prescott, and I was unsuccessful. I was forced back to Lexington, and there the sound of shots frightened the British and they took my horse and fled.

PAUL III: And you never got to Concord that night?

PAUL: No, but Dr. Prescott did.

PAUL III: And that's the end?

RACHEL: Hardly. That was little more than the beginning.

PAUL: Then there was much to do after that. Rides for the Committee of Safety, printing paper money for the soldiers, supplying the Continental Army with gunpowder, fixing the cannon at Castle William for General Washington . . .

RACHEL: And sleepless nights and anxiety, worry and hard times, Paul.

PAUL: And great jubilation when it was over and we were free.

RACHEL: Free, yes. But your grandfather, Paul, became the busiest free man in the country. I was left dazed just trying to keep up with him.

PAUL III: What did you do, grandfather?

PAUL: Oh, I opened a hardware store opposite the Liberty Tree, then a foundry for the casting of bells and cannon, and in 1801 your Uncle Joseph and I erected copper rolling mills at Canton. . . . We were the first to do it. . . .

PAUL III: I wish I were older and could work with you, grandfather. When I grow up there won't be anything for me to do.

RACHEL: Bless you, child, there'll always be problems to solve in this world of ours. And you just follow in your grandfather's footsteps and I dare say you'll be a very busy man.

PAUL: Why, son, there's so much for you to do. This is a new country and you must work to make it the greatest in the world; a country free of tyrants. You must work to win the respect of the rest of the world and show them by our government, our industries, our inventions, and our very lives that we really had something to fight for.

PAUL III: And that was, grandfather?

PAUL: And that was Liberty, son.

PAUL III: And will we get to be the greatest country in the world because we have liberty?

PAUL: Yes, son. Some day great foundries and mills and industries will crop up all over this great country, past the Appalachians, and the Louisiana Purchase. And our ships will sail the seven seas. And England, and France, and Spain will talk of that great country, the United States of America, where people are all free —

PAUL III: Free, grandfather, is just like having liberty?

PAUL: Yes, son. Liberty, the sweetest word that man has ever breathed. Liberty! (*In the distance bells ring and again the sound of distant hoofs.*)

THE END

DOLLY SAVES THE DAY

by Helen Louise Miller

Characters

Captain Livingston
Mrs. Livingston
A Hessian Captain
David Livingston
Dolly Livingston
General Washington
Mary Anne, *the doll.*

Setting: *A corner of the yard of the Livingston farmhouse.*

At Rise: Dolly Livingston *is hopping up and down screaming for help as her brother pretends to drown her favorite rag doll in the well.*

Dolly: Help! Help! Oh, please, Davy, please don't drown my Mary Anne. Please! Please! Oh, help, help!

David: Stop screaming, you little goose; 'twon't do a mite of good. Mary Anne is not a patriot and I am going to drown her dead for good and all.

Dolly: She is! She is! Please! Oh, you wouldn't dare do this if Father were here.

David: Wouldn't I? And why not, pray tell? I'd dare to drown a wretched Tory no matter who was here.

Dolly: You would not. Father wouldn't let you. And he'd punish you good and proper if he knew how you teased me.

David: And I suppose you're going to be a tattle tale and tell him when he comes home so I'll get a birching. In that case, I might as well be thrashed for something as nothing. So here goes your precious Mary Anne . . . down . . . down . . . down . . . to a watery grave. You better say goodbye to her forever.

Dolly: Oh, Davy, please spare her life. (*Kneeling before him*) I'll give you anything you want or do anything you want.

DAVID: Can I trust you to keep your word?

DOLLY (*Jumping up in relief*): Of course, Davy, just give me back my darling Mary Anne. (MR. LIVINGSTON *enters, sees what is going on, and stands quietly left stage, watching the following scene.*)

DAVID: Nope! Girls always tell.

DOLLY: But I wouldn't tell. Honest, I wouldn't.

DAVID: Oh, yes, you would. And if you didn't tell about this, you'd tell how I ran away yesterday to go swimming instead of working in the field.

DOLLY: No, I wouldn't, Davy. Cross my heart and hope to die.

MR. LIVINGSTON: Your sister won't have to tell me about your wrong-doings, David, and I think I came home just in time to administer a litle justice. (*Brandishing his riding crop in a threatening manner.*)

DAVID: Father!

DOLLY (*Running to his side*): Oh, Father! I'm so glad to see you.

MR. LIVINGSTON (*Patting her head*): I'm sure you are, my dear. But I fear your brother will not be so glad when I have finished with him. Come, sir, take that wretched doll baby out of the well bucket and return it to your sister. Then you and I will settle our accounts.

DAVID (*Obeying his father's orders*): Here's your toy, Dolly. I wasn't going to drown her for real.

MR. LIVINGSTON: Just going to tease your little sister, and make her cry, eh! Humph! I daresay she'll be able to hear you yelling a-plenty till I get through with you. Now, march!

DOLLY (*Taking hold of her father's arm*): Oh, please, Father. Don't be harsh with Davy. All boys love to tease and he is no worse than the rest. Besides Davy worked hard while you were away.

MR. LIVINGSTON: Worked hard, did he? I heard him boasting just now of going swimming, when he was needed on the farm. That is something else he must answer for. Sorry, my dear, your plea for mercy won't do your brother a bit of good this time. (*He crosses to* DAVID, *seizes him by the collar and prepares to march him off stage when* MRS. LIVINGSTON *enters, very much out of breath from excitement.*)

MRS. LIVINGSTON: Oh, George, hurry, hurry. You must leave at once. The hired boy just told me the Hessian soldiers are coming up the road. They are as far as the spring house and headed this way. You must escape at once.

MR. LIVINGSTON (*Releasing his hold on* DAVID): I guess you are not sorry to hear that, are you, my boy?

DAVID (*Quickly*): I wouldn't want to see the Hessians catch you, sire.

MR. LIVINGSTON (*Relenting*): But you are glad enough to have them save you from punishment.

DAVID: I know I shouldn't tease Dolly the way I do, but she is such a little goose about that old rag doll. And as for the swimming, it was such a hot day, and I had worked hard all morning.

MRS. LIVINGSTON: Davy is a good lad, George.

MR. LIVINGSTON: Well, I hope so, for now I must have someone to help me now that the Hessians are so close.

DAVID: Oh, please, Father, let me help you. I know I am an idler and a tease, but there is nothing I wouldn't do for our noble cause.

MR. LIVINGSTON: I believe you mean every word you say, lad, and I am going to place my confidence in you as if you were a grown man. Your mother will have to go with me as far as the old mill so she can bring my horse back. You and Dolly will have to face the enemy alone.

DOLLY: I am not afraid.

MR. LIVINGSTON: I don't think you will have cause to be afraid, Dolly. Surely the enemy would not harm a little mite like you. But there is something you and David must do for me.

DOLLY: I hope it is something big and brave.

MR. LIVINGSTON: General Washington is coming here this afternoon.

DAVID: To this house?

DOLLY: Goody! goody! Just listen to that, Mary Anne.

MRS. LIVINGSTON: My patience! How am I to entertain such a fine gentleman on such short notice?

MR. LIVINGSTON: The general is not looking for entertainment, my dear. He is to use this house as a meeting place with General Wayne. There are important plans on foot and I have the papers in my dispatch case.

DAVID: Are they very important, sir?

MR. LIVINGSTON (*Seating himself at the table and producing the papers*): I cannot even describe their importance. General Wayne has been ordered to attack tomorrow morning. But these papers order him to postpone his attack because of the increasing number of the enemy. Unless he receives these orders, he will make the attack and be wiped out. He must get these papers within the hour and report here to form new plans with General Washington. Now do you understand how important it is?

DAVID: Indeed I do. But where shall I find General Wayne?

MR. LIVINGSTON: He is staying with Mr. McClellan at the top of the hill. The old stone house in the oak grove. If I am captured these papers will never reach him and his army will be destroyed.

DAVID: Give them to me, sir. Dolly and I will see that they are delivered safely.

MR. LIVINGSTON: I don't see how you will manage, for all the roads will be guarded. Even the most innocent looking people will be searched. You cannot afford to let these papers fall into enemy hands.

DOLLY: Davy and I will look after everything.

MR. LIVINGSTON (*Rising*): You are a brave little maid, and your brother is a staunch lad, even if he is a rascal at times. Now I must leave you. Good luck to you and to our righteous cause. (FATHER *exits left.*)

MRS. LIVINGSTON: Good-bye, my dears. I trust you will be safe. I will see your father to the old mill. As soon as the soldiers are gone, Uncle Peter will kindle a fire in the wash house and when Father sees the smoke signal, he will come home. (MOTHER *exits left.*)

DOLLY (*Perching herself on the table with* MARY ANNE): How long will it be till the soldiers come, Davy?

DAVID (*Busy reading the plans*): I don't know. But we must think of a way to fool them and find a place to hide these papers.

DOLLY: As long as I have Mary Anne and you, Davy, I am not one bit afraid, and Mary Anne isn't afraid either. Aren't you ashamed, Davy, that you called her a Tory? Why, there isn't a more loyal doll in the colonies than Mary Anne.

DAVID (*Getting idea as he looks at the doll*): Say, Dolly, I have an idea! We'll use Mary Anne to fool the soldiers.

DOLLY (*Jumping off table*): How?

DAVID (*Producing pen knife from pocket*): You run and get Mother's sewing basket. Be sure to bring a needle with a good strong thread. We'll cut a slit in Mary Anne's back and sew the papers inside with her stuffings.)

DOLLY (*Screaming*): No, no, no! Not my Mary Anne! Oh, Davy, you're a cruel, wicked boy! Why, that's a million times worse than drowning her in the well.

DAVID: Now, listen, Dolly. Be sensible. Mary Anne is only a rag doll. She can't feel a thing!

DOLLY: She can too. She's my very own child and I'm her mother. I won't stay here to see her tortured.

DAVID (*Catching hold of* DOLLY *as she tries to run away*): Aw shucks, Dolly. Give me that doll and let me hide those papers. (*Kneels before her and speaks in a coaxing voice.*) Look, then she'd be a hero and save the whole army. You said just now she was loyal to the cause. Now's her chance to suffer for her country just like a soldier on the battlefield.

DOLLY: Would she really be a hero, Davy?

DAVID: Sure she would. And maybe General Washington would even give her a medal for bravery. Now be a good girl and let me have her before the soldiers arrive.

DOLLY (*Kissing* MARY ANNE *before she hands her over to* DAVID): Now don't you be scared, Mary Anne. Davy says it won't hurt a bit. Here she is, now mind you be careful. I'll go get the needle and thread. (DOLLY *exits left.*)

DAVID (*Pretending to slit the doll and stuff the papers inside*): There, Mistress Mary Anne, you have a brand new set of insides. Now you are a servant of General Washington under his orders. I must say you were a brave patient. Not a peep out of you. (DOLLY *enters with needle and thread.*) You better do the sewing, Dolly, you'll do a neater job.

DOLLY (*Covering her eyes as she sits at the table*): Oh, I couldn't. You do it, Davy. Her dress will hide the stitches. I can't bear to look.

DAVID (*Sits on floor and sews up the doll*): I always said you were a silly little goose. Now I am sure of it. I bet I'll sew her so that she stays sewed for good. (*As he is sewing,* DOLLY *becomes conscious of the sound of riding. She crosses right to listen.*)

DOLLY: Hurry, Davy, someone is coming. Someone is riding up the drive.

DAVID (*Runs right to look out*): You're right, Dolly. It's a Hessian Captain. Now remember — not a word about Father's being here.

DOLLY: Oh, Davy, I'm scared.

DAVID: Nonsense! I have a plan and you must show me what a good little play actress you can be.

DOLLY: I don't know how to be an actress.

DAVID: Oh, yes you do. Look, I'm going to pretend to drown Mary Anne in the well, just as I did before. And I want you to scream and holler and carry on for dear life — just the way you did when Father caught me.

DOLLY: Oh, I will. I will.

DAVID: Mind — if you don't, I'll throw her in the well for real.

DOLLY: Oh, I'll scream and cry as loud as I can.

DAVID: You let me do the talking. I'm going to pretend that you are not my sister at all. I'll say your name is Betty McClellan. Understand?

DOLLY: No, but I know enough to scream and cry. (*Offstage — "Squad, halt. Ground arms. Surround the house. Let no one escape. I'll search the yard myself."* DAVID *seizes* MARY ANNE *and approaches the well.* DOLLY *goes into her act, paying no attention to the* CAPTAIN *who enters and stares at them in amazement.*)

DOLLY: Help! Help! Oh, please, Davy, please don't drown my Mary Anne. Please, please. Oh, help, help!

DAVID: Stop screaming, you little goose. 'Twon't do a mite of good. Mary Anne is not a patriot and I'm going to drown her in the well for sure.

DOLLY: Oh, please, please. Oh, you wicked boy. You'll pay for this. I'll tell your father. Oh, please, help, help, help.

CAPTAIN: Well, upon my word! What goes on here? Stop, you wretched boy! What are you doing with this child's doll?

DAVID: I'm going to drown her in the well because she's a wicked Tory and loyal to King George, that's what I'm going to do.

CAPTAIN (*Rescuing doll*): You're going to do nothing of the sort. Here, child, take your doll (*Seizing* DAVID *by the collar*) and tell me what to do with this young ruffian. I think the flat of my sword is what he needs, and he shall have it, if you say the word.

DOLLY: Oh, thank you, kind sir. (*Curtsies*) Thank you very much.

CAPTAIN (*Shaking* DAVID): Speak up, you young rascal, and tell me what you mean by such treatment. Is this the way George Washington teaches his rebels to behave?

DAVID: You let me go. You're on *her* side. That's Betty McClellan and she has no business playing in our yard. I was only teasing her so she'd take her old doll and go home.

CAPTAIN: And so she shall. (*To* DOLLY) Where do you live, little maid?

DAVID (*Quickly*): In the big stone house on the hill near the oak grove.

CAPTAIN: Are you sure you can find the way there safely?

DOLLY: Oh, yes, sir.

CAPTAIN: I have a little maid at home about your age. She has a whole family of dolls. Now run along. Don't be afraid of the soldiers. They will do you no harm. Just tell them you have Captain Parr's permission to go to your home.

DOLLY: Thank you, sir.

CAPTAIN (*Examining the doll, much to* DAVID'S *alarm*): What a pretty doll you have there! What is her name?

DOLLY: Mary Anne, sir. Mother gave her to me last Christmas.

CAPTAIN: No wonder you love her so dearly.

DOLLY: She's my favorite child, sir. Thank you for saving her.

CAPTAIN: You're welcome, child. Don't dawdle on the road. Your mother will be worried about you.

DAVID: Yes and run all the way or I'll catch that old doll and drown her in the deepest well I can find. (DOLLY *runs off left.*)

CAPTAIN: Are all you rebels so bloodthirsty? Aren't you ashamed to tease so small a child? But 'tis none of my business how you savages treat each other. Come, what is your name and where are your folks?

DAVID: My name is David Livingston and my mother and father are not at home.

CAPTAIN: Where are they?

DAVID: They took the road to Philadelphia.

CAPTAIN: I don't mind telling you, boy, we are on the lookout for some important papers which we have reason to believe are in this neighborhood. Do you know anything about them?

DAVID: Nothing, sir. And Father and Mother are really not at home. You are welcome to go into the house and see for yourself.

CAPTAIN: I'll soon make a thorough search. As for you — if you stir from that spot, I'll skin you alive. (CAPTAIN *exits left calling over his shoulder, "This way, men. We'll search the house."*)

DAVID (*Wiping his brow*): Phew! That was a close call. I wonder if Dolly will reach the McClellan home in safety. If only there was some way to be sure. Oh, well, I must appear cool and collected. Poor Father. If they catch him, it will go hard with him. I believe my friend, the Captain, is returning. (*Hastily sits on chair.*) Did you find anyone at home?

CAPTAIN (*Reëntering left*): No. Perhaps you are telling the truth after all. You can tell your father when he comes home that he has furnished the Hessian army with five hams and two saddle horses.

DAVID (*Rising in anger*): You thief.

CAPTAIN: Be careful of your language, son. War is war. You should have thought of that when your patriots started this war.

DAVID: That's all right. We patriots are ready to sacrifice anything for our independence.

CAPTAIN (*Laughing*): Independence! What does a lad your size know about independence?

DAVID: I know plenty about it. I know that just last year in Philadelphia our statesmen signed a paper that declared our colonies free and independent of the British crown. But you wouldn't understand that, since you are being paid to fight for King George.

CAPTAIN: And whom would you fight for?

DAVID: For General George Washington and Freedom.

CAPTAIN: You are as likely to find freedom in this war as I am to find a fortune in this old well. One of these days we'll catch your fancy General and send him back to England in a cage. In the meantime, don't let me catch you teasing any more little girls or I'll give you the trouncing you deserve.

DAVID: I guess my father can take care of that.

CAPTAIN: And I hope he does — with a good stout switch. Sorry I can't be here to see it done. Until then — my compliments. (*Bows stiffly.*) Good day to you. (CAPTAIN *exits right. Off stage—"Squad—attention! Shoulder arms! Forward march!"*)

DAVID (*Watching them from right*): Thank goodness, they are going. Really going! Now I can tell Uncle Pete to light the signal in the wash house for father. (*In a few seconds after* DAVID *has made his exit right,* GENERAL WASHINGTON *enters right.*)

GENERAL: What a pleasant spot to rest awhile. Surely my old friend will not keep me waiting long. (*Gets a drink from the dipper at the well.*) In the meantime, I can sit down here and go over these dispatches. (*As he goes over his papers,* DAVID *enters right.*)

DAVID: Good afternoon, sir. Are you waiting for someone?

GENERAL: As a matter of fact, I am. Is this not the home of Captain Livingston?

DAVID: Indeed, it is, sir, and I am his son, at your service, sir.

GENERAL: I had no idea the Captain had so grown-up a son. I am General Washington, at *your* service, sir.

DAVID: General Washington!

GENERAL: You seem surprised. Perhaps your father was keeping my visit a military secret.

DAVID: I am surprised and overwhelmed, sir. I have long waited to meet you and be of service to you.

GENERAL: Well, now that you have met me, you can be of real service to me by calling your father.

DAVID: Oh, that I have already done, sir. At least I have signalled for him to come home.

GENERAL: Signalled? I do not understand.

DAVID: Well, you see, sir, just before you came, a detachment of Hessian soldiers was here looking for Father. He had to hide in the old mill until they had gone. Just now I gave the signal that the coast was clear.

GENERAL: But the dispatches for General Wayne? Did your father deliver them safely?

DAVID: Alas, no, sir. He had to flee before he could reach the general.

GENERAL: Then it is too late! Wayne will attack. We stand to lose everything.

DAVID: I don't think so, sir — not if my plans turn out all right.

GENERAL: Your plans! What do you have to do with it?

DAVID: Well, sir, you see, I sent my little sister.

GENERAL (*In disgust*): Your little sister! Lad, lad, this war is for men and boys, not for little sisters.

DAVID: But you see, sir, she had her doll. . . .

GENERAL: Her doll! Boy, have you lost your senses?

DOLLY (*Entering from left stage — very much excited. She runs straight to* DAVID *without noticing the* GENERAL.): Oh Davy, I did it! I did it! I gave Mary Anne to the General and he ripped her open and read the paper and told me to tell you to tell the General that everything will be all right. (*Catching sight of* WASHINGTON) Oh, I beg your pardon, sir. I did not see we had a guest.

DAVID: Dolly, this is General Washington.

DOLLY (*Dropping a curtsey*): How do you do, sir. Mary Anne and I are at your service.

GENERAL: Delighted, my child. And who is Mary Anne?

DOLLY (*Showing him the doll*): Mary Anne is my favorite child. And she has done a brave deed for you this day. She let herself be cut by a cruel knife and never cried once.

GENERAL: Indeed! I wish all my military plans might turn out so successfully. I am greatly indebted to you young patriots. By your wit and courage you have done our cause a great service. I scarcely know how to thank you.

DOLLY: Oh, I do, sir.

DAVID (*Reproachfully*): Dolly! Remember your manners.

GENERAL: Let the child speak.

DOLLY: Well, you see, sir, it was really my dollie, my precious Mary Anne, who had all the pain and suffering to bear. Davy said that she would be a hero and that you might decorate her for bravery, just the way you do your own soldiers. That would thank us very, very much.

GENERAL: Would it indeed, child? Then it shall be done. (*He picks up* DOLLY *and* MARY ANNE *and perches them on the table beside him. Removes medal from his own coat.*) It gives me great pleasure to be able to present this medal of my own to Mary Anne, the bravest doll in the colonies, for her courage under the knife and for her devotion to her country.

DOLLY: Oh, thank you, sir. Mary Anne and I will treasure it forever.

DAVID (*Solemnly*): And I promise on my sacred word of honor never to try to drown or in any way molest this doll that has been decorated by our General — the doll that saved an army.

THE END

NOT ONLY THE STRONG

by Helen E. Waite and Elbert M. Hoppenstedt

Characters

MRS. REYNOLDS, *a girl of any desired age, but she should be taller than others.*
PRISCILLA REYNOLDS, *about 12, but somewhat small for her age*
DEBBIE BARNES, *her friend*
CAPTAIN REYNOLDS
WILLIAM REYNOLDS, *about 14*
HULDA, JANE, ALICE, DORCAS — *friends of Priscilla's, and about her age*
SIRAS WITCHFIELD, *an Indian scout, an older boy*
PREACHER MCBRIDE

SETTING: *The family room of a Kentucky blockhouse, an August day, 1783.*

AT RISE: PRISCILLA REYNOLDS *is arranging flowers at the table, anr her friend* DEBBIE BARNES, *a sturdy girl, is dusting.*

DEBBIE (*Glancing at* PRISCILLA): You are the queerest girl in Bryan's Station — and perhaps in all Kentucky! This makes the sixth time today you've been moping over those blackeyed susans and bluegrass!

PRISCILLA: I do want them to look just right when Father arrives. (*Moves from table.*) Now how do you like it?

DEBBIE (*Dubiously*): It's not a bit the way Mistress Gallen makes her bouquets.

PRISCILLA (*Quickly*): Oh, no! Mistress Gallen crowds her flowers together into a wad, like this — (*She clasps her hands tightly.*)

DEBBIE (*Nodding*): And then she puts a frilly paper around them, and it is so pretty.

PRISCILLA (*Looking at her own arrangement thoughtfully*): Perhaps that *is* the proper way to fix flowers, but oh, Debbie, I'm always sorry for flowers when I see them stand so straight and prim! I want them to look happy, as though the breeze was playing with them.

DEBBIE (*Laughing*): I said you were queer! Sometimes you want to mope over bluegrass all morning, and not do a single useful thing; and then you're all in a dither because you're a girl, and can't have adventures as an Indian scout, like your brother.

PRISCILLA (*Slowly*): It isn't the adventures I crave so much, Debbie. But I would like to *do* things for Kentucky! I love this wilderness. It makes you feel as though you ought to do brave things for it, and (*Her voice drops tiredly.*) I'm the most useless and helpless person at Bryan's Station. My mother won't even let me work in the fields with the other girls.

DEBBIE (*Coming across to comfort her*): That's because you were so ill with the fever this spring. It was no fault of yours.

PRISCILLA: But my father says that every person here at Bryan's Station should prove himself valuable to the settlement. And William was stricken with the fever too — (PRISCILLA'S *mother,* MISTRESS REYNOLDS, *enters with fresh candles for the candlesticks. She glances about the room approvingly.*)

MISTRESS REYNOLDS: Praise is not good for children, but I *will* say that I am well pleased with the look of the house. You girls will be neat housewives within a few years.

DEBBIE (*Curtseying*): Thank you, ma'am. (MISTRESS REYNOLDS, *having replaced candles, touches* PRISCILLA'S *shoulder affectionately.*)

MISTRESS REYNOLDS: You have done well with your flowers, Cilla. They make a bright spot for our eyes, and we must endeavor to do everything in our power to provide cheer and comfort for the new preacher. He comes from Philadelphia, a most elegant city, and I fear he'll find our wilderness life very wild and hard.

PRISCILLA: I really meant the flowers for Father —

MRS. REYNOLDS: He will be pleased to see them. And you have found his favorite black-eyed susans and bluegrass. But when the preacher arrives you will offer them to him as a welcoming gift, I hope?

PRISCILLA (*Wistfully*): I did pick them especially for Father. (*With determination*) Oh, Mother, there's something I want to do — oh, so much!

MRS. REYNOLDS: Something you want to do, dear? What is it?

PRISCILLA: Mother, I — I — oh, I've been penned up in Bryan's Station so long — I — I — want to go with Father tomorrow when he rides to town to fetch the Preacher! (MRS. REYNOLDS *is plainly taken aback. She stiffens and stares at her daughter disapprovingly.* PRISCILLA *sees it and squirms uncomfortably, but she plunges on breathlessly.*) I — I could ride my pony, Mother! He — he can keep up with Father's horse!

MRS. REYNOLDS: Priscilla! Such talk is unseemly. Why should you, a little girl, go out with the Captain of Bryan's Station to greet the new Preacher? It would be a very forward thing for you to do. (PRISCILLA'S *head droops.*) Yes, hang your head, my child, and remember a girl's place. Your father has well-nigh spoiled you by allowing you to accompany him on short expeditions. But now, when your Father goes with an escort to meet the Preacher, it is unthinkable! Home, Priscilla, is the proper place for all women, and *little* girls, especially, belong at home. They should think of little else besides obeying and pleasing their elders.

PRISCILLA (*Meekly*): Yes, ma'am.

MRS. REYNOLDS: I know you have a brave spirit, child, but meekness is more becoming to a girl. It is nearly time for your father to return, and I must see that all is going well with the dinner. (*She leaves stage. When she is out of hearing,* DEBBIE *speaks eagerly.*)

DEBBIE: *My* mother said those very words to Hulda and me when she chanced to hear Hulda wishing to be an Indian scout.

PRISCILLA (*Impatiently*): But there ought to be opportunities for girls to do great things for their country —

DEBBIE (*Doubtfully*): God didn't mean us to do noble things — (*She is interrupted by the entrance of* CAPTAIN REYNOLDS *and his son,* WILLIAM, *a boy about 14. The* CAPTAIN *is expected, but the boy's arrival is a surprise. Both girls curtsey to the* CAPTAIN.)

CAPTAIN (*Glancing about room*): Everything ready for our honored guest? You will make a fine housewife, Cilla. I am proud of you. (*Touches* WILLIAM'S *shoulder.*) And you will be proud of your brother: All alone he has journeyed from Fort Lexington, over dangerous roads and through lonely forests, to bring me word from Siras Witchfield—a good two days before I looked for his return. (*He crosses to table, seats himself, and busies himself with papers.*)

WILLIAM (*Swaggering a little*): Where have you left your manners, girls? You've certainly been taught to curtsey to your betters, and now that I'm a scout, trusted with important messages of Indian doings —

PRISCILLA (*Scornfully*): Our betters! Poof!

DEBBIE (*Alarmed*): Indians? Oh, is there — will there be new trouble with the Indians?

CAPTAIN (*Who has been listening*): No, Debbie, I think not. The message Siras sent with William was that the Indians are unusually quiet and peaceful. That is right, William?

WILLIAM (*Rather meekly*): Yes, sir.

CAPTAIN: The Indians are learning we mean to hold our own in this wilderness. They'll not molest us soon, I think. We've given them some sharp lessons — (*Suddenly sees flowers.*) Well, Cilla, you have been finding my favorite black-eyed susans again. Thank you, child. I may be a rough soldier, but I do confess I love the sight of flowers in our dark blockhouse.

PRISCILLA: Thank you, sir. (*Pause.*) Father —

CAPTAIN: Yes, Priscilla?

PRISCILLA: I — I want to do something very much. (*Twists her fingers nervously.*) Oh, Father, when — when you go into town to fetch the Preacher, won't you please let me ride Flash and go with you? (DEBBIE *gives a start, and makes a sound of protest, while* WILLIAM *laughs scornfully.* PRISCILLA *ignores them both. She steps nearer her Father, and speaks appealingly.*) *Please,* Father! I — I haven't been beyond this clearing for weeks.

CAPTAIN (*Thoughtfully*): Yes, I know. It *is* hard for you here in the wilderness. I have been anxious about you lately, Priscilla, and I have almost decided this Kentucky is no fit place for you. At my first opportunity I think I shall send you to your grandparents in Philadelphia.

PRISCILLA (*Alarmed*): Oh, Father — *no!* I *love* the wilderness! I'd stifle in Philadelphia! Don't send me away. I want to see this marvelous Kentucky grow into a great country!

CAPTAIN: Do you feel that way about our Kentucky? Yes, it *is* a marvelous country.

PRISCILLA (*Eagerly*): Some day it will have rich farms and fine cities — like Boston and Philadelphia. (CAPTAIN *nods.*) And *I* want to help make it grow, Father! I want people to remember that I did something for God and Kentucky! That I was as important as William —

CAPTAIN (*Sternly*): *Priscilla!*

PRISCILLA: But I *do,* sir!

CAPTAIN: Cilla, you must not indulge in such thoughts. They are not wholesome for girls. And do not let me think you envy William. Valor is not meant for girls.

PRISCILLA (*Wistfully*): Then why are we born?

CAPTAIN: To make homes, my dear, gladden men, and inspire them to do valiant things, but to help mold the country — no!

WILLIAM: How *can* girls be so silly, sir? And do you know what I heard Mr. Caldwell say the other week? It was after I had brought the first message from Siras Witchfield. He remarked it was a pity you couldn't have had two brave sons, in place of a delicate daughter, like Priscilla —

CAPTAIN (*Gravely*): I do not care for that speech, my son. It is not kind to your sister, and no true man needs to boast of being brave. Now, Priscilla, I am sorry for your disappointment, but I certainly cannot take you with me when I go to meet Preacher McBride. The roads are rough and dangerous, and we will need to ride at top speed, for I dare not be absent from my post here for more than a few hours. Besides it would be a most unseemly thing for you to go on such an errand. Someday, perhaps, when there is not so much need for haste, I will take you. But if you return to Philadelphia, you will journey to your heart's content. (*Enter* MRS. REYNOLDS.)

MRS. REYNOLDS: I thought I heard your voice — why, William! How glad I am you have returned safely! Just in time for the venison steak you like so well.

WILLIAM: I hope it is large!

MRS. REYNOLDS (*Laughing*): It is. Come now, all of you, and prepare for dinner.

CAPTAIN (*Rising*): I am very ready to do so. (CAPTAIN, MRS. REYNOLDS, *and* WILLIAM *leave stage. Girls linger.*)

PRISCILLA (*Despairingly*): He *will* send me away to Philadelphia, Debbie! I *know* he will!

DEBBIE: But wouldn't you like that? I thought you said you felt so shut in?

PRISCILLA: Yes, I do, sometimes. But—(*Throws out her hands*) Kentucky is so big and beautiful and — and free! I *belong* here, Debbie! But I can't prove it to Mother or Father.

DEBBIE: God can prove it for you, Cilla.

PRISCILLA (*Wistfully*): Do you think God considers girls? No one else seems to think we're worth taking into account.

DEBBIE (*Hugging her*): God thinks of everyone, Priscilla. And if you really do belong here in Kentucky, He'll give you an opportunity to prove it.

PRISCILLA: I hope He'll do it very soon! (*They walk toward door.*)

MRS. REYNOLDS (*Calling off stage*): Cilla! Debbie! Make haste!

PRISCILLA: Yes, Mother. We're coming.

CURTAIN

* * *

SCENE 2

SETTING: *The same, the next afternoon.*

AT RISE: MRS. REYNOLDS *is seated in the best chair, and* PRISCILLA *sits opposite, at work on a sampler. She seems dejected.*

MRS. REYNOLDS: The girls will be here any minute now, I imagine. Now, my dear, remember that you are the daughter of the Captain of Bryan's Station, and must be a leader to the others. When your Father arrives with the Preacher, you are to give the signal to rise and make your curtseys. Then tell him how grateful we are that he is honoring Bryan's Station with his presence, and nod to Dorcas Gallen to present her flowers.

PRISCILLA (*Without spirit*): Yes, Mother.

MRS. REYNOLDS (*Looking at her sharply*): You are not in your usual spirits, today, child. Are you quite well?

PRISCILLA: Yes, Ma'am.

MRS. REYNOLDS (*Doubtfully*): These past few days have been most oppressive. And if you should have another bout of fever —

PRISCILLA: Truly I am well, Mother.

MRS. REYNOLDS (*Unconvinced*): I hope so. And I trust that you do appreciate your father's arranging this little gathering of your friends to make up for your disappointment in not going into town? I very much fear he pampers you far too much. A proper girl is demure, and retiring, Priscilla.

PRISCILLA (*Sighing*): Yes, Mother.

MRS. REYNOLDS: See you remember — (*She is interrupted by the entrance of* DEBBIE *and* HULDA.) Ah, my dears, I am glad you could come. (*Girls curtsey, and murmur thanks, and* MRS. REYNOLDS *makes a gracious gesture.*) Take your seats, girls. (*She watches with interest while* HULDA *takes her knitting from her pocket.*) You have work to keep your fingers from being idle this afternoon, too, I see, Hulda.

HULDA: Yes, ma'am. My knitting. Silly to work on it these sticky days, but I always break and snarl the threads when I sew, and Mother says I *must* be doing *some* worthy work.

MRS. REYNOLDS: A very wise mother, Hulda.

HULDA: I would sooner be at work in the garden. (MRS. REYNOLDS *gazes at her disapprovingly.*)

DEBBIE (*Warningly*): Hulda!

HULDA: To work in the gardens is a worthy work, I am certain!

MRS. REYNOLDS (*Reprovingly*): It is not for little girls to decide which work is best for them. What is it you are making, child?

HULDA (*Shrugging*): It is supposed to be a muffler — it makes me hot just to think of a muffler today!

MRS. REYNOLDS: It is a cheerful color. Perhaps you will finish it for Priscilla to wear if she journeys back to Philadelphia this year — (*She is startled by a sudden, suspicious sound from* PRISCILLA, *and turns to see the girl dabbing at her eyes.*) Priscilla, you are crying! What ails you, child? (PRISCILLA *gulps, tries to speak, and only shakes her head.* DEBBIE *speaks impulsively.*)

DEBBIE: She is so afraid Captain Reynolds *will* send her back to Philadelphia, ma'am. Oh, ma'am, *please* don't do it! Cilla *loves* the wilderness. She says she'd smother back East —

MRS. REYNOLDS (*Sternly*): Priscilla must allow her father to be the judge of what is best for her, Deborah. He has not quite decided to send her to her grandparents, but if he does, Priscilla must remember that even the grown men and women of Bryan's Station obey the Captain's commands, and his own daughter must not murmur! (*To* PRISCILLA *in a softer tone.*) I know you are no scared bunny, my child, but your father fears the frontier life may be too severe a strain for your strength. (WILLIAM'S *voice is heard saying, "The others are in here," and then he appears, with* DORCAS, JANE *and* ALICE. DORCAS *carries two typical, tight, round Colonial bouquets. She is a charming child, with dainty ways and a pretty voice.*)

WILLIAM: Here are the other girls, Mother.

MRS. REYNOLDS: You are very welcome, my dears. I am glad you will be here to greet Preacher McBride.

DORCAS: We were glad to come, ma'am. Mother sent you this nosegay with her compliments. The other is for the Preacher. (*She presents flowers to* MRS. REYNOLDS *with a curtsey.*)

MRS. REYNOLDS (*Much pleased*): My compliments to your mother, Dorcas, and please tell her I am much flattered to receive a gift of her prized flowers. (*Rises.*) Now I'll leave you to your own devices, and have a happy afternoon. (*The girls all stand while she leaves stage.* WILLIAM *remains long enough to say impishly.*)

WILLIAM: Mind your manners well, when the Preacher arrives, girls! (*Exit.*)

PRISCILLA: Of course your own manners are already nicely polished! (*But he has gone before her retort is finished.*)

ALICE (*Sighing*): I wish *my* brother was old enough to be an Indian scout! They are so important in Kentucky. William was telling me all about it.

HULDA (Dryly): Oh, William is a very noble scout! (*The girls take up their various work, sewing, knitting or sampler-stitching.*)

JANE: Oh, Priscilla, aren't you thrilled to think of entertaining the Preacher?

DORCAS: It is a great honor that Captain Reynolds asked us to be here with Priscilla to be the first to greet Preacher McBride when he arrives. I was so excited when William brought the message this morning!

ALICE: Captain Reynolds came to our door himself. And after he asked my mother if I might come this afternoon, he talked a long time with my brother James and his wife. He was much interested in their plans for their journey next month.

DORCAS: Oh, does your brother James mean to leave Kentucky?

ALICE: N-no. Just for several months. They're going to Philadelphia to help my grandmother dispose of her house and things, and bring her back to Bryan's Station to live with us. (*At the word "Philadelphia"* PRISCILLA *starts and drops several stitches of her knitting. She and* DEBBIE *exchange frightened glances. Then* PRISCILLA *bends her head over work.*)

DEBBIE: How — how soon does — does your brother plan to go?

ALICE: Oh, after the hot weather is gone, and before the autumn storms begin. *Your* grandparents live in Philadelphia, don't they, Priscilla? (*Before* PRISCILLA *can answer* WILLIAM *bursts in upon the group. He is excited and panting.*)

WILLIAM: Cilla, where — where is Mother? Quick! (*Girls stare at him.*)

PRISCILLA: She left us just after Jane and Dorcas came. I don't know where she is now. What happened? Is anyone hurt?

WILLIAM: I can't find her anywhere! And there's no time to lose! (*Girls exchange frightened glances.*)

PRISCILLA: William, what is it? (*Sharply*) William, has something happened to Father?

WILLIAM: No — no! But — oh, it isn't anything for *girls* to hear! (PRISCILLA *is on her feet now. Despite being small, she seems suddenly commanding.*)

PRISCILLA: William Reynolds, tell us at once what awful thing has happened!

WILLIAM (*Desperately*): Well — if you *must* know — Siras Witchfield has just come in with word that the Indians are planning an attack on Bryan's Station — today. Since Father's away I must take Siras to Mother. (DORCAS *gives a frightened cry.* JANE *claps her hands over her mouth.* HULDA *has been standing near window. Now she turns.*)

HULDA: Your mother has just entered the gate. (WILLIAM *darts off.*)

JANE: An Indian attack! (*She shivers.*)

DEBBIE: And the Captain away!

DORCAS: What *will* we do?

PRISCILLA (*With sudden determination*): Girls, I mean to go hear what Siras Witchfield has to say. If there are preparations to be made, there *must* be something we can do to help. (*She hurries off.*)

DEBBIE: And only yesterday Siras Witchfield sent word by William that the Redskins were unusually quiet and peaceful! The Captain never would have left the Station had he had a suspicion of this!

JANE: Do — do you think the Indians knew he was to be away?

ALICE (*Shuddering*): Most likely they did. They are crafty creatures. Oh — oh — (*Her voice rises in fear.*) I wish I had never seen this miserable Kentucky!

HULDA: Don't be silly, Alice! This isn't the first time the Indians have tried to attack Bryan's Station! We can defend the Station even in the Captain's absence — (*Enter* PRISCILLA. *She is plainly excited, and yet controlled.*)

PRISCILLA: Girls, Siras says we have a good chance of beating off the attack if we can summon the men from the fields in time. William has gone to call them. And we have plenty of food and ammunition. But, girls, we *must* have more water, and we must have it at once.

DEBBIE: But — but our well is outside the stockade! if the men go for water now — the Indians would surely —

PRISCILLA: They would swoop down upon the men. But if *we* go after the water, they'll never guess we know their plans, and they wouldn't dare attack us for fear of giving the alarm, before they want us to know they are about. (*Girls glance at one another in fear and doubt.*)

DORCAS (*Tearfully*): You — you mean that *we* girls must go for the water?

PRISCILLA: We always go in the morning. The Indians will never suspect that this is different.

JANE: But suppose they do? Oh, Priscilla, we *mustn't!*

PRISCILLA: Bryan's Station needs water. There is no one else to go. It's for God and Kentucky.

ALICE: I — I just *can't!* I'd die of fright before I was halfway to the well! I tell you I can't, Priscilla. (*Others shake their heads.* PRISCILLA *looks at them steadily. Then she turns to* HULDA.)

PRISCILLA: My father said once that you had courage, Hulda. Will you come with me?

HULDA (*Rising*): For months I've been pining for a chance to test my courage against my brothers'. Yes — I'm ready.

DEBBIE (*Stands*): And so am I. (*As they start from stage, other girls hesitate, then rise.*)

ALICE: Wait — wait, Priscilla. We're all going! (*Her voice trembles and* PRISCILLA *slips an arm about her.*)

PRISCILLA: We'll each take two buckets. God will let us save Bryan's Station. I'm sure He means we should.

CURTAIN

* * *

SCENE 3

SETTING: *By rearranging the furniture, and removing one or two articles, the stage should be made to represent another room from the one in which the first two scenes have been played.*

AT RISE: MRS. REYNOLDS *is seated in a high-backed chair, toward the left of stage, and* SIRAS WITCHFIELD *standing before her.* WILLIAM *stands by her chair.*

MRS. REYNOLDS: An Indian attack is frightful enough at any time, but now — with the Captain away — !

SIRAS: Take heart, Ma'am. Our commander may be away, but all the men of Bryan's Station are brave soldiers, and William will warn those who are in the fields. You say you have fresh supplies of food and ammunition. If only your wells were within the stockade, everything would be safe.

MRS. REYNOLDS: But they're *not* inside the stockade!

SIRAS (*Glancing from window*): No. It is a goodly distance from the gates to the well. And over exposed fields.

MRS. REYNOLDS (*Shuddering*` : And anyone we sent would be at the full mercy of the Indians!

SIRAS: Yet we must have the water!... (*Turns to* WILLIAM Well, boy, be on your way to the fields. Don't show excitement. Whistle and sing as you go, but make your rounds as speedily as possible. Tell the men not to run for the fort, but to reach their posts quickly. Understand?

WILLIAM: Yes, sir. (*Starts toward door.*)

MRS. REYNOLDS: And God be with you, my son. (*She is silent as* WILLIAM *leaves stage, then looks at* SIRAS.) Now, Mr. Witchfield, what may we do — what *must* we do about the water? I fear our water barrels are very low — it goes so quickly these hot days. (SIRAS *runs his fingers through his hair, looks away and shakes his head.*) Come, Mr. Witchfield, you must tell me what to do. I depend on you.

SIRAS (*Soberly*): I don't know how to advise you, Mrs. Reynolds. We are in a grave plight. Water we must have, yet how to get it —

MRS. REYNOLDS: When the men come in from the fields we must risk sending them —

SIRAS: You dare not send the men or boys, ma'am. It would be a certain signal for the Redskins' attack. The Indians know the girls go to fetch the water.

MRS. REYNOLDS (*Springing up*): And we dare not send the girls! (SIRAS *shrugs, and turns away from her.*)

SIRAS: The water must be brought — (MRS. REYNOLDS *looks from window and suddenly shrieks.*)

MRS. REYNOLDS: Siras! See! Priscilla and the other girls! Out there, past the gate!

SIRAS (*Striding to window*): *What!* Yes — yes, I see them! One — two — six in all. But it's a marvel the sentry allowed them to pass.

MRS. REYNOLDS: Priscilla is free to pass any hour during the day; he would never question her errand. Siras, they must have heard us! *They* are going for the water!

SIRAS: And see how Priscilla urges on the two laggards.

MRS. REYNOLDS (*Hysterically*): Oh, Siras, *stop* them! If the Indians *are* lurking about, the girls will be killed or captured! (*She starts from window, but* SIRAS *detains her.*)

SIRAS: You cannot stop them now, Mrs. Reynolds. See, they are already at the well, drawing water. I think we have little cause to fear for their safety. The Indians wish to take us by surprise, so they are not likely to harm the girls. I did not dare suggest sending them, but it was the only way for us to fetch the water — see, they are turning. In only a little while —

MRS. REYNOLDS: Why don't they *hurry?*

SIRAS: The worst possible thing for them to do.

MRS. REYNOLDS: Jane is looking back. Perhaps the Redskins — Oh, will they ever reach the stockade! Someone stumbled!

SIRAS: They are almost here, now. See how Priscilla laughs and talks with them. She is a brave girl.

MRS. REYNOLDS (*Who, now that danger to the girls is over, realizes that* PRISCILLA *has not been behaving like a self-effacing, demure child*): She is more foolhardy than brave.

SIRAS: If this was her idea, she may have saved the Station.

MRS. REYNOLDS (*Disapprovingly*): She should not have gone without my permission! (*Presses nearer window, speaking excitedly*) Siras, look! Isn't that — isn't that —

SIRAS: It is! — It *is* the Captain and the Preacher! Thank God. Everything favors us today. (*The girls enter. They are breathless and somewhat disheveled.*)

PRISCILLA: We — we brought in more water, Mother. Two buckets apiece.

MRS. REYNOLDS: Yes, I know. Siras and I watched from the window. It was a desperate and foolhardy thing to do.

SIRAS: Save your scolding, ma'am. We have too much to thank her for. You were a brave girl, Priscilla —

PRISCILLA: So were the other girls!

SIRAS: The Captain will be proud of what you've done this day. (*Enter* CAPTAIN *and* PREACHER, *quickly.*)

CAPTAIN: What has been happening here? We sighted the girls returning from the well — in mid-afternoon, and knew something was wrong.

SIRAS: Your daughter and her friends have shown much courage, Captain. I brought word that the Indians are surrounding the Station for an attack, and we were low on water —

CAPTAIN: And do I understand, sir, that you *sent* the *girls* —?

SIRAS (*Drawing himself up stiffly*): No, sir. They went of their own accord.

CAPTAIN: Your pardon, Siras. I should have known you would not expose young girls to such dangers. (*Turning to* PRISCILLA) You have courage, child, and all Bryan's Station will be grateful to you. You wished for an opportunity to be of service to Kentucky, and when the time came, you were equal to it.

DEBBIE (*Eagerly*): She *was* brave, sir. Some of us were frightened, and tried to run back, but Priscilla made us go on, and she laughed and sang —

PRISCILLA: I asked God to give us all courage.

PREACHER: Is this the child you told me you were so anxious about, Captain Reynolds?

CAPTAIN: This is Priscilla, yes.

PREACHER: You gave me to understand you would ask my advice about her future. I think, sir, she has earned her right to remain in Kentucky.

PRISCILLA (*Awed*): Oh! God did send me the opportunity to prove that girls can be of value and service in this wilderness, and now He's going to let me stay in Kentucky! I — I wish I could thank Him properly.

MRS. REYNOLDS: Perhaps Preacher McBride can do that. Will you, sir?

PREACHER: Gladly will I give thanks for both your courage and the successful accomplishment of your errand, Priscilla. (*All bow heads. He begins prayer as the curtain falls.*) Father, we thank Thee for the courage and strength which were given to this lass and to her friends to brave danger for the good of the people of Bryan's Station....

THE END

PRODUCTION NOTES

Make Him Smile

Characters: 4 male; 5 female.

Playing Time: 20 minutes.

Costumes: Mrs. Bimilie is dressed in quaint, rather dowdy clothes—a long black dress, and later a bonnet and shawl. The dolls are dressed to represent the various kinds mentioned. Mr. Crossby is dressed in everyday dress.

Properties: Address book, letter, pen, envelope.

Setting: At rear center and diagonally at either side are placed low flights of steps covered with striped or gaily colored papers upon which the dolls stand. There is a door left center, and down left stands a closed Jack-in-the-Box. Near it is a rocking chair.

China Comes to You

Characters: 8 male; 8 female; 2 characters dressed like lions, and one as a dragon.

Playing Time: 20 minutes.

Costumes: Dorothy wears a school dress. The Chinese children wear trousers of gay colors, with contrasting jackets. The tightly fitting, small black caps of the boys top long queues which may be made from strips of black silk, braided together and tied at the ends with gay ribbons or string and sewed to the caps. The girls wear large Chinese hats, or they may wear flowers in their hair. The gods are elaborately attired in silk gowns and many jewels. May Ling wears a flowered pajama suit over which she may wear a silk kimono coat. The servant's garb is more somber. Flo Flo and the lions wear animal costumes and masks.

Properties: Sets of chopsticks, bowls of rice, plates, bowls of tea, straw pallet, pin, American flag pins.

Setting: Chinese screens may be switched for the two different interiors. For the screens, Chinese pictures may be tacked to frames. Chinese lanterns may be used for decorations. There is a raised dais at wall center, on which stands a large frame, behind which sits the Kitchen God. The Dragon sits beside him. There is a Chinese screen at right, which conceals the place where May Ling and the servant prepare the meal. A lighted incense burner stands on a small table in front of the Kitchen God. In scene 2, the screens are removed and there is nothing on the stage except the throne of the Sun God, which should be a gilded chair decorated with dragons.

What's a Penny?

Characters: 5 male; 4 female.

Playing Time: 10 minutes.

Costumes: Thrift wears a costume with dollar signs all over it. Pennies are glued on a white band around her hair. Children wear everyday school clothes.

Properties: Five pennies, three piggy banks.

Setting: None required.

The Dulce Man

Characters: 3 male; 2 female; male and female extras.

Playing Time: 20 minutes.

Costumes: Simple Mexican costumes. Jose's costume is more elaborate than the others.

Properties: Coins, small table filled with various pieces of candy and covered with a white cloth, strings, top, balls, spoon, colored handkerchiefs, small toy mouse on a string; large stone jar, letter in an envelope, flags, flowers, cape for Jose.

Setting: There are trees, shrubs and seats as in a small park. To the left, upstage is a stone fountain.

The Talent Tree

Characters: 6 male; 2 female.

Playing Time: 20 minutes.

Costumes: Bobbins wears everyday clothes. Sundown is in a frayed and rather wrinkled suit. The Talents should be dressed to suggest their arts. Art's dress may be a long, flowing one of beautiful colors. The Whistler is dressed in overalls and a straw hat. The Poet wears a long, white robe. Acrobat wears a brilliantly-colored Harlequin costume with full sleeves and

legs, caught in at the wrists and ankles. Culinary Art is in a chef's apron and hat and may carry a mixing bowl and ladle. Gardener wears overalls.
Properties: Flute, notebook, pencil, mixing bowl, ladle, garden tools.
Setting: Shrubs and the Talent Tree are at right center. The tree is an odd-looking one, wide enough at the base to hide the Talents. Shrubbery may be extended to entrance if desired. The moss-covered rocks placed downstage right, in front of tree and left provide seats.
Lighting: A red spot from the wings may be used to reflect the glow from the setting sun. This is gradually dimmed and blue overheads and spots are used for the approach of night.
Note: Suitable tunes may be selected for entrance of Talents.

A CHINESE RIP VAN WINKLE

Characters: 9 male, 3 female; male and female extras.

Playing Time: 20 minutes.

Costumes: May vary from hand dyed and decorated pajamas to real Chinese robes. Chorus should wear a good deal of red. Male characters wear conventional Chinese skirt and skullcap. The women wear loose fitting coats and trousers. Both male and female wear soft-soled slippers. Papier-mache mask for Dragon's head. Property Man wears black. White Hare wears white rabbit suit or white Chinese costume.
Properties: Cymbals for musicians, lanterns, long fake cigarette for Property Man, basket and axe, which can crumble later, for Wang Chih. Chinese fan. Baskets for other laborers. Sweetmeats and artificial beards which can unroll for Old Men. Artificial beard and hump for Wang Chih. Lanterns for people in procession. Bottle full of water for Property Man, who later gives it to Wang Chih, gold paper ball representing sun for Property Man. Stick and feather, representing White Crane, for Wang Chih. White and red tissue paper streamers for Sky Dragon. Gilt moon for Property Man. Dish and stick, and water representing Elixir of Life, for White Hare. Match for Wang Chih. Property Man holds up sparklers to represent fireflies.
Note: With exception of lanterns carried in procession, and streamers blown from Sky Dragon's mouth, all properties are placed in and around property box at left, for Property Man to get and pass on to other actors.
Setting: Bare stage, backdrop of houses and rice fields, table, chair.

GREY GHOSTS

Characters: 4 male; 2 female.

Playing Time: 25 minutes.

Costumes: Lewis, Alice and John are dressed in camping clothes. Dave wears a khaki shirt and pants.

Properties: Scene 1: Box of marshmallows, long sticks. Scene 2: Guest book, pencil, a pair of binoculars, canteen of water, paper cups.
Setting: Scene 1: A clearing in the woods. There is a tent in the background. A campfire of red coals is "burning" center stage. A bathing suit is hanging on a line at one side and duffle bags and a carton of supplies are on the ground at the other side. Scene 2: The fire warden's lookout. It is furnished with a table, four straight chairs. Maps and charts hang on the wall. On the table is a clock, a telephone, more maps, the guest book.
Lighting: Scene 1: The lighting is quite dim and becomes dimmer after the fire is put out. Scene 2: As bright as possible.

OLD MAN RIVER

Characters: 2 male, 5 female.

Playing Time: 20 minutes.

Costumes: Everyday clothes. Mr. Peters wears an old cap and a raincoat. Jim wears a raincoat, rain helmet and high boots. Miss Marsh wears a dark coat, hat and rubbers.
Properties: Knitting, magazine, flashlight, three candles and candlesticks, book, dress box, blanket, small bag for Miss Marsh, umbrella, cane, winter coats for Betty and Rose, lantern, two cups and saucers, a jar of coffee.

Setting: Modern American living room in a modest home. Exits are at right and left rear. There is a window at side. Kitchen and back porch are reached through right door; telephone, bedrooms and attic through left door.
Lighting: At rise stage is rather dim. Lights go off on cue.

One-Ring Circus

Characters: 6 male; 3 female.

Playing Time: 20 minutes.

Costumes: Modern, everyday dress.

Properties: Dishpan of sawdust, small wooden or metal box containing an imaginary or toy mouse, mouth organ, jump rope, stack of books, key collections, cardboard box containing a piece of wire and some gadgets and two linked rings which can be separated.
Setting: All that is required is several odd crates and boxes about the stage.

Special Edition

Characters: 4 male; 4 female.

Playing Time: 20 minutes.

Costumes: Everyday modern dress.

Properties: Stack of papers, account books, worn black notebook, bag of cookies, coins.
Setting: The stage is divided into three parts. Down the middle is a strip representing a hallway in a large house. At the end of the hall is a telephone and stand. To the right of the hall is Patsy's room. A sign, "Neighborhood News" is tacked on the door. There is a typewriter on a table in this room. To the left of the hall is Chuck's room. A sign, "What's Up," is tacked on the door. The rooms need not have partitions. They can be marked off with lines on the stage, with screens serving as doors between the halls and both rooms. Simple furniture suggesting a combination study-room and office is used. Note: Actors in each room, of course, pay no attention to what happens elsewhere on the stage.

The Way to Norwich

Characters: 6 male, 4 female, 1 male or female.

Playing Time: 20 minutes.

Costumes: The Children, the Boy and the Girls wear everyday modern dress. The Man in the Moon wears a long cape and dark hat. Chair Mender wears old suit as does Old Clothes Man. The Pony wears brown suit and a mask made of cardboard.
Properties: Four porridge dishes, notebook and pencil, chair for Chair Mender, bag of clothes for Old Clothes Man.
Setting: None required.

Louisa Alcott's Wish

Characters: 4 male; 3 female.

Playing Time: 20 minutes.

Costumes: The players wear clothes of the period. In Scene 2 Louisa is dressed in a pink dress, white hat and green shoes. The O'Rourkes are shabbily clothed. Giant wears a one-piece brown garment which covers his entire body. He may also wear an animal head or large brown ears.
Properties: Books, paper, pencil, hoop, tin can with a string tied to it, scraggly fur piece, paper bag, food wrapped in waxed paper, dinner bell, cord.
Setting: Scene 1 is a comfortably furnished room. A sofa, chairs, tables, lamps, etc., may be used as desired. There are a great many books about, in bookcases and on the tables. Scene 2 may be played before a painted backdrop or a plain cyclorama. There is a bench in the center of the stage and various shrubs and trees here and there. Scene 3 is the same as Scene 1.

Grandma and the Pampered Boarder

Characters: 5 male; 4 female; lion and gorilla (non-speaking), either male or female.

Playing Time: 20 minutes.

Costumes: Simple everyday clothes. Mrs. Vandemark wears expensive-looking dress, Joseph a chauffeur's uniform. Lollypop and Gorilla wear appropriate animal outfits.

Properties: Scrapbook, snapshots, paste, recipe card, bowl of custard, bowl of milk, ball, jump rope, two packages of meat, broom, books, a check, knitting.

Setting: The Bascom kitchen. Downstage, a refrigerator and cupboard; center, a table and chairs; up right, a rocker; down right a bird cage with an artificial bird. A sign, BASCOM BOARDING HOUSE FOR PETS, hangs on wall.

THE LANGUAGE SHOP

Characters: 12 male; 5 female. Boys or girls may be used for all the parts (except Fifi and the citizens) as desired.

Playing Time: 15 minutes.

Costumes: Principal wears a black dress, wears glasses, and carries a book. Fifi wears a party dress. The Messenger boy wears a messenger's uniform. The Greek Citizen and the Roman Citizen may wear tunics. The Soldier wears a uniform. The rest of the characters wear everyday dress and carry the appropriate signs as indicated.

Properties: Many boxes of different shapes and sizes. A number of cardboard signs are required reading, "Slightly Used Adectives," "Adverbs — Shopworn," "Reduced in Price." Sign containing excerpt from Constitution indicated in play, "Someone," "Everybody," "Anyone," "Anybody," "Done," "Have," "His," "Swell," etc.

Setting: There is a long counter across the stage. Behind it are shelves piled with various types of boxes. There are a number of boxes open on the counter.

THE TRIAL OF BILLY SCOTT

Characters: 7 male; 6 female.

Playing Time: 20 minutes.

Costumes: All the characters are in everyday clothes, except the Judge who may wear a black robe.

Properties: Toy wagon, gavel.

Setting: The Judge's desk is on a raised platform at the center rear of the stage. There is a table at the right where the accused and his lawyer sit, and another at the left for the plaintiff and his attorney. Chairs for the witnesses are at right, and a table for the court reporter is just in front of the Judge's desk. The witness stand is at the immediate right of the Judge's desk.

CHILDREN OF THE CALENDAR

Characters: 7 male; 6 female.

Playing Time: 10 minutes.

Costumes: Father Time wears a long robe and has a grey beard. January, a boy, is dressed in winter clothing. Christmas tree icicles and artificial snow (soap flakes) are on his shoulders. February, a very short boy, also wears winter clothing with a cap pulled low over his face. March, April and May wear bright spring dresses with mayflowers and apple blossoms in their hair. June, July and August wear fluffy summer dresses. June has roses in her hair. July has a flag draped about her. August has summer flowers in her hair. September, a boy, is dressed in a bright suit. October wears a yellow or orange suit with a Halloween hat. November wears a dark suit with a wide paper collar and a Pilgrim hat. December is dressed in a Santa Claus costume or regular winter clothing.

Properties: Scythe for Father Time, paper for the children's pictures, basket of apples.

Setting: All that is required is a long, low table with chairs around it. Paper, scissors, paste, paints, crayons are on the table. Down right is a fireplace.

MUCH ADO ABOUT ANTS

Characters: 4 male; 3 female.

Playing Time: 20 minutes.

Costumes: Everyday modern clothes.

Properties: Catcher's mitt, bundle of mail, magazine, jump rope, vacuum cleaner, two trumpets, plate of doughnuts.

Setting: Modern American living room. There are doors at left and right. A desk with a typewriter and paper on it is at right. There is a table in the center of the room. A rocking chair with arms is at the left. Other chairs, lamps, and a couch make up the furnishings.

MIDNIGHT BURIAL

Characters: 8 female.
Playing Time: 15 minutes.
Costumes: Modern camp costumes.
Properties: Large, square parcel wrapped in brown paper and containing a cake; hoe, pail of water.
Setting: A night out-of-doors setting. A few bushes and small trees may be placed about the stage.
Lighting: Lighting should be dim throughout the play.

THE LITTLE CIRCUS DONKEY

Characters: 10 male.
Playing Time: 10 minutes.
Costumes: Clowns wear traditional clown suits. The Music Maker, the Piper, and the two Drummers wear regular clothes. The animals wear Dr. Denton suits painted the appropriate color. The animal faces may be cut from cardboard and colored and tied around the actor's face like a mask.
Properties: Drums, pipe, harmonica for Music Maker.
Setting: Boxes, covered with crepe paper to resemble tree stumps, and greens are placed about the stage. If desired, a backdrop of a woodland scene may be used.

HOW WE GOT OUR NUMBERS

Characters: 7 male; 2 female.
Playing Time: 15 minutes.
Costumes: Everyday modern clothes for Aunt Polly, Bill, and Mary Ann. The Hindu wears a colorful turban, long white tunic which buttons high at the throat and white trousers. The Grand Vizier dresses like a character in Arabian Nights. Ali wears a traditional Arab costume, wide trousers, gathered at the ankles, flowing robe and an Arabian headdress. Leonardo wears a doublet, short velvet cape, velvet hat with plume. Antonio and Roberto are dressed in a similar fashion.
Properties: School books, pencils, paper, Oriental gong, scroll, old clock with Roman numbers on face.
Setting: A modern living room. There is a long table, an easy chair for Aunt Polly, footstool, an old clock, and other tables and chairs. The center part of the stage only is used, leaving space on the sides for dramatized episodes.
Lighting: Spotlights should be used for the scenes played on the side of the stage.

PIFFLE! IT'S ONLY A SNIFFLE!

Characters: 7 male; 3 female; male and female extras.
Playing Time: 20 minutes.
Costumes: Everyday modern dress for school children, Teacher, Principal, Doctor, Mother, Father and Johnny. In Scene 1 Johnny is wearing outdoor clothes. The Mighty Germ is dressed in a sickly green costume. On his head he wears a dunce cap similar in color to his tight-fitting costume. The Sun wears a bright yellow costume.
Properties: Long feather for the Germ, handkerchief for Father; large red polka dot handkerchief for Johnny; different colored handkerchiefs for the children, and small white one for the Principal.
Setting: Scene 1: Hall of Johnny's home. Nothing is required; however, if desired, appropriate furniture may be used. Scene 2: The classroom. Three rows of four seats each face the right. There is a table at the left and a blackboard behind it. Scene 3: All that is required is two chairs. A desk may be used. Scene 4: Same as Scene 2.

TOMMY'S ADVENTURE

Characters: 6 male; 5 female.
Playing Time: 10 minutes.
Costumes: Modern dress for Tommy and Ellie. The Cat wears a gray costume; the Dog, a brown costume. The Red Hen wears a red costume. The Butterfly wears a long, full dress of soft yellow. Wings made of cardboard and attached to her arms are covered by the dress. The Bee wears a bright yellow costume. The Sunflower Twins are dressed in short, straight green dresses with yellow ruffs. The wind wears a full, grey cloak and the Sun a bright yellow one.
Properties: A spade.
Setting: No setting is required. If desired, a backdrop of a farm house may be used.

THE CLOCK'S SECRET

Characters: 2 male; 4 female.

Playing Time: 20 minutes.

Costumes: Everyday modern dress.

Properties: Large egg; a large amount of paper money; glass of water.

Setting: Scene 1: A comfortable living room in a country house. In a prominent position is a large grandfather's clock. (There must be a place at bottom big enough to conceal a child. The clock could be made of heavy cardboard or built over an exit.) The room contains comfortable furniture. Scene 2: The living room of a home in the city. Again the clock is in a prominent position. The furniture in this scene is more formal. Scene 3: Same as Scene 2.

SHADY SHADOWS

Characters: 2 male; 3 female; male voice.

Playing Time: 30 minutes.

Costumes: Nip and Tuck are simply dressed, and their shadows must wear clothes identical with theirs, but of black material. The shadows should have black arms, legs, faces.

Properties: Bottle of glue; brushes; desk lamp; bedroom slippers.

Setting: The room is furnished with small twin beds, two small desks, a little table, radio, book shelf, and a screen covered with plain light material. The screen must be right in front of the center entrance.

Lighting: No special effects, except for lights going out and coming on full again near end of play.

IF WISHES WERE HORSES

Characters: 5 male; 3 female.

Playing Time: 20 minutes.

Costumes: Everyday country dress. The men and boys wear overalls. Emmie and the girls wear simple cotton dresses. Hiram wears an old hat.

Properties: Rake, stick, small table, blanket, rumpled dollar bill, scarecrow dressed in an overcoat with moth balls in the pockets, pencil, paper, cotton waste, lantern, spade, package filled with money, cap, flashlight, a worn wallet.

Setting: The yard of a farm house. If desired, a backdrop may be used. The yard is covered with leaves. There is a large rock upstage left. Note: the rock may be made of bunches of newspapers tied with long strings and covered with dark material. In Scene 2 when the rock falls down, someone under the table can pull the strings of the newspapers, collapsing the rock.

Lighting: In Scene 2 a spot of moonlight on the characters and the rock may be used.

NOT ON THE MENU

Characters: 3 male; 5 female.

Playing Time: 20 minutes.

Costumes: The Anderson children wear their regular school clothes, but have chosen the gayest things they have with the intention of appearing as gypsies by adding various bright scarves, sashes and jewelry. Tommy's friends are in everyday clothes. Aunt Martha is well dressed in dark clothes. Mrs. Anderson wears an ordinary house dress.

Properties: Large sticks; knives and forks; pieces of white and brown paper; jelly glasses; rubber bands; burlap; kitchen stool; sofa pillow; bracelets; necklaces; bright sashes; handkerchiefs; earrings; two flashlights; kettle; broom stick; piece of note paper.

Setting: The sun porch is furnished with wicker pieces, its cushions covered in gay materials and there are a few potted plants here and there. The various accessories the children use are piled on a chair.

A FAMILY IN SPACE

Characters: 16 male; 6 female; 1 female extra.

Playing Time: 30 minutes.

Costumes: Everyday modern clothes for the students. Lonely Star wears a white suit with a red cape. The planets are all dressed in bright clothes and each carries a stick with a red ribbon. The airplane pilot is dressed in flying clothes.

Properties: Hand mirror and comb for Venus, picture for Professor, long scroll, small model airplane, handkerchief.
Setting: A school room. Upstage left is a large desk. The students sit in a semi-circle downstage right.

ALL IN FAVOR

Characters: 4 male; 3 female.
Playing Time: 15 minutes.
Costumes: Modern, everyday dress.
Properties: Handkerchief, several slips of paper.
Setting: The front of a shack in a backyard. There is a door leading into the shack and a bench outside the shack.

TWIN COUSINS

Characters: 3 male; 2 female.
Playing Time: 15 minutes.
Costumes: The two girls wear colorful summer dresses. Eddie wears a long-sleeved sweater of a light solid color, and a bright green cap. He also has a bright red cap for when he plays the role of Freddie. The other boys wear slacks and sweaters.
Properties: Suitcase, pin-button badge, long rope.
Setting: There may be a backdrop of houses to indicate a street scene, or no furnishings at all. Entrances are right and left.

THE KING'S CREAMPUFFS

Characters: 5 male; 4 female.
Playing Time: 30 minutes.
Costumes: All characters are in traditional costumes. The Baker wears a white apron and a cook's hat.
Properties: Tray of creampuffs; large spectacles for Queen; book; long spoon; handkerchief; boxing gloves; bottle.
Lighting: No special effects for Scenes 1 and 3, but the stage should be very dim for Scene 2, with perhaps a red or blue lantern near the cauldron to give an eerie effect.

THE DAY IS BRIGHT

Characters: 6 male; 3 female.
Playing Time: 30 minutes.
Costumes: Murillo and the students may wear solid color smocks. The Duchess is an over-dressed person, wearing highly styled clothes of the period. Sebastion and Carlos may wear brown or black trousers and blouses.
Properties: Paint brushes, apple for Sebastion, handkerchief, piece of cloth to cover easel, orange, paints, bag.
Setting: There are a number of easels and canvases scattered about the room. Sebastion's easel is at right, and Murillo's at the left. The pupils' easels are distributed at random between these two. The easels of Ricardo, Carmen, and Francisco should be grouped together, with Ricardo's in the middle. Slightly to the left of Murillo's easel is a raised platform upon which is the subject's chair. There is a chair in front of each easel. There are two windows at the rear, and a door at the left.

A LETTER TO LINCOLN

Characters: Seven female.
Playing Time: 30 minutes.
Costomers: Mrs. Baxter and the four girls wear the quaint costumes of Civil War time. In Scene 3, Medora and Betty are in simple, modern dresses.
Properties: Old-fashioned doll with scraps of silk and sewing box for Caroline. A copy of "Uncle Tom's Cabin" for Medora, knitting for Mrs. Baxter, letter on desk for Medora. Scene 3: Knitting for Betty, letter in drawer of desk for Medora.
Setting: Living room in Baxter home. At back, right of center, is a lovely old mahogany desk. At left, a window with dotted Swiss curtains. Mantel at back with fireplace. Andirons on hearth and simulated fire in fireplace. Brass candlesticks for mantel. Family portrait above mantel. Large chair with hassock. Smaller chair down left. Old-fashioned settee down right. A door at left and one at right. Scene 3: The room is a bit modernized, with bright drapes, rugs, etc.

THE LINCOLN COAT

Characters: 4 male; 4 female; male and female extras.
Playing Time: 30 minutes.
Costumes: Miss Roberts is dressed in a modern dress. Mr. Abrams

wears dark pants and a shabby jacket. Mrs. Abrams wears a clean white apron over a housedress. The Abrams children are dressed in clean but shabby clothes.
Properties: Erasers, blackboard, suit box, long-tailed black coat, coat and hat for Miss Roberts; cap and mackinaw for Joey, books, paper for Joey's note.
Setting: The first two scenes are in the schoolroom. There may be as much or as little as is feasible to indicate the scene. A blackboard stands upstage center, with a desk facing the audience to one side of it. The third scene is a crowded living room which also serves as a dining room. There is a couch at the left. A table stands on the right of the stage. A small mirror hangs on a wall. There are some chairs placed about the room.

THE QUEEN WITH THE BROKEN HEART

Characters: 2 male; 4 female.
Playing Time: 10 minutes.
Costumes: The Queen wears a long robe trimmed with red hearts. The King is dressed similiarly. The Lady-in-Waiting wears a long dress with a tall pointed hat. The Page is dressed in Knave of Hearts costume. The Fairy Godmother is dressed in grey and wears a tall, peaked grey hat. Spring wears a long white dress with flowers.
Properties: Knitting for Queen; handkerchief for Queen; locket; wand; colorful Valentine box with Valentines; spoon and flask; floral handbag.
Setting: All that is required is two large chairs with a small table holding a plant beside one, and a pile of large books on the floor beside the other. A hassock stands in front of the King's chair.

WHAT HAPPENED TO THE CAKES

Characters: 5 male; 3 female; extras.
Playing Time: 10 minutes.
Costumes: The animals may wear hoods to represent what they are. The other characters wear traditional costumes.
Properties: Mixing bowl, spoon, cup, flour, four eggs, heart-shaped cakes or cookies, butter, cookie sheet, cupcake pans, small cakes
Setting: There is a large round kitchen table in the center, on which are the ingredients for the cakes, a mixing bowl, spoon, and cup, and pans for baking. At rear wall there is a simulated oven. A cabinet or an orange crate may be used for this. There are one or two chairs beside the table.
Note: The song, "Good Morning, It Is St. Valentine's Day," used near end of play, is a traditional air.

A GUIDE FOR GEORGE WASHINGTON

Characters: 3 male; 3 female.
Playing Time: 25 minutes.
Costumes: George Washington and the Captain are both in worn Colonial uniforms. In the first two scenes they are wrapped in heavy, long, dark cloaks. Winchester is in plain uniform of the time. Elizabeth is in plain dress of Colonial style while Mrs. Winchester is in a formal gown covered by a full-length cape. The Maid is in uniform. When Elizabeth appears as the Stranger in Scene 3 she has on high riding-boots, men's pants and a jacket, a long cape, and wears a cap pulled low over her forehead. In Scene 4, Winchester has a large white bandage around his head, and his arm is in a sling.
Properties: An oil lantern, sound of a pistol shot offstage.
Setting: Scenes 1 and 3 are played either on a bare stage or before a plain dark cyclorama. Scene 2 requires an interior set with Colonial furnishings: a secretary, a turn-top table, several beautiful chairs, if possible a canopied bed. There is a door at back and one at right. Near the door is a curtained window. Scene 4 is a simple interior set, plainly and sparsely furnished with a table and a few chairs. At right there is a door.
Lighting: Scenes 1 and 3 are played on an almost dark stage. A single blue overhead spot is the only lighting and it is concentrated on the actors. In the first part of Scene 1

the stage is completely dark except for a faint indication of light from offstage. This should be just enough to give the outlines of the characters. Later the oil lamp is uncovered, and that is the only light other than the baby spot. Scenes 2 and 4 are played with regular daylight overheads and footlights.

DAVID AND THE SECOND LAFAYETTE

Characters: 10 male; 3 female; extras.

Playing Time: 30 minutes.

Costumes: The children are all dressed in everyday modern clothes, except Jean, who is dressed in a French black school smock. Miss Farnsbee wears everyday clothes. Grandpapa Cohen wears a dark suit and a scholar's cap. Lafayette is in elaborate military costume, and carries gloves.

Properties: Books, paper, etc., normally to be found in a schoolroom; a ball; large books for Scene 2; eye-glasses; papers.

Setting: Scenes 1 and 2 are in a typical American schoolroom. Maps, globe, blackboard are in evidence. There is a door at the left. In front of the room and near the teacher's desk is a big costume box containing a sword, a cocked hat, and various other bits of costumes of the revolutionary period, which are to be used in the school play. Scene 2 is a book-lined room, containing a table, several chairs, lamps, etc.

Lighting: No special effects required, except in Scene 2 where the light becomes faint, and then comes on bright again.

THE MAGIC EGG

Characters: 8 male; 9 female.

Playing Time: 20 minutes.

Costumes: The bunnies' costumes can be made from different colored snow suits with long ears to match, held up on wires. Mama Bunny wears a large, bright-colored apron; Polly wears a smaller bright-colored apron, and the boy bunnies wear bright-colored capes. Papa Bunny wears spectacles on his nose. Mrs. Feathers wears a feathery costume with cardboard wings covered with feathers attached to each arm. Mr. Feathers wears a feathery costume of bright colors with cardboard wings over his arms. The children wear everyday modern dress.

Properties: Easter bonnets, feathers, flowers, several bowls, some colored and some uncolored eggs, dough, small oven, bouquet, Easter lilies, baking tray, handkerchief for Papa Bunny.

Setting: There are entrances left and right between the trees. If desired, a backdrop of a forest may be used. Under a spreading tree upstage right is a small log and a big toadstool that is used for a table. Upstage center is a fallen tree which is used for another table. A sawed-off tree stump stands downstage left. Upstage left is a small bonfire over which is a small oven.

A PRESENT FOR MOTHER

Characters: 2 male; 1 female; 4 male or female.

Playing Time: 10 minutes.

Costumes: Bill and Janie wear everyday clothes. The animals are dressed in costumes suggestive of the type they represent.

Properties: None required.

Setting: Scene 1: All that is required is a large log in the center of the stage, with some bushes around it. Scene 2: A hollow tree stands in center. Other trees and bushes surround it.

MOTHER'S GIFT

Characters: 3 male; 4 female.

Playing Time: 15 minutes.

Costumes: Dicky and his mother wear everyday clothes. The other characters should be suggested by their costumes. Hoods or caps with ears, wiskers, and bill for the bird (made with construction paper or buckram and colored with crayons) may be used. Feelers for bees may be made from pipe cleaners.

Properties: Long weeds for reeds; nuts; red ribbon with a little silver bell; artificial clover.

Setting: There may be potted trees at back and right center. If possible some patches of grass and moss

should be placed around the trees. There is a small flowering bush (a large plant in bloom may be used) at the left.
Lighting: Stage should be brightly lighted to indicate bright sun.

A GOLDEN BELL FOR MOTHER

Characters: The six mice may be represented by girls, and the six kittens by boys. Other than these one male and one female are required.

Playing Time: 12 minutes.

Costumes: The mice should be dressed in gray and the kittens in various shades of brown and tan. The whiskers for both may be made from pipe cleaners. Mother Mouse is also dressed in gray, but a much larger child should play this part. The storeman wears a white apron and a white jacket.
Properties: String; piece of sewing; piece of knitting; knitting needles; needle and thread; a large round piece of heavy gray cardboard may be used for the coin; if possible, this may be covered with silver-colored paper; a golden bell. (A large cow bell may be used for this.)
Setting: There is nothing required for Scenes 1 and 4 except a large sign on the wall reading, "Mice Working." The mice sit on the floor. In Scene 2 a large box at the right may be used as a counter to suggest a store. There is a door left with a bell hanging on it, which rings as door is opened. For the third scene there may be a table in the center. There is a door left, and the entrance to the mouse hole at the right.
Note: The old song, "The Frog in the Well," or any other version of this song may be substituted for "A Frog He Would A-Wooing Go." All these songs have familiar tunes.

THE DO-NOTHING FROG

Characters: 10 male; 6 female; as many extras as desired for other children.

Playing Time: 15 minutes.

Costumes: Boys and girls wear everyday clothes. Shopkeeper may wear a hat reading, "Shopkeeper".
Properties: A collection of items representing the various trades and professions mentioned in the play. Sign reading, *The I'm-Going-To-Be Shop* and a large bell for Shopkeeper; hat labeled *Zoo.*
Setting: The I'm-Going-To-Be Shop. Tables representing counters are upstage. A stool is down right. Exits are left and right.

Lighting: No special effects.

THE PINK PARASOL

Characters: 3 male; 6 female.

Playing Time: 40 minutes.

Costumes: Mrs. Marshall and Sally Marshall are in modern dress; the rest of the characters are in costumes of the Civil War period. Clayton is dressed in a shabby gray Confederate uniform; the Yankee soldier is dressed in the blue uniform of the North.
Properties: Lots of artificial flowers or baskets of flowers; a pink parasol, first wrapped in brown paper; a long skirt with ruffles; thread and needle; plate of sandwiches; a cake; plates; knife; forks; shawl; napkins.
Setting: The first and last scenes require no setting except a bench in front of the curtain. For Scene 2 there is a garden table and some garden chairs.

COLUMBUS SAILS THE SEA

Characters: 4 male; 1 female; sailors and Indians.

Playing Time: 20 minutes.

Setting: One setting with several changes of stage properties. First scene requires no stage properties, but only a soft background. For Scene 2 there should be a throne-chair on an elevated platform which can be made from a large box. A rail and some rope and rigging can be used to suggest the third scene. Palms and trees against the backdrop should be used for Scene 4.

Costumes: Rough dark suits for Columbus and the sailors. Elaborate court robes and jewels for Isabella. Conventional court costumes for courtiers. The Indians may be clothed in shorts and feathered headdress.

Properties: Map; branch with berries; standard with flag of Spain.

THE MAGIC SPELL

Characters: 1 male; 5 female.

Playing Time: 15 minutes.

Costumes: Teena and her mother are dressed as witches in long black cloaks and tall black pointed hats. Jimmy is dressed as a clown, and Betty as a gypsy. Mrs. Lane wears a simple street dress. Jenny wears a maid's uniform.

Properties: A pumpkin jack-o'-lantern, a tea tray with a cup and saucer, napkin, sugar bowl, and teaspoon, books, toys.

Setting: The room is simply furnished. In the center is an armchair with a table at the right of it. There is a chair on either side of the stage. The doorway on the left leads outside; the one on the right leads to the other rooms. A few toys and books are on the table.

THE WITCH'S PUMPKIN

Characters: 3 female

Playing Time: 15 minutes.

Costumes: Betty wears a regular school dress. Anne is dressed in some appropriate Hallowe'en costume. Cindy wears a long, black cloak, mask and pointed hat.

Properties: Small pumpkin, pencils, paper, scissors, broom, package containing a Hallowe'en costume.

Setting: A plainly furnished room. There are two doors, one opening on the porch, the other leading to a hall. In the center of the room is a table with a chair behind it, and one near either side. Other furnishings may be added.

GOBLIN PARADE

Characters: 6 male; 2 female; extras.

Playing Time: 20 minutes.

Costumes: The Janitor, the Boy, Harry and Jack are in everyday clothes. The Scarecrow is dressed in shabby, patched overalls and tattered straw hat. The Witch wears a long, black dress and peaked hat. The Goblins are in dark, tightly fitting suits. Animal heads may be procured for the others or they may be dressed to resemble as much as possible the animals they represent.

Properties: Broom, step-ladder, large orange sun, two corn-shocks, jack-o'-lantern, knife, huge yellow moon.

Setting: This play can be produced in the schoolroom itself or on a bare stage with entrances at right and left. The only furnishing is a teacher's chair, preferably a wooden armchair.

Lighting: Bright overheads and footlights can be used at the beginning of the play and dimmed when the Goblins enter. They can then be brought on full again when the Goblins have left the stage.

THE MAGIC JACK-O-LANTERN

Characters: Six male or female; extras, if desired.

Playing Time: 10 minutes.

Costumes: The elves are dressed in colored shorts with matching jerkins and pointed hats. They wear long colored hose, the toes of which are stuffed and made to curl up beyond the end of the foot. The goblins are dressed in shorts with matching jerkins, colored differently from the elves' costumes. Trappy wears a large, red leaf on his hat. Micky wears a large red feather in his cap. Flappy should have large cardboard ears placed over his own ears. These may be attached with adhesive tape.

Properties: Jack-o-lantern, broomstick, scarlet leaf, large red feather.

Setting: This may be a bare stage with no furnishings, or a wooded scene may be suggested by the backdrop.

THE MAGIC PUMPKIN

Characters: 10 male; 6 female.

Playing Time: 10 minutes.

Costumes: Minstrel wears tight-fitting jersey costume and stocking cap. Little bells are attached to cap and to jacket. The King's guards are dressed in royal soldiers' costumes and the King himself may wear a long, full gown and a crown on his head. The Mother and children may wear simple everyday clothes.
Properties: Large white handkerchief, a number of brown stones, a large pumpkin, whistle, hunting knife.
Setting: A bench.

WONDERS OF STORYBOOK LAND

Characters: 11 male; 8 female.
Playing Time: 25 minutes.
Costumes: Billy and Betty in clothes of modern boy and girl. Little Red Riding Hood, red hooded cape. White Rabbit, white rabbit suit with black waistcoat. Captain Hook, blue cape, black pirate hat, black patch over eye and hook for claw. Alice-in-Wonderland, starched, full-length, white apron over dress, narrow black ribbon with tiny bow on hair. Smee, pirate costume, Snow White, blue skirt, white blouse, black laced bodice and pretty white bow in hair. Peter Pan, brown cap with feather, brown belted blouse, short brown pants and three-quarter stockings. Tiger Lily, beautiful white beaded Indian Princess costume. Lost Boy, boy's outfit. Raggedy Ann, wig of yarn, rag doll's dress. Raggedy Andy, wig of yarn, rag doll's costume and cap. Sleepy and Happy, dwarf costume. Blue Fairy, pale blue gown, golden star in hair. Pinocchio, conical hat, yellow blouse, red pants, large, blue bow tie. Cinderella, ragged costume and small broom. Little Lame Prince, full-sleeved blouse and skull cap.
Properties: Living-room table, chairs, pictures, books, sewing basket. Front of white cottage, picket fence, paper flowers, tree, package.
Setting: Scene 1 is living room of Robertson home. Necessary properties are living-room table and chairs, but pictures, flowers, lamps, etc., may be used as desired to give room attractive appearance. Scene 2 is Storybook Land and should be as colorful as possible. White, green trimmed cottage with picket fence, a garden and large tree will be required. Bird houses, benches or other properties may be used.
Lighting: No special effects for Scene 1, but soft colored lights for Scene 2.

OFF THE SHELF

Characters: 5 male; 3 female.
Playing Time: 25 minutes.
Costumes: These may be simple or elaborate for the book characters. A simple placard on the front of each character may indicate the name of the book. Or there may be back and sides of cardboard with holes for the head, arms, and legs.
Properties: Ruler, eight white posters of stiff cardboard.
Setting: The upstage wall is completely covered with books on shelves. These can be painted on the backdrop. On the side walls the ends of the book shelves are seen with rows of books running off left and right. There are openings between these stacks which serve as entrances. At center is a long table of the sort used in libraries, with chairs set at the ends and sides. There are green reading lamps on the table. Upstage center against the back wall is the librarian's desk.
Lighting: The lights are low but grow gradually brighter as the action of the play progresses.

MR. LONGFELLOW OBSERVES BOOK WEEK

Characters: 6 male; 5 female.
Playing Time: 20 minutes.
Costumes: Longfellow and his daughters wear clothes of the times. Joseph is in Polish dress and wears a medal around his neck. Two children inside a horse costume may play Smoky, or one child may play this character wearing just an animal head and tail. Smoky also has a medal around his neck. Dr. Doolittle is dressed in a tall hat and long-tailed coat. Younger Brother wears an Indian costume, and Young Fu Chinese dress of blue coat and trousers. Hitty is dressed in the style of

a century ago, and Lucinda in the clothes of her time. The books in which characters appear may be consulted for costuming if desired.
Properties: Horn, roller skates.
Setting: Longfellow's desk is at left, a comfortable armchair in front of it. There is a grandfather clock in the background. A round table nearby is covered with books and bookshelves line the walls.

HUBBUB ON THE BOOKSHELF

Characters: 7 male; 2 female.
Playing Time: 30 minutes.
Costumes: The eight young Bookworms are clothed in sheaths of white or pale gray, and from their tightly-fitting hoods spring antennae or feelers. They speak in unison much of the time, act as a group instead of as individuals, and have no distinguishing marks at all. The old Bookworm is dressed like the others, with the addition of a long white beard. Costumes for the Bookworms when they emerge from the volumes during the play are described in the text.
Properties: Scrap of paper; lorgnette; basket filled with groceries and containing a napkin; spectacles for Mr. Wise; hatchet; sword; suitcase; spray-gun, handkerchief for Gangster.
Setting: Eight large books provide the background. Reading from left to right they are Encyclopedia, Fairy Tales, American History, Etiquette, King Arthur and His Knights, My Book of Poems, Travel Stories and Arithmetic.

THE BOOK HOSPITAL

Characters: 4 male; 4 female.
Playing Time: 10 minutes.
Costumes: Dr. Librarian and Nurse Mary wear white uniforms. The book characters wear shabby, torn cardboard book covers. King Arthur wears a crown.
Properties: Hospital cart or tea wagon, glass of water, pills, thermometer, pliers, cotton, sponge, scissors, binding tape, mending tape, stethoscope, blanket, and containers marked "Glue," Shellac," "Mending Tape," "Pain Pills," and "Alcohol."
Setting: The book hospital. There are three cots and five chairs.
Sound: Hospital bell.

I'LL SHARE MY FARE

Characters: 4 male; 2 female.
Playing Time: 10 minutes.
Costumes: The Farmer wears overalls and straw hat; the Butcher wears a long, white apron. The Baker wears a white coat and high baker's hat. The Storekeeper wears a short apron over his trousers. The Basketweaver wears a shawl over her long dress.
Properties: Wares for the booths (may be made of cardboard); hobby horse for Farmer; large basket.
Setting: Three small booths decorated with wares.

THANKS TO SAMMY SCARECROW

Characters: 3 male; 1 female.
Playing Time: 10 minutes.
Costumes: Sammy is dressed as the usual scarecrow — a shabby black coat and pants, a bunch of straw showing out from under a black high hat. Long sticks may be pushed into his sleeves to give him the stiff, scarecrow look. Sandy is dressed in a gray flannel costume and hood. Pipe cleaners may be used for his whiskers, and a large bushy or furry tail should be attached to his back. The children wear everyday play clothes.
Properties: Nuts; basket, gaily decorated; corn stalks.
Setting: The stage is bare except for the scarecrow in the center, leaning haphazardly on crossed sticks. At right center there are some corn shocks to indicate the field.

MR. THANKS HAS HIS DAY

Characters: 7 male; 4 female.
Playing Time: 20 minutes.
Costumes: Mr. Thanks is shabbily dressed and wears an old slouch hat. The policemen are in uniform. The boys and girls and man and woman wear everyday clothes. Granny wears a housedress and apron. The Mayor wears a dark suit and derby.
Properties: A large sack containing a wool scarf, shoes, bag of flour, hair-ribbon, and other sundries; sticks for policemen; pair of shoes in child's size; notebook and pencil.
Setting: A backdrop of painted trees may be used to indicate park. At

left center is a park bench. Right wall should represent a street facing the park, which may be indicated through one or two outside doorways. The same setting may be used throughout.

JONATHAN'S THANKSGIVING

Characters: 6 female; 5 male.
Playing Time: 15 minutes.
Costumes: Opatuck and Punkapoag in full Indian attire; chief with feathered headgear. All others in Pilgrim costumes.
Properties: Rough furniture of time: benches, stools, crib, table, spinning wheel, hornbook, bible, sewing pieces, bow and arrows, sickle, ears of corn, spider, crier's bell, scroll of paper, musket, pumpkin, stick, bread, knife, jug, mug, baskets, jars, hour glass, hamper, kettle, turkey, tomahawk, doll, grapes and cranberries, red leaves, roots, knives.
Setting: Kitchen of Pilgrim log cabin. Door to outside right back, fireplace left back. Window right. Inner door left. Furniture of the period.
Lighting: Daylight foot and overhead.

THE HOLLY HANGS HIGH

Characters: 3 male; 4 female.
Playing Time: 20 minutes.
Costumes: Modern everyday clothes. Rose wears a heavy coat, tall boots and a beret. Tom wears a dark suit and a leather jacket. The Ranger is dressed in mountain clothes with boots. Hannah wears a plain print dress with a white apron over it.
Properties: Large tray, chocolate pot, two cups and saucers, presents to be placed under Christmas tree.
Setting: Main room of a mountain cabin. At the back is a fireplace in which there is a simulated fire. A box filled with fire wood is at the right along side of a fireside bench. At the left of the fireplace is a tall screen hiding the Christmas tree which is decorated with lights. To the right is a low table and a comfortable chair. A bunch of holly hangs over the mantle. At lower right is a desk with desk chair and telephone. At the right is a door leading to other parts of the house. The door leading outside at left.

MERRY, MERRY, MERRY

Characters: 13 male; 11 female.
Playing Time: 25 minutes.
Costumes: All adults and the children wear straight costumes from everyday life. The Fairy is dressed in white, with a silver cap. Her dress is trimmed in red, and she carries a wand with a sparkling star at the end of it. The elves are all in green and gold. Santy is a little man in a red suit, but without a beard. Santa Claus is in traditional costume with long white, beard.
Properties: Sofa, easy chairs, table, end tables, lamps for tables and also floor, rugs, pictures on the wall, radio, telephone, and other livingroom furniture depending on the elaborateness of the set; a Christmas tree completely decorated, stockings for the fireplace, white shawl, newspaper, basket, gaily-wrapped boxes of presents in various shapes and sizes, jew's harp or harmonica, clock, pipe, a wand, tremendous bag for Santy, fruit and knives and dolls for the stockings, three cowboy outfits.
Setting: Simple interior living-room set. This may be furnished like a living room in any home of an American family of moderate income. There is a festive air about it, particularly evidenced by the Christmas tree, and if possible holly wreaths and electric candles in the windows rear. A fireplace in the rear wall between the two windows is also essential. Other than that, the set may be left entirely to the discretion of the Director.
Lighting: Dim evening light, footlights and overhead. All lamps on in the room, tree lighted, and candles in window. Spotlight follows Fairy. Lights all up bright at end of play particularly on entrance of Santa Claus.

Note: The school glee club, or a selected chorus, may do the singing of the carols offstage. The volume must be carefully controlled to give effect of receding and approaching carollers.

THE FIRST NEW ENGLAND CHRISTMAS TREE

Characters: 6 male; 2 female; male extras.
Playing Time: 25 minutes.
Costumes: Clothes of the Colonial period. Cynthia, George and William wear outdoor clothes at their entrance. Captain Harcus wears a sea captain's outfit.
Properties: Sack; a small doll; several silver paper stars, six wishing nuts each marked plainly with a white name tag and each containing a slip of paper; candles.
Setting: The entire play takes place in a simply furnished room of the Harcus cottage. Colonial furniture, including a table and a rocker, is placed about the room. There are two doors and a window in the room. Scene 3: A blanket is fastened across the window. A small, partly decorated spruce stands in one corner of the room.

THE LITTLE CAKE

Characters: 2 male; 6 female; extras.
Playing Time: 40 minutes.
Costumes: The Old Man wears an old hooded cloak over royal purple robes. The Captain is dressed in scarlet and gold court costume. Marie wears ragged dress. Other girls are richly dressed in clothes of the period.

Properties: Dish containing pudding; sausages, basket, little cake, a package representing Sonia's gift.
Setting: Up center are deep casement windows through which can be seen castle towers silhouetted against the night sky. There is snow on the branches outside and in the corners of the frosted window panes. There is a fireplace at left. Up right is a doorway leading to a hallway which is the way to the rest of the house, and also to the outside. The room is furnished with the usual benches and rough table, which are adorned with colorful and rich-looking draperies and hangings.
Lighting: There is a red light in the fireplace to represent a fire. The room is in shadow except for the glow of a candle on the table and the red light from the fireplace.

CHRISTMAS COMES TO HAMELIN

Characters: 13 male; 13 female; male and female extras.
Playing Time: 20 minutes.
Costumes: Suggestion of medieval clothes. The men wear knickers, soft hats with plumes, and swords. The Mayor wears an elaborate cape. The Stranger is dressed simply and carries a staff. The Toyman wears a long apron. The women wear long, bright full dresses with shawls or capes. Some wear caps and aprons. The children are dressed very plainly; the boys in knickers; girls in long dresses, or rain capes.
Properties: A large book, a ruler or pointer, an oilcan.
Setting: All that is required for the first scene is a table, a sofa, a few easy chairs, and a fireplace. The scenes in the orphanage only require a few chairs or stools, perhaps some old toys, a blackboard or a globe. A large framed sampler, reading "God Bless Our Home," hangs on a wall.

HAPPY CHRISTMAS TO ALL

Characters: 3 male; 3 female.
Playing Time: 20 minutes.
Costumes: Dr. Moore wears a long black coat of clerical cut, and spectacles on his nose. At first he wears slippers, but changes to shoes when he goes out. He also then puts on an overcoat, a black stove-pipe hat, and a black woolen muffler. He wears gloves. Mrs. Moore wears a white apron over her dark house-dress. She wears a neat white cap on her head. The boys are dressed in warm winter clothes, as is the girl. Emily is smartly dressed according to the fashion of the early Nineteenth century. At end children wear white flannel nightgowns.
Properties: Books, quill pen, paper, tall red candle, covered basket, packages with Christmas wrappings, simulated turkey, black toy kitten, newspaper, bowl and spoon.
Setting: There is an old-fashioned desk upstage right. Left upstage is a fireplace where light may be hidden to represent a fire. Over the fireplace is a mantel. The room is cheerful. There are several comfortable chairs scattered about the

room, and a table in the center. There is a pile of books on the desk. There is an armchair near the fireplace with a footstool in front of it. There is a window and door in the rear wall, and a door in the left wall beyond the fireplace.
Lighting: Lighting is furnished by candles which are on the fireplace mantel. At the end of each scene, just before the reading of the poems, the light may be dimmed.

NO ROOM AT THE INN

Characters: 15 male; 1 female; extras.

Playing Time: 20 minutes.

Costumes: The players wear the traditional flowing garments of the Orient, not necessarily white. The Boy is dressed in a short tunic. Sandals are worn by all.
Properties: Pitchers, staffs for the Shepherds, three coffers.
Setting: On two sides of the stage, rear and left, runs the wall of the courtyard. This is about six feet high and is broken by two arched gateways. One arch is at the center of the rear wall and leads to the stables. It has a wooden gate. The other arch is at the center of the left wall and is the entrance to the inn yard from the highway. It has no gate. On the right of the stage is the wall of the inn. There is a door in the center of the wall; to the right of the door, a bench; to the left, a small window. The stage is bare save for the bench and at the rear left a circular well-curb of stone wide enough to use as a seat. Above the wall sky is seen.
Lighting: Red overheads and footlights are used in Scene 1, with most of the light from the overheads concentrated at left or perhaps additional red spots shining from the left wings. For Scene 2 dark blue overheads and footlights are desirable. A white spot from offstage can be placed to shine directly over the stable to represent the star; or the desired effect can also be attained by hanging a silver star above the stable and using a white spot on it.
Note: This play can be combined effectively with a musical program by preceding and following it with the singing of carols. One verse of a carol could be sung also while the curtain is lowered to denote passage of time. Nothing longer should be introduced here as it would break the continuity of the play.
Appropriate carols are "O Little Town of Bethlehem," "While Shepherds Watched Their Flocks," "Away in a Manger," "We Three Kings," "Silent Night," "All my Heart this Night Rejoices," "It Came Upon a Midnight Clear," "First Noel," "In Bethlehem 'neath Starlit Skies," "Adeste Fidelis."

CHRISTMAS HOUSE

Characters: 4 male; 6 female.

Playing Time: 30 minutes.

Costumes: Everyday modern dress.
Properties: A magazine for Margery, Christmas decorations for the tree, including lights, logs for fireplace, paper for Margery's sketch.
Setting: A fireplace, flanked by two easy chairs stands upstage center. Against one wall is a couch. Occasional chairs and tables with lamps are placed here and there. The Christmas tree stands near fireplace.

THE CRYSTAL FLASK

Characters: 2 male; 6 female.

Playing Time: 18 minutes.

Costumes: The Princess wears an elaborate satin robe with a crown on her head in Scenes 2 and 3. The King and Queen wear long robes and crowns. The Godmothers are dressed in long, bright-colored gowns. One carries a silver flask and the other, a crystal flask. The Prince wears bright satin trousers, long white stockings, a blue velvet cape and matching hat. The Nurse is dressed in a long gray dress, white apron and cap.
Properties: A large baby doll that can be used for the Princess in Scene 1; silver flask, crystal flask, handkerchief.
Setting: The stage should represent a room in the palace. This may be as elaborate as desired. Two large chairs should be in the center of the stage for the thrones.

LITTLE HERO OF HOLLAND

Characters: 7 male; 14 female.

Playing Time: 20 minutes.

Costumes: The girls wear very full skirts, starched white aprons and caps, white stockings and, if possible, wooden shoes, which may be made out of white cardboard glued to old shoes. The boys wear long wide breeches (ski-pant style) and close-fitting jackets of some dark material. They wear little round dark caps. The flower fairies' costumes may be made of crêpe paper, or they may wear short white dresses trimmed with gummed tulip and hyacinth cut-outs. Flowers bind their hair and trim their slippers. Tipsey and Topsey are dressed in bright green, close-fitting costumes with bright spangle trimmings, peaked caps with tassels, and sneakers, painted green.

Properties: Pails and scrub brushes; basket covered with a white napkin; artificial tulips, toy windmill, lanterns, a few wads of paper or corks for plugs.

Setting: The Dutch background may be painted on large sheets of heavy paper tacked to beams. Or pictures of windmills, green fields dotted with tulips and other flowers and quaint flowers may be pasted on this paper. The hole in the dike is at the right. Artificial flowers may be used for stage decorations. At right there is a large oblong box covered with green paper, representing a boulder.

RUMPLESTILTSKEN

Characters: 7 male; 2 female.

Playing Time: 20 minutes.

Costume: The King wears a long purple robe and a crown. The huntsmen are dressed in breeches and hunting caps. The Miller wears dark trousers and shirt. Marilyn wears a simple, plain long dress in the first two scenes; in the last two scenes she wears a long robe and a crown. The servant is dressed in a long, dark dress with a white apron and cap. The Dwarf is dressed in brown, long, tight-fitting pants which fit over his feet and curl up at the toes. Little bells are attached to the feet. A pointed matching cap completes his outfit.

Properties: Scroll, gold colored bits of paper, tube, necklace.

Setting: Scene 1: All that is required is a large chair on a platform for the throne. Scene 2: The room can be bare except for a spinning wheel and piles of straw. Last two Scenes: Large chair for the Queen; other furniture, if desired.

SLEEPING BEAUTY

Characters: 6 male, 11 female.

Playing Time: 20 minutes.

Costumes: King and Queen in royal attire with long robes and crowns; Fairies in long, flowing dresses; Wicked Fairy dressed to resemble a witch; Princess in long party-type dress; Spinning Woman in ordinary clothes of older working woman; Guard could wear a red vest to denote a costume; Prince, ordinary clothes; Hunters, ordinary clothes.

Properties: Thrones for King and Queen to sit in; 8 magic wands; perambulator trimmed with ribbons and bows; Spinning wheel and spindle; Guard carries spear; Hunters carry bows and arrows; glass of water for Spinner.

Settings: Room in King's palace, may be ordinary room with two thrones. Spinner's room may have two or three stools and spinning wheel and spindle. In the forest, may be woods scenery, or plain stage as dialogue sets the stage for audience.

THE LION AND THE MOUSE

Characters: 1 male; 1 female.

Playing Time: 10 minutes.

Costumes: The Lion may be dressed in long yellow or tan pants with matching jerkin with long sleeves. A lion's face may be made of cardboard and attached to the player's head. The Mouse is dressed in grey shorts and matching jerkin.

Properties: None required.

Setting: All that is necessary is some bushes in the background with a net caught in them. A tennis net could be used. If desired, a backdrop of a woody scene may be used.

THE THREE WISHES

Characters: 5 male; 4 female.
Playing Time: 20 minutes.
Costumes: All characters are in modern dress. Mrs. Kehoe wears a print dress trimmed with lace, and earrings. Patrick may wear a cap with a visor and working clothes. Col. Moore is elegantly dressed.
Properties: Cake with white icing and ten birthday candles; basket with pieces of lace; salt-cellar; salt box; bottle of milk; bowls; pot porridge; violets and leaves; towels; glasses; spoons; string of coral-colored beads; bowl of goldfish; lace collar; green tickets; hat; cape; flags; noise-makers.
Setting: The room for Scene 1 is furnished as a combination dining-room, kitchen, and living-room. A cot covered with a homespun bedspread is seen at one end. A large crayon picture of a man about thirty-five, with a Union Jack and an American flag crossed above it, stands on a homemade easel. Scene 2 consists merely of a few tables covered around three sides with cloth to make booths. There is one with odd pieces of costume jewelry on it, and another with only one lace collar pinned to the cord stretched across the booth. This booth has a sign on it, "The Mountain Home Industries' Booth". There are several stools around and one behind the booth.

THE SALT IN THE SEA

Characters: 15 male; 2 female.
Playing Time: 30 minutes.
Costumes: All characters are dressed in clothes of the times, each according to rank.
Properties: Quill pen, cap with long feather for Giles, sack of meal, ham, bag of gold, mill, jug of milk, cake, cheese, little cakes, pack for Miller, silver basket, new mill, faggots, jug of ale, two mugs.
Setting: Scene 1 is very bare with stacks of casks and sacks of food piled high around the walls. The Dwarfs' workshop in Scene 2 needs only a rough table and a few chairs. In Scene 3 there is a door, left front; another, right back; and an empty fireplace, center back. An open Welsh cupboard is at right of left door with four mugs on the shelves. Scene 4 is the same as Scene 1 except that the walls are now hung with tapestries, cloth covers the table. For Scene 5 two sea chests are placed at right and left back. Ropes and ship paraphernalia are scattered about. This scene can also be produced before a plain cyclorama if desired.

CINDERELLA

Characters: 17 male; 9 female.
Playing Time: 30 minutes.
Costumes: First sister wears old-fashioned pink satin and lace, and the Second Sister, old-fashioned blue satin and lace. Cinderella, in fireside scenes, wears ragged, patched dress; in ballroom scene and finale, silver and white gown and silver Juliet head piece. Godmother wears dark cloak and conical hat, gray wig. Prince is in white and gold full sleeved jacket, white knee breeches and stockings, Romeo cap with jaunty gold feather. Trumpeters are in green and gold. Attendants to Prince wear various colored costumes similar to that of Prince, but less elaborate. Guests at ball are dressed in old-fashioned costumes.
Properties: Table, chairs, box, fireplace, broom, pumpkin, toy mice, throne.
Setting: Scene 1 is by the fireplace in Cinderella's home. Two chairs, a table, a box and a fireplace will suffice to set this scene. Scene 2 is the scene of the ball and the throne should occupy the center of attention as all available space should be left for dancing. Scene 3, same as Scene 1.
Lighting: Scenes 1 and 3 require an artificial fire in fireplace. Scene 2 colored lights.
Music: Selections for dancing and entrances are optional. Music to which rights have expired may be used. If amateur orchestra is available effect would add color to production. If not, records offstage may be used.

THE FLOATING STONE

Characters: 6 male; 4 female.

Playing Time: 10 or 12 minutes.

Costumes: These may be copied from any book of fairy tales. The King and Princess have gilt crowns, his rather more elaborate. The ladies should have Juliet caps or simple silver bands about their hair. The Shepherd wears a brown tunic and carries a crook made from cardboard. The Herald wears a tabard to which heraldic animals or fleur-de-lis cut from gay paper have been pinned. He should hold a trumpet; if there are none in the school band, one may be cut from cardboard and gilded. The Princes wear crowns and gay colors; if possible they have capes clasped with jewels from the useful Woolworth. The Wizard has flowing robes to which are pasted stars, moons, etc.

Properties: A bag for the Princess, preferably a chatelaine, containing a folded piece of paper for the King's message and a tiny mirror. A table, cloth, and pebble for the Herald to bring in. A bundle for the Shepherd containing a mortar and pestle; there must be ground-up chalk or flour darkened with a little soot in the mortar, as the grinding of the stone has to be tricked a little. A handkerchief for the Prince of Tripota, made of bright-colored cloth. Two thrones, which may be draped chairs.

Setting: This may be played before a plain cyclorama.

JACK AND JILL

Characters: 4 male; 3 female.

Playing Time: 10 minutes.

Costumes: Jack wears a play suit with a large tie. Jill is dressed in a print dress and large white apron which she takes off when she is playing. Mother wears a long full skirt and apron. She may also wear a grey wig or a dust cap. The Fairy wears a long pastel gown with wings.

Properties: Toy pails and shovels, wand.

Setting: A plain brown cottage should be indicated on the backdrop with a door and window opening off the stage. Flowers made of crepe paper or real potted plants are set in beds along the house. A walk of flat stones leads from door to right of stage and off stage. A carpet of green paper matting may be used to give the effect of grass.

BROOM MARKET DAY

Characters: 5 male; 4 female.

Playing Time: 20 minutes.

Costumes: Costumes may be suggestive of early colonial days in New England. For the women, a long, plain-colored frock with white cap, apron and neckerchief. Dame Dickens, however, wears a high-crowned hat with a brown dress and an apron of giddy calico patchwork. The men may have knee trousers, plain coats, and broad-brimmed hats. A frock coat is worn by the Parson.

Properties: Coat for Granther — also hat and white parcel, dustcloth, penny, coins, scarecrow broom with carrot nose, corn silk hair and a shawl. Note: Prop brooms may be fashioned from heavy wrapping paper, fringed and fastened to stock handles. Small, straight tree branches may be used for the scare-crow and hobby-horse brushes. Be sure that there is a distinct difference in the size of the brooms of various sorts.

Setting: The broom maker's cottage. Center back is a large fireplace with a kettle on the hob. Pewter candlesticks, mugs and plates are on the high mantel. There is an open door at the right. Small alcove is at left back. Several three-legged stools are placed about the room with a stool by the fireplace. There are many brooms about.

JENNY-BY-THE-DAY

Characters: 4 male; 3 female.

Playing Time: 20 minutes.

Costumes: Margery Daw wears a dark, bodiced gown with a long, full skirt and a white apron and cap. Dally wears doublet and hose. Dilly wears a long, full dress. The twins wear dust-mop wigs and their clothes are generally disheveled. Jenny wears a long, bodiced dress with a tiny white apron and cap. The Trumpeter and Herald are dressed in doublet and hose. The King wears dark hose and a plain maroon doublet and plumed hat.

Properties: Trumpet, paper roll for proclamation, faggots, apple blossoms, huge crock.

Setting: The inn. There is a casement window at left. The door at left rear opens into the courtyard. There is a huge fireplace center rear, with a large pot over simulatd fire. Another kettle sits on the ashes. Cooking pans, skillets, ladles, spoons, long-handled fork and a broom hang on the sides of the fireplace. There is a small pile of faggots to right of fireplace. Bowls, mugs and plates are on the ledge above the fireplace. There is a large chest at right. In the chest are pudding bag and string, polishing cloths and scrub brush. Down center are a trestle table and two backless benches. In the upper corner of the door is a spider in a web. (Dyed pipe cleaner may be used to make the spider which should be suspended from the door frame with a light thread. Dark netting may be fashioned into a web.)

THE WISE MAN OF GOTHAM

Characters: 8 male; many extras, both male and female.

Playing Time: 20-25 minutes.

Costumes: The costumes are of the period of Robin Hood, all brightly colored.

Properties: Baskets, sacks, eggs, apples, bowl of water, horn, heavy rocks, branches of trees, a door either of wood or made from large strips of cardboard nailed to a light frame, and painted to look very real.

Setting: Scenes 1, 2, and 3 take place in the market place of Gotham. This entire play may be staged with a plain cyclorama. Otherwise, these scenes are played with a countryside picture of trees and hills painted on the backdrop. Scene 4 is set in a field near Gotham and also may be played on a bare stage. It is necessary, however, to have a thicket or bushes of some kind in upper right corner of stage, so that references may be made to the cuckoo which is just offstage. Then when the villagers mention that the bird has flown away, the audience merely takes their word for it. Visible from the audience, therefore, is only one side of the fence the villagers are building from tree branches.

Lighting: Scene 1 is daylight, with amber overhead, and white footlights. Scene 2 is night; use blue overheads and dim or no footlights. Scene 3 at dawn, slight tinge of pink in lights overhead. Footlights dim. It is not yet full daylight lighting. Scene 4 is same as Scene 1.

THE PIED PIPER OF HAMELIN

Characters: 5 male; 1 female lead. Many female extras to make up The Crowd. At least a dozen children.

Playing Time: 30 minutes.

Costumes: The Piper wears the traditional costume: with one leg yellow, the other blue, one sleeve scarlet, the other dune, the back purple, and the front green. During the opening part of the play he also wears a peaked hat and a dusty black cloak concealing his multicolored costume. Obie is dressed in very ragged boy's pants and sweater. Stempernickel wears a lovely red cloak; Bumperkopf a beautiful green cloak; and The Mayor a gorgeous one of royal purple. Katrinka is dressed as a simple housewife with apron, and kerchief over her hair.

Properties: A wooden cat, a knife, crutches, a bun, brooms and mops for The Crowd, cardboard signs, a pipe for the Piper, gold coins, an enormous lollipop, a vine in two pots with caramels attached to it.

Lighting: Daylight stage, with footlights and overheads up full at beginning. Amber baby spot on Piper as he plays tune that rids the city of the rats. Fade on green baby spot on Piper as he plays tune that leads the children away. At this point stage darkens gradually for a moment while Obie calls for the Piper and then lights go up full again as he appears in amber spot. Lights full up at end.

THE MIXING STICK

Characters: 6 male; 5 female.

Playing Time: 10 minutes.

Costumes: Simple everyday clothes.

Properties: Large stick, salt, two onions, potatoes, some turnips, a jar of drippings, large bone, sprig of parsley, few carrots, a cane for Tommy, some bowls.

Setting: The kitchen of the Brown home. It is a large, old-fashioned room. At right is a fireplace with a big pot hanging in it. An almost empty table and some chairs are at left. Against back wall is a cupboard with some bowls in it.

THE MAGIC COOKIE JAR

Characters: 2 male; 2 female.
Playing Time: 30 minutes.
Costumes: The Prince wears a long dark cloak and a mask over his clothes. The others are in uniform according to rank.
Properties: Rolling pin, dough or something that resembles it, tray of burned cookies, large stone jar, glass of milk, plate of cookies, cake turner, gold coins, paper and pencil.
Setting: There is a door right, and another entrance at left. The stage is set with a large table, several chairs and cupboards along the walls, right and left. These are lined with dishes, pots, pans, etc., and there are also a great many cookie jars and tins.

THE TOWN MOUSE AND HIS COUNTRY COUSIN

Characters: 4 male; 2 female; 2 others (cat and the dog).
Playing Time: 15 minutes.
Costumes: Costumes for the mice may be made by dyeing old long underwear, and attaching wired rope tails. Mouse masks with humorously painted white eyes and perky ears can be made of crepe paper for the heads. The hands may be clad in mouse-colored gloves and held in paw-like positions throughout. The cat and dog are clad in adapted brownie suits, and wear dog and cat masks. The Mayor's Mouse should be dressed in a frock coat, opera hat, white vest, gloves. He wears oxford glasses, and carries a cane. He also wears gray spats. Ma Mouse wears a sunbonnet and also an apron and a shawl when she goes out.
Properties: Cane, broom, scraps of food, two watches, dishes of candy and of nuts.
Setting: Scene 1 is a shabbily furnished corner of a barn. There are a few rough chairs and a table. Scene 2 is a well-furnished dining room. Long drapes hang over windows at right. There is a door at left. The table is covered with a lace tablecloth, on which are the remains of a banquet. Several chairs are around the table, and one large chair is at the head. There are two candles burning on the table, just burning down into the golden sockets of the candlesticks.
Lighting: For Scene 1 try to give effect of sunbeams coming through cracks in barn. In Scene 2, the burning candles supply the light.

HANS WHO MADE THE PRINCESS LAUGH

Characters: 7 male; 6 female; extras.
Playing Time: 20 minutes.
Costumes: Henrik, Nils, Maria and Hans in peasant dress. Hans wears a red wig. Fru Beek and Gertrude: bodices, brightly colored skirts, caps and aprons. Johan Koeller in buff breeches and black coat. He wears a wide brimmed black hat. Peder Jesson in uniform; red coat, buff breeches, gaiters and a hat suggesting a shako. The Fairy Godmother wears a long, dark cloak and a kerchief tied over her head. The Princess wears a long dark cloak with a hood. She throws the cloak off for the final scene. The costume disclosed should be worthy of a Princess. The Princess's attendant is in gray. Page in tunic and long hose. Street sweeper in nondescript garments but clothed with the air of authority which street sweepers have. Extras in variations of the above costumes. Dog wears all-over gray or brown, and walks on all fours.
Properties: Stuffed cloth pigs; basket; eggs (for which ping pong balls may be used); basket scroll; handkerchiefs; simulated white goose; pop gun; balloon; confetti.
Setting: The Palace is in the upstage part of the marketplace. A balcony looks out on the square. Around the square are various stalls. There is a fruit stall, egg stall, vegetable stall. Not a great deal of each article is needed. The contents of the stalls may be suggestive and colorful, and crêpe paper may be used

to give appearance of larger amounts. The facade of the palace may be made of grey crêpe paper, and a pattern of masonry can be drawn on it in black and white crayon. The balcony may be simulated by covering a screen with the same grey crepe paper and placing behind it a table on which two children can stand. An entrance to the balcony either of steps from the stage or through the rear wall must be arranged.

A PRECEDENT IN PASTRIES

Characters: 14 male; 5 female; extras as desired.

Playing Time: 15 minutes.

Costumes: The judge's costume may be as elaborate or as simple as circumstances dictate. It can range from the official ermine-trimmed robe and the judicial wig to a plain black gown. The costumes of the men are divided between the smocks, heavy brogans and wide-brimmed hats of the farmers and the gaiters and frock coats of the men of the village. John Chubb is in his shirt sleeves and wears a baker's apron and cap. The women should wear bright colors to give life to the scene. Their costumes are those of housewives — plain dresses with long full skirts, relieved by white kerchiefs, mopcaps and aprons.

Properties: A small cake or bun; a fairly long plank and a substantial trestle; a sack filled with anything at all to represent the buns and a long piece of rope to bind the sack to the plank. The trumpet announcing the judge's entrance is traditional. Papers and pen and ink on the clerk's table.

Setting: It should follow the traditional arrangement of a Court room. The judge's bench should be on a dais and if possible there should be a canopy representing wood above his chair. The rest of the furniture should be very plain and have a look of long use. The benches of the spectators should be well to the sides of the stage to allow space for setting up the "scales of justice."

THE THREE AUNTS

Characters: 5 male; 10 female. Extras as desired.

Playing Time: 25 minutes.

Costumes: The maids are dressed in medieval peasant costume. The court ladies are in peaked caps and wimples. Tapestries would offer excellent suggestions for details. Doublets and hose for the men. The three aunts are dressed in black with touches of white. A false face or nose for Gros Bec; a hump for Bossu; red eye make-up for Oeil Rouge.

Properties: Broom and dusters; a spinning wheel or a spindle; a basket full of flax (untwisted rope may be used for this). A spindle full of twine to represent the spun flax. The loom may be improvised from odds and ends of lumber with slight attention to details. A white cloth is stretched on it. A white "linen" shirt with full sleeves.

Setting: If possible, there should be two sets. However, it is not necessary. A change of scene may be made simply by a change of stage properties. The Throne Room should give an effect of spaciousness. The throne is on a dais. A carpet leads to the dais. A small bench on which the aunts may be seated during the last scene should be just offstage. If screens are available, they may be set up in front of the Throne Room scene in such a way as to suggest a small tower room. The second scene requires a bench on which Julie sleeps and a chair before the spinning wheel. The third scene is the same except for the substitution of the loom for the spinning wheel.

Lighting: The play may be produced without special lighting, but if possible the dimming of lights while the three aunts are at work will add to the effectiveness of the scenes.

HANSEL AND GRETHEL

Characters: 2 male; 3 female.

Playing Time: 10 minutes.

Costumes: All the characters may be dressed in simple, poor peasant dress, except the witch, who wears traditional witch's costume.

Properties: Wood logs, bone, candy, stick for witch, bags with coins, colored stones to represent jewels, cloak.
Setting: The Woodcutter's home in Scenes 1 and 5 is very sparsely furnished with a rough table and a few chairs. There is a fireplace upstage left. No set is needed for Scene 2, except a simple backdrop with a few trees to indicate a forest scene, and the outside of the witch's house at right. The witch's house for Scenes 3 and 4 is simply furnished. There is a cupboard with a door at the right and a large stove door at left. There are cots for the children, and a fireplace in center of rear wall.

PETER RABBIT

Characters: 3 male; 3 female.
Playing Time: 15 minutes.
Costumes: Flopsy and Mopsy are dressed in gingham; Cotton-Tail and Peter in little suits with short pants and jackets. Mother Rabbit wears a house dress with a large white apron over it. The children taking the part of the rabbits wear large brown ears and have large wads of cotton tacked to the back of their dresses or suits for tails. Cotton-Tail should be quite a bit smaller than the other rabbits and have a larger tail than the others. Farmer McGregor is in blue overalls and tattered straw hat. He has a beard.
Properties: Handkerchief bonnet, cape, market basket, rake, baskets of berries, buns, botttle, spoon.
Setting: Scene 1 is furnished with a rough table and several chairs. A lantern, or two, may hang on the walls. There is a cupboard at the rear filled with dishes, silverware, etc. The table is set for breakfast. There is an entrance at right. For Scene 2, a fence is placed at the rear of the stage. This may be a cardboard affair and at one end there should be an aperture large enough for Peter to crawl through. Bunches of carrots, radishes and other vegetables are lined against the fence to give the appearance of growing there. A large watering pot or bucket is at left. Scene 3 is the same as Scene 1 except that the dishes are not on table.

THE POT OF GOLD

Characters: 1 male; 8 female,
Playing Time: 10 minutes.
Costumes: The fairies all wear dresses of the colors they represent. Other characters wear everyday, modern clothes.
Properties: Pot of Gold (this may be a gilded kettle or one covered with yellow paper), yellow flowers.
Setting: None is required. However, a backdrop of an outdoor scene may be used.

THE TEST

Characters: 11 male; male and female extras.
Playing Time: 30 minutes.
Costumes: All characters wear medieval costumes. Each prince wears a cap of his special color.
Properties: Books, scroll, bugle, piece of wire.
Setting: The first and last scenes take place in the throne room of the king. A canopied throne stands at the center back. Very little other furniture is needed as the cast fills the stage. The second scene, a library in the palace, may be played before the curtain to avoid a change of scene. A table and chairs may be arranged to suggest the scene. A few books are on the table, and there is a large clock on the curtain to indicate the passage of time. It should be arranged to have the hands of the clock move slowly so that by the end of the scene, the clock shows the hour to have passed.

PUSS-IN-BOOTS

Characters: 10 male; 1 female; male and female extras.
Playing Time: 15 minutes.
Costumes: Puss-in-Boots may wear an animal head. The others are in costumes of the time, each according to rank. Two players are required to wear the donkey suit. A lion's head is needed for the Ogre.
Properties: Rope for donkey; bag; clothing; toy rabbit; bugles; spears; fan; fine suit of clothes for Tom; scythe; sickle; rake; sword.

Setting: Act 1 is an interior set with a wide open door at rear. Sacks of "flour" are piled on the floor. In the corner is a pair of boots, and a hat, jacket and an empty flour sack hang on pegs nearby. An invisible thread or wire runs across floor and is attached to toy mouse concealed in wings. Act 2 is played before a painted backdrop with a river bank in the background and beyond it a view of trees. A castle tower rises above them in the distance. There is a large tree trunk on the river bank which concals the rear entrance. In Act 3 there is a small door in side wall behind the Ogre's chair, in an interior set.
Lighting: Daylight overheads and footlights if desired.

THE THREE SILLIES

Characters: 6 male; 4 female; male and female extras.
Playing Time: 10 minutes.
Costumes: Mr. Fuddyman wears a black suit. The farmers wear plaid shirts and overalls. The women wear long, flowing dresses, gathered at the waist, with aprons. The Cat wears black pants and jerkin with a black hood. The Cow wears spotted pants, jerkin and hood.
Properties: Ring; axe; cider jug; large, shiny boots; a switch.
Setting: There is a porch or shed across the rear of the stage, connecting the house and barn, corners of which are seen on either side. Door to the house is at the left end of porch; door to the barn is at the right. Near the house door is a woodpile, chopping block, and nails in the wall. In the center of the porch stands a large barrel on a stand with a stool at the right. Hoes, rakes, and other farm tools hang on the wall near the barn door. In the part of the barn visible, an upper door to hay loft, with a ladder leading to it and projecting into yard is seen.

A KETTLE OF BRAINS

Characters: 2 male; 2 female.
Playing Time: 7 minutes.
Costumes: Boys wear shabby play clothes. Noodle has a soft boy's hat. The Wise Woman may wear a long dress with an apron over it. Betsy wears a simple dress with a pocket in which she has a handkerchief.
Properties: Large kettle, large burlap bag, small bag.
Setting: A forest scene with the doorway to a hut indicated. There are some sticks and logs set like a fire, on which the kettle may be set.

THE FLAG OF THE UNITED STATES

Characters: 10 male; 4 female; extras.
Playing Time: 10 minutes.
Costumes: Costumes of the Colonial period.
Properties: A large American flag set in a standard. Another flag with thirteen alternate red and white stripes with a British Jack in the corner is required for Episode 1.
Setting: In Episode 1 a background of ropes and sails to suggest a ship. In Episode 2 a small table and a few chairs are all that is required. Episode 6 also has a ship background and a large wheel.

NO BRAVER SOLDIER

Characters: 8 male; 3 female.
Playing Time: 20 minutes.
Costumes: The characters are dressed in clothes of the period — traditional colonial costumes for all but the two British officers, who wear red coats with gilded buttons, and three-cornered hats over wigs.
Properties: Bible, kettle, handkerchiefs, pile of clean clothes, cream bucket, logs, keg, muskets (these may be cut out of cardboard), pewter jug, quilts, cloths.
Setting: There is a large fireplace in the rear of the room with a crane and iron kettle. At the right side hangs a warming pan and tongs, and on the other side an array of long-handled spoons and ladles. On the mantle stands a clock, pewter candlesticks, and a powder horn. To the right of the fireplace stands a spinning wheel, and to the left a high-backed settle. A space must be left between the settle and the fireplace to show piled logs of wood. The dresser is upstage right, and on it is the usual assortment of pewter and willowware. At the extreme right downstage is a door leading to the entry-way. Left downstage is a window and window bench. At the left

downstage is a door leading to the woodshed. A gate-legged table and rushbottom chairs are arranged center left to allow a good view of the hearth.

THE HEROINE OF WREN

Characters: 4 male; 2 female.
Playing Time: 20 minutes.
Costumes: Cynthia, her Grandmother and Grandfather and the Rider are dressed in Colonial Quaker costumes. Colonel Day and his Orderly wear British uniforms of the period.
Properties: Parcel wrapped in cloth; sheet of paper; two more parcels, cloaks and hoods for Cynthia and Grandmother; market basket covered with a white cloth; sword for Colonel; a sack of coins.
Setting: Simple interior of a Quaker home. There are two exits. The room is furnished to give a Colonial effect. There are a rocking chair, several straight chairs and a table holding an old-fashioned quill pen in a bottle of sand, a large ink well, several sheets of paper, candlesticks holding tall white candles.

HEARTS OF OAK

Characters: 6 male; male extras.
Playing Time: 15 minutes.
Costumes: The men are clad in plain, homespun garments, and broad-brimmed hats. In the first scene the boys are in torn dirty clothes. The Governor and his guards are dressed in red military uniforms, trimmed with gold braid. The guardsmen carry swords, bellows, wood.
Properties: A rolled document representing the charter.
Setting: A rather large, sparsely furnished room. A door at the back leads to entrance hall. At the left is an open fireplace. On the mantel above, the unlighted candles. There are also candles on the long table which occupies the center of the room. Rude benches and an armchair are scattered about in disorderly confusion. There is a fireplace at rear.
Lighting: Provided by candlelight, and extinguished as indicated in end of first scene.

SON OF LIBERTY

Characters: 5 male; 2 female.
Playing Time: 30 minutes.
Costumes: All characters wear traditional colonial costumes.
Properties: Bouquet of flowers, vase of water, large silver spoon, piece of knitting and knitting needles, copperplates, silverware, jewelry, etc., ledger, tray with cups and saucers and teapot, book, journal, teapot, straw basket.
Setting: There is a settee at right; various rockers and straight colonial chairs and small tables are about the room. In Scene 2 there is a display case with jewelry, copperplates, silverware, etc. There is a table holding the ledger before which is a rough wooden bench. There are one or two other chairs about the room. Scene 3 may be the same as Scene 1.

DOLLY SAVES THE DAY

Characters: 4 male; 2 female.
Playing Time: 20 minutes.
Costumes: Characters may be dressed in clothes of the period. Washington wears the uniform of a Continental General, and the Captain that of the Hessians.
Properties: A rag doll; riding crop; papers for the plans; pen knife; dipper; medal.
Setting: There is an old well at the right, and a rustic table and chair at the left.

NOT ONLY THE STRONG

Characters: 4 male; 7 female.
Playing Time: 30 minutes.
Costumes: The costumes for Mrs. Reynolds and the six girls must be Colonial in type, but simple and plain. The clothing worn by the Captain, Siras Witchfield, and William is the Daniel Boone garb. The Preacher should wear an old-fashioned black coat and high collar.
Properties: Flowers, bowl, two Colonial-style bouquets, knitting and sewing for girls, musket.
Setting: The furnishings are extremely simple. A plain, rather rough table, upon which rests a large Bible and a pair of brass candlesticks, stands at one side. The chairs are rush-bottomed. A wool-wheel may be included, and a small window at back of stage is absolutely necessary.